Lecture Notes in Computer Science   16343

Founding Editors

Gerhard Goos
Juris Hartmanis

Editorial Board Members

Elisa Bertino, *Purdue University, West Lafayette, IN, USA*
Wen Gao, *Peking University, Beijing, China*
Bernhard Steffen, *TU Dortmund University, Dortmund, Germany*
Moti Yung, *Columbia University, New York, NY, USA*

The series Lecture Notes in Computer Science (LNCS), including its subseries Lecture Notes in Artificial Intelligence (LNAI) and Lecture Notes in Bioinformatics (LNBI), has established itself as a medium for the publication of new developments in computer science and information technology research, teaching, and education.

LNCS enjoys close cooperation with the computer science R & D community, the series counts many renowned academics among its volume editors and paper authors, and collaborates with prestigious societies. Its mission is to serve this international community by providing an invaluable service, mainly focused on the publication of conference and workshop proceedings and postproceedings. LNCS commenced publication in 1973.

Fiona Fui-Hoon Nah · Keng Leng Siau
Editors

HCI International 2025 – Late Breaking Papers

27th International Conference on
Human-Computer Interaction, HCII 2025
Gothenburg, Sweden, June 22–27, 2025
Proceedings, Part XIII

 Springer

Editors
Fiona Fui-Hoon Nah
Singapore Management University
Singapore, Singapore

Keng Leng Siau
Singapore Management University
Singapore, Singapore

ISSN 0302-9743   ISSN 1611-3349 (electronic)
Lecture Notes in Computer Science
ISBN 978-3-032-13166-9   ISBN 978-3-032-13167-6 (eBook)
https://doi.org/10.1007/978-3-032-13167-6

This Springer imprint is published by the registered company Springer Nature Switzerland AG
The registered company address is: Gewerbestrasse 11, 6330 Cham, Switzerland

If disposing of this product, please recycle the paper.

Foreword

The HCI International (HCII) conference was founded in 1984 by Gavriel Salvendy (Purdue University, USA, Tsinghua University, P.R. China, and University of Central Florida, USA) and the first event of the series, "1st USA-Japan Conference on Human-Computer Interaction", was held in Honolulu, Hawaii, USA, on 18–20 August. Since then, HCI International has been held jointly with several Thematic Areas and Affiliated Conferences, with each one under the auspices of a distinguished international Program Board and under one management and one registration. Twenty-seven HCI International Conferences have been organized so far (every two years until 2013, and annually thereafter).

Last year, we celebrated 40 years since the establishment of the HCII conference, which has been a hub for presenting groundbreaking research and novel ideas and collaboration for people from all over the world. Over the years, this conference has served as a platform for scholars, researchers, industry experts, and students to exchange ideas, connect, and address challenges in the ever-evolving HCI field. The conference has evolved itself, adapting to new technologies and emerging trends, while staying committed to its core mission of advancing knowledge and driving change.

The 27th International Conference on Human-Computer Interaction, HCI International 2025 (HCII 2025), was held as an 'on-site' conference at the Gothia Towers Hotel and Swedish Exhibition & Congress Centre, in Gothenburg, Sweden, on June 22–27, 2025, with the additional option for 'on-line' participation. It incorporated the 21 thematic areas and affiliated conferences listed below.

A total of 7972 individuals from academia, research institutes, industry, and government agencies from 92 countries submitted contributions. 1430 papers and 355 posters (as short research papers) were included in the volumes of the proceedings published just before the start of the conference. Additionally, 439 papers and 104 posters were included in the volumes of the proceedings published after the conference, as "Late Breaking Work". The contributions thoroughly cover the entire field of human-computer interaction, highlight the evolving role of computers in diverse contexts, and demonstrate how HCI research is shaping and improving user experiences across a wide range of domains, influencing technological progress and its effective integration into various sectors. The volumes constituting the full set of the HCII 2025 conference proceedings are listed on the following pages.

I would like to thank the Program Board Chairs and the members of the Program Boards of all thematic areas and affiliated conferences for their contribution towards the high scientific quality and overall success of the HCI International 2025 conference. Their manifold support including paper reviews (via a single-blind review process, with a minimum of two reviews per submission), session organization, and their willingness to act as goodwill ambassadors for the conference is most highly appreciated.

This conference would not have been possible without the continuous and unwavering support and advice of Gavriel Salvendy, founder, General Chair Emeritus, and Scientific Advisor. For his outstanding efforts, I would like to express my sincere appreciation to Abbas Moallem, Communications Chair and Editor of HCI International News.

September 2025   Constantine Stephanidis

HCI International 2025 Thematic Areas and Affiliated Conferences

- HCI: Human-Computer Interaction Thematic Area
- HIMI: Human Interface and the Management of Information Thematic Area
- EPCE: 22nd International Conference on Engineering Psychology and Cognitive Ergonomics
- AC: 19th International Conference on Augmented Cognition
- UAHCI: 19th International Conference on Universal Access in Human-Computer Interaction
- CCD: 17th International Conference on Cross-Cultural Design
- SCSM: 17th International Conference on Social Computing and Social Media
- VAMR: 17th International Conference on Virtual, Augmented and Mixed Reality
- DHM: 16th International Conference on Digital Human Modeling & Applications in Health, Safety, Ergonomics & Risk Management
- DUXU: 14th International Conference on Design, User Experience and Usability
- C&C: 13th International Conference on Culture and Computing
- DAPI: 13th International Conference on Distributed, Ambient and Pervasive Interactions
- HCIBGO: 12th International Conference on HCI in Business, Government and Organizations
- LCT: 12th International Conference on Learning and Collaboration Technologies
- ITAP: 11th International Conference on Human Aspects of IT for the Aged Population
- AIS: 7th International Conference on Adaptive Instructional Systems
- HCI-CPT: 7th International Conference on HCI for Cybersecurity, Privacy and Trust
- HCI-Games: 7th International Conference on HCI in Games
- MobiTAS: 7th International Conference on HCI in Mobility, Transport and Automotive Systems
- AI-HCI: 6th International Conference on Artificial Intelligence in HCI
- MOBILE: 6th International Conference on Human-Centered Design, Operation and Evaluation of Mobile Communications

Conference Proceedings – Full List of Volumes

1. LNCS 15766, Human-Computer Interaction — Part I, edited by Masaaki Kurosu and Ayako Hashizume
2. LNCS 15767, Human-Computer Interaction — Part II, edited by Masaaki Kurosu and Ayako Hashizume
3. LNCS 15768, Human-Computer Interaction — Part III, edited by Masaaki Kurosu and Ayako Hashizume
4. LNCS 15769, Human-Computer Interaction — Part IV, edited by Masaaki Kurosu and Ayako Hashizume
5. LNCS 15770, Human-Computer Interaction — Part V, edited by Masaaki Kurosu and Ayako Hashizume
6. LNCS 15771, Human-Computer Interaction — Part VI, edited by Masaaki Kurosu and Ayako Hashizume
7. LNCS 15772, Human-Computer Interaction — Part VII, edited by Masaaki Kurosu and Ayako Hashizume
8. LNCS 15773, Human Interface and the Management of Information: Part I, edited by Hirohiko Mori and Yumi Asahi
9. LNCS 15774, Human Interface and the Management of Information: Part II, edited by Hirohiko Mori and Yumi Asahi
10. LNCS 15773, Human Interface and the Management of Information: Part III, edited by Hirohiko Mori and Yumi Asahi
11. LNAI 15776, Engineering Psychology and Cognitive Ergonomics: Part I, edited by Don Harris and Wen-Chin Li
12. LNAI 15777, Engineering Psychology and Cognitive Ergonomics: Part II, edited by Don Harris and Wen-Chin Li
13. LNAI 15778, Augmented Cognition, Part I, edited by Dylan D. Schmorrow and Cali M. Fidopiastis
14. LNAI 15779, Augmented Cognition, Part II, edited by Dylan D. Schmorrow and Cali M. Fidopiastis
15. LNCS 15780, Universal Access in Human-Computer Interaction: Part I, edited by Margherita Antona and Constantine Stephanidis
16. LNCS 15781, Universal Access in Human-Computer Interaction: Part II, edited by Margherita Antona and Constantine Stephanidis
17. LNCS 15782, Cross-Cultural Design: Part I, edited by Pei-Luen Patrick Rau
18. LNCS 15783, Cross-Cultural Design: Part II, edited by Pei-Luen Patrick Rau
19. LNCS 15784, Cross-Cultural Design: Part III, edited by Pei-Luen Patrick Rau
20. LNCS 15785, Cross-Cultural Design: Part IV, edited by Pei-Luen Patrick Rau
21. LNCS 15786, Social Computing and Social Media: Part I, edited by Adela Coman and Simona Vasilache

85. CCIS 2772, HCI International 2025 — Late Breaking Posters: Part II, edited by Constantine Stephanidis, Margherita Antona, Stavroula Ntoa, George Margetis and Gavriel Salvendy
86. CCIS 2773, HCI International 2025 — Late Breaking Posters: Part III, edited by Constantine Stephanidis, Margherita Antona, Stavroula Ntoa, George Margetis and Gavriel Salvendy

https://2025.hci.international/proceedings

27th International Conference on Human-Computer Interaction (HCII 2025)

The full list with the Program Board Chairs and the members of the Program Boards of all thematic areas and affiliated conferences of HCII 2025 is available online at:

http://www.hci.international/board-members-2025.php

HCI International 2026 Conference

The 28th International Conference on Human-Computer Interaction, HCI International 2026, will be held jointly with the affiliated conferences at the Montréal Convention Centre (Palais des congrès de Montréal), in Montreal, Canada, 26–31 July 2026. It will cover a broad spectrum of themes related to Human-Computer Interaction, including theoretical issues, methods, tools, processes, and case studies in HCI design, as well as novel interaction techniques, interfaces, and applications. The proceedings will be published by Springer (part of Springer Nature) in a multi-volume set. More information will become available on the conference website: https://2026.hci.international/.

General Chair
Constantine Stephanidis
University of Crete and ICS-FORTH
Heraklion, Crete, Greece
Email: general_chair@2026.hci.international

https://2026.hci.international/

Contents

Advances in Commerce, Marketing, and Consumer Behavior

Human-Centered Perspectives on New Technologies Adoption and Impact

Tackling Global AI-Driven Hiring Bias:
A Literature Review from an HCI Perspective

Huaigu Li[1(✉)], Sanjay Damodaran[2], and Michael L. Best[1,2]

[1] School of Interactive Computing, Georgia Institute of Technology, Atlanta, GA 30332, USA
`{hli723,mikeb}@gatech.edu`
[2] Sam Nunn School of International Affairs, Georgia Institute of Technology, Atlanta,
GA 30332, USA
`sjdamgr@gatech.edu`

Abstract. As artificial intelligence (AI) technologies are increasingly integrated into hiring processes, concerns about AI-driven bias issues have become prominent across disciplines. This paper presents a systematic literature review of 37 Human-Computer Interaction (HCI) studies on the topic of AI-driven hiring bias, published between 2018 and 2024. Using both qualitative and quantitative approaches, we identify and summarize the trends and focus of HCI research on this topic. We also uncover how regional affiliation influences the prioritization of research globally. We conclude the article by outlining future research opportunities for the HCI community to support more equitable and governable AI-driven hiring systems.

Keywords: Human Resource · AI-driven Hiring · AI Ethics · AI Governance

1 Introduction

Artificial intelligence (AI) has become increasingly integrated into hiring workflows. Organizations are adopting AI-driven tools to streamline recruitment processes, enhance hiring efficiency, and reduce the operational burden on human recruiters. However, despite their potential, AI-driven hiring systems have been found to reinforce and even amplify biases present in traditional hiring processes [1]. These biases, often embedded in training data and algorithmic decision-making, can lead to discriminatory hiring outcomes, disproportionately affecting candidates based on their gender, race, educational background, age, and other factors. As AI-driven recruitment methods become globally adopted, concerns over AI-driven hiring bias have escalated worldwide, with governments, enterprises, and researchers across different regions recognizing it as a significant ethical challenge. The implications of AI-driven hiring bias extend beyond individual hiring decisions, influencing workforce diversity, economic opportunities, and broader social equity. Addressing these issues requires multidisciplinary efforts that combine technological, regulatory, and ethical perspectives.

Research studies across disciplines have raised critical concerns about the implications of the AI-driven hiring systems. In the field of computer science, scholars have documented how biased datasets and algorithms can lead to disparate impact [2], spurring

© The Author(s), under exclusive license to Springer Nature Switzerland AG 2026
F. F.-H Nah and K. L. Siau (Eds.): HCII 2025, LNCS 16343, pp. 3–21, 2026.
https://doi.org/10.1007/978-3-032-13167-6_1

a wave of work on fairness-aware and explainable AI-hiring algorithms [3, 4]. Legal and public policy scholars, meanwhile, have examined how these systems challenge existing anti-discrimination laws and accountability structures, especially when proprietary algorithms lack transparency or mechanisms for appeal [5–8]. Social science researchers have emphasized that AI hiring tools do not operate in a vacuum but reflect and reinforce broader structural inequalities [9], and their acceptance by users depends heavily on perceived fairness, procedural clarity [10], and cultural context [11]. A recurring concern across these domains is the opacity of algorithmic hiring decisions. Most of the AI-driven hiring systems operate as "black boxes" [12], offering little explanation for their outputs to either applicants or recruiters, which undermines trust and impedes scrutiny. Moreover, accountability is often diffused between human resource departments and AI application developers, making it difficult to assign responsibility for discriminatory recruitment outcomes. Despite recent regulatory interventions, such as the European Union's AI Act [13], significant regulatory enforcement gaps remain. Although various countries and regions have implemented laws and regulations to minimize discrimination and bias in hiring practices, AI-driven hiring bias remains inadequately addressed [14, 15]. Additionally, enforcement of these laws varies significantly across different jurisdictions, resulting in inconsistencies in how AI-driven hiring bias issues are addressed globally [16]. While significant research in law and public policy has focused on mitigating AI hiring bias through regulatory frameworks and accountability mechanisms, these approaches alone have limitations. Against this backdrop, Human-Computer Interaction (HCI) research offers a distinct and complementary perspective on exploring how AI-driven hiring tools are utilized in practice and how biases manifest in real-world user interactions. By integrating insights from both technical and human factors perspectives. Unlike legal and policy-based approaches, which often operate at a systemic level, HCI research allows for direct engagement with end users, facilitating design improvements and bias mitigation strategies for AI-driven technologies.

To our knowledge, there is still limited HCI research that discusses bias issues in AI-driven hiring systems from a global perspective. Current literature focuses on specific regions, user groups, or industry sectors, leaving gaps in understanding the broader, cross-cultural implications of AI-driven hiring bias research. This review aims to contribute to the field by synthesizing recent HCI research studies to explore how HCI research worldwide addresses this topic. Specifically, we analyze the research focus, trends, and key findings within the field. 37 selected HCI research papers are analyzed by combining qualitative and quantitative approaches. Our analysis aims to provide a clearer understanding of the strengths and gaps in existing HCI research and highlight opportunities for future work in mitigating AI-driven hiring bias.

The study is guided by two primary research questions:

RQ1: How have different HCI research studies across the globe examined AI-driven hiring bias issues?

RQ2: How have the regional affiliations influenced the focus and approaches of HCI research on AI-driven hiring bias?

Our study contributes to the existing body of research in several ways. First, we provide a comprehensive synthesis of HCI research on the AI-driven hiring bias topic, offering insights into how the field has evolved. Second, we identify methodological patterns and thematic trends in AI hiring bias-related research, highlighting prevalent research focus and approaches. Third, by mapping the key research findings and proposed solutions, our review informs future research directions and practical efforts aimed at mitigating bias in AI-driven recruitment. By summarizing the existing HCI literature on AI hiring bias, this study helps bridge knowledge gaps and facilitates the development of fairer and more accountable AI hiring systems. Additionally, our findings underscore the importance of interdisciplinary collaboration in addressing AI hiring bias, highlighting the need for continuous dialogue between AI application developers, policymakers, HCI researchers, and human resource professionals from different regions.

2 Methodology

2.1 Literature Search and Strategy

To conduct a comprehensive and systematic literature review, a structured selection process was adopted. This collecting process was divided into two rounds: the first round focused on identifying studies related to AI hiring bias, while the second round refined the selection to include only studies within the HCI domain.

The first round started from an extensive search across Google Scholar, IEEE Xplore, and the ACM Digital Library using the following keywords, including their synonyms or related terms: "artificial intelligence/algorithm" + "hiring/recruitment/workplace/employment" + "discrimination/bias/inequity". The inclusion criteria required studies to be published in English, explicitly focus on AI-driven hiring bias, present a clear methodology, and provide full-text availability. The search yielded 289 papers in total. Then, duplicated and off-topic papers were removed, resulting in a refined dataset of 229 papers for further evaluation (Fig. 1).

In the second round, the goal was to identify HCI research studies. Papers were selected based on the following criteria: they were peer-reviewed; involved human subjects; employed HCI research methods; focused on the design, evaluation, or implementation of algorithms, applications, or other computing systems; and explicitly examined AI-driven hiring bias or discrimination issues. Studies failing to meet these criteria were excluded. The final set of 37 papers, deemed relevant to both AI hiring bias and HCI research, constituted the corpus of this literature review (Fig. 1).

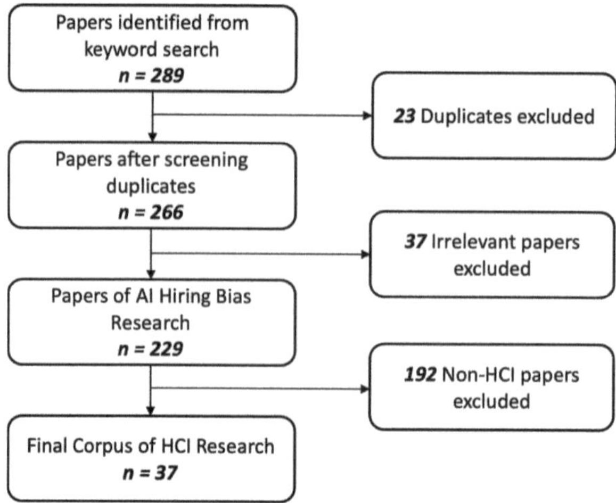

Fig. 1. Publication Collecting Process.

2.2 Data Analysis

Qualitative Analysis. We employed qualitative content analysis, using a deductive coding approach to systematically identify and categorize patterns from the collected corpus. The categories in the codebook were developed through a structured, theory-informed process grounded in the study's research questions and a preliminary scan of representative papers in the corpus. Each category reflects recurring dimensions in the literature on AI-driven hiring bias, including well-established typologies in recruitment research, HCI studies, and algorithmic bias analysis. The categories were iteratively refined through multiple rounds of discussion between the two researchers to ensure clarity, relevance, and applicability across diverse sources. The high intercoder agreement (Cohen's Kappa $= 0.89$) further supports the reliability and operational consistency of the final codebook structure. The following items were the categories coded for each paper:

- *Hiring Processes.* The hiring processes that facilitated by AI. The use of AI-driven hiring processes in the selected studies was categorized into four main types based on the commonly accepted four stages of hiring [17]: AI outreach, AI screening, AI assessment, and AI facilitation.
- *Bias Types.* The bias or discrimination issues that the research studies focus on [18]. We categorized the five types of bias based on the corpus: gender bias, racial bias, educational bias, age bias, and general bias.
- *Human Subject Roles.* In the HCI research on AI hiring bias, study participants take on various roles, reflecting different perspectives in the hiring process. The most common roles in the corpus include job candidates, recruiters, and organization managers.
- *Research Methodologies.* The research methodologies are categorized into three main types: quantitative methods, qualitative methods, and mixed methods [19].
- *Recommended Intervention Types.* The recommended levels of intervention in the research. We categorized the four types of recommendations based on the corpus: policy recommendations, candidate recommendations, AI developer recommendations, and organization recommendations.

- *Regional Affiliations.* The primary region or country associated with the research, typically based on the authors' institutional locations.

To handle cases where a single paper suits multiple codes under a certain category, the one-hot encoding approach is employed. From this method, we coded all publications within the collected corpus, preventing data conflation and allowing for more granular insights into how researchers studied the AI-driven hiring bias. We also conducted a thematic synthesis of the research focus and reported findings across the reviewed corpus. This process involved extracting the research topics from each research study and grouping them into emergent thematic categories through iterative review and comparative analysis.

Quantitative Analysis.   Based on the qualitative coding results, quantitative analysis was conducted to examine the trends of research on the AI-driven hiring bias topic (RQ1) and to identify correlations between the categorized elements and their corresponding research affiliations to identify regional variations (RQ2).

3   Results

3.1   RQ1: Global AI-Driven Hiring Bias HCI Research

Corpus Description. Our final corpus consists of 37 peer-reviewed publications from 2018 to 2024, reflecting a growing research interest in algorithmic hiring within the HCI and adjacent communities. Figure 2A shows that the volume of publications increased after 2020, peaking in 2022 and remaining high thereafter.

A thematic breakdown of the corpus reveals several noteworthy patterns from a global perspective. First, across categories such as Hiring Processes, Human Subject Roles, and Bias Types, the distribution of subcategories is relatively balanced (Fig. 2). For example, studies address AI screening, assessment, facilitation, and outreach at comparable rates, suggesting an equal-level concern with bias throughout the hiring pipeline. Similarly, researchers examine diverse stakeholder perspectives equally rather than focusing exclusively on one kind of stakeholder. In terms of research methodologies, while independent qualitative or quantitative approaches are both well represented, mixed-methods studies have become increasingly dominant. Moreover, there has been a noticeable rise in publications proposing policy-level intervention recommendations since 2021. This reflects a broader turn in the HCI-related fields contributing to public policy and AI governance [20, 21].

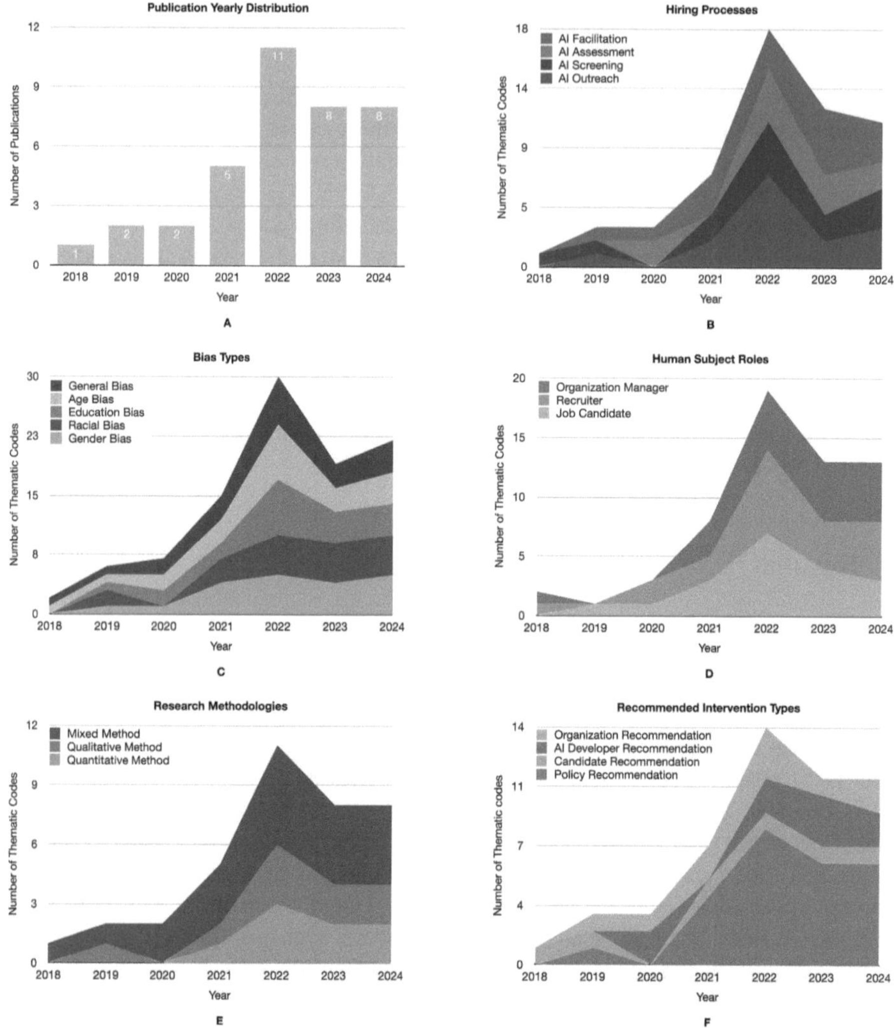

Fig. 2. (A) Yearly Distribution of the Corpus; (B–F) Yearly Distribution of Thematic Codes by Categories.

The global distribution of research on AI-driven hiring bias is regionally concentrated and only partially collaborative across regions. The geographic heatmap (Fig. 3) shows that author affiliations are concentrated in the United States, Western Europe, and East Asia, leading in publication counts. In contrast, contributions from Oceania are modest, and no affiliated studies were identified from Africa, Latin America, or the Middle East. The co-authoring heatmap (Fig. 4) further illustrates cross-regional collaboration trends: publications are produced within a single region, with North America, Europe, and Asia each demonstrating strong internal research activities. Only a smaller number of studies span multiple regions. This suggests that while the field is increasingly investigated worldwide, cross-regional collaboration remains limited.

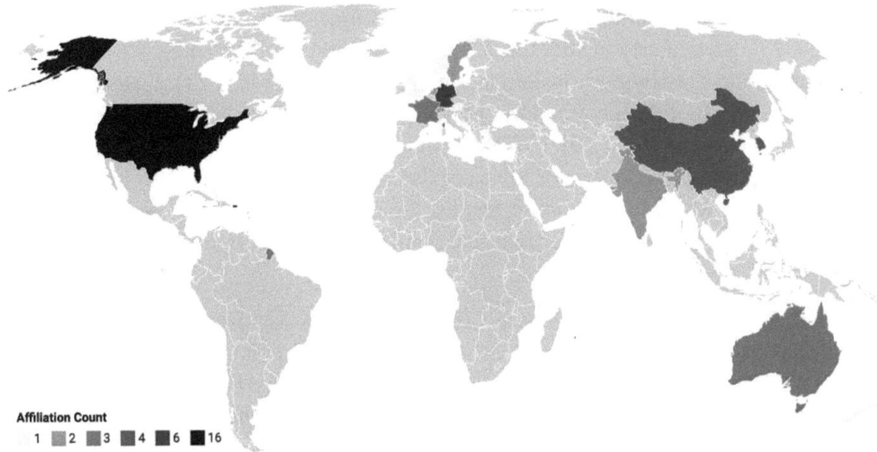

Fig. 3. Frequency of Author Affiliations by Region

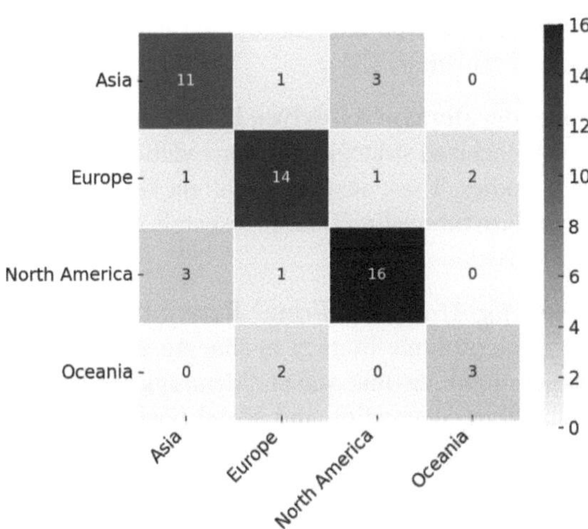

Fig. 4. Research Collaboration Heatmap by Continent.

Research Focuses. Through the thematic synthesis of the collected research works, we identified two overarching themes of the research topics. These themes reflect the dominant discourse patterns and concentration within the HCI research of the AI-driven hiring bias topic.

Concerns Around Bias, Transparency, and Explainability. Across the reviewed corpus, the algorithmic bias, as well as the transparency and explainability design of the hiring systems, consistently emerged as central concerns shaping user perceptions of fairness and legitimacy in AI-driven hiring. Participants with different roles expressed uncertainty not only about the fairness of outcomes but also about the processes that produced them

[3, 22, 23]. While some studies suggested that algorithmic tools may reduce overt human biases [24, 25], particularly in structured tasks such as resume screening [26], this technical potential did not always translate into perceived fairness [25, 27]. Instead, opaque AI model logic, algorithmic decision criteria, and unexplainable error patterns often heightened user distrust [28, 29]. While existing studies have examined how different stakeholder roles (e.g., recruiters or job candidates) prioritize transparency and explainability in distinct ways, less attention has been paid to how expectations around them may diverge across cultural [30] or regional contexts, even within the same stakeholder role.

Emotional Responses and Stakeholder Expectations. A significant portion of HCI research has explored how different participant groups respond to varying forms and degrees of explainability and transparency in AI hiring systems. For example, job candidates frequently reported discomfort, alienation, or aversion when engaging with fully automated hiring systems, especially in the context of video interviews or automated assessments [31–33]. At the same time, human resource professionals and organizational stakeholders emphasized the need for explainable and transparent system capabilities [34–36] and human-AI collaboration rather than full automated systems [37]. Across studies, stakeholders highlighted the importance of governance structures, ethical accountability [38], and design approaches that balance efficiency with fairness, trust, and user emotional sensitivity [34].

Future Research Considerations of AI-driven Hiring Bias. In addition to the research focuses reported, we synthesized strategic recommendations and reflective insights proposed by the research studies. These insights highlight key sociotechnical issues in AI-driven hiring and can inform future directions in research, system design, and governance efforts.

Education and Training for AI-Driven Hiring. Recent HCI literature has increasingly emphasized the role of algorithmic literacy in shaping user experience with AI-based hiring systems. Studies highlight that stakeholders engage with these systems from varied levels of technical understanding and social positioning [27, 39, 40]. Existing work has examined educational strategies such as tutorials for applicants undergoing asynchronous video interviews [41], fairness audit training for recruitment teams [22, 34, 38, 42, 43], and explainability education for developers of AI models [42]. These efforts are often motivated by concerns over "digital resignation" or passive acceptance of opaque algorithmic outcomes. However, the literature remains sparse on how such education or training can be made culturally adaptive, inclusive for users with disabilities, and scalable across diverse hiring contexts. HCI researchers may explore how interactive interfaces, participatory training environments, or localized AI-literacy frameworks can support equitable engagement with AI-driven hiring tools.

User Trust and Adoption for AI-Driven Hiring. A recurring finding across the HCI research corpus is that trust in AI-driven hiring systems is contingent on a range of social, procedural, and contextual factors. Candidates are more likely to accept hiring decisions when those decisions are accompanied by transparency in hiring logic and processes, and when the systems provide explanations that align with user expectations [24]. However, even successful applicants sometimes report discomfort with AI-driven hiring judgments, reporting concerns over depersonalization and fairness [25]. Notably, cross-cultural research in the corpus suggests that the trust and adoption of AI-driven hiring tools vary across regions, calling attention to the need for design practices that accommodate cultural specificity [38]. HCI scholars can contribute by examining how design elements could further mediate trust and adoption differently across user populations, and by testing adaptive trust-building mechanisms in real-world hiring scenarios.

Hybrid Oversight and Human-AI Collaboration for AI-Driven Hiring. Among the various strategies proposed by the research in corpus, human oversight design emerges as the most widely endorsed and contextually robust approach. On the one hand, some technical solutions, such as fairness-aware algorithms or data debiasing techniques [27], are often reported to fall short in addressing socially complex hiring decisions [44]. On the other hand, several studies emphasize that human involvement provides the necessary contextual reasoning, ethical judgment, and interpretive flexibility that algorithmic systems currently are deficient. Especially in high-stakes or ambiguous situations, human oversight is seen as critical for ensuring fairness, transparency, and accountability. Most studies converge on the view that hybrid decision-making, where humans either monitor (on-the-loop) or participate in (in-the-loop) algorithmic judgments, could enhance perceived fairness [22, 24]. However, open questions remain about how best to design and communicate the presence and extent of human involvement. For example, few studies explore how applicant perceptions shift when the oversight is disclosed proactively versus retroactively. Additionally, while some work explores error auditing and explainability mechanisms, little is known about how these practices scale across organizational sizes or hiring cultures. For HCI researchers, these gaps suggest opportunities to investigate collaborative decision interfaces, workflows, and visualization techniques for AI-driven hiring systems.

3.2 RQ2: Geographical Differences in Global AI-Driven Hiring Bias HCI Research

Our analysis examined the relationship between several thematic category variables and the affiliation of the research articles.

Regional Differences in Bias Types Focus. Firstly, findings indicate that bias types examined are significantly associated with the regional affiliation of the research. A Fisher's exact test yielded a p-value of 0.006, confirming a statistically significant relationship ($p < 0.05$). This suggests that the types of biases emphasized in AI hiring research differ by regions, reflecting regional priorities and social concerns. Specifically, in the United States, racial bias is the most scrutinized, given the country's strong emphasis on racial diversity and inclusion. In Europe, gender bias is the most prominent concern, indicating the region's heavy commitment to gender equality. In Asia, however, age bias remains a significant issue, reflecting that age-related inequality in hiring continues to be a persistent societal challenge in Asian countries [45, 46].

Regional Differences in Hiring Processes Focus. In contrast, we found no statistically significant association between the hiring processes examined and their research regional affiliations. A Fisher's exact test yielded a p-value of 0.092 ($p > 0.05$), indicating that AI hiring processes are likely studied globally without significant regional variation. This finding implies that AI-driven hiring bias is a global issue rather than a region-specific problem.

Regional Differences in Intervention Level Focus. Another key finding relates to the types of recommendations proposed in AI-driven hiring bias research across different regions. A Fisher's exact test yielded a p-value of 0.039, indicating a statistically significant relationship ($p < 0.05$) between recommendation type and regional affiliation. The researchers from the United States primarily focus on organizational recommendations, analyzing how AI-driven hiring tools impact companies and recruiting practices. In contrast, the research from European countries and Asian countries/regions emphasizes proposing more policy recommendations, advocating for regulatory frameworks to mitigate AI-driven hiring bias. This statistical significance indicates that different regions prioritize distinct aspects of AI-driven hiring bias, reflecting local regulatory and corporate governance concerns. Furthermore, recommendations proposed for job candidates are notably absent across all regions, suggesting a gap in research regarding how to support job candidates in the new era of AI-driven hiring. Our analysis also explored the relationship between bias types and research methodologies, with no statistically significant association between research methodology types and bias type variables ($p > 0.05$), This suggests that HCI researchers have applied diverse methodological approaches to a range of bias topics without a dominant methodological pattern. As the field matures, future work may consider whether certain bias types are better suited to specific methodological lenses, offering opportunities for more targeted empirical designs.

4 Discussion

4.1 From Interface Trust to Governance Trust

While much of the HCI research has focused on the user trust in AI-driven hiring tools, it is equally important to address trust issues at a governance level. From the corpus, the research studies mostly approached the user trust issue as a computing system-level problem: improve the system's explainability or accountability, make the AI more transparent or user-friendly [47]. These factors are indeed important, but they are not sufficient for high-stakes domains like recruitment. Users (both candidates and hiring managers) also need confidence in the institutional and legal frameworks surrounding the system. A recurring finding from the corpus is that the lack of accountability of the AI-driven hiring systems erodes trust in both employee and employer [48]. If an applicant receives an unfair rejection from the AI-driven hiring systems, but there is no clear way to appeal or no responsible party to hold to account, the system will be perceived as fundamentally untrustworthy regardless of its transparency. HCI research must therefore expand its notion of "trustworthiness" beyond the interface of the AI. This includes factoring in institutional trust as well as legal trust, meaning the AI's operation aligns with societal norms and regulations. In the context of hiring, this could translate to practices like third-party audits of hiring systems' algorithms, regulatory compliance audits, or providing candidates with explanations and recourse as legal rights. Rather than treating trust as solely a user experience to be influenced by design tweaks, researchers should treat it as an outcome of socio-technical systems. Building truly trustworthy AI-driven hiring systems will require collaboration with policymakers and a sensitivity to AI governance issues.

4.2 Limited Engagement with Multilevel Intervention Exploration

HCI research has just started to engage with the complexities of multilevel governance of AI-driven hiring. Real-world AI hiring systems operate at the intersection of overlapping regimes: the local level of organizational hiring practices, the national (or regional) level of labor and anti-discrimination laws, and the platform level policies of the AI vendors or platforms providing the technologies. Each level can profoundly influence the recruitment outcomes, yet current HCI studies often consider these levels isolated. In practice, tensions between these governance layers are already evident. At the organizational level, some forward-thinking companies and AI providers have created internal ethics guidelines or fairness committees [49]. However, self-regulation by platforms or firms, while laudable, has no binding force; without external enforcement, it can easily become toothless "ethics washing." As the current AI-driven hiring practices create ethical issues unless backed by third-party oversight and formal regulations, the HCI community has an important role in navigating this complexity. We need research that examines how design recommendations or fairness interventions play out under different levels. For example, how might a user interface for contesting a hiring decision integrate with an organization's legal compliance workflow? What happens when a platform's algorithmic ranking policy conflicts with a particular employer's diversity commitments or a country's affirmative action laws?

4.3 Limitations

This literature review has several limitations. First, it does not examine the technical implementations of AI systems described in the literature, such as specific AI models or training data. This limits the ability to understand how system-level design decisions influence observed research trends and topic emergence in AI-driven hiring bias research. Second, the number of relevant publications remains limited, which constrains the depth of qualitative analysis due to incomplete reporting and reduces the potential for meaningful quantitative comparisons. Future reviews should consider incorporating gray literature, technical documentation to offer a more comprehensive account of how AI-driven hiring systems are developed and studied in practice.

5 Conclusion

This literature review examines how HCI researchers across regions have engaged with the growing challenges of bias in AI-driven hiring systems. Through a systematic analysis of 37 peer-reviewed publications, we identified research focuses and regional disparities on this topic. As AI becomes more deeply embedded in hiring practices worldwide, HCI scholars are uniquely positioned to contribute not only technical interventions but also culturally and contextually grounded design insights. Future work should expand cross-regional collaboration and engage more directly with AI governance structures across multiple levels. Addressing these gaps will be essential to advancing equitable and accountable AI-driven hiring systems that are responsive to diverse user needs and societal values.

Acknowledgments. The author would like to thank the conference and all the reviewers.

Disclosure of Interests. All authors declared that they have no conflict of interest relevant to the content of this paper.

Appendix: Codebook of Thematic Categories and Definitions

Category 1: Hiring Processes

(See Table 1)

Table 1. Codebook for Hiring Processes.

Code Name	Definition	Sample Papers
AI Outreach	AI outreach enhances talent acquisition by automating targeted outreach via social media and online platforms to identify potential active or passive candidates. Additionally, AI outreach includes generating and posting job descriptions by analyzing role expectations from the hiring team	[50, 51]
AI Screening	AI screening is the process to filter, rank, and evaluate job candidates based on their resumes, applications, and other relevant data	[52, 53]
AI Assessment	AI assessment refers to evaluate job candidates beyond resume screening. It includes AI-driven video interviews, psychometric tests and skill tests, which analyze speech, facial expressions, and behavioral patterns to predict a candidate's potential job performance	[54, 55]
AI Facilitation	AI facilitation refers to streamline administrative tasks in the hiring process, improving efficiency for both recruiters and candidates	[56, 57]

Category 2: Bias Types

(See Table 2)

Table 2. Codebook for Bias Types.

Code Name	Definition	Sample Papers
Gender Bias	AI-driven hiring decisions influenced by gender stereotypes, leading to unequal opportunities for women, and non-binary individuals	[23, 58]
Racial Bias	AI and human recruiters exhibited favoritism or disadvantages toward candidates based on specific racial, ethnic, nationality backgrounds	[28, 59]
Education Background Bias	Candidates from certain institutions or certain educational backgrounds being favored over those from non-traditional paths, potentially overlooking skills and potential	[38, 60, 61]
Age Bias	Certain candidates within certain age range faced discrimination based on assumptions about experience, adaptability, or technological proficiency	[23, 55, 62–64]
General Bias	Bias types not specified	[42, 43, 57, 65–67]

Category 3: Human Subject Roles

(See Table 3)

Table 3. Codebook for Human Subject Roles.

Code Name	Definition	Sample Papers
Job Candidate	Human subjects either acted as job candidates during the experiment or had previously experienced AI-driven hiring tools as actual applicants	[3, 68, 69]
Recruiter	Human subjects either acted as recruiters during the experiment or had previously experienced AI-driven hiring tools as actual recruiters	[63, 70, 71]
Organization Manager	Human subjects either acted as organization managers during the experiment or had previously experienced AI-driven hiring tools as organization managers	[22, 23, 72]

Category 4: Research Methodologies

(See Table 4)

Table 4. Codebook for Research Methodologies.

Code Name	Definition	Sample Papers
Quantitative Method	Quantitative approaches such as examining numerical data derived from surveys, experimental evaluations, or coded textual sources	[25, 28, 73]
Qualitative Method	Qualitative approaches such as semi-structured interviews, focus groups, ethnographic observation, and qualitative content	[24, 38, 63]
Mixed Method	Mixed methods combine quantitative and qualitative approaches	[29, 35, 64]

Category 5: Recommended Intervention Types

(See Table 5)

Table 5. Codebook for Recommended Intervention Types.

Code Name	Definition	Sample Papers
Policy Recommendation	Policy recommendations are identified when the papers provide guidelines and regulatory interventions to mitigate biases in AI-driven hiring systems	[27, 29, 38, 61, 74]
Candidate Recommendation	Candidate recommendations are identified when the papers provide recommendations or interventions for job applicants	[31, 37]
Organizational Recommendation	Organizational recommendations are identified when the papers provide recommendations or interventions for organizations and human resource departments	[40, 41, 64, 75]
AI Developer Recommendation	AI developer recommendations are identified when the papers provide recommendations or interventions for engineers and designers of AI-driven hiring tools	[26, 31]

References

1. Wilson, K., Caliskan, A.: Gender, Race, and Intersectional Bias in Resume Screening via Language Model Retrieval. In: Proceedings of the 2024 AAAI/ACM Conference on AI, Ethics, and Society. AAAI Press, pp. 1578–1590 (2025)
2. Fabris A, et al.: Fairness and bias in algorithmic hiring: a multidisciplinary survey. ACM Trans. Intell. Syst. Technol. **16**, 16:1–16:54 (2025). https://doi.org/10.1145/3696457
3. Hofeditz, L., Clausen, S., Rieß, A., Mirbabaie, M., Stieglitz, S.: Applying XAI to an AI-based system for candidate management to mitigate bias and discrimination in hiring. Electron Mark. **32**, 2207–2233 (2022). https://doi.org/10.1007/s12525-022-00600-9

4. Schumann, C., Foster, J.S., Mattei, N., Dickerson, J.P: We need fairness and explainability in algorithmic hiring. In: Proceedings of the 19th International Conference on Autonomous Agents and MultiAgent Systems. International Foundation for Autonomous Agents and Multiagent Systems, pp 1716–1720. Richland, SC, (2020)

5. Jibril, M., Florentina, T.A.: Governing AI in hiring: an effort to eliminate biased decision. In: Suzumura, T., Bono, M. (eds.) New Frontiers in Artificial Intelligence, pp 49–63. Springer Nature, Singapore (2024). https://doi.org/10.1007/978-981-97-3076-6_4

6. Raub, M.: Bots, bias and big data: artificial intelligence, algorithmic bias and disparate impact liability in hiring practices comment. Ark L Rev. **71**, 529–570 (2018)

7. Moss, H.: Screened out onscreen: disability discrimination, hiring bias, and artificial intelligence. Denv L Rev. **98**, 775–806 (2020)

8. Houser, K.A.: Can AI solve the diversity problem in the tech industry: mitigating noise and bias in employment decision-making. Stan. Tech. L Rev. **22**, 290–354 (2019)

9. Njoto, S., Cheong, M., Lederman, R., McLoughney, A., Ruppanner, L., Wirth, A.: Gender bias in AI recruitment systems: a sociological-and data science-based case study. In: 2022 IEEE International Symposium on Technology and Society (ISTAS), pp 1–7(2022)

10. Drage, E., Mackereth, K.: Does AI debias recruitment? race, gender, and AI's "eradication of difference." Philos. Technol. **35**, 89 (2022). https://doi.org/10.1007/s13347-022-00543-1

11. Zheng, F., Zhao, C., Usman, M., Poulova, P.: From bias to brilliance: the impact of artificial intelligence usage on recruitment biases in China. IEEE Trans. Eng. Manage. **71**, 14155–14167 (2024). https://doi.org/10.1109/TEM.2024.3442618

12. Xiong, Y., Kim, J.K.: Who wants to be hired by AI? How message frames and AI transparency impact individuals' attitudes and behaviors toward companies using AI in hiring. Comput. Hum. Behav.: Artific. Hum. **3**, 100120 (2025). https://doi.org/10.1016/j.chbah.2025.100120

13. Voigt, P., Hullen, N.: The EU AI act: answers to frequently asked questions. Springer, Berlin, Heidelberg (2024)

14. Poe, R.L.: Why fair automated hiring systems breach EU non-discrimination law. In: Meo, R., Silvestri, F. (eds.) Machine Learning and Principles and Practice of Knowledge Discovery in Databases. ECML PKDD 2023. Communications in Computer and Information Science, vol. 2133. Springer, Cham (2025). https://doi.org/10.1007/978-3-031-74630-7_34

15. Kwan, M.: Regional discrimination as a quasi-form of racial discrimination: comparing the protection under anglo-american, p. 39. American University International Law Review, International and Chinese Laws (2024)

16. Shaffer, M.A., Joplin, J.R.W., Bell, M.P., Lau, T., Oguz, C.: Gender discrimination and job-related outcomes: a cross-cultural comparison of working women in the United States and China. J. Vocat. Behav. **57**, 395–427 (2000). https://doi.org/10.1006/jvbe.1999.1748

17. Hunkenschroer, A.L., Kriebitz, A.: Is AI recruiting (un)ethical? A human rights perspective on the use of AI for hiring. AI Ethics **3**, 199–213 (2023). https://doi.org/10.1007/s43681-022-00166-4

18. Adamovic, M.: Analyzing discrimination in recruitment: a guide and best practices for resume studies. Int. J. Sel. Assess. **28**, 445–464 (2020). https://doi.org/10.1111/ijsa.12298

19. Van Turnhout K, et al.: Design patterns for mixed-method research in HCI. In: Proceedings of the 8th Nordic Conference on Human-Computer Interaction: Fun, Fast, Foundational, pp. 361–370. Association for Computing Machinery, New York, NY, USA, (2014)

20. Phillips R, et al.: Design Futures, Ecological Citizenship and Public Interest Technologies = HCI Regenerative Interaction Opportunities …? In: Kurosu, M., Hashizume, A. (eds.) Human-Computer Interaction. HCII 2024. NCS, vol. 14687. Springer, Cham (2024). https://doi.org/10.1007/978-3-031-60441-6_8

21. Gairola, R., Gray, C.M.: How is "Public Policy" used in HCI scholarship? In: Proceedings of the Extended ABSTRACTS of the CHI Conference on Human Factors in Computing Systems, pp. 1–8. Association for Computing Machinery, New York, NY, USA, (2025)

22. Lee, C., Cha, K.: FAT-CAT—explainability and augmentation for an AI system: a case study on AI recruitment-system adoption. Int. J. Hum Comput Stud. **171**, 102976 (2023). https://doi.org/10.1016/j.ijhcs.2022.102976
23. Laurim, V., Arpaci, S., Prommegger, B., Krcmar, H.: Computer, whom should i hire? – acceptance criteria for artificial intelligence in the recruitment process (2021)
24. Girona, A.E., Yarger, L.: To impress an algorithm: minoritized applicants' perceptions of fairness in AI hiring systems. In: Sserwanga, I., et al. (eds.) Wisdom, Well-Being, Win-Win. iConference 2024. LNCS, vol. 14597. Springer, Cham (2024). https://doi.org/10.1007/978-3-031-57860-1_4
25. Lee, M.K.: Understanding perception of algorithmic decisions: Fairness, trust, and emotion in response to algorithmic management. Big Data Soc. **5**, 2053951718756684 (2018). https://doi.org/10.1177/2053951718756684
26. Cai, F., Zhang, J., Zhang, L.: The impact of artificial intelligence replacing humans in making human resource management decisions on fairness: a case of resume screening. Sustainability **16**, 3840 (2024). https://doi.org/10.3390/su16093840
27. Awad, E., Balafoutas, L., Chen, L., Ip, E., Vecci, J.: Artificial intelligence and debiasing in hiring: impact on applicant quality and gender diversity (2023)
28. Vaishampayan, S., Farzanehpour, S., Brown, C.: Procedural justice and fairness in automated resume parsers for tech hiring: insights from candidate perspectives. In: 2023 IEEE Symposium on Visual Languages and Human-Centric Computing (VL/HCC), pp 103–108 (2023)
29. Dargnies, M.-P., Hakimov, R., Kübler, D.: Aversion to hiring algorithms: transparency, gender profiling, and self-confidence. Manage. Sci. (2024). https://doi.org/10.1287/mnsc.2022.02774
30. Peters, U., Carman, M.: Cultural bias in explainable AI research: a systematic analysis. J. Artific. Intell. Res. **79**, 971–1000 (2024). https://doi.org/10.1613/jair.1.14888
31. Fister, T., Thiruvathukal, G.: Exploring perceptions of algorithmic bias in video interviewing software: the importance of AI hiring education. RESPECT 2024 (2024)
32. Zhang, L., Yencha, C.: Examining perceptions towards hiring algorithms. Technol. Soc. **68**, 101848 (2022). https://doi.org/10.1016/j.techsoc.2021.101848
33. Avery, M., Leibbrandt, A., Vecci, J.: Does artificial intelligence help or hurt gender diversity? evidence from two field experiments on recruitment in tech (2023)
34. Park, H., Ahn, D., Hosanagar, K., Lee, J.: Human-AI interaction in human resource management: understanding why employees resist algorithmic evaluation at workplaces and how to mitigate burdens. In: Proceedings of the 2021 CHI Conference on Human Factors in Computing Systems, pp. 1–15. Association for Computing Machinery, New York, NY, USA, (2021)
35. Park, H., Ahn, D., Hosanagar, K., Lee, J.: Designing fair AI in human resource management: understanding tensions surrounding algorithmic evaluation and envisioning stakeholder-centered solutions. In: Proceedings of the 2022 CHI Conference on Human Factors in Computing Systems, pp. 1–22. Association for Computing Machinery, New York, NY, USA (2022)
36. Ochmann, J., Laumer, S.: Fairness as a determinant of AI adoption in recruiting: an interview-based study. DIGIT 2019 Proceedings (2019)
37. Figueroa-Armijos, M., Clark, B.B., da Motta Veiga, S.P.: Ethical perceptions of AI in hiring and organizational trust: the role of performance expectancy and social influence. J. Bus. Ethics **186**, 179–197 (2023). https://doi.org/10.1007/s10551-022-05166-2
38. Kim, J.-Y., Heo, W.: Artificial intelligence video interviewing for employment: perspectives from applicants, companies, developer and academicians. Inf. Technol. People **35**, 861–878 (2021). https://doi.org/10.1108/ITP-04-2019-0173

39. Suen, H.-Y., Chen, M.Y.-C., Lu, S.-H.: Does the use of synchrony and artificial intelligence in video interviews affect interview ratings and applicant attitudes? Comput. Hum. Behav. **98**, 93–101 (2019). https://doi.org/10.1016/j.chb.2019.04.012
40. Bankins, S., Formosa, P., Griep, Y., Richards, D.: AI decision making with dignity? contrasting workers' justice perceptions of human and AI decision making in a human resource management context. Inf. Syst. Front. **24**, 857–875 (2022). https://doi.org/10.1007/s10796-021-10223-8
41. Gonzalez, M.F., et al.: Allying with AI? Reactions toward human-based, AI/ML-based, and augmented hiring processes. Comput. Hum. Behav. **130**, 107179 (2022). https://doi.org/10.1016/j.chb.2022.107179
42. Chen, Z.: Collaboration among recruiters and artificial intelligence: removing human prejudices in employment. Cogn. Tech. Work **25**, 135–149 (2023). https://doi.org/10.1007/s10111-022-00716-0
43. Soleimani, M., Intezari, A., Pauleen, D.J.: Mitigating cognitive biases in developing AI-assisted recruitment systems: a knowledge-sharing approach. Int. J. Knowl. Manage. **18**, 1–18 (2021). https://doi.org/10.4018/IJKM.290022
44. Deshpande, K.V., Pan, S., Foulds, J.R.: Mitigating demographic bias in AI-based resume filtering. In: Adjunct Publication of the 28th ACM Conference on User Modeling, Adaptation and Personalization, pp. 268–275. Association for Computing Machinery, New York, NY, USA (2020)
45. Hou J, Chen X, Zhang W, Liao L, Zhu H (2024) Age Discrimination, Employment Barriers During the Prime Working Age and Career Behaviours
46. de Paula Couto M.C., et al.: Do we all perceive experiences of age discrimination in the same way? Cross-cultural differences in perceived age discrimination and its association with life satisfaction. Eur. J. Ageing **20**, 43 (2023). https://doi.org/10.1007/s10433-023-00790-x
47. Bach, T.A., Khan, A., Hallock, H., Beltrão, G., Sousa, S.: A systematic literature review of user trust in AI-enabled systems: an HCI perspective. Int. J. Hum.-Comput. Interact. **40**, 1251–1266 (2024). https://doi.org/10.1080/10447318.2022.2138826
48. Starke, C., Baleis, J., Keller, B., Marcinkowski, F.: Fairness perceptions of algorithmic decision-making: a systematic review of the empirical literature. Big Data Soc. **9**, 20539517221115188 (2022). https://doi.org/10.1177/20539517221115189
49. Chen, Z.: Ethics and discrimination in artificial intelligence-enabled recruitment practices. Humanit. Soc. Sci. Commun. **10**, 1–12 (2023). https://doi.org/10.1057/s41599-023-02079-x
50. Van Esch, P., Black, J.S.: Factors that influence new generation candidates to engage with and complete digital, AI-enabled recruiting. Bus. Horiz. **62**, 729–739 (2019). https://doi.org/10.1016/j.bushor.2019.07.004
51. Walker, D.O.H., Larson, M.: Leveraging generative Artificial Intelligence (AI) for human resource management: the AI job description assignment. J. Manag. Educ. **49**, 113–141 (2025). https://doi.org/10.1177/10525629241294075
52. Lacroux, A., Martin-Lacroux, C.: Should i trust the artificial intelligence to recruit? recruiters' perceptions and behavior when faced with algorithm-based recommendation systems during resume screening. Front. Psychol. **13** (2022). https://doi.org/10.3389/fpsyg.2022.895997
53. Rąb-Kettler, K., Lehnervp, B.: Recruitment in the times of machine learning. Manage. Syst. Product. Eng. **27**, 105–109 (2019). https://doi.org/10.1515/mspe-2019-0018
54. Rhea, A.K., et al.: An external stability audit framework to test the validity of personality prediction in AI hiring. Data Min. Knowl. Disc. **36**, 2153–2193 (2022). https://doi.org/10.1007/s10618-022-00861-0
55. Booth, B.M., Hickman, L., Subburaj, S.K., Tay, L., Woo, S.E., D'Mello, S.K.: Bias and fairness in multimodal machine learning: a case study of automated video interviews. In: Proceedings of the 2021 International Conference on Multimodal Interaction, pp. 268–277. Association for Computing Machinery, New York, NY, USA (2021)

56. Johnson, R.D., Stone, D.L., Lukaszewski, K.M.: The benefits of eHRM and AI for talent acquisition. J. Tour. Futures **7**, 40–52 (2020). https://doi.org/10.1108/JTF-02-2020-0013

57. Rosenthal-von der Pütten, A.M., Sach, A.: Michael is better than Mehmet: exploring the perils of algorithmic biases and selective adherence to advice from automated decision support systems in hiring. Front. Psychol. **15** (2024). https://doi.org/10.3389/fpsyg.2024.1416504

58. Andrews, L., Bucher, H.: Automating discrimination: AI hiring practices and gender inequality. Cardozo L Rev. **44**, 145–202 (2022)

59. Armstrong, L., Liu, A., MacNeil, S., Metaxa, D.: The silicon ceiling: auditing GPT's race and gender biases in hiring. In: Proceedings of the 4th ACM Conference on Equity and Access in Algorithms, Mechanisms, and Optimization, pp. 1–18. Association for Computing Machinery, New York, NY, USA (2024)

60. Baker, R.S., Hawn, A.: Algorithmic bias in education. Int. J. Artif. Intell. Educ. **32**, 1052–1092 (2022). https://doi.org/10.1007/s40593-021-00285-9

61. Choung, H., Seberger, J.S., David, P.: When AI is perceived to be fairer than a human: understanding perceptions of algorithmic decisions in a job application context. Int. J. Hum.-Comput. Interact. **40**, 7451–7468 (2024). https://doi.org/10.1080/10447318.2023.2266244

62. Batinovic, L., Howe, M., Sinclair, S., Carlsson, R.: Ageism in hiring: a systematic review and meta-analysis of age discrimination. Collabra: Psychol. **9**, 82194 (2023). https://doi.org/10.1525/collabra.82194

63. Liu, Q., Jiang, H., Pan, Z., Han, Q., Peng, Z., Li, Q.: BiasEye: a bias-aware real-time interactive material screening system for impartial candidate assessment. In: Proceedings of the 29th International Conference on Intelligent User Interfaces, pp. 325–343. Association for Computing Machinery, New York, NY, USA (2024)

64. Schulte Steinberg, A.L., Hohenberger, C.: Can AI close the gender gap in the job market? Individuals' preferences for AI evaluations. Comput. Hum. Behav. Reports **10**, 100287 (2023). https://doi.org/10.1016/j.chbr.2023.100287

65. Teodorescu, M.H.M., Ordabayeva, N., Kokkodis, M., Unnam, A., Aggarwal, V.: Identifying Systematic Bias in Human Graders for Automated Hiring Systems (2022)

66. Cruz, I.F.: Rethinking artificial intelligence: algorithmic bias and ethical issues| how process experts enable and constrain fairness in AI-driven hiring. Int. J. Commun. **18**, 21 (2023)

67. Acikgoz, Y., Davison, K.H., Compagnone, M., Laske, M.: Justice perceptions of artificial intelligence in selection. Int. J. Sel. Assess. **28**, 399–416 (2020). https://doi.org/10.1111/ijsa.12306

68. Mirowska, A., Mesnet, L.: Preferring the devil you know: Potential applicant reactions to artificial intelligence evaluation of interviews. Hum. Resour. Manag. J. **32**, 364–383 (2022). https://doi.org/10.1111/1748-8583.12393

69. Lavanchy, M., Reichert, P., Narayanan, J., Savani, K.: Applicants' fairness perceptions of algorithm-driven hiring procedures. J. Bus. Ethics **188**, 125–150 (2023). https://doi.org/10.1007/s10551-022-05320-w

70. Li, L., Lassiter, T., Oh, J., Lee, M.K.: Algorithmic hiring in practice: recruiter and HR professional's perspectives on AI use in hiring. In: Proceedings of the 2021 AAAI/ACM Conference on AI, Ethics, and Society, pp. 166–176. Association for Computing Machinery, New York, NY, USA (2021)

71. Teodorescu, M.H.M., Ordabayeva, N., Unnam, A., Aggarwal, V.: Determining systematic differences in human graders for machine learning-based automated hiring

72. Black, J.S., van Esch, P.: AI-enabled recruiting: what is it and how should a manager use it? Bus. Horiz. **63**, 215–226 (2020). https://doi.org/10.1016/j.bushor.2019.12.001

73. Horodyski, P.: Applicants' perception of artificial intelligence in the recruitment process. Comput. Hum. Behav. Reports **11**, 100303 (2023). https://doi.org/10.1016/j.chbr.2023.100303

74. Fumagalli, E., Rezaei, S., Salomons, A.: OK computer: worker perceptions of algorithmic recruitment. Res. Policy **51**, 104420 (2022). https://doi.org/10.1016/j.respol.2021.104420
75. Nørskov, S., Damholdt, M.F., Ulhøi, J.P., Jensen, M.B., Ess, C., Seibt, J.: Applicant fairness perceptions of a robot-mediated job interview: a video vignette-based experimental survey (2020). https://doi.org/10.3389/frobt.2020.586263

Reflective Questioning by AI-Powered Virtual Assistants and Human Visitors in Digital Museums

Jiatong Liu[1] (iD), Yingru Ji[2] (iD), and Bo Lu[3(✉)] (iD)

[1] The Ohio State University, Columbus, OH 43210, USA
[2] University of British Columbia, Vancouver, BC V6T 1Z4, Canada
[3] Shenyang Normal University, Shenyang 110034, Liaoning, China
luboguavarian@outlook.com

Abstract. This study investigates the impact of reflective questioning by human visitors and AI-powered virtual assistants in digital museums. Reflective questioning, which encourages deeper engagement with exhibits, enhances cognitive processing and emotional involvement. The study consists of two parts. In Study 1, a one-factor between-subjects design is used to compare the effectiveness of reflective questioning posed by either human visitors or AIVAs in a controlled online museum environment. Study 2 further explores the mediating roles of emotional engagement and mental cognition that contribute to attitudes toward the conversation. The results show that emotional engagement plays a partially mediating role in the reflective questioning and attitudes toward the conversation. Human-initiated reflective questioning fosters stronger emotional engagement, whereas AIVA-driven questioning has a less effect. This research advances the understanding of AI-mediated engagement in digital museums and offers practical insights for designing interactive museum experiences that foster deeper visitor involvement.

Keywords: Reflective Questioning · AI-Powered Virtual Assistants · Digital Museums

1 Introduction

In recent years, Artificial Intelligence (AI) technologies have reshaped the digital museum landscape, introducing innovative tools that enhance accessibility, engagement, and interactivity for visitors. Among these advancements, AI-powered virtual assistants (AIVAs) have gained prominence for their ability to provide real-time guidance, personalized recommendations, and interactive storytelling. AIVAs function as intelligent systems that assist museum visitors by answering inquiries, offering relevant information, and facilitating exhibit navigation, thereby enhancing the overall visitor experience [1]. By delivering tailored tours and dynamic content, AIVAs seek to create more engaging and interactive museum experiences. Traditional AIVAs have already been adopted in museum environments. For instance, AI-powered chatbots with embodiment and reflection features have been found to enhance visitor learning and interaction with museum exhibits [2].

F. F.-H Nah and K. L. Siau (Eds.): HCII 2025, LNCS 16343, pp. 22–31, 2026.
https://doi.org/10.1007/978-3-032-13167-6_2

Reflective questioning, which prompts visitors to think more deeply about their experiences or the content being presented, has been shown to enhance engagement and cognitive processing [3]. Unlike conventional answer-seeking questions, which focus on factual information retrieval, reflective questions encourage individuals to analyze, evaluate, and form personal connections with the subject matter [3, 4]. In digital museums, this questioning approach shifts visitors from passive information consumption to active engagement, allowing them to interact more meaningfully with exhibits [5]. Despite the growing use of AIVAs in museum settings, little is known about how the source of reflective questioning—a human visitor versus an AIVA—affects visitor attitudes toward the conversation in digital museums. This study specifically examines the role of reflective questioning in AI-human interactions within the context of online museum tours. To address this gap, the study aims to compare the effectiveness of reflective questioning posed by a human visitor versus an AIVA and examines the underlying psychological mechanisms—emotional engagement and mental cognition—that mediate these effects. By doing so, this study contributes to theoretical discussions on AI-mediated engagement in digital museums and provide practical insights for designing interactive museum experiences that optimize visitor attitudes and engagement.

2 Literature Review and Hypotheses Development

2.1 AI-Powered Virtual Assistants in Digital Museum

AI-powered virtual assistants (AIVAs) in digital museums leverage artificial intelligence technologies—such as natural language processing, machine learning, and computer vision—to enhance visitor experiences [6]. These intelligent systems interact with visitors via text or voice, offering personalized guidance and support. AIVAs assist with a range of tasks, including answering questions, delivering educational content, recommending exhibits based on visitor preferences, and generating reflective or thought-provoking questions to foster deeper engagement with art and exhibits [7].

As digital transformation continues to reshape museums, AIVAs are increasingly integrated into websites, mobile apps, and on-site installations, enabling interactive and immersive exhibit exploration. The adoption of AI and Mixed Reality (MR) technologies has further expanded the possibilities for visitor engagement [7]. Similarly, the National Museum of Australia employs a voice-enabled AI assistant powered by Amazon Alexa [8]. By utilizing natural language processing, Alexa interprets and responds to spoken commands, enabling hands-free interaction and improving accessibility for exhibit navigation. Echo, another voice assistant, enhances museum navigation by providing visitors with exhibit information and answering questions on historical topics [9]. Unlike screen-based interactions, Echo facilitates a more immersive and accessible experience, particularly benefiting visitors with visual impairments or those who prefer voice-based interaction.

2.2 Reflective Questioning

Reflective questioning is a technique designed to stimulate deeper thinking, self-reflection, and engagement with a topic or experience [3]. The primary purpose of reflective questioning is to provoke critical thinking, enhance learning, and foster deeper understanding by addressing both the emotional and intellectual experiences [4]. This active engagement can increase the perceived value and enjoyment of an experience, leading to more positive feedback and fostering an interactive environment. In digital museums, reflective questioning serves as a specialized engagement strategy that extends the traditional role of AIVAs and interactive systems [4]. These systems are designed to provide information and to encourage deeper reflection and personal connection with museum content.

Reflective questioning can be applied across various digital museum contexts. In VR/AR environments, it prompts visitors to reflect on the historical, emotional, or thematic significance of immersive digital reconstructions [9]. In digital art museums, reflective questioning encourages visitors to think critically about the emotional content and deeper meaning behind artworks [4]. The integration of reflective questioning enhances visitor interaction in digital museums. Unlike traditional answer-seeking questions, which have dominated question generation and conversational AI systems [5], reflective questions play a key role in improving engagement. By shifting the focus from mere information retrieval to active meaning-making, reflective questioning fosters a more immersive and cognitively engaging museum experience.

2.3 Hypotheses Development

We expect that reflective questioning by human visitors will have a more positive influence on attitudes toward the conversation compared to reflective questioning by AIVAs in digital museums for several reasons. First, human visitors are capable of asking reflective questions, which can provoke deeper thinking and reflection [3]. This deeper thinking often leads to more positive attitudes towards the interaction [10]. In addition, visitors may experience a stronger positive attitude toward the conversation when their engagement is increased through reflective questioning. By actively involving visitors in the conversation, rather than letting them passively receive information, reflective questioning encourages them to share their ideas, opinions, and thoughts [11], leading to a greater sense of involvement and increased positive attitude toward the conversation. Third, the human touch in communication enhances perceptions of authenticity and credibility, making the conversation feel more meaningful and relatable [12]. Given these factors, reflective questioning by human visitors is likely to be provoke more reflecting, engaging, and credible resonant compared to AIVA-led questioning.

Based on this reasoning, we propose the following hypothesis:

H1: Reflective questioning by human visitors will bring more positive attitudes towards the conversation compared with reflective questioning by AIVAs in digital museums.

We further expect that emotional engagement will mediate the effect of reflective questioning on attitudes toward the conversation in digital museums. When visitors engage in reflective questioning, they are more likely to be emotionally stimulated as they connect with the exhibits on a deeper level. Reflective questions encourage visitors to explore their thoughts and emotions related to the exhibits, making their experience more meaningful and impactful [4]. This thereby leads to an increased positive attitude toward the conversation as visitors feel more emotionally invested in the conversation.

Furthermore, visitors are more likely to notice the emotional aspects of the exhibits when they engage in reflective questioning. They are prompted to consider the emotional layer conveyed by the exhibits. Enabling a deeper, more personal connection with the content [13]. Such a connection may result in a greater positive attitude toward the conversation. Therefore, we propose:

H2: *In digital museums, emotional engagement will act as a mediator between reflective questioning and the human visitor's positive attitude toward the conversation.*

We expect that mental cognition will mediate the effect of reflective questioning on attitudes toward the conversation in digital museums. First, reflective questioning encourages visitors to engage in deeper thought and critical analysis of the exhibits, prompting cognitive processing that enhances understanding and engagement with the content [3]. As visitors process the information more deeply, they are more likely to appreciate the complexity and relevance of the exhibits, which can enhance their evaluation of the conversation itself. Second, mental cognition fosters greater interest in the subject, as visitors consider the historical context, underlying themes, and various perspectives related to the exhibits. This deeper cognitive involvement helps visitors form more thoughtful and positive attitudes toward the conversation, as they are better able to appreciate the significance and value of the exhibits [14]. Third, as visitors engage more cognitively with the content, they are likely to develop a more thoughtful and intellectual connection to the conversation [14], which contributes to more positive attitudes toward the interaction. Therefore,

H3: *In digital museums, mental cognition will act as a mediator between reflective questioning and the human visitor's positive attitude toward the conversation.*

3 Methodology

This research aims to explore the effects of reflective questioning by an AIVA versus human visitors in an online museum setting. In Study 1, we examine the effect of reflective questioning on attitudes towards conversation using a one-factor between-subjects design with two conditions (AIVA vs. human visitor) in a controlled online museum environment. In Study 2, we build upon Study 1 by examining the mediating processes underlying the effects of reflective questioning. We focus on the roles of emotional engagement and mental cognition as mediators of the impact on attitude towards the conversation. The aim is to understand how these psychological processes contribute to the change in attitude observed in Study 1, providing insight into the mechanisms behind the effect of reflective questioning by an AIVA and a human visitor. The procedures for these studies were approved by ethics committees.

3.1 Study 1: Main Effect: Reflective Questioning in an Online Museum Setting

In Study 1, we test the effect of reflective questioning on attitude towards conversation using a one-factor between-subjects design with two agents (AIVA vs. human visitor) in a controlled online museum setting. Specifically, we examine whether exposure to reflective questions from either an AIVA or a human visitor influences participants' attitude towards the conversation during a museum tour.

Participants and Procedure. We recruited 62 participants through the Credamo platform, but could not record the responses of 12 participants who failed attention checks during the study, leading to a final sample of $N = 50$ ($M_{age} = 29.4$years, $SD_{age} = 8.22$; 66% female, 34% male). Participants received monetary compensation for their participation and were randomly assigned to one of two conditions: reflective questioning by an AIVA or by a human visitor. Each participant was instructed to explore a digital artwork while engaging in an interaction conversation with an AIVA or a human visitor. The conversation was designed to encourage reflective thinking about the artwork, and participants were unaware of the experimental manipulation until debriefed at the end of the study. Participants viewed one artwork displayed in the virtual museum environment. The AIVA or human visitor engaged them with reflective questioning, such as: "What is the theme of this painting?", "What feelings are conveyed in this painting?" and "What is the message of the artwork?" [4].

We measured attitude toward the presented conversation using a validated 7-point Likert scale (1 = "strongly disagree," and 7 = "strongly agree") adapted form [15] (e.g., "The AIVA is good.", "The AIVA is favorable." and "The AIVA assistant is likable."). Participants rated how positively or negatively they felt about the conversational experience. Additionally, we included a manipulation check, asking participants whether they perceived the AIVA's questions as reflective or as simple question-and-answer.

The questionnaire also collected demographic information, including: frequency of museum visits, knowledge of art, familiarity with AIVA, gender, age group, highest level of education, and occupation type.

Results and Discussion. To ensure the manipulation check, we asked participants whether they perceived the questions posed by an AIVA or human visitor as reflective or as simple question-and-answer. A chi-square test confirmed the effectiveness of the reflective questioning manipulation ($\chi^2(1) = 2.885, p = 0.089$, Cramer's V $= .088$). We identify $p < 0.1$ because the sample size in this study may not have been large enough to achieve the typical $p < 0.05$ level of statistical significance, suggesting the need for future studies with larger sample sizes.

We tested the effect of reflective questioning on attitude towards the conversation using an analysis of variance (ANOVA), with condition (AIVA vs. human visitor) as the independent variable and attitude towards the conversation as the dependent variable. As shown in Fig. 1, the results indicate the expected pattern. Specifically, participants in the human visitor condition ($M = 6.013$, SD $= 0.597$) reported significantly more positive attitudes towards the conversation than those in the AIVA condition ($M = 5.280$, SD $= 1.197$). The ANOVA revealed a significant effect of condition on attitude towards the conversation ($F(1, 48) = 7.517, p = 0.009, \eta^2 = 0.135$), indicating that reflective questioning by human visitor led to more favorable attitudes towards the conversation, supporting *H1*.

3.2 Study 2: Emotional Engagement and Mental Cognition as Potential Underlying Processes

Study 2 consists of two parts. The first part examines the effect of reflective questioning on attitude towards the conversation during an online museum tour, using a one-factor

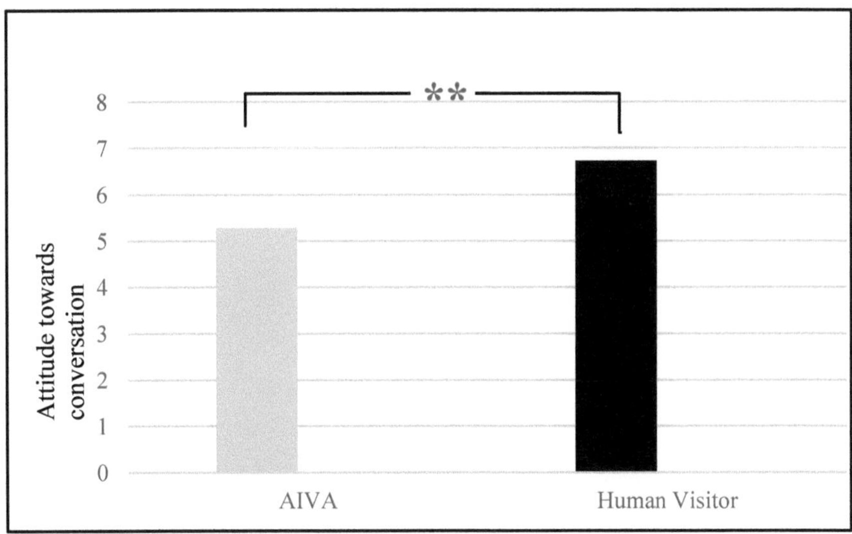

Fig. 1. Results Study 1. **$p < .01$.

between-subjects design with two experimental conditions (reflective questioning by an AIVA vs. reflective questioning by a human visitor). In this part of the study, participants were randomly assigned to one of the two experimental conditions, where they interacted with an AI assistant or a human visitor who posed reflective questions related to the artwork in the virtual museum.

The second part of the study investigates potential mediators that could explain the effect of reflective questioning on attitude towards the conversation. Specifically, we explore the roles of emotional engagement and mental cognition as mediating variables. The goal is to understand how emotional engagement (feeling emotionally connected to the artwork) and mental cognition (reflecting on the meaning and personal relevance of the artwork) contribute to the positive change in attitude towards the conversation.

Participants and Procedure. A total of 93 participants (68% female, 32% male) were recruited through the Credamo platform, with a final sample of $N = 88$ ($M_{age} = 28.64$ years, $SD_{age} = 7.64$). Participants received monetary compensation for their participation. The study was conducted in an online setting, where participants presented interaction with either AIVA or a human visitor who posed reflective questions related to the artwork in the virtual museum.

The main dependent variable was attitude towards the conversation, measured with a 7-point Likert scale. We measured participants' emotional engagement and mental cognition using a 7-point Likert scale (1 = "strongly disagree," and 7 = "strongly agree"). Emotional engagement was assessed with items adapted from [14], such as "The artwork's elements evoke profound emotions in me.", "The artwork fills me with happiness." and "The AIVA's questions made me connect more deeply with the artwork". Mental cognition was assessed with items adapted from [14], such as "I have a clear understanding of the artwork.", "Understanding the artwork is effortless for me." and "I actively think about and analyze the deeper meaning of the artwork". Table 1 shows the items used to measure the variables in the study.

Table 1. Items of variables.

Variables	Adapted items	Reference
Emotional engagement	EE1: The artwork's elements evoke profound emotions in me EE2: The artwork fills me with happiness EE3: The questions made me connect more deeply with the artwork	(Ahmed et al., 2024) [14]
Mental cognition	MC1. I have a clear understanding of the artwork MC2. Understanding the artwork is effortless for me MC3. I actively think about and analyze the deeper meaning of the artwork	
Attitude toward the conversation	ATT1: The conversation is good ATT2: The conversation assistant is likable ATT3: The conversation is favorable	(Li & Sung, 2021) [15]

Results and Discussion. First, we conducted three separate ANOVAs to test the effect of condition (AIVAs vs. human visitors) on the attitude and the two mediators (emotional engagement and mental cognition). Participants in the reflective questioning by AIVA group ($M_{AIVA} = 5.222$, $SD_{AIVA} = 1.099$) scored lower than those the reflective questioning by human visitor group ($M_{HV} = 5.967$, $SD_{HV} = 0.494$; $F(1, 86) = 15.696$, $p < .001$, $\eta2 = 0.154$) on attitude. Similarly, the reflective questioning by AIVA ($M_{AIVA} = 5.528$, $SD_{AIVA} = 0.792$) led to lower mental cognition compared to human visitor questioning ($M_{HV} = 5.858$, $SD_{HV} = 0.687$; $F(1, 86) = 4.277$, $p = .042$, $\eta2 = 0.047$). Likewise, emotional engagement was significantly lower in the AIVA group ($M_{AIVA} = 5.410$, $SD_{AIVA} = 0.800$) than in the human visitor group ($M_{HV} = 5.742$, $SD_{HV} = 0.634$; $F(1, 86) = 4.522$, $p = .036$, $\eta2 = 0.050$).

We then proceeded with a mediation analysis. The correlation between mental cognition and the dependent variable (Attitude) is $r = .5374$ ($p < .001$), indicating a significant positive relationship between mental cognition and attitude. The correlation between the mental mediator and the dependent variable is $r = .373$, $p < .001$, while the correlation between the emotional mediator and the dependent variable is $r = .720$, $p < .001$. Furthermore, discriminant validity was confirmed as the heterotrait-monotrait (HTMT) ratio of correlations among all constructs remained below the recommended .85 cutoff [16].

A parallel mediation analysis was conducted using PROCESS (Model 4; Hayes, 2018 [17]) with bias-corrected bootstrapping and 10,000 subsamples to estimate the indirect effects, with a 95% confidence interval (CI). As illustrated in Fig. 2, reflective questioning by AIVA significantly reduced both mental cognition and emotional engagement ($\beta_{Mental} = -0.331$, $p_{Mental} = .042$; $\beta_{Emotional} = -0.332$, $p_{Emotional} = .036$), indicating that participants in the AIVA condition reported lower scores on both mediators compared to those in the human visitor condition. Furthermore, only emotional engagement significantly predicted attitude ($\beta = 0.903$, $p < .001$), whereas mental cognition did not have a significant effect on attitude ($\beta = -0.097$, $p = .369$). Importantly, the indirect effect of condition (AIVA vs. human visitor) on attitude is significant through emotional engagement (indirect effect = -0.300, BootSE = 0.147, 95% CI: [-0.610, -0.030]) supporting *H2*, but not through mental cognition (indirect effect = 0.032, BootSE = 0.047, 95% CI: [-0.064, 0.131]), which provides no support for *H3*. The direct effect of condition on attitude remains significant (direct effect = -0.477, $p = .0009$, 95% CI: [-0.752, -0.201]), suggesting that reflective questioning by AIVA negatively affects attitude, partially mediated by emotional engagement.

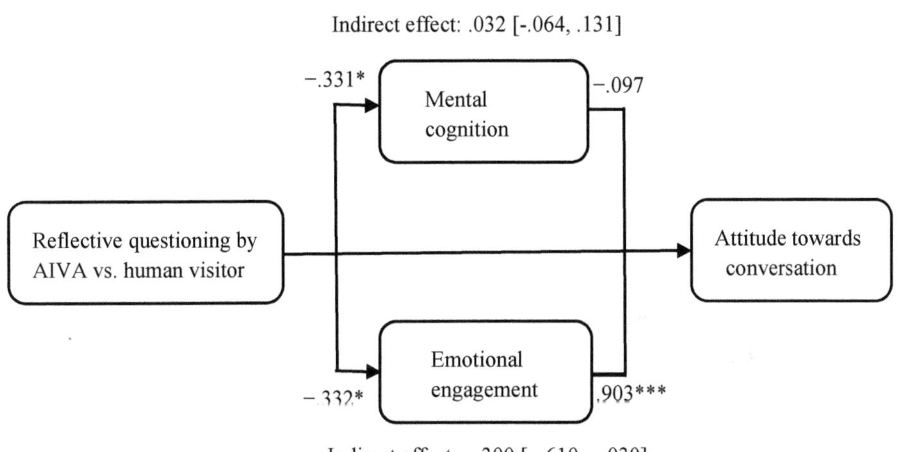

Fig. 2. Parallel Mediation Analysis. *p < .05. ***p < .001.

4   Methodology

Existing research on digital museums focuses on immersive experiences [18], tour guide systems [7], and AR/VR technologies [19], with comparatively less emphasis on the role of visitor-initiated questioning in conversational interactions. This study introduces the concept of reflective questioning, derived from educational psychology, into the human-AI dialogue context of digital museums, providing theoretical insights into the design of AI-driven conversational interactions to foster deeper visitor engagement.

Furthermore, this study examines how visitor-initiated reflective questioning, compared to AIVA-driven reflective questioning, influences attitude, with a particular focus on the mediating role of emotional engagement. By identifying the mechanisms, this study advances the understanding of emotional engagement in digital museum interactions.

Practically, this research offers actionable insights for museum designers and AI developers, highlighting the potential benefits of granting visitors in the questioning process. When visitors have the autonomy to pose reflective questions, their conversational attitude may improve. Therefore, in designing AIVA, museums should consider interface design and functional settings that encourage visitors to formulate their own inquiries, rather than relying solely on system-generated questions. This study also reveals that when visitors actively formulate reflective questions, they are more likely to develop positive emotional engagement. For digital museums, this suggests that interactive platforms, Q&A spaces, or online communities can facilitate visitor engagement by enabling them to freely express inquiries, curiosities, and insights.

Our research objective has been to introduce reflective questioning in virtual museum and begin to shed light on its effects and underlying processes, an effort that can produce additional questions and avenues for future research. For instance, the sample size and the selection of participants could introduce some biases, as participants were recruited from a single platform, which may not be fully representative of the broader museum-going population. Additionally, the study's controlled online setting, while allowing for a rigorous experimental design, may not capture the complexities of real-world museum visits. The findings might differ when applied in physical museum contexts, where environmental and social factors play a larger role. Future studies could include more diverse participant groups and explore both virtual and physical museum settings to validate the findings in different contexts. Moreover, there are likely many moderators that still need to be uncovered to better understand when reflective questioning is effective or not. Clearly, there are powerful moderators such as the type of reflective questioning used (e.g., open-ended vs. closed-ended questions), and the perceived credibility or empathy of the agent posing the questions, that could amplify or attenuate the effects of reflective questioning on corresponding behaviors.

Acknowledgments. The authors thank the anonymous reviewers.

Disclosure of Interests. The authors have no competing interests to declare that are relevant to the content of this article.

References

1. Pandey, P., Rai, A.K.: Consumer adoption of AI-powered virtual assistants (AIVA): an integrated model based on the SEM–ANN approach. FIIB Bus. Rev. (2023). https://doi.org/10.1177/23197145231196066
2. Noh, Y.G., Hong, J.H.: Designing reenacted chatbots to enhance museum experience. Appl. Sci. **11**(16), 1–15 (2021). https://doi.org/10.3390/app11167420

3. Malthouse, R., Watts, M., Roffey-Barentsen, J.: Reflective questions, self-questioning and managing professionally situated practice. Res. Educ. **94**(1), 71–87 (2015). https://doi.org/10.7227/RIE.0024

4. Gollapalli, S., Das, M., Du, M., Ng, S.-K.: Generating reflective questions for engaging gallery visitors in ArtMuse. In: Procccdings of the 37th AAAI Conference on Artificial Intelligence (AAAI 2023), pp. 16434–16436. https://doi.org/10.1609/aaai.v37i13.27070 (2023)

5. Gao, J., Galley, M., Li, L.: Neural approaches to conversational AI: Question answering, task-oriented dialogues and social chatbots. Now Foundations and Trends (2019)

6. Trichopoulos, G., Konstantakis, M., Alexandridis, G., Caridakis, G.: Large language models as recommendation systems in museums. Electronics **12**(18), 1–16 (2023). https://doi.org/10.3390/electronics12183829

7. Li, J., Zheng, X., Watanabe, I., Ochiai, Y.: A systematic review of digital transformation technologies in museum exhibition. Comput. Hum. Behav. **161**, 108407 (2024). https://doi.org/10.1016/j.chb.2024.108407

8. Shih, W., Rivero, E.: Virtual voice assistants. ALA TechSource (2020). https://doi.org/10.5860/ltr.56n4

9. Yu, T.-C., Huang, M.-X., Liu, Y.-H., Wu, H.-Y.: A systematic review of integrating mixed reality and artificial intelligence in museums: Enhancing visitor experiences and innovating exhibit design. In: Proceedings of the 58th Hawaii International Conference on System Sciences (2025), pp. 1533–1542

10. Gibbs, G.: Learning by doing: a guide to teaching and learning methods. Further Education Unit (1998)

11. Lombardi, B.M.M., Oblinger, D.G.: Authentic learning for the 21st century: an overview. Educause Learn. Initiat. **1**, 1–12 (2007). https://doi.org/10.7748/ns.29.52.8.s5

12. McLean, G., Osei-Frimpong, K., Wilson, A., Pitardi, V.: How live chat assistants drive travel consumers' attitudes, trust, and purchase intentions: the role of human touch. Int. J. Contemp. Hosp. Manag. **32**(5), 1795–1812 (2020). https://doi.org/10.1108/IJCHM-07-2019-0605

13. Elliot, A.J., Dweck, C.S.: Handbook of competence and motivation. Guilford Publications (2013)

14. Ahmed, S., Sharif, T., Ting, D.H., Sharif, S.J.: Crafting emotional engagement and immersive experiences: comprehensive scale development for and validation of hospitality marketing storytelling involvement. Psychol. Mark. **41**(7), 1514–1529 (2024). https://doi.org/10.1002/mar.21994

15. Li, X., Sung, Y.: Anthropomorphism brings us closer: the mediating role of psychological distance in User–AI assistant interactions. Comput. Hum. Behav. **118**, 106680 (2021). https://doi.org/10.1016/j.chb.2021.106680

16. Voorhees, C.M., Brady, M.K., Calantone, R., Ramirez, E.: Discriminant validity testing in marketing: an analysis, causes for concern, and proposed remedies. J. Acad. Mark. Sci. **44**(1), 119–134 (2016). https://doi.org/10.1007/s11747-015-0455-4

17. Hayes, A.F.: Introduction to mediation, moderation, and conditional process analysis: a regression-based approach. The Guilford Press, New York; London (2018)

18. Guo, K., Fan, A., Lehto, X., Day, J.: Immersive digital tourism: The role of multisensory cues in digital museum experiences. J. Hospit. Tour. Res. **47**, 1017–1039 (2023). https://doi.org/10.1177/10963480211030319

19. Bachiller, C., Monzo, J.M., Rey, B.: Augmented and virtual reality to enhance the didactical experience of technological heritage museums. Appl. Sci. **13**(6) (2023). https://doi.org/10.3390/app13063539

Beyond Words
Exploring User Engagement with AI-Generated Visual News Summaries

Julia Christine Mittermayr and Martin Stabauer[(✉)]

Johannes Kepler University, Linz, Austria
`martin.stabauer@jku.at`

Abstract. In an increasingly visual and fast-paced media landscape, traditional text-heavy news formats struggle to maintain user engagement, especially among mobile and social media users. This study explores the potential of generative artificial intelligence (AI) tools to create image-based news summaries that are semantically accurate and emotionally resonant. Specifically, we investigate how current text-to-image models perform in summarizing real-world news content, and how users perceive the resulting visuals.

We conducted a quantitative survey with 63 participants who were shown AI-generated images corresponding to short news articles. The participants rated the images in four dimensions: content accuracy, emotional tone, visual quality, and independent comprehensibility. ChatGPT 4o consistently outperformed other models, receiving the highest scores in all categories. However, no model succeeded in conveying the full complexity of the article without limitations. In addition, we collected data on news consumption habits and AI usage frequency. The results indicate strong correlations between positive image ratings and demographic factors such as age, gender, and education level. Younger university-educated users, particularly those who frequently use AI tools, responded most positively to the generated visuals.

In general, our findings highlight both the promise and current limitations of AI-generated news images. Although editorial oversight remains necessary, the tools under review offer a valuable opportunity to improve accessibility, inclusion, and engagement, especially in the context of digital transformation in journalism.

Keywords: Artificial Intelligence · Image Generation · News Summarization · Visual Communication · User Perception · Accessibility

1 Introduction

In a digital information landscape shaped by mobile usage, social media platforms, and short attention spans, traditional text-based news formats face increasing limitations. Readers are frequently overwhelmed by the volume of

F. F.-H Nah and K. L. Siau (Eds.): HCII 2025, LNCS 16343, pp. 32–44, 2026.
https://doi.org/10.1007/978-3-032-13167-6_3

information presented to them, leading to selective attention, reduced engagement, and even avoidance of important but text-heavy content. According to recent studies, more than half of Internet users in German-speaking countries report feeling overwhelmed by the flood of digital news and updates [7]. In parallel, a recent study shows that a considerable share of the adult population lacks basic reading competencies, making it difficult for them to engage meaningfully with news content [10]. In particular, on social networks and mobile platforms, text-heavy content faces declining user engagement, while visually appealing elements, such as images and emojis, consistently drive higher interaction rates [1].

In response to these developments, media organizations and news agencies are under growing pressure to create content that is more accessible, emotionally engaging, and digestible in a short time. An emerging solution is the use of visual communication strategies, particularly images generated by artificial intelligence (AI), to visually summarize news content. These images are not just illustrations, but are intended to represent the key takeaways of a news story in a single aesthetically appealing frame. The goal is for viewers to understand the main message of the article in a glance, without reading the full text, thus supporting rapid orientation, emotional engagement, and inclusive access to information.

This study investigates how AI-based tools can support the automated creation of such image-based news summaries. Specifically, we want to understand:

RQ1: How capable are current text-to-image models in generating semantically accurate and visually appealing representations of news articles?

And further,

RQ2: How do users perceive and evaluate the resulting images in terms of representativeness, emotional tone, and design quality?

The target audience for such formats includes everyday news consumers, but especially those who rely on mobile interfaces and are accustomed to image-based information processing on platforms like Instagram, TikTok, and mobile news apps.

The motivation for this research is two-fold: First, a research gap in how generative AI can be used in applied journalism and media production, and second, to understand how such formats can enhance accessibility and inclusiveness. The European Union Directive 2019/882 ("Accessibility Act") requires digital content providers, including news media, to offer formats that are understandable for people with cognitive or linguistic limitations. Visually summarized news stories could be one way to fulfill this obligation while also improving user engagement and content visibility.

2 Related Work

2.1 Generative AI in Journalism and News Summarization

The emergence of powerful generative AI models has caused significant transformations in journalism and news production. OpenAI's release of ChatGPT in late 2022 famously captured the imagination of both the public and the news industry. Its success encouraged other tech companies to introduce competing large language models (e.g., Google's Bard, Anthropic's Claude, Meta's LLaMA) and AI-assisted tools in 2023. Throughout 2023, news organizations around the world scrambled to understand what generative AI would mean for news gathering, production, and distribution. Several international initiatives were launched, from the LSE JournalismAI survey to the WAN-IFRA global survey, to map this impact. Empirical research by the Associated Press in late 2023 found that almost three-quarters of the journalists surveyed had already experimented with generative AI in their work [3].

Such rapid uptake underscores a global trend: journalists in regions as diverse as sub-Saharan Africa and Latin America have begun to integrate generative AI into their workflows [9]. This momentum reflects optimism about the potential of AI to improve newsroom efficiency and production, but is accompanied by early cautionary discussions about ethics and best practices [3].

One major application of AI in journalism is news summarization and content creation. Generative models can help draft articles, write headlines, and summarize complex information into digestible updates. In fact, news organizations have experimented with automated summaries for years – for example, the Associated Press uses natural language generation to produce brief story summaries for wire releases [6]. Earlier "automated journalism" systems relied on template-based techniques and structured data (e.g., for financial earnings or sports scores), but modern generative models markedly expand these capabilities. Models like GPT-3 and GPT-4 are adept at abstractive summarization, translation, and other language tasks, often performing at a level approaching human-written coherence. This has led some outlets to use AI to write news content. For example, CNET and Men's Journal drew attention by publishing AI-generated news pieces (with human oversight) in early 2023. These cases demonstrated both the promise and the pitfalls of AI-written journalism – while AI could produce fluent news copy, articles were later found to contain factual errors, highlighting ongoing concerns about accuracy [5].

In general, generative AI is already being used to support a range of newsroom tasks, including content creation, fact checking, data analysis, summarization, image generation, and even translation. News organizations report efficiency gains from these tools, but also face new challenges in maintaining transparency and editorial standards [9]. As industry observers note, generative AI offers "opportunities for productivity and new experiences" even as it raises serious questions about accuracy, source attribution, and the potential spread of misinformation [3]. These dual considerations of potential and risk set the stage for examining how AI can be responsibly deployed in news summarization and reporting.

2.2 Text-To-Image Generation for Visual Communication

Alongside text generation, advances in text-to-image models have opened new possibilities for visual communication in journalism. Recent multimodal generative AI systems such as DALL-E 2, Midjourney, and Stable Diffusion can produce high-quality images from textual prompts, often in a manner comparable to human-created visuals. For example, Cosmopolitan magazine garnered attention in 2022 for publishing a cover generated entirely by an AI model a novel illustration of a female astronaut to demonstrate the creative potential of these tools [6]. Such systems enable newsrooms to instantly generate custom illustrations or concept art that align with the content of a story. Researchers have begun to develop pipelines to integrate text-to-image generation into news workflows; for example, Liu et al. (2022) introduced the "Opal" system to automatically create news illustrations from article text [4].

The appeal of generative visuals is clear: they provide completely unique images on demand, reducing the need to rely on stock photos or wire photography. This is especially advantageous for abstract or underphotographed topics (e.g. cybersecurity threats, future scenarios) and for smaller newsrooms with limited budgets, which can now obtain custom graphics at minimal cost [6]. In fact, producing an image via an AI service like Midjourney is much cheaper and faster than commissioning a human illustrator, a fact that budget conscious editors do not miss [12]. By mid-2023, some online news sites were even using AI-generated pictures mixed with real stock photos to accompany articles [6]. Generative visual tools offer a new degree of flexibility and creative control in news design and illustration.

However, these benefits come with significant challenges and ethical implications. The photorealism of modern AI-generated images can blur the line between reality and fabrication, raising concerns about misinformation. Notwithstanding their creative uses, "the potential misuse and dangers of AI-generated news images are high", as noted by Paik et al. (2023), including the dissemination of fake news and the spread of misinformation/disinformation through synthetic visuals [6]. Several high-profile incidents have already been reported that illustrate these risks. In one instance, an AI-generated image that purported to show a former US president being arrested went viral on social media, garnering millions of views before it was debunked. In another case, a series of fake but highly realistic images of a nonexistent earthquake were widely upvoted on Reddit, with captions formatted like real news updates that misled users about the event. These examples demonstrate how easily a completely fabricated visual narrative can gain traction when produced by advanced generative models.

Since tools like DALL-E 2 and Midjourney can create images virtually indistinguishable from authentic news photographs, there is a tangible risk that unscrupulous actors (or even well-intentioned but careless users) could produce misleading visuals that erode public trust. News organizations are acutely aware that their credibility rests on conveying truth; if AI-generated illustrations are mistaken for real photojournalism or used to fabricate events, the integrity of news imagery as a 'objective' witness to reality could be fundamentally undermined [6]. This has prompted calls for strict editorial guidelines on how generative images should be used and labeled in news contexts. In summary, text-to-image generation offers exciting new storytelling tools for journalism, but it also forces the field to grapple with issues of authenticity, verification, and reader trust in the visual domain.

2.3   User Perception of AI-Generated Visuals

As generative AI becomes more integrated in journalism, audience perception has emerged as a key area of concern. Studies indicate that news labeled as "AI-generated" is often perceived as less trustworthy than human-authored content, even when the content is accurate [13]. This "AI disclosure dilemma" reflects a tension between transparency and credibility. With images, the issue is further amplified. Photorealistic AI-generated visuals can be difficult to distinguish from real photographs, leading to misinformation incidents when fake images circulated widely before being debunked [6]. Once viewers learn that an image was made by AI, trust may decline, not just in the image but also in the publisher.

However, not all effects are negative. Paik et al. (2023) found that AI-generated news visuals can evoke emotional responses similar to traditional photojournalism [6]. Visual novelty can improve engagement, though it can also raise concerns about sensationalism or bias. In general, acceptance depends on context, disclosure, and image design. Further research is needed to understand how visual style, labeling, and content relevance affect user trust and comprehension.

2.4   Accessibility and Inclusive Design

AI-generated visuals also raise important questions of accessibility and inclusion. Currently, text-to-image models do not generate alt text, limiting access for visually impaired users who rely on screen readers. Research by Bennett et al. (2024) shows that standard prompt text often does not produce alt text that blind users find meaningful [2]. Moreover, generative models have been found to reflect and amplify biases. A study by Sun et al. (2024) revealed that DALL·E 2 underrepresents women in high-status occupations and overrepresents stereotypical traits, such as submissive body language. This raises concerns about journalistic integrity, especially when such images accompany public-interest stories [11]. To ensure inclusive AI use, newsrooms must actively verify and curate AI-generated visuals, provide accessible descriptions, and monitor representational fairness. Responsible implementation can support broader access without sacrificing accuracy or equity.

2.5   Research Gap

The review above highlights that while interest in generative AI for journalism has increased, there are critical gaps in our understanding, particularly with regard to user engagement with AI-generated visual news summaries, which is the focus of this study. Most existing research to date has examined generative AI in news from the production side (e.g., how journalists use AI, how AI impacts newsroom workflows) or has debated normative issues such as accuracy and ethics [9]. Far less scholarly attention has been paid to the consumption side, that is, how audiences actually interact with and interpret news content produced with AI assistance.

Thomson and Thomas (2023) emphasize that AI-driven text-to-image tools "pose profound questions" about the value and impact of images in journalism, yet these questions are only beginning to be explored in research [12]. Similarly, Paik et al. (2023) note that few studies have investigated the applications of generative AI in public-interest news domains [6]. We have evidence that readers approach AI-generated news with a skeptical eye and that AI visuals can evoke emotional responses, but we lack focused studies on user engagement outcomes, for example, does an AI-generated visual summary of a news story improve audience understanding or retention of information compared to a traditional text summary? Does it affect their willingness to share or discuss the news? How do factors such as the style of the image or the presence of explanatory captions influence engagement and trust? These practical questions remain unanswered.

3 Methodology

Fig. 1. Image generated by Gemini 2.0 Flash on 27 April 2025.

3.1 Text-to-Image Generation for News Articles

Technologically, this research builds on state-of-the-art diffusion models and transformer architectures. Principally, these models are capable of generating high-quality images based on short text prompts, which makes them potentially useful for summarizing articles in visual form [8]. However, their actual performance in this specific domain, i.e. summarizing real-world news in a meaningful, emotionally appropriate, and visually coherent way, remains largely untested.

To address this gap, our research follows a multistage methodology. In the first stage, we selected a set of news articles covering various topics (e.g., politics, lifestyle, environment). The articles were sourced from media websites provided by our industry partner Pinpoll[1], who offers a polling tool which is used on these sites. The primary objective of the tool is to improve user engagement and generate valuable first-party customer insights. To consider linguistic differences, we selected quite a variety of outlets in German and English, originating from Austria and South Africa.

In a preliminary test, we experimented with a wide range of different AI models currently on the market. The most promising ones were incorporated into the further experimental setup. The prompt used for the articles in German language was *"Erzeuge ein einzelnes Bild, das die Kernaussage des folgenden Nachrichtenartikels visuell zusammenfasst. Das Bild soll die wichtigsten Inhalte des Artikels semantisch korrekt widerspiegeln, emotional ansprechend sein und eine hochwertige visuelle Gestaltung aufweisen. Vermeide die Einbettung von Text oder Logos im Bild. Hier ist der Artikel"*, which translates to *"Generate a single image that visually summarizes the core message of the following news article. The image should accurately reflect the main content of the article in a semantically correct way, be emotionally engaging, and feature high-quality visual design. Avoid embedding any text or logos in the image. Here is the article"*.

To give an example, Figs. 1 to 3 show the three images generated for one of the news articles included in the study, i.e. "Health Minister calls for a sugar tax on drinks", published on an Austrian media website.[2]

3.2 Online Questionnaire

In the second stage, we conducted a quantitative survey with potential readers of these news articles. The participants were presented with three news articles. In addition to the article presented in the previous section, those were "Mayoral candidate criticizes lack of crosses in schools", published on the web presence of an Austrian newspaper[3], and "Karma? Woman wins the lottery after family's rejection", published by a South African radio station.[4]

In the survey, all articles were accompanied by three images generated by different AI models. Participants were asked to read the articles and then evaluate

---

[1] https://pinpoll.com.

[2] https://www.vol.at/gesundheitsminister-rauch-fordert-zuckersteuer-auf-getranke/9168028 (last access on 2 June 2025).

[3] https://www.nachrichten.at/oberoesterreich/linz/raml-kritisiert-fehlende-kreuze-in-linzer-schulen;art66,4017767 (last access on 2 June 2025).

[4] https://www.ecr.co.za/lifestyle/karma-woman-wins-lottery-after-familys-rejection (last access on 2 June 2025).

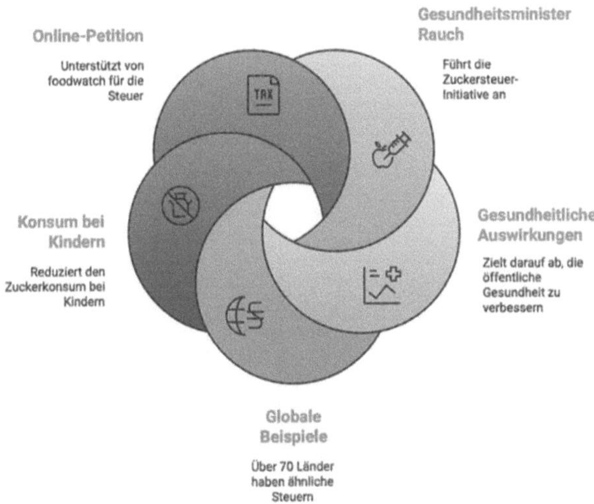

Fig. 2. Image generated by Napkin.AI on 27 April 2025.

the images according to four main dimensions: (1) how well the image represents the article, (2) how visually appealing the image is, (3) how emotionally resonant the image is, and (4) which AI tool produced the most effective results, that is, which image best conveys the content of the article without having read it. These dimensions were surveyed using a 5-point Likert scale from 1 = very poor to 5 = very good. These assessments were supplemented with demographic questions, as well as questions regarding general attitudes toward news consumption and the use of AI tools. The questionnaire was distributed to news consumers in May 2025.

4   Results

A total of 63 fully completed questionnaires were collected, which provided a variety of insights.

In general and across all news articles, younger participants rated the generated images more positively. While the average rating among those under 18 years was 3.18, this average dropped to, for example, 2.75 among those aged 25–34 years and 2.67 among those aged 45–54 years. The female participants gave an average rating of 2.77, while the male participants gave a lower average of 2.68.

Educational background also proves to be a significant influencing factor: Participants with only compulsory schooling rated the generated images at around 2.52; This value increases to 3.00 for those with higher secondary education, then drops to 2.68 for those with a completed bachelor's or master's degree, and further decreases to 2.54 for those with a doctorate.

Fig. 3. Image generated by ChatGPT 4o on 27 April 2025.

We can also observe clear differences between the AI models used: While the images generated by ChatGPT 4o received an average rating of 3.51, those from Gemini 2.0 Flash lag significantly behind at 2.53. The other models used performed considerably worse, with an average rating of only 2.13.

A focused comparison of the aforementioned "sugar tax" images further highlights the qualitative differences between the AI models. Figure 3, created by ChatGPT 4o, received the highest ratings in all dimensions of the evaluation: content ($M = 4.18$, 85.7% $\geq$ 4), quality ($M = 4.03$, 76.2% $\geq$ 4), emotional tone ($M = 4.26$, 85.7% $\geq$ 4), and independent understanding of the article ($M = 4.07$, 79.4% $\geq$ 4). The overall mean score was 4.13, with a negatively skewed distribution, indicating a higher frequency of positive ratings.

In contrast, Fig. 1, generated by Gemini 2.0 Flash, was evaluated less favorably in all dimensions. It achieved significantly lower scores for content ($M = 1.92$, 6.3% $\geq$ 4), emotional expression ($M = 1.73$) and grasp ($M = 1.75$). The total average was 1.89, with only 8.3% of the responses scoring any dimension 4 or higher (Fig. 4).

Qualitative feedback from participants further supports these findings. The difficulty in grasping the content of the articles based solely on the images is evident, as illustrated by the following participant comment: *"Fig. 1 shows only girls. One might assume it is about litter on the playground. Fig. 2: The icons do not contribute to better understanding. Fig. 3: The topic of tax is missing here."* Although ChatGPT 4o scored highest overall, this remark highlights a recurring challenge: Even well-rated images do not always succeed in conveying the full complexity of the news content.

We also examined general user behavior and attitudes toward news consumption and the use of AI tools. The results provide valuable context for understanding how participants interact with digital content and emerging technologies in everyday life.

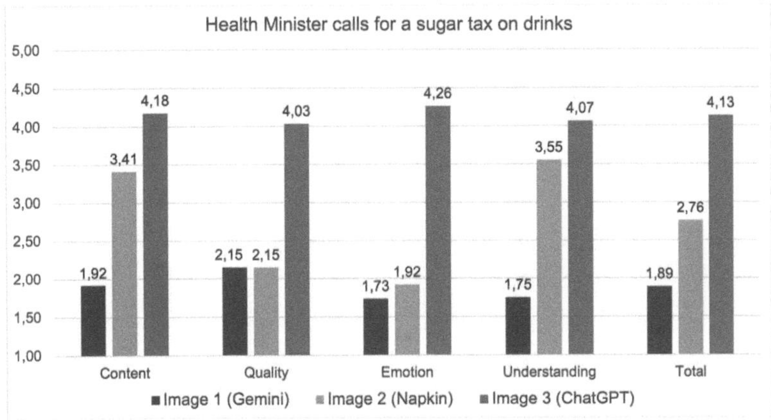

Fig. 4. User Ratings for Images (1 = very poor, 5 = very good).

Most of the respondents regularly engage with online news, and most indicating that they read digital news articles multiple times a day or several times per week (92%). Traditional news websites and social media platforms were the most frequently cited sources. In contrast, news apps, YouTube, and podcasts played a less prominent role. Only a small number of participants reported not consuming news at all (1.59%).

When it comes to the use of AI tools, such as ChatGPT, Perplexity, or Gemini, a significant proportion of respondents reported using them daily or several times a week (71.43%). These tools are used predominantly in academic and professional contexts, such as to prepare presentations or support study-related tasks. A considerable number of participants (79.37%) also stated that they use AI tools out of curiosity or for entertainment, while fewer applied them to creative projects or content on social networks. Only a small minority explicitly avoided AI-generated imagery (6.35%).

Notable differences emerged across education level, gender, and age. Participants with a university degree were significantly more likely to be frequent users: 78% of those with a master's or doctorate reported using AI tools daily or several times a week, compared to only 38% among those without a university degree.

Regarding gender differences, we see that 65.63% of the male respondents used AI tools frequently, compared to 80% of the female participants. However, many men reported occasional or exploratory use, 25% said they use AI once or twice a month, 6.25% have tried it once, and 3.13% have never tried it.

The differences in age are illustrated in Fig. 5: the highest intensity of use was reported among the respondents aged 25–34 years and 35–44 years, where a substantial proportion indicated daily or several times a week of engagement. In contrast, younger participants (1824 years) showed more varied patterns, with fewer daily users and a noticeable number of respondents who had only tried AI tools once or rarely used them. For the age group 45–54 years, AI usage was

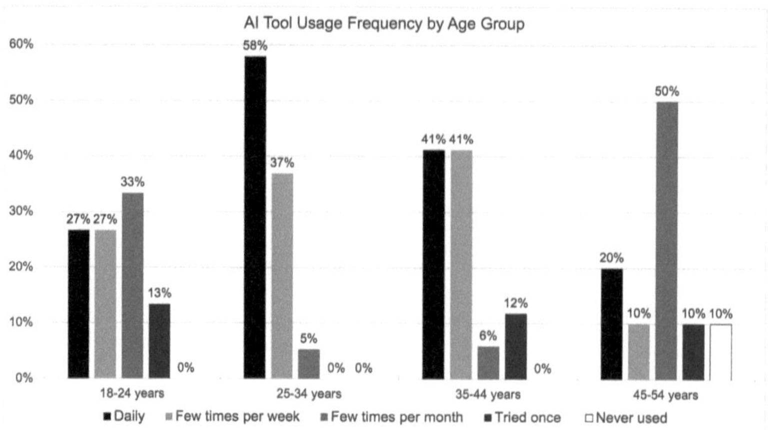

Fig. 5. AI Tool Usage Frequency by Age Group.

significantly lower overall and most of the respondents used AI only occasionally, if at all.

5   Conclusion

This study aimed to explore how generative AI can support visual summarization of news content in a way that is accessible and engaging. In an information environment, increasingly dominated by mobile consumption and visual stimuli, AI- generated images offer new potential to reach audiences who might otherwise disengage from text-heavy formats.

The results show that image generation tools like ChatGPT 4o can produce emotionally resonant and semantically accurate visuals that significantly out-perform other models such as Gemini 2.0 Flash, Midjourney, and Napkin.AI. Across all dimensions, including emotional tone, content representation, and overall quality, ChatGPT achieved the highest average scores. However, none of the tools consistently conveyed the full complexity of a news article without missing key elements.

Differences in user ratings also reveal that demographic factors such as age, gender, and educational background shape the way AI-generated visuals are perceived. Younger and more highly educated participants generally rated the images more positively, and AI usage patterns reflect this trend: those more familiar with generative tools tend to assess the visuals more favorably. These insights underscore the importance of AI literacy as a key enabler of trust and acceptance in digital journalism.

As part of the survey, we also examined user behavior around news consumption and AI usage. Most participants regularly consume digital news, especially via traditional websites and social networks. AI tools are already integrated into the academic and professional routines of many users, indicating a broader change in the way digital content is created, accessed, and understood.

In general, the automatic generation of images for news articles proved to be challenging. Tools and prompts that work well for a particular article can produce very poor results for others. The results presented in this paper are based on a consistent prompt applied to all news topics and a selection of tools that produce usable results across several outlets. However, capturing the content of a news article without having read it is possible only to a limited extent. Details such as chronological sequences, names, or similar elements may be lost. Currently, manual intervention by editors appears to be indispensable. However, AI models are evolving rapidly, and this limitation may no longer apply in the future.

Even today, the average user ratings for the generated images range between 1.89 and 4.13 on a 5-point scale. These values can certainly be improved if the generation process is optimized for a specific news outlet. It is also conceivable that editorial intervention will only be necessary in certain cases, while other articles can be processed fully automatically.

Looking ahead, the integration of AI-generated visuals into journalistic workflows holds real promise, not only to improve engagement but also to meet accessibility requirements. Considering the Accessibility Act of the European Union, visual summaries can provide a valuable supplement for people with cognitive or linguistic limitations. When implemented transparently and responsibly, such tools can help make quality journalism more inclusive, efficient, and visually compelling – truly expanding communication beyond words.

References

1. Chang, H., et al.: Muse: text-to-image generation via masked generative transformers. Google Research (2023). http://arxiv.org/abs/2301.00704
2. Das, M., Fiannaca, A.J., Morris, M.R., Kane, S.K., Bennett, C.L.: From provenance to aberrations: image creator and screen reader user perspectives on alt text for ai-generated images. In: Conference on Human Factors in Computing Systems. ACM (2024). https://doi.org/10.1145/3613904.3642325
3. Diakopoulos, N., et al.: Generative AI in journalism: the evolution of Newswork and ethics in a generative information ecosystem. Technical report April, Associated Press (2024). https://doi.org/10.13140/RG.2.2.31540.05765, https://www.researchgate.net/publication/379668724
4. Liu, V., Qiao, H., Chilton, L.: Opal: Multimodal image generation for news illustration. In: 35th Annual ACM Symposium on User Interface Software and Technology. ACM (2022). https://doi.org/10.1145/3526113.3545621
5. Nishal, S., Diakopoulos, N.: Envisioning the applications and implications of generative AI for news media. In: CHI 2023 Generative AI and HCI Workshop, pp. 1–7 (2023). https://nishalsach.github.io/pdfs/2023-genaihci-chi.pdf
6. Paik, S., et al.: The affective nature of AI-generated news images: impact on visual journalism. In: 11th International Conference on Affective Computing and Intelligent Interaction. IEEE (2023). https://doi.org/10.1109/ACII59096.2023.10388166
7. Paulsen, N., Peveling, K.: Nachrichtenflut im Netz: Jeder und jede Zweite fühlt sich überfordert. Technical report, Bitkom (2024). https://www.bitkom.org/

Presse/Presseinformation/Nachrichtenflut-im-Netz-Jeder-und-jede-Zweite-fuehlt-sich-ueberfordert

8. Ramesh, A., et al.: Zero-Shot text-to-image generation. Proc. Mach. Learn. Res. **139**, 8821–8831 (2021)
9. Shi, Y., Sun, L.: How generative AI is transforming journalism: development application ethics. Journalism Media **5**(2), 582–594 (2024). https://doi.org/10.3390/journalmedia5020039
10. Stöger, E., Deichman, F., Mayerl, M.: PIAAC Grundkompetenzen von Erwachsenen. Tech. rep., Statistik Austria (2022). https://www.statistik.at/fileadmin/publications/PIAAC_1_Web-barrierefrei.pdf
11. Sun, L., et al.: Smiling women pitching down: auditing representational and presentational gender biases in image-generative AI. J. Comput. Mediated Commun. **29**(1) (2024). https://doi.org/10.1093/jcmc/zmad045
12. Thomson, T.J., Thomas, R.J.: Generative visual AI in newsrooms. Considerations related to production, presentation, and audience interpretation and impact. Journalism Res. **6**(March), 318–328 (2023). https://doi.org/10.1453/2569-152X-3
13. Toff, B., Simon, F.M.: "Or they could just not use it?": the dilemma of AI disclosure for audience trust in news. Int. J. Press/Politics (2025). https://doi.org/10.1177/19401612241308697

Education 5.0 and Metaverses: Teachers' Reflections on Opportunities and Challenges in Pedagogical Transformation

Iris Cristina Peláez-Sánchez[1] (iD), Leonardo David Glasserman-Morales[2]([⊠]) (iD), and Gustavo de la Cruz Martínez[3] (iD)

[1] School of Humanities and Education, Tecnologico de Monterrey, Eugenio Garza Sada Avenue 2501 South, Tecnológico, 64700 Monterrey, Nuevo León, Mexico
[2] Institute for the Future of Education, Tecnologico de Monterrey, Eugenio Garza Sada Avenue 2501 South, Tecnológico, 64700 Monterrey, Nuevo León, Mexico
glasserman@tec.mx
[3] Institute for Applied Sciences and Technology, Universidad Nacional Autónoma de México, Circuito Exterior S/N, Ciudad Universitaria Coyoacán, 04510 Mexico City, Mexico

Abstract. The industry's rapid advancement towards digital environments has significantly changed workplace and educational dynamics. Industry 5.0 introduces a new focus on collaboration between humans and machines, leading to a shift towards Education 5.0. This educational approach aims to prepare future professionals for the constantly evolving job market, emphasizing the importance of digital skills, especially in communication and collaboration, for effective interaction in these environments. Education 5.0 incorporates advanced technologies like immersive environments to enhance these skills, promoting a more inclusive and personalized education that aligns with the needs of the modern digital economy.

In the current scenario, teachers are experiencing significant changes and must adjust to new teaching methods. Reflective teaching is essential for teachers to adapt to these changes effectively. It involves acquiring technical skills, critically analyzing their teaching methods, and understanding how new technological tools impact student learning. Reflective teaching allows educators to question, evaluate, and adjust their didactic strategies. This ensures that emerging technologies are not used superficially but are integrated coherently and meaningfully into the curriculum.

This study analyzed teachers' reflections at the end of a course focused on their training in immersive environments within a framework of Education 5.0. After completing the course, 26 teachers' reflections were collected and analyzed using a qualitative approach based on a multiple case study supported by ATLAS.ti software. The study evaluated the teachers' final reflections on how these technologies impacted their pedagogical practices and student learning.

The research identified two main categories in the teachers' final reflections on implementing emerging technologies and metaverses in Education 5.0: challenges and opportunities. Among the opportunities, it was found that these technologies allow for creating more dynamic and interactive learning experiences. Additionally, immersive environments offer personalized learning tailored to individual student needs, fostering their autonomy and control over the learning process.

F. F.-H Nah and K. L. Siau (Eds.): HCII 2025, LNCS 16343, pp. 45–59, 2026.
https://doi.org/10.1007/978-3-032-13167-6_4

Teachers also noted that using metaverses increases student motivation and participation, leading to greater engagement in educational activities and improved content retention. However, the teachers also reflected on the challenges of integrating these emerging technologies into their pedagogical practices, such as limited technological infrastructure and the need for continuous teacher training.

In conclusion, this study underscores adopting new educational approaches and integrating emerging technologies, such as metaverses, present challenges, and opportunities, especially from the perspective of one of the key players in education: the teachers. Their role is crucial in educational transformation, as their ability to critically reflect on their practice and adapt to new technological demands will be decisive for the successful implementation of Education 5.0. While this study provides valuable insights into the opportunities and challenges perceived by teachers, the classroom implementation phase remains a crucial step in evaluating the real impact of these emerging technologies on the teaching and learning process.

Keywords: Metaverses · Education 5.0 · Immersive environments · Reflective teaching · Higher education · Innovation in education

1 Introduction

In the context of Industry 5.0, where collaboration between humans and machines redefines productive paradigms, education faces the challenge of adapting to meet the demands of a highly technical labor market [1, 2]. Industry 5.0, centered on the customization and optimization of processes through integrating advanced intelligence, necessitates rethinking the traditional educational model [3, 4]. This shift has given rise to Education 5.0, positioned as an essential response to technological needs and as a crucial requirement for developing competencies that enable effective synergy between human capabilities and advanced machines [5].

Within this framework, Education 5.0 seeks to transform learning environments by integrating emerging technologies such as metaverses [6, 7]. These immersive environments are notable for their capacity to simulate real and complex scenarios, facilitating the development of practical skills and problem-solving abilities in contexts similar to those students will encounter in the future workforce [8]. The successful implementation of these technologies depends not on more than just the tools themselves but on how educators reflect upon and adapt their pedagogical practices to achieve genuine educational transformation [9, 10].

From this perspective, reflective teaching practice becomes a fundamental pillar, allowing educators to assess, adapt, and improve their teaching methods through critical introspection of their practice [11]. Based on this context, the study aimed to explore teachers' perceptions at the end of a course that promoted metaverses in secondary and higher education in Mexico from the Education 5.0 perspective. The goal was to understand how educators perceived the potential integration of this approach and metaverses into their classes, identifying the opportunities and challenges they anticipated for incorporating metaverses or immersive environments into their pedagogical practices from the perspective of Education 5.0.

2 Theorical Framework

2.1 Industry 5.0

Industry 5.0 marks a significant advancement in the evolution of industrial revolutions, emphasizing a return to the human element within production processes, previously dominated by the automation of Industry 4.0 [4, 12]. This new industrial phase is characterized by a synergistic collaboration between human capabilities and autonomous machines, moving beyond simple automation to foster a personalized, human-centered work environment [13, 14].

Industry 5.0 aims to center humans in production processes, highlighting cooperation between people and intelligent machines [3]. This approach seeks to improve productivity and efficiency and values human creativity and skills—fundamental elements that machines cannot replicate [15, 16].

The transition to Industry 5.0 also implies a significant cultural shift, where sustainability and personalization become central objectives [17]. This shift reflects a deeper commitment to social and environmental responsibility, viewing technology as a tool to enhance the quality of life and overall well-being rather than solely production efficiency [18, 19].

In conclusion, Industry 5.0 envisions a future in which technology and humanity advance together, optimizing innovative solutions that benefit society and the global economic environment and redefining the interaction between technological progress and human development [12, 20].

As with previous industrial transitions, in which each phase spurred a corresponding shift in pedagogical approaches, Industry 5.0 underscores the need for an educational model aligned with the demands of a highly technical and human-centered work environment [21–23]. Education 5.0 emphasizes the integration of advanced technologies, such as metaverses, to create richer and more personalized learning experiences. This approach helps develop essential skills for navigating and thriving in the evolving professional landscape of Industry 5.0, including creativity, collaboration, and critical thinking. [5].

2.2 Education 5.0

Education 5.0 emerges as an innovative pedagogical model, essential in adapting educational systems to Industry 5.0 [23, 24]. This approach aims to develop an educational system that is efficient, equitable, and capable of adaptively responding to the evolving needs of society, focusing on the development of digital competencies and essential soft skills in today's technological context [5, 25]. Drawing inspiration from the principles of Industry 5.0, this educational approach places the individual at the center of learning, using advanced technologies to enhance educational accessibility and flexibility [26, 27].

Methodologies characterizing Education 5.0 include personalized learning, which adapts teaching to the individual characteristics of each student, and collaborative learning, which promotes interaction and teamwork, strengthening the social skills required in contemporary work environments [28, 29]. Additionally, adaptive and analytical learning enhances problem-solving and critical thinking skills, equipping students to face the current challenges of the labor market [30, 31].

While implementing Education 5.0 involves challenges—such as adapting curricula and integrating technologies like artificial intelligence and robotics—it offers significant opportunities for collaboration between the educational sector and industry [25, 32]. This approach facilitates access to personalized, real-time information through technologies like Virtual Reality, Augmented Reality, and the Internet of Things. It prepares students to excel in a constantly evolving labor market [5, 33].

In the context of Education 5.0, metaverses are highly relevant learning platforms, providing immersive environments that foster personalized and deeply active educational interactions [6, 7]. These virtual spaces enable students to explore and learn in contexts that simulate reality, preparing them for today's world's technological and social demands [34, 35].

2.3 Metaverses in Education

Metaverses, conceived as immersive environments or virtual worlds, allow users to create and customize avatars that act as their digital representations to interact within a three-dimensional virtual space [36, 37]. The term was coined in the novel Snow Crash [38]. Since then, it has become a central component of modern video games and social networks, with platforms like Facebook's Meta Platforms and devices like the Oculus Rift or the Apple Vision pro providing a fully immersive experience [39, 40]. Likewise, platforms such as Roblox, which hosts over 199 million active users, and Second Life, with a community of around 10 million users, exemplify the expansion and popularity of these virtual worlds [41, 42].

These virtual worlds create scenarios that range from realistic to fantastic, providing a boundless digital space for immersion and interaction, where avatars serve as virtual extensions of users [43]. Metaverses are becoming the new frontier for social interaction, encompassing a broad spectrum of activities, including economic, political, social, cultural, and educational spheres [44, 45]. Notably, access to these environments can vary from simple desktop interfaces to complex immersive virtual reality setups utilizing goggles and motion sensors for a more authentic and physical interaction [36, 46, 47].

In the educational sector, metaverses have been incorporated into prestigious institutions such as Harvard and Indiana in the USA and applied in fields ranging from medicine to language learning and information systems [48]. These environments promote active and collaborative learning, removing physical limitations and allowing seamless student interaction [34, 35]. These immersive platforms are invaluable for personalizing and enriching the educational experience, enhancing both individual student engagement and collaborative learning [49–52].

2.4 Reflective Teaching

Reflective teaching is an essential process for professional development in education. It involves a critical and ongoing review of pedagogical experiences to improve and adapt teaching strategies [53, 54]. This methodology allows educators to critically examine their assumptions and the motivations behind their pedagogical decisions, assessing how these influence student learning [55, 56].

This approach facilitates observation and demands in-depth analysis that promotes adaptive, student-centered teaching. Reflection becomes indispensable for developing creative and adaptable learning environments that align with contemporary sociocultural and technological demands [57, 58]. Through reflection before, during, and after teaching, educators continuously adjust and personalize their pedagogical methods to meet the specific needs of their students [59].

Moreover, reflective teaching is fundamental to fostering innovation. Educators can significantly transform their pedagogical practices by engaging in reflection throughout all stages of teaching activities [60]. Research highlighting the importance of reflection in teacher professional development supports this transformation, helping adapt teaching strategies to specific cultural and disciplinary contexts and facilitating the identification of innovative solutions to respond to the changing needs of the educational environment [61, 62].

In this context, the study's primary objective was to analyze teachers' perceptions and reflections after participating in a workshop designed to promote the integration of metaverses in secondary and higher education in Mexico from the perspective of Education 5.0. Through this analysis, the study aimed to understand how educators perceived the potential incorporation of these advanced technologies into their pedagogical practices and identify the opportunities and challenges that emerged when adapting these tools in the classroom.

3 Methodology

This study adopted a qualitative methodological approach based on a multiple case study design to deepen the understanding of teachers' perceptions regarding incorporating metaverses in secondary and higher education in Mexico. This methodological choice responds to the need to capture, in a comprehensive and detailed manner, teachers' reflections and expectations about the pedagogical potential of metaverses within the principles of Education 5.0.

An exploratory-descriptive design was employed, suitable for examining the teachers' perceptions and expectations regarding this educational innovation in depth. Thematic analysis was chosen as the technique to organize and extract significant patterns from the information gathered, allowing the identification of recurring themes and trends in participants' responses.

The research began with designing and implementing a 40-h online workshop. This course targeted secondary and higher education teachers interested in integrating immersive technologies into their pedagogical practices, combining theory and practice to facilitate the direct application of the concepts taught. Throughout the course, various units were explored, from transitioning to Education 5.0 to integrating emerging technologies such as virtual reality and metaverses, examining their potential to transform the educational environment, and highlighting successful implementation examples in immersive contexts.

The central objective of the workshop was to foster in-depth reflective teaching on implementing metaverses in their pedagogical practices and adopting the pedagogical principles of Education 5.0. This reflective teaching exercise was essential, enabling educators to critically analyze the implications of integrating emerging technologies into their pedagogical practices [10]. To facilitate and guide this reflection, online forums, and synchronous sessions via Zoom were established, providing spaces for teachers to exchange experiences, discuss concerns, and collaboratively reflect on the challenges and opportunities of implementing metaverses from the perspective of Education 5.0 in their classrooms. At the end of the workshop, a final reflection session was held where teachers shared their conclusions on applying the knowledge acquired to their subjects, exploring concrete strategies for incorporating immersive environments into their courses.

This study specifically analyzed the discussion forum on the possibilities and limitations of immersive environments and the final reflections shared by each teacher. This forum focused on exploring the potential of these spaces to transform teaching and learning dynamics and the barriers teachers might face in implementing them in their subjects. Additionally, the analysis of teachers' final reflections captured the individual perspectives of each participant regarding the real applicability of metaverses in the educational context, as well as their plans and concrete strategies for integrating these technologies into their classes following the principles of Education 5.0.

The workshop participants were secondary and higher education teachers from Mexico City, representing 17 teachers (65.38%) at the secondary level and nine (34.62%) at the higher education level. Regarding gender, most participants were women, with 21 teachers (80.77%), while men represented 19.23% (n = 5). In terms of the highest level of education, 8 participants (30.77%) held a doctorate, 13 (50.00%) held a master's degree, and 5 (19.23%) held a bachelor's degree. Regarding their field of study, the teachers came from diverse disciplines: the largest proportion were from Physical-Mathematical Sciences and Engineering with ten teachers (38.46%), followed by Humanities and Arts with 8 participants (30.77%). Additionally, six teachers (23.08%) had training in biological, chemical, and health sciences, while the fields of actuarial science and social sciences each had one teacher (3.85%) (see Table 1).

3.1 Study Procedure

The study was structured into four consecutive phases. In the first phase, the workshop was implemented, with its content and activity distribution previously validated by a group of instructional designers. This team reviewed the workshop activities to ensure they promoted deep and structured reflection on the part of the teachers regarding the adoption of immersive environments in their educational practices.

In the second phase, teachers' forum contributions were collected, where they explored the pedagogical implications of using immersive environments. Additionally, each teacher presented a final reflection in a video format (three to five minutes) on the feasibility of implementing these technologies in their subjects, providing detailed insights into their perceptions and plans.

The third phase involved transcribing all final reflections and forum contributions to ensure content fidelity for subsequent analysis. Thematic analysis was conducted using the software, Atlas.ti, allowing the identification of patterns, recurring themes, and key dimensions in teachers' perceptions of implementing immersive environments.

Table 1. Participant Characteristics

Characteristics		N	%
Gender	Female	21	80.77%
	Male	5	19.23%
Highest Degree	Doctorate	8	30.77%
	Master's Degree	13	50.00%
	Bachelor's Degree	5	19.23%
Field of Study	Actuarial Science	1	3.85%
	Biological, Chemical, and Health Sciences	6	23.08%
	Physical-Mathematical Sciences and Engineering	10	38.46%
	Social Sciences	1	3.85%
	Humanities and Arts	8	30.77%
Teaching educational Level	Secondary Education	17	65.38%
	Higher Education	9	34.62%
Total		26	100.00%

Finally, in the fourth phase, the results of thematic coding were established. This phase consisted of organizing and consolidating the identified themes, allowing for structuring findings around the experiences, perceived benefits, and challenges identified by teachers. This process provided a comprehensive framework for interpreting the results, highlighting the possibilities and limitations of metaverses from the participants' perspectives.

4 Results

This section presents the findings from the thematic analysis of teachers' final reflections and contributions in the forum. The analysis was organized into two main categories: Opportunities and Challenges, each broken down into different subcategories that reflect specific aspects teachers perceive regarding implementing metaverses in their educational practices.

4.1 Opportunities

Within the Opportunities category, the thematic analysis identified four main subdimensions: a) Dynamic and Interactive Learning Experiences (n = 46), b) Personalized and Adaptive Learning (n = 70), c) Increased Student Motivation and Engagement (n = 55), and d) Collaborative Spaces (n = 43) (see Fig. 1).

Analyzing the opportunities subdimensions, it was recognized that the subdimension Dynamic and Interactive Learning Experiences (n = 46) focuses on teachers' perceptions

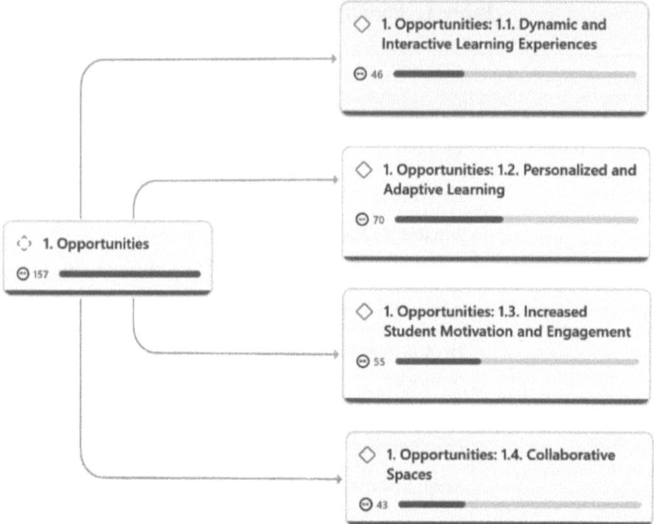

Fig. 1. Thematic Network of Opportunities Perceived by Teachers in the Implementation of Metaverses in Education.

of the value of metaverses in creating learning experiences that are active and interactive, facilitating student participation in real-time simulations and activities that promote more engaged learning. For instance, a teacher mentioned in their final reflection, "The integration of immersive environments not only sparks students' interest and curiosity but also enhances their understanding of complex technological concepts, such as the components of a computer and their practical functions."

On the other hand, the Personalized and Adaptive Learning subdimension (n = 70) centers on the ability of metaverses to offer customized learning experiences, adapting to each student's needs, styles, and paces, enabling more inclusive and tailored instruction. A teacher commented, "These environments facilitate personalized learning; students can interact with materials according to their needs and learning styles, promoting a more inclusive learning experience." Another noted, "Personalization in immersive environments allows each student to delve into content at their own pace, achieving a more adaptive and meaningful understanding of complex topics."

Likewise, the Increased Student Motivation and Engagement subdimension (n = 55) highlights the potential of metaverses to boost students' interest and motivation, capturing their attention through visually engaging and interactive experiences that foster greater involvement in the learning process. One teacher stated, "The use of avatars and interaction in virtual environments enables students to engage in debates on topics such as mining actively, increasing their motivation by assuming fictional yet critical roles in their arguments." Similarly, another teacher explained, "Virtual tours on physics in everyday life captivate students' attention by allowing them to see practical applications, which increases their interest and motivation."

Finally, the Collaborative Spaces subdimension (n = 43) focuses on creating virtual spaces that encourage teamwork and collaboration among students, enabling them to develop essential interpersonal and communication skills in both academic and professional contexts. Relevant comments include: "Immersive environments provide a space where students can work together on collaborative projects, such as virtual galleries of computing elements, reinforcing collaboration and problem-solving," and "Students can visit their peers' virtual exhibits on coastal erosion, fostering meaningful collaboration and enhancing their understanding of the topic."

In conclusion, the findings in the Opportunities dimension highlight the recognition of metaverses as versatile and effective pedagogical tools within Education 5.0. The analyzed subdimensions illustrate a variety of benefits perceived by teachers, who emphasize how these technologies foster active student participation and engagement while allowing them to tailor their learning processes according to their pace and needs.

These results underscore the potential of metaverses to transform pedagogical practices and meet the demands of an education focused on the holistic development of students' skills, emphasizing the role of Education 5.0 in creating meaningful and personalized educational experiences. However, implementing these metaverses in education also presents challenges, as described in the following dimension.

4.2 Challenges

The second dimension of analysis, Challenges, highlights the barriers teachers perceive regarding implementing metaverses within the framework of Education 5.0. This dimension is divided into two key categories: Technological Infrastructure Limitations (n = 18) and the Need for Continuous Teacher Training (n = 16) (see Fig. 2).

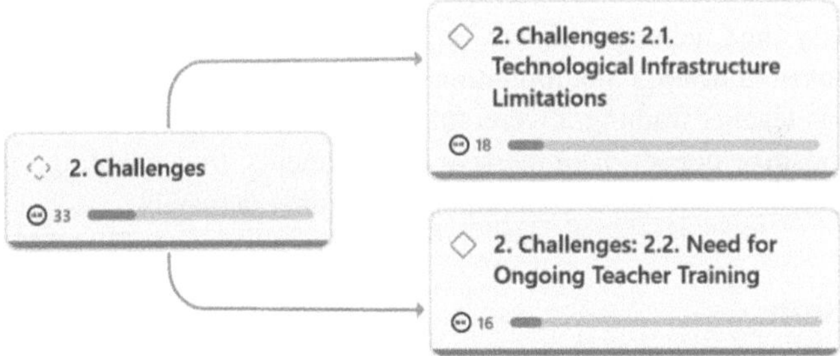

Fig. 2. Thematic Network of Challenges Perceived by Teachers in the Implementation of Metaverses in Education.

The first subdimension, Technological Infrastructure Limitations (n = 18), emphasizes the lack of adequate infrastructure as a critical barrier to adopting metaverses in educational institutions. Teachers pointed to challenges related to internet connectivity, the availability of suitable technological devices, and insufficient financial resources to invest in these tools. The lack of infrastructure limits the accessibility and quality of immersive environments, creating disparities in access and restricting their potential in the classroom.

One secondary education teacher noted, "The use of platforms like Spatial is promising, but often frustrating due to slow connection speeds and the lack of well-functioning equipment, which disrupts the immersive educational experience and causes stress among students." A higher education teacher shared a similar view: "Although virtual reality environments provide unique educational experiences, institutions often lack the necessary funding to acquire the required equipment, affecting the continuous and effective implementation of these resources." These technological limitations unevenly impact educational institutions depending on their context, influencing the equity and sustainability of immersive technology implementation across different educational realities.

The second subdimension, the Need for Continuous Teacher Training ($n = 16$), reveals the demand for ongoing, specialized training that equips teachers with the technical and pedagogical skills necessary to integrate metaverses into their educational practice effectively. Teachers expressed insecurity and a lack of specific skills to maximize the potential of these technologies in the classroom, limiting the adoption and positive impact of immersive environments. In the context of Education 5.0, continuous teacher development is crucial for metaverses to fulfill their purpose of significantly enhancing the teaching-learning process. Consequently, the lack of adequate training becomes an obstacle that hinders the integration of these resources and limits their effectiveness in developing advanced digital and pedagogical competencies.

In this context, two teacher reflections in the forum highlighted the importance of continuous training: "To leverage immersive environments fully, proper training is essential, as many teachers feel uncertain about using these tools, which affects the quality of educational activities they can develop," and "Teachers must receive ongoing support and training to adapt to the rapid evolution of immersive technologies. The lack of this support creates a gap between the potential of metaverses and their effective application in teaching."

In summary, the Challenges dimension identifies two primary barriers to implementing metaverses in Education 5.0: limitations in technological infrastructure and the need for continuous teacher training. Overcoming these challenges is fundamental to maximizing the positive impact of immersive environments, thus enabling innovative and accessible education that meets contemporary learning demands.

5 Discussion

The study's findings illuminate the implications of the thematic analysis across the two main identified categories: Opportunities and Challenges. In the Opportunities dimension, metaverses in Education 5.0 emerge as catalysts for dynamic and interactive learning experiences, where students can actively participate in simulations and real-time activities, fostering meaningful learning. From these reflections, teachers from secondary and higher education institutions in Mexico concur on perceiving these environments as spaces that facilitate dynamic and cooperative learning, overcoming physical barriers and enabling continuous and effective student interaction [34, 35].

Additionally, the customization potential of these environments allows students to progress at their own pace and according to their individual needs, promoting inclusive learning adapted to various styles. These benefits align with the principles of a student-centered education, where autonomy and engagement increase within an interactive digital framework that prepares students for the demands of a technologically advanced world, as proposed by Education 5.0 with its emphasis on highly personalized and active educational interaction [6, 7]. Teachers also recognize the benefits of integrating emerging technologies consistent with Education 5.0 principles and technologies such as metaverses [34].

However, implementing these environments also reveals significant challenges, most notably technological infrastructure limitations, as highlighted in teachers' reflections. The lack of stable connectivity and suitable devices in some institutions hinders the uniform integration of metaverses, as noted by the teachers. This situation urgently requires institutional investments and policies to ensure robust and accessible technological infrastructure for all stakeholders. Supporting teachers' reflections, a study conducted in universities in Mexico and Spain identifies the digital divide as a determining obstacle to achieving equitable and high-quality education [63].

Another critical challenge identified by teachers through reflection is the need for continuous training, which is essential for teachers to maximize the pedagogical potential of immersive environments. This need for training underscores the importance of developing teacher development programs that strengthen technical skills and pedagogical abilities, enabling more effective and meaningful implementation of immersive technologies in Education 5.0. To achieve meaningful technology implementation, the relevance of ongoing teacher updates that promote using these technologies through reflective teaching practices is acknowledged [60].

6 Conclusion

In conclusion, the study's findings underscore that metaverses offer significant opportunities to transform learning experiences, enabling the creation of dynamic and interactive environments where students can actively participate, increasing their engagement and motivation. Teachers play a crucial role in this transformation process, as their ability to critically reflect on their practices and adapt to current technological demands directly influences the successful implementation of these environments in the classroom. Nonetheless, the study also identifies relevant limitations, particularly in infrastructure and training. The lack of adequate connectivity and devices restricts the uniform implementation of these technologies across educational institutions. Furthermore, the need for continuous training in immersive tool use is evident, as teachers express insecurity in effectively applying these technologies in their pedagogical practice.

Finally, it is essential to highlight certain limitations of the study, such as the sample size, which consisted of only 26 teachers, limiting the generalizability of the findings. Although these teachers come from diverse areas, the results reflect the experiences and perceptions of a restricted sample. Additionally, the geographical context of the study was limited to Mexico, so the conclusions may only partially represent the educational realities of other countries or regions with different levels of technological and cultural development.

Future research could focus on evaluating the impact of metaverses on student performance and exploring strategies to overcome technological access barriers in the participants' real contexts. Furthermore, it is recommended to delve into the role of reflective practice in teacher training, as this emerges as an essential component for the coherent and meaningful integration of emerging technologies into the teaching-learning process, promoting adaptive, student-centered education in the era of Industry 5.0.

Acknowledgements. The authors would like to acknowledge the financial support of Writing Lab, Institute for the Future of Education, Tecnologico de Monterrey, Mexico, in the production of this work.

References

1. Rosalina, D., Yuliari, K., Setianingsih, D., Zati, M.R.: Factors influencing the digital literacy competency of college students in the industrial revolution era 4.0. Int. J. Econ. Bus. Appl. **6**, 81 (2021). https://doi.org/10.31258/ijeba.6.2.81-92

2. Pacher, C., Woschank, M., Zunk, B.M.: The role of competence profiles in industry 5.0-related vocational education and training: exemplary development of a competence profile for industrial logistics engineering education. Appl. Sci. **13**, 3280 (2023). https://doi.org/10.3390/app13053280

3. Leng, J., et al.: Towards resilience in Industry 5.0: a decentralized autonomous manufacturing paradigm (2023). https://doi.org/10.1016/j.jmsy.2023.08.023

4. Pelaez-Sanchez, I.C., Glasserman-Morales, L.D., Rocha-Feregrino, G.: Exploring digital competencies in higher education: design and validation of instruments for the era of Industry 5.0. Front. Educ. (Lausanne) **9** (2024). https://doi.org/10.3389/feduc.2024.1415800

5. Tavares, M.C., Azevedo, G., Marques, R.P.: The challenges and opportunities of era 5.0 for a more humanistic and sustainable society—a literature review. Societies **12**, 149 (2022). https://doi.org/10.3390/soc12060149

6. Ahmad, S., Umirzakova, S., Mujtaba, G., Amin, M.S., Whangbo, T.: Education 5.0: requirements, enabling technologies, and future directions (2023)

7. Lee, H., Hwang, Y.: Technology-enhanced education through VR-making and metaverse-linking to foster teacher readiness and sustainable learning. Sustainability **14**, 4786 (2022). https://doi.org/10.3390/su14084786

8. Azevedo, G., Tavares, M.C., Bastos, M.A., Vale, J., Bandeira, A.M.: Universities in era 5.0: the future accountant. in: iberian conference on information systems and technologies, CISTI (2023). https://doi.org/10.23919/CISTI58278.2023.10211963

9. Larrivee, B.: Transforming teaching practice: becoming the critically reflective teacher. Reflect. Pract. **1** (2000). https://doi.org/10.1080/713693162

10. Yuksel, D.: Technology use in reflective teaching: a practicum research project. Anthropologist **16**, 145–152 (2013). https://doi.org/10.1080/09720073.2013.11891343

11. Nunan, D.: Thomas farrell: reflective language teaching: from research to practice. Appl. Linguist. **31** (2010). https://doi.org/10.1093/applin/amq013

12. Kemendi, Á., Michelberger, P., Mesjasz-Lech, A.: Industry 4.0 and 5.0 – organizational and competency challenges of enterprises. Polish J. Manage. Stud. **26**, 209–232 (2022). https://doi.org/10.17512/pjms.2022.26.2.13

13. Xu, X., Lu, Y., Vogel-Heuser, B., Wang, L.: Industry 4.0 and Industry 5.0—inception, conception and perception. J. Manuf. Syst. **61**, 530–535 (2021). https://doi.org/10.1016/j.jmsy.2021.10.006

14. Mezgebe, T.T., Gebreslassie, M.G., Sibhato, H., Bahta, S.T.: Intelligent manufacturing ecosystem: a post COVID-19 recovery and growth opportunity for manufacturing industry in Sub-Saharan countries. Sci. Afr. **19**, e01547 (2023). https://doi.org/10.1016/j.sciaf.2023.e01547

15. Carayannis, E.G., Morawska, J.: University and education 5.0 for emerging trends, policies and practices in the concept of industry 5.0 and society 5.0. In: Industry 5.0 (2023). https://doi.org/10.1007/978-3-031-26232-6_1
16. Breque, M., De Nul, L., Petridis, A.: Industry 5.0 - towards a sustainable, human- centric and resilient European industry (2021)
17. Aheleroff, S., Huang, H., Xu, X., Zhong, R.Y.: Toward sustainability and resilience with Industry 4.0 and Industry 5.0. Front. Manuf. Technol. 2 (2022). https://doi.org/10.3389/fmtec.2022.951643
18. Ghobakhloo, M., Iranmanesh, M., Morales, M.E., Nilashi, M., Amran, A.: Actions and approaches for enabling Industry 5.0-driven sustainable industrial transformation: a strategy roadmap. Corp. Soc. Responsib. Environ. Manag. 30, 1473–1494 (2023). https://doi.org/10.1002/csr.2431
19. Ungureanu, A.V.: The transition from industry 4.0 To industry 5.0. The 4Cs of the Global Economic Change. Presented at the August (2020). https://doi.org/10.18662/lumproc/ncoe4.0.2020/07
20. Wolniak, R.: Industry 5.0 – characteristic, main principles, advantages and disadvantages. Scientific Papers of Silesian University of Technology. Organ. Manage. Ser. 2023, 663–678 (2023). https://doi.org/10.29119/1641-3466.2023.170.40
21. Leng, J., et al.: Industry 5.0: Prospect and retrospect. J. Manuf. Syst. 65, 279–295 (2022). https://doi.org/10.1016/j.jmsy.2022.09.017
22. Andres, B., Sempere-Ripoll, F., Esteso, A., Alemany, M.D.M.E.: Mapping between industry 5.0 and education 5.0. In: EDULEARN22 Proceedings (2022). https://doi.org/10.21125/edulearn.2022.0739
23. Gürdür Broo, D., Kaynak, O., Sait, S.M.: Rethinking engineering education at the age of industry 5.0. J. Ind. Inf. Integr. 25, 100311 (2022). https://doi.org/10.1016/j.jii.2021.100311
24. Bakkar, M.N., Kaul, A.: Education 5.0 serving future skills for industry 5.0 era. In: Advanced Research and Real-World Applications of Industry 5.0 (2023). https://doi.org/10.4018/978-1-7998-8805-5.ch007
25. Adel, A.: Future of industry 5.0 in society: human-centric solutions, challenges and prospective research areas. J. Cloud Comput. 11, 40 (2022). https://doi.org/10.1186/s13677-022-00314-5
26. Ahmad Zukarnain, Z., Abdul Rahman, N., Sudin, R., Jamaludin, M.: Implementation of A.D.A.B model in technology -based subjects. Int. J. Educ. Psychol. Counsel. 7 (2022). https://doi.org/10.35631/ijepc.746042
27. Mustafa Kamal, N.N., Mohd Adnan, A.H., Arifuddin Yusof, A., Khairul Ahmad, M., Mohd Kamal, M.: Immersive interactive educational experiences-adopting education 5.0, industry 4.0 learning technologies for Malaysian universities. In: Proceedings of the International Invention, Innovative & Creative (InIIC) Conference, pp. 190–196 (2020)
28. van der Linden, J., Erkens, G., Schmidt, H., Renshaw, P.: Collaborative Learning. In: New Learning, pp. 37–54. Springer Netherlands, Dordrecht (2000). https://doi.org/10.1007/0-306-47614-2_3
29. Zhang, L., Basham, J.D., Yang, S.: Understanding the implementation of personalized learning: a research synthesis. Educ. Res. Rev. 31, 100339 (2020). https://doi.org/10.1016/j.edurev.2020.100339
30. Walkington, C.A.: Using adaptive learning technologies to personalize instruction to student interests: the impact of relevant contexts on performance and learning outcomes. J. Educ. Psychol. 105, 932–945 (2013). https://doi.org/10.1037/a0031882
31. Waragai, I., Ohta, T., Raindl, M., Kurabayashi, S., Kiyoki, Y., Tokuda, H.: Examining and supporting online writing – a qualitative pre-study for an analytic learning environment. In: Critical CALL – Proceedings of the 2015 EUROCALL Conference, pp. 543–548. Research-publishing.net, Padova, Italy (2015). https://doi.org/10.14705/rpnet.2015.000390

32. Marlinton, M.: Transformation of Education in the Era 5.0: challenges of innovation and opportunities for change. In: The 2nd International Conference on Education Innovation and Social Science, pp. 448–453 (2023)
33. Fricticarani, A., Hayati, A., R, R., Hoirunisa, I., Rosdalina, G.M.: Strategi pendidikan untuk sukses di era teknologi 5.0. Jurnal Inovasi Pendidikan dan Teknologi Informasi (JIPTI) 4, 56–68 (2023). https://doi.org/10.52060/pti.v4i1.1173
34. Kye, B., Han, N., Kim, E., Park, Y., Jo, S.: Educational applications of metaverse: possibilities and limitations (2021). https://doi.org/10.3352/jeehp.2021.18.32
35. Guo, H., Gao, W.: Metaverse-Powered experiential situational english-teaching design: an emotion-based analysis method. Front Psychol. 13 (2022). https://doi.org/10.3389/fpsyg.2022.859159
36. Jamei, E., Mortimer, M., Seyedmahmoudian, M., Horan, B., Stojcevski, A.: Investigating the role of virtual reality in planning for sustainable smart cities. Sustainability. 9, 2006 (2017). https://doi.org/10.3390/su9112006
37. Mujica-Sequera, R.M.: El Metaverso como un Escenario Transcomplejo de la Tecnoeducación. Revista Tecnológica-Educativa Docentes 2.0. 13, 20–28 (2022). https://doi.org/10.37843/rted.v13i1.268
38. Stephenson, N.: Snow Crash (1992)
39. Egliston, B., Carter, M.: Critical questions for Facebook's virtual reality: data, power and the metaverse. Internet Policy Rev. 10 (2021). https://doi.org/10.14763/2021.4.1610
40. Waisberg, E., et al.: Apple Vision Pro and the advancement of medical education with extended reality. Can. Med. Educ. J. (2023). https://doi.org/10.36834/cmej.77634
41. Ordoñez Valencia, M.L., Ordoñez-Zúñiga, N.L., Mantilla-Ordóñez, J.C., Garcés Wila, M.E., Vera Apoyo, D.M., Coronel Mendez, W.J.: Análisis de herramientas del metaverso y su impacto en contextos educativos. Int. J. Interdiscipl. Stud. 3, 610–630 (2022). https://doi.org/10.51798/sijis.v3i2.366
42. Suh, W., Ahn, S.: Utilizing the metaverse for learner-centered constructivist education in the post-pandemic era: an analysis of elementary school students. J. Intell. 10 (2022). https://doi.org/10.3390/jintelligence10010017
43. Márquez Díaz, J.E.: Virtual world as a complement to hybrid and mobile learning. Int. J. Emerg. Technol. Learn. 15, 267–274 (2020). https://doi.org/10.3991/ijet.v15i22.14393
44. Davis, F.D., Bagozzi, R.P., Warshaw, P.R.: User acceptance of computer technology: a comparison of two theoretical models. Manage Sci. 35 (1989). https://doi.org/10.1287/mnsc.35.8.982
45. Hwang, G.-J., Chien, S.-Y.: Definition, roles, and potential research issues of the metaverse in education: an artificial intelligence perspective. Comput. Educ.: Artific. Intell. 3 (2022). https://doi.org/10.1016/j.caeai.2022.100082
46. Vasarainen, M., Paavola, S., Vetoshkina, L.: A systematic literature review on extended reality: virtual, augmented and mixed reality in working life. Int. J. Virtual Real. 21, 1–28 (2021). https://doi.org/10.20870/ijvr.2021.21.2.4620
47. Pérez, S., Muñoz, A., Stefanoni, M.E., Carbonari, D.: Realidad virtual, aprendizaje inmersivo y realidad aumentada: Casos de Estudio en Carreras de Ingeniería. In: XXIII Workshop de Investigadores en Ciencias de la Computación, pp. 963–968 (2021)
48. Huang, Y.C., Backman, S.J., Backman, K.F., McGuire, F.A., Moore, D.W.: An investigation of motivation and experience in virtual learning environments: a self-determination theory. Educ. Inf. Technol. (Dordr). 24, 591–611 (2019). https://doi.org/10.1007/s10639-018-9784-5
49. Anacona Ortiz, J.D., Millán Rojas, E.E., Gómez Cano, C.A.: Aplicación de los metaversos y la realidad virtual en la enseñanza. Entre ciencia e ingeniería. 13, 59–67 (2019). https://doi.org/10.31908/19098367.4015

50. Duan, H., Li, J., Fan, S., Lin, Z., Wu, X., Cai, W.: Metaverse for social good: a university campus prototype. In: MM 2021 - Proceedings of the 29th ACM International Conference on Multimedia, pp. 153–161. Association for Computing Machinery, Inc (2021). https://doi.org/10.1145/3474085.3479238

51. George-Reyes, C.E., Peláez-Sánchez, I.C., Glasserman-Morales, L.D.: Digital Environments of Education 4.0 and complex thinking: communicative Literacy to close the digital gender gap. J. Interact. Media Educ. **2024** (2024). https://doi.org/10.5334/jime.833

52. George-Reyes, C.E., Peláez Sánchez, I.C., Glasserman-Morales, L.D., López-Caudana, E.O.: The Metaverse and complex thinking: opportunities, experiences, and future lines of research. Front. Educ. (Lausanne) **8** (2023). https://doi.org/10.3389/feduc.2023.1166999

53. Brevis-Yéber, M., Mas-Torelló, Ó., Bueno, C.R.: Reflective teaching practice as a strategy to encourage school innovation. Logos: Revista de Linguistica, Filosofia y Literatura **32** (2022). https://doi.org/10.15443/RL3216

54. Sevilla Muñoz, T.C., Sánchez Diaz, S., Nauca Guzmán, R.A., Martínez Rueda, E.M., Vidal Sevilla, J.M.: Acompañamiento pedagógico y la práctica reflexiva docente. Ciencia Latina Revista Científica Multidisciplinar **5**, 4430–4447 (2021). https://doi.org/10.37811/cl_rcm.v5i4.630

55. Korthagen, F.A.J.: In search of the essence of a good teacher: Toward a more holistic approach in teacher education. Adv. Res. Teach. **19** (2013). https://doi.org/10.1108/S1479-3687(2013)0000019015

56. Loughran, J.J.: Effective reflective practice in search of meaning in learning about teaching. J. Teach. Educ. **53** (2002). https://doi.org/10.1177/0022487102053001004

57. Navaneedhan, C.G.: Reflective teaching-learning process of integrating metaphorical thinking and visual imagery. J. Behav. Brain Sci. **02**, 407–410 (2012). https://doi.org/10.4236/jbbs.2012.23047

58. Zahid, M., Khanam, A.: Effect of reflective teaching practices on the performance of prospective teachers. Turkish Online J. Educ. Technol. **18** (2019)

59. Rawani, D., Putri, R.I.I., Zulkardi, Z., Susanti, E.: The reflective teaching practices using PMRI and collaborative learning. Jurnal Pendidikan Matematika **17**, 69–88 (2023). https://doi.org/10.22342/jpm.17.1.17208.69-88

60. Harvey, M., Vlachopoulos, P.: What a difference a day makes: reflection retreats as academic development in higher education. J. Furth. High Educ. **44** (2020). https://doi.org/10.1080/0309877X.2018.1541976

61. Rojas, M.T.: La investigación acción y la práctica docente. Cuaderno de Educación (2012)

62. Zeichner, K.M., Liston, D.P.: Reflective teaching: an introduction (2014)

63. Rodríguez-Abitia, G., Martínez-Pérez, S., Ramirez-Montoya, M.S., Lopez-Caudana, E.: Digital gap in universities and challenges for quality education: a diagnostic study in Mexico and Spain. Sustainability **12**, 9069 (2020). https://doi.org/10.3390/su12219069

Citizens' Perceptions and Acceptance of Drone Delivery Services

Madalena Pita[1] and Sofia Kalakou[2]([✉]) [iD]

[1] ISCTE, Avenida das Forças Armadas, Edifício II, Gabinete D402, 1649-026 Lisboa, Portugal
madalena_pita@iscte-iul.pt
[2] ISCTE, Business Research Unit, Avenida das Forças Armadas, Edifício II, Gabinete 402,
1649-026 Lisboa, Portugal
sofia.kalakou@iscte-iul.pt

Abstract. As e-commerce expands rapidly, companies seek solutions to inefficiencies in last-mile logistics, with drone delivery services emerging as a potential answer. This study explores how awareness impacts consumer perceptions and acceptance of drone delivery services while exploring the relatively underexplored impact on corporate reputation. Based on survey data from 229 residents of Lisbon, the study investigates three key areas: (1) how demographic factors such as age, gender, education, and income influence perceptions of drone delivery benefits and concerns; (2) how online shopping behaviour shapes these perceptions; and (3) how awareness of drone delivery services affects both consumer attitudes and company reputation. The findings indicate that younger consumers are more favourable toward drone delivery, particularly regarding its environmental impact and efficiency, while older respondents are more sceptical. Frequent online shoppers view drone services as operational improvements, though concerns about reliability and costs remain. Awareness is critical in shaping positive perceptions of drone delivery and enhancing a company's reputation as innovative and trustworthy. This research provides strategic insights for companies, suggesting that raising awareness, addressing operational concerns, and targeting younger consumers can improve both acceptance and corporate reputation.

Keywords: Drone delivery · Awareness · Consumer behavior · Company reputation · Consumer acceptance

1 Introduction

The introduction of commercial drones has generated interest in employing drones for home deliveries, providing faster, cheaper, and more efficient delivery solutions, mainly to online businesses. This transformation has the potential to transform multiple sectors and consumer behaviors. While technological innovations have transformed corporate operations, research into user acceptance of new technological innovations, such as drones, remains limited to several industries. (Hwang et al. 2021). The rapid technological and regulatory advances in autonomous unmanned aerial vehicles (UAVs or drones) may soon make them appropriate for last-mile product deliveries. This idea can reduce

F. F.-H Nah and K. L. Siau (Eds.): HCII 2025, LNCS 16343, pp. 60–77, 2026.
https://doi.org/10.1007/978-3-032-13167-6_5

delivery costs, mitigate the adverse effects of road traffic, and eliminate missed deliveries, potentially changing the parcel delivery sector. As a result, numerous transportation and delivery companies are testing drones. However, the existing literature must provide a full market potential analysis for this system (Aurambout et al. 2022). To contribute to this initiative, this study's focus is to comprehend further the interaction between users (consumers) with drones, specifically, the general perception and intention to use drone delivery services and the role that awareness and information play in determining customer perception. Building on the points above, this study aims to address the following research questions:

1. How do demographic factors (such as age, gender, education, and income) shape consumers' perceptions of the benefits and concerns related to drone delivery services?
2. How does consumer´s online shopping behaviour shape their perceptions of the benefits and concerns related to drone delivery services?
3. How does consumer awareness of drone delivery services and a company's use of them influence perceptions of the service and its reputation?

A theoretical framework was developed to assess whether consumers in the Lisbon Metropolitan area would accept this innovation, assessing 18 hypotheses to answer the research questions specific to this region. This framework was built upon a thorough analysis of the existing literature. For the analysis, the study employs a quantitative descriptive research design, allowing for the collection of measurable data in numbers and statistics. The goal is to use a survey to collect data on people's views on drone delivery services.

2 Literature Review

The public perception of drones has evolved significantly and remains a key factor in their adoption. In the UK, for example, the public is in the "persuasion" phase, reconsidering their stance on drones, but the decisive "adoption" phase is still pending (Miron et al. 2023). The commercial drone market is expanding rapidly, yet integrating drones into last-mile delivery systems presents regulatory and governance challenges. National strategies are needed to leverage drones' economic and environmental benefits, including airspace integration and greener logistics (Smith et al. 2022). Despite their potential to reduce traffic and pollution, drone delivery remains unfamiliar to many, hindered by regulatory uncertainty and privacy concerns (Chen et al. 2022). To foster acceptance, companies should target tech-inclined individuals. Studies show that familiarity and direct experience with drones correlate with positive attitudes, though privacy concerns persist (Smith et al. 2022).

Drone integration into urban environments is accelerating due to numerous expected benefits. One of the most prominent is its potential to transform logistics and transportation. Drones offer faster, more efficient, and often cheaper alternatives to traditional delivery methods, especially in congested urban areas (Sabino et al. 2022). Drones, beyond their economic value, fulfill critical societal roles by accessing hard-to-reach areas to deliver medical supplies and support search and rescue operations, thereby reducing risks to human responders (Kellermann et al. 2020). Drones also enhance urban mobility by reducing road congestion and offering potential for passenger transport, such as air taxis (Sabino et al. 2022). In healthcare, drones deliver supplies to remote areas and transport samples for testing, improving patient outcomes (Kellermann et al. 2020). They also improve traffic management by monitoring violations and alerting drivers (Raj & Sah 2019). They also drive innovation in fields like AI and robotics creating new jobs and economic opportunities (Raj & Sah 2019). As regulatory frameworks evolve, drones are poised to become a transformative force in modern urban life (Sabino et al. 2022; Kellermann et al. 2020; Raj & Sah 2019).

H1: Different demographic factors, such as age, gender, education, and residential location, significantly influence how consumers perceive the benefits of drone delivery services.

H1.1- Age influences the perception of the benefits of drone delivery services.

H1.2 – Gender influences the perception of the benefits of drone delivery services.

H1.3 - Academic Background influences the perception of the benefits of drone delivery services.

H1.4 – Residential Location influences the perception of the benefits of drone delivery services.

Recent studies reveal growing concerns about drones in civilian settings, particularly regarding privacy, misuse, malfunction, safety, noise and legal liability. Privacy is a major issue for rural residents. Gender plays a significant role in drone acceptance: men are generally more optimistic about drone services, while women express greater concern over malfunctions and privacy, perceive fewer benefits, and are more supportive of regulation. This may stem from women's limited experience with drones and under-representation in technical roles (Smith et al. 2022). Age also influences attitudes. Older adults (65+) show lower awareness and support for drones, perceiving higher risks due to unfamiliarity with the technology (Smith et al. 2022; Reddy & DeLaurentis). Geographical location matters too as urban residents are more open to drone use, focusing on safety and performance, while rural and suburban populations emphasize privacy. Industrial zones show the highest acceptance, while residential areas show the least due to concerns about intrusion (Sabino et al. 2022). Education and technical knowledge correlate with acceptance. More informed individuals support drone use but are cautious about deployment in sensitive areas. Educated users are also more concerned about environmental impacts (Sabino et al. 2022). Privacy concerns are heightened by drones' data collection capabilities, including facial recognition and thermal imaging, prompting calls for stricter regulation and pilot identification (Ramadan et al. 2017). Legal concerns include drone flights over private property and the difficulty of identifying operators. Public support exists for pilot registration to ensure accountability (Sabino et al. 2022). Demographic factors—gender, age, education, and location—significantly shape public attitudes toward drones (Wang et al. 2023; Smith et al. 2022; Yaprak et al.; Hwang & Kim). As drone use expands, addressing these concerns through regulation and public education is essential for broader acceptance.

H2: Demographic factors play a significant role in shaping consumers' concerns about drone delivery services.

H2.1 - Age influences the perception of concerns about drone delivery services.

H2.2 - Gender influences the perception of concerns about drone delivery services.

H2.3 Academic Background influences the perception of concerns about drone delivery services.

H2.4 - Residential Location influences the perception of concerns about drone delivery services.

Drones´ adoption is influenced by both rational and emotional consumer behavior, shaped by psychological, social, and economic factors such as gender, education, income, and lifestyle (Makarewicz 2013). Gender differences are notable, women express more concern about drone malfunctions and privacy, while men are more optimistic and experienced with drones (Smith et al. 2022). Consumer behavior evolves with technology. Online shopping habits, influenced by convenience, trust, and price, significantly shape perceptions of drone delivery (Ayalew & Zewdie 2022; Mircea Fuciu 2015). Digital behavior, including social media use, also affects how consumers perceive drone benefits and risks (Efendioğlu 2024). Emotional and intellectual responses to drones are shaped by marketing, peer influence, and product design (Ayalew & Zewdie 2022). As drones become central to retail experiences, they are increasingly seen as part of brand identity (Ramadan et al. 2017). Understanding evolving consumer behavior, especially online, is essential for predicting acceptance of drone delivery. Sociodemographic factors like age, gender, and digital literacy continue to influence consumer trust, expectations, and concerns about drone technology (Makarewicz 2013; Smith et al. 2022).

H4: Consumer's online shopping behavior significantly impacts their perception of the concerns of drone delivery services.

Awareness, broadly defined as being informed or alert, varies by context ranging from public health knowledge (Gafoor 2012) to self-perception in psychology (Fitzgerald 2003). In technology adoption, social influence and awareness are crucial, as shown in the extended Technology Acceptance Model (Venkatesh & Davis 2000). Social and perspective awareness also enhance collaboration (Steinfield et al. 1999). Emotional awareness, often stronger in women, enables better emotional articulation without implying greater intensity (Feldman Barrett et al. 2000). In marketing, brand awareness—especially through advertising—drives customer loyalty (Han 2012; Khan 2012). Awareness influences consumer perceptions of drone delivery services, with functional, emotional, and brand awareness shaping attitudes (Gafoor 2012; Fitzgerald 2003; Ramadan et al. 2017).

H5: Increased awareness of drone delivery services positively influences consumers' perception of the benefits associated with these services.

Numerous authors provide research supporting the premise that increasing awareness of drone delivery services increases perceptions of related concerns. According to Gafoor (2012) and Fitzgerald (2003), customers can better identify potential dangers and challenges as they become more knowledgeable. Venkatesh and Davis (2000) emphasize the importance of awareness and social influences in generating worries about new technology. In contrast, Steinfield et al. (1999) argue that different levels of awareness increase understanding of potential risks. Feldman Barrett et al. (2000) argue that enhanced emotional awareness can amplify risk perceptions, and Khan (2012) demonstrates that brand awareness can also increase worry about new technology.

H6: As consumers become more aware of drone delivery services, their perception of the concerns associated with these services also increases.

Corporate reputation is a dynamic, multidimensional construct shaped by stakeholder perceptions of a company's identity, innovation, and values (Santos, 2018). In high-tech sectors, innovation, such as drone delivery, plays a crucial role in enhancing reputation and competitiveness (Ou & Hsu 2013). Drones exemplify technological advancement that can improve customer experience, operational efficiency, and brand perception. As drone delivery becomes more visible, it contributes to a company's innovative image, fostering trust and loyalty (Santos 2018). Reputation built on innovation can lead to increased customer engagement, though it may not always translate into higher prices or retention (Santos 2018). Awareness driven by advertising also strengthens reputation (Fitzgerald 2003; Khan 2012). Studies suggest that consumer knowledge of drone applications positively influences brand perception (Ramadan et al. 2017). As drones become integral to service delivery, companies must align innovation with strategic communication to build reputation. Future research should explore how specific innovations like drones impact reputation across industries (Breitenbach 2015), reinforcing the link between technological advancement and stakeholder trust.

H7: A company's reputation is positively impacted by consumers' awareness of its use of drone delivery services.

A conceptual model was developed to understand the structure of the study better. Demographic Information, Online Consumer Behavior, Awareness, Perception of Benefits, Concerns, and Company Reputation are the variables considered (Fig. 1).

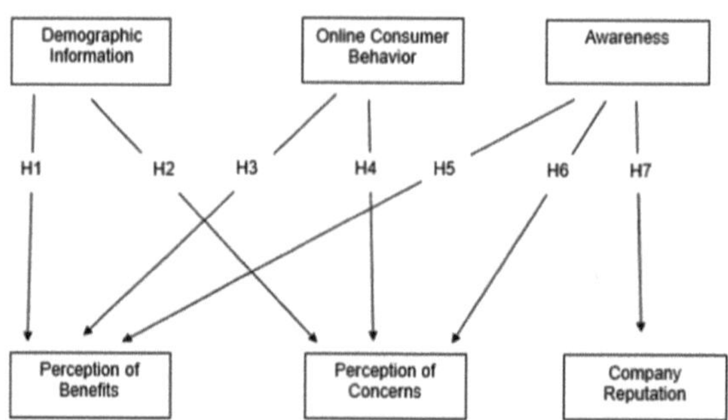

Fig. 1. Conceptual Model

3 Methodology

This study employs a quantitative descriptive research design, allowing for the collection of measurable data in numbers and statistics. A web-based survey was selected as the research instrument for its numerous advantages. The MANOVA Test was used to conduct this analysis as it provides a more robust overall significance test and is more efficient in calculation and interpretation, making it the better option when simultaneously dealing with multiple dependent variables (Parsad 1987). Since the sample size for each dependent and independent variable combination exceeds 20, we may use the Multivariate Central Limit Theorem. The web survey is structured into six sections to gather data on consumer perceptions, awareness, and the impact of drone delivery services. Each section is tied to specific hypotheses and research questions. The survey is designed to comprehensively test each hypothesis and research question by connecting demographic factors, behaviour, awareness, perceptions, and company reputation. It was organized in the following sections: (1) Socioeconomic Information: Collects demographic data (age, gender, education) to test how these factors influence perceptions of drone delivery benefits and concerns (H1, H2); (2) Consumer u in Online Shopping: Examines online shopping habits and delivery preferences to analyze their impact on perceptions of drone delivery (H3, H4); (3) Awareness: Measures awareness of drones beyond military uses to explore their connection to perceptions of benefits and concerns (H5, H6); (4) Perception of Benefits: Evaluate views on the advantages of drone delivery, such as environmental impact and cost efficiency, linked to demographics, consumer behaviour, and awareness (H1, H3, H5); (5) Perception of Concerns: Assesses concerns related to privacy, safety, and reliability to test how demographics, shopping behaviour, and awareness shape these perceptions (H2, H4, H6); (6) Impact on Company Reputation: Examines how drone delivery affects a company's reputation, testing H7.

4 Results and Discussion

4.1 Sample

The data collection for this research was conducted through a quantitative web-based survey utilizing the Google Forms platform. The survey was open for responses over 30 days, from May 1 to May 31 2024. This timeframe was chosen to allow ample opportunity for many participants to engage with the survey. In total 244 replies were collected. The target population for this research includes adults aged 18 to 44 living in Lisbon. This age group was chosen based on a Eurostat article highlighting a surge in e-commerce across the EU, mainly driven by individuals aged 25–34 and 35–44. In 2023, 87% and 85% of people in these age groups, respectively, purchased or ordered goods or services online (Eurostat 2024). This makes them the most relevant demographic for studying the adoption of innovations like drone delivery services.

Within the final sample, 51.1% of the participants were female, while 48.9% were male. The age distribution showed that most respondents fell within the 25–34 age group (28.8%), indicating strong representation from this demographic. Additionally, 50.2% of the respondents had an academic background in bachelor's degree, offering valuable insights into how education level may influence perceptions and attitudes toward drone delivery services. These characteristics were essential for providing a well-rounded perspective to the research findings (Table 1).

Table 1. Descriptive statistics

	Mean	Median	Std. Dev
A2 - How important is fast delivery (same-day or next-day delivery) when making online purchases?	3,11	3,00	0,823

(continued)

Table 1. (*continued*)

	Mean	Median	Std. Dev
A3 - Have you ever opted to pay an additional fee for expedited shipping when making online purchases?	2,28	2,00	0,875
A4 - How likely are you to try new delivery methods, such as drone delivery, if they promise a faster delivery?	2,92	3,00	0,880
B1 - I am aware that drones can be employed to deliver items	3,85	4,00	1,122
B2 - I am aware of the way drones operate	3,63	4,00	1,248
B3 - My first reply when hearing about drone delivery service is positive	3,64	4,00	0,752
B4 - I am aware that drones have uses outside military application	3,44	3,00	1,014
C1 - Drone delivery service is more environmentally friendly than the traditional delivery methods	3,56	4,00	0,849
C2 - Drone delivery service is going to reduce traffic congestion	3,82	4,00	1,004
C3 - Drone delivery service helps to lower the delivery costs	3,18	3,00	0,837
C4 - Drone delivery service increases the delivery efficiency	3,24	3,00	0,864
C5 - Drone delivery service has a lower maintenance	3,49	4,00	1,029
C6 - Drone delivery systems improve the responsiveness of the service	3,38	3,00	0,832
C7 - Drone delivery services have more scheduling flexibility	3,51	4,00	1,020
D1 - Drone delivery services may violate privacy	3,24	3,00	0,812
D2 - Drone delivery services may malfunction throughout the service	3,34	3,00	0,847
D3 - Throughout Drone Delivery Services It is more probable that the delivery may arrive damaged	3,70	4,00	0,983
D4 - Drone delivery services are noisier than the traditional delivery methods	3,04	5,00	1,127
D5 - Drone delivery services have a transport limitation (size of the delivery items)	4,25	5,00	0,897
D6 - Drone delivery services have a transport limitation (dependability of the weather)	4,20	5,00	0,948
D7 - Drone delivery services have a higher upfront cost	3,86	4,00	0,960
E1 - How do you think the adoption of drone delivery service would impact a company's reputation?	4,09	4,00	0,925
E2 - How important is a company's reputation to you when deciding whether to use its products or services?	3,33	3,00	1,032
E3 - Would you be more likely to trust a company that implements innovative delivery methods like drone delivery?	3,07	3,00	0,991

(continued)

Table 1. (*continued*)

	Mean	Median	Std. Dev
E4 - How do you perceive the reputation of a company that employs drone delivery services compared to companies utilizing traditional delivery methods?	3,81	4,00	0,929
E5 - Have you ever changed your opinion of a company based on its adoption of new technologies or innovative services?	2,71	3,00	1,007

Reliability refers to the consistency of measures. A reliability of 1 implies that all variability is due to fundamental differences with no measurement error, while a reliability of 0 suggests that all variability is caused by measurement error. A reliability of 0.5 represents equal contributions from fundamental differences and measurement errors. This means that someone whose actual value is the same as the group average will have measured values overlapping with the entire population's exact value distribution. To improve reliability, either minimize measurement error or increase natural variability within the sample, reducing error (Matheson 2019).

Table 2 presents the reliability analysis conducted for each segment to demonstrate the validity of the group of statements. The results indicate that Cronbach's alpha exceeded 0.70 for each category, confirming that the findings are highly reliable.

Table 2. Reliability Statistics

Segment analyzed	Number of items	Cronbach's Alpha
Online Consumer Behaviour	5	0,755
Awareness	4	0,711
Perception of Benefits	7	0,871
Perception of Concerns	7	0,763
Company Reputation	5	0,872

4.2 Impact of Demographics on the Perception of Benefits

The research on demographic parameters that influence people's perceptions of the benefits of drone delivery services yields various outcomes. First, age statistically significantly influences how consumers perceive the benefits of drone delivery services (Wilks' Lambda = 0.659, p-value = 0.035). This suggests that age substantially impacts how consumers evaluate the advantages of drone delivery, such as environmental benefits, financial efficiency, and operational efficiencies. Thus, H1.1 is validated.

In contrast, gender has no statistically significant effect on perceptions of drone delivery benefits, as evidenced by a Wilks' Lambda of 0.926 and a p-value of 0.064. While the result is close to significance, it is not less than the standard threshold of 0.05, implying that gender does not play a significant influence in shaping how customers perceive the advantages. Consequently, H1.2 is rejected. Similarly, academic education has no bearing on how people perceive the benefits of drone delivery. With a Wilks' Lambda of 0.848 and a p-value of 0.752, the data reveal no significant association between academic background and perceived benefits of drone delivery services. Therefore, H1.3 is rejected. Finally, residential location has no significant impact on how consumers perceive the benefits of drone delivery services, as evidenced by a Wilks' Lambda of 0.927 and a p-value of 0.505. This finding implies that where a consumer lives has no substantial effect on their perception of the advantages, leading to the conclusion that H1.4 is rejected. In conclusion, the study reveals that age is a significant factor in shaping opinions of the benefits of drone delivery services, but gender, academic background, and residential location have little influence.

To extract more information on the age variable, a correlation analysis of age and perceived benefits of drone delivery services indicates several significant unfavorable relationships. Older people are less likely to think drone delivery is environmentally benign, with a Pearson's correlation of -0.150 (p = 0.023). A more significant negative association is shown for the opinion that drone delivery will lessen traffic congestion (-0.182, p = 0.006), implying that older respondents are less sure of this benefit. Similarly, older people are less likely to view drone delivery as a cost-cutting measure, with a correlation coefficient of -0.138 (p = 0.036). Furthermore, older respondents are less likely to perceive that drone improve service responsiveness (-0.133, p = 0.044) or provide better schedule flexibility, as evidenced by a significant negative correlation of -0.194 (p = 0.003). However, there is no significant link between age and perceptions of drone delivery efficiency (-0.035, p = 0.597) or lower maintenance costs (0.033, p = 0.614), indicating that these benefits are perceived identically across age groups. To summarize, as people get older, their perceptions of the benefits of drone delivery services decrease, especially in terms of environmental impact, traffic reduction, cost savings, responsiveness, and flexibility.

4.3 The Impact of Demographics on the Perception of Concerns

Results of the analysis reveal that demographic factors have differing effects on consumers' perceptions of concerns about drone delivery services. First, age is found to have a statistically significant impact on how consumers perceive concerns, with a Wilks' Lambda value of 0.749 and a p-value of 0.005. This shows that older and younger consumers may have different perspectives on potential concerns with drone delivery. As a result, H2.1 is validated, demonstrating that age considerably influences the perceptions for concerns. In contrast, gender does not substantially impact consumers' perceptions of concerns. The Wilks' Lambda value of 0.944 and p-value of 0.189 indicate that gender has a minor effect in shaping these concerns. Therefore, H2.2 is rejected. Similarly, academic background has no statistically significant effect on the perception of concerns, as evidenced by a Wilks' Lambda value of 0.773 and a p-value of 0.111. This result suggests that H2.3 is likewise rejected. Finally, the research shows that residential location considerably impacts the perception of concerns, with a Wilks' Lambda value of 0.861 and a p-value of 0.024. This suggests that where consumers live influences their concerns regarding drone delivery services, which validates H2.4. In conclusion, the study reveals that age and residential location substantially impact consumers' impressions of concerns about drone delivery services, although gender and academic background do not.

The link between age and concerns concerning drone delivery services was further analysed demonstrating variable effects across topics. A substantial negative relationship exists between age and privacy concerns ($r = -0.138$, $p = 0.037$), implying that older people are less concerned about privacy infractions. Concerns about drone delivery failures show a more significant negative connection ($r = -0.208$, $p = 0.002$), indicating that older respondents are less concerned about system malfunctions. Although the correlation between age and concerns about damaged delivery is negative ($r = -0.124$), it is not statistically significant ($p = 0.061$), reflecting weaker evidence that age influences this concern. Similarly, concerns regarding drone noise reveal a very modest negative association ($r = -0.077$, $p = 0.246$), indicating that age has no meaningful bearing on this problem. Transport limits, such as item size and weather reliability, show a higher negative connection with age ($r = -0.260$ and $r = -0.252$, respectively, $p < 0.001$), indicating that older people are less concerned about these limitations. However, age does not significantly affect concerns about increased upfront expenditures ($r = -0.109$, $p = 0.0101$). In conclusion, age considerably impacts concerns regarding privacy, malfunctions, and transportation limits, with older people often being less concerned about these issues. However, age does not affect concerns regarding loudness, damaged goods, or expenses.

4.4   The Impact of Resident Location on the Perception of Concerns

There is a minor positive association between residential features and privacy concerns ($r = 0.036$, $p = 0.585$), indicating no substantial relationship between where people live and their concerns about privacy infringement. Concerns regarding weather-related transportation limits reveal a stronger positive association ($r = 0.132$, $p = 0.046$), indicating that residency has a tiny but statistically significant impact. Concerns about higher upfront costs have a weak negative association ($r = -0.043$, $p = 0.517$) but no substantial relationship to residential qualities. Most concerns about drone delivery services are unaffected by resident characteristics, except for a minor but statistically significant correlation with concerns about weather-dependent transportation limits. Where people live have little impact on privacy, malfunctions, noise, and expenses.

The research found that age and residency substantially influence consumers' concerns about drone delivery services, although gender and academic background do not. The MANOVA results show that age ($p = 0.005$) and residency ($p = 0.024$) statistically influence these issues. In contrast, gender ($p = 0.189$) and academic background ($p = 0.111$) have no significant effect on consumer concerns.

Correlation analysis supports these findings, revealing that older respondents are often less concerned about privacy infringement, service malfunctions, and transportation limits (including item size and weather dependability). Similarly, residency has a significant impact, particularly in influencing worries about the reliability of drone delivery services in different weather situations. In conclusion, H2 is partially supported because age and residency are key demographic characteristics impacting consumers' concerns about drone delivery services, whereas gender and academic background have no significant impact. These findings indicate that certain demographic factors have a more substantial effect on determining consumer concerns than others.

4.5 Impact of Online Behavior on the Perception of Benefits

Analyzing the relationship between online purchasing and drone delivery services' perceived benefits finds several significant correlations, supporting Hypothesis 3 (H3). Consumers' online buying habits are related to how they perceive the benefits of drone delivery services. First, there is a substantial but slight correlation between the frequency of online purchasing and the opinion that drone delivery services are more environmentally friendly ($r = 0.137$, $p = 0.039$) and that drones improve delivery efficiency ($r = 0.130$, $p = 0.050$). This shows that people who shop online frequently are more inclined to see drone delivery services as environmentally friendly and operationally effective. Rapid delivery is substantially and continuously linked to various perceived benefits of drone delivery. Drones are associated with reduced traffic congestion ($r = 0.204$, $p = 0.002$), lower maintenance costs ($r = 0.263$, $p < 0.001$), and improved service responsiveness ($r = 0.151$, $p = 0.022$). These findings suggest that consumers who value fast delivery view drones as a feasible solution to reduce logistical issues while increasing service flexibility and speed. Additionally, individuals willing to pay for accelerated shipment associate drone delivery with lower maintenance ($r = 0.215$, $p = 0.001$) and better responsiveness, underscoring the belief that drones have operational advantages over traditional delivery methods.

The most significant correlations occur among consumers willing to explore innovative delivery methods, such as drones. There are substantial relationships observed across a range of perceived benefits, including reduced traffic congestion ($r = 0.143$, $p = 0.031$), lowered delivery costs ($r = 0.269$, $p < 0.001$), increased delivery efficiency ($r = 0.170$, $p = 0.010$), reduced maintenance ($r = 0.246$, $p < 0.001$), and improved responsiveness. This suggests that early adopters of new delivery systems view drones as having several logistical and operational advantages.

Finally, satisfaction with online shopping experiences correlates to various perceived benefits of drone delivery, such as reduced traffic congestion ($r = 0.199$, $p = 0.020$), lower delivery costs ($r = 0.199$, $p = 0.002$), and less maintenance ($r = 0.198$, $p = 0.003$). This shows that customers happy with their online purchasing experiences are more likely to see drone delivery as a credible alternative for improving logistics and operational efficiency.

In conclusion, H3 is valid, as multiple significant correlations were discovered between online buying behavior and the perceived benefits of drone delivery services. Consumers who value fast delivery, are open to innovative delivery methods and are satisfied with their online purchasing experiences are likelier to see drones as applicable for traffic reduction, cheaper maintenance costs, increased responsiveness, and overall efficiency.

4.6 Impact of Online Behavior on Perception of Concerns

The study of the correlation between purchasing habits on the internet and concerns about drone delivery services reveals conflicting results for Hypothesis 4 (H4). Consumers' online shopping habits are significantly associated with fears of drone delivery services.

Prioritizing speedy delivery correlates with concerns about damaged deliveries ($r = 0.247$, $p < 0.001$). The desire to pay for accelerated shipment correlates with many issues, such as damaged deliveries ($r = 0.289$, $p < 0.001$), delivery item size constraints ($r = 0.243$, $p < 0.001$), and more excellent upfront prices ($r = 0.294$, $p < 0.001$). According to these data, buyers who prioritize or pay for speedier delivery are more likely to be concerned about potential difficulties such as damage, size constraints, and increased expenses related to drone delivery.

Furthermore, consumers who are willing to try new delivery methods exhibit significant correlations with concerns about damaged deliveries ($r = 0.140$, $p = 0.034$) and higher upfront costs ($r = 0.137$, $p = 0.038$), implying that those who adopt new technologies may have specific concerns about these issues. Other purchasing behaviors, such as online shopping frequency, show little or no significant correlation with most concerns, implying that certain activities are not strongly linked to perceptions of drone delivery risks.

In conclusion, H4 is valid. While some online shopping behaviors, such as the necessity of fast delivery and readiness to test novel delivery methods, have a considerable impact on concerns regarding drone delivery services, others, such as online buying frequency, have less influence. This shows that some features of online shopping behavior are more influential in determining consumers' fears about drone delivery.

4.7 The Effect of Awareness on the Perception of Benefits

The analysis of the relationship between awareness and perception of drone delivery benefits provides data to support Hypothesis 5 (H5), which states that higher awareness of drone delivery services improves consumers' perception of the associated benefits.

The results reveal multiple substantial relationships between different dimensions of awareness and customers' perceptions of the advantages. A general understanding of drone technology and its utilization correlates with judgments of better efficiency ($r = 0.219$, $p < 0.001$), improved responsiveness ($r = 0.192$, $p < 0.001$), and cheaper delivery costs ($r = 0.155$, $p = 0.019$). Drone awareness correlates with benefits such as environmental friendliness ($r = 0.229$, $p < 0.001$), reduced traffic congestion ($r = 0.262$, $p < 0.001$), and improved responsiveness. Furthermore, understanding drones' non-military applications is substantially associated with environmental benefits ($r = 0.209$, $p = 0.001$) and lower delivery costs ($r = 0.171$, $p = 0.009$).

The results demonstrate that consumers who are more knowledgeable about drone technology and its possible uses are more likely to recognize the advantages of drone delivery services, particularly in terms of environmental impact, efficiency, responsiveness, and cost savings. Although some awareness components have weaker or non-significant associations with specific advantages, the general findings support the idea.

In conclusion, H5 is valid. Increased customer awareness of drone delivery services has a beneficial impact on their perceived benefits, notably in terms of environmental friendliness, traffic reduction, efficiency, responsiveness, and cost savings. These findings highlight the role of customer awareness in influencing positive attitudes toward drone delivery technology.

4.8 The Impact of Awareness on Perception of Concerns

According to the correlation analysis, Hypothesis 6 (H6) indicates, "As consumers become more aware of drone delivery services, their perception of the concerns associated with these services also increases." Research results reveal considerable beneficial links between dimensions of awareness and specific concerns. For example, awareness of drone activities is substantially connected with worries about malfunctions ($r = 0.167$, $p = 0.011$) and weather-related transportation limits ($r = 0.133$, $p = 0.044$). Awareness of drone applications correlates with concerns about malfunctions ($r = 0.219$, $p < 0.001$) and transportation limits ($r = 0.143$, $p = 0.030$). These findings show that as consumers become more aware of drone services, their concerns regarding specific operational and logistical hazards, such as failures and transport, tend to increase. However, no significant correlations were identified between damaged deliveries, noise levels, and upfront prices. This implies that while awareness raises some concerns, it does not affect all potential issues uniformly. Since awareness considerably impacts some concerns but not others, the theory is only sometimes applicable. As a result, H6 is rejected because raising awareness does not reliably improve concerns about drone delivery services.

4.9 The Impact of Awareness on Companies' Reputation

The analysis explores the relationship between consumers' awareness of drone delivery services and their perception of a company's reputation to assess Hypothesis 7 (H7). Consumers are more aware of a company's use of drone delivery services, which benefits its reputation. The research results establish substantial positive relationships between awareness and reputation. Awareness of drone operations has a positive impact on a company's reputation, including perceptions of innovation ($r = 0.155$, $p = 0.019$), trustworthiness ($r = 0.248$, $p < 0.001$), and high-quality service ($r = 0.246$, $p < 0.001$). Similarly, general awareness of drone technology is significantly positively related to assessing the company's trustworthiness ($r = 0.153$, $p = 0.021$). Awareness of how drones work is also positively correlated with the perception that the company provides high-quality service ($r = 0.203$, $p = 0.002$), implying that consumers who understand the operational aspects of drone delivery are more likely to perceive companies that use drones as providing high-quality services.

4.10 Summary

The respondents´ replies to the collected information allow to conclude that they favor drone delivery, especially for environmental benefits and reducing traffic, but are more uncertain about cost savings and efficiency. The most significant concerns are operational limits seen as critical barriers to drone delivery success while damage to goods is also a notable issue, and concerns about privacy, malfunctions, and noise are less prominent. Respondents who shop online frequently, value fast delivery moderately, and are open to innovations like drone delivery but are less willing to pay extra for expedited shipping. In addition, high awareness of drones in delivery services and a positive attitude toward drone delivery. Knowledge gaps exist in understanding drone operations and non-military applications, suggesting opportunities for further education. With regard to a company´s reputation, it was found that drone delivery services enhance a company's reputation, though its impact on trust and changing perceptions is more moderate. Finally, reputational value is important, but innovation alone may not shift public opinion without clear benefits.

The results of the statistical analysis are summarized as follows and the hypothesis results are in Table 3:

1. As age increases, perceptions of drone delivery benefits generally decline, particularly regarding environmental friendliness, traffic reduction, cost savings, service responsiveness, and scheduling flexibility. However, age does not significantly impact views on delivery efficiency or maintenance costs, suggesting these benefits are seen consistently across age groups.
2. The study reveals that age and residential location substantially impact consumers' perceptions of concerns about drone delivery services, although gender and academic background do not.
3. Age considerably impacts concerns regarding privacy, malfunctions, and transportation limits, with older people often being less concerned about these issues. However, age does not affect concerns regarding loudness, damaged goods, or expenses.
4. Most concerns about drone delivery services are unaffected by resident characteristics, except for a minor but statistically significant correlation with concerns about weather-dependent transportation limits. Where people live has little impact on privacy, malfunctions, noise, and expenses.
5. Online buying behavior significantly correlates with positive perceptions of drone delivery benefits. Consumers who value quick delivery, are open to innovation and enjoy their online shopping experience view drones as beneficial for traffic reduction, reduced costs, increased responsiveness, and improved efficiency.
6. Certain online shopping behaviors, like the need for fast delivery and willingness to try new delivery methods, strongly influence concerns about drone delivery services, while behaviors like the frequency of online purchases have a lesser impact. This suggests that specific aspects of online shopping behavior play a more significant role in shaping consumer concerns about drone delivery.
7. Increased customer awareness of drone delivery services has a beneficial impact on their perceived benefits, notably in terms of environmental friendliness, traffic reduction, efficiency, responsiveness, and cost savings. These findings highlight the role of customer awareness in influencing positive attitudes toward drone delivery technology.
8. Research findings indicate that higher awareness of drone services is linked to increased concerns about specific operational risks, such as malfunctions and weather limitations, while it has little effect on concerns like damaged deliveries, noise, and upfront costs.

9. The analysis finds that consumer awareness of drone delivery services generally enhances a company's reputation, particularly in perceptions of innovation, trustworthiness, and service quality. Positive correlations exist between awareness of drone operations and increased reputation. The findings indicate that general awareness of drone delivery services positively affects a company's reputation

Table 3. Hypothesis Results.

Hypothesis	Test	Conclusion
H1.1: Influence that age has on the perception of benefits of drone delivery services	MANOVA	Validated
H1.2: Influence that gender has on the perception of benefits of drone delivery services	MANOVA	Rejected
H1.3: Influence that academic background has on the perception of benefits of drone delivery services	MANOVA	Rejected
H1.4: Influence that residential location has on the perception of benefits of drone delivery services	MANOVA	Rejected
H2.1: Influence that age has on the perception of concerns of drone delivery services	MANOVA	Validated
H2.2: Influence that gender has on the perception of concerns of drone delivery services	MANOVA	Rejected
H2.3: Influence that academic background has on the perception of concerns of drone delivery	MANOVA	Rejected
H2.4: Influence that residential location has on the perception of concerns of drone delivery	MANOVA	Validated
H3: Consumers' online shopping behavior significantly impacts their perception of the benefits of drone delivery services	Correlation	Validated
H4: Consumer's online shopping behavior significantly impacts their perception of the concerns of drone delivery services	Correlation	Validated
H5: Increased awareness of drone delivery services positively influences consumers' perception of the benefits associated with these services	Correlation	Validated
H6: As consumers become more aware of drone delivery services, their perception of the concerns associated with these services also increases	Correlation	Rejected
H7: A company's reputation is positively impacted by consumers' awareness of its use of drone delivery services	Correlation	Validated

5   Conclusion

This study provides a comprehensive analysis of the role of consumer awareness and perception in the acceptance of drone delivery services and its impact on a company's reputation. It addresses the primary research objectives by evaluating customer perceptions, examining how drone delivery relates to changes in corporate reputation, and investigating the factors influencing these perceptions. The study also answers the three research questions concerning demographic factors, online shopping behavior, and consumer awareness by integrating insights from a detailed literature review and empirical findings.

The literature review laid the theoretical foundation by identifying critical factors influencing the adoption of drone delivery services, such as consumer awareness, demographics, and online shopping behavior. It emphasized the potential reputational benefits for companies adopting innovative delivery methods while highlighting the importance of addressing consumer concerns, particularly regarding privacy, reliability, and safety. These theoretical insights were supported by the empirical analysis based on data from 229 respondents in the Lisbon Metropolitan area.

In response to the first research question, the study demonstrates that demographic factors, particularly age and residential location, significantly shape consumer perceptions of drone delivery services. Younger consumers and those in urban areas tend to view drone delivery more favorably, particularly regarding environmental sustainability, cost-efficiency, and faster delivery times. In contrast, older consumers and those in rural areas express more concerns about privacy, reliability, and safety.

The second research question, concerning online shopping behavior, reveals that frequent online shoppers and those who value fast delivery are more open to trying drone delivery services. However, they also express concerns about potential issues such as damaged deliveries and higher upfront costs. These findings suggest that online shopping habits are crucial in shaping drone delivery services' perceived benefits and concerns.

The third research question, focusing on consumer awareness, shows that higher levels of awareness are associated with more positive evaluations of drone delivery benefits. However, increased awareness also amplifies concerns about privacy and safety. Importantly, the study demonstrates that companies implementing drone delivery can enhance their reputation, mainly if consumers know about their innovative initiatives. Yet, these reputational benefits can be mitigated by consumer concerns, emphasizing the need for companies to address these issues to capitalize on the positive impact fully.

Despite its contributions, this study has several limitations. The sample is confined to the Lisbon Metropolitan area, limiting the generalizability of the findings to other regions or countries. The reliance on self-reported data may introduce bias, and the cross-sectional design does not allow for observing changes in consumer perceptions over time. Additionally, some consumer concerns, particularly those related to privacy and safety, require further exploration to understand the underlying causes of skepticism.

Future research should address these limitations by expanding the scope to include more diverse and representative samples across different regions and countries. Longitudinal studies provide insights into how consumer perceptions evolve as drone delivery services become more widespread. Furthermore, qualitative research could delve deeper into the reasons behind consumer concerns and identify strategies to mitigate them effectively. Investigating how companies can better communicate the benefits of drone delivery, particularly regarding privacy and safety, would further enrich understanding in this field.

In conclusion, this study achieves its research objectives. It provides straightforward answers to the research questions by showing how consumer awareness, demographics, and online shopping behavior shape the acceptance of drone delivery services and their impact on corporate reputation. By addressing consumer concerns and leveraging positive perceptions of innovation, companies can successfully integrate drone delivery into their operations, enhancing efficiency and market position. Integrating theoretical insights from the literature and empirical findings offers a robust framework for understanding and addressing the factors that influence the adoption of drone delivery services and their potential impact on business success.

Acknowledgments. A third level heading in 9-point font size at the end of the paper is used for general acknowledgments, for example: This study was funded by X (grant number Y).

Disclosure of Interests. The authors have no competing interests to declare that are relevant to the content of this article.

References

Aurambout, J.P., Gkoumas, K., Ciuffo, B.: A drone hop from the local shop? Where could drone delivery as a service happen in Europe and the USA, and how many people could benefit from it? Transport. Res. Interdiscipl. Perspect. **16**, 100708 (2022). https://doi.org/10.1016/J.TRIP.2022.100708

Ayalew, M., Zewdie, S.: What factors determine the online consumer behavior in this digitalized world? a systematic literature. Hum. Behav. Emerg. Technol. **2022** (2022). https://doi.org/10.1155/2022/1298378

Chen, C., Leon, S., Ractham, P.: Will customers adopt last-mile drone delivery services? An analysis of drone delivery in the emerging market economy. Cogent Bus. Manage. **9**(1) (2022). https://doi.org/10.1080/23311975.2022.2074340

E-commerce statistics for individuals - Statistics Explained. (n.d.). Retrieved August 17, 2024, from https://ec.europa.eu/eurostat/statistics-explained/index.php?title=E-commerce_statistics_for_individuals

Efendioğlu, İ.H.: digital consumer behavior: a systematic literature review. Prizren Soc. Sci. J. **8**(1) (2024). https://doi.org/10.32936/PSSJ.V8I1.479

Fitzgerald, B.: The role of social awareness in technology acceptance of groupware in virtual learning (2003). https://www.academia.edu/73883983/The_role_of_social_awareness_in_technology_acceptance_of_groupware_in_virtual_learning

Foreign population Lisbon 2022 | Statista. (n.d.). Retrieved August 17, 2024. https://www.statista.com/statistics/1456505/number-of-foreign-population-lisbon/

Gafoor, A.: Considerations in measurement of awareness Natl. Seminar Emerg. **2** (2012)

Hassanalian, M., Abdelkefi, A.: Classifications, applications, and design challenges of drones: a review. Prog. Aerosp. Sci. **91**, 99–131 (2017). https://doi.org/10.1016/j.paerosci.2017.04.003

Hwang, J., Kim, J.J., Lee, K.W.: Investigating consumer innovativeness in the context of drone food delivery services: its impact on attitude and behavioral intentions. Technol. Forecast. Soc. Chang. **163**, 120433 (2021). https://doi.org/10.1016/J.TECHFORE.2020.120433

Janse, R.J., et al.: Conducting correlation analysis: important limitations and pitfalls. Clin. Kidney J. **14**(11), 2332 (2021). https://doi.org/10.1093/CKJ/SFAB085

Kellermann, R., Biehle, T., Fischer, L.: Drones for parcel and passenger transportation: a literature review. Transport. Res. Interdiscipl. Perspect. **4** (2020). https://doi.org/10.1016/J.TRIP.2019.100088

Khan, S.: Contribution of brand awareness and brand characteristics towards customer loyalty (A Study of Milk Industry of Peshawar Pakistan). J. Asian Bus. Strat. (2012). https://www.academia.edu/61061815/Contribution_of_Brand_Awareness_and_Brand_Characteristics_towards_Customer_Loyalty_A_Study_of_Milk_Industry_of_Peshawar_Pakistan_

Makarewicz, A.: Consumer behavior as a fundamental requirement for effective operations of companies. J. Int. Stud. **6**(1), 103–109 (2013). https://doi.org/10.14254/2071-8330.2013/6-1/10

Miron, M., Whetham, D., Auzanneau, M., Hill, A.: Public drone perception. Technol. Soc. **73**, 102246 (2023). https://doi.org/10.1016/J.TECHSOC.2023.102246

Ou, Y.-C., Hsu, L.-C.: How does corporate reputation affect innovative performance? Int. Bus. Res. **6**(12) (2013). https://doi.org/10.5539/IBR.V6N12P46

(PDF) multivariate analysis of variance. (n.d.). Retrieved September 19, 2024. https://www.researchgate.net/publication/237227650_MULTIVARIATE_ANALYSIS_OF_VARIANCE

Raghunatha, A., Thollander, P., Barthel, S.: Addressing the emergence of drones – a policy development framework for regional drone transportation systems. Transport. Res. Interdiscipl. Perspect. **18**, 100795 (2023). https://doi.org/10.1016/J.TRIP.2023.100795

Raj, A., Sah, B.: Analyzing critical success factors for implementation of drones in the logistics sector using grey-DEMATEL based approach. Comput. Ind. Eng. **138**, 106118 (2019). https://doi.org/10.1016/J.CIE.2019.106118

Ramadan, Z.B., Farah, M.F., Mrad, M.: An adapted TPB approach to consumers' acceptance of service-delivery drones. Technol. Anal. Strat. Manage. **29**(7), 817–828 (2017). https://doi.org/10.1080/09537325.2016.1242720

Breitenbach, R.: The services innovation contribution to formation of corporate reputation: a systematic literature review (2015). https://www.researchgate.net/publication/336107325_The_Services_Innovation_Contribution_to_Formation_of_Corporate_Reputation_A_Systematic_Literature_Review

Sabino, H., et al.: A systematic literature review on the main factors for public acceptance of drones. Technol. Soc. **71**, 102097 (2022). https://doi.org/10.1016/J.TECHSOC.2022.102097

Smith, A., Dickinson, J.E., Marsden, G., Cherrett, T., Oakey, A., Grote, M.: Public acceptance of the use of drones for logistics: the state of play and moving towards more informed debate. Technol. Soc. **68**, 101883 (2022). https://doi.org/10.1016/J.TECHSOC.2022.101883

Susana Silva Santos. O Impacto da Reputação por Inovação nos Consumidores (n.d.). Retrieved June 11, 2024 https://www.researchgate.net/publication/329844068_O_Impacto_da_Reputacao_por_Inovacao_nos_Consumidores

Wang, N., Mutzner, N., Blanchet, K.: Societal acceptance of urban drones: a scoping literature review. Technol. Soc. **75**, 102377 (2023). https://doi.org/10.1016/J.TECHSOC.2023.102377

Can We Read AI's Mind? A Quest for Transparency

Santhosh Kumar Ravindran[1]([✉]) [iD], Estera Kot[2] [iD], and Fiona Fui-Hoon Nah[3] [iD]

[1] Microsoft, One Microsoft Way, Redmond, WA 98052, USA
Santhosh.Ravindran@microsoft.com
[2] Faculty of Electrical Engineering, Warsaw University of Technology, Pl. Politechniki 1, 00-661 Warsaw, Poland
estera.kot@pw.edu.pl
[3] Singapore Management University, Singapore 178903, Singapore
fionanah@smu.edu.sg

Abstract. Although Artificial Intelligence (AI) systems are playing an increasing role in critical domains such as healthcare, finance, and autonomous systems, their decision-making processes remain largely opaque. This paper examines the challenges of AI transparency, addressing the "black box" problem using Explainable AI (XAI) techniques such as SHapley Additive exPlanations (SHAP) and Local Interpretable Model-agnostic Explanations (LIME). It also examines the ethical, regulatory, and societal implications of AI opacity and proposes a Comprehensive AI Observability (CAO) Framework that integrates deep explainability, provenance tracking, and real-time monitoring to enhance AI accountability. By bridging technical solutions with governance structures, this research emphasizes the necessity for adaptive, transparent AI-based solutions that align with ethical norms and expectations. The findings underscore the importance of interdisciplinary collaboration in making AI decisions interpretable, ensuring trust, fairness, and responsible deployment in practical applications.

Keywords: Explainable AI · Trust and Ethics in AI · Human-AI Collaboration · Data Security and Provenance · AI in Healthcare and Decision-Making

1 Introduction

As Artificial Intelligence (AI) rapidly evolves, it is also increasingly integrated into daily life, impacting sectors such as healthcare, finance, and robotics. While AI systems demonstrate remarkable capabilities that often surpass human intelligence in specific narrow domains, they also present a significant challenge due to the 'black box' nature of AI. This lack of transparency, as highlighted in [1–4], makes it difficult to understand how these systems arrive at their decisions, raising concerns about accountability and ethical implications. Hence, the focus of this paper is to address this critical issue associated with the "black box" nature of AI by examining the use of Explainable AI (XAI) to increase AI transparency.

F. F.-H Nah and K. L. Siau (Eds.): HCII 2025, LNCS 16343, pp. 78–93, 2026.
https://doi.org/10.1007/978-3-032-13167-6_6

1.1 Background

By developing methods to interpret and understand AI decision-making processes, we can empower users, regulators, and stakeholders to interact more confidently with emerging AI technologies. The broader field of XAI is crucial for enhancing transparency and identifying the most suitable techniques for different AI systems [5, 6].

The benefits of achieving AI transparency are paramount. Increased transparency can help mitigate biases, improve accountability, and protect individuals impacted by AI-driven decisions. Furthermore, establishing a common framework for analyzing societal requirements and AI norms is essential. This research not only provides valuable theoretical insights but also offers practical guidance for developing effective governance and policy frameworks for AI [7, 8].

The similarities between human and AI decision-making underscore the importance of understanding and controlling these processes, especially as we develop increasingly intelligent systems that govern daily life. The topics explored in this paper have significant implications as they reflect the growing movement towards responsible and transparent AI.

1.2 Importance of Transparency in AI Decision-Making

As AI increasingly permeates critical sectors such as healthcare, finance, and autonomous systems, the need for explainable AI becomes paramount. Deep learning models, often referred to as 'black boxes,' are notoriously difficult to understand, making it challenging to grasp how they arrive at their decisions. This lack of transparency poses significant challenges, particularly when AI systems make decisions with real-world consequences for individuals and societies.

This section delves into the core question: How can we open up these opaque systems to gain a deeper understanding of their inner workings? We explore ways to improve AI transparency, evaluate existing interpretability techniques, and identify best practices that align with ethical guidelines.

Transparency is not merely a technical issue; it is crucial for building public trust and empowering decision-makers to make informed choices. By improving transparency, we can address concerns like algorithmic bias and discrimination while upholding ethical principles in technology development. Increased transparency enhances user acceptance, improves regulatory compliance, and increases organizational accountability, particularly in sectors where decisions have significant ethical dimensions [5, 6].

Furthermore, emphasizing the need for AI transparency sends a powerful message to policymakers, developers, and users. It encourages the development of systems that are transparent, understandable, and aligned with societal needs and legal frameworks [9, 10]. Techniques like SHAP and LIME offer promising avenues for explaining AI decisions, shifting the focus from purely algorithmic models towards human-centered approaches that integrate ethical ramifications into the advancement and deployment of AI [7, 8].

The need to explain AI decisions is not a new concept. It is a fundamental principle of ethical AI development, ensuring respect for individual rights and the well-being of society.

With the rise of AI in decision-making, understanding the inner workings of these complex systems becomes paramount. This section addresses the challenge of 'reading the mind' of AI, essentially trying to decipher how AI models arrive at their conclusions – the so-called 'black box' problem [1]. The primary objective is to systematically investigate solutions to achieve AI transparency by evaluating existing interpretability frameworks, identifying the role of XAI in fostering trust and accountability, and proposing actionable strategies for increasing AI transparency. Through this structured approach, we aim to develop a deeper understanding of how to bridge the gap between computational systems and human comprehension [2, 11].

The findings from this research have significant practical implications for policy-makers, developers, and industry leaders in the ethical design and deployment of AI applications [12]. Transparency is crucial to ensure that decisions made by AI systems are understandable, justifiable, and ultimately build public trust in these technologies [5, 6].

Developing AI within the context of human values can inform governance practices, ensuring that AI addresses societal needs while upholding ethical considerations. This paper is organized into several interconnected sections. It begins with a literature review that provides the context for the current discourse on AI transparency and then delves into an in-depth analysis of various interpretability techniques and case studies that illustrate both the successes and limitations of the current methods [9, 10]. This investigation aims to contribute both theoretically and practically to the ongoing discourse on the ethical implications and societal impact of AI technologies.

2 Literature Review

In this section, we provide a review of the literature on XAI and AI transparency. We also briefly introduce two state-of-the-art XAI techniques: SHapley Additive exPlanations (SHAP) [12] and Local Interpretable Model-agnostic Explanations (LIME) [13].

2.1 Foundations

Given the rapid development and deployment of AI, it has become increasingly important to be able to explain the underlying reasoning that drives these systems. The growing interest in XAI, or the explanation of AI models, has become a crucial and indispensable topic due to the increasing societal concerns about the use of AI applications in high-stakes areas such as healthcare, finance, and justice. The inability to explain the reasoning behind AI's decisions can have serious consequences, underscoring the urgent need for frameworks that promote transparency, understanding, and accountability in AI decision-making.

The concept of AI transparency has been explored in the literature from various perspectives, including the technical challenges of interpreting models, the ethical implications of algorithms, and the societal calls for greater accountability and trust. Various approaches have been proposed to address these issues, ranging from models that help end users understand how AI functions to policies that emphasize transparency as a primary focus in AI development. However, there are critical gaps that need to be addressed.

One such gap is the integration of sociological, psychological, and policy perspectives into discussions about AI transparency. Most studies tend to focus on the technical or ethical aspects, creating a disconnect between the technical solutions and the psychosocial needs of users, as well as between theoretical work and real-world applications. Additionally, it remains unclear how transparency and accountability can be enforced, particularly in high-stakes industries.

Further investigation is warranted to establish standardized benchmarks that define transparency in AI and to explore the diverse perspectives that shape the understanding of what it means to "read AI's mind." By examining the intersection of technology, ethics, and human behavior, researchers can uncover the nuanced implications of AI transparency and contribute to the development of frameworks that enhance interpretability and foster trust. The search for transparency in AI is not merely a technological challenge but also a complex socio-ethical problem that necessitates an integrative approach. Through a comprehensive examination of these challenges, this review sets the stage for future research aimed at bridging the existing knowledge gaps and fostering meaningful dialogue surrounding AI transparency.

2.2   Evolution of the Quest for AI Transparency

The quest for AI transparency has evolved significantly over the past two decades, primarily driven by advancements in machine learning and the growing deployment of AI systems in critical domains. In the early 2000s, AI was often viewed as a "black box," with decision-making processes that were opaque to both users and developers. This opacity led to concerns about accountability, fairness, and bias. As the limitations of black-box models became more apparent, researchers began to advocate for interpretability, marking the onset of XAI. This shift was evident by 2016, when methods such as LIME [13] emerged, which allowed users to understand individual model predictions by approximating black-box models with simpler, interpretable ones. By 2018, the conversation around XAI grew more robust with the introduction of SHAP [12], which formalized the process of understanding feature contributions to model outputs. These developments highlighted the importance of transparency not only in fostering trust but also in adhering to ethical guidelines in AI deployment.

The integration of AI in sensitive sectors, such as healthcare and finance, further necessitated the creation of more rigorous governance frameworks focused on accountability and ethical considerations. As research on responsible AI advanced, privacy-preserving technologies and stronger regulatory frameworks have become increasingly important to ensure that AI systems balance effectiveness with ethical integrity.

2.3   Introduction of SHAP and LIME

As AI models continue to grow in complexity, the need for techniques that can explain their decision-making processes becomes increasingly important. Two key approaches—**LIME (Local Interpretable Model-agnostic Explanations)** and **SHAP (SHapley Additive exPlanations)**—have emerged as leading methods for enhancing the transparency of AI models.

LIME (Local Interpretable Model-agnostic Explanations). LIME is a widely used XAI technique designed to explain individual predictions of black-box machine learning models by approximating them locally with interpretable models. The fundamental idea behind LIME is that complex models (e.g., deep neural networks) can be difficult to understand as a whole, but their behavior can be approximated through simpler, more transparent models in the local vicinity of a specific data point. For a given instance to be explained, LIME generates a set of perturbed data points by modifying the original instance's features. The complex model's predictions are then observed for these perturbed samples, and a simple model (often linear regression) is trained on this data to approximate the complex model's behavior for that specific instance.

One of the key advantages of LIME is that it is model-agnostic, meaning it can be applied to any machine learning model regardless of its underlying architecture. This makes LIME highly versatile, as it can be used to interpret both traditional models (like logistic regression) and more complex, non-interpretable models (such as deep neural networks). By explaining individual predictions, LIME helps users understand the factors influencing specific outcomes, fostering trust in the AI system. However, LIME's reliance on surrogate models means that its explanations are inherently local and may not fully reflect the global behavior of the underlying black-box model.

SHAP (SHapley Additive exPlanations). SHAP, in contrast, is a method that provides a global explanation by assigning an importance value to each feature based on its contribution to the model's output. Drawing on cooperative game theory, SHAP uses Shapley values to determine how each feature contributes to the prediction of a specific instance. The Shapley value is calculated by considering all possible combinations of features and assessing the marginal contribution of each feature in these combinations. This process ensures that SHAP provides a fair and consistent measure of feature importance.

SHAP has a significant advantage over other XAI techniques because it offers both local and global interpretability. While it can explain the contribution of each feature to a specific prediction (local explainability), it can also summarize the importance of features across an entire dataset (global explainability). This flexibility makes SHAP a powerful tool for understanding both individual predictions and broader model behavior. Its theoretical foundation in game theory ensures that the explanations are consistent and satisfy fairness properties, making SHAP a more robust and reliable method compared to others.

Despite its computational complexity, SHAP has gained widespread popularity due to its ability to provide deep, consistent, and mathematically sound explanations. It has been widely adopted for use in both industry and academia, especially in high-stakes domains where transparency is critical.

2.4 Interdisciplinary Approaches to AI Transparency

While technical advancements in XAI, such as LIME and SHAP, have made great strides in enhancing the interpretability of AI systems, addressing AI transparency requires more than just technical solutions. It necessitates an interdisciplinary approach that incorporates insights from sociology, psychology, and ethics. These disciplines help bridge the gap between technical methods and the human need for understanding.

The theoretical foundation of ethical AI plays a critical role in discussions of transparency, as ethical considerations are vital for mitigating risks such as bias, discrimination, and unfairness [6]. Furthermore, incorporating insights from psychology and cognitive science can lead to the design of AI systems that align with human cognitive processes and foster better understanding. Social constructivist theories, which emphasize the role of human interpretation in understanding AI decisions, suggest that transparency must not only be technically feasible but also meaningful in the context of human experience and societal norms [5].

Thus, while XAI techniques like LIME and SHAP are important tools, true transparency in AI requires integrating these technical methods with a broader understanding of human behavior, societal needs, and ethical considerations.

2.5 Industry Review

The industry of new technologies based on AI is shaped and defined by scientists, and at the same time, the industry leaders and companies are heavily influencing the laws, principles, and regulations. Many leading world-wide companies have recognized and prioritized the role of ethical AI solutions by defining their responsible AI frameworks. These frameworks aim to ensure that AI-based products are designed, developed, and deployed with a broader ethical and transparent view, and with consideration for societal and long-lasting impact. While there are commonalities across these frameworks, each company's approach has its unique focus. In the next section of this paper, we examine Responsible AI frameworks across fifteen companies that are perceived to be leading in the AI area.

The key Responsible AI framework elements across various organizations focus on fairness and bias mitigation, ensuring AI systems promote inclusion, diversity, and non-discrimination. Explainability and transparency are emphasized to make AI decisions interpretable and accountable. Many frameworks prioritize robustness and security, safeguarding AI systems against cyber threats and adversarial attacks. Privacy protection and user control are central themes, ensuring ethical data usage and compliance with regulations. Companies align AI with human values, emphasizing reliability, safety, and responsible deployment. Accountability and governance structures are implemented to oversee AI ethics, while ethical use of AI in business solutions ensures AI benefits industries without unintended consequences. AI risk management, crisis mitigation, and governance frameworks are established to handle unforeseen challenges. Organizations also explore adversarial machine learning research and open standards for AI communication to improve AI reliability and steerability. Throughout the AI lifecycle, privacy controls, ethical integration, and responsible AI testing ensure compliance with regulatory and ethical requirements, supporting the long-term trustworthiness of AI technologies.

Static frameworks are inadequate to meet the ever-expanding scope of AI applications and their evolving societal impacts. The rapid pace at which new models are being developed and deployed—coupled with their increasing capabilities across diverse sectors—demands continuous updates and evaluations of these frameworks. As benchmarks for AI models advance at an accelerating rate, what was once considered state-of-the-art can quickly become outdated. This underscores the necessity for frameworks that are agile and capable of adapting to these shifting standards. As AI-based solutions continue to permeate various industries and influence an ever-widening array of decisions, the ethical considerations and potential risks associated with these technologies evolve in tandem.

This dynamic landscape requires a proactive, forward-thinking approach to AI governance. Responsible AI frameworks should go beyond simply outlining ethical guidelines; they must anticipate and address the underlying mechanisms of AI systems before unintended consequences arise. By incorporating regular evaluation cycles—perhaps annually or even semi-annually—framework providers can ensure that their principles and products remain relevant, effective, and aligned with the evolving technological and ethical landscape. These evaluations should not only consider the latest technical advancements but also reflect insights gained from real-world applications, emerging ethical concerns, and changing societal expectations. The increased focus on AI safety in 2024, marked by the creation of new AI safety institutes, demonstrates just how quickly the priorities in the field can shift. Such agility is crucial in ensuring that frameworks keep pace with these rapid changes and continue to serve their intended purpose effectively.

Understanding the nuances of AI decision-making is imperative in a landscape where AI systems pervade critical sectors such as healthcare, finance, and autonomous driving. Consequently, the demand for transparency in AI has intensified, necessitating a rigorous examination of these systems' interpretability and accountability mechanisms. Comparative analysis with prior studies corroborates those models utilizing techniques like SHAP and LIME significantly enhance user understanding, enabling more informed decision-making [11, 12]. Previous literature has pointed toward the inherent biases present in opaque systems, reinforcing the notion that transparent AI can mitigate these risks by fostering trust among users and stakeholders [5, 6].

3 Responsible AI Extended Framework by Comprehensive AI Observability

The proposed framework described in [8] adds to the growing body of literature advocating for interpretability frameworks, including call-to-action documents from leading AI ethics organizations that emphasize the importance of transparency as a fundamental principle of ethical AI systems. In essence, it underscores that fostering transparency is not merely an academic inquiry but carries substantial real-world implications that could redefine how AI systems are designed, implemented, and governed to align them with human-centric decision-making paradigms [13].

User trust and model interpretability are intricately linked in human-AI collaborations. Achieving transparency in AI is not just a technical challenge but a necessary step towards responsible innovation that safeguards user rights and enhances accountability, thereby fostering an environment where AI can be "read" not only by its creators but also by its users [7, 10]. Such transformations are crucial as societies increasingly rely on AI technologies in pivotal sectors, driving home the importance of transparency as a cornerstone of public trust and acceptance in this rapidly evolving domain [8].

3.1 Extended Core Principles

Recent literature stresses that explainability in AI is crucial for robust AI governance. A multi-faceted approach combining technical methods with governance practices has emerged to ensure AI systems are transparent, accountable, and ethically aligned. This review covers key strategies: retrospective analysis, provenance tracking, visualization, ethical checkpoints, contextual reasoning, interactive feedback, and holistic governance.

3.2 Retrospective Analysis

Retrospective analysis examines AI decisions after deployment to understand outcomes and uncover errors or biases [13]. By auditing model logs and decision pathways, organizations can investigate anomalous results, attributing outcomes to model behavior or data conditions and strengthening accountability. Such audits yield lessons from failures and inform models and policies on improvements [14].

3.3 Provenance Tracking

Provenance tracking documents the origins and transformations of data and models throughout the AI lifecycle [15]. Maintaining detailed records of datasets, training processes, and model versions allows each decision to be traced back to its source, enabling thorough investigations of outputs and supporting transparency and accountability. In practice, data lineage tools and model documentation facilitate provenance tracking and build trust in AI systems.

3.4 Visualization

Visualization techniques help interpret complex deep learning models by presenting their inner workings in human-understandable form [16]. Methods such as heatmaps, saliency maps, and attention graphs highlight which features influence a model's decisions, demystifying the "black box" by revealing patterns in its reasoning. Studies show that visual explanations improve understanding and trust in AI outcomes [17].

3.5 Ethical Checkpoints

Ethical checkpoints are control gates in the AI development lifecycle dedicated to evaluating and mitigating ethical risks [18]. During key phases (e.g., design, deployment, post-deployment), teams review systems for biases, fairness, privacy, and compliance, ensuring potential harms are addressed early and models adhere to ethical and legal requirements.

3.6 Contextual Reasoning

Contextual reasoning means AI systems consider context when explaining their decisions. Rather than providing one-size-fits-all justifications, models tailor explanations to the situation or domain, making them more relevant. Studies suggest that context-aware explanations help users understand why an AI acts a certain way, improving acceptance and perceived fairness [19].

3.7 Interactive Feedback

Interactive feedback mechanisms engage users in explaining and refining a model's behavior. Through interfaces, stakeholders can query the AI, adjust inputs, or provide feedback. This two-way interaction allows users to test "what-if" scenarios and correct the system's understanding. Studies indicate that these tools enhance transparency and help calibrate model behavior, using feedback to iteratively improve performance and alignment with user expectations [20].

3.8 Holistic AI Governance

Holistic AI governance is an overarching framework that integrates all components into a unified strategy [21]. Rather than addressing explainability and ethics in isolation, a holistic approach combines technical transparency measures (logging, provenance, visualization) with organizational policies (ethics committees, audits) and regulatory compliance. This comprehensive model ensures AI oversight is systemic and continuous throughout the AI lifecycle. Such synergistic integration of retrospective analysis, contextual reasoning, and feedback loops creates a more adaptable AI ecosystem, helping organizations uphold trust, fairness, and accountability [22].

3.9 Case Study – Computer Vision in Healthcare to Detect Brain Tumors Based on MRIs

The integration of AI in medical imaging has revolutionized brain tumor detection, particularly in MRI-based segmentation. This cutting-edge approach combines deep learning algorithms with multimodal MRI scans to identify and highlight potential tumors with unprecedented accuracy. The system's high-sensitivity design ensures that even subtle anomalies are flagged, prioritizing patient safety over the risk of false positives. At the heart of this technology lies a sophisticated explanation framework. Techniques such as Gradient-weighted Class Activation Mapping (Grad-CAM) [27] visually highlight the pixels that most significantly contribute to tumor classification (see Fig. 1). It allows radiologists to see exactly which areas of the scan the AI considers suspicious. Additionally, Activation Atlases – methods for visualizing the neural network activations – provide insights into filter-level features, such as indicators of edema or necrosis, offering a more nuanced understanding of AI's reasoning and decision-making.

The system's robustness is further enhanced by meticulous metadata tracking. Every aspect of the MRI process - from scanner type and sequence parameters to patient records - is carefully logged and encrypted. This comprehensive approach ensures consistency across different healthcare facilities while maintaining strict patient privacy standards. Moreover, detailed records of model versions and training datasets are maintained, facilitating quick error tracing and meeting regulatory requirements for audit trails. Interpretability remains a key focus in the ongoing development of this technology. Advanced visualization techniques allow for a layered view of the AI's analysis, enabling radiologists to observe how the model builds its understanding of the scan from initial pixel clusters to final tumor boundary predictions. This transparency is crucial in building clinical confidence and allowing for timely interventions when necessary. The system also

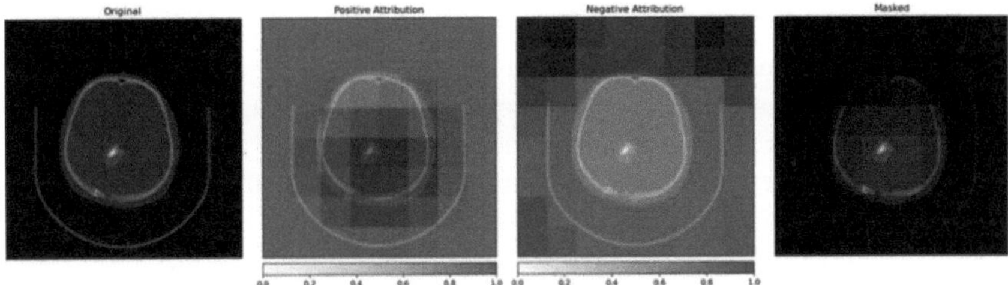

Fig. 1. An example of predictions of brain tumors explained by Grad-CAM (LayerGradCam), where glioma was predicted with 65% with the usage of the Mask R-CNN model with ResNet 50 trained only on 349 images [28].

incorporates ethical considerations through layer-wise checkpoints and evaluates intermediate convolutional layers to ensure there is no systematic bias against any particular patient subgroups, such as older individuals or those with atypical tumor presentations. When significant deviations in detection accuracy are identified, the system triggers corrective measures, including data rebalancing or hyperparameter adjustments. Contextual verification is another critical component of the AI's decision-making process. The system cross-references its findings with established patterns of tumor progression and vascular infiltration. When unusual shapes or locations are detected, additional verification routines are activated to distinguish between genuine anomalies and potential misinterpretations of scanner artifacts. The implementation of this advanced AI system in clinical settings has been complemented by a robust governance framework. Oversight committees continuously monitor quality indices such as dice coefficients and sensitivity, alongside newly developed "explainability metrics." This holistic approach to governance ensures that AI not only maintains high accuracy but also evolves in transparency and fairness. The system's interactive design allows for real-time feedback from radiologists, SMEs and MDs. When experts identify potential overestimations in tumor boundaries, they can query the AI about specific image features influencing its segmentation. This collaborative approach leads to continuous refinement of the model, reducing false positives and improving overall diagnostic accuracy.

3.10 Operationalization of Principles

To assess the effectiveness of Responsible AI practices across machine learning pipelines, we propose a 10-point scorecard that quantifies readiness, transparency, and responsiveness (see Table 1). During the data ingestion stage, Provenance Tracking Coverage examines the consistency of documentation for data sources and transformations, while Bias Detection Rigor assesses the thoroughness of demographic distribution analysis to prevent bias. In the training and validation stages, Layer-Wise Ethical Checks Frequency indicates how frequently fairness assessments are integrated into the Continuous Development and Deployment (CDD) pipeline, and Contextual Reasoning Verification Completeness verifies the presence of domain-specific safeguards that can halt deployment in cases of logical inconsistencies. Regarding transparency, Visual Interpretability Clarity measures how easily stakeholders can comprehend attention or Grad-CAM outputs, while Real-Time Instrumentation Coverage outlines the range of micro-services that disclose the model's internal processes and can be utilized for online debugging or compliance verification. Proactive Bias Detection Responsiveness evaluates the speed at which the tool identifies and rectifies performance issues affecting specific demographic groups, and Governance and Oversight Engagement assesses the effectiveness of boards responsible for overseeing fairness, transparency, and the overall integrity of the models. Lastly, interactive feedback mechanisms are evaluated through Stakeholder Interface Adoption, which gauges how effectively non-technical users can utilize dashboards to modify outputs, and Retraining Iteration Speed, which focuses on the frequency with which user insights are integrated into future model updates. This scorecard provides a comprehensive overview of maturity within the Responsible AI framework, assisting organizations in making technical choices aligned with ethical standards.

To quantitatively assess the extended Responsible AI framework, each of the 10 metrics—from "Provenance Tracking Coverage" to "Retraining Iteration Speed"—is rated on a scale from 1 (minimal) to 5 (exemplary), yielding a total score that can range from 10 to 50 points. Within this framework, a cumulative score below 20 reflects processes characterized by limited rigor and sporadic oversight, while a score between 20 and 30 denotes foundational yet incomplete practices that may neglect demographic biases and inadequately document data transformations. Scores between 31 and 40 denote moderate to advanced maturity, where protocols and tools are largely automated, fairness assessments are routinely integrated into CI/CD pipelines, and domain experts actively interact with interpretability dashboards. A score exceeding 40 denotes an exemplary environment characterized by real-time monitoring, strong governance, and ongoing stakeholder feedback, creating a continuous cycle of ethical, data-driven enhancement. Periodic re-evaluation of this quantitative score not only monitors progress over time but also highlights opportunities for enhanced investment—whether in monitoring infrastructure, interactive feedback systems, or domain-specific evaluations—that can markedly strengthen trust and accountability in AI deployments.

Within an MLOps pipeline, automated alert systems act as vigilant monitors that continuously track performance metrics in real time, promptly notifying stakeholders whenever predefined thresholds are breached. These alerts can be delivered through various channels, including Slack or Teams notifications, color-coded dashboards, or email/SMS messages sent to the relevant teams. For example, if the "Contextual Reasoning Verification Completeness" score falls below three, the system may automatically generate a remediation ticket in the project management tool and suspend further deployments until domain experts can investigate potential issues such as emerging biases or misaligned training data. In sectors with stringent regulations, organizations can strengthen this safety mechanism by linking alerts to semi-automated rollback capabilities, allowing for a seamless return to a previously validated model version. By integrating these notifications into both continuous integration processes and post-deployment monitoring, teams can gain early insights into any significant drops in fairness, transparency, or performance, thus maintaining accountability and trust in operational AI systems. The rise of foundation models in AI has made the proposed extended Responsibility framework increasingly vital.

These complex, pre-trained models serve as starting point, but the real value appears through transfer learning and fine-tuning as well as final deployment which is part of

Table 1. Proposed metrics with key focus (with scores from 1–5 for each metric).

Metric (Dimension)	Key Focus (Fact)
Provenance Tracking Coverage (Data Ingestion and Preparation)	Guarantees uniform documentation of data sources and transformations from the initial phases
Bias Detection Rigor (Data Ingestion and Preparation)	Assesses demographic distributions for possible biases; verifies the comprehensiveness of bias detection
Layer-Wise Ethical Checks Frequency (Model Training and Validation)	Evaluates the frequency of fairness probes conducted in CI/CD processes and the thoroughness of their analyzes
Contextual Reasoning Verification Thoroughness (Model Development and Assessment)	Evaluates the robustness of domain-specific or causal rule sets that prevent deployment in the event of inconsistencies arising
Clarity in Visual Interpretability (Transparency)	The effectiveness of interpreting attention maps, Grad-CAM overlays, or other visualization outputs is assessed
Real-Time Instrumentation Coverage	Analyzes the scope of microservices and dashboards that reveal model internals for debugging or compliance purposes
Proactive Bias Identification and Response (Deployment and Monitoring)	Evaluates the responsiveness and efficiency of alerts in relation to performance changes for specific demographics
Governance and Oversight Involvement (Implementation and Supervision)	Evaluates the extent to which oversight boards monitor and respond to metrics related to fairness, transparency, and accuracy
Implementation of Stakeholder Interface (Interactive Feedback Loops)	Evaluates the frequency of interaction with interactive dashboards among domain experts, developers, and end-users
Retraining Iteration Speed (Interactive Feedback Loops)	Assesses the speed at which user feedback impacts future updates, maintaining ongoing alignment

the operationalization. Online training keeps these models current and updated, while transfer learning lets them tackle new tasks and domains. The operationalization part that is often overlooked is vital. It involves setting up cross-components logging and monitoring, lineage and governance, and feedback loops to ensure the model behaves as expected, ethically and effectively in use.

4 Conclusion and Implications

In the swiftly advancing field of AI, ensuring transparent decision-making has become essential for both ethical deployment and the cultivation of public trust. Findings from this literature review highlight a significant gap between users' expectations of AI interpretability and the reality of its often-opaque workings.

While frameworks like SHAP and LIME show promise in elucidating individual predictions by attributing feature contributions, these methods are not uniformly effective across all AI models and applications, particularly in areas characterized by complex interactions among numerous variables such as healthcare where the recommendations and their causal reasoning carry significance due to the scale of their impact on human life [11, 12]. Comparatively, prior research has documented instances where opacity led to significant reluctance among users to engage with AI systems, ultimately hindering adoption [5, 6]. The objective of this paper centers on addressing these concerns, indicating a pressing need for improved methodologies/frameworks that can provide breadth and depth in interpretability across diverse AI applications, particularly in sensitive domains like healthcare [9, 10]. Ultimately, achieving transparency is not merely an aspirational goal but an essential component of responsible AI practices that aim to serve societal interests while safeguarding individual rights and fostering trust [15, 29]. The proposed Comprehensive AI Observability (CAO) Framework will shape the future trajectory of AI development as stakeholders seek a more comprehensive, deep and yet broad understanding of AI's decision-making landscape.

4.1 Implications for Future Research and Practice

The exploration of transparency within AI systems has unveiled critical insights into the interpretability and accountability required for ethical AI deployment. This paper reviews the complexities surrounding AI decision-making, emphasizing the importance of methodologies like SHAP and LIME in demystifying the processes by which AI arrives at conclusions [1]. Central to resolving the research problem—whether we can truly "read AI's mind"—is the integration of core principles for responsible AI and comprehensive AI observability, which helps users see through the inherent opacity that is found in AI applications that poses significant challenges to user trust and ethical application [2]. The implications of this framework extend both academically and practically; they provide a foundation for future discourse on AI ethics and establish a framework for practitioners seeking to enhance AI transparency in everyday applications such as recommendation systems, virtual assistants and automated decision-making agents in customer service or healthcare [11].

Significant insights have been gleaned from the exploration of transparency in AI systems throughout this paper. The key points discussed underline the crucial role of interpretability frameworks, such as SHAP and LIME, in illuminating AI's reasoning while addressing the challenges posed by algorithmic opacity [1]. The resolution of the research problem—the ability to "read" AI's mind—was achieved by systematically evaluating existing technologies and methodologies that enhance transparency, indicating that while current AI models demonstrate remarkable performance, their black-box nature raises substantial ethical and accountability concerns [2].

Hence, this paper sets the stage for ongoing dialogue and exploration in the realm of AI transparency, urging stakeholders to collectively strive for systems that reflect societal values and ethical standards [8]. Furthermore, the necessity for adaptive governance structures that can keep pace with rapid technological advancements is essential for addressing concerns of bias and misuse of AI [12, 31]. Future work is critical in this field; longitudinal studies examining the effectiveness of transparency frameworks across varied contexts will offer deeper insights into their impact on user trust and AI functionality [5]. Interdisciplinary approaches (model and domain agnostic) that combine insights from cognitive psychology and ethics will enrich the understanding of human-AI interaction, leading to better design principles that prioritize user cognition and accountability [6]. Additionally, addressing the emerging need for dynamic consent models that can evolve alongside AI technologies will be crucial in protecting patient data and ensuring ethical use in healthcare applications [9].

The gaps identified in the literature concerning low-resource settings and the specific challenges these environments face should inform future research explorations, pushing for solutions that foster equitable AI access [10]. By advancing these areas of inquiry, researchers can contribute to the conversation on ethical AI deployment, ensuring that AI serves not only as a powerful tool but also as a responsible and accountable partner in decision-making [7]. By integrating the CAO Framework as part of the AI instrumentation framework, it is possible for enterprise users to gain deeper insights into their AI systems, identify and mitigate biases, improve the accuracy and reliability of AI-powered decisions, and ultimately achieve more trustworthy and responsible AI solutions.

Disclosure of Interests. The authors have no competing interests to declare that are relevant to the content of this article.

References

1. Al-Akayleh, F., Ali Agha, A.S.A.: Trust, ethics, and user-centric design in AI-integrated genomics. In: 2nd International Conference on Cyber Resilience, pp. 1–6 (2024). https://doi.org/10.1109/ICCR61006.2024.10532890
2. Ennis-O'Connor, M., O'Connor, W.T.: Charting the future of patient care: a strategic leadership guide to harnessing the potential of artificial intelligence. Healthcare Manage. Forum **37**, 290–295 (2024). https://doi.org/10.1177/08404704241235893
3. Nah, F.F.H., Cai, J., Zheng, R., Pang, N.: An activity system-based perspective of generative AI: challenges and research directions. AIS Trans. Hum.-Comput. Interact. **15**(3), 247–267 (2023). https://doi.org/10.17705/1thci.00190
4. Nah, F.F.H., Zheng, R., Cai, J., Siau, K., Chen, L.: Generative AI and ChatGPT: applications, challenges, and AI-human collaboration. J. Inform. Technol. Case Appl. Res. **25**(3), 277–304 (2023). https://doi.org/10.1080/15228053.2023.2233814
5. Kostopoulos, N., Antonopoulou, H.: The intersection of blockchain technology and data security in e-business. Techn. Bus. Manage. **10**, 109–122 (2024). https://doi.org/10.47577/business.v10i.11997
6. Kim, J.Y., et al.: Development and preliminary testing of health equity across the AI lifecycle (HEAAL): a framework for healthcare delivery organizations to mitigate the risk of AI solutions worsening health inequities. PLOS Dig. Health **3**(5), e0000390 (2024). https://doi.org/10.1371/journal.pdig.0000390

7. Nguyen, T.N., Jamale, K., Gonzalez, C.: Predicting and understanding human action decisions: insights from large language models and cognitive instance-based learning. In: Proceedings of the AAAI Conference on Human Computation and Crowdsourcing, vol. 12, pp. 126–136 (2024). https://doi.org/10.1609/hcompv12i1.31607.

8. Omar, M.: From generative AI to objective-driven systems: a paradigm shift in artificial intelligence. Indonesian J. Comput. Sci. (2024). https://doi.org/10.33022/ijcs.v13i5.4381

9. Durga, N., Nidamanuri, S.: A study on the adoption challenges and solutions for transforming healthcare with generative AI. World J. Adv. Res. Rev. 13(3), 533–542 (2022). https://doi.org/10.30574/wjarr.2022.13.3.0169

10. Yang, Y.: Visual abstract reasoning in computational imagery. In: Proceedings of the AAAI Conference on Artificial Intelligence, vol. 38(21), pp. 23431–23432 (2024). https://doi.org/10.1609/aaai.v38i21.30416

11. Aldosari, B., Alanazi, A.: Pitfalls of artificial intelligence in medicine. Stud. Health Techn. Inform. 316, 554–555 (2024). https://doi.org/10.3233/SHTI240474

12. Nasar, I., Nassar, D., Hayajneh, J.: The influence of ChatGPT on decision-making: a theoretical approach. In: 2024 International Conference on Decision Aid Sciences and Applications, pp. 1–4 (2024). https://doi.org/10.1109/DASA63652.2024.10836487

13. Kale, A., Nguyen, T., Harris, F.C., Li, C., Zhang, J., Ma, X.: Provenance documentation to enable explainable and trustworthy AI: a literature review. Data Intell. 5(1), 139–162 (2023). https://doi.org/10.1162/dint_a_00119

14. Athanasiou, M., Sfrintzeri, K., Zarkogianni, K., Thanopoulou, A.C., Nikita, K.S.: An explainable XGBoost-based approach towards assessing the risk of cardiovascular disease in patients with type 2 diabetes mellitus. In: IEEE 20th International Conference on Bioinformatics and Bioengineering, pp. 859–864. Cincinnati, OH, USA (2020). https://doi.org/10.1109/BIBE50027.2020.00146

15. Gautam, S.: Bridging multimedia modalities: enhanced multimodal AI understanding and intelligent agents. In: Proceedings of the 25th International Conference on Multimodal Interaction (2023). https://doi.org/10.1145/3577190.3614225

16. Oltramari, A.: Enabling high-level machine reasoning with cognitive neuro-symbolic systems. arXiv:abs/2311.07759 (2023). https://doi.org/10.48550/arXiv.2311.07759

17. Li, C., Bing, Y.: Investigating relational reasoning performance: a comparative analysis of humans and MRNet network. In: 8th International Conference on Computational Intelligence and Applications, pp. 97–101 (2023). https://doi.org/10.1109/ICCIA59741.2023.00025

18. Saeed, W., Omlin, C.: Explainable AI (XAI): a systematic meta-survey of current challenges and future opportunities". Knowl.-Based Syst. 263, 110273 (2021). https://doi.org/10.1016/j.knosys.2023.110273

19. Riveiro, M., Thill, S.: The challenges of providing explanations of AI systems when they do not behave like users expect. In: Proceedings of the 30th ACM Conference on User Modeling, Adaptation and Personalization (2022). https://doi.org/10.1145/3503252.3531306

20. Heikkilä, M.: It's high time for more AI transparency. MIT Technology Review (2023). https://www.technologyreview.com/2023/07/25/1076698/its-high-time-for-more-ai-transparency/

21. Muhammad, D., Bendechache, M.: Unveiling the black box: a systematic review of explainable artificial intelligence in medical image analysis. Comput. Struct. Biotechnol. J. 24, 542–560 (2024). https://doi.org/10.1016/j.csbj.2024.08.005

22. Bhattacharya, S., Khanna, A., Ganapaneni, S., Najana, M.: Attention-based deep learning frameworks for network intrusion detection: an empirical study. Int. J. Global Innov. Solut. (2024). https://doi.org/10.21428/e90189c8.eb32676c

23. Longpre, S., et al.: Data authenticity, consent, and provenance for AI are all broken: what will it take to fix them?" In: An MIT Exploration of Generative AI, March (2024). https://doi.org/10.21428/e4baedd9.a650f77d

24. Dai, W., Berleant, D.: Benchmarking contemporary deep learning hardware and frameworks: a survey of qualitative metrics. In: IEEE First International Conference on Cognitive Machine Intelligence, pp. 148–155. Los Angeles, CA, USA (2019). https://doi.org/10.1109/CogMI4 8466.2019.00029

25. Agarwal, A., Agarwal, H., Agarwal, N.: Fairness score and process standardization: framework for fairness certification in artificial intelligence systems. AI Ethics **3**, 267–279 (2023). https://doi.org/10.1007/s43681-022-00147-7

26. Bommasani, R., et al.: The foundation model transparency index, v1.1: May 2024. arXiv: 2407.12929 (2024). https://arxiv.org/abs/2407.12929

27. Latha, M., Kumar, P.S., Chandrika, R.R., Mahesh, T.R., Kumar, V.V., Guluwadi, S.: Revolutionizing breast ultrasound diagnostics with efficientNet-B7 and explainable AI. BMC Med. Imaging **24**(1), 230 (2024). https://doi.org/10.1186/s12880-024-01404-3

28. Kot, E.: Multimodal medical image processing methods for computer-aided diagnosis support system of brain tumors. PhD Thesis, Warsaw University of Technology (2024). https://www.bip.pw.edu.pl/Postepowania-w-sprawie-nadania-stopnia-naukowego/Doktor aty/Wszczete-po-30-kwietnia-2019-r/Rada-Naukowa-Dyscypliny-Informatyka-Techniczna-i-Telekomunikacja/mgr-inz.-Estera-Kot

29. Cao, S., Gomez, C., Huang, C.-M.: How time pressure in different phases of decision-making influences human-AI collaboration. In: Proceedings of the ACM on Human-Computer Interaction, vol. 7, pp. 1–26 (2023). https://doi.org/10.1145/3610068

AI-Empowered Ageing, Education, and Healthcare

Using Large Language Models and Prompt Strategies to Annotate Healthcare Posts on Social Media

Lucas Aust[1](✉) and Anthony Fu[1,2] (iD)

[1] University of South Carolina, Columbia, SC, USA
LAUST@email.sc.edu
[2] Dutch Fork High School, Irmo, SC, USA

Abstract. Using youth vaping as a use case, this paper explores the feasibility of applying the latest large language models (LLMs) to automatically annotate social media posts, especially on Reddit. Youth vaping poses serious health risks, and social media offers key insights into user behavior. This study evaluates the capacity of the latest LLMs—including GPT-o1, GPT-o3-mini, Gemini 2.0 Flash, Gemma 2, LLaMA 3.3, DeepSeek R1, and Grok-2—to detect user quit intentions and cessation stages from social media posts. Model outputs were benchmarked against human annotations using various prompting strategies. Preliminary results indicate OpenAI's GPT-o1 is the best-performing model, followed by LLAMA 3.3; the worst was Gemma 2. Although the current preliminary results demonstrate the potential of LLMs, none of them can replace human annotators yet.

Keywords: Vaping Cessation · Large Language Models · Social Media Analytics · Annotations

1 Introduction

Today's social media provides dynamic real-time user-generated content and has become a useful public health surveillance tool to understand public sentiment, popular health topics, public perceptions, and trends. Researchers have started to pay attention to massive social media data and also make efforts to efficiently identify patterns of social media posts in healthcare. In this study, we aim to explore the feasibility of using the latest large language models (LLMs) to automatically annotate social media posts and use youth vaping as a use case. Electronic-cigarette (e-cigarette) aerosol delivers carbonyls, ultrafine particles, and high-dose nicotine that can inflame airways, raise blood pressure, and damage vascular endothelium. Repeated exposure is now linked to chronic bronchitis, impaired lung function, and early markers of cardiovascular disease [12]. Additionally, researchers conducting longitudinal studies have asserted that people who vape face higher risk of chronic bronchitis, wheezing and shortness of breath as they get older [17, 20]. Nicotine is known to spike users' heart rate and blood pressure, which induces strain on the circulatory system. There is evidence that shows the toxic chemicals and addictive nicotine in these vaping devices cause an increase in cardiovascular

F. F.-H Nah and K. L. Siau (Eds.): HCII 2025, LNCS 16343, pp. 97–107, 2026.
https://doi.org/10.1007/978-3-032-13167-6_7

risk for young people that vape [1]. Users can expect reduced eNOS activity, arterial stiffening, pro angiogenic remodeling, and right ventricular fibrosis. On the metabolic level, nicotine is proven to cause insulin resistance, dyslipidemia, higher fasting glucose, and elevated free fatty acids. These factors cause an increase of Atherogenesis [5], which is the process of plaque formation in the arteries. Atherogenesis can lead to additional heart complications [18].

Adolescents have adopted e-cigarettes at an alarming rate. National surveys show current (past-30-day) vaping among U.S. high-school students rose from roughly 11% in 2017 to 27% in 2019 [22]. This rapid rise, featuring a substantial increase from 2017 to 2018, caused youth e-cigarette use to be declared a national epidemic by the FDA Commissioner and the U.S. Surgeon General in 2018 [3]. This high level of usage shows that millions of adolescents are at risk of health consequences from e-cigarette use, showing the need for effective prevention and support.

The goal of this study is to utilize the latest artificial intelligence (AI) techniques to identify youth who have exhibited the desire to quit vaping on social media so that they can be assisted with their vaping cessation attempt. It is known that nicotine addiction in young people can be extremely difficult to overcome. However, surveys indicate that many of these young vapers want to quit. For example, one national study found that over half of adolescent and young-adult vapers intend to quit vaping, and about 15% even plan to quit within the next 30 days following the study [2]. About 33% of users in this study reported that they had already made at least one quit attempt in the year leading up to the study [2]. Another survey reported that 60% of vapers aged between 15 and 24 say that they want to quit vaping within a year after the survey [8].

Social media offers a real-time window into vaping trends and health concerns due to its accessibility and the candidness of user-generated content. Mining millions of posts on platforms such as X, Reddit, and TikTok has already revealed geographic hotspots, symptom reports, and pro-vaping marketing faster than traditional surveillance methods [24]. During the EVALI outbreak, one team showed that Twitter posts could be used to identify "at-risk" vapers and suggested that those users be signed up for a digital cessation intervention [9].

Recent advances in LLMs make it feasible to analyze large amounts of content without time-consuming and lengthy manual annotations by clinicians. Studies show transformer-based models including GPT-4 match or exceed human coders in identifying health themes and sentiment in public-health corpora [10]. Leveraging today's LLMs' capability could more efficiently identify youth who are actively considering cessation for early intervention programs. This study will compare seven state-of-the-art LLMs, i.e., GPT-o1, GPT-o3-mini, Gemini 2.0 Flash, Gemma 2, LLAMA 3.3, Deepseek R1, and Grok-2, on their ability to detect quit-intent signals in social-media posts. By benchmarking F1 score accuracy, precision, and recall, we seek the most reliable model for triggering digital interventions that help adolescents reduce or quit vaping.

2 Methodology

The social media platform Reddit has subreddits (i.e., communities focused on specific discussion topics) that focus on the discussion of vaping. We built our dataset out of 2,311 Reddit posts. Out of these 2,311, we collected 1,101 from the Quit Vaping subreddit, 655 posts from subreddits focused on vaping but not Quit Vaping, 450 posts from subreddits about quitting substances other than vaping, and 115 posts from random subreddits. We selected this dataset to mimic the large array of content that can be found on Reddit. This large dataset was narrowed down to a more representative subset. We gave this representative sample to clinicians who specialize in youth vaping, along with the seven state-of-the-art LLMs as described in Sect. 1, asking each to assign binary labels to the posts. The clinicians' labels served as the gold standard to be compared against the models' accuracy. Finally, we used these analyses to compare the performance of the different models to draw conclusions.

2.1 Data Preparation

We stored the subreddit, subreddit description, post body, and post title for each extracted post for analysis. We developed a python program to narrow down the dataset. This program used API calls to send each post to GPT-o1, GPT-o3-mini, Gemini 2.0 Flash, Gemma 2, LLAMA 3.3, Deepseek R1, and Grok-2 respectively. Each call gave the post title, body, and subreddit it was posted in, and that subreddit's description. Each model was required to classify the post into precontemplation, contemplation, preparation, action, maintenance, and withdrawal, based on the transtheoretical model of behavior change [13, 15, 16]. For each post, if a majority of the models agreed on a stage, then this post was classified into this stage. We repeated this process until there were one hundred posts for each stage. We chose this number of posts for each stage to ensure that the models analyzed posts from users in a variety of stages in their vaping cessation journey. However, due to the nature of the subreddits in which the users posted, there were only 6 posts for the precontemplation phase.

2.2 Human Annotation

The clinicians with expertise in evaluating vaping behaviors labelled each post as 'yes' or 'no' based on whether the user was currently attempting to quit vaping. The labels 'yes' and 'no' were to make this classification binary. The human annotation was done by two clinical experts from Washington University School of Medicine. The annotators independently reviewed the dataset and coded all the sentences, removing any discrepancies that may have occurred through internal discussion.

2.3 Large Language Model Detection

Model Selection. We chose OpenAI GPT-o1, GPT-o3-mini, Gemini 2.0 Flash, Gemma 2, LLAMA 3.3, DeepSeek R1, and Grok-2 because each is the newest model with a publicly available API from its creator company. GPT-o1 is OpenAI's leading reasoning model. GPT-o1 can complete harder problems than earlier versions [14]. GPT-o3-mini delivers similar reasoning power faster and more efficiently [6]. This model excels in science and math. Gemini 2.0 flash is the latest release from Google, optimized for high-speed task automation [7]. Gemma 2 is the current open-source alternative to Gemini [21]. LLAMA 3.3 is the newest model from Meta that can outperform previous LLAMA versions

[23]. DeepSeek R1 is a fully open-source model trained with multi-stage reinforcement learning and cold-start data [4]. Finally, Grok 2 is xAI's latest model that is powered with real-time knowledge and a large performance jump over Grok-1 [25].

Prompt Strategy. The LLMs were tasked with analyzing each post to determine whether the user was currently attempting to quit vaping at the time of the post. To do this successfully, we had to craft two types of prompts for LLMs. The first is the system instructions which are used to give context to LLMs. This context includes general instructions on how to complete the task and the role that the model is supposed to assume [11]. For this study, we used the basic prompt of "You are an assistant analyzing user posts about vaping cessation." It was kept intentionally short for efficient use of tokens. The second type of prompt is the user prompt, which is used to provide specific instructions to the LLMs and pass user input [11], or the posts in our case. We used a simple prompting strategy to keep the instructions clear and simple for the model. The base of the prompt read: "Consider this post that has this title: ['title'] and this body: ['body'] that was posted to this subreddit ['subreddit'] that has this description ['public_description'] using this strategy:" We inserted this base into the prompt that reads: "You are an assistant analyzing user posts about vaping cessation. Whenever you receive a user's post, determine which stage of the Transtheoretical Model (TTM) that the user is in: precontemplation, contemplation, preparation, action, maintenance, or relapse. The user can only be in one stage. If there is no stage, then report NONE. Then decide if the user is currently trying to quit vaping. This must be yes or no. Include a percentage between 0–100 with how confident you are with each response and add your reasoning. Answer with the following format, any deviations create an invalid response.

DO NOT ADD ANY SPECIAL CHARACTERS LIKE * OR # AND PRINT ALL PARTS OF THE RESPONSE ON THE SAME LINE THE LABEL IS ON. 1 row for each part of the response Stage: {Stage} Stage Confidence: {confidence %} Stage Reasoning: {Reasoning} Intention To Quit: {YES/NO} Intention To Quit Confidence: {confidence %} Intention Input Reasoning Input To Quit Reasoning: {Reasoning}."

Evaluation. The clinical experts' manual annotations were considered as the ground truth. By cross-referencing each model's results, we calculated the accuracy, precision, recall, and F1 score for intention to quit by separating the "yes" and "no" instances and combining them. Our focus was on the f1 score as it is effective in comparing predicted results to a gold standard [19]. We then evaluated which model worked the best, delving into the different reasoning paths that may have caused models to come up with conflicting responses for the same post.

3   Results

To gain in-depth insights into what the different models are thinking, we performed quantitative evaluation to compare the performance of the models against the ground truth. Then, we will break down the different models' reasoning paths to gain further insights on what caused the models to get the right insights and what may have caused them to go astray. For the evaluations, we calculated the accuracy, precision, recall, and f1 score for yes or no separate and combined for each model.

Overall, the models performed well for binary classification tasks (See Fig. 1). The best performing model at binary classification was OpenAI GPT-o1. OpenAI GPT-o1 had the highest F1 score for binary classification at 0.852. GPT-o1 had an accuracy of .856, a precision of .857, and a recall of .850, displaying strong performance across all statistics. The next best model is LLAMA 3.3 with an F1 score of 0.820. LLAMA 3.3 had an accuracy of .823, a precision of .841, and a recall of .814. Next highest was Deepseek R1 with an F1 score of .816. Deepseek R1 had an accuracy of .824, a precision of .840, and a recall of .810. Figure 2 displays the confusion matrix for the binary classification by the different prompt levels for the strongest performing model, OpenAI GPT-o1. Although not as strong, the rest of the models still performed at a high standard. Annotating the posts with Gemini 2.0 Flash resulted in an F1 score of .767, an accuracy of .784, a precision of .818, and a recall of .763. Gemma 2 had an F1 score of .764, an accuracy of .774, a precision of .783, and a recall of .760. GPT o3-mini had an F1 score of .757m an accuracy of .774, a precision of .802, and a recall of .752. The lowest performing model for the binary classification task was Grok 2 with an F1 score of .707, an accuracy of .740, a precision of .795, and a recall of .710. Figure 3 shows the confusion matrix for Grok 2, to highlight the difference in performance between the best model (GPT o1) and the worst model (Grok 2).

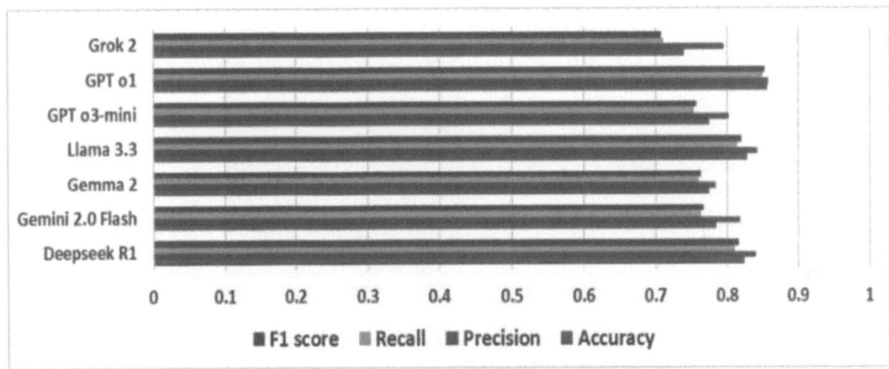

Fig. 1. Performance statistics across the various models.

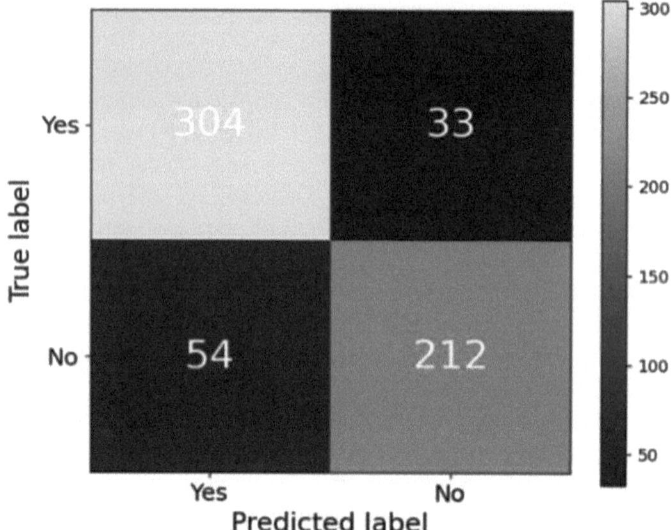

Fig. 2. Confusion matrix for GPT-o1.

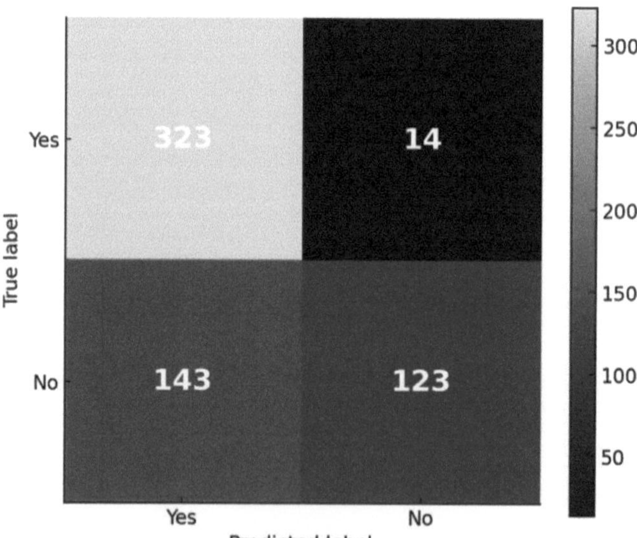

Fig. 3. Confusion matrix for Grok 2.

4 Discussion

4.1 Binary Classification

LLMs were capable of performing this binary classification task at a high level. However, further fine-tuning is required, as the models were not performing at full accuracy.

There were some instances in which all the models correctly identified that the user was attempting to quit vaping. For example, a post with the title "Quitting tips pleeeease 😵" and body "Hi I'm Flo. I started vaping to help me quit smoking and now it's time to quit vaping. I hate that I rely on it and need it by my side at all times otherwise I get stressed out, it's totally controlling me. Not to mention all the money I'm throwing down the drain! I've tried going down nicotine percentage but I always fold and go back up, no motivation! Anyone know any apps I could download or just any useful tips you may of found work for you? Thanks and good luck to you too 😊" was posted to the QuitVaping subreddit, which "is a place for redditors to motivate each other to quit vaping." The annotation of this post resulted in all models responding that the poster does want to quit vaping. This is an example of how the models can take all elements of a post (title, body, and subreddit) into account to correctly identify a user that wants to quit vaping.

There were also instances in which every model was able to successfully identify that the user does not want to quit vaping. For example, a post with the title "Best disposable vapes and where to buy them?" and body "Best disposable vapes and where to buy them? I've been looking around for vapes to buy online, hopefully wholesale if there's one I like, but I can't seem to find any good ones to buy online. Any help is awesome! Puff plus are always good if you have the right ones. The Pink Lemonade Airbar is also super bomb but it's sold out everywhere. If anyone has any suggestions, I'm all ears, just not sure where to start." was posted into the VapeDisposable subreddit where users can learn about disposable vaporizers or share their experience. Each model was able to successfully identify that this user does not want to quit vaping due to the explicit contents of the post, even though it was posted in a vaping related subreddit.

While the models did correctly identify many posts, they struggled with others. There were even instances where every model responded that the poster wanted to quit vaping when they did not. For example, one post in the subreddit leaves, which is for support and recovery while quitting cannabis with the title "Can't f****** do it, seriously want to blow my f****** head off." And body "Quitting due to being drug tested in a CPS case. I've been slacking the past week or two and decided 2 days ago, f*** this. This isn't worth it. I'd rather have my child and be a productive father than sit around with a foggy head all day. It's day 2 and I can't even function properly. I'm constantly screaming, absolutely f***ing enraged at the wind blowing the wrong way, I can't play video games with my friends which is literally one of the only things I genuinely enjoyed. I'm not relapsing or planning on smoking, but holy shit. How long is this going to last??? I thought about slitting my wrists open and I actually felt sharp pains in my arm for an hour after thinking about it for .5 s. I know it gets better, but f***. Right now I just want to curl up with a 12 gauge and not wake up tomorrow. I hate my f***ing job, I can't see my f***ing kid, my life is in f***ing shambles and the one escape I had from this shit, is gone for good. The world being in the state it's in right now doesn't help either. I can't go five f***ing feet without absolutely snapping at something so small it doesn't even matter. Not seeking advice, judgement or anything along those lines. I'm just irritated as F*** and need to vent. Thank you to anyone who reads, hopefully the post doesn't get removed as somehow all of my posts on this SubReddit do." This post is about a user attempting to quit marijuana for a child-protection case. All the models assumed quit intention because of the intense emotional plea, however the models failed to notice the fact that the user was talking about quitting marijuana. The strong emotions outweighed the context for this post.

There were all instances where every model resulted in a false positive. For example, one post was posted into quitvaping with a title of "I don't know if this is withdrawal or not". This post described how the user is dealing with body-image issues and suicidal thoughts. They ponder if these symptoms are withdrawal. The models failed to tie in the context of where the user created this post along with the content of the post. If the models did, then they would have been able to see that the user did in fact want to quit vaping.

4.2 Model Differences

It is evident that some models performed much better than others, creating a ranking of sorts. OpenAI GPT-o1 performed the best. The next best performer was LLAMA 3. Gemini 2.0 flash, OpenAI o3-mini, and Gemma 2 were close behind, and Grok 2 clearly brought up the rear. Based on these results, four tiers of models emerge. GPT-o1 is the sole model in the top tier. We recommend using GPT-o1 as a primary model for classification tasks similar to ours. In the next tier is LLAMA 3.3 and Deepseek R1. These models were remarkably close together in performance. Either model could be used as a strong fallback if needed. In the third tier falls Gemini 2.0 Flash, Gemma 2, and GPT o3-mini. These models are usable if additional fine tuning is employed. In the bottommost tier is Grok 2, we do not recommend using Grok 2 for tasks similar to ours.

A trend that we noticed was that the models performed well when posters were explicit about their desire to quit vaping. For example, the title of one post was "Day 2 Sucked Like A B**** In A Cops Car Outside of Denny's" This was posted into the subreddit quittingjuul and read "(sloppy and emotional) I made it to day 3… And its been challenging my dudes. Ive been tempted to buy pods, search for refries, or pretty much anything to smoke. The only thing that helps is smoking that green. I put the money I wouldve spent into stocks and use that as motivation to quit. Being in quarintine makes it easier to avoid people who vape and smoke cigs so imma use this opportunity to better myself I believe in all of you. Use this time to stop like me and have better odds fighting the beer virus. Use this as an excuse to quit and never go back ever again. Think of nicotine as a narcissistic ex. Inclined to cheat, when you do her it puts you down, and your better off without her." This post had slang and emotional language, and the model was able to pick up on all of that as well as the mentions of withdrawal and temptation to correctly identify intention to quit. The models' performance was hindered when there was uncertainty in the post. Following multiple different themes in a single post proved challenging for the model. For example, the title of one post in quitvaping was "4 years of vaping all day every day. Want to quit but do not see life without it." In this post the user is talking about how they have heavy addiction, they state their desire to quit, and they also show that they are nervous to quit indicating ambivalence. Following all these distinct patterns made it difficult for models to ascertain the posters' true feelings, leading to disagreement across the models.

Across all models, one trend we identified was that there were many more false positives than false negatives. This means that the model was much more likely to indicate that the user wanted to quit vaping than the humans. This can be caused by the models hallucinating and assuming context that is not actually present. It can also indicate that the models placed too much of an emphasis on key words such as "quit" or "stop", so whenever the models see words like this in a post, they assume that the user is quitting vaping. Finally, unclear cues such as asking for advice, talking about previous quit attempts, or discussing the quit attempts of others can confuse the models, leading to false positive markings when the user may not be talking about themselves or their current quit attempts.

4.3 Limitations

There are two limitations to this study. (1) Representative Dataset. While we took careful randomization steps to ensure that the dataset was representative of all the various stages of behavior change, it still ended up that there were much less posts in the precontemplation phase. This can lead to skewed results if they are not managed properly. In the future, we will continue to improve our methods to ensure that the dataset is representative of each class equally. (2) Small and focused dataset. Our dataset focuses on a small portion of Reddit and only contains a few hundred posts. Expanding this study to include more posts from a wider array of subreddits will subject the models to a more contextualized environment.

5 Conclusion

In this study, we systematically evaluated the feasibility of using seven latest LLMs including OpenAI's GPT-o1 and GPT-o3-mini, Google's Gemini 2.0 Flash and Gemma 2, Meta's LLAMA 3.3, Deepseek's R1, and xAI's Grok-2 to complete binary classification to determine whether a user's Reddit post exhibited a current intention to quit vaping. While the preliminary results show potential, none of these models are ready to replace human annotators. When used with simple prompting techniques, GPT-o1 proved to be the best performer, with an F1 score of 0.852. In last place was Grok 2. It had a binary classification F1 score of 0.707.

In the future, we plan to expand this study to a larger, more representative dataset. In doing so, we will continue to improve prompting techniques and adapt the study to utilize state-of-the-art LLMs. The ultimate goal of this study is to identify potential users for a secondary study that will provide participants with a mobile app intervention, specifically designed to assist them throughout their vaping cessation journey.

Acknowledgements. The authors would like to thank Dr. Ming Huang at UT Health Houston, Texas, USA for his guidance and advice for this research project. We also appreciated the clinicians from Washington University in St. Louis for their help with expert annotations.

References

1. American Heart Association. People Who Vape Had Worrisome Changes in Cardiovascular Function, Even as Young Adults. American Heart Association, 31 Oct. 2022. newsroom.heart.org/news/people-who-vape-had-worrisome-changes-in-cardiovascular-function-even-as-young-adults

2. Cuccia, A., et al.: Quitting E-cigarettes: quit attempts and quit intentions among youth and young adults. Prevent. Med. Reports **21**(21), 101287 (2021). www.sciencedirect.com/science/article/pii/S221133552030245X, https://doi.org/10.1016/j.pmedr.2020.101287

3. Cullen, Karen A., et al.: E-cigarette use among youth in the united states, 2019. JAMA **322**(21), 2095–2103 (2019). jamanetwork.com/journals/jama/article-abstract/2755265, https://doi.org/10.1001/jama.2019.18387

4. deepseek-ai/DeepSeek-R1·Hugging Face. (2001). https://huggingface.co/deepseek-ai/DeepSeek-R1

5. Espinoza-Derout, J., et al.: Electronic cigarette use and the risk of cardiovascular diseases. Front. Cardiovasc. Med. **9**(879726) (2022). www.ncbi.nlm.nih.gov/pmc/articles/PMC9021536/, https://doi.org/10.3389/fcvm.2022.879726

6. Franzen, C.: OpenAI confirms new frontier models o3 and o3-mini. VentureBeat (2024). https://venturebeat.com/ai/openai-confirms-new-frontier-models-o3-and-o3-mini/

7. Gemini 2.0 Flash. (n.d.). Google Cloud. https://cloud.google.com/vertex-ai/generative-ai/docs/models/gemini/2-0-flash

8. Initiative, Truth. Most Young E-Cigarette Users Say They Want to Quit Vaping in 2021. Truth Initiative, 27 Jan. 2021. truthinitiative.org/research-resources/quitting-smoking-vaping/most-young-e-cigarette-users-say-they-want-quit-vaping

9. Kasson, E., et al.: Using a mixed methods approach to identify public perception of vaping risks and overall health outcomes on twitter during the 2019 EVALI outbreak. Int. J. Med. Inform. **155**, 104574 (2021). www.sciencedirect.com/science/article/pii/S1386505621002008?via%3Dihub, https://doi.org/10.1016/j.ijmedinf.2021.104574

10. Li, K.D., et al.: Comparing GPT-4 and human researchers in qualitative analysis of healthcare data: qualitative description study (Preprint). J. Med. Internet Res. **26**, e56500 (2024). https://doi.org/10.2196/56500

11. LLM System Prompt vs. User Prompt. (n.d.). https://www.nebuly.com/blog/llm-system-prompt-vs-user-prompt

12. Marques, P., Piqueras, L., Sanz, M.: An updated overview of e-cigarette impact on human health. Respirat. Res. **22**(1) (2021). https://doi.org/10.1186/s12931-021-01737-5

13. Martinasek, M., et al.: Predictors of vaping Behavior Change in Young Adults using the Transtheoretical Model: a Multi-Country study. Tobacco Use Insights **14**, 1179173X2098867 (2021). https://doi.org/10.1177/1179173x20988672 (NOW 13

14. OpenAI. OpenAI O1 and new tools for developers (2024). https://openai.com/index/o1-and-new-tools-for-developers/

15. Park, M., An, B.: Comparison of the predictors of smoking cessation plans between adolescent conventional cigarette smokers and e-cigarette smokers using the transtheoretical model. Children **11**(5), 598 (2024). https://doi.org/10.3390/children11050598

16. Psychology, P.: Transtheoretical model and stages of change (Examples). Practical Psychology (2023). https://practicalpie.com/transtheoretical-model-stages-of-change-examples/

17. Samuels, M.: Vaping could make you 40 percent more likely to get respiratory disease. Boston University (2020). www.bu.edu/articles/2020/vaping-could-make-you-40-percent-more-likely-to-get-respiratory-disease/

18. Santanam, N., et al.: Nicotinic acetylcholine receptor signaling in atherogenesis. Atherosclerosis **225**(2), 264–273 (2012). https://doi.org/10.1016/j.atherosclerosis.2012.07.041

19. Sokolova, M., Lapalme, G.: A systematic analysis of performance measures for classification tasks. Inf. Process. Manage. **45**(4), 427–437 (2009). https://doi.org/10.1016/j.ipm.2009.03.002

20. Tackett, A.P., et al.: Prospective study of e-cigarette use and respiratory symptoms in adolescents and young adults. Thorax **79**(2) (2023). thorax.bmj.com/content/thoraxjnl/early/2023/08/17/thorax-2022-218670.full.pdf, https://doi.org/10.1136/thorax-2022-218670

21. Team, G., et al.: Gemma 2: Improving open language models at a practical size (2024). arXiv.org. https://arxiv.org/abs/2408.00118
22. Wang, T.W., et al.: Tobacco product use and associated factors among middle and high school students — United States. MMWR Surveillance Summ. **68**(12), 1–22 (2019). https://doi.org/10.15585/mmwr.ss6812a1
23. Wiggers, K.: Meta unveils a new, more efficient Llama model. TechCrunch (2024). https://techcrunch.com/2024/12/06/meta-unveils-a-new-more-efficient-llama-model/
24. Wilson, A.E., Lehmann, C. U., Saleh, S. N., Hanna, J., Medford, R.J.: Social media: a new tool for outbreak surveillance. Antimicrobial Stewardship Healthcare Epidemiol. **1**(1) (2021). https://doi.org/10.1017/ash.2021.225
25. xAI. Grok-2 Beta release (2024). https://x.ai/news/grok-2

Active Ageing with Generative AI, Agentic AI, Humanoid Robots, and the Metaverse: Opportunities, Challenges, and Risks

Yuxin Liu[1] and Keng Leng Siau[2]([✉])

[1] City University of Hong Kong, Hong Kong SAR, China
`yliu2324-c@my.cityu.edu.hk`
[2] Singapore Management University, Singapore, Singapore
`klsiau@smu.edu.sg`

Abstract. The rapid global aging population necessitates innovative approaches to enhance the quality of life for older adults, with artificial intelligence (AI), humanoid robots, and the Metaverse emerging as transformative tools for active ageing. This study systematically investigates the opportunities, challenges, and risks associated with integrating these technologies to support elderly health, cognitive function, emotional well-being, and social engagement. AI demonstrates potential in personalized health monitoring, cognitive training, and emotional support through adaptive algorithms, while humanoid robots offer functional assistance and companionship, mitigating social isolation. The Metaverse facilitates immersive telemedicine, remote rehabilitation, and virtual social interactions, bridging physical limitations. However, critical challenges persist in the successful implementation of gerontechnology, including technical, personal, and social barriers. Serious ethical risks (e.g., AI bias and privacy breaches) further complicate the ethical deployment of these technologies. The study proposes future research directions to address these issues. By advocating for diverse, equal, and inclusive design, this research contributes theoretical insights and practical guidelines for effectively and ethically deploying technologies to empower aging populations while minimizing inequalities.

Keywords: Active ageing · Artificial Intelligence · Humanoid robots · Metaverse

1 Introduction: AI and Human-AI Interaction

The aging population is becoming one of the most pressing global issues, with its pace accelerating in recent decades. By 2030, one in six people worldwide will be 60 years or older, and the number of seniors is expected to rise from 1 billion in 2020 to 1.4 billion (World Health Organization 2024). This demographic shift necessitates substantial efforts to address the challenges faced by the elderly population, including physical decline, cognitive impairments, and social isolation (Netuveli & Blane 2008), all of which diminish their quality of life. The concept of active ageing has emerged as a crucial framework, advocating for "optimizing opportunities for health, participation,

F. F.-H Nah and K. L. Siau (Eds.): HCII 2025, LNCS 16343, pp. 108–120, 2026.
https://doi.org/10.1007/978-3-032-13167-6_8

and security in order to enhance the quality of life as people age" (World Health Organization 2002). It extends beyond physical well-being to encompass mental and social well-being, ensuring older adults remain engaged in social, economic, cultural, spiritual, and civic affairs.

Achieving successful and active ageing requires more than traditional caregiving methods. Technological advancements play a pivotal role in enhancing the lives of seniors. Emerging technologies such as wearable health devices, telemedicine, Artificial Intelligence (AI) companions, and assistive robots have shown significant potential in enhancing seniors' well-being by improving healthcare access, promoting social engagement, and supporting independent living (Cantone et al. 2023). However, the integration of advanced technologies into ageing societies is still in its early stages, with numerous challenges to overcome. The key issue lies in harnessing their full potential while addressing challenges and potential risks. This study aims to provide valuable insights into how advanced technologies, specifically generative AI (GenAI), agentic AI, humanoid robots, and the Metaverse, can be effectively leveraged to promote active ageing.

We begin by reviewing current applications of these technologies in enhancing seniors' physical health, cognitive capabilities, emotional well-being, and social participation in Sect. 2. The challenges in their successful implementation, including technological, personal, and social barriers, are discussed in Sect. 3. Furthermore, in Sect. 4, we analyze the potential threats associated with the integration of gerontechnology, particularly concerns related to AI bias, unequal access, social isolation, privacy breaches, and autonomy violations. Finally, we suggest future research directions in Sect. 5, focusing on how current technologies can be optimized to better serve the ageing population.

2   Current Development: Technological Innovations for Promoting Active Ageing

2.1   Generative AI in Enhancing Active Ageing

GenAI refers to AI systems that can produce new and original content, such as text, images, audio, or video, based on patterns learned from large-scale datasets (Nah et al. 2023; Stephanidis et al. 2025). In the context of active ageing, GenAI offers significant potential to enhance emotional well-being, cognitive engagement, and social interaction for older adults through personalized, adaptive, and interactive experiences.

GenAI offers valuable opportunities for cognitive training in the elderly. GenAI can enhance cognitive training by providing personalized, adaptive learning paths (Wang & Zhang 2024). By continuously monitoring cognitive states, GenAI facilitates real-time adjustments to training and enables the early detection of cognitive decline, allowing for timely interventions.

In addition to supporting cognitive health, GenAI also plays a vital role in improving the emotional well-being of the elderly. Using speech and behavioral analysis, GenAI-powered virtual assistants can detect emotional states and identify psychological issues such as depression and anxiety at early stages (Qian et al. 2021), providing tailored responses to improve social engagement and emotional well-being. GenAI-powered virtual assistants also offer significant potential to alleviate social isolation and loneliness in the elderly by enhancing social connections and providing companionship (Corbett et al. 2021).

2.2 Agentic AI in Supporting Active Ageing

Agentic AI refers to "autonomous systems designed to pursue complex goals with minimal human intervention" (Acharya et al. 2025, p. 18912). Unlike traditional reactive systems that require user input to function, agentic AI can initiate actions, learn from user behavior, and adapt its strategies over time, making it especially promising for supporting autonomy, safety, and personalized care in ageing populations.

Traditional AI has shown considerable value in health prevention, health screening, and activities of daily living (ADL) assistance for the elderly (Lee et al. 2023). In the realm of health prevention, one notable application is in elderly fall detection systems, where machine learning and deep learning algorithms analyze sensor data to improve accuracy, reduce false alarms, and enhance real-time detection and response (Wang et al. 2020). Furthermore, in health screening, AI is increasingly employed in diagnosing chronic diseases such as diabetes, heart disease, and liver disease, leveraging various machine learning methods to enhance early detection and diagnostic accuracy (Battineni et al. 2020).

While the current deployment of agentic AI in these areas remains limited, its potential to enhance and extend traditional AI applications is significant. Rather than passively analyzing data, agentic AI systems can proactively identify risks, initiate responses, and autonomously adapt to users' evolving needs (Acharya et al. 2025). For instance, rather than merely detecting a fall, an agentic system could autonomously contact emergency services, notify caregivers, and adjust the environment to prevent further incidents. Similarly, in chronic disease management, agentic AI could monitor daily health patterns and independently recommend behavioral adjustments or suggest scheduling a medical consultation. As these technologies mature, integrating agentic AI into elderly care systems holds great promise for promoting proactive, adaptive, and person-centered support, shifting the paradigm from assistance to empowerment in active ageing.

2.3 Humanoid Robots in Promoting Active Ageing

Robots are playing an increasingly important role in supporting active ageing by providing both functional assistance and emotional support (Broekens et al. 2009). Service-type robots (e.g., Nurse Bot Pearl) provide essential support in daily activities, like navigation and safety monitoring (Pollack et al. 2002). Companion-type robots, such as Huggable, focus on emotional well-being by offering interactive and therapeutic companionship, reducing feelings of loneliness and stress (Stiehl et al. 2006). While earlier robots often mimicked animal appearances, such as dogs and bears (Broekens et al. 2009), recent advancements in technologies have led to the development of humanoid robots that are designed to more closely resemble humans.

Humanoid robots are anthropomorphic robots designed to emulate human physical characteristics and behaviors (Valenzuela et al. 2024). Humanoid robots can mimic human gestures and speech patterns, enabling more intuitive and engaging interactions with older adults. By incorporating human-like characteristics, these robots can foster trust and reduce the impact of operational errors, as users tend to prefer robots that communicate expressively rather than those that focus solely on efficiency (Hamacher et al. 2016). Moreover, existing research indicates that the effectiveness of human-robot interaction (HRI) is influenced by factors such as empathy, professionalism, and personality alignment between the user and the robot. A lower difference in empathy between a user and a robot correlates with higher satisfaction levels, suggesting that humanoid robots can be designed to adapt their interactions based on the emotional needs of older individuals (Kwon et al. 2018). The increasing applications of humanoid robots can transform the dynamics of human interaction, creating a synthetic society where humans and robots coexist and communicate in new ways. For older adults, especially those experiencing social isolation, this interaction has the potential to enhance emotional engagement and promote social integration (Zhao 2006).

2.4 Metaverse for Active Ageing

The Metaverse is an immersive virtual environment powered by augmented reality (AR), virtual reality (VR), and other digital technologies, enabling individuals to interact with each other and digital objects in real time through avatars (Liu & Siau 2024; H. Wang et al. 2023a, b). Within this virtual space, older adults can access a range of virtual healthcare services remotely, such as medical advice and therapy sessions (Yang et al. 2022). VR enhances telehealth by offering solutions like VR-assisted biofeedback and immersive environments for telerehabilitation, teleconsultation, and telementoring (Worlikar et al. 2023).

VR has also shown significant potential in cognitive training for the elderly, offering a flexible and engaging platform for enhancing cognitive functions. In VR environments, older individuals can practice tasks such as walking or crossing the street--scenarios that would be unfeasible or risky in the real world (Bauer & Andringa 2020). This flexibility not only aids cognitive improvement but also reduces reliance on healthcare professionals, enabling remote rehabilitation and continuous care (Amorim et al. 2018). Additionally, VR can provide rich, high-resolution data that aids in tracking subtle individual changes, offering real-time feedback for corrective actions (Bauer & Andringa 2020).

Beyond telehealth and cognitive training, the metaverse has also shown promise in enhancing social connections among the elderly, particularly those facing cognitive decline or physical limitations. Studies suggest that VR can help reduce loneliness and improve social engagement by allowing older adults to connect with family, friends, and new people with shared interests (Mois et al. 2024). For individuals with dementia, co-designed VR environments have proven effective in enhancing social connectedness (Flynn et al. 2023). In long-term care settings, VR programs can effectively enhance social engagement among residents with varying cognitive and physical impairments (Hung et al. 2023).

3 Barriers to Effective Implementation of Technologies for Active Ageing

While GenAI, agentic AI, humanoid robots, and the Metaverse offer significant potential for enhancing active ageing, their widespread integration into the lives of older adults is obstructed by a range of barriers. It is crucial to identify the challenges to ensure the successful implementation of these technologies.

3.1 Technological Barriers

Inapplicability of Technologies Trained Using Younger Populations. A significant technological barrier in elderly care technologies is the inapplicability of models and systems that are trained using younger populations. For instance, fall detection systems often rely on simulated datasets from young, healthy volunteers, which fail to capture the unique movement patterns and fall characteristics of older adults (Wang et al. 2020). This leads to high false-positive rates in real-world applications involving the elderly (Maray et al. 2023). Similarly, while immersive VR shows great potential for cognitive training in older adults, most studies have been conducted with younger participants, leaving a gap in research tailored to older populations at various stages of cognitive decline (Bauer & Andringa 2020). These limitations highlight the need for models and technologies specifically designed and tested for the elderly.

Safety Design with Robotics for Older Adults. The safety design of robots for elderly care presents significant technological challenges. Such technological barriers, like improper navigation, can increase the risk of physical injury. For instance, environmental factors such as hallway clutter can interfere with the robot's sensors, hindering its movement and increasing the likelihood of collisions with residents or entry into restricted areas. These issues can lead to falls or confusion among cognitively impaired individuals (Hung et al. 2022). Additionally, technical failures, such as sensor malfunctions or system crashes, pose further safety concerns. Robots may also struggle to handle complex scenarios that human caregivers manage easily, potentially resulting in safety hazards if they fail to respond appropriately in emergencies (He 2024). These technological barriers underscore the need for robust safety designs, comprehensive risk assessments, and clear guidelines to ensure the safe and effective use of robots in elderly care environments.

VR Motion Sickness. VR motion sickness represents a key technological barrier in the use of VR for active ageing, impacting its usability and acceptance. Research suggests that hardware factors, such as variations in resolution and refresh rate of head-mounted displays (HMDs), as well as content features like game-based content, can exacerbate motion sickness symptoms (Saredakis et al. 2020). Individual differences, such as gender, age, and motion sickness history, also influence the severity of symptoms (Chang et al. 2020). While some studies have indicated that older users report lower levels of motion sickness compared to younger users, this finding is based on a limited older population, highlighting the need for more in-depth studies in this area (Saredakis et al. 2020). Furthermore, other health issues prevalent among older adults may also affect their susceptibility to motion sickness. As a result, it is crucial to develop VR experiences tailored specifically for older adults, considering their unique physiological responses to technology.

3.2 Personal Barriers

Low Digital Literacy. Digital literacy, defined as individuals' ability to find, evaluate, and use information through appropriate digital technologies (Reddy et al. 2020), is crucial for older adults to engage with advanced gerontechnologies that support active ageing. Research shows that higher ICT (Information and Communication Technology) usage among elderly individuals is linked to better health outcomes, including fewer chronic diseases, less physical decline, and greater life satisfaction (Oh & Bae 2024). However, older adults often face significant challenges in acquiring digital skills compared to younger generations, which can limit their participation in a digital society. Previous research indicates that as individuals age, their reaction times increase, error rates rise, and they experience greater subjective fatigue and difficulty in completing tasks involving ICT (Susło et al. 2018). Even basic digital skills can be difficult for older individuals with limited prior digital experience (Vercruyssen et al. 2023). These barriers highlight the importance of addressing digital literacy as a key component in the effective implementation of gerontechnologies for active ageing.

Privacy Concerns. The use of gerontechnologies often involves the collection of sensitive personal information, raising significant Health Information Privacy Concerns (HIPCs). For example, AI-powered health monitoring systems, such as wearable devices that track vital signs and physical activity, collect sensitive health data, including heart rate, sleep patterns, and blood pressure. These privacy concerns negatively impact the perceived usefulness and perceived ease of use of technologies, significantly hindering technology adoption (Dhagarra et al. 2020). Personal characteristics, such as age and health status, play a crucial role in shaping HIPCs. As individuals age, their HIPC tends to increase. Furthermore, those in poorer health exhibit higher HIPC, indicating that individuals with more health challenges are particularly sensitive to the potential misuse of their health data (Fox & James 2021). Therefore, addressing privacy directly is crucial for encouraging older adults to engage with innovations for active ageing.

3.3 Social Barriers

The lack of social support poses a critical barrier to older adults' adoption of gerontechnologies. The ability to access and effectively utilize these innovations largely depends on attitudes and assistance from family members, caregivers, and broader societal networks. Therefore, pervasive age-related stereotypes that older individuals inherently lack the capacity to master complex technologies such as VR cognitive training systems often limit older users' access (Comunello et al. 2017). Even when the elderly have the opportunity to use these technologies, such social bias and exclusion can increase their psychological burden, reducing their willingness to adopt these technologies (Spencer et al. 2016). Furthermore, the lack of digital literacy education and training exacerbates this issue, restricting their opportunities to engage with gerontechnologies. These barriers highlight the significance of fostering a more supportive and inclusive environment for active ageing.

4 Potential Risks in the Integration of Technologies for Active Ageing

As the integration of GenAI, agentic AI, humanoid robots, and the Metaverse in promoting active ageing progresses, it is essential to consider the potential risks associated with these technologies. While these innovations offer numerous benefits for older adults, their widespread adoption may give rise to ethical and social risks that could potentially harm ageing populations.

4.1 AI Bias

AI bias represents a significant ethical issue in the application of gerontechnologies. AI systems are trained on large datasets, which can unintentionally reflect biases present in the data (Wang & Siau 2018; Wang et al. 2025). One serious AI bias is digital ageism. For example, training data may overlook atypical manifestations of diseases in older adults, which can impact the accuracy of medical devices (Van Kolfschooten 2023). Existing research has introduced the concept of the "AI Cycle of Health Inequality", revealing how AI systems can replicate and reinforce existing age discrimination patterns in healthcare, leading to health disparities in health outcomes across different demographic groups (Van Kolfschooten 2023). Furthermore, current technologies targeting older adults primarily focus on health management and chronic disease treatment, while neglecting their needs in areas such as entertainment, socialization, and education. This narrow focus not only restricts older adults' opportunities to benefit from technologies but may also lead to their further marginalization in society (Chu et al. 2022). Therefore, it is essential to ensure that AI systems are designed and implemented to minimize bias, address the diverse needs of older adults, and foster a more equitable and inclusive technological environment.

4.2 Unequal Access

The application of gerontechnologies leads to significant inequalities in resource distribution. While technologies like AI and VR can improve seniors' lives, high costs and internet infrastructure requirements may make these innovations inaccessible to parts of the ageing population. This inequality manifests in three key ways: First, many older adults cannot afford essential smart devices; second, poor internet connectivity in rural areas limits access to cloud-based health monitoring services; third, existing technologies rarely account for health-related challenges such as declining vision or slower motor skills (McLean 2011). Gerontechnologies may inadvertently widen quality-of-life disparities between seniors of different socioeconomic statuses, underscoring the urgency of addressing systemic inequities to ensure technological advancements benefit all ageing populations equitably (Zhu et al. 2022).

4.3 Social Isolation

The integration of advanced technologies to promote active ageing raises social isolation concerns. While innovations such as humanoid robots and GenAI companions aim to provide social support, overreliance on these tools may yield counterproductive outcomes. For instance, excessive use of AI-based caregiving systems or robotic companions may diminish meaningful interactions between older adults and their families or friends, potentially leading to emotional neglect (Vogan et al. 2020). Similarly, smart home technologies (e.g., automated household devices) could reduce necessary interactions with caregivers or neighbors, weakening older adults' connections to their communities and exacerbating social alienation (Zhu et al. 2022). Existing research emphasizes that technologies should serve as complementary tools rather than substitutes for human interaction (Liu et al. 2025). Efforts should be made to integrate these technologies into broader community networks to maintain social well-being.

4.4 Privacy Breach

Privacy and data security concerns constitute a critical ethical challenge in applying intelligent technologies to ageing societies (Vogan et al. 2020). Older adults often lack sufficient awareness of the scope and purposes of data collection by AI systems, robotics, and virtual platforms. Their sensitive data may be excessively collected or inappropriately shared, posing risks of privacy breaches. For instance, smart home technologies, which continuously gather users' daily activity data (e.g., movement frequency and medication schedules), may infringe on both physical privacy (e.g., monitoring personal routines) and informational privacy (e.g., exposing health records) without proper data protection measures like encryption and anonymization (Zhu et al. 2022).

4.5 Autonomy Violation

Autonomy is a fundamental aspect of ageing with dignity. Advanced gerontechnologies can play a crucial role in helping older adults maintain independence in their daily activities, thereby preserving their sense of self-worth and dignity (Zhu et al. 2022). However, ensuring informed consent of older adults is a key challenge in protecting autonomy. Informed consent requires older individuals to fully understand the purpose, use, benefits, and potential risks of technologies. However, due to limited awareness, familiarity, knowledge, and skills regarding technologies, older adults, particularly those who may be cognitively impaired, may struggle to make informed decisions (R. H. Wang et al. 2023). This raises concerns about the adequacy of consent processes and the ethical implications of monitoring and data collection practices, which may not always respect the autonomy of older individuals (Bowes et al. 2012). Furthermore, autonomy is not only about making choices regarding one's own life but also involves the impact on others. For instance, in shared living situations, decisions regarding remote home monitoring may infringe upon the privacy of others (Bowes et al. 2012). Therefore, balancing individual autonomy with collective interests becomes crucial to ensure that decisions respect the rights and needs of all parties involved.

5 Future Research Directions

Based on the barriers and risks identified in the last two sections, this study proposes the following research directions to advance the successful and ethical integration of technologies for active ageing.

1. Addressing Technological Barriers	
Adaptation of Technologies and Models for Older Adults	How to construct multimodal datasets that capture older adults' unique behavioral patterns to enhance AI models' generalization capabilities?
	How to effectively adapt existing models to accommodate older adults' physiological and cognitive traits?
	How to design differentiated VR cognitive training content tailored to varying levels of cognitive decline?
Safety Design for Elderly Care Robots	How to design robust navigation algorithms to handle dynamic environments?
	How to mitigate safety risks caused by hardware failures?
	How to train robots to respond to emergencies in ways that align with care ethics and safety protocols?
Mitigating VR-Induced Motion Sickness in Older Adults	How to adjust VR hardware parameters and interaction modes to lower motion sickness incidence?
	How to dynamically adapt VR content for older adults with diverse health conditions?
	How to integrate multimodal feedback (e.g., tactile cues, breath-synchronized audio) to alleviate motion sickness symptoms?
2. Addressing Personal Barriers	
Enhancing Digital Literacy in Older Adults	How to design age-friendly digital training tools to help older adults master the basic operations of smart devices?
	Can gamified learning increase seniors' motivation to acquire digital skills?
	How to design progressive learning pathways tailored to older adults' cognitive traits to reduce frustration?
Elderly-Friendly Interface Design	How to simplify interaction processes using natural interaction methods?

(continued)

(continued)

	How to optimize design elements to improve information recognition efficiency for older adults?
	How to implement error-tolerant guidance mechanisms (e.g., real-time voice prompts) to reduce interaction errors?
Privacy Protection and Trust Building	How to simplify privacy settings interfaces to empower older adults to control personal data effortlessly?
	Can transparent data usage explanations enhance seniors' trust in technologies?
	How to balance health monitoring accuracy with data minimization principles?
3. Addressing Social Barriers	
Combating Social Bias and Strengthening Social Support	Can family-shared technologies (e.g., health monitoring platforms managed collaboratively with family members) encourage collective engagement in seniors' technology use?
	How to provide ongoing technical support for older adults through public infrastructure?
	How to shift societal perceptions of older adults' technological adaptability?
4. Addressing Ethical Concerns	
Ensuring Diversity, Equity, and Inclusion	How can improvements in data collection and algorithm design reduce "digital ageism"?
	How to design "human-machine collaborative" intelligent systems that provide convenience while avoiding the erosion of authentic social interactions among older adults?
	How to design transparent informed consent processes that adapt to older adults' cognitive abilities?

6 Conclusion

As global ageing accelerates, emerging technologies present new opportunities for promoting active ageing. This study focuses on the role of GenAI, agentic AI, humanoid robots, and the Metaverse in supporting the ageing population. We provide a comprehensive overview of how these technologies can enhance elderly health, cognitive abilities, social participation, and emotional well-being. However, the successful integration of gerontechnology faces several challenges and potential risks. We discuss key technical, personal, and social barriers to the adoption of these technologies, along with the ethical concerns that may arise. Future research directions and questions are proposed targeting these challenges and risks.

This study offers valuable theoretical insights and practical implications. It provides actionable guidelines for researchers and practitioners, such as simplifying user interfaces for older adults and capturing their unique behavioral patterns to improve adaptability. These contributions aim to advance human-centered gerontechnology that supports elderly health and dignity, fosters greater social engagement, and addresses inequalities in access and use.

Acknowledgements. This research is partially supported by the Lee Kong Chian Professorship and Singapore MoE Tier 1A funding.

References

Acharya, D.B., Kuppan, K., Divya, B.: Agentic AI: autonomous intelligence for complex goals–a comprehensive survey. IEEE Access **13**, 18912–18936 (2025)

Amorim, J.S.C.D., Leite, R.C., Brizola, R., Yonamine, C.Y.: Virtual reality therapy for rehabilitation of balance in the elderly: a systematic review and Meta-analysis. Adv. Rheumatol. **58**, 18 (2018)

Battineni, G., Sagaro, G.G., Chinatalapudi, N., Amenta, F.: Applications of machine learning predictive models in the chronic disease diagnosis. J. Personal. Med. **10**(2), 21 (2020)

Bauer, A.C.M., Andringa, G.: The potential of immersive virtual reality for cognitive training in elderly. Gerontology **66**(6), 614–623 (2020)

Bowes, A., Dawson, A., Bell, D.: Ethical implications of lifestyle monitoring data in ageing research. Inf. Commun. Soc. **15**(1), 5–22 (2012)

Broekens, J., Heerink, M., Rosendal, H.: Assistive social robots in elderly care: a review. Gerontechnology **8**(2), 94–103 (2009)

Cantone, A.A., Esposito, M., Perillo, F.P., Romano, M., Sebillo, M., Vitiello, G.: Enhancing elderly health monitoring: achieving autonomous and secure living through the integration of artificial intelligence, autonomous robots, and sensors. Electronics **12**(18), 3918 (2023)

Chang, E., Kim, H.T., Yoo, B.: Virtual reality sickness: a review of causes and measurements. Int. J. Hum.-Comput. Interact. **36**(17), 1658–1682 (2020)

Chu, C.H., et al.: Digital ageism: challenges and opportunities in artificial intelligence for older adults. Gerontologist **62**(7), 947–955 (2022)

Comunello, F., Fernández Ardèvol, M., Mulargia, S., Belotti, F.: Women, youth and everything else: age-based and gendered stereotypes in relation to digital technology among elderly Italian mobile phone users. Media Cult. Soc. **39**(6), 798–815 (2017)

Corbett, C.F., Wright, P.J., Jones, K., Parmer, M.: Voice-activated virtual home assistant use and social isolation and loneliness among older adults: mini review. Front. Public Health **9**, 742012 (2021)

Dhagarra, D., Goswami, M., Kumar, G.: Impact of trust and privacy concerns on technology acceptance in healthcare: an Indian perspective. Int. J. Med. Inform. **141**, 104164 (2020)

Flynn, A., Reilly, G., Barry, M., Brennan, A., Redfern, S., Casey, D.: Co-designing a virtual reality social connecting space for older adults living with dementia. Alzheimers Dement. **19**, e067826 (2023)

Fox, G., James, T.L.: Toward an understanding of the antecedents to health information privacy concern: a mixed methods study. Inf. Syst. Front. **23**(6), 1537–1562 (2021)

Hamacher, A., Bianchi-Berthouze, N., Pipe, A.G., Eder, K.: Believing in BERT: using expressive communication to enhance trust and counteract operational error in physical Human-robot interaction. In: 25th IEEE International Symposium on Robot and Human Interactive Communication (RO-MAN) (2016)

He, J.: AI robots in elderly care: opportunities, challenges, and ethical concerns. UC Merced Undergraduate Res. J. **17**(1) (2024)

Hung, L., Mann, J., Perry, J., Berndt, A., Wong, J.: Technological risks and ethical implications of using robots in long-term care. J. Rehabil. Assist. Technol. Eng. **9**, 20556683221106916 (2022)

Hung, L., Wong, J., Upreti, M., Kan, W.: Using virtual reality in long-term care to reduce social isolation. Innov. Aging **7**(Suppl 1), 317 (2023)

Kwon, O., Kim, J., Jin, Y., Lee, N.: Impact of human-robot interaction on user satisfaction with humanoid-based healthcare. Int. J. Eng. Technol. **7**(2), 68–75 (2018)

Lee, C.-H., Wang, C., Fan, X., Li, F., Chen, C.-H.: Artificial intelligence-enabled digital transformation in elderly healthcare field: scoping review. Adv. Eng. Inform. **55**, 101874 (2023)

Liu, Y., Siau, K.L.: Generative artificial intelligence and metaverse: future of work, future of society, and future of humanity. In: Zhao, F., Miao, D. (eds.) AI-generated Content. AIGC 2023. Communications in Computer and Information Science, vol. 1946. Springer, Singapore (2024).https://doi.org/10.1007/978-981-99-7587-7_10

Liu, Y., Wang, R., Siau, K.: FinTech digital transformation: generative AI, humanoid robots, metaverse, human—AI collaboration, and Industry 5.0. In: Huang, K.W., Cao, Q., Su, R. (eds.) Financial Technology. ICFT 2024. Communications in Computer and Information Science, vol. 2437. Springer, Singapore (2025). https://doi.org/10.1007/978-981-96-3811-6_12

Maray, N., Ngu, A.H., Ni, J., Debnath, M., Wang, L.: Transfer learning on small datasets for improved fall detection. Sensors **23**(3), 1105 (2023)

McLean, A.: Ethical frontiers of ICT and older users: cultural, pragmatic and ethical issues. Ethics Inf. Technol. **13**(4), 313–326 (2011)

Mois, G., et al.: Understanding older adults' interest in using virtual reality to support social engagement activities. Innov. Aging **8**(Supplement_1), 1224–1224 (2024)

Nah, F., Zheng, R., Cai, J., Siau, K., Chen, L.: Generative AI and ChatGPT: applications, challenges, and AI-human collaboration. J. Inform. Technol. Case Appl. Res. **25**(3), 277–304 (2023)

Netuveli, G., Blane, D.: Quality of life in older ages. Br. Med. Bull. **85**(1), 113–126 (2008)

Oh, E.-A., Bae, S.-M.: The relationship between the digital literacy and healthy aging of the elderly in Korea. Curr. Psychol. **43**(18), 16160–16169 (2024)

Pollack, M.E., et al.: Pearl: A mobile robotic assistant for the elderly. AAAI Workshop on Automation as Eldercare (2002)

Qian, K., Zhang, Z., Yamamoto, Y., Schuller, B.W.: Artificial intelligence internet of things for the elderly: from assisted living to health-care monitoring. IEEE Signal Process. Mag. **38**(4), 78–88 (2021)

Reddy, P., Sharma, B., Chaudhary, K.: Digital literacy: a review of literature. Int. J. Technoethics **11**(2), 65–94 (2020)

Saredakis, D., Szpak, A., Birckhead, B., Keage, H.A., Rizzo, A., Loetscher, T.: Factors associated with virtual reality sickness in head-mounted displays: a systematic review and meta-analysis. Front. Hum. Neurosci. **14**, 96 (2020)

Spencer, S.J., Logel, C., Davies, P.G.: Stereotype threat. Annu. Rev. Psychol. **67**(1), 415–437 (2016)

Stephanidis, C., et al.: Seven HCI grand challenges revisited: five-year progress. Int. J. Hum.-Comput. Interact. 1–49 (2025)

Stiehl, W.D., et al.: The huggable: a therapeutic robotic companion for relational, affective touch. In ACM SIGGRAPH 2006 Emerging Technologies, pp. 15-es (2006)

Susło, R., Paplicki, M., Dopierała, K., Drobnik, J.: Fostering digital literacy in the elderly as a means to secure their health needs and human rights in the reality of the twenty-first century. Family Med. Primary Care Rev. **3**, 271–275 (2018)

Valenzuela, K.L., Roxas, S.I., Wong, Y.-H.: Embodying intelligence: humanoid robot advancements and future prospects. In: Degen, H., Ntoa, S. (eds.) Artificial Intelligence in HCI. HCII 2024. LNCS, vol. 14736. Springer, Cham (2024). https://doi.org/10.1007/978-3-031-60615-1_20

Van Kolfschooten, H.: The AI cycle of health inequity and digital ageism: Mitigating biases through the EU regulatory framework on medical devices. J. Law Biosci. **10**(2), lsad031 (2023)

Vercruyssen, A., Schirmer, W., Geerts, N., Mortelmans, D.: How "basic" is basic digital literacy for older adults? Insights from digital skills instructors. Front. Educ. **8**, 1231701 (2023)

Vogan, A.A., Alnajjar, F., Gochoo, M., Khalid, S.: Robots, AI, and cognitive training in an era of mass age-related cognitive decline: a systematic review. IEEE Access **8**, 18284–18304 (2020)

Wang, H., et al.: A survey on the metaverse: the state-of-the-art, technologies, applications, and challenges. IEEE Internet Things J. **10**(16), 14671–14688 (2023)

Wang, R.H., Tannou, T., Bier, N., Couture, M., Aubry, R.: Proactive and ongoing analysis and management of ethical concerns in the development, evaluation, and implementation of smart homes for older adults with frailty. JMIR Aging **6**(1), e41322 (2023)

Wang, X., Ellul, J., Azzopardi, G.: Elderly fall detection systems: A literature survey. Frontiers in Robotics and AI **7**, 71 (2020)

Wang, W., Siau, K.: Ethical and moral issues with AI. In: Americas Conference on Information Systems (AMCIS) (2018)

Wang, Y., Wang, L., Siau, K.L.: Human-centered interaction in virtual worlds: a new era of generative artificial intelligence and metaverse. Int. J. Hum.-Comput. Interact. **41**(2), 1459–1501 (2025)

Wang, Y., Zhang, Y.: Enhancing cognitive recall in dementia patients: Integrating generative ai with virtual reality for behavioral and memory rehabilitation. In: Proceedings of the 6th International Conference on Big-data Service and Intelligent Computation (2024)

World Health Organization. Active Ageing: A Policy Framework. World Health Organization (2002). https://extranet.who.int/agefriendlyworld/wp-content/uploads/2014/06/WHO-Active-Ageing-Framework.pdf

World Health Organization. Ageing and Health. World Health Organization (2024). https://www.who.int/news-room/fact-sheets/detail/ageing-and-health

Worlikar, H., et al.: Mixed reality platforms in telehealth delivery: scoping review. JMIR Biomed. Eng. **8**, e42709 (2023)

Yang, Y., Siau, K., Xie, W., Sun, Y.: Smart health: intelligent healthcare systems in the metaverse, artificial intelligence, and data science era. J. Organ. End User Comput. **34**(1), 1–14 (2022)

Zhao, S.: Humanoid social robots as a medium of communication. New Media Soc. **8**(3), 401–419 (2006)

Zhu, J., et al.: Ethical issues of smart home-based elderly care: a scoping review. J. Nurs. Manag. **30**(8), 3686–3699 (2022)

Generative AI in Sports Management Education: A Systematic Review and Pilot Study

Xinyu Liu and Xiaodong Qu[⊠]

The George Washington University, Washington, USA
`x.qu@gwu.edu`

Abstract. Generative Artificial Intelligence (GenAI) is reshaping the landscape of higher education, with growing applications in specialized fields such as sports management. This paper presents a systematic literature review (SLR) of 92 peer-reviewed studies published between 2019 and 2025, examining how GenAI tools—including ChatGPT, Bing Copilot, and Google Gemini—are being integrated into sports management education. The review synthesizes evidence across themes of curricular integration, industry readiness, and student perceptions, highlighting how GenAI supports authentic, data-rich learning experiences that bridge academic theory with professional practice. A small-scale pilot study in an undergraduate sports management course further illustrates potential benefits, with students using GenAI to conduct case studies and interpret sports analytics data, leading to improved project performance. While the findings point to significant educational value, the review also identifies gaps in empirical evaluation, large-scale implementation, and ethical integration frameworks. The paper concludes with recommendations for curriculum design, industry-academic collaboration, and future research to ensure that GenAI adoption in sports management education is both pedagogically effective and ethically responsible.

Keywords: Generative Artificial Intelligence · Sports Management Education · Systematic Literature Review · Sports Analytics · Curriculum Design · Higher Education

1   Introduction

Sports management education is undergoing a rapid transformation as Artificial Intelligence (AI) technologies reshape how students acquire, apply, and refine professional skills. In particular, Generative AI (GenAI) tools—such as ChatGPT, Bing Copilot, and Google Gemini—are enabling sports management students to integrate real-time data analysis, scenario simulation, and automated content generation into their coursework and professional training. These capabilities are especially valuable in preparing students for an industry that is increasingly data-driven, competitive, and global in scope.

F. F.-H Nah and K. L. Siau (Eds.): HCII 2025, LNCS 16343, pp. 121–133, 2026.
https://doi.org/10.1007/978-3-032-13167-6_9

Despite the growth of sports analytics and AI-assisted decision-making in professional sports, sports management education faces persistent challenges. Students often lack opportunities to apply classroom knowledge to authentic industry contexts, encounter barriers in accessing and interpreting complex datasets, and receive limited personalized guidance in developing business and operational strategies. These gaps can hinder graduates' readiness for roles that demand both strategic thinking and technical literacy.

Generative AI tools offer unique solutions to these challenges. By enabling natural-language interaction with large datasets, automating repetitive tasks, and generating tailored strategic insights, GenAI can act as both a cognitive assistant and a creative partner. When integrated into sports management curricula, these tools can bridge the gap between theory and practice, allowing students to engage in experiential learning that mirrors real-world professional demands.

This study examines how business students specializing in sports management leverage GenAI tools to enhance learning outcomes and prepare for careers in the sports industry. Through both literature synthesis and ongoing classroom experiments, we explore the pedagogical, cognitive, and practical impacts of GenAI integration in sports-focused business education. Case examples include a student using AI to develop data-driven marketing strategies for a golf influencer business, and another employing AI-assisted analytics in ski coaching and sports event planning (Fig. 1).

1.1   Research Questions

This research addresses the following key questions:

1. How can Generative AI tools improve learning outcomes for business students specializing in sports management?
2. What role does GenAI play in preparing these students for real-world challenges in the sports industry?

2   Related Works

2.1   AI in Sports Management Education

The integration of Artificial Intelligence (AI) into sports management education is gaining momentum as both the sports industry and higher education increasingly adopt data-driven decision-making practices. Keiper et al. [10] demonstrated how ChatGPT can be incorporated into sport management curricula to simulate real-world decision-making scenarios, enabling students to develop practical problem-solving skills. Zhou et al. [31] provided a comprehensive review of AI applications in sports, identifying opportunities in performance analysis, strategic planning, and fan engagement.

Recent applied studies extend these insights to more advanced generative and multimodal AI technologies. Baughman et al. [1] examined the use of large-scale generative AI text systems for live sports events such as the US Open and

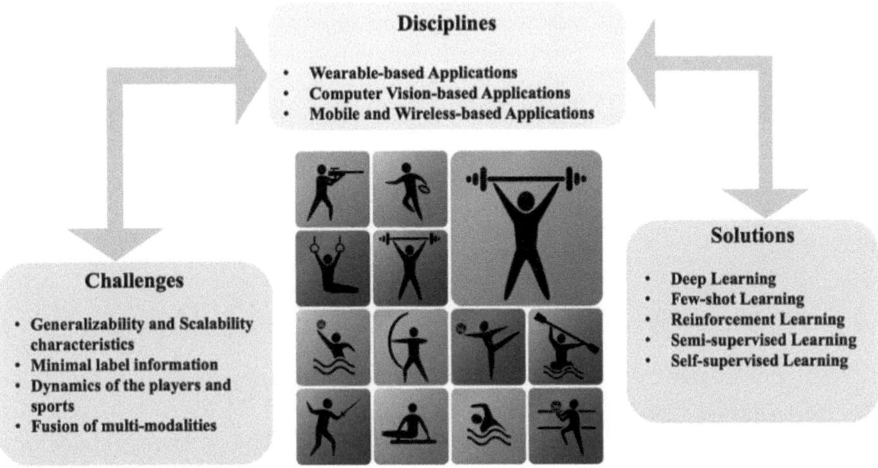

Fig. 1. Overview of AI applications in sports analytics and education [5].

Wimbledon, illustrating how AI can create real-time, context-specific narratives. Lin et al. [13] introduced *SportsBuddy*, an AI-powered sports video storytelling tool evaluated through real-world deployment, showing its potential as a teaching resource for sports media and analytics. Merilehto [15] demonstrated how large language models (LLMs) can convert semi-structured sports database content into structured datasets, significantly reducing manual processing.

Domain-specific applications broaden the educational landscape. Ma et al. [14] developed a multimodal LLM-based table tennis coaching system that combines tactical and technical feedback, offering possibilities for sports analytics education. Dindorf et al. [3] examined psychological and perceptual factors affecting the acceptance of AI-driven sports coaches, while Nalbant and Aydin [18] explored the intersection of AI technologies, digital sports marketing, and sports management, highlighting implications for management curricula. Swim et al. [24] designed a sport management course to improve students' digital literacy, demonstrating curriculum integration strategies relevant to AI adoption.

Qu et al. [20] offer a relevant parallel from computer science education, showing how project-based learning can integrate real-world datasets and AI tools, a model that could inform AI-enhanced sports management curricula. Yunoki et al. [30] similarly reviewed AI integration in music generation for undergraduate researchers, demonstrating how domain-specific AI reviews can inform curricular strategies across disciplines.

Haghparast et al. [8] applied AI language models to foresight planning in sports businesses, combining them with financial management strategies. Jokela [9] analyzed AI's impact on business and management processes in the sports industry, while Glebova et al. [6] emphasized AI's role as part of a suite of digital technologies transforming the sports sector. Tan et al. [25] examined digital management and smart technologies in sports education, linking them to employment, sustainability, and tourism—dimensions that could inform broader educational objectives.

Survey-based and domain-specific evidence reinforces AI's potential. Krämer et al. [11] found that sports students generally expect AI to improve performance and manage complexity, but remain cautious about ethics and over-reliance. Ha et al. [7] documented ChatGPT's opportunities and limitations in kinesiology education.

2.2   Generative AI in Higher Education and Sport Science

Beyond sports management, the role of GenAI in higher education and sport science is rapidly evolving. Krause et al. [12] identified AI literacy, bias awareness, and prompt engineering as essential competencies, while Wang [26] demonstrated that scaffolding GenAI with real-world projects enhances creativity and relevance. Gately [4] synthesized the potential of GenAI in educational research, emphasizing adaptive learning and automated feedback. Qu et al. [21] provide a meta-analysis of GenAI's cognitive impact in higher education, offering cross-domain evidence of AI's effect on learning outcomes.

In sport science and medicine, Connor and O'Neill [2] reviewed LLM opportunities and risks, while Xia et al. [29] introduced *SportQA*, a benchmark for LLM performance in sports question answering. Naughton et al. [19] identified challenges and opportunities for AI implementation in sports science and medicine teams. Murungi et al. [17] and Qu et al. [20] highlight trends in machine learning and EEG as well as AI-assisted research processes, offering methodological parallels for structured reviews in emerging fields. Saunders et al. [22] further demonstrate how GenAI can support the literature review process, a technique relevant to systematic reviews in sports management.

Skinner et al. [23] provided foundational methodologies for sport management research, relevant for designing and evaluating AI integration in curricula. Wang and Wang [27] reviewed AI in physical education teacher training, offering lessons for sports management pedagogy.

2.3   Synthesis and Gaps

The reviewed literature suggests that GenAI can bridge the gap between theoretical learning and practical, industry-ready skills in sports management education. Research demonstrates promise in areas such as AI-powered storytelling, live event content generation, database automation, coaching systems, digital literacy training, foresight planning, and AI-enhanced marketing analytics. Parallel evidence from other disciplines shows similar integration patterns, reinforcing the transferability of AI-enhanced pedagogical strategies.

Nonetheless, gaps remain. Few empirical studies focus specifically on sports management students' use of GenAI, and mixed-methods research linking quantitative outcomes to qualitative experiences is rare. Comprehensive frameworks for integrating GenAI into curricula—balancing technical training with ethical and strategic competencies—are still underdeveloped. This review addresses these gaps by synthesizing recent, domain-specific studies alongside cross-disciplinary precedents to form a foundation for evaluating both educational and industry-preparatory impacts of GenAI tools.

3   Methods

This study employed the Preferred Reporting Items for Systematic Reviews and Meta-Analyses (PRISMA) methodology [16] to systematically review recent literature on the use of Generative Artificial Intelligence (GenAI) in sports management education for business students. The focus was on peer-reviewed works and reputable preprints examining how platforms such as ChatGPT, Bing Copilot, and Google Gemini enhance learning outcomes, provide personalized feedback, support real-time data analysis, and assist in decision-making within sports-focused educational contexts.

3.1   Study Selection

The review included studies published between January 2019 and March 2025, targeting AI applications in sports management education, sports analytics education, and AI-driven learning environments with direct relevance to business students specializing in sports. To ensure comprehensive coverage, the literature search was conducted across multiple databases:

– *Google Scholar, ResearchGate, arXiv.org*
– *IEEE Xplore, ACM Digital Library, Web of Science, Scopus,* and *SpringerLink*

We used an expanded set of search strings to address gaps identified by reviewers, including:

("Generative AI" OR "Large Language Model" OR ChatGPT OR "Bing Copilot" OR "Google Gemini") AND ("sports management education" OR "sports analytics education" OR "sports business education" OR "sports business learning" OR "sports data analysis")

The initial search retrieved 512 records. After removing duplicates, 374 unique records were screened by title and abstract. Of these, 142 papers were selected for full-text review, and 92 met the inclusion criteria. Figure 2 illustrates the PRISMA-based selection process.

3.2   Inclusion and Exclusion Criteria

Studies were included if they:

– Presented peer-reviewed or reputable preprint research available in full text.
– Focused directly on the application of Generative AI or large language models in sports management education or closely related sports business training contexts.

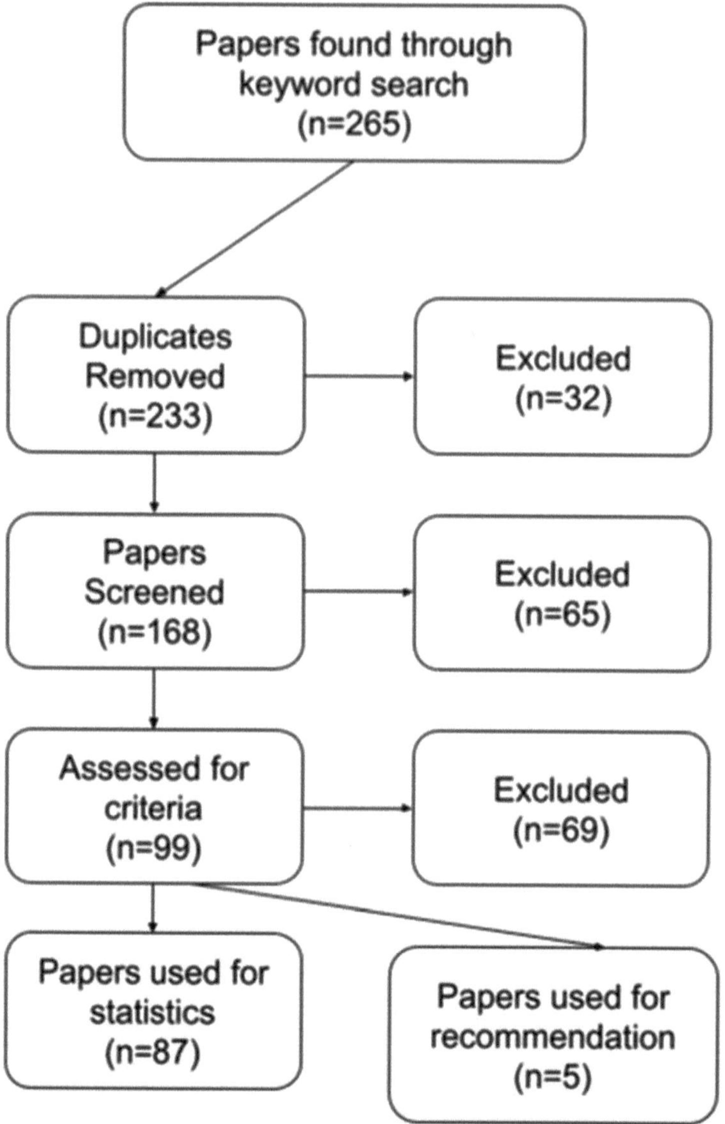

Fig. 2. PRISMA selection process for the reviewed papers.

- Were published in English between January 2019 and March 2025.

  Studies were excluded if they:

- Were inaccessible in full text.
- Mentioned AI only tangentially without substantive educational or sports-related relevance.
- Were non-English publications.

3.3 Data Collection and Evaluation

For each included study, the following information was extracted:

- **Bibliographic metadata:** authors, year, venue.
- **AI tool focus:** platform(s) studied (e.g., ChatGPT, Bing Copilot).
- **Educational context:** sports management, sports analytics, or sports business education.
- **Reported outcomes:** learning gains, skill development, industry readiness.
- **Challenges and opportunities:** ethical issues, technical barriers, adoption strategies.

The studies were then thematically coded into categories such as *Curricular Integration*, *Performance Analytics Education*, and *Experiential Learning with GenAI*, allowing synthesis of findings across diverse settings.

3.4 Ongoing Experiments

In parallel with the literature review, we are conducting classroom-based experiments in undergraduate sports management courses. These involve business students specializing in sports using GenAI tools for tasks such as data-driven marketing plan development, sports performance analytics interpretation, and event planning simulations. Observations and qualitative feedback from these experiments will be analyzed and reported in the Results section to complement the systematic review.

4 Results

Our analysis of 92 selected studies, supplemented with recent domain-specific and cross-disciplinary contributions, shows that Generative AI (GenAI) tools such as ChatGPT, Bing Copilot, and Google Gemini are increasingly embedded in sports management education. The literature reveals three recurring themes: curricular integration, industry readiness, and student perceptions and ethics. While the emphasis here is on synthesizing published work, we also include findings from a small-scale classroom pilot to illustrate potential applications.

4.1 Theme 1: Curricular Integration of GenAI Tools

Studies consistently show that embedding GenAI into sports management curricula enhances authenticity and practical relevance. Examples include *Sports-Buddy* [13], which enables students to produce AI-powered storytelling and video analyses for sports media and analytics training, and large-scale text generation systems applied to live event coverage at major tournaments [1]. Merilehto [15] demonstrates how large language models can automate the structuring of sports databases, lowering technical barriers to advanced analytics.

Domain-specific applications broaden the scope of integration. Ma et al. [14] developed a multimodal table tennis coaching system combining tactical and technical feedback, adaptable to broader analytics education. Swim et al. [24] designed a digital literacy course in sport management, illustrating how digital competencies can be systematically embedded. Cross-disciplinary parallels strengthen these findings: Qu et al. [20] integrated HCI datasets into project-based machine learning courses, offering a transferable model for AI-enhanced sports management curricula, while Yunoki et al. [30] reviewed AI in music generation, providing another example of domain-specific AI integration into undergraduate research contexts. Skinner et al. [23] provide methodological guidance that can underpin rigorous evaluation of such curricular innovations.

4.2   Theme 2: Industry Readiness and Skills Development

Evidence suggests that GenAI enhances industry readiness by equipping students with skills in strategic decision-making, marketing analytics, and fan engagement [28,31]. Baughman et al. [1] illustrate how real-time narrative generation can be applied to sports media, while Haghparast et al. [8] show how AI can be used in foresight planning with financial strategies. Jokela [9] emphasizes AI's transformative role in sports business processes, and Glebova et al. [6] situate it within a wider digital transformation landscape. Nalbant and Aydin [18] specifically link AI to digital sports marketing strategies, while Tan et al. [25] extend this to sustainability and tourism in sports education.

Operational realities also matter. Naughton et al. [19] detail barriers to AI adoption in sports science and medicine teams, highlighting the need for graduates to be skilled in interdisciplinary collaboration and change management. Murungi et al. [17] provide a review of trends in machine learning for EEG analysis, offering a parallel case of emerging technical skills and adoption challenges in another applied field.

4.3   Theme 3: Student Perceptions, Ethics, and Adoption Barriers

Survey data from Krämer et al. [11] show optimism about AI's educational benefits tempered by concerns over ethics, over-reliance, and transparency. Dindorf et al. [3] explore trust and acceptance of AI-driven coaching, while Ha et al. [7] find similar tensions in kinesiology education. Connor and O'Neill [2] emphasize governance and ethical safeguards for LLM adoption in sport science, echoed by Krause et al. [12]. From a process perspective, Saunders et al. [22] demonstrate how GenAI can improve literature review workflows, a capability that can be applied to student projects requiring critical source evaluation.

4.4   Keyword Trend Analysis

An analysis of keywords from reviewed papers reveals three clusters: educational integration terms such as "curriculum," "training," and "experiential learning";

technical references including "ChatGPT," "large language model," and "analytics"; and industry application terms like "sports marketing," "fan engagement," and "performance analysis." Google NGram analysis shows a sharp rise in the co-occurrence of "Generative AI" and "sports analytics" starting in 2022, reflecting growing interest in both research and practice. Qu et al. [21] provide meta-analytic evidence of GenAI's broader cognitive impact in higher education, reinforcing the relevance of this trend.

4.5 Pilot Study: Classroom Experiment

To complement the literature review, a pilot study was conducted in an undergraduate sports management course with five students. Participants used ChatGPT to design a market entry strategy for a hypothetical sports franchise and interpret a sports analytics dataset. Projects completed with AI assistance demonstrated greater clarity and depth in data-driven decision-making compared to previous assignments. While these results are promising, the small sample size limits generalization. Plans are in place to expand the study to approximately 15 students in the next academic term.

4.6 Summary

Across the literature and our preliminary observations, GenAI emerges as a catalyst for authentic, data-rich learning experiences that link theory to industry practice. It supports technical, analytical, and strategic competencies while prompting engagement with ethics and responsible use. Insights from cross-disciplinary AI integration studies in computing [17,20] and creative domains [30] underscore the transferability of these strategies to sports management education. Despite growth in the literature, there remains a shortage of large-scale, mixed-methods studies that can link educational interventions to sustained industry readiness.

5 Discussion

This study set out to investigate how Generative AI (GenAI) tools can improve learning outcomes for students in sports management education, and the role these tools play in preparing learners for the realities of the sports industry. The synthesis of 92 studies, supplemented by a small pilot classroom experiment, provides a multi-faceted picture of GenAI's current and potential impact.

In relation to the first research question, the literature consistently demonstrates that embedding GenAI tools into sports management curricula can create more authentic, data-rich learning experiences. Examples such as *SportsBuddy* [13] and large-scale sports event coverage systems [1] show how AI can enable students to engage directly with sports media, analytics, and real-time decision-making tasks. Domain-specific tools like the multimodal table tennis coaching system developed by Ma et al. [14] illustrate how AI-based feedback mechanisms could be adapted for broader analytics education, while database automation [15] helps remove technical barriers to hands-on data analysis. Together, these applications align with competency frameworks in sports management education, which emphasize both technical skills and applied problem-solving.

Addressing the second research question, GenAI appears to be a strong enabler of industry readiness. Studies highlight its value in developing capabilities for strategic planning, marketing analytics, and fan engagement [28,31]. Haghparast et al. [8] add a foresight perspective by combining AI language models with financial management strategies, while Jokela [9] underscores the transformative impact of AI on business and management processes in the sports industry. Glebova et al. [6] situate AI within a broader digital transformation context, and Naughton et al. [19] identify the operational and cultural challenges that graduates may face when entering AI-augmented professional environments. These insights reinforce the importance of preparing students not only for technical tasks, but also for navigating change management, interdisciplinary collaboration, and technology adoption processes in their future careers.

The role of student perceptions and ethical considerations is equally important. Surveys [7,11] show enthusiasm for GenAI's educational potential but caution about ethical risks, over-reliance, and the need for transparency. Dindorf et al. [3] highlight psychological and perceptual factors that influence trust and acceptance of AI-driven coaching, while Connor and O'Neill [2] and Krause et al. [12] emphasize the need to embed AI literacy, bias mitigation, and responsible use into curricula. Naughton et al. [19] add that without adequate governance frameworks, AI adoption can encounter resistance within sports organizations, underscoring the importance of preparing students to address such barriers.

The findings from our pilot study, although limited in scale, provide practical evidence relevant to both research questions. For RQ1, students using ChatGPT to complete a market entry case study and perform sports data analysis demonstrated greater clarity and depth in applying theoretical knowledge, suggesting that GenAI can directly enhance learning outcomes in applied coursework. For RQ2, the same students showed improved capacity to analyze and communicate actionable insights—skills closely tied to industry readiness—indicating that even short-term exposure to GenAI-supported tasks can foster competencies valued in the sports business sector.

The implications for curriculum design are clear. GenAI should not be positioned as an occasional enhancement, but rather integrated as a core element of teaching and assessment in sports management education. Embedding AI tools into projects, simulations, and case studies can help students apply theoretical knowledge to realistic, complex scenarios. Partnerships with sports organizations—providing authentic datasets, live projects, and mentorship—can further strengthen this connection. At the same time, explicit instruction in AI ethics, transparency, and bias awareness must accompany technical training, ensuring that graduates are not only competent users of AI but also responsible stewards of its application.

Despite these promising developments, significant gaps remain. Much of the existing research is descriptive, with few large-scale, longitudinal studies that measure the sustained impact of GenAI on learning outcomes and career readiness. The small pilot conducted for this study suggests potential benefits in improving the clarity and depth of student work, but its limited scale prevents broad generalization. More robust, mixed-methods research is needed to establish causality, track long-term effects, and explore how GenAI integration interacts with other pedagogical and institutional factors.

This review is also limited by its focus on English-language publications and reliance on academic databases, potentially excluding relevant industry reports and non-English research. While the search strategy was broadened to include multiple disciplinary databases and recent domain-specific work, there remains scope for incorporating grey literature and practice-based case studies.

Taken together, the findings support a strategic, critical, and ethically grounded integration of GenAI into sports management education. When implemented thoughtfully, these tools can enhance curriculum relevance, strengthen alignment with industry demands, and foster both technical expertise and ethical awareness in graduates. However, realizing this potential will require sustained research, deliberate curriculum design, and ongoing dialogue between academia and the sports industry.

6   Conclusion

This study examined the role of Generative AI tools in sports management education for business students, combining a systematic literature review with a small-scale classroom pilot. The synthesis of recent research indicates that tools such as ChatGPT, Bing Copilot, and Google Gemini are increasingly used to bridge the gap between academic theory and professional practice. In both the literature and our pilot study, GenAI platforms supported authentic, data-driven learning activities and helped students develop skills in analytics, strategic decision-making, and communication.

The review also highlights critical factors for successful adoption. Effective integration of GenAI requires deliberate curriculum design that embeds these tools into core teaching activities, fosters collaboration with industry partners, and addresses ethical considerations such as bias, transparency, and responsible use. While the potential benefits are clear, the current evidence base remains limited, with a shortage of large-scale, empirical studies and few comprehensive frameworks for structured integration.

Our findings suggest several priorities for future research and practice. Longitudinal, mixed-methods studies are needed to assess the sustained impact of GenAI on student learning outcomes and career readiness. Closer partnerships between universities and the sports industry could provide students with richer, more authentic datasets and problem scenarios. Finally, curriculum development should balance technical proficiency in AI tools with the cultivation of critical thinking and ethical awareness, ensuring that graduates are prepared to navigate an AI-augmented sports business environment.

By addressing these areas, educators and researchers can help ensure that the integration of Generative AI in sports management education is not merely a technological enhancement, but a catalyst for producing graduates who are innovative, adaptable, and equipped for the evolving demands of the sports industry.

References

1. Baughman, A., et al.: Large scale generative AI text applied to sports and music. In: Proceedings of the 30th ACM SIGKDD Conference on Knowledge Discovery and Data Mining, pp. 4784–4792 (2024)
2. Connor, M., O'Neill, M.: Large language models in sport science and medicine: opportunities, risks and considerations. arXiv preprint arXiv:2305.03851 (2023)
3. Dindorf, C., et al.: Characteristics and perceived suitability of artificial intelligence-driven sports coaches: a pilot study on psychological and perceptual factors. Front. Sports Active Living **7**, 1548980 (2025)
4. Gately, L.: A narrative review of the potential use of generative artificial intelligence in educational research practices in higher education. Studies Technol. Enhanced Learn. **4**(1) (2024)
5. Ghosh, I., Ramasamy Ramamurthy, S., Chakma, A., Roy, N.: Sports analytics review: artificial intelligence applications, emerging technologies, and algorithmic perspective. Wiley Interdisc. Rev. Data Mining Knowl. Discov. **13**(5), e1496 (2023)
6. Glebova, E., Su, Y., Desbordes, M., Schut, P.O.: Emerging digital technologies as a game changer in the sport industry. Front. Sports Active Living **7**, 1605138 (2025)
7. Ha, T.: Using ChatGPT in the field of kinesiology: opportunities and considerations. J. Phys. Educ. Sport **24**(1), 3–12 (2024)
8. Haghparast, M., Hoseini, S.M., Esfahani, N.D.: Foresight in sports businesses: Exploring emerging scenarios based on AI-language models and financial management strategies. Sports Business J. (2025)
9. Jokela, S.: Impact of artificial intelligence on business and management processes in the sports industry (2024)
10. Keiper, M.C., Fried, G., Lupinek, J., Nordstrom, H.: Artificial intelligence in sport management education: playing the AI game with ChatGPT. J. Hospitality Leisure Sport Tourism Educ. **33**, 100456 (2023)
11. Krämer, D., Bosold, A., Minarik, M., Schyvinck, C., Hajek, A.: Artificial intelligence in sports: insights from a quantitative survey among sports students in Germany about their perceptions, expectations, and concerns regarding the use of AI tools. arXiv preprint arXiv:2503.05785 (2025)
12. Krause, S., Dalvi, A., Zaidi, S.K.: Generative AI in education: student skills and lecturer roles. arXiv preprint arXiv:2504.19673 (2025)
13. Lin, T., et al.: SportsBuddy: designing and evaluating an AI-powered sports video storytelling tool through real-world deployment. In: 2025 IEEE 18th Pacific Visualization Conference (PacificVis), pp. 214–223. IEEE (2025)
14. Ma, W., et al.: Table tennis coaching system based on a multimodal large language model with a table tennis knowledge base. PLoS ONE **20**(2), e0317839 (2025)
15. Merilehto, J.: From pdfs to structured data: Utilizing LLM analysis in sports database management. arXiv preprint arXiv:2410.17619 (2024)
16. Moher, D., Liberati, A., Tetzlaff, J., Altman, D.G.: Preferred reporting items for systematic reviews and meta-analyses: the Prisma statement. BMJ **339** (2009)

17. Murungi, N.K., Pham, M.V., Dai, X., Qu, X.: Trends in machine learning and electroencephalogram (EEG): a review for undergraduate researchers. In: International Conference on Human-Computer Interaction, pp. 426–443. Springer (2023)
18. Nalbant, K.G., Aydın, S.: Literature review on the relationship between artificial intelligence technologies with digital sports marketing and sports management. Indonesian J. Sport Manag. **2**(2), 135–143 (2022)
19. Naughton, M., Salmon, P.M., Compton, H.R., McLean, S.: Challenges and opportunities of artificial intelligence implementation within sports science and sports medicine teams. Front. Sports Active Living **6**, 1332427 (2024)
20. Qu, X., Key, M., Luo, E., Qiu, C.: Integrating HCI datasets in project-based machine learning courses: a college-level review and case study. In: International Conference on Human-Computer Interaction, pp. 124–143. Springer (2024)
21. Qu, X., Sherwood, J., Liu, P., Aleisa, N.: Generative AI tools in higher education: a meta-analysis of cognitive impact. In: Proceedings of the Extended Abstracts of the CHI Conference on Human Factors in Computing Systems, pp. 1–9 (2025)
22. Saunders, T., Aleisa, N., Wield, J., Sherwood, J., Qu, X.: Optimizing the literature review process: evaluating generative AI models on sum-marizing undergraduate data science research papers. In: Proceedings of the 30th ACM SIGKDD Conference on Knowledge Discovery and Data Mining (2024)
23. Skinner, J., Smith, A.C., Read, D., Burch, L.M., Mueller, J.: Research methods for sport management. Routledge (2024)
24. Swim, N., Presley, R., Thompson, E.: Digital development and technology in sport: a course to improve digital literacy in the sport management curriculum. Sport Manag. Educ. J. **18**(1), 87–93 (2023)
25. Tan, X., Abbas, J., Al-Sulaiti, K., Pilař, L., Shah, S.A.R.: The role of digital management and smart technologies for sports education in a dynamic environment: employment, green growth, and tourism. J. Urban Technol. **32**(1), 133–164 (2025)
26. Wang, N.C.: Scaffolding creativity: Integrating generative AI tools and real-world experiences in business education. In: Proceedings of the Extended Abstracts of the CHI Conference on Human Factors in Computing Systems, pp. 1–9 (2025)
27. Wang, Y., Wang, X.: Artificial intelligence in physical education: comprehensive review and future teacher training strategies. Front. Public Health **12**, 1484848 (2024)
28. Westerbeek, H.: Algorithmic fandom: how generative AI is reshaping sports marketing, fan engagement, and the integrity of sport. Front. Sports Active Living **7**, 1597444 (2025)
29. Xia, H., et al.: SportQA: a benchmark for sports understanding in large language models. arXiv preprint arXiv:2402.15862 (2024)
30. Yunoki, I., Berreby, G., D'Andrea, N., Lu, Y., Qu, X.: Exploring AI music generation: a review of deep learning algorithms and datasets for undergraduate researchers. In: International Conference on Human-Computer Interaction, pp. 102–116. Springer (2023)
31. Zhou, D., et al.: Artificial intelligence in sport: a narrative review of applications, challenges and future trends. J. Sports Sci, 1–16 (2025)

The Impact of Feedback Timing on Metacognition in AI-Mediated Language Learning

Asikaer Nadila, Sylvain Senecal, Constantinos K. Coursaris[✉], and Pierre-Majorique Léger

HEC Montreal, Montreal, QC 3T27, Canada
{asikaer.nadila,sylvain.senecal,constantinos.coursaris,
pierre-majorique.leger}@hec.ca

Abstract. This research examines the impact of feedback timing on metacognition in the context of AI-mediated language learning. The study addresses a gap in the literature, since most previous works have primarily focused on human-to-human interactions, overlooking the influence of AI-mediated feedback on metacognition. Thus, the objective of this research is to explore how feedback timing affects emotional and cognitive states (namely, valence, arousal, and cognitive load) and how these states mediate the relationship between feedback timing and metacognitive judgment. A between-subjects experiment involved 30 adult English speakers learning French at the A2 French language proficiency level. Participants were randomly assigned to an experimental condition involving either immediate or delayed feedback during a reading-aloud task in French, where an AI tutor provides pronunciation feedback. Data collection involved both self-reported and physiological measure. The results indicate that feedback timing did not have an impact on valence, arousal or cognitive load, nor in metacognitive judgment accuracy. However, emotional valence was positively associated with higher metacognitive accuracy in comprehensibility, while increased cognitive load was associated with improved accuracy in metacognitive judgments for accentedness. This implies that, although feedback timing may not have a direct effect on metacognitive outcomes, emotional valence and cognitive load were found to have a significant effect on improving metacognitive accuracy.

Keywords: Metacognition · Feedback · Valence · Arousal · Cognitive Load · Conversation AI

1 Introduction

As Artificial Intelligence (AI) continues to drastically change industry and daily personal life alike, it comes with no surprise that its global user base exceeded 250 million in 2023, more than double the penetration rate from 2020, and expected to exceed 700 million users by 2030 [1]. In education, AI-driven voice technologies are challenging traditional teaching methods by offering real-time, adaptable feedback. Unlike other conventional

F. F.-H Nah and K. L. Siau (Eds.): HCII 2025, LNCS 16343, pp. 134–148, 2026.
https://doi.org/10.1007/978-3-032-13167-6_10

e-learning methods that are less dynamic, generative AI (GenAI) like ChatGPT provides flexible, engaging experiences. This is particularly valuable for language learners who need precise, responsive feedback to master pronunciation.

Yet critical questions remain about how these systems affect learning processes. While research shows corrective feedback enhances verbal learning [2], there's ongoing debate about optimal timing. Behaviorists argue feedback must be immediate to be effective [3], while others find delayed feedback beneficial [4]. Most studies, however, focus on human-to-human interactions, leaving a gap in understanding how feedback timing functions in AI-mediated environments.

This study examines how feedback timing (immediate vs. delayed) affects metacognitive judgments - learners' ability to evaluate their own pronunciation accuracy. We focus on two specific aspects: comprehensibility (how easily others can understand the learner) and accentedness (how native-like the learner's pronunciation sounds). These are particularly challenging for learners to self-assess accurately [5]. Hence, our research addresses two main questions:

RQ1: To what extent does feedback timing impact metacognitive judgment accuracy?

RQ2: To what extent do the cognitive (cognitive load) and emotional (valence, arousal) states of a learner mediate the relationship between feedback timing and metacognitive judgement accuracy?

2   Literature Review and Theoretical Foundation

2.1   Feedback and Metacognition

Metacognition, a fundamental aspect of self-regulated learning, refers to the process of monitoring and regulating one's own cognitive performance [6]. Feedback, defined as information provided by an agent (e.g., teacher, peer, book, parent, self, or experience) regarding aspects of a learner's performance or understanding [7], plays a critical role in this process. It informs learners about their performance, and it can significantly shape how learners evaluate their own learning – metacognitive judgment [8].

Nelson and Naren's [9] Metacognitive Model provide a framework for understanding how feedback operates within metacognitive processes. The model distinguishes between two levels of cognitive processing: the object-level and the meta-level. In the context of this study, the former corresponds to participants completing the task of reading French sentences, while the latter involves evaluating how well the task is being performed. In this study, participants complete a metacognitive judgment questionnaire, where they assess their own performance. According to the model, information flows between these two levels in both directions. Monitoring refers to information flow from the object-level to the meta-level, where participants evaluate their performance based on internal cues (self-assessment) and external feedback (whether immediate or delayed). This process forms the basis of their metacognitive judgments. On the other hand, information flowing from the meta-level to the object-level is called control and informs what to do next at the object-level. Metacognitive judgments, which assess one's own learning and performance, fall under the monitoring aspect of this model.

Existing research on feedback and metacognition has yielded inconsistent results. For example, Haddara [10] found that feedback had no effect on metacognitive sensitivity in a study on perceptual decision-making. In contrast, Luo and Liu [8] found that trial-by-trial feedback enhanced metacognition in easy perceptual judgments but impaired it in difficult ones. Another study by Callender, Franco-Watkins, & Roberts [11] showed that feedback in classroom settings helped students adjust their performance and judgments more effectively, leading to better calibration. Similarly, Geurten and Meulemans [12] demonstrated that feedback improved the accuracy of children's metacognitive judgments by anchoring their predictions closer to their actual performance, particularly in memory tasks. Additionally, Urban & Urban [13] found that performance feedback improves accuracy in predictive judgments, helping children adjust their expectations after incorrect answers.

Building on this existing research, this study aims to further explore the role of feedback in metacognitive judgments, specifically looking into how the timing of feedback (immediate versus delayed) affects the accuracy of these judgments. While many studies have examined feedback content, relatively few have explored how the timing of feedback might change learners' self-evaluations. On the one hand, delayed feedback may give learners time for reflection, encouraging deeper self-assessment and potentially more thoughtful metacognitive judgments. On the other hand, immediate feedback may provide learners with instant correction, allowing them to adjust their judgments in real time, potentially leading to better calibration between confidence and accuracy. Given the increasing use of AI-based tutoring systems—where feedback timing can be precisely controlled—and the abovementioned benefits of GenAI in affording real-time, personalized, engaging interactions, we hypothesize that:

H1: Immediate feedback will result in more accurate metacognitive judgments than delayed feedback.

2.2 Emotion, Cognitive Load, and Feedback

Prior research suggests that feedback influences learners' affective states. For example, learners' affective states were significantly influenced by feedback from AutoTutor, an Intelligent Tutoring System (ITS) [14]. Specifically, it was found that positive feedback tends to induce "delight," while negative feedback often evokes "surprise." Meanwhile, in a study examining the effects of corrective feedback (CF) on learner affect in a computer-assisted language learning system, no significant difference in valence was found between a no-feedback group and a corrective feedback group [15].

Prior research, however, has not examined the role of feedback timing. Since immediate feedback may feel more salient, while delayed feedback allows emotional processing, the potential directionality of this effect is unclear. Thus, we hypothesize:

H2a: There will be a difference in valence between immediate and delayed feedback.

Arousal—the intensity of emotional response—may also vary based on feedback characteristics. Kluger, Lewinsohn, & Aiello [16] found that extreme feedback (highly positive or negative) increases arousal more than moderate feedback. Whether the effect of feedback intensity is shared by feedback timing remains unexplored. It is reasonable to expect that interrupting the learner while speaking might evoke a more intense reaction. At the same time, delayed feedback might be more difficult to reconcile and thereby causing a more intense reaction. Given this plausible effect of feedback timing on arousal but the competing mechanisms involved, we hypothesize:

H2b: There will be a difference in arousal between immediate and delayed feedback.

Feedback also influences cognitive states, particularly in terms of cognitive load. According to Cognitive Load Theory, cognitive resources are limited [17], and feedback plays a role in how learners allocate these resources during learning. Moreno [18] found that explanatory feedback can reduce extraneous load, while corrective feedback can increase it by offering limited guidance. Fyfe et al. [19] noted that strategy feedback is cognitively demanding, while outcome feedback imposes a lighter load. However, Lin et al. [20] found no link between feedback type and cognitive load in multimedia learning. Given that numerous feedback characteristics have been found to affect cognitive load, it is reasonable to expect a similar effect to be observed by feedback timing. As the learner is interrupted mid-stream a speaking or reading-aloud task, the cognitive switch might lead to greater cognitive demands. On the other hand, attempting to recall the speaking or reading behavior for which delayed feedback has been provided might lead to a more cognitively demanding state. Thus, we hypothesize:

H2c: There will be a difference in cognitive load between immediate and delayed feedback.

2.3 Emotion, Cognitive Load, and Metacognition

The relationship between emotion and metacognition is still underexplored in the literature, and the findings that do exist tend to be context dependent. Massoni [21] noted that negative emotions may sometimes enhance metacognitive processes. Similarly, Agadzhanyan and Castel [22] found that negative valence could improve both memory and metacognitive accuracy. However, they did not explore the effects of positive valence. Further, Undorf, Söllner, & Bröder [23] showed that both positive and negative words increase judgments of learning compared to neutral words. Thus, we propose:

H3a: Valence is associated with the accuracy of metacognitive judgments.

Garfinkel et al. [24] suggested that high arousal may impair memory and metacognition, depending on an individual's sensitivity to internal states. Thus, we propose:

H3b: Arousal is associated with the accuracy of metacognitive judgments.

A meta-analysis by Baars et al. [25] found that cognitive load negatively impacts metacognitive judgments when learners use data-driven regulation. However, under goal-driven strategies, the relationship may reverse. Therefore, we hypothesize that:

H3c: Cognitive load is associated with the accuracy of metacognitive judgments.

2.4 Proposed Research Model

Based on the earlier discussion and proposed hypotheses, Fig. 1 presents the proposed conceptual model. The model shows the hypothesized relationship between feedback timing, emotional state (valence and arousal), cognitive state (cognitive load), and metacognitive judgment. It examines the direct impact of feedback timing on metacognitive judgment (H1), as well as its mediated effects through valence (H2a), arousal (H2b), and cognitive load (H2c), and the subsequent effects by these states on metacognitive judgment (H3a, H3b, H3c).

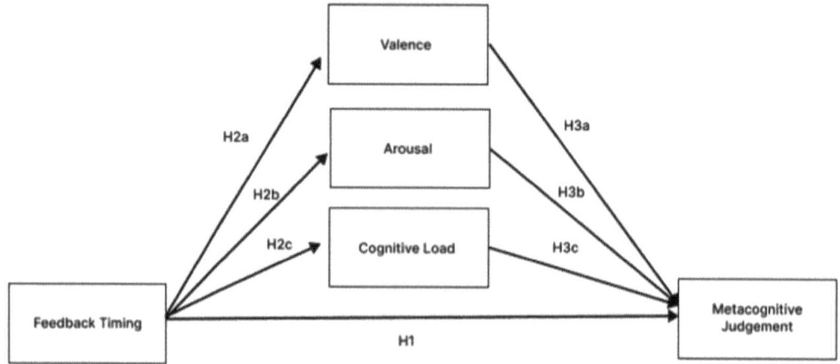

Fig. 1. Proposed Research Model Illustrating the Relationships Between Feedback Timing, Emotional and Cognitive States, and Metacognitive Judgment.

3 Method

This study used a between-subjects design in a controlled laboratory setting to test the extent to which feedback timing (immediate versus delayed) may impact metacognitive judgments while reading-aloud French sentences. Participants were randomly assigned to two conditions: either to a group that received feedback immediately after completing each sentence, or to a group that received all corrective feedback at the end of the read-aloud task. Three factors – valence, arousal, and cognitive load - pertaining to the emotional and cognitive states of the users were measured using a combination of self-reported scales and psychophysiological assessments. The goal was to estimate whether and to what extent these three factors mediate the relationship between feedback timing and metacognitive judgment.

3.1 Participants

This study recruited a convenience sample of 30 adult English speakers (18 years or older) living in Quebec with A2-level French proficiency, based on the Common European Framework of Reference for Languages (CEFR). At this level, participants can understand common expressions related to everyday needs and perform simple, routine communication on familiar topics. Convenience sampling was used to recruit participants who were at the beginning stages of learning French—not necessarily as a second language, but as an additional one. Individuals with intermediate or advanced proficiency were excluded to maintain a focus on novice learners. Recruitment was conducted both online and in person through language institutions, cafes, and personal contacts to reach the target population. Those who expressed interest in the study completed a CEFR-based French self-assessment to confirm eligibility. Participants who met the inclusion criteria were invited to take part in the experiment and were compensated with a $30 honorarium.

3.2 Stimuli

The stimuli used in this were French sentences created in Tobii Pro Lab with the help of ChatGPT to ensure consistency across the three trials. Full texts and prompt details are provided in the Appendix. Figures 2 and 3 show sample stimuli; Fig. 4 shows the delayed feedback view. The experimental manipulation focused solely on feedback timing—not content. All participants received the same prompts to correct four specific words, regardless of whether they had made an error. In the immediate feedback condition, participants received correction after each sentence, heard the correct pronunciation from the AI tutor, and repeated the sentence before continuing. In the delayed feedback condition, feedback was delivered only after all 10 sentences were completed. The feedback content remained identical across both conditions.

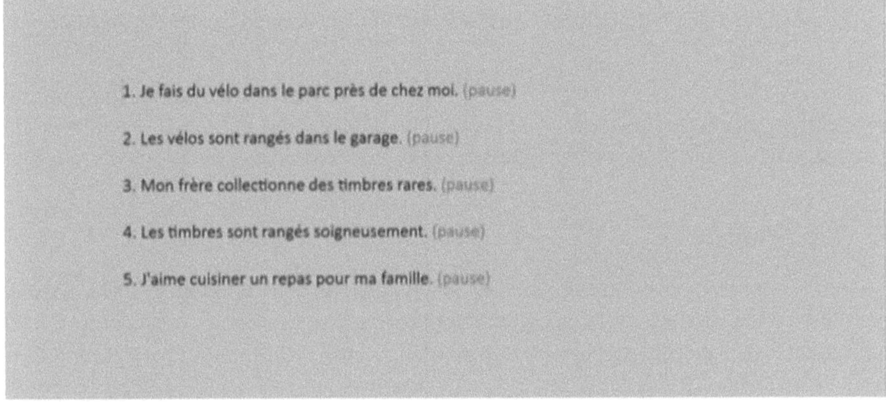

Fig. 2. Screenshot of an Experimental Stimulus (5 French sentences).

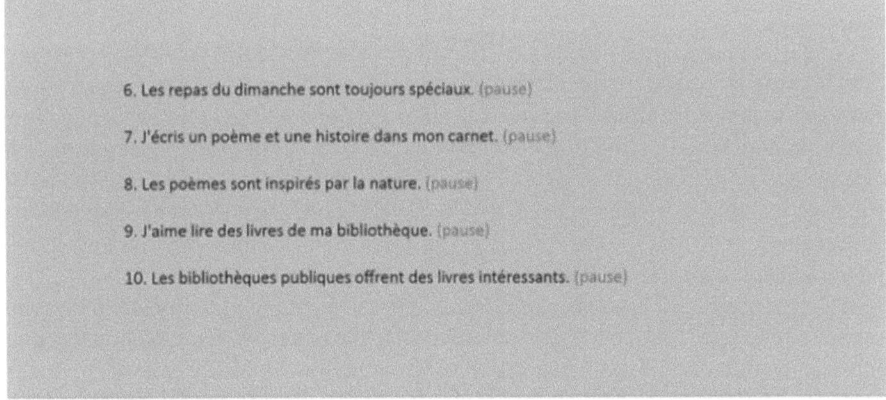

Fig. 3. Screenshot of Another Experimental Stimulus (5 French sentences).

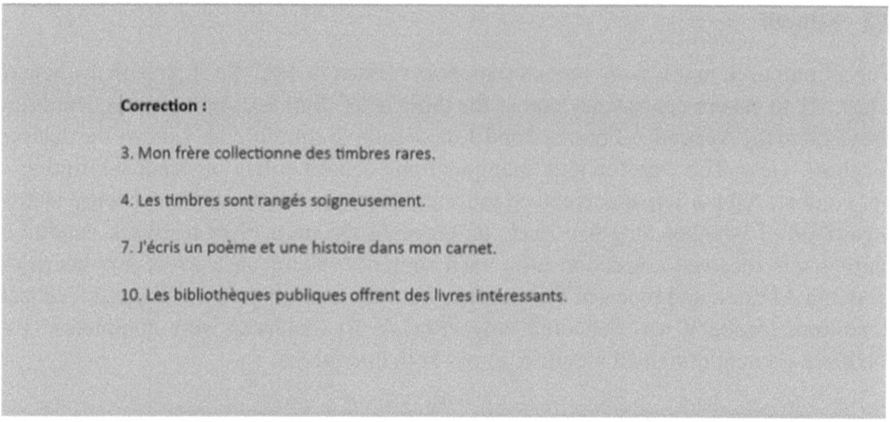

Correction :

3. Mon frère collectionne des timbres rares.

4. Les timbres sont rangés soigneusement.

7. J'écris un poème et une histoire dans mon carnet.

10. Les bibliothèques publiques offrent des livres intéressants.

Fig. 4. Correction Page Displayed to Participants in the Delayed Feedback Condition.

The AI tutor used was OpenAI's GPT-4 via ChatGPT, configured through prompt engineering. Spoken interaction was enabled using GPT-4's voice function. The Appendix details the final prompts used to generate feedback.

3.3 Procedure

When participants arrived at the lab, they were greeted by the researcher, who gave an overview of the study. After reviewing and signing the informed consent form, each participant was randomly assigned to one of two conditions: immediate feedback or delayed feedback. Detailed instructions were provided, and any questions were answered to ensure clarity. Participants were seated at a Tobii Pro Lab eye-tracking system (Tobii AB, Danderyd, Sweden), where a calibration process was conducted to ensure accurate tracking. A brief baseline task—counting white squares—was completed, followed by a demographic questionnaire covering language background, education, and employment. Participants also completed a short warm-up by reading three lines of French sentences on the screen.

For the main task, participants read 10 French sentences, displayed over two screens (5 per screen). In the immediate feedback condition, participants received feedback right after each sentence that contained one of four target words. The AI tutor provided the correct pronunciation of the mispronounced word, and participants repeated the full sentence before moving on. In the delayed feedback condition, participants read all 10 sentences without interruption. Then, they received a correction page showing only the four sentences with target words. The AI tutor then provided the correct pronunciation, and participants repeated the full sentence using the correction.

After the reading-aloud task, participants completed a short questionnaire measuring emotional responses and metacognitive judgments. The metacognitive questions focused on pronunciation, specifically comprehensibility (how easy their speech was to understand) and accentedness (how closely it matched a native speaker). These dimensions were chosen because pronunciation is particularly difficult for learners to self-assess [5], unlike listening or reading [26]. Self-assessments were completed using two slider scales: 0 = hard to understand, 100 = easy to understand for comprehensibility; and 0 = not accented at all, 100 = heavily accented for accentedness [27].

This entire procedure was repeated three times, each using a new set of 10 French sentences to allow for variability in task performance and to collect sufficient data. All sentences were generated using ChatGPT. Details are available in the Appendix: Stimuli Creation. At the end of the session, participants were thanked, given a compensation form, and escorted out of the lab.

3.4 Measures

Perceived cognitive load was assessed using a self-reported slider questionnaire based on the NASA TLX [28], including questions such as: 1) 'How mentally demanding was the task?' and 2) 'How hard did you have to work to accomplish your level of performance?' Psychophysiological cognitive load was measured using pupillometry [29].

Perceived valence and arousal were measured with affective sliders [30], while psychophysiological valence was assessed using FaceReader [31]. Psychophysiological arousal was captured through average phasic electrodermal activity using the Cobalt Bluebox [32].

Retrospective and prospective metacognitive judgments were calculated based on the difference between participants' self-reported performance on comprehensibility and accentedness and their actual performance, which was rated by three French speakers using the same scale. The average of the three raters' scores was taken as the actual performance since the inter-rater reliability ICC = 0.88. The inter-rater reliability was assessed using intraclass correlation.

4 Analysis and Results

4.1 Data Analysis

All statistical analyses were conducted using SAS (v3.81). To assess the effects of feedback timing and internal states on metacognitive accuracy, a combination of logistic and linear regressions was used. Metacognitive judgment accuracy (for comprehensibility and accentedness) was analyzed using logistic regression, as the data were not normally distributed; median splits were applied (cutoffs: 16 for comprehensibility, 14 for accentedness). This approach was also used to examine the influence of valence, arousal, and cognitive load on metacognitive accuracy. To test for differences in emotional and cognitive states (valence, arousal, and cognitive load) between immediate and delayed feedback conditions, linear regressions with random intercepts were performed, as these dependent variables were normally distributed. A significance threshold of $\alpha = .05$ was applied throughout, and all p-values, estimates, and standard errors were reported.

4.2 Descriptive Statistics

Table 1 presents the descriptive statistics for both the immediate and delayed feedback conditions across various measures. It provides a summary of how participants' emotional states, cognitive load, and self-assessment of their pronunciation varied between the immediate and delayed feedback conditions.

Table 1. Descriptive Statistics.

Variable	Immediate feedback		Delayed feedback	
	M	SD	M	SD
Perceived Arousal	61.55	14.11	64.54	21.22
Physiological Arousal	−4.63	4.12	−3.92	3.45
Perceived Valence	63.37	17.42	67.00	19.42
Physiological Valence	−.062	.15	−.104	.117
Perceived Cognitive Load	31.59	19.36	40.01	21.53
Physiological Cognitive Load	2.89	.28	2.88	.26
Prospective Metacognitive Judgment (comprehensibility)	18.18	16.29	19.40	15.26
Prospective Metacognitive Judgment (accentedness)	22.64	20.17	18.45	15.71
Retrospective Metacognitive Judgment (comprehensibility)	20.15	15.12	19.75	14.99
Retrospective Metacognitive Judgment (accentedness)	22.57	20.41	17.31	16.94

4.3 Results

The results showed that feedback timing did not significantly affect learners' metacognitive judgment accuracy. Logistic regression analyses indicated no significant difference between the immediate and delayed feedback groups in predicting metacognitive accuracy for either comprehensibility ($\beta = -0.31$, SE $= 0.737$, p $= .675$) or accentedness ($\beta = 0.089$, SE $= 0.868$, p $= .919$).

Similarly, feedback timing was not found to significantly influence participants' emotional or cognitive states. Linear regression analyses revealed no significant differences between conditions in either perceived or physiological measures of valence, arousal, or cognitive load. For valence, the effects were not significant for both perceived ($\beta = -3.91$, p $= .537$) and physiological ($\beta = 0.029$, p $= .547$) indicators. Arousal also did not differ significantly across conditions, whether measured subjectively ($\beta = -3.33$, p $= .579$) or physiologically ($\beta = -0.719$, p $= .631$). For cognitive load, no effect was found on either perceived ($\beta = -7.81$, p $= .263$) or physiological ($\beta = 0.023$, p $= .813$) measures.

However, emotional valence and cognitive load are associated with the accuracy of metacognitive judgments. Higher perceived valence was significantly associated with improved metacognitive accuracy in judging comprehensibility ($\beta = 0.047$, SE $= 0.020$, p $= .024$, a similar association was found for accentedness but merely approaching statistical significance ($\beta = 0.04$, SE $= 0.022$, p $= .07$). In contrast, cognitive load—measured physiologically—was significantly associated with metacognitive accuracy for accentedness ($\beta = 3.79$, SE $= 1.81$, p $= .042$), but not for comprehensibility. Table 2 provides a summary of the hypothesis testing results conducted for this study.

5 Discussion

5.1 Findings

The main findings showed that feedback timing (immediate versus delayed) did not significantly impact learners' emotional states (valence and arousal), cognitive load, or the accuracy of metacognitive judgments for comprehensibility and accentedness in language learning. However, an interesting result was observed in that higher perceived emotional valence was associated with higher metacognitive judgment accuracy, suggesting that learners who experienced higher positive emotions tended to evaluate their pronunciation performance more accurately. Additionally, cognitive load showed a significant relationship with metacognitive accuracy for accentedness, implying that higher cognitive effort might enhance learners' awareness of their pronunciation. These results highlight that while the timing of feedback might not directly influence metacognitive judgments, emotional states and cognitive load are indeed important factors in learners' metacognitive evaluation processes.

Table 2. Hypothesis Testing.

Hypothesis	From	To	Estimate	p-value	Status
H1	Feedback Timing	Metacognitive Judgment - Comprehensibility	−.3109	0.663	no support
H1	Feedback Timing	Metacognitive Judgment - Accentedness	.089	0.459	no support
H2a	Feedback Timing	Perceived Valence	−3.91	.537	no support
H2a	Feedback Timing	Valence	.029	.547	no support
H2b	Feedback Timing	Perceived Arousal	−3.33	.579	no support
H2b	Feedback Timing	Arousal	−.719	.631	no support
H2c	Feedback Timing	Perceived Cognitive Load	−7.81	.263	no support
H2c	Feedback Timing	Cognitive Load	.023	0.813	no support
H3a	Perceived Valence	Metacognitive Judgment - Comprehensibility	.047	.024	supported

(*continued*)

Table 2. (continued)

Hypothesis	From	To	Estimate	p-value	Status
H3a	Perceived Valence	Metacognitive Judgment - Accentedness	.04	.07	appr. Sign
H3a	Valence	Metacognitive Judgment - Comprehensibility	0.999	.738	no support
H3a	Valence	Metacognitive Judgment - Accentedness	−.894	.794	no support
H3b	Perceived Arousal	Metacognitive Judgment - Comprehensibility	.023	.205	no support
H3b	Perceived Arousal	Metacognitive Judgment - Accentedness	.017	.403	no support
H3b	Arousal	Metacognitive Judgment - Comprehensibility	−.086	.365	no support
H3b	Arousal	Metacognitive Judgment - Accentedness	1.08	.353	no support
H3c	Perceived Cognitive Load	Metacognitive Judgment - Comprehensibility	.021	.215	no support
H3c	Perceived Cognitive Load	Metacognitive Judgment - Accentedness	−.019	.338	no support
H3c	Cognitive Load	Metacognitive Judgment - Comprehensibility	−1.62	.269	no support
H3c	Cognitive Load	Metacognitive Judgment - Accentedness	3.791	.042	supported

5.2 Limitations

This study can be further built-upon in two main areas. Firstly, the relatively short trials duration might have limited the difference observed between immediate and delayed conditions. Since participants only read 10 French sentences per trial in both conditions, the study design may not have provided enough opportunities to observe a sufficient variation between the two feedback timing approaches. Future studies could extend the trials' duration, which may result in a more noticeable difference. Secondly, the sample size of 30 participants, constrained by resources (namely, time and funding), may have influenced the statistical power of the results. In future research, recruiting a larger sample might allow for any present effects to be observed.

6 Conclusion

This study aimed to explore the impact of feedback timing on metacognitive judgment in AI-mediated language learning. It addressed the gap in understanding how immediate and delayed feedback may influence emotional states, cognitive load, and self-assessment in pronunciation. Using conversational AI, the study showed that while feedback timing itself may not significantly affect metacognitive accuracy, emotional valence and cognitive load have a significant effect on learners' self-assessment. In the future, AI in language learning could focus on emotional and cognitive engagement to increase metacognitive accuracy. By creating more personalized feedback that takes into account learners' emotional and cognitive states, AI learning tools can better support self-guided learning and improve the overall learning experience.

Acknowledgements. This work was supported by the Natural Sciences and Engineering Research Council of Canada (NSERC) Alliance Sénécal (ALLRP 565704-21) and PROMPT (Prompt Projet 176, Sénécal).

Appendix

Stimuli Creation. We used ChatGPT to generate all the text that the participants will read. Below are the specific texts for each trial and an explanation of how they were created. Note that even though the prompt asked for 15 sentences (or 5 sentences in the case of Prompt 4) each with 10 words, the generated result comprised only 10 sentences, each with a slightly different number of words albeit of similarly short length. Hence, the ChatGPT-generated stimuli were used verbatim.

Prompt 1. (masculine/feminine).

Instruction: Please create a 15-sentence paragraph in French (the theme is introducing yourself and your family). Each pair of sentences should contain one word that appears in both masculine and feminine forms. For example, in sentence one: "un étudiant," and in sentence two: "une étudiante." Number each sentence and ensure that each sentence has exactly 10 words. The text should be easy to understand for A1-level French learners.

Sentence

1. Bonjour, je m'appelle Marie et je suis **étudiante**.
2. Mon frère Pierre est **étudiant**.
3. J'ai une sœur qui est **gentille**.
4. Mon père est un homme **gentil** et **intelligent**.

 5. Ma mère, une femme **intelligente**, travaille dans une école.
 6. Ma tante médecin est très **occupée.**
 7. J'ai un cousin qui est **sportif**.
 8. Ma cousine **sportive** joue au tennis.
 9. Mon ami est un garçon **sérieux** qui travaille beaucoup.
10. Mon amie, une fille **sérieuse**, aime étudier.

Prompt 2. (singular/plural).

Instruction: Please create a 15-sentence paragraph in French (the theme is about hobby). Each pair of sentences should contain one word that appears in singular form in one sentence, and plural forms in another sentence. Number each sentence and ensure that each sentence has exactly 10 words. The text should be easy to understand for A1-level French learners.

Sentence

 1. Je fais du **vélo** dans le parc près de chez moi.
 2. Les **vélos** sont rangés dans le garage.
 3. Mon frère collectionne des **timbres** rares.
 4. Les **timbres** sont rangés soigneusement.
 5. J'aime cuisiner un **repas** pour ma famille.
 6. Les **repas** du dimanche sont toujours spéciaux.
 7. J'écris un **poème** et une histoire dans mon carnet.
 8. Les **poèmes** sont inspirés par la nature.
 9. J'aime lire des livres de ma **bibliothèque**.
10. Les **bibliothèques** publiques offrent des livres intéressants.

Prompt 3. (Contractions).

Instruction: Please create a 15-sentence paragraph in French (the theme is where I live) where each sentence contains the word "au", "à la", "à l'" or "aux". Number each sentence. Each sentence must contain exactly 10 words. The text should be easy to understand for A1-level French learners.

Sentence

 1. J'habite dans un petit village **au** bord de la mer.
 2. Il y a un grand parc **au** centre de la ville.
 3. Les enfants jouent souvent **aux** jeux dans ce parc.
 4. Je vais **au** marché chaque samedi.
 5. À **l'**école, les élèves apprennent le français et les mathématiques.
 6. Nous dînons souvent **au** restaurant près de la maison.
 7. Les voisins se retrouvent **au** café pour discuter.
 8. Le dimanche, nous allons **à la** plage.
 9. Il y a une bibliothèque **au** coin de ma rue.
10. J'adore me promener **au** parc avec mon chien.

Prompt 4. (warm up - number).

Instruction: Please create a 5-sentence paragraph in French (the theme is the address) where all the sentences must contain numbers written in French. Number each sentence. Each sentence must contain exactly 10 words. The text should be easy to understand for A1-level French learners.

Sentence

1. J'habite au numéro **vingt** de la rue principale.
2. Ma voisine vit au numéro **trente-deux**, juste à côté.
3. Mon immeuble compte **huit** étages.

References

1. Statista: Generative Artificial Intelligence (AI) (2023). https://www.statista.com/study/133 112/generative-artificial-intelligence-ai/. Accessed 3 Oct 2024
2. Metcalfe, J., Kornell, N.: Principles of cognitive science in education: the effects of generation, errors, and feedback. Psychon. Bull. Rev. **14**, 225–229 (2007)
3. Saltzman, I.J.: Delay of reward and human verbal learning. J. Exp. Psychol. **41**(6), 437 (1951)
4. Butler, A.C., Roediger, H.L.: Feedback enhances the positive effects and reduces the negative effects of multiple-choice testing. Mem. Cognit. **36**(3), 604–616 (2008)
5. Trofimovich, P., Isaacs, T., Kennedy, S., Saito, K., Crowther, D.: Flawed self-assessment: Investigating self-and other-perception of second language speech. Bilingualism Lang. Cogn. **19**(1), 122–140 (2016)
6. Kuhn, D., Dean, D., Jr.: Metacognition: a bridge between cognitive psychology and educational practice. Theor. Pract. **43**(4), 268–273 (2004)
7. Hattie, J., Timperley, H.: The power of feedback. Tijdschrift voor Medisch Onderwijs **27**(1), 50–51 (2008). https://doi.org/10.1007/BF03078234
8. Luo, T., Liu, C.: The impact of feedback on metacognition: enhancing in easy tasks, impeding in difficult ones. Conscious. Cogn. **116**, 103601 (2023)
9. Nelson, T. O. (1990). Metamemory: A theoretical framework and new findings. In Psychology of learning and motivation (Vol. 26, pp. 125–173). Academic Press
10. Haddara, N., Rahnev, D.: The impact of feedback on perceptual decision-making and metacognition: Reduction in bias but no change in sensitivity. Psychol. Sci. **33**(2), 259–275 (2022)
11. Callender, A.A., Franco-Watkins, A.M., Roberts, A.S.: Improving metacognition in the classroom through instruction, training, and feedback. Metacogn. Learn. **11**, 215–235 (2016)
12. Geurten, M., Meulemans, T.: The effect of feedback on children's metacognitive judgments: a heuristic account. J. Cogn. Psychol. **29**(2), 184–201 (2017)
13. Urban, K., Urban, M.: Anchoring effect of performance feedback on accuracy of metacognitive monitoring in preschool children. Europe's J. Psychol. **17**(1), 104–118 (2021). https://doi.org/10.5964/ejop.2397
14. Aghaei Pour, P., Hussain, M.S., AlZoubi, O., D'Mello, S., Calvo, R.A.: The impact of system feedback on learners' affective and physiological states. In: Aleven, V., Kay, J., Mostow, J. (eds.) Intelligent Tutoring Systems. ITS 2010. Lecture Notes in Computer Science, vol. 6094, pp. 264–273. Springer, Heidelberg (2010). https://doi.org/10.1007/978-3-642-13388-6_31

15. Bodnar, S., Cucchiarini, C., de Vries, B.P., Strik, H., van Hout, R.: Learner affect in computerised L2 oral grammar practice with corrective feedback. Comput. Assist. Lang. Learn. **30**(3–4), 223–246 (2017)
16. Kluger, A.N., Lewinsohn, S., Aiello, J.R.: The influence of feedback on mood: linear effects on pleasantness and curvilinear effects on arousal. Organ. Behav. Hum. Decis. Process. **60**(2), 276–299 (1994)
17. Sweller, J.: Cognitive load theory (2011)
18. Moreno, R.: Decreasing cognitive load for novice students: effects of explanatory versus corrective feedback in discovery-based multimedia. Instr. Sci. **32**(1), 99–113 (2004)
19. Fyfe, E.R., DeCaro, M.S., Rittle-Johnson, B.: When feedback is cognitively-demanding: the importance of working memory capacity. Instr. Sci. **43**, 73–91 (2015)
20. Lin, L., Atkinson, R.K., Christopherson, R.M., Joseph, S.S., Harrison, C.J.: Animated agents and learning: Does the type of verbal feedback they provide matter? Comput. Educ. **67**, 239–249 (2013)
21. Massoni, S.: Emotion as a boost to metacognition: how worry enhances the quality of confidence. Conscious. Cogn. **29**, 189–198 (2014)
22. Agadzhanyan, K., Castel, A.D.: The effect of emotional valence and font size on metacognition and memory. Memory **32**(2), 252–263 (2024)
23. Undorf, M., Söllner, A., Bröder, A.: Simultaneous utilization of multiple cues in judgments of learning. Mem. Cogn. **46**, 507–519 (2018). https://doi.org/10.3758/s13421-017-0780-6
24. Garfinkel, S.N., Barrett, A.B., Minati, L., Dolan, R.J., Seth, A.K., Critchley, H.D.: What the heart forgets: cardiac timing influences memory for words and is modulated by metacognition and interoceptive sensitivity. Psychophysiology **50**(6), 505–512 (2013)
25. Baars, M., Wijnia, L., de Bruin, A., Paas, F.: The relation between students' effort and monitoring judgments during learning: a meta-analysis. Educ. Psychol. Rev. **32**, 979–1002 (2020)
26. Li, M., Zhang, X.: A meta-analysis of self-assessment and language performance in language testing and assessment. Lang. Test. **38**(2), 189–218 (2021)
27. Tsunemoto, A., Trofimovich, P., Blanchet, J., Bertrand, J., Kennedy, S.: Effects of benchmarking and peer-assessment on French learners' self-assessments of accentedness, comprehensibility, and fluency. Foreign Lang. Ann. **55**(1), 135–154 (2022)
28. Hart, S.G., Staveland, L.E.: Development of NASA-TLX (Task Load Index): results of empirical and theoretical research. Adv. Psychol. **52**, 139–183 (1988)
29. Krejtz, K., Duchowski, A.T., Niedzielska, A., Biele, C., Krejtz, I.: Eye tracking cognitive load using pupil diameter and microsaccades with fixed gaze. PLoS ONE **13**(9), e0203629 (2018)
30. Betella, A., Verschure, P.F.: The affective slider: a digital self-assessment scale for the measurement of human emotions. PLoS ONE **11**(2), e0148037 (2016)
31. Skiendziel, T., Rösch, A.G., Schultheiss, O.C.: Assessing the convergent validity between the automated emotion recognition software Noldus FaceReader 7 and facial action coding system scoring. PLoS ONE **14**(10), e0223905 (2019)
32. Bluebox: Courtemanche, F., Sénécal, S., Fredette, M., Léger, P.M. In: Montréal, H. (ed.) COBALT-Bluebox: Multimodal User Data Wireless Synchronization and Acquisition System (2022)

Human-Computer Interaction and Artificial Intelligence for Ageing Population

Keng Leng Siau[1]([✉]) [iD], Hailiang Wang[2] [iD], Fiona Fui-Hoon Nah[1] [iD],
Runyu Wang[3] [iD], Jiaan Li[2] [iD], Ruitong Che[2] [iD], and Can Liu[3] [iD]

[1] Singapore Management University, Singapore, Singapore
{klsiau,fionanah}@smu.edu.sg
[2] The Hong Kong Polytechnic University, Hong Kong, China
hailiang.wang@polyu.edu.hk, {jiaan.li,
cherry.che}@connect.polyu.hk
[3] City University of Hong Kong, Hong Kong, China
runyuwang2-c@my.cityu.edu.hk, canliu@cityu.edu.hk

Abstract. As the global population ages rapidly, the field of human-computer interaction (HCI) is in urgent need of innovation, redesign, and reengineering to meet the evolving needs of older adults. The older demographic faces a range of challenges—including physical limitations, cognitive decline, reduced social integration, and varying levels of technological literacy—that can hinder effective engagement with digital technologies. In response to these challenges, researchers and designers are using inclusive and adaptive approaches to enhance accessibility, usability, and emotional well-being. This paper reviews key design principles in HCI for the ageing population and discusses how artificial intelligence (AI) tools, such as voice assistants, social robots, and cognitive training platforms, can enhance autonomy, support daily living, and foster social connectivity among older adults. Drawing on recent empirical studies and case examples, we highlight both the opportunities and limitations of current AI-driven interventions. This research identifies critical research gaps related to long-term engagement, ethical concerns, and personalization. This paper also proposes future research directions that emphasize user-centered design, cross-generational collaboration, and responsible innovation. By reimagining HCI with the ageing population in mind, this paper contributes to the development of technologies that promote dignity, independence, and quality of life for older adults.

Keywords: Human-Computer Interaction · Ageing Population · Artificial Intelligence · Assistive Technologies · Inclusive Design · Digital Health

1 Introduction

1.1 Importance of Human-Computer Interaction for Ageing Population

Human-computer interaction (HCI) is a multidisciplinary field focused on the design and use of computer technology, such as artificial intelligence, to facilitate, ease, and transform the interaction between people and digital systems. With the rapid ageing of

F. F.-H Nah and K. L. Siau (Eds.): HCII 2025, LNCS 16343, pp. 149–164, 2026.
https://doi.org/10.1007/978-3-032-13167-6_11

the global population, HCI research tailored for older adults has become increasingly important. Countries like Thailand, Korea, China, Japan, Singapore, Italy, Germany, Spain, and Monaco are experiencing significant demographic shifts, and by 2050, over 2 billion people will be over the age of 60 [1, 2]. This demographic transformation presents both critical challenges and unique opportunities for technology design. Older adults often face age-related changes in cognition, mobility, and perception, which demand more accessible, inclusive, and user-friendly digital systems. Therefore, designing HCI solutions that support healthy and independent ageing has become increasingly critical to improve the quality of life for older adults and enable successful ageing by creating accessible and user-friendly systems.

Despite the growing needs of the elderly, most technologies have been designed for younger, tech-savvy users, overlooking the specific needs, limitations, and preferences of older adults. Nevertheless, older adults can benefit significantly from digital technologies, such as health monitoring systems, social networking platforms, and smart home devices. Among these technologies, immersive virtual technologies have shown promise in promoting physical and mental well-being [3]. These technologies provide interactive and customizable environments, making them valuable for health interventions such as physical training, cognitive stimulation, and social engagement [4, 5]. However, the design of such systems often fails to account for the unique challenges faced by older adults. For example, 40% of older adults over 65-year-old struggle with touchscreen accuracy due to arthritis [6]. In addition, many older adults report feelings of loneliness and social isolation [7]. Yet most platforms fail to prioritize intuitive social connectivity for non-tech-savvy users. Compounding these issues, only 42% of older adults use smartphones regularly, with complexity cited as a key barrier [8].

To address these limitations, emerging technologies, such as AI and immersive extended reality (XR), including virtual reality (VR) and augmented reality (AR), offer promising directions. AI-powered tools like large language models (LLMs) can provide cognitive support and companionship, while VR-based applications have been shown to enhance physical health and emotional well-being [9]. Hybrid approaches, such as narrative-driven spatial visualizations [10], also demonstrate the potential to make complex information more comprehensible and engaging. These technologies can enhance independence, improve social connectivity, and facilitate access to information and services. Technology designs that take ageing population into consideration become increasingly important.

However, the behavioral interaction patterns between older adults and AI within immersive virtual environments remain underexplored. Technologies that fail to consider the unique characteristics of ageing users during the design process can hinder usability and even pose risks to this group of vulnerable population. This paper aims to examine the specific needs and limitations of older adults and address the design challenges in developing human-computer interaction systems for this demographic. With rapid advances in artificial intelligence, such as GenAI and Agentic AI, we also consider how technologies can support more meaningful and accessible interactions for older users.

1.2 Challenges Faced by Older Adults in HCI

In general, the ageing population faces four main challenges that affect their interactions with digital systems: physical, cognitive, social, and technological skill-related. Understanding these challenges is essential for designing inclusive and supportive HCI solutions tailored to older users' needs.

Physical Challenges. Older adults experience significant physiological changes that create barriers to technology adoption. First, visual impairments (e.g., cataracts) increase for older adults. One study found that 27.5% of older adults in a Polish sample exhibited visual impairment, with increasing age being a notable risk factor [11]. Another study reported that 17% of American adults aged 45 and older self-reported visual impairments, which increased to 26.5% among those aged 75 and older [12]. Considering the difficulties faced by the visually impaired population, a study found that reading time was minimized and mental workload was the least when using the 14-point font size [13]. In terms of color contrast, the Web Content Accessibility Guidelines stipulate that text and line graphs should maintain a minimum contrast ratio of 4.5:1 for standard text and 3:1 for larger text [14]. This is crucial for ensuring that individuals with varying levels of visual acuity can effectively engage with the content. These changes necessitate interface designs with a minimum of 14-point font size and a 3:1 contrast ratio for older adults. Second, older people face the problem of declining motor skills, particularly reduced finger dexterity due to conditions such as osteoarthritis, which poses significant challenges for standard touchscreen interactions. Research indicates that optimal target sizes for touchscreen activation are crucial for users with diminished dexterity. Parhi et al.'s study focused on one-handed thumb use of mobile devices and found that while speed improved with larger target sizes, a target size of 9.6 mm was recommended for reliable activation during discrete tasks, such as pressing buttons or checkboxes [15]. This finding aligns with the need for accessible design in mobile interfaces, particularly for elderly users with motor skill impairments. Thirdly, hearing loss is a significant concern among older adults, as it affects approximately 25% of this demographic [16]. The need for effective communication strategies and assistive technologies is underscored by the challenges faced by individuals with hearing loss in various settings. Emerging solutions like pressure-sensitive touchscreens [17] and adaptive gesture recognition [18] demonstrate promising approaches to overcoming these physical barriers.

Cognitive Challenges. Age-related cognitive changes follow distinct patterns that impact technology use. Research indicates that working memory capacity does indeed decline with age, particularly from young adulthood into later life. A study assessing visual working memory (VWM) across a large sample of individuals aged 8 to 75 found that VWM abilities peak around age 20, followed by a sharp decline that results in adults aged 55 exhibiting poorer immediate visual memory than younger children [19]. There is a significant reduction in working memory capacity as individuals age. The decline in working memory capacity frequently results in measurable cognitive impairments in daily functioning, significantly compromising the quality of life for older adults [20]. Consequently, targeted cognitive rehabilitation interventions have become increasingly crucial for this population. However, conventional cognitive training approaches often suffer from poor long-term adherence and limited effect sustainability [21]. In contrast, immersive virtual technologies offer distinct advantages through reminiscence therapy (capitalizing on relatively preserved episodic memory systems) while providing engaging multisensory stimulation. Mao et al.'s [9] systematic review of VR reminiscence therapy demonstrated this potential, showing immersive environments leveraging episodic memory achieved greater engagement than traditional paper-based cognitive exercises.

Social Integration Challenges. Social isolation is a significant concern for many older adults, impacting their mental health and overall well-being. Khosravi et al. [22] argued that technology can be used to reduce social isolation among older adults. They discovered eight different technologies that have been used to alleviate social isolation, namely, general information and communication technology, video games, robotics, personal reminder information and social management systems, asynchronous peer support chat rooms, social networking sites, telemedicine, and 3D virtual environments. While technology can help bridge the gap between older adults and their families or communities, it must be designed with social contexts in mind. Successful social technologies for older adults should employ: (1) simplified contact initiation workflows, (2) integrated emergency alert systems, and (3) intergenerational interaction designs that facilitate natural communication patterns [23–25]. The integration of AI-mediated conversation support with human oversight appears to be a promising approach to addressing loneliness, particularly among older adults. Research indicates that technologies such as voice assistants can play a significant role in reducing feelings of loneliness and social isolation [26]. These systems facilitate easier and more natural human-computer interactions, which may help overcome barriers associated with traditional digital technologies.

Technical Knowledge Challenges. Older adults may have varying attitudes toward technology, often influenced by their prior education, experiences, and their perceived usefulness of digital tools. Some may feel intimidated by technology or skeptical about its benefits. Recent studies suggest that training programs combining (1) hands-on practice, (2) error normalization techniques, and (3) peer learning components achieve greater retention among older adults than traditional instructional methods [27, 28]. Longitudinal data analysis indicates that successful initial experiences with technology significantly predict long-term adoption patterns.

With the limitations of and the challenges faced by the ageing population in mind, the next section discusses the design considerations for the ageing population.

2 Design Considerations for Ageing Population

Contemporary gerontechnology, an interdisciplinary field that studies ageing and technology to help improve the lives of older adults, uses a multidimensional approach to address the complex interplay between age-related capabilities and digital interaction paradigms. Recent meta-analyses indicate that effective solutions must simultaneously account for physiological changes, cognitive processing patterns, and sociotechnical contexts [29]. Doing so necessitates moving beyond conventional accessibility guidelines to develop adaptive systems that respond dynamically to users' evolving needs.

2.1 Inclusive Interaction Interfaces to Address Physical and Sensory Constraints

Older adults often experience reduced vision, hearing, dexterity, and strength, which can significantly impair their ability to engage with digital technologies. For instance, age-related macular degeneration can hinder the ability to read small text or differentiate colors, while conditions like arthritis may affect fine motor control, complicating the use of touchscreens and keyboards.

To address these challenges, design solutions must prioritize simplicity, clarity, and adaptability. Research demonstrates that interface elements should maintain 12mm minimum touch targets with 5mm spacing to accommodate reduced finger dexterity [30]. Current best practices also recommend implementing dynamic text resizing options and avoiding pure color coding due to the increased prevalence of color vision deficiencies in this population [31]. In addition, the use of larger fonts, high-contrast color schemes, and consistent layout structures can enhance both readability and navigability, reducing cognitive load and fostering user confidence.

Customizability also plays a critical role in enhancing accessibility. Interfaces that allow users to personalize font sizes, contrast settings, and input modes enable alignment with diverse physical and cognitive needs. For instance, the integration of voice control, screen readers, or Braille displays expands usability for those with sensory impairments. These features, when thoughtfully implemented, transform one-size-fits-all interfaces into adaptive ecosystems for elderly users.

2.2 Multimodal Inputs Leveraging Voice, Touch, and Gesture Technologies

Alternative input modalities, such as voice commands, touch interfaces, and gesture recognition, present both opportunities and challenges for elderly users. For instance, voice assistants like Siri and Alexa can be used to control devices and access information without needing to interact with a graphical user interface [32]. While voice interfaces show high initial acceptance rates, longitudinal studies reveal declining usage due to issues such as difficulty recalling activation phrases and interference from ambient noise [33, 34].

To enhance usability and task success rates, researchers have proposed hybrid interaction systems that combine simple gestures with confirmatory voice feedback. They have demonstrated promises, achieving higher completion rates for complex tasks than single-modality approaches [35]. Multimodal interaction systems should be designed to accommodate various sensory impairments, incorporating adaptive timeout thresholds and context-aware assistance prompts to support users with slower response times.

Further, Che et al. [36] found that virtual reality systems with intuitive hand-interaction modes significantly improved usability for older adults. However, they also identified persisting challenges, such as reduced precision during controller-free tasks, further underscoring the importance of refining gesture-based input systems for the older population.

2.3 Participatory and Elderly-Centered Design

Effective systems for older adults must be grounded in participatory design methodologies that treat users as co-creators rather than passive recipients. Engaging older adults throughout the design process, from needs assessment and prototyping to usability testing, ensures that resulting technologies align with their daily practices, values, and preferences [37, 38].

This user-centered approach is elderly-centered and is especially vital in domains such as healthcare where technology-enhanced systems can empower older individuals to monitor their chronic conditions, adhere to medication schedules, and stay connected with caregivers. However, these systems must reflect not only medical utility but also emotional and social needs to foster sustained use.

2.4 Training, Support, and Digital Confidence

Despite thoughtful design, older adults may still experience anxiety or uncertainty when adopting new technologies. Therefore, educational interventions and technical support play a crucial role in promoting digital inclusion. Training programs should incorporate scaffolded instruction, step-by-step demonstrations, and hands-on practice tailored to varying levels of prior experience [39].

In addition, integrating good help resources, such as built-in tutorials, FAQs, and real-time assistance, can enhance users' confidence and reduce abandonment. Research also shows that peer-based learning environments, where older users can share experiences and problem-solve collectively, further improve digital literacy and motivation [40].

Establishing positive early interactions is key to long-term engagement. Systems should offer quick and rewarding initial experiences that demonstrate tangible benefits and reinforce a sense of competence and autonomy.

By addressing the ageing population's physical, cognitive, and emotional needs through inclusive design, participatory methods, and ongoing support, technology can become a powerful enabler of autonomy, health, and social connection in later life.

3 AI Tools to Support Ageing Population

AI technologies increasingly play a pivotal role in enhancing the quality of life for older adults. They foster autonomy, improve health outcomes, and facilitate communication and cognitive functioning. Below are several categories of AI tools that have shown promise in promoting user empowerment among the ageing population.

3.1 AI Voice Assistants

AI-powered voice assistants enable older adults to interact with digital services using natural language. These tools, such as Amazon Alexa, Google Assistant, Apple Siri, and Microsoft Cortana, reduce reliance on complex interfaces and support multimodal accessibility. These AI tools also enable users to control smart home devices, set reminders, and access information such as news or weather updates with simple voice commands.

Further, AI-powered voice assistants can perform a variety of health-related tasks. For example, emotion recognition through vocal prosody analysis enables a more appropriate response generation, while proactive health check-in features use biomedical voice markers to detect potential wellness issues [41, 42]. These capabilities contribute to early intervention and reinforce users' confidence in managing their health independently.

Voice assistants also improve social connectivity. Studies show that older adults using smart speakers experience reduced loneliness and greater perceived control over daily routines [43, 44]. However, long-term engagement may be challenged by concerns over privacy, ambient noise, and difficulty remembering activation phrases. Continued system refinement and enhancement are necessary.

3.2 Health Monitoring Apps

Health monitoring applications, such as MySugr and Medisafe, leverage AI capabilities to assist users in managing their health conditions through various innovative features. These applications are designed to enhance patient engagement and facilitate effective self-management of chronic diseases. AI-driven health monitoring apps provide personalized treatment plans and real-time monitoring capabilities, which are essential for managing conditions like diabetes and cardiovascular diseases [45]. By utilizing predictive analytics, these applications can offer tailored recommendations based on individual health data, thereby improving adherence to treatment regimens and promoting positive health outcomes [46, 47]. The integration of AI allows for continuous data collection and analysis, enabling users to receive timely feedback and support, which is crucial for maintaining health behaviors [47]. Moreover, features such as virtual health coaching and community support are integral to these applications. They foster user engagement by providing real-time feedback and personalized interventions, which have been shown to enhance adherence and motivation among users managing noncommunicable diseases [46]. The applications also facilitate access to healthcare professionals and simplify complex medical information, empowering users to make informed decisions about their health.

3.3 Robot Companions

Socially assistive robots, such as Paro and ElliQ, provide companionship and promote emotional and cognitive stimulation. Designed for older adults living independently, ElliQ can initiate conversations, suggest health-promoting activities, and facilitate communication with caregivers and family members. ElliQ's AI-driven interaction engine adapts over time to user preferences, which fosters a sense of familiarity and emotional bonding. Research shows that long-term interactions with such robots can reduce feelings of isolation and improve users' mood and social well-being [48–50]. The robot's proactive engagement model encourages users to stay mentally and physically active, aligning with behavioral activation principles in geriatric health.

Challenges remain regarding ethical design, user data privacy, and cultural adaptability. Nevertheless, pilot studies have shown positive responses to robot companionship, particularly among users with mild cognitive impairment or limited mobility.

3.4 AI Home Technologies

AI home or smart home technologies, such as Philips Hue and Google Nest, enhance independence and safety by automating environmental controls and monitoring health-related behaviors. The Internet of Things (IoT), integrated with AI in systems like Nest and Philips Hue, allows users to adjust lighting, climate, and security using voice commands or mobile apps, minimizing physical strain.

For older adults with limited mobility or memory impairments, these systems support ageing-in-place by enabling environmental personalization, fall detection, and emergency alerts. As highlighted by Qian and Siau [51], IoT-driven smart home solutions not only optimize energy efficiency and sustainability but also create adaptive environments tailored to users' real-time needs, bridging gaps between autonomy and caregiving. Some systems incorporate machine learning algorithms that detect behavioral anomalies, such as changes in movement patterns, which may indicate health issue [52, 53].

AI homes also offer peace of mind to caregivers through remote monitoring features. By balancing autonomy and oversight, these technologies foster a supportive living environment that adapts to users' evolving needs.

3.5 AI-Driven Cognitive Training Apps

AI-driven cognitive training platforms deliver personalized mental exercises aimed at maintaining or improving cognitive functioning in older adults [54, 55]. Programs like Lumosity and BrainHQ tailor difficulty and content based on user performance through adaptive algorithms.

Evidence suggests that regular use of computerized cognitive training programs can enhance memory, attention, and processing speed among older adults [56]. The gamified elements foster engagement, while progress-tracking features promote a sense of achievement and motivation. Some studies have shown that these interventions can delay cognitive decline in older adults with mild cognitive impairment (MCI) when used consistently. While their clinical efficacy continues to be debated, particularly for general cognitive transfer, users report high satisfaction due to personalization, ease of use, and the ability to track cognitive progress over time.

3.6 Digital Health Platforms

Digital health platforms reduce barriers to care by enabling older adults to access medical services from home. Systems such as Teladoc and Doxy.me integrate AI tools to improve diagnostic accuracy, triage decision-making, and patient education.

For users with mobility or transportation limitations, these platforms offer timely medical consultations and continuity of care. AI chatbots embedded in systems assist in symptom checking, medication management, and follow-up scheduling, enhancing engagement and adherence [57, 58].

Digital health has also been linked to improved outcomes in chronic disease management, particularly when combined with remote monitoring tools. Ensuring that platforms are user-friendly and incorporate accessible features, such as large text, clear navigation, and voice input, is crucial to maximizing their impact among older adults.

4 Research Directions for HCI to Support Ageing Population

As the need for technology that accommodates the ageing population grows, several research directions can be pursued to enhance HCI for older users.

4.1 Adaptive and Personalized Interfaces

Older adults demonstrate diverse and evolving needs due to age-related changes in vision, hearing, cognition, and motor abilities. Research into adaptive interfaces, i.e., systems that respond dynamically to users' real-time conditions, offers significant potential for personalization. Biocybernetic adaptation, which integrates physiological data (e.g., galvanic skin response, heart rate, pupil dilation), enables real-time monitoring and adjustments of the interfaces to fit individuals and circumstances [59, 60]. For example, a reading interface might slow down scrolling or increase font sizes in response to signs of cognitive fatigue or visual strain.

In addition to real-time adaptation, longitudinal personalization is critical. Interfaces could learn from repeated use, building profiles to accommodate user preferences for input styles (e.g., touch, voice, gesture), notification timing, and content layout. Such systems would not only improve accessibility but also foster digital confidence among older users.

4.2 Assistive and Immersive Technologies

Assistive technologies, such as AR, VR, and wearable devices, provide new avenues for compensating age-related limitations. AR can overlay contextual prompts in physical space, for instance, reminding users to take medication when they enter the kitchen or guiding them through complex appliance usage. VR has shown promise in delivering immersive experiences that combat isolation, stimulate cognitive function, and encourage physical activity, such as virtual travel, exergaming, and reminiscence therapy.

Despite their promise, these technologies still face adoption challenges. Research on how to reduce the physical discomfort that is associated with head-mounted displays, as well as how to simplify calibration and navigation processes, is warranted. As highlighted by Wang et al. [61], human-centered design frameworks for the Metaverse can inform these efforts by prioritizing intuitive interaction paradigms and minimizing the cognitive load for older adults. Importantly, future systems should not only compensate for impairments but also promote dignity and agency through inclusive interaction design.

4.3 Social and Companion Robots

Socially Assistive Robots (SARs) are increasingly developed to offer emotional support, daily reminders, and light household assistance. Designed to foster companionship, robots like ElliQ or PARO can initiate conversations, encourage routines, and respond empathetically to users' affective states.

Yet, social robots must do more than simulate companionship. Adaptation to cultural norms, privacy preferences, and emotional expectations of older adults is necessary. Future research should examine how these robots can navigate the complexities of relational boundaries while encouraging engagement. Moreover, longitudinal studies are needed to evaluate whether SARs meaningfully alleviate loneliness or merely offer short-term novelty effects.

4.4 Health Monitoring and Digital Health Interfaces

Remote health monitoring and telemedicine have become essential tools for older adults managing chronic illnesses or mobility limitations. These systems must deliver clinically relevant data, such as blood pressure, glucose levels, or sleep patterns, while maintaining simplicity and clarity in user interaction. Effective interface design should avoid overwhelming users with data and instead focus on emphasizing key trends, alerts, and actionable suggestions.

Moreover, these systems should provide seamless integration with care teams and family members while respecting data sovereignty. Research should explore how conversational agents, or explainable AI, can support shared decision-making, helping older adults interpret medical advice and make informed choices. The challenge lies in developing interfaces that are both technically robust and emotionally reassuring, particularly for populations with limited digital literacy.

4.5 Privacy, Security, and Ethical Design

AI-powered eldercare solutions often require collecting and analyzing sensitive health, location, and behavioral data, which can raise ethical concerns around surveillance, consent, and autonomy. Information privacy (e.g., data sharing and storage) and physical privacy (e.g., in-home camera monitoring) must be addressed simultaneously [62, 63]. The lack of transparency in many AI systems compounds these concerns, leaving older users unsure about how their data is used and by whom.

Future HCI research can study user-centered privacy frameworks, including privacy-by-design principles and customizable consent interfaces. Equally important is designing for "informed refusal," allowing users to selectively opt out of certain data-sharing functions without compromising the core utility of the system. Developers should consider accountability structures to ensure that ethical responsibilities are clearly assigned or designated when systems fail or are misused.

4.6 Autonomy, Decision-Making, and Algorithmic Fairness

While AI can enhance autonomy by offering personalized support, it may be risky if decisions are automated without sufficient explanation or control. Decision-support systems, particularly in healthcare, should be designed to augment, and not replace, human judgment. HCI researchers must investigate interface strategies that empower users to understand, question, and override AI-generated recommendations.

Algorithmic fairness remains a significant challenge. Older adults are often under-represented in training datasets, which can lead to biased predictions or suboptimal recommendations. Research must prioritize inclusive data practices and explore transparency tools (e.g., visual explanations and confidence indicators) that allow users to understand how AI arrives at its conclusions, which is especially crucial in contexts like fall detection or medication adherence, where biased errors may have consequences.

4.7 Emotional, Social, and Intergenerational Design

HCI can play a central role in supporting the emotional and social needs of older adults. Socioemotional Selectivity Theory [64, 65] suggests that as people age, they prioritize emotionally meaningful interactions. Technologies that promote intergenerational engagement, such as shared digital storytelling platforms or collaborative games, can strengthen family bonds while reducing feelings of isolation [66].

Designers must be careful to foster connection rather than replace it [67]. AI systems should be used to supplement, not substitute, human contact. Emotional design principles, such as empathetic feedback, customizable interaction styles, and recognition of user affect, are essential in maintaining a sense of emotional resonance. Researchers should also explore how technology can preserve identity and agency in later life, enabling users to share memories, preferences, and life narratives.

4.8 Long-Term Impact, Sustainability, and Policy Integration

The long-term implications of AI systems in eldercare must be systematically evaluated. Too often, technologies are assessed only during short-term deployments, ignoring issues such as habit formation, emotional fatigue, or shifting expectations. Longitudinal studies provide valuable insights into evolving user needs and sustained engagement.

Beyond the individuals, researchers must consider how widespread adoption of AI might alter family dynamics, caregiving roles, and healthcare policy. The following questions need to be investigated: Will reliance on digital care reduce institutional burdens or introduce new dependencies? Will it reinforce inequalities for those without access or digital literacy? These broader societal questions require interdisciplinary collaboration, integrating HCI, ethics, public health, and gerontology.

5 Conclusion

As the elderly population grows, the importance of HCI in supporting older adults becomes increasingly evident. Technologies tailored to this demographic can enhance independence, improve access to services, and enrich quality of life. However, realizing these benefits requires a user-centered approach that acknowledges the diverse capabilities, preferences, and needs of older users.

Emerging research in adaptive interfaces, assistive technologies, and social robotics highlights the transformative potential of technology to support ageing in place, maintain cognitive and physical health, and foster social engagement. These innovations can empower older adults to manage daily activities with greater autonomy and confidence, provided they are designed with inclusivity and accessibility in mind.

The integration of artificial intelligence into eldercare technologies introduces important ethical challenges. Concerns around privacy, algorithmic transparency, user autonomy, and fairness must be addressed to ensure that such systems uphold the dignity and well-being of older adults. Inclusive design processes that actively engage older users, along with transparent communication about data use and system functionality, are essential for building trust and promoting meaningful adoption. Technologies for the older population should be SMART – i.e., **S**ensible, **M**odern, **A**daptable, **R**esponsive, and **T**angible – to meet the needs of the population [68].

Ultimately, the intersection of ageing and technology presents both challenges and opportunities. By combining technical innovation with ethical awareness and deep empathy for the ageing experience, researchers and designers can shape an inclusive digital future, empowering and enriching people of all ages and not just the elderly with trust and enjoyment to embrace these technologies as part of their lives [69]. The success of these efforts will be measured not only by usability but also by the degree to which older adults embrace these technologies as valuable parts of their everyday lives.

Acknowledgements. This research is partially supported by the Lee Kong Chian Professorship at Singapore Management University, Singapore Ministry of Education Tier 1A funding, and Hong Kong Polytechnic University grants [P0050656 and P0049595].

References

1. World Health Organization: Ageing and health. (2024). https://www.who.int/news-room/fact-sheets/detail/ageing-and-health
2. United Nations: World population prospects 2024: summary of results (2024). https://population.un.org/wpp/assets/Files/WPP2024_Summary-of-Results.pdf
3. Doré, B., et al.: Acceptability, feasibility, and effectiveness of immersive virtual technologies to promote exercise in older adults: a systematic review and meta-analysis. Sensors **23**, 2506 (2023)
4. Chen, P.-J., Du, Y.-C., Shih, C.-B., Yang, L.-C., Lin, H.-T., Fan, S.-C.: Development of an upper limb rehabilitation system using inertial movement units and kinect device. In: Proceedings of the 2016 International Conference on Advanced Materials for Science and Engineering (ICAMSE), pp. 275–278. IEEE (2016)
5. Lange, B.S., et al.: The potential of virtual reality and gaming to assist successful aging with disability. Phys. Med. Rehabil. Clin. **21**, 339–356 (2010)
6. Czaja, S.J., et al.: Factors predicting the use of technology: findings from the Center for Research and Education on Aging and Technology Enhancement (CREATE). Psychol. Aging **21**, 333 (2006)
7. Pinquart, M., Sorensen, S.: Influences on loneliness in older adults: a meta-analysis. Basic Appl. Soc. Psych. **23**, 245–266 (2001)
8. Zhou, Z., Zhou, J., Liu, F.: Fewer steps the better? Instructing older adults' learning and searching in smartphone apps. Int. J. Hum. Comput. Interact. **38**, 789–800 (2022)

9. Mao, Q., Zhao, Z., Yu, L., Zhao, Y., Wang, H.: The effects of virtual reality–based reminiscence therapies for older adults with cognitive impairment: systematic review. J. Med. Internet Res. **26**, e53348 (2024)

10. Li, J., Wang, H.: Designing and evaluating a narrative-driven spatial visualization for improving patient-centered communication among older adults. In: Proceedings of the Extended Abstracts of the CHI Conference on Human Factors in Computing Systems, pp. 1–11 (2025)

11. Nowak, M.S., Smigielski, J.: The prevalence and causes of visual impairment and blindness among older adults in the city of Lodz, Poland. Medicine **94**, e505 (2015)

12. Horowitz, A., Brennan, M., Reinhardt, J.P.: Prevalence and risk factors for self-reported visual impairment among middle-aged and older adults. Res. Aging **27**, 307–326 (2005)

13. Banerjee, J., Bhattacharyya, M.: Selection of the optimum font type and size interface for on screen continuous reading by young adults: an ergonomic approach. J. Hum. Ergol. (Tokyo) **40**, 47–62 (2011)

14. Behler, A.C., Koelling, G.: Journal content accessibility: considerations and best practices. Portal Libr. Acad. **24**, 679–687 (2024)

15. Parhi, P., Karlson, A.K., Bederson, B.B.: Target size study for one-handed thumb use on small touchscreen devices. In: Proceedings of the 8th Conference on Human-computer Interaction with Mobile Devices and Services, pp. 203–210 (2006)

16. De Iorio, M.L., Rapport, L.J., Wong, C.G., Stach, B.A.: Characteristics of adults with unrecognized hearing loss. Am. J. Audiol. **28**, 384–390 (2019)

17. Dempsey, S.J., Szablewski, M., Atkinson, D.: Tactile sensing in human–computer interfaces: the inclusion of pressure sensitivity as a third dimension of user input. Sens. Actuators A Phys. **232**, 229–250 (2015)

18. Hung, I.-C., Wang, S.-C., Chiang, Y.-H.V., Yang, J., Kinshuk, Chen, N.-S.: The effects of a dual adaptive strategy with gesture recognition and perceived exertion on training efficiency of elders' functional fitness. Smart Learn. Environ. **6**, 1–24 (2019)

19. Brockmole, J.R., Logie, R.H.: Age-related change in visual working memory: a study of 55,753 participants aged 8–75. Front. Psychol. **4**, 12 (2013)

20. Cantarella, A., Borella, E., Carretti, B., Kliegel, M., de Beni, R.: Benefits in tasks related to everyday life competences after a working memory training in older adults. Int. J. Geriatr. Psychiatry **32**, 86–93 (2017)

21. He, Z., et al.: New opportunities for the early detection and treatment of cognitive decline: adherence challenges and the promise of smart and person-centered technologies. BMC Digit. Health **1**, 7 (2023)

22. Khosravi, P., Rezvani, A., Wiewiora, A.: The impact of technology on older adults' social isolation. Comput. Human Behav. **63**, 594–603 (2016)

23. Müller, J., Zhao, X., Foran, H.M.: A technology-supported psychoeducational intervention for older adults and their families to improve social isolation, loneliness, and intergenerational connectedness—a randomized controlled study. Cyberpsychol. Behav. Soc. Netw. **27**, 835–845 (2024)

24. Tsai, T.-H., Chang, H.-T., Ho, Y.-L.: Perceptions of a specific family communication application among grandparents and grandchildren: an extension of the technology acceptance model. PLoS ONE **11**, e0156680 (2016)

25. Conde, M., Mikhailova, V., Döring, N.: "I have the feeling that the person is here": older adults' attitudes, usage intentions, and requirements for a telepresence robot. Int. J. Soc. Robot. **16**, 1619–1639 (2024)

26. Marziali, R.A., et al.: Reducing loneliness and social isolation of older adults through voice assistants: literature review and bibliometric analysis. J. Med. Internet Res. **26**, e50534 (2024)

27. Tan, Y.Y., Neo, M., Asran, I.N.M.: Breaking barriers: designing digital inclusion and digital literacy learning programs for senior citizens. In: Proceedings of the 7th International Conference on E-Society, E-Education and E-Technology, pp. 68–74. IEEE (2023)

28. Bahadori, F., Abolfathi Momtaz, Y., Mohammadi Shahboulaghi, F., Zandieh, Z.: Information and communication technology adoption strategies among Iranian older adults: a qualitative evaluation. Gerontol. Geriatr. Med. **10**, 23337214241246316 (2024)
29. Warner, C.H., Fortin, M., Melkonian, T.: When are we more ethical? A review and categorization of the factors influencing dual-process ethical decision-making. J. Bus. Ethics **189**, 843–882 (2024)
30. Guo, J., Cheng, R., Zhang, W., Xia, T.: Influence of size and location of buttons on the usability of interface on large touch screens. Ergonomics **66**, 2025–2038 (2023)
31. Geddes, C., Flatla, D.R., Connelly, C.L.: 30 Years of solving the wrong problem: how recolouring tool design fails those with colour vision deficiency. In: Proceedings of the 25th International ACM SIGACCESS Conference on Computers and Accessibility. pp. 1–13 (2023)
32. Hoy, M.B.: Alexa, Siri, Cortana, and more: an introduction to voice assistants. Med. Ref. Serv. Q. **37**, 81–88 (2018)
33. Klein, A.M., Kölln, K., Deutschländer, J., Rauschenberger, M.: Design and evaluation of voice user interfaces: what should one consider?. In: Salvendy, G., Wei, J. (eds.) Design, Operation and Evaluation of Mobile Communications . HCII 2023. Lecture Notes in Computer Science, vol. 14052, pp. 167–190. Springer, Cham (2023). https://doi.org/10.1007/978-3-031-35921-7_12
34. Chung, J., Mansion, N., Viceconte, M., Syros, R., Winship, J.: User challenges and preferences for voice interface design on smart speakers among low income minority older adults. Innov. Aging **8**, 581–582 (2024)
35. Bradwell, H.L., et al.: Implementation of virtual reality motivated physical activity via omnidirectional treadmill in a supported living facility for older adults: a mixed-methods evaluation: virtual reality to motivate physical activity for older adults. In: Proceedings of the 2024 CHI Conference on Human Factors in Computing Systems, pp. 1–13 (2024)
36. Che, R., Li, J., Wang, H.: Comparative analysis of hand-interaction modes for older adults in virtual reality: a pilot study on freehand and controller-based interactions. In: The 22nd Triennial Congress of the International Ergonomics Association, Korea (2024)
37. Lindsay, S., Jackson, D., Schofield, G., Olivier, P.: Engaging older people using participatory design. In: Proceedings of the SIGCHI Conference on Human Factors in Computing Systems, pp. 1199–1208 (2012)
38. Fischer, B., Peine, A., Östlund, B.: The importance of user involvement: a systematic review of involving older users in technology design. Gerontologist **60**, e513–e523 (2020)
39. Charness, N., Boot, W.R.: Aging and information technology use: potential and barriers. Curr. Dir. Psychol. Sci. **18**, 253–258 (2009)
40. Xie, B.: Older adults, e-health literacy, and collaborative learning: an experimental study. J. Am. Soc. Inform. Sci. Technol. **62**, 933–946 (2011)
41. Agrawal, R., Pandey, N.: Developing rapport between humans and machines: emotionally intelligent AI assistants. Int. J. Res. Appl. Sci. Eng. Technol. **12**, 1473–1480 (2024)
42. Asha, P., Suresh, L.P., Gani, A.M.I., Sai, A.D., Mathivanan, G.: Employing intelligence for detecting the emotions using efficient machine learning algorithms. In: Proceedings of the 2024 International Conference on Science Technology Engineering and Management, pp. 1–5. IEEE (2024)
43. Pradhan, A., Mehta, K., Findlater, L.: "Accessibility Came by Accident" use of voice-controlled intelligent personal assistants by people with disabilities. In: Proceedings of the 2018 CHI Conference on Human Factors in Computing Systems, pp. 1–13 (2018)
44. Astell, A., Clayton, D.: "Like another human being in the room": a community case study of smart speakers to reduce loneliness in the oldest-old. Front. Psychol. **15**, 1320555 (2024)

45. Yang, Y., Siau, K., Xie, W., Sun, Y.: Smart health: intelligent healthcare systems in the metaverse, artificial intelligence, and data science era. J. Organ. End User Comput. **34**, 1–14 (2022)
46. Muthineni, S.R.: AI in mobile health apps: transforming chronic disease management. Int. J. Sci. Res. Comput. Sci. Eng. Inf. Technol. **11**, 108–116 (2025)
47. Patel, P.M., et al.: Beyond the pain management clinic: the role of AI-integrated remote patient monitoring in chronic disease management–a narrative review. J Pain Res., 4223–4237 (2024)
48. Odekerken-Schröder, G., Mele, C., Russo-Spena, T., Mahr, D., Ruggiero, A.: Mitigating loneliness with companion robots in the COVID-19 pandemic and beyond: an integrative framework and research agenda. J. Serv. Manag. **31**, 1149–1162 (2020)
49. Scoglio, A.A.J., Reilly, E.D., Gorman, J.A., Drebing, C.E.: Use of social robots in mental health and well-being research: systematic review. J. Med. Internet Res. **21**, e13322 (2019)
50. Robinson, H., MacDonald, B., Broadbent, E.: The role of healthcare robots for older people at home: a review. Int. J. Soc. Robot. **6**, 575–591 (2014)
51. Qian, Y., Siau, K.L.: IoT in sustainability and IoT in the AI and Metaverse age. IEEE Internet Things Mag. **8**, 92–98 (2025)
52. Demiris, G., Hensel, B.K., Skubic, M., Rantz, M.: Senior residents' perceived need of and preferences for "smart home" sensor technologies. Int. J. Technol. Assess. Health Care **24**, 120–124 (2008)
53. Peek, S.T.M., Wouters, E.J.M., Van Hoof, J., Luijkx, K.G., Boeije, H.R., Vrijhoef, H.J.M.: Factors influencing acceptance of technology for aging in place: a systematic review. Int. J. Med. Inform. **83**, 235–248 (2014)
54. Khalid, U.B., Naeem, M., Stasolla, F., Syed, M.H., Abbas, M., Coronato, A.: Impact of AI-powered solutions in rehabilitation process: recent improvements and future trends. Int. J. Gen. Med., 943–969 (2024)
55. Jiao, D.: AI-enhanced digital therapeutics for cognitive impairment: integrating mobile applications, virtual reality, and wearable devices. Discover Artif. Intell. **5**, 1–13 (2025)
56. Lampit, A., Hallock, H., Valenzuela, M.: Computerized cognitive training in cognitively healthy older adults: a systematic review and meta-analysis of effect modifiers. PLoS Med. **11**, e1001756 (2014)
57. Xu, L., Sanders, L., Li, K., Chow, J.C.L.: Chatbot for health care and oncology applications using artificial intelligence and machine learning: systematic review. JMIR Cancer **7**, e27850 (2021)
58. Aggarwal, A., Tam, C.C., Wu, D., Li, X., Qiao, S.: Artificial intelligence–based chatbots for promoting health behavioral changes: systematic review. J. Med. Internet Res. **25**, e40789 (2023)
59. Ye, G.C.: Review of VREED in eye tracking-based VR emotion detection. In: Proceedings of the 2024 4th International Conference on Artificial Intelligence, Virtual Reality and Visualization, pp. 60–66. IEEE (2024)
60. Sáiz-Manzanares, M.C., Marticorena-Sánchez, R., Sáez-García, J., González-Díez, I.: Analysing virtual labs through integrated multi-channel eye-tracking technology: a proposal for an explanatory fit model. Appl. Sci. **14**, 9831 (2024)
61. Wang, Y., Wang, L., Siau, K.L.: Human-centered interaction in virtual worlds: a new era of generative artificial intelligence and metaverse. Int. J. Hum. Comput. Interact. **41**, 1459–1501 (2025)
62. Zhu, J., et al.: Ethical issues of smart home-based elderly care: a scoping review. J. Nurs. Manag. **30**, 3686–3699 (2022)
63. Bouchlaghem, M.A., et al.: Ethical issues raised in the care of the elderly during the SARS-CoV-2 pandemic and possible solutions for the future: a systematic review of qualitative scientific literature. BMC Med. Ethics **26**, 10 (2025)

64. Charles, S.T.: Socioemotional selectivity theory. In: Encyclopedia of Gerontology and Population Aging, pp. 4708–4710. Springer (2022)
65. Siette, J., Pomare, C., Dodds, L., Jorgensen, M., Harrigan, N., Georgiou, A.: A comprehensive overview of social network measures for older adults: a systematic review. Arch. Gerontol. Geriatr. **97**, 104525 (2021)
66. Yuan, J., Xiang, J., Liu, F.: Intergenerational support and subjective well-being of older adults in China. J. Appl. Gerontol., 07334648241292970 (2024)
67. Liu, Y., Siau, K.L.: Generative artificial intelligence and metaverse: future of work, future of society, and future of humanity. In: Zhao, F., Miao, D. (eds.) AI-generated Content. AIGC 2023. Communications in Computer and Information Science, vol. 1946, pp. 118–127. Springer, Singapore (2024). https://doi.org/10.1007/978-981-99-7587-7_10
68. Sharma, R., et al.: Smart living for elderly: design and human-computer interaction considerations. In: Zhou, J., Salvendy, G. (eds.) Human Aspects of IT for the Aged Population. Healthy and Active Aging. ITAP 2016. Lecture Notes in Computer Science, vol. 9755, pp. 112–122. Springer, Cham (2016). https://doi.org/10.1007/978-3-319-39949-2_11
69. Zhu, W., Nah, F., Zhao, F.: Factors influencing users' adoption of mobile computing. In: Managing E-commerce and Mobile Computing Technologies, pp. 260–271. IGI Global (2003)

AI Systems for Physicians: A Review from Socio-technical and Human-Computer Interaction Perspectives

Jiaqi Wu Young[✉] and Fiona Fui-Hoon Nah

School of Computing and Information Systems, Singapore Management University, Singapore, Singapore
{jq.wuyoung.2023,fionanah}@smu.edu.sg

Abstract. The adoption of artificial intelligence (AI) in healthcare is accelerating, yet successful implementations of physician-facing AI systems remain limited and uneven. This paper presents a literature review of 40 peer-reviewed studies published between November 2022 and November 2024, spanning clinical, technical, and human-computer interaction (HCI) domains. Anchored in a socio-technical perspective, the review examines our existing understanding of how technical design, user expertise, and organizational factors shape the effectiveness of AI systems in real-world clinical settings. Our analysis identifies two meta-themes: (1) context as a dynamic, multi-level influence that actively reshapes AI system behavior, and (2) trust as an emergent property that evolves over time through clinician experience, team dynamics, and institutional feedback. These insights challenge static models of implementation and highlight the need for adaptive governance mechanisms that support continuous monitoring, runtime oversight, and trust calibration. We propose actionable recommendations for healthcare leaders, implementation teams, and assurance functions, and propose future research directions grounded in control theory, organizational learning, and complex adaptive systems theory. By integrating perspectives from HCI and clinical informatics, this review provides a foundation for designing AI systems that not only are technically robust, trustworthy, and sustainable but also have contextual awareness capabilities in high-stakes healthcare environments.

Keywords: Human-AI interaction · Physician-facing AI · Socio-technical systems · Adaptive governance

1 Introduction

Artificial Intelligence (AI) demonstrates remarkable potential for transforming the healthcare sector, particularly through physician-facing systems that support clinical decision-making, and for streamlining healthcare operations. In specific domains such as medical imaging and pathology analysis, AI has demonstrated diagnostic accuracy comparable to human specialists [1, 2]. These capabilities have attracted substantial investment, with U.S. healthcare AI venture funding projected to reach $11 billion US dollars in 2024 [3].

F. F.-H Nah and K. L. Siau (Eds.): HCII 2025, LNCS 16343, pp. 165–180, 2026.
https://doi.org/10.1007/978-3-032-13167-6_12

Despite their technical capabilities, physician-facing AI systems frequently underperform in real-world clinical settings. For instance, Google Health's evaluation of AI diagnostic tools revealed that even highly accurate models struggle with practical implementation due to workflow misalignment and resource constraints [4]. Beyond technical issues like data quality and model generalizability [2], challenges arise from insufficient attention to workflow integration, clinician trust, staff training, and organizational readiness [1, 3]. Many AI project efforts prioritize algorithmic innovation while underinvesting in the human and organizational infrastructure needed to enable and sustain a growing adoption.

This gap reflects a broader implication: the successful implementation of AI in clinical practice requires addressing not only technical performance but also the complex interplay of technical design, human expertise, and organizational systems. This aligns with the socio-technical systems perspective, originally introduced in the management information systems (MIS) literature by Bostrom and Heinen (1977), which argues that technologies are only effective when they are jointly optimized with the social and organizational systems where they operate [5]. Recent regulatory developments also reflect this socio-technical view. The European Union's AI Act (Articles 14, Annex III) mandates human oversight and governance measures for high-risk AI systems—a category under which physician-facing AI systems are likely to fall [6]. Similarly, the U.S. Food and Drug Administration's guidance on Software as a Medical Device (SaMD) emphasizes real-world performance monitoring and change control governance [7]. These policies underscore the need for implementation frameworks that go beyond model performance to include clinician trust calibration, system usability, and institutional accountability.

Motivated by these challenges, we review research from the fields of health informatics and human-computer interaction (HCI) to identify implementation patterns across a diverse set of countries and markets (e.g., Europe, the US, China, Australia, South Korea, etc.) to inform practice and future research. Our scope focuses on physician-facing systems—as opposed to patient-facing applications or administrative tools—reflecting the high-stakes nature of human-AI collaboration where clinical accuracy, trust, and organizational governance intersect. Three research questions guide our literature review:

RQ1: How do technical design characteristics of physician-facing AI systems shape human-AI interaction patterns?
RQ2: How do domain expertise and team factors influence the adoption and effectiveness of physician-facing AI systems?
RQ3: What governance mechanisms enable the responsible deployment and the ongoing use of physician-facing AI systems?

The remainder of this paper is structured as follows: Sect. 2 presents our methodology; Sect. 3 summarizes findings across technical implementation, human factors, and organizational governance; Sect. 4 synthesizes meta-themes and practical implications; and Sect. 5 outlines future research directions.

2 Methodology

We conducted a literature review to identify and synthesize research on the implementation of physician-facing AI systems. Our goal is to understand how technical, human, and organizational factors shape the latest trend of real-world use, and to inform both practice and research from a socio-technical and HCI perspective. As shown in Fig. 1, our analysis followed a structured three-step synthesis process: (1) Evidence Synthesis (Sect. 3) for identifying findings from the literature across three dimensions—technical implementation, human factors, and organizational governance—focusing on observable patterns in system implementation, adoption and evaluation. (2) Theme Development (Sect. 4) for synthesizing cross-cutting meta-themes, with particular attention to how contextual factors and trust dynamics influence implementation outcomes. We define context as the multi-level situational factors—task, social, and institutional—that influence how physician-facing AI systems are used and governed [8, 9]. These factors are not static but interact dynamically with AI system behavior over time. We conceptualized context as both a situational illuminator and causal influence to interpret our findings. (3) Future Research Directions (Sect. 5) for outlining theoretical and methodological opportunities for addressing identified knowledge gaps, advancing the responsible and sustainable adoption of physician-facing AI systems.

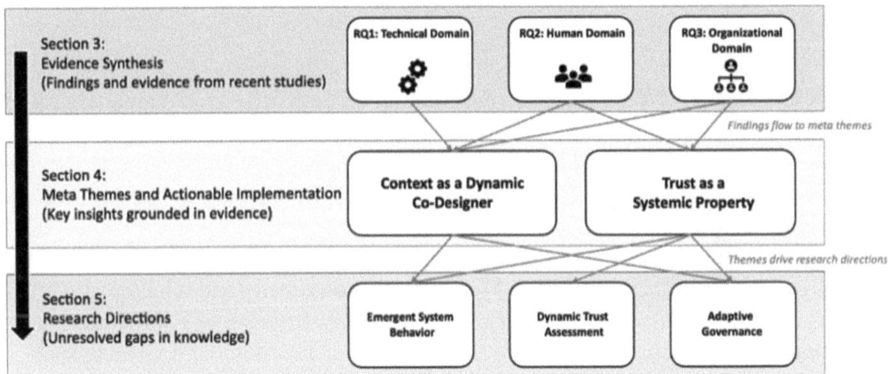

Fig. 1. Analysis Process for Synthesizing Health Informatics and HCI Literature.

2.1 Search Strategy

To reflect the interdisciplinary and socio-technical nature of this domain, we selected three major databases: (1) PubMed: To capture studies and evaluations in medical and clinical research that focus on physician-facing AI systems; (2) IEEE Xplore: To include engineering and technical design research on AI system development for clinical settings; (3) ACM Digital Library: To access research from the HCI community.

We iteratively refined our query to reflect three core domains: (1) Technological advancements in AI ("AI", "machine learning"). (2) Human-centered and socio-technical aspects ("human-AI interaction", "collaboration"). (3) physician-facing ("clinical", "medical"). We also included terms such as "performance", "ethics" and "bias" to ensure we captured both outcome-oriented studies and those emphasizing context-aware implementation.

To ensure relevance to current deployment environments, we limited our search to peer-reviewed, English-language studies published between November 2022 and November 2024. This time frame captures the rapid evolution of explainable AI, the emergence of generative AI, and the latest responses to regulatory frameworks such as the EU AI Act [6] and FDA SaMD guidance [7]. It also corresponds to a critical period for examining how HCI literature has addressed long-standing gaps in the treatment of contextual and socio-technical factors during a time of accelerated investment, public attention, and technical advancement in AI adoption [8, 10].

Inclusion Criteria. We included studies that (i) focus on the implementation or real-world use of AI systems in clinical settings, (ii) describe physician-facing AI systems— i.e., systems designed to support physicians in diagnosis and clinical decision-making, and (iii) address at least one of the following dimensions: (a) Human factors in AI implementation, (b) Human-AI interaction and interface design, (c) Evaluation metrics for clinical tasks, and (d) Organizational-level contextual factors affecting AI adoption, including cross-level influences such as workflow alignment, institutional readiness, and trust dynamics [8].

Exclusion Criteria. We excluded studies that (i) focus solely on technical algorithm development or model validation in isolation, (ii) do not involve clinical professionals as direct users (e.g., patient-facing applications, administrative automation tools), and (iii) lack clear methods for evaluating implementation, interaction, or impact from the socio-technical perspective.

The initial database search returned 107 articles from PubMed, 6 from IEEE Xplore, and 43 from the ACM Digital Library. After removing duplicates and screening titles and abstracts against our criteria, 57 articles remained for full-text review. Following detailed assessment, 40 publications met all criteria and were included in the final analysis.

2.2 Key Definitions and Concepts

To provide clarity, we define key concepts that frame our analysis:

Adaptive Governance. A structured approach for dynamic oversight. It enables AI systems to remain safe, effective, and contextually aligned in complex and evolving environments. Informed by control theory [74], socio-technical systems theory [5, 13], and organizational learning frameworks [24], adaptive governance emphasizes continuous monitoring, feedback loops, and policy adjustment mechanisms to account for emergent risks and evolving use patterns. Instead of relying solely on static rules or pre-deployment validation, adaptive governance structures use runtime signals—such as trust erosion, override patterns, or drift in workflow alignment—to recalibrate decision thresholds, escalate reviews, or adjust AI-human interaction protocols [7, 8].

Context. The situational conditions—spanning individual, task, social, and organizational levels—that shape the adoption and use of physician-facing AI systems. We distinguish between two conceptualizations of context: (1) context that illuminates phenomena to describe background conditions that help interpret human-AI interaction; and (2) context that affects phenomena, referring to situational factors that directly influence user behavior, system effectiveness, or organizational outcomes. In clinical settings, relevant contextual factors include clinician expertise, workload, explanation style, team dynamics, workflow structure, institutional governance and compliance requirements [8, 10].

Emergent Properties. System-level effects that arise from interactions among AI technologies, users, and organizational workflows. Rooted in socio-technical and complex systems theory, these properties—such as bias amplification or role shifts—require adaptive governance responses that evolve with usage patterns and context. This is drawing on socio-technical systems principles [5, 13], event system theory [12], and complex adaptive systems thinking [11, 12].

Physician-Facing AI Systems. Machine-based systems that combine algorithmic models, data infrastructure, and operational components and are deployed to support clinical decision-making via prediction, classification, or recommendation. These systems vary in their levels of autonomy and adaptability. Their effectiveness depends not only on technical performance but also on integration with human workflows, governance structures, and organizational context. This definition aligns with ISO/IEC 22989:2022 Artificial intelligence—Concepts and terminology and the Organization for Economic Cooperation and Development (OECD) AI system taxonomy, which emphasize adaptability and varying levels of autonomy [15, 18].

Human-AI Interaction Protocols. Structured rules, guidelines, user interface design elements, and technical characteristics that guide and facilitate interactions between clinicians and AI systems during clinical decision-making. These protocols define when and how AI assistance is provided, specify the presentation and format of outputs to ensure usability and workflow alignment, and address algorithmic features such as explainability and adaptability. These protocols influence explainability, usability, and trust calibration during clinical use [19–21].

Trust Calibration. The process of aligning clinicians' trust with AI system reliability—avoiding both over-reliance and under-utilization. Trust calibration occurs dynamically through use experience, social learning, and organizational culture, and is critical for effective human-AI teaming in clinical environments [22, 23].

3 Findings

3.1 Research Methods and Use Case Distribution

Our analysis of the 40 publications [30–69] in the literature review reveals variations in research approaches and use cases (see Fig. 2). Empirical studies (11 publications - 27.5%) provided direct evidence of implementation challenges but were largely limited to single-institution experiences. Simulation studies (15 publications - 37.5%) offered controlled investigation of specific factors but may not capture the full complexity of clinical environments. Conceptual and systematic reviews (14 publications - 35%) synthesized existing knowledge but highlighted the need for more empirical validations. This gap is particularly pronounced in long-term impact on clinical expertise development, and the evolution of team dynamics and workflows.

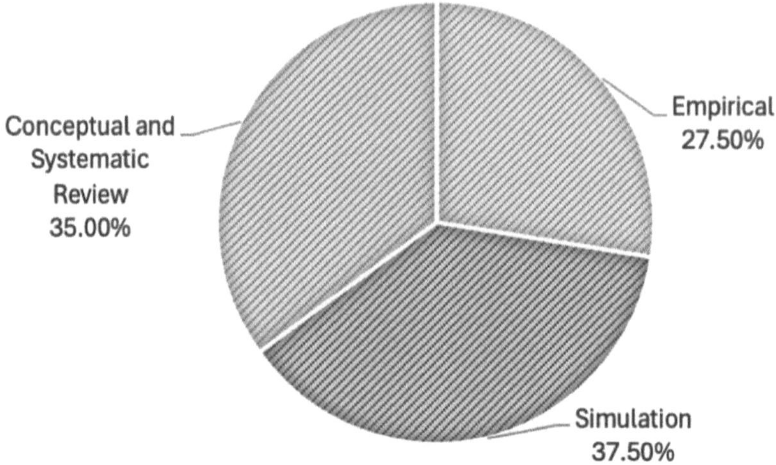

Fig. 2. Research Methods Used.

As shown in Fig. 3, most of these studies (24, 60%) focused on medical image analysis and diagnostic decision support, which is likely due to AI's maturity in these domains. The remaining studies examined clinical risk prediction (5, 13%), workflow optimization (6, 15%), quality improvement (9, 23%), which covered multiple dimensions of AI system quality, such as improving accuracy and interpretability. This distribution highlights a potential bias toward areas where AI performance is more easily quantified, such as accuracy and efficiency, while potentially overlooking less measurable aspects, such as the integration of AI into existing workflows, trust building in AI systems, and the emergence of runtime risks and error monitoring.

The methodological landscape and use cases inform our subsequent analysis of technical, human, and organizational factors, while also highlighting where current evidence may be lacking for definitive conclusions.

3.2 Technical Factors

The Effects of Design and Interface. Interface design functions as a key socio-technical junction in physician-AI interaction. One key design decision is choosing different ways—such as "Prescriptive" and "Descriptive"—that AI systems offer recommendations or information to a human user. The reviewed studies [60, 68] show that how AI outputs are framed—not just their predictions—affects clinician autonomy, trust calibration, and likelihood of appropriate use. Prescriptive approach tells the user what they

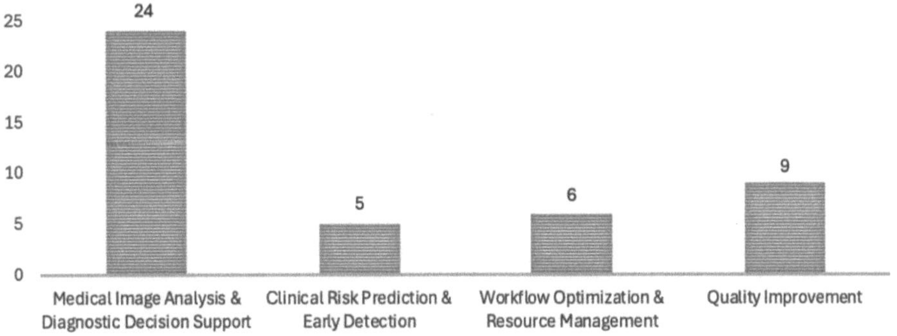

Fig. 3. Distribution of Use Cases for Physician-facing AI Systems

should do. This format involves the AI offering direct advice or a specific course of action, leading to higher adherence to AI advice, even when biased, while descriptive formats presenting findings as observations enabled clinicians to maintain independent judgment. In contrast, descriptive approach provides information or flags a potential issue without explicitly recommending a specific action. This format allows users enough flexibility to use their own judgment and potentially disregard or correct for shortcomings of a biased AI model, thereby helping them to maintain their original, unbiased decision-making.

Another example is visualization choices that affect clinicians' ability to understand and validate AI outputs. Clear presentations connecting AI findings to specific clinical contexts improved decision quality, while complex statistical representations often hindered effective use [40, 42, 44, 53, 57, 62, 63, 67]. Several studies [35, 39, 44, 45] revealed that even when AI systems could explain their decisions, poorly designed interfaces prevented clinicians from detecting potential biases or errors.

Workflow Integration. Different interaction protocols create distinct trade-offs between efficiency and cognitive load. Studies examining concurrent AI assistance, where systems provide real-time feedback during clinical tasks, found improvement in speed but increased risks of cognitive overload [62]. Sequential protocols, where an AI reviews cases before clinician involvement, showed better clarity but could impede workflow in time-sensitive situations [36]. Clinician-triggered protocols preserved autonomy but potentially missed opportunities for proactive assistance [34, 40].

The relationship between technical integration and clinical workflow is more complex than previously assumed. Studies across clinical domains [35, 48, 49, 51, 61] show that technically accurate AI systems often struggle with workflow disruptions and complex decision-making requirements. Clinicians frequently need to perform additional "repair work" to integrate AI output into their existing practices, balancing standardized protocols with clinical judgment and emphasizing that successful integration depends as much on adaptation to existing clinical processes and team dynamics as it does on technical performance. These findings highlight the need for adaptive system designs that anticipate variations in the clinical context [8].

Algorithm-Specific Effects
Multiple studies described specific algorithms and models employed in healthcare settings [31, 34, 35, 37, 40, 42, 53, 54, 58, 60, 63, 66, 68]. Notable implementations include the Paige BLN system, which employs a ResNet-34 Convolutional Neural Network (CNN) for tumor detection [31], and YOLOv4, a CNN-based architecture for real-time colonoscopy object detection [53]. However, most of these studies primarily served to provide contextual background rather than offering systematic analysis of how different algorithmic architectures influence system design or impact clinical users. The choice of algorithms is also often treated as a purely technical decision, with limited discussion of its downstream effects on human interaction or system usability. Differences in model transparency, adaptability, and error patterns can significantly influence clinician trust, explainability, and error recovery strategies. Yet few studies systematically evaluate how algorithmic architecture shapes interface design, user experience, or interpretability protocols in clinical workflows. These gaps suggest the need for a socio-technical framing of algorithm design that considers not only performance but also how clinicians interpret, engage with, and calibrate trust in AI outputs.

3.3 Human Factors

Expertise. Clinician expertise is a core contextual factor influencing system success. Less experienced clinicians showed more accuracy improvements with AI support, particularly in specialized tasks like skin cancer diagnosis, gastrointestinal endoscopy, and fracture detection [50, 53, 54]. However, this improved performance often came with an increased risk of overreliance, possibly due to limited prior experience and lower confidence in independent judgment.

Experienced clinicians exhibited distinctly different interaction patterns. While they demonstrated stronger critical evaluation skills, they showed higher algorithm aversion after encountering AI errors [32, 55]. Studies examining diagnostic workflows found that giving clinicians control over system parameters, such as sensitivity thresholds, helped build trust and improved collaboration effectiveness [40, 58, 59].

Technology familiarity emerged as a distinct factor from clinical expertise. For example, research on AI-assisted polyp detection [53] found that nurses with greater familiarity with computer-aided detection systems showed more significant performance improvements than expert endoscopists, suggesting the importance of technological literacy alongside clinical knowledge.

Team and Workflow Dynamics. AI not only supports individual cognition but also reconfigures team coordination and role distribution, reflecting broader patterns of role reconfiguration observed in socio-technical systems, where the introduction of new technologies prompts shifts in responsibilities, communication patterns, and interdependencies across clinical teams [73]. Studies in complex care environments [33, 46, 67] revealed that successful deployment requires AI outputs to support both individual decision-making and collective awareness across care teams. The impact on team communication is particularly significant, as it is critical for AI recommendations to be integrated into collaborative decision-making processes.

3.4 Organizational Context

Governance Mechanisms. Organizations face significant challenges in establishing effective oversight of AI systems while maintaining operational efficiency. Several studies [33, 48] have highlighted the need for clear protocols covering error management, disagreement resolution, and ethical oversight. Successful implementations featured decision-referral approaches where AI systems appropriately deferred uncertain cases to human experts, enhancing collaboration without undermining clinician autonomy. Training programs are critical for preparing both clinicians and other users for effective AI integration in organizations [30, 35, 49, 52, 56, 61, 68]. Research revealed the importance of role-specific training, as nurses, physicians, and technicians often require distinct types of AI support. However, studies also identified concerns about potential deskilling through over-reliance on AI systems [30, 38, 45, 51], suggesting the need for approaches that preserve core clinical skills while leveraging AI for efficiency. These findings suggest that organizations will need not only oversight mechanisms but also adaptive governance structures capable of responding to emergent behavior—consistent with feedback-based control theory and dynamic trust models.

Evaluation. Current evaluation approaches reveal a fundamental misalignment between how AI systems are assessed prior to deployment and how they perform in dynamic clinical environments. Most studies rely on static validation metrics such as accuracy metrics (sensitivity and specificity), and diagnosis and task completion time [37, 38, 41, 42, 47, 50, 55], which offer limited insight into real-world performance with contextual complexity. While qualitative evaluations begin to address user satisfaction, trust development, interpretability, and operational fit [30, 35, 38, 39, 44, 47–49, 52, 54, 58–61, 68], they too often occur outside the context of sustained system use. Several studies [47, 67] highlight how pre-deployment testing fails to anticipate performance drift, emergent risks, or unintended consequences arising from evolving workflows. Others [60, 65] reveal ethical blind spots—such as fairness and bias—that only surface during longitudinal use. These gaps underscore the need for rethinking evaluation as a continuous, context-aware process. Rather than relying solely on static thresholds or once-time testing, effective system governance must integrate runtime monitoring, adaptive feedback mechanisms, and longitudinal evaluation frameworks—core principles of adaptive governance and control-informed design.

Collectively, these findings reveal that technical performance, human interaction, and organizational context are deeply interdependent. As the next section shows, these dynamics give rise to cross-cutting themes that inform the design, deployment, and governance of physician-facing AI systems.

4 Meta-Theme Discussion and Implications

4.1 Meta-Themes

Our analysis reveals two cross-cutting meta-themes that characterize the real-world implementation of physician-facing AI systems: (1) context as a dynamic, multilevel force, and (2) trust as a systemic and emergent property. These themes challenge traditional assumptions that AI behavior is shaped primarily by technical design and suggest that effective implementation depends on adaptive responses to evolving socio-technical conditions.

First, we find that context functions not as a static backdrop but as a dynamic influence that shapes human-AI interaction and system behavior over time. Across studies, clinicians modified workflows in ways that diverged from system design assumptions [35, 49]; teams developed novel patterns for interpreting and validating AI out-puts [33, 46]; and institutions adapted their procedures, escalation protocols, and training approaches in response to AI system deployment [61]. These findings reflect what socio-technical theorists describe as context affecting phenomena, rather than simply describing them [8, 9].

Second, trust emerges not as a static user attitude but as a property of the broader socio-technical environment. While initial trust may correlate with individual expertise [50, 53, 55], long-term trust is shaped through collective experience, institutional learning, and interaction with system behavior over time [59, 64]. In line with control theory and organizational learning literature [33], we view trust as an outcome of feedback processes—where clinicians' beliefs are revised based on system performance, override experience, and peer interpretation. These dynamics require active trust calibration mechanisms, including transparent override processes, real-time monitoring of adherence patterns, and team-based feedback integration [66].

Together, these meta-themes suggest that AI implementation in healthcare must be understood as a process of dynamic adaptation rather than linear deployment. Static policies, rigid training, or one-time evaluations are insufficient. Instead, implementation strategies must anticipate emergent behaviors, evolving workflows, and shifting trust relationships [36, 62]. Without this adaptive lens, organizations risk misalignment between AI capabilities and real-world usage.

4.2 Actionable Recommendations

To address these meta-themes, we propose actionable recommendations across three levels of the healthcare delivery system: leadership, implementation, and assurance.

Leadership. Leaders play a critical role in creating an organizational environment where adaptive patterns can emerge. It requires (1) hosting cross-functional feedback sessions to identify workflow tensions and AI misalignments; (2) supporting the development of living documentation (e.g., learning logs) that track how clinicians adapt to AI tools over time [47]; (3) embracing a paradox mindset [25] to balance efficiency with safety, standardization with clinician autonomy, and innovation with accountability [14].

Implementation Teams. Implementation should focus not only on technical deployment but also on system-wide adaptation. It includes (1) designing responsive AI systems that adjust explanations, thresholds, or escalation protocols based on usage patterns [42]; (2) institutionalizing co-design processes between AI developers and clinicians to iteratively refine system behavior [45]; (3) establishing clear interaction protocols for when clinicians can override, query, or modify AI outputs, especially in high-stakes decisions.

Assurance Teams. Traditional evaluation metrics often fail to capture runtime system behavior. Assurance teams should (1) track context-specific trust signals, such as changes in override frequency, delayed response patterns, or selective AI adherence; (2) evolve performance metrics beyond accuracy to include human override rates, AI verification time, and longitudinal fairness assessments [66]; (3) leverage explanation approaches that align with cognitive models of decision support, enabling more robust trust calibration at both individual and team levels.

To address evolving regulatory requirements for AI governance [6, 7], healthcare organizations need internal frameworks for safe and context-sensitive deployment. They should include (1) rapid learning channels that propagate post-deployment lessons across departments and institutions, such as in Google Health's study showing real-world performance divergence [4]; (2) controlled pilot phases that allow systems to evolve before full-scale rollout, aligned with quality improvement models [47]; (3) resource reallocation strategies based on real-time metrics, such as escalation volume or override justification frequency.

Together, these practices move beyond checklist compliance and toward adaptive governance—a model grounded in socio-technical systems thinking and control theory.

5 Future Research Directions and Conclusion

5.1 Modeling Emergent Behavior and Trust Dynamics in Physician-Facing AI Systems

Healthcare AI systems behave as complex adaptive systems, where local human-AI interactions can give rise to nonlinear, unpredictable, and often unanticipated organizational effects. Current frameworks in AI for healthcare and HCI lack sufficient capacity to account for these emergent dynamics. We propose extending Bar-Yam's Complex Adaptive Systems Theory [17] to study how clinical content, technical design, user practices, workflows, and institutional governance co-evolve. This research requires longitudinal studies of Electronic Health Records (EHR) to track patterns of adaptation, comparative case studies across institutions, and simulation-based experimentation around decision points under uncertainty and time pressure. A key objective is not only prediction but explanation and anticipation of system behavior under real-world constraints.

Trust, in this context, must be treated as a dynamic, context-sensitive, and socially distributed phenomenon. Our findings confirm that trust evolves not only through individual use but also via peer influence, local workarounds, and institutional policies [66]. To model trust, we propose a conceptual and methodological agenda that draws from: (1) Control Theory to model trust calibration through real-time feedback loops, signal thresholds, and override mechanisms [27]. (2) Safety-II Theory to study how successful trust is maintained and adapted under variability, rather than only during failure [28]. (3) Organizational Learning Theory and Trust Development Models to examine how trust is collectively shaped over time within teams and institutions [22, 29]. We recommend multi-modal trust sensing, including: (1) Behavioral signals such as override frequency, hesitation delays, or explanation click-through patterns. (2) Physiological indicators (e.g., galvanic skin response, eye-tracking, heart rate variability) to detect cognitive load and uncertainty in real time. (3) Discourse analysis from team communication logs or EHR interaction traces, reflecting evolving narratives of trust or doubt.

Importantly, trust must be modeled both as a response to system behavior ("context as illuminator") and a driver of system evolution ("context as causal") [8, 9], enabling systems that not only respond to user confidence, but also reshape workflows and escalation norms through trust-aware adaptation.

5.2 Engineering Adaptive Governance Through Control-Theoretic Frameworks

Traditional governance models—built around pre-deployment reviews, compliance audits, and static rules—struggle to accommodate the real-time behavior of AI systems in clinical environments. Such systems must be governed not as static artifacts but as dynamically evolving agents operating within socio-technical ecosystems. We propose reframing AI governance using control-theoretic principles—a foundation well-established in engineering but underutilized in HCI and health informatics. Control theory offers tools to model system state estimation, feedback-driven adaptation, and intervention thresholds, enabling governance agents that monitor risk and comprehension in real time, and adjust system behavior accordingly [16, 72].

This control-based approach to adaptive governance can be enriched by integrating: (1) Adaptive Management Theory to support systematic learning and real-time policy adjustment [71]. (2) High Reliability Organization Theory to maintain operational safety amid complexity and risk [70]. (3) Institutional Theory to examine how new governance norms and practices can be embedded, legitimated, and sustained over time [26].

This new governance paradigm enables runtime adaptation—not just catching errors, but co-evolving with clinicians' needs, stressors, and trust signals. It requires participatory design to align governance mechanisms with user mental models, scenario-based pilots to simulate emergent behaviors and evaluate feedback designs, and longitudinal organizational studies to assess how governance logic integrates into clinical routines and regulatory structures.

5.3 Limitations

This review has several limitations. First, the two-year time frame (2022–2024), while focused on capturing recent developments, may have excluded foundational or longitudinal studies that provide historical or trend-based insights. Second, the English-language restriction introduces potential language bias, possibly omitting perspectives from non-English-speaking healthcare systems. Third, our focus on HCI and implementation teams may have underrepresented technically focused studies, particularly those analyzing algorithm design and performance. These limitations suggest opportunities for future reviews to broaden the scope, incorporate additional socio-technical perspectives, and engage with more diverse healthcare contexts.

5.4 Conclusion

This review synthesizes findings from 40 studies and reveals that the success of physician-facing AI systems depends not only on technical performance but also on their interaction with clinician expertise, workflows, and institutional contexts. AI implementation must be understood as a dynamic socio-technical process. We highlight two critical insights: (1) Context is active and evolving, shaping how AI systems function in practice. (2) Trust is not a fixed input but an emergent property, requiring continuous calibration and oversight. These themes hold relevance across all high-stakes, human-in-the-loop domains. To advance safe and effective AI adoption, we call for deeper integration of control theory, socio-technical systems thinking, and adaptive governance. Future research should combine theoretical grounding with participatory and measurement-driven approaches to co-design AI systems that are resilient, trustworthy, and contextually aligned with clinical realities.

References

1. Olawade, D.B., David-Olawade, A.C., Wada, O.Z., Asaolu, A.J., Adereni, T., Ling, J.: Artificial intelligence in healthcare delivery: prospects and pitfalls. J. Med. Surg. Pub. Health **3**, Article 100108 (2024)
2. Shuaib, A.: Transforming healthcare with AI: promises, pitfalls, and pathways forward. Int. J. Gen. Med. **17**, 1765–1771 (2024)
3. Goldsack, J., Overgaard, S.: Billions of dollars have been invested in healthcare AI. But are we spending in the right places? World Econ. Forum (2024). https://www.weforum.org/sto ries/2024/11/healthcare-health-ai/
4. Heaven, W.D.: Google's medical AI was super accurate in a lab. Real life was a different story. MIT Technol. Rev. (2020), https://www.technologyreview.com/2020/04/27/1000658/ google-medical-ai-accurate-lab-%20real-life-clinic-covid-diabetes-retina-disease/
5. Bostrom, R.P., Heinen, J.S.: MIS problems and failures: a socio-technical perspective, part I: the causes. MIS Q. **1**(3), 17–32 (1977)
6. European Parliament and Council.: Regulation (EU) 2024/1689 of 12 July 2024 on laying down harmonised rules on artificial intelligence (Artificial Intelligence Act) and amending certain Union legislative acts. Official J. Eur. Union (2024)
7. U.S. Food and Drug Administration: Artificial Intelligence/Machine Learning (AI/ML)-Based Software as a Medical Device (SaMD) Action Plan. https://www.fda.gov/media/145 022/download. Accessed 22 Mar 2024
8. Addas, S.: A call for engaging context in HCI/MIS research with examples from the area of technology interruptions. AIS Trans. Hum.-Comput. Interact. **2**(4), 178–196 (2010)
9. Johns, G.: The essential impact of context on organizational behavior. Acad. Manag. Rev. **31**(2), 386–408 (2006)
10. Johns, G.: Advances in the treatment of context in organizational research. Annu. Rev. Organ. Psychol. Organ. Behav. **5**(1), 21–46 (2018)
11. Holland, J.H.: Complex adaptive systems. Daedalus **121**(1), 17–30 (1992)
12. Morgeson, F.P., Mitchell, T.R., Liu, D.: Event system theory: an event-oriented approach to the organizational sciences. Acad. Manag. Rev. **40**(4), 515–537 (2015)
13. Sittig, D.F., Singh, H.: A new socio-technical model for studying health information technology in complex adaptive healthcare systems. Qual. Saf. Health Care **19**(Suppl 3), i68–i74 (2010)
14. Gharajedaghi, J.: Systems Thinking: Managing Chaos and Complexity – A Platform for Designing Business Architecture, 3rd edn. Elsevier, Amsterdam (2011)
15. International Organization for Standardization: ISO/IEC 22989:2022 Artificial Intelligence—Concepts and Terminology. ISO, Geneva (2022)
16. Danks, D., London, A.J.: Regulating autonomous systems: beyond standards. IEEE Intell. Syst. **32**(1), 88–91 (2017)

17. Bar-Yam, Y.: Making Things Work: Solving Complex Problems in a Complex World. NECSI Knowledge Press, Cambridge (2004)
18. Organization for Economic Co-operation and Development: Explanatory memorandum on the updated OECD definition of an AI system. https://www.oecd.org/content/dam/oecd/en/publications/reports/2024/03/explanatory-memorandum-on-the-updated-oecd-definition-of-an-ai-system_3c815e51/623da898-en.pdf
19. DECIDE-AI Steering Group: DECIDE-AI: New reporting guidelines to bridge the development-to-implementation gap in clinical artificial intelligence. Nat. Med. **27**(2), 186–187 (2021)
20. Wang, L., et al.: Human-centered design and evaluation of AI-empowered clinical decision support systems: a systematic review. Front. Comput. Sci. **5**, Article 108 (2023)
21. Ghassemi, M., Oakden-Rayner, L., Beam, A.L.: The false hope of current approaches to explainable artificial intelligence in health care. Lancet Digit. Health **3**(11), e745–e750 (2021)
22. Lee, J.D., See, K.A.: Trust in automation: designing for appropriate reliance. Hum. Factors **46**(1), 50–80 (2004)
23. Madhavan, P., Wiegmann, D.A.: A new look at the dynamics of human-automation trust: Is trust in humans comparable to trust in machines? Proc. Hum. Factors Ergon. Soc. Annu. Meet. **48**(3), 582–586 (2004)
24. Farjoun, M.: Beyond dualism: Stability and change as a duality. Acad. Manag. Rev. **35**(2), 202–225 (2010)
25. Smith, W.K., Lewis, M.W.: Toward a theory of paradox: a dynamic equilibrium model of organizing. Acad. Manag. Rev. **36**(2), 381–403 (2011)
26. Scott, W.R.: Institutions and Organizations: Ideas and Interests, 3rd edn. SAGE, Thousand Oaks (2008)
27. Woods, W., Grushin, A., Khan, S., Velasquez, A.: Combining AI control systems and human decision support via robustness and criticality. Manuscript in preparation (2024)
28. Hollnagel, E.: Safety-I and Safety-II: The Past and Future of Safety Management. CRC Press, Boca Raton (2014)
29. Argote, L., Miron-Spektor, E.: Organizational learning: from experience to knowledge. Organ. Sci. **22**(5), 1123–1137 (2011)
30. Agrawal, A., Khatri, G.D., Khurana, B., Sodickson, A.D., Liang, Y., Dreizin, D.: A survey of ASER members on artificial intelligence in emergency radiology: trends, perceptions, and expectations. Emerg. Radiol. **30**(3), 267–277 (2023)
31. Retamero, J.A., et al.: Artificial intelligence helps pathologists increase diagnostic accuracy and efficiency in the detection of breast cancer lymph node metastases. Am. J. Surg. Pathol. **48**(7), 846–854 (2024)
32. Wang, D.Y., et al.: Artificial intelligence suppression as a strategy to mitigate artificial intelligence automation bias. J. Am. Med. Inform. Assoc. **30**(10), 1684–1692 (2023)
33. Jansson, M., et al.: Artificial intelligence-enhanced care pathway planning and scheduling system: content validity assessment of required functionalities. BMC Health Serv. Res. **22**(1), Article 1513 (2022)
34. Jung, M., et al.: Augmented interpretation of HER2, ER, and PR in breast cancer by artificial intelligence analyzer: enhancing interobserver agreement through a reader study of 201 cases. Breast Cancer Res. **26**(1), Article 31 (2024)
35. Zając, H. D., Li, D., Dai, X., Carlsen, J. F., Kensing, F., Andersen, T. O.: Clinician-facing AI in the wild: taking stock of the sociotechnical challenges and opportunities for HCI. ACM Trans. Comput.-Hum. Interact. **30**(2), Article 33 (2023)
36. Leibig, C., Brehmer, M., Bunk, S., Byng, D., Pinker, K., Umutlu, L.: Combining the strengths of radiologists and AI for breast cancer screening: a retrospective analysis. Lancet Digit. Health **4**(7), e507–e519 (2022)

37. Frazer, H.M.L., et al.: Comparison of AI-integrated pathways with human-AI interaction in population mammographic screening for breast cancer. Nat. Commun. **15**(1), Article 7525 (2024)

38. Thieme, A., et al.: Designing human-centered AI for mental health: developing clinically relevant applications for online CBT treatment. ACM Trans. Comput.-Hum. Interact. **30**(2), Article 27 (2023)

39. Carmichael, J., Costanza, E., Blandford, A., Struyven, R., Keane, P.A., Balaskas, K.: Diagnostic decisions of specialist optometrists exposed to ambiguous deep-learning outputs. Sci. Rep. **14**(1), Article 6775 (2024)

40. Kritharidou, M., et al.: Ethicara for responsible AI in healthcare: a system for bias detection and AI risk management. In: AMIA Annual Symposium Proceedings 2023, pp. 2023–2032 (2023)

41. Novak, A., et al.: Evaluating the impact of artificial intelligence-assisted image analysis on the diagnostic accuracy of front-line clinicians in detecting fractures on plain X-rays (FRACT-AI): protocol for a prospective observational study. BMJ Open **14**(9), e086061 (2024)

42. Famiglini, L., Campagner, A., Barandas, M., La Maida, G.A., Gallazzi, E., Cabitza, F.: Evidence-based XAI: an empirical approach to design more effective and explainable decision support systems. Comput. Biol. Med. **170**, Article 108042 (2024)

43. Reverberi, C., et al.: Experimental evidence of effective human-AI collaboration in medical decision-making. Sci. Rep. **12**(1), Article 14952 (2022)

44. Gomez, C., Smith, B.L., Zayas, A., Unberath, M., Canares, T.: Explainable AI decision support improves accuracy during telehealth strep throat screening. Commun. Med. **4**(1), Article 149 (2024)

45. Nagendran, M., Festor, P., Komorowski, M., Gordon, A.C., Faisal, A.A.: Eye tracking insights into physician behaviour with safe and unsafe explainable AI recommendations. NPJ Digit. Med. **7**(1), Article 202 (2024)

46. Ghosh, P., et al.: Framing machine learning opportunities for hypotension prediction in perioperative care: A socio-technical perspective. ACM Trans. Comput.-Hum. Interact. **30**(5), Article 79 (2023)

47. de Hond, A.A.H., et al.: Guidelines and quality criteria for artificial intelligence-based prediction models in healthcare: a scoping review. NPJ Digit. Med. **5**(1), Article 2 (2022)

48. Procter, R., Tolmie, P., Rouncefield, M.: Holding AI to account: challenges for the delivery of trustworthy AI in healthcare. ACM Trans. Comput.-Hum. Interact. **30**(2), Article 31 (2023)

49. Knop, M., Weber, S., Mueller, M., Niehaves, B.: Human factors and technological characteristics influencing the interaction of medical professionals with artificial intelligence-enabled clinical decision support systems: literature review. JMIR Hum. Factors **9**(1), e28639 (2022)

50. Krakowski, I., et al.: Human-AI interaction in skin cancer diagnosis: a systematic review and meta-analysis. NPJ Digit. Med. **7**(1), Article 78 (2024)

51. Campion, J.R., O'Connor, D.B., Lahiff, C.: Human-artificial intelligence interaction in gastrointestinal endoscopy. World J. Gastrointest. Endosc. **16**(3), 126–135 (2024)

52. Tahri Sqalli, M., Aslonov, B., Gafurov, M., Nurmatov, S.: Humanizing AI in medical training: ethical framework for responsible design. Front. Artif. Intell. **6**, Article 1189914 (2023)

53. Lee, J., et al.: Impact of user's background knowledge and polyp characteristics in colonoscopy with computer-aided detection. Gut Liver **18**(5), 857–866 (2024)

54. Gu, H., et al.: Improving workflow integration with xPath: design and evaluation of a human-AI diagnosis system in pathology. ACM Trans. Comput.-Hum. Interact. **30**(2), Article 28 (2023)

55. Tong, W.J., et al.: Integration of artificial intelligence decision aids to reduce workload and enhance efficiency in thyroid nodule management. JAMA Netw. Open **6**(5), e2313674 (2023)

56. Zhang, J., Wu, J., Qiu, Y., Song, A., Li, W., Li, X., Liu, Y.: Intelligent speech technologies for transcription, disease diagnosis, and medical equipment interactive control in smart hospitals: a review. Comput. Biol. Med. **153**, Article 106517 (2023)

57. Cálem, J., Moreira, C., Jorge, J.: Intelligent systems in healthcare: a systematic survey of explainable user interfaces. Comput. Biol. Med. **180**, Article 108908 (2024)

58. Xu, Q., et al.: Interpretability of clinical decision support systems based on artificial intelligence from technological and medical perspective: a systematic review. J. Healthc. Eng. **2023**, Article 9919269 (2023)

59. van Berkel, N., Bellio, M., Skov, M.B., Blandford, A.: Measurements, algorithms, and presentations of reality: framing interactions with AI-enabled decision support. ACM Trans. Comput.-Hum. Interact. **30**(2), Article 32 (2023)

60. Adam, H., Balagopalan, A., Alsentzer, E., Christia, F., Ghassemi, M.: Mitigating the impact of biased artificial intelligence in emergency decision-making. Commun. Med. **2**(1), Article 149 (2022)

61. Barry, B., et al.: Provider perspectives on artificial intelligence-guided screening for low ejection fraction in primary care: qualitative study. JMIR AI **1**(1), e41940 (2022)

62. Duncan, S.F., et al.: Radiograph accelerated detection and identification of cancer in the lung (RADICAL): a mixed methods study to assess the clinical effectiveness and acceptability of Qure.ai artificial intelligence software to prioritise chest X-ray (CXR) interpretation. BMJ Open **14**(9), e081062 (2024)

63. Yang, J., et al.: RDmaster: a novel phenotype-oriented dialogue system supporting differential diagnosis of rare disease. Comput. Biol. Med. **169**, 107924 (2024)

64. Al-Bazzaz, H., Janicijevic, M., Strand, F.: Reader bias in breast cancer screening related to cancer prevalence and artificial intelligence decision support—a reader study. Eur. Radiol. **34**(8), 5415–5424 (2024)

65. Wies, C., Hauser, K., Brinker, T.J.: Reply to: False conflict and false confirmation errors are crucial components of AI accuracy in medical decision making. Nat. Commun. **15**(1), 6897 (2024)

66. Sáez, C., Ferri, P., García-Gómez, J.M.: Resilient artificial intelligence in health: synthesis and research agenda toward next-generation trustworthy clinical decision support. J. Med. Internet Res. **26**, e50295 (2024)

67. Zhang, S., et al.: Rethinking human-AI collaboration in complex medical decision making: a case study in sepsis diagnosis. Proc. CHI Conf. Hum. Factors Comput. Syst., Article 445 (2024)

68. Nazir, S., Dickson, D.M., Akram, M.U.: Survey of explainable artificial intelligence techniques for biomedical imaging with deep neural networks. Comput. Biol. Med. **156**, 106668 (2023)

69. Hernández-Aceituno, J., Méndez-Pérez, J.A., González-Cava, J.M., Reboso-Morales, J.A.: Towards intelligent supervision of operating rooms using stencil-based character recognition. Comput. Biol. Med. **162**, 107071 (2023)

70. Weick, K.E., Sutcliffe, K.M.: Managing the Unexpected: Resilient Performance in an Age of Uncertainty, 2nd edn. Jossey-Bass, San Francisco (2007)

71. Williams, B.K., Brown, E.D.: Adaptive Management: The U.S. Department of the Interior Technical Guide. U.S. Department of the Interior, Washington D.C. (2012)

72. Åström, K.J., Murray, R.M.: Feedback Systems: An Introduction for Scientists and Engineers. Princeton University Press, Princeton (2008)

73. Barley, S.R.: The alignment of technology and structure through roles and networks. Adm. Sci. Q. **35**(1), 61–103 (1990)

Advances in Commerce, Marketing, and Consumer Behavior

Digital Catalogs and Digital Marketing Strategies for Product Promotion in the Popular and Solidarity Economy: A Community Engagement Experience

Carlos Borja-Galeas[1]([✉]) [iD], Hugo Arias-Flores[2] [iD], Ivanna Sanchez[3] [iD], Andrés Palacio-Fierro[4] [iD], and Viviana Cajas[5] [iD]

[1] Carrera de Marketing Digital, Facultad de Ciencias Económicas, Administrativas y Negocios, Universidad Indoamérica, 170103 Quito, Ecuador
carlosborja@uti.edu.ec

[2] Centro de Investigación de Ciencias Humanas y de la Educación (CICHE), Universidad Indoamérica, 170103 Quito, Ecuador

[3] Carrera de Administración de Empresas, Facultad de Ciencias Económicas, Administrativas y Negocios, Universidad Indoamérica, 170103 Quito, Ecuador

[4] Universidad Internacional del Ecuador (UIDE), 170595 Quito, Ecuador

[5] UISEK Business and Digital School, Universidad Internacional SEK, Quito, Ecuador

Abstract. This article analyzes the development of digital catalogs as a strategic marketing tool for promoting products within the popular and solidarity economy (EPS), as part of a community engagement project carried out by sixth-semester students from the Digital Marketing program at Universidad Indoamérica. The students, who had already gained experience in web development, worked on creating interactive digital catalogs for 12 local businesses from the province of Pichincha, whose products were already equipped with labels and packaging ready for commercialization. In addition to designing the catalogs, digital marketing elements such as visual content optimization and linking the catalogs to e-commerce platforms and social media were integrated. The results show that the use of digital catalogs not only facilitated the professional presentation of the products but also enhanced consumer interaction and expanded the reach of these businesses in the digital marketplace. This study demonstrates how the collaboration between academia and community can strengthen small businesses, fostering their growth in digital environments.

Keywords: digital catalogs · digital marketing · graphic design · popular and solidarity economy · community engagement

1 Introduction

The popular and solidarity economy (PSE) has been a key tool for the economic development of the most vulnerable sectors in Ecuador. This model, based on cooperation and equity, aims to create opportunities for micro and small enterprises that often face

F. F.-H Nah and K. L. Siau (Eds.): HCII 2025, LNCS 16343, pp. 183–192, 2026.
https://doi.org/10.1007/978-3-032-13167-6_13

challenges in accessing the formal market [1]. Despite its potential to contribute to economic and social well-being, many of these enterprises face significant barriers, such as limited access to technological and marketing tools that would allow them to compete on equal terms in a globalized market. In this context, digitalization emerges as an effective solution to overcome these limitations and open new opportunities for PSE entrepreneurs.

The digitalization of commerce has transformed the way consumers interact with products and services, creating the need for enterprises to adapt to new market dynamics [2]. One of the most effective mechanisms to facilitate this adaptation is the creation of digital catalogs. These tools allow entrepreneurs to showcase their product offerings in an organized and professional manner, facilitating consumer interaction and increasing the likelihood of sales conversions [3]. Additionally, digital catalogs provide small businesses with the opportunity to reach wider audiences through digital platforms, which can significantly increase their visibility and competitiveness.

Digital catalogs have become an essential tool for companies, especially small and medium-sized enterprises, as they enable the structured and attractive presentation of their products in the digital environment [2]. These catalogs not only facilitate consumer access but also offer the ability to integrate interactive elements, such as links to e-commerce platforms, which increase conversion rates and enhance the user experience. Their market presence but also enhances competitiveness by optimizing how their products are presented and marketed online [4]. In fact, digital catalogs have proven to be especially effective in sectors with limited resources, where digitalization plays a key role in accessing broader markets.

Moreover, integrating digital marketing strategies with catalogs optimized for search engines (SEO) is crucial for improving product visibility and online positioning. In the digital age, a company's ability to stand out largely depends on its capacity to implement technological tools and optimize them for the digital environment [5]. Digital catalogs that use high-quality visual content and are well integrated with SEO strategies have a positive impact on customer perception, increasing trust and, consequently, purchase decisions [6]. The ability of catalogs to foster consumer interaction is key in creating value, as it enhances customer engagement with the brand and its products, which in turn leads to higher conversion rates [7].

The use of digital catalogs also allows for the integration of digital marketing strategies, such as search engine optimization (SEO) and linking with social media, which amplifies the impact of these tools in the digital marketplace [8]. Through the proper implementation of these strategies, PSE entrepreneurs can improve their online positioning and attract more consumers, which is particularly important for businesses that lack significant resources to invest in traditional advertising. Thus, the digital catalog becomes an accessible and effective tool for promoting products and services in the digital realm [9].

This article stems from a community engagement project carried out by sixth-semester students of the Digital Marketing program at Universidad Indoamérica. The students, who had already developed skills in web development during the fifth semester, worked on creating interactive digital catalogs for 12 PSE businesses in the province of Pichincha. These businesses already had marketable products, including packaging and labels [2, 9], but lacked adequate digital platforms to promote their products. The main objective of the project was to design and develop catalogs that could be used on digital platforms, while also integrating digital marketing strategies to maximize their effectiveness.

Visual content production was one of the key components in the development of the digital catalogs. The students conducted product photography sessions and created high-quality images that reflected the value and unique characteristics of the products offered by the entrepreneurs. These images were optimized for use in the digital catalogs, as well as on websites and social media, to improve consumer perception and increase trust in the products [10]. In addition, graphic design tools were used to make the resulting catalogs visually appealing and easy to navigate.

Another fundamental aspect of the project was the training provided to the entrepreneurs. The students not only designed the catalogs but also taught the entrepreneurs how to manage and update their own digital catalogs autonomously. This training was essential for ensuring the long-term sustainability of the project, as it enabled the entrepreneurs to keep their catalogs updated with new products and changes in their offerings [11]. In this way, the digital catalogs not only became a promotional tool but also a dynamic and adaptable resource to meet the changing needs of the market.

The results of the project demonstrated that the use of digital catalogs had a significant impact on the visibility and competitiveness of PSE businesses. The entrepreneurs reported that, following the implementation of the catalogs, they were able to increase customer interaction and improve the perception of their products in terms of quality and professionalism. Additionally, the integration of digital marketing strategies allowed the businesses to reach wider audiences, enhancing their presence in the digital marketplace [12].

In conclusion, the development of digital catalogs as part of a community engagement project not only benefited the entrepreneurs, who gained access to effective digital tools for promoting their products, but also provided students with valuable practical experience in the fields of digital marketing and graphic design. This project highlights the importance of collaboration between academia and the community to drive local economic development and the digitalization of small businesses, particularly in vulnerable sectors such as the PSE [13].

2 Methods and Materials

2.1 Methodological Approach

This study was developed using a qualitative and applied approach, focused on creating digital catalogs as a strategic marketing tool for 12 businesses from the popular and solidarity economy (PSE) in the province of Pichincha, Ecuador. The project was carried out by sixth-semester students from the Digital Marketing program at Universidad Indoamérica, who worked closely with local entrepreneurs to develop digital catalogs that accurately reflected their products and brand value. The primary objective of the project was to enhance the visibility and competitiveness of these businesses in the digital environment by creating interactive catalogs that could be used on websites and social media.

2.2 Participants

The project involved the active participation of sixth-semester students who, having completed a previous course on web development in the fifth semester, applied their knowledge of graphic design and digital marketing to create digital catalogs. The 12 selected businesses belonged to various sectors of the PSE, such as artisanal products, processed foods, and agricultural goods, and already had market-ready products with labels, packaging, and professional presentations. These entrepreneurs were selected in coordination with the Prefecture of Pichincha, prioritizing those who already had products in the market but lacked an adequate digital platform for their promotion.

2.3 Ethical Considerations

The ethical standards established in the Declaration of Helsinki [14] were followed for the research. Informed consent agreements were guaranteed with all the entrepreneurs involved in the project, in which, among other elements, the objectives of the study, the voluntary nature of their participation and the confidentiality of data management were made explicit. It was informed that the rights over the contents and materials created will be the property of the entrepreneurs. In addition, the confidentiality of the commercial information provided during the development of the catalogs was respected. The students also received guidance on the ethical handling of product and brand information, ensuring that the project was developed in accordance with the ethical principles established at Universidad Indoamérica.

2.4 Procedure

The development of the project followed several clearly defined stages:

1. Selection of Businesses: The Prefecture of Pichincha, in collaboration with Universidad Indoamérica, identified and selected 12 businesses that met the criteria to participate in the project. These businesses had marketable products but lacked a digital presence or an effective marketing strategy to reach more consumers.
2. Information Gathering and Needs Analysis: The students conducted interviews and visits to the businesses to gather key information about their products, target markets, and marketing needs. Through these interactions, specific strategies were designed for each business, based on the analysis of their products and the creation of differentiated value propositions. This information served as the basis for the design of the digital catalogs.
3. Graphic Design and Visual Content Production: Visual content production was a fundamental part of the process. The students organized photography sessions to capture professional images of the products, which were optimized for inclusion in the digital catalogs. Additionally, graphic elements such as covers, banners, and visually appealing descriptions were designed for each of the products presented. The use of professional editing software like Adobe Photoshop and Illustrator enabled the students to create high-quality digital catalogs [10].

4. Development of Digital Catalogs: Using graphic design tools such as Adobe InDesign, the students developed interactive catalogs that included detailed information about each product, such as descriptions, prices, and availability. These catalogs were designed with a responsive approach to facilitate viewing on mobile devices and integration with digital platforms, such as websites and social media [8]. The catalogs also included direct links to contact forms and purchase buttons.
5. Implementation of Digital Marketing Strategies: To maximize the impact of the catalogs, search engine optimization (SEO) strategies and social media integration were implemented. The students conducted keyword research and optimized the catalog content to improve its search engine ranking. Additionally, the catalogs were integrated into the entrepreneurs' websites, and specific social media campaigns were designed to attract more traffic and generate interest in the products [3].
6. Entrepreneur Training: Once the catalogs were completed, the entrepreneurs received personalized training on how to manage and update their digital catalogs autonomously. These sessions included guidance on how to modify the catalogs based on changes in products, prices, or availability, as well as how to use them effectively in their digital marketing strategies. The training was crucial to ensure the long-term sustainability of the project and the digital independence of the entrepreneurs [11].

2.5 Tools Used

1. Adobe InDesign: It was the main design tool used for the creation of the digital catalogs. Its ability to design interactive and visually appealing catalogs allowed the students to produce high-quality materials, as shown in Fig. 1.

Fig. 1. Images from one of the catalogs designed in Adobe InDesign featuring products from the producers of the popular and solidarity economy.

2. Adobe Photoshop and Adobe Illustrator: Used for editing and optimizing product images, ensuring that the visual content was appealing and suitable for the catalogs, as shown in Fig. 2.
3. Google Analytics and Google Search Console: Tools used to evaluate the performance of the implemented digital marketing strategies and measure the traffic generated through the digital catalogs.
4. Social Media: Platforms such as Facebook and Instagram were used to integrate the digital catalogs and enhance interaction with consumers, implementing specific advertising campaigns.

Fig. 2. Images created with photographic composition and edited using graphic design programs such as Adobe Illustrator and Adobe Photoshop.

2.6 Data Analysis

The analysis of the results was conducted through satisfaction surveys directed at the entrepreneurs, who evaluated the usability, aesthetics, and functionality of the digital catalogs, as well as their impact on the visibility of their products. Additionally, web analysis tools such as Google Analytics were used to measure the traffic and interaction generated by the catalogs, identifying improvements in the online positioning of the products. The success of the project was evaluated in terms of increased product visibility and greater interaction with customers on digital platforms [12].

3 Proposed Model

The proposed model aims to strengthen the digital presence of businesses within the popular and solidarity economy (PSE) through the creation of interactive digital catalogs and the implementation of digital marketing strategies. This approach, developed as part of a community engagement project, is structured around three key pillars: high-quality graphic design, content optimization for digital platforms, and continuous training for the autonomous management of digital tools. Through this methodology, the goal was to provide entrepreneurs with not only a visually appealing solution to showcase their products, but also the skills needed to manage their own digital resources in the long term.

3.1 Model Components

Design of Personalized Digital Catalogs. The first element of the model is the creation of personalized digital catalogs that allow businesses to display their product offerings in a clear, organized, and attractive manner. These catalogs are designed using professional graphic design tools, ensuring visual quality and consistency with each brand's identity. The catalogs were optimized for viewing on various devices, from desktop computers to smartphones, ensuring a smooth and adaptable user experience [6]. Additionally, the catalogs include interactive links that allow customers to navigate through different sections, providing easy access to relevant product information and, in some cases, direct connection to e-commerce platforms.

PDF Product Catalog Design. A WordPress plugin was implemented within the website to generate personalized digital catalogs directly from the product information uploaded to the platform. This plugin connects with WooCommerce, allowing all product information, such as descriptions, images, and prices, to be automatically converted into PDF files. These digital catalogs can be downloaded and provided by entrepreneurs to their customers in both physical and digital formats, offering them an additional sales tool. This functionality not only optimizes the catalog update process but also provides entrepreneurs with a practical solution for sharing their product offerings in accessible and portable formats.

Search Engine Optimization (SEO) and Digital Marketing Strategies. The second component of the model focuses on content optimization for search engines (SEO) and integration with social media to maximize the online visibility of the digital catalogs. The catalogs were designed not only to present products but also to be optimized with relevant keywords to improve their search engine ranking [7]. By linking to social media platforms like Facebook and Instagram, the catalogs leverage these channels to extend product reach and capture the attention of a broader audience. Digital marketing, centered on creating attractive visual content, increases user engagement and enhances consumer interaction, generating greater potential for sales conversion [5].

Training and Sustainability in Digital Management. The third pillar of the proposed model is continuous training for entrepreneurs so they can manage and update their digital catalogs autonomously. After the catalogs were delivered, the students organized training sessions where entrepreneurs were taught how to use editing tools necessary to modify the catalogs as their products or sales strategies changed. This approach not only ensures the long-term sustainability of the project but also gives entrepreneurs the independence needed to adapt to new market conditions or launch new products [4].

Model Impact Evaluation. The impact of this model was evaluated through metrics analysis such as increased online visibility of products and customer interaction with the digital catalogs. Entrepreneurs reported significant improvements in product perception and an increase in customer inquiries after the catalogs were implemented. The websites and social media where the catalogs were shared experienced increased traffic and longer user session times, key indicators of the success of the digital marketing strategies applied. Additionally, satisfaction surveys conducted among the entrepreneurs showed a high acceptance of the model, highlighting the ease of use and effectiveness of the digital catalogs in driving sales [6].

Innovation and Replicability of the Model. This model represents a significant innovation by combining high-quality graphic design with affordable digital marketing strategies, making it especially relevant for popular and solidarity economy businesses, which often lack access to advanced technological resources. The possibility of replicating this approach in other contexts is feasible, as it uses accessible digital tools that can be easily adapted to various sectors. Furthermore, the methodology can be expanded to include new functionalities, such as integrating advanced e-commerce platforms or data analysis to improve business decisions based on consumer behavior [6].

Future Applications of the Model. The proposed model can continue to evolve through the incorporation of emerging technologies such as e-commerce, which would allow entrepreneurs not only to display their products in catalogs but also to sell directly from the same platform. Additionally, linking with digital advertising campaigns on social media can further enhance the impact of digital marketing in promoting PSE products. The integration of new data analysis tools would also allow entrepreneurs to more accurately measure the performance of their catalogs and adjust their strategies to maximize their market effectiveness [5].

4 Discussion

The use of digital catalogs as part of a digital marketing strategy has proven to be an effective tool for improving the visibility and reach of products in businesses within the popular and solidarity economy (PSE). By implementing these catalogs, entrepreneurs were not only able to showcase their products more professionally, but they also optimized their visual presentation to attract and retain more customers in the digital environment. Digital catalogs, when integrated with platforms like WooCommerce, allowed for product information to be kept up-to-date and generated downloadable PDF versions that entrepreneurs could share directly with their customers. This approach facilitated inventory management and improved the flow of information between businesses and consumers.

The use of digital marketing strategies linked to the catalogs also played a key role in the success of this initiative. The integration of search engine optimization (SEO) techniques and promotion through social media significantly increased the online exposure of the products, enabling entrepreneurs to reach wider audiences. Previous research highlights that the implementation of digital tools, such as interactive catalogs, not only enhances consumer perception of product quality but also increases customer trust and interest in the brand, which translates into higher conversion rates [6].

One of the greatest achievements of this project was the training of entrepreneurs in the autonomous management of their digital catalogs. This component of the model not only allowed entrepreneurs to easily update their products but also provided them with long-term independence, as they can now modify their catalogs without relying on third parties. The training enabled entrepreneurs to acquire key skills in digital content management, which is crucial in a constantly evolving market environment. This autonomy is essential for ensuring the sustainability of the implemented digital strategies.

Finally, the results obtained through this model show that the combination of attractive visual design, accessible technology, and well-planned marketing strategies can radically transform how PSE businesses present their products and connect with their customers. The implementation of digital catalogs optimized for mobile devices and synchronized with product management systems, such as WooCommerce, not only improved the user experience but also simplified operational management for entrepreneurs. This methodology can serve as a reference for future applications in other sectors that seek to enhance visibility and competitiveness in the digital environment [5].

5 Conclusions

The implementation of a comprehensive digitalization model, which includes the development of personalized websites and the creation of high-quality graphic content, has proven to be an effective strategy for improving the visibility and competitiveness of businesses in the popular and solidarity economy (PSE) in Pichincha. The adoption of accessible digital tools, such as WordPress, allowed entrepreneurs to establish a professional online presence, facilitating access to new markets and enhancing consumer perception of their products. This approach not only optimized product commercialization but also empowered entrepreneurs to independently manage and update their platforms, increasing their digital autonomy.

Moreover, the collaboration between academia and the community, through the participation of students in the design and development of websites and digital catalogs, highlights the importance of the connection between teaching and community service. This project allowed students to apply theoretical knowledge in a practical context, benefiting both their education and the strengthening of local businesses. In conclusion, digitalization represents a key opportunity for the transformation and growth of PSE businesses, and this model can be replicated and adapted in other regions, promoting digital inclusion and economic development in vulnerable sectors.

Acknowledgments. To the entrepreneurs who participated in the project, the sixth-semester students who worked on the development of the project, the faculty members who supported the process, and the Production Support Directorate of the Prefecture of Pichincha.

References

1. Saiz-Álvarez, J.M., Palma-Ruiz, J.M.: Entrepreneurship in the solidarity economy: a valuation of models based on the quadruple helix and civil society, pp. 33–50 (2019). https://doi.org/10.1007/978-3-030-11542-5_4
2. Borja-Galeas, C., Arias-Flores, H., Piedra, M.: Development of a model for the construction of corporate manuals with QR codes, pp. 685–692 (2024). https://doi.org/10.1007/978-981-99-0333-7_50
3. Barbosa, B., Saura, J.R., Bennett, D.: How do entrepreneurs perform digital marketing across the customer journey? A review and discussion of the main uses. J. Technol. Transf. **49**(1), 69–103 (2024). https://doi.org/10.1007/s10961-022-09978-2
4. Alford, P., Page, S.J.: Marketing technology for adoption by small business. Serv. Ind. J. **35**(11–12), 655–669 (2015). https://doi.org/10.1080/02642069.2015.1062884
5. Leeflang, P.S.H., Verhoef, P.C., Dahlstrom, P., Freundt, T.: Challenges and solutions for marketing in a digital era. Eur. Manag. J. **32**(1), 1–12 (2014). https://doi.org/10.1016/j.emj.2013.12.001

6. Hollebeek, L.D., Macky, K.: Digital content marketing's role in fostering consumer engagement, trust, and value: framework, fundamental propositions, and implications. J. Interact. Mark. **45**, 27–41 (2019). https://doi.org/10.1016/j.intmar.2018.07.003

7. Kannan, P.K., "Alice" Li, H.: Digital marketing: a framework, review and research agenda. Int. J. Res. Mark. **34**(1), 22–45 (2017). https://doi.org/10.1016/j.ijresmar.2016.11.006

8. Wilk, V., Soutar, G.N., Harrigan, P.: Online brand advocacy and brand loyalty: a reciprocal relationship? Asia Pacific J. Mark. Logist. **33**(10), 1977–1993 (2021). https://doi.org/10.1108/APJML-05-2020-0303

9. Borja-Galeas, C., Arias-Flores, H.: Participatory design as an audiovisual strategy in brand manuals, pp. 811–817 (2023). https://doi.org/10.1007/978-981-99-3091-3_66

10. Loewenstein, G.: Out of control: visceral influences on behavior. Organ. Behav. Hum. Decis. Process. **65**(3), 272–292 (1996). https://doi.org/10.1006/obhd.1996.0028

11. Rosenbaum, M.S., Otalora, M.L., Ramírez, G.C.: How to create a realistic customer journey map. Bus. Horiz. **60**(1), 143–150 (2017). https://doi.org/10.1016/j.bushor.2016.09.010

12. Ariely, D., Berns, G.S.: Neuromarketing: the hope and hype of neuroimaging in business. Nat. Rev. Neurosci. **11**(4), 284–292 (2010). https://doi.org/10.1038/nrn2795

13. Chatterjee, S., Kumar Kar, A.: Why do small and medium enterprises use social media marketing and what is the impact: empirical insights from India. Int. J. Inf. Manage. **53**, 102103 (2020). https://doi.org/10.1016/j.ijinfomgt.2020.102103

14. Carlson, R.V., Boyd, K.M., Webb, D.J.: The revision of the declaration of Helsinki: past, present and future. Br. J. Clin. Pharmacol. **57**(6), 695–713 (2004)

Development of Websites as an Academic Integrative Project to Strengthen Businesses in the Popular and Solidarity Economy

Carlos Borja-Galeas[1]([✉]) [iD], Hugo Arias-Flores[2] [iD], Ivanna Sanchez[3] [iD],
Andrés Palacio-Fierro[4] [iD], and Viviana Cajas[5] [iD]

[1] Carrera de Marketing Digital, Facultad de Ciencias Económicas, Administrativas y Negocios, Universidad Indoamérica, 170103 Quito, Ecuador
`carlosborja@uti.edu.ec`
[2] Centro de Investigación de Ciencias Humanas y de la Educación (CICHE), Universidad Indoamérica, 170103 Quito, Ecuador
[3] Carrera de Administración de Empresas, Facultad de Ciencias Económicas, Administrativas y Negocios, Universidad Indoamérica, 170103 Quito, Ecuador
[4] Universidad Internacional del Ecuador (UIDE), 170595 Quito, Ecuador
[5] UISEK Business and Digital School, Universidad Internacional SEK, Quito, Ecuador

Abstract. This article explores the development of websites as an academic integrative project aimed at strengthening businesses within the popular and solidarity economy (EPS) in the province of Pichincha, Ecuador. Fifth-semester students from the Digital Marketing program at Universidad Indoamérica, as part of their integrative project, worked on creating customized websites for 12 local businesses that already had marketable products, including labels, packaging, and other presentation tools. Using the WordPress platform, the students developed websites tailored to the specific needs of each business, with the goal of improving their digital presence, facilitating access to broader markets, and increasing the competitiveness of their products and services. In addition to the technical development, graphic design elements such as professional product photography and promotional videos were integrated, along with digital marketing strategies that included search engine optimization and social media integration. The results indicate that the creation of these customized websites significantly increased the online visibility of the businesses and enhanced consumer perception of professionalism and trust. This study highlights the importance of applied academic projects as tools for community engagement and local economic development in vulnerable sectors.

Keywords: Integrative project · web design · WordPress · popular and solidarity economy · digital marketing · entrepreneurship

1 Introduction

The popular and solidarity economy (EPS) has been a fundamental model for the economic development of vulnerable sectors in Latin America, particularly in Ecuador, where it has promoted the creation of businesses based on principles of cooperation and

F. F.-H Nah and K. L. Siau (Eds.): HCII 2025, LNCS 16343, pp. 193–203, 2026.
https://doi.org/10.1007/978-3-032-13167-6_14

sustainability [1]. However, despite its potential to generate employment and improve living conditions, EPS entrepreneurs face numerous challenges in a globalized market, where digitalization plays a key role in competitiveness [2]. The lack of adequate technological tools limits these businesses' access to new markets, restricting their growth potential [3].

Nowadays, having an effective digital presence is essential for small businesses to survive and thrive in an increasingly competitive economic environment. Various studies have shown that micro and small enterprises that adopt digital platforms, such as websites, significantly improve their visibility and relationship with customers, increasing their chances of success [4]. In this sense, the creation of websites for EPS businesses not only improves their access to broader markets but also provides them with an indispensable tool to implement digital marketing strategies tailored to their needs.

The community engagement project between Universidad Indoamérica and local EPS entrepreneurs, developed as part of the integrative project for fifth-semester students of the Digital Marketing program, had the primary objective of creating personalized websites for 12 businesses. These businesses already had marketable products, with labels, packaging, and other elements that needed to be integrated into a digital strategy to improve their competitiveness [2, 5]. The development of these websites provided students with an opportunity to apply their classroom knowledge, while the entrepreneurs benefited from a digital tool designed to increase their market presence [6].

The choice of WordPress as the platform for website development was key due to its flexibility and ease of use, as presented in Table 1. WordPress has been widely adopted by small and medium-sized enterprises as an accessible tool that does not require extensive technical knowledge, allowing entrepreneurs to manage their websites independently after receiving appropriate training [7]. This approach not only gave them the ability to update their products and content but also helped them save on future web maintenance costs.

In addition to the technical development, the students worked on content optimization and the integration of digital marketing strategies, such as search engine optimization (SEO) and social media integration, which are crucial for improving product visibility online and increasing customer engagement [8]. Online visibility is essential for EPS businesses, which generally lack the resources to compete with larger companies through traditional marketing channels.

Another fundamental component of this project was graphic design, which included the creation of high-quality visual content, such as product photography and promotional videos. Research has shown that attractive visual content not only enhances consumers' perception of products but also increases conversion rates on digital commerce platforms [9]. The inclusion of professional images and videos on the websites helped build customer trust in EPS products, reflecting a higher level of professionalism.

Finally, entrepreneur training was a key aspect to ensure the long-term sustainability of the websites. After the students completed the website development, training sessions were conducted to teach the entrepreneurs how to manage and update their platforms independently. This is crucial, as it allows entrepreneurs to maintain their digital presence without constantly relying on external services, giving them greater autonomy and control over their digital marketing strategies [10].

Table 1. Comparison summarizing the advantages of WordPress over other similar platforms.

Criteria	WordPress	Wix	Shopify	Joomla	Webflow
Flexibility and Customization	★★★★★ Open source, thousands of plugins and themes.	★★ Limited to templates and proprietary tools.	★★★ Focused solely on eCommerce, moderate customization.	★★★★ Flexible but with a steep learning curve.	★★★★ Great control over design, but fewer extensions.
Ease of Use	★★★ Intuitive interface, but requires initial learning.	★★★★★ Visual drag-and-drop editor.	★★★★ Easy for online stores, but limited outside that scope.	★★ More complex than WordPress.	★★★ Powerful visual editor, but with a learning curve.
Costs	★★★★ Free platform, but requires hosting and optional plugins.	★★ Paid plans with hosting included, less control.	★★ Monthly fees and sales commissions.	★★★ Free, but with hosting and development costs.	★★ More expensive plans than WordPress.
SEO and Performance	★★★★★ Advanced plugins like Yoast and Rank Math.	★★ Less control over advanced SEO.	★★★ Optimized for eCommerce, but less flexible.	★★★ Good SEO, but with fewer tools.	★★★★★ Advanced control over SEO and speed.
Scalability and Features	★★★★★ Adapts to blogs, eCommerce, forums, and more.	★★ Ideal for small sites, less scalable.	★★★★ Perfect for eCommerce, but not for other types of sites.	★★★ Powerful, but with fewer extensions.	★★★★ Scalable, but more design-focused.
Community and Support	★★★★★ Large community, support forums, and documentation.	★★ Official technical support, but smaller community.	★★★ Specialized support for eCommerce.	★★★ Active technical community, but smaller.	★★★ Growing community.

In conclusion, the creation of websites as part of the academic integrative project not only provided students with valuable practical experience in a real-world context but also strengthened EPS businesses by equipping them with essential digital tools for growth in a digitalized economic environment. The collaboration between academia and the community, as demonstrated by this project, is essential for promoting local economic development and ensuring that small entrepreneurs can compete on equal terms in the digital marketplace [11].

2 Methods and Materials

2.1 Methodological Approach

This study adopted a qualitative and applied approach, focusing on the creation of websites for 12 businesses within the popular and solidarity economy (EPS) in the province of Pichincha, Ecuador. The project was developed as part of the integrative project for fifth-semester students in the Digital Marketing program at Universidad Indoamérica, which allowed students to apply their academic knowledge in a practical context. The main goal was to equip entrepreneurs with digital tools to improve their online visibility and, in turn, increase their competitiveness in the market.

2.2 Participants

The project involved fifth-semester students who developed websites for the 12 selected businesses. These businesses were identified and chosen in collaboration with the Prefecture of Pichincha, prioritizing those that already had marketable products, including labels, packaging, and presentation materials, and that required a digital strategy to improve their market reach. The businesses represented various sectors, including artisanal products, processed foods, and consumer goods.

2.3 Ethical Considerations

The research adhered to the ethical standards set forth in the Declaration of Helsinki [12]. Informed consent was obtained from all entrepreneurs participating in the project, clearly outlining the study's objectives, the voluntary nature of their involvement, and the confidentiality of data management. All participants, including both entrepreneurs and students, signed informed consent agreements that guaranteed the appropriate use of the provided information and respect for the intellectual property of the products and content generated. Additionally, the entrepreneurs received full ownership of the websites and visual content produced, along with the necessary training to manage and update their digital platforms. The information collected during the project was handled confidentially, respecting the privacy of the businesses' commercial data.

2.4 Procedure

The project development followed a sequence of clearly defined stages:

- **Selection of Businesses:** Through a call organized by the Prefecture, 12 EPS businesses that already had market-ready products were selected. These businesses lacked an established digital presence and were chosen based on their growth potential through digital marketing strategies.
- **Information Gathering:** The students conducted interviews and meetings with the entrepreneurs to collect key information about their products, target audiences, brand values, and specific needs. Tools such as the Business Model Canvas were used to define the strategic aspects of each business, including value propositions, distribution channels, and customer segments [3].
- **Website Development:** Using WordPress as a content management system (CMS), the students designed and developed customized websites for each business, as shown in Fig. 1. WordPress was chosen for its flexibility and ease of use, allowing the students to create functional websites that could be easily managed by the entrepreneurs after receiving the appropriate training [7].

- **Graphic Design and Visual Content Production:** In addition to the technical development of the websites, the students integrated graphic design elements, including product photography sessions and the production of promotional videos, as shown in Fig. 2. The visual content was optimized for use on both websites and social media to enhance the presentation and appeal of the products, contributing to an improved perception of professionalism and quality [8].
- **Search Engine Optimization (SEO):** The students also implemented SEO strategies to improve the websites' rankings in search engine results, increasing the visibility of the products. Keyword research was conducted, and the site content was optimized to improve online performance.
- **Entrepreneur Training:** After the websites were delivered, training sessions were conducted to teach the entrepreneurs how to manage and update their websites independently. The training included basic use of WordPress, product updates, and management of visual and textual content [10].

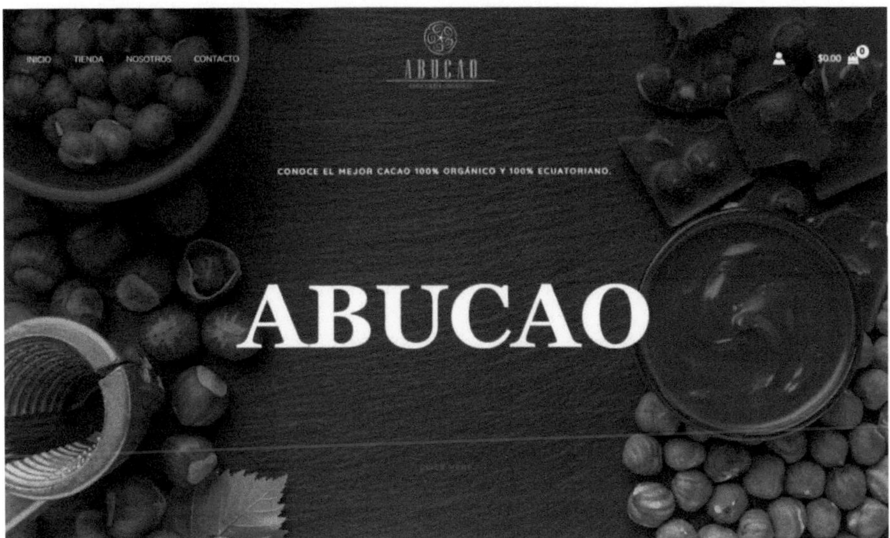

Fig. 1. Image of a website designed by the students according to the type of business.

Fig. 2. Frame from a video produced as part of the presentation for an artisanal beer.

2.5 Tools Used

- **WordPress:** As the web development platform, WordPress was used for its user-friendly interface and flexibility. This allowed the students to create fully functional websites tailored to each entrepreneur's needs, enabling them to manage and update content without advanced technical knowledge.
- **DSLR Cameras and image/video editing software:** Students used professional photography equipment and software to create visual content, such as product photos and promotional videos. These tools were essential for improving product presentation online and creating appealing content for consumers [9].
- **Google Analytics and SEO Tools:** Tracking and analysis tools, such as Google Analytics, were implemented to measure website traffic and evaluate the performance of the SEO strategies.

2.6 Data Analysis

The analysis included an evaluation of the websites by the entrepreneurs and end users. Satisfaction surveys were used to measure the entrepreneurs' perceptions of the usability and effectiveness of the websites, as well as the quality of visual content and the integration of digital marketing strategies. Additionally, project instructors conducted technical evaluations using a rubric that measured the usability, functionality, and design of the developed websites [11].

3 Proposed Model

The proposed model for improving the competitiveness and visibility of businesses within the popular and solidarity economy (EPS) is based on three fundamental pillars: custom web development, comprehensive graphic design, and autonomous training for digital management. This model was implemented and validated as part of the integrative project for fifth-semester students in the Digital Marketing program at Universidad Indoamérica, who created websites for 12 local businesses in the province of Pichincha. The model not only includes the creation of a functional digital platform but also the training of entrepreneurs so they can independently manage their online presence.

3.1 Model Components

1. Custom Web Development

     The first component of the model focuses on creating custom websites using WordPress as the content management system (CMS). WordPress was chosen for its flexibility and ease of use, allowing entrepreneurs to manage their websites independently after receiving the necessary training, without relying on external services [7]. The development process includes:

   - *Information Gathering:* The students conducted initial interviews with the entrepreneurs to gather key business data, such as value propositions, the products they sell, and their target audience, using tools such as the Business Model Canvas [3].
   - *Tailored Web Design:* Based on the information gathered, the students designed custom websites that reflect each business's visual and commercial identity. The sites include product galleries, contact forms, social media links, and, in some cases, e- commerce functionalities for direct product sales.
   - *Mobile Optimization:* All websites were designed with a responsive approach, ensuring proper viewing and functionality on mobile devices an essential feature to attract and retain users in the digital age.

2. Comprehensive Graphic Design

     The second key component of the model is the integration of high-quality visual content into the websites. This includes product photography, graphic design, and promotional videos, which significantly improve the business presentation and consumer perception [9]. The students were responsible for:

   - *Product Photography:* The entrepreneurs participated in photography sessions organized by the students, where professional images of the products were captured and optimized for inclusion on the websites.
   - *Video Production:* In some cases, promotional videos were produced to highlight the business values, the artisanal production process, and product quality, thus increasing the visual appeal and customer trust [8].
   - *Digital Catalogs:* Although digital catalogs are the focus of another article, some websites integrated this tool as a visual supplement for presenting products and facilitating inventory navigation.

3. Digital Management Training

The third pillar of the model is the training of entrepreneurs to manage their websites independently. Since WordPress is a user-friendly platform, the students trained the entrepreneurs in basic site administration tasks, such as:

- *Product Updates:* Entrepreneurs were taught how to upload new product images, modify descriptions, and adjust prices.
- *Content Management:* Entrepreneurs learned how to update the visual and textual content of their websites, allowing them to keep their platforms current and relevant to customers.
- *Basic SEO and Social Media*: As part of the training, the students instructed entrepreneurs on basic search engine optimization (SEO) and linking their websites to social media, maximizing their reach in the digital marketplace [10].

3.2 Model Evaluation

The model's impact was evaluated through satisfaction surveys administered to the entrepreneurs, who reported a significant improvement in the visibility of their products and an enhanced perception of professionalism in their businesses. Additionally, the instructors evaluated the websites in terms of usability, functionality, and design, using a predefined rubric that measured the technical quality of the development [11]. The results indicated that the model's implementation not only improved the competitiveness of the businesses but also strengthened the entrepreneurs' ability to manage their businesses in the digital environment.

3.3 Innovation and Sustainability

The main innovation of this model lies in its comprehensive approach, combining web development, visual content production, and entrepreneur training to ensure the long-term sustainability of the digital tools created. Furthermore, this model fosters collaboration between students and the community, providing practical experience for the former and direct benefits for the latter [13]. This academic engagement not only contributes to the development of the students but also reinforces the university's social commitment to local entrepreneurs.

3.4 Future Applications

This model can be replicated and adapted to other communities or regions, especially those where businesses lack sufficient resources to implement complex digital solutions. The integration of accessible technologies like WordPress and digital training allows the model to be scalable and flexible, facilitating digital inclusion and economic growth in the most vulnerable sectors [14].

4   Discussion

The results obtained in this project demonstrate that the digitalization of businesses within the popular and solidarity economy (EPS), through the creation of personalized websites and the integration of high-quality graphic content, significantly improves the visibility and competitiveness of these businesses in the digital marketplace. By providing entrepreneurs with tools such as well-designed websites, digital catalogs, and visual marketing strategies, the products and services offered reached a broader audience, increasing commercialization opportunities. This is consistent with previous studies that have highlighted the importance of digitalization and the use of accessible platforms, like WordPress, to facilitate technology adoption by small businesses with limited resources [4, 7].

Moreover, the continuous training provided to the entrepreneurs was a crucial component to ensure the long-term sustainability of the digital platforms. By empowering business owners to manage and update their websites autonomously, they gained technological independence, enhancing their ability to adapt in an ever-evolving market environment. These findings emphasize the importance of combining accessible digital tools with the development of technical skills among entrepreneurs, which aligns with research highlighting the need to provide technical support and training to vulnerable sectors to close the digital divide [13, 14].

5   Conclusions

The development of websites as part of the academic integrative project has proven to be an effective strategy for improving the visibility and competitiveness of businesses within the popular and solidarity economy (EPS). The results of this project indicate that the implementation of digital platforms not only allowed entrepreneurs to increase their online presence but also improved the perception of professionalism of their businesses. This finding is consistent with previous studies that emphasize the importance of digitalization in small businesses, particularly in vulnerable sectors where access to technology and digital marketing tools can make the difference between subsistence and growth [4]. The creation of personalized websites enabled entrepreneurs to present their marketable products more attractively, and the use of WordPress proved to be an accessible, adaptable, and sustainable solution for local businesses [7].

Another key aspect was the integration of graphic design and high-quality visual content into the websites, which had a positive impact on consumers' perception of the products. The inclusion of professional photography and promotional videos not only enhanced the aesthetics of the websites but also increased customer trust and conversion potential, aligning with research that highlights the value of visual content in user experience [8, 9]. Furthermore, the training provided to entrepreneurs to manage and update their websites ensured the long-term sustainability of the project, granting business owners greater digital autonomy. This comprehensive approach, which combines web development, digital marketing, and technical training, underscores the value of collaboration between academia and the community in digital transformation projects, offering a replicable framework for other regions and sectors with similar characteristics [14].

Acknowledgments. To the entrepreneurs who participated in the project, the sixth-semester students who worked on the development of the project, the faculty members who supported the process, and the Production Support Directorate of the Prefecture of Pichincha.

References

1. Saiz-Álvarez, J.M., Palma-Ruiz, J.M.: Entrepreneurship in the solidarity economy: a valuation of models based on the quadruple helix and civil society. In: Ratten, V., Jones, P., Braga, V., Marques, C.S. (eds.) Subsistence Entrepreneurship. Contributions to Management Science, pp. 33–50. Springer, Cham (2019). https://doi.org/10.1007/978-3-030-11542-5_4

2. Borja-Galeas, C., Arias-Flores, H.: Participatory design as an audiovisual strategy in brand manuals. In: Yang, XS., Sherratt, R.S., Dey, N., Joshi, A. (eds.) Proceedings of Eighth International Congress on Information and Communication Technology. ICICT 2023. Lecture Notes in Networks and Systems, vol. 694, pp. 811–817. Springer, Singapore (2023). https://doi.org/10.1007/978-981-99-3091-3_66

3. Morales-Urrutia, X., Naranjo-Gaibor, A., Espinoza-Guano, M., Morales-Urrutia, D., Simbaña-Taipe, L.: A retrospective and prospective analysis of social entrepreneurship: popular and solidarity economy in ecuador. In: Botto-Tobar, M., Cruz, H., Díaz Cadena, A. (eds.) Artificial Intelligence, Computer and Software Engineering Advances. CIT 2020. Advances in Intelligent Systems and Computing, vol. 1327, pp. 178–189. Springer, Cham (2021). https://doi.org/10.1007/978-3-030-68083-1_14

4. Barbosa, B., Saura, J.R., Bennett, D.: How do entrepreneurs perform digital marketing across the customer journey? A review and discussion of the main uses. J. Technol. Transf. **49**(1), 69–103 (2024). https://doi.org/10.1007/s10961-022-09978-2

5. Borja-Galeas, C., Arias-Flores, H., Piedra, M.: Development of a model for the construction of corporate manuals with QR codes. In: Reis, J.L., Del Rio Araujo, M., Reis, L.P., dos Santos, J.P.M. (eds.) Marketing and Smart Technologies. ICMarkTech 2022. Smart Innovation, Systems and Technologies, vol. 344, pp. 685–692. Springer, Singapore (2024). https://doi.org/10.1007/978-981-99-0333-7_50

6. Xie, C., Zhu, Y., Zhao, Q.: How digital business penetration influences farmers' sense of economic gain: the role of farmers' entrepreneurial orientation and market responsiveness. IEEE Access **8**, 187744187753 (2020). https://doi.org/10.1109/ACCESS.2020.3031110

7. Kumar, A., Kumar, A., Hashmi, H., Khan, S.A.: WordPress: a multi-functional content management system. In: Proceedings of the 2021 10th International Conference on System Modeling & Advancement in Research Trends (SMART), pp. 158–161, December 2021. https://doi.org/10.1109/SMART52563.2021.9675311

8. Wilk, V., Soutar, G.N., Harrigan, P.: Online brand advocacy and brand loyalty: a reciprocal relationship? Asia Pacific J. Mark. Logist. **33**(10), 1977–1993 (2021). https://doi.org/10.1108/APJML-05-2020-0303

9. Loewenstein, G.: Out of control: visceral influences on behavior. Organ. Behav. Hum. Decis. Process. **65**(3), 272–292 (1996). https://doi.org/10.1006/obhd.1996.0028

10. Rosenbaum, M.S., Otalora, M.L., Ramírez, G.C.: How to create a realistic customer journey map. Bus. Horiz. **60**(1), 143–150 (2017). https://doi.org/10.1016/j.bushor.2016.09.010

11. Ariely, D., Berns, G.S.: Neuromarketing: the hope and hype of neuroimaging in business. Nat. Rev. Neurosci. **11**(4), 284–292 (2010). https://doi.org/10.1038/nrn2795

12. Carlson, R.V., Boyd, K.M., Webb, D.J.: The revision of the Declaration of Helsinki: past, present and future. Br. J. Clin. Pharmacol. **57**(6), 695–713 (2004)

13. Leal Filho, W., Shiel, C., Paco, A.: Implementing and operationalising integrative approaches to sustainability in higher education: the role of project-oriented learning. J. Clean. Prod. **133**, 126–135 (2016). https://doi.org/10.1016/j.jclepro.2016.05.079
14. Chatterjee, S., Kumar Kar, A.: Why do small and medium enterprises use social media marketing and what is the impact: empirical insights from India. Int. J. Inf. Manage. **53**, 102103 (2020). https://doi.org/10.1016/j.ijinfomgt.2020.102103

An Exploratory Study on the Effects of Dynamic Pricing on Customers' Online Purchase Journeys

Samuel Elharrar, Sylvain Senecal, Constantinos K. Coursaris[✉], and Pierre-Majorique Léger

HEC Montréal, Montréal, QC H3T 2A7, Canada
{samuel.elharrar,sylvain.senecal,constantinos.coursaris,
pierre-majorique.leger}@hec.ca

Abstract. Dynamic pricing is now a standard practice in digital commerce, yet the impact of unannounced price reductions on customer experience remains underexplored. While most research has focused on price increases and perceived unfairness, this study investigates how price reductions, introduced dynamically during online journeys without explicit communication, shape users' emotional, cognitive, and behavioural responses. Using a mixed-methods design, 22 participants completed tasks on a real telecommunications website while interacting with a multi-step purchase process that included a subtle mid-journey price reduction. Participants were categorized post hoc based on whether they noticed the price change. Their responses were captured through physiological data, self-reported measures, behavioural tracking, and post-task interviews. While both groups completed the purchase, their experiences diverged. Participants who became aware of the price drop reported increased cognitive strain, fairness concerns, and reduced confidence. In contrast, unaware participants experienced a smoother, less effortful journey with more stable emotional states. These findings challenge the assumption that lower prices universally enhance experience. Instead, they highlight the moderating role of awareness in shaping user perception and engagement. The study reframes dynamic pricing as a touchpoint within user experience design rather than a purely economic lever. It contributes to the literature on pricing fairness, emotional engagement in digital services, and consumer behaviour under algorithmic pricing. Practically, it offers actionable insights for designing dynamic pricing strategies that account for transparency, awareness, and emotional impact.

Keywords: Dynamic Pricing · Price Reduction · Price Fairness Perception · Customer Journey · Decision-Making · Consumer Behaviour · User Experience · Digital Service Design

1 Introduction

1.1 Background and Research Context

Dynamic pricing has become a standard feature of today's digital economy. Enabled by real-time consumer data and machine learning, platforms can now adjust prices instantly based on individual behaviour, market demand, and contextual signals [1, 2]. While once

© The Author(s), under exclusive license to Springer Nature Switzerland AG 2026
F. F.-H Nah and K. L. Siau (Eds.): HCII 2025, LNCS 16343, pp. 204–223, 2026.
https://doi.org/10.1007/978-3-032-13167-6_15

reserved for sectors like travel and hospitality, these pricing models are now embedded across a range of industries, including online retail, streaming, and telecommunications [3].

Simultaneously, consumers have developed greater expectations around pricing transparency and fairness. Pricing is no longer just a number; it's a cue that shapes trust and brand perception [4, 5]. Research shows that price changes impact not only purchasing decisions but also emotional and cognitive processing [6]. Consumers actively interpret and react to price changes, especially when they appear unclear or hidden [7].

As online services become more experience-driven, pricing plays a growing role in the overall user journey. Companies compete not just on product features but on how pricing is presented [8, 9]. In digital interfaces, price isn't static; it evolves with interaction flow, shaped by page layout, timing, and interface cues [10]. Even subtle differences in when and how prices are revealed can influence attention, emotional response, and fairness perception [11]. Dynamic pricing often unfolds invisibly during a digital experience, with contextual or behavioural triggers adjusting prices mid-journey, frequently without the user's awareness. These shifts raise important UX questions around decision-making, emotional engagement, and perceived value.

1.2 Research Gap

Existing research on dynamic pricing has largely focused on price increases and their impact on consumer perceptions of fairness, trust, and satisfaction. Studies have shown that when prices rise unexpectedly or appear personalized, consumers are more likely to view the pricing as exploitative or manipulative, which can damage brand trust and reduce purchase intentions [6, 7, 12, 13]. This has led to a growing body of literature examining algorithmic price discrimination, perceived unfairness, and consumer resistance in dynamic pricing environments [14, 15].

While much of the existing literature has focused on price increases and their effect on fairness perceptions and consumer trust, the effects of price reductions within dynamic pricing ecosystems remain underexplored [13, 16]. Although price drops are often assumed to benefit user experience, little is known about how they are processed when they occur dynamically and without explicit communication during the purchasing process. The extent to which users notice these reductions is still uncertain, as is how their subtle and unannounced presence can influence emotional responses, perceived value, and decision-making.

2 Research Question and Study Objectives

This research explores how unannounced, dynamic price reductions affect consumer behaviour and user experience during online purchases. Rather than treating pricing as a static element, the study considers it as an embedded touchpoint, one that influences emotional engagement, perception of fairness, and trust.

Using a multi-method approach that includes physiological measures, self-reports, behavioural tracking, and interviews, this research evaluates the role of user awareness. Do users who detect the price reduction respond differently from those who do not? What does this imply for decision-making confidence and final purchase choices? Hence, this research aimed to answer the following question:

RQ – What are the effects of price reduction tactics in online dynamic pricing on consumer purchase decisions?

By investigating this question through a UX lens, the study uncovers how dynamic pricing mechanisms shape perception, emotion, and behaviour in real time.

2.1 Key Contributions

This research offers theoretical contributions and practical implications. From a theoretical standpoint, it contributes to the literature on dynamic pricing by shifting the focus away from commonly studied price increases and toward the underexplored area of price reductions [13, 16]. It advances understanding of how these reductions are perceived within the flow of a customer journey, especially in the context where they occur without explicit user awareness. By integrating physiological, behavioural, and qualitative data, the study advances multi-method approaches in UX research and demonstrates the value of capturing both lived and perceived user experience [8, 9]. The findings offer insights into the role of user awareness in pricing perception, suggesting that the emotional and behavioural effects of dynamic pricing cannot be fully understood without considering whether or not users detect the change [5, 17].

From a practical standpoint, the results offer actionable guidance for designers, marketers, and digital strategists involved with dynamic pricing models. They emphasize the significance of timing, transparency, and emotional impact when presenting price changes [18]. Subtle reductions that go unnoticed may still influence decisions and user experiences, but the effects vary based on awareness. These insights can inform the design of pricing strategies that balance optimization with user trust [4, 15]. Viewing pricing as a component of the customer experience rather than merely a transactional variable allows organizations to better align their digital pricing strategies with user expectations and behaviours.

3 Related Work

3.1 Price Fixation and Consumer Expectations

Consumer price evaluations are anchored by internal and external reference prices, which act as benchmarks against which new prices are judged [19, 20]. Internal reference prices (IRPs) are developed through personal experience, while external reference prices (ERPs) are drawn from contextual cues such as competing offers, past promotions, or interface prompts [21]. These mental anchors play a foundational role in shaping price perceptions and behavioural thresholds.

Digital environments intensify the role of pricing as a visual and cognitive stimulus. Techniques like "starting at" messaging, limited-time offers, and triptych presentations (e.g., "good–better–best") manipulate ERPs and direct user attention [22, 23]. Anchoring effects are pronounced in interface design, where the first visible price can influence judgments, even if that anchor is arbitrary [24]. Research shows that such framing strategies influence emotional engagement and value assessments at early decision stages [25], setting the tone for the rest of the user journey.

3.2 Price Discrimination and Fairness Perception

Dynamic pricing frequently involves price discrimination, charging different prices to different consumers for the same product based on behavioural, contextual, or demographic data [2]. This can take the form of personalized offers (first-degree), tiered plans (second-degree), or group-based segmentation (third-degree) [26, 27]. These strategies allow firms to extract maximum willingness to pay and have become common in industries such as travel, e-commerce, and telecommunications.

Despite their efficiency, these tactics raise fairness concerns, especially when pricing differences are not transparent or appear arbitrary [28]. Perceived fairness hinges not just on the price paid, but on comparisons to others and on whether users believe pricing differences are justified [5, 6]. Studies have shown that when users perceive a violation of fairness norms, especially in environments where personal data drives pricing, they often react negatively by withdrawing, switching brands, or vocalizing dissatisfaction [7, 29]. These effects are amplified in digital contexts where transparency is limited and interface design conceals pricing logic.

The literature has heavily focused on consumer backlash to price increases, with less attention given to how price reductions are processed. Although often presumed to improve customer satisfaction, reductions that occur dynamically and without user awareness may also trigger fairness concerns or diminish perceived value [13, 16]. This asymmetry in the literature leaves open questions about whether price drops are experienced as rewards, anomalies, or signals of unreliability.

3.3 Awareness and Emotional Response

Consumer awareness of pricing strategies plays a critical role in moderating emotional and behavioural responses. Transparency has been shown to improve acceptance of dynamic pricing, especially when accompanied by a clear rationale [30, 31]. In contrast, opaque or hidden pricing logic can provoke suspicion, even if the final price benefits the user.

Interestingly, some research suggests that a lack of awareness may simplify decision-making by reducing cognitive effort [32], while awareness, particularly mid-task, may reintroduce deliberation, emotional conflict, or doubt [33]. In practice, many digital pricing changes occur during checkout steps or location validation, which users may overlook or misattribute to design noise.

Few studies, however, have empirically examined how awareness unfolds in real-time or how it interacts with emotional states during live decision-making. Most rely on post-task surveys or simulated vignettes. The emotional texture of such experiences, particularly how users feel and act upon noticing or not noticing a change, is rarely captured through physiological measures. As such, the literature lacks a multimodal perspective on how price interventions are lived, interpreted, and integrated into digital purchase journeys.

3.4 Dynamic Pricing as a UX Touchpoint

Recent work in digital service design has emphasized that price should not be viewed solely as a transactional variable, but rather as a design component that shapes trust, perceived control, and brand perception [8, 9]. In sectors like telecommunications, where offerings are complex and comparisons are multi-layered, pricing plays an integral role in structuring the user journey and influencing long-term customer relationships.

This reframing positions dynamic pricing as a UX-sensitive interaction, subject to the same principles of emotional design and cognitive load management as other interface elements. Studies have called for customer-centric pricing models that balance optimization with transparency and fairness [18]. Yet few address the moment-to-moment emotional and cognitive fluctuations users experience when confronted with subtle pricing shifts. Even fewer isolate the role of awareness, a factor this study treats as both a perceptual variable and a moderator of trust and confidence.

These insights are especially relevant to the HCI community, which is increasingly engaged in the ethics of personalization, algorithmic transparency, and behavioural nudging. Dynamic pricing systems, when experienced without clarity, can act as disruptive interventions that alter user engagement in unintended ways. Understanding how users respond emotionally and behaviorally, both when they detect a change and when they do not, is key to designing pricing strategies that are both effective and experientially sound.

4 Method

4.1 Study Design

This study employed a mixed-method experimental protocol to investigate how unannounced price reductions influence users' emotional and behavioural responses during a digital purchase journey. The design simulated a realistic e-commerce interaction within the telecommunications sector by having participants complete structured tasks on an authentic telecom website in a controlled lab environment (Fig. 1).

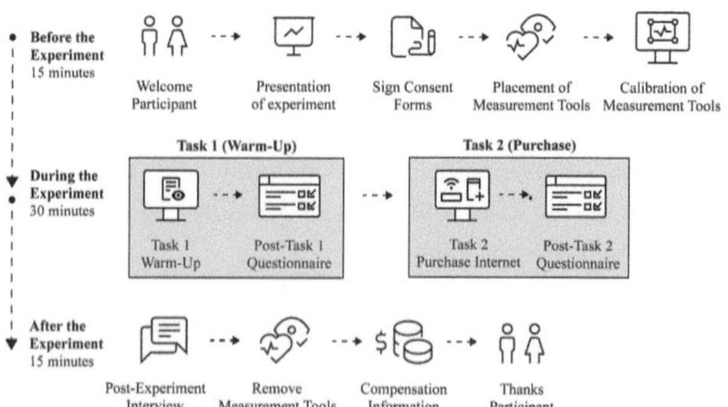

Fig. 1. Visual Representation of the Experimental Design.

A key manipulation was introduced mid-journey: after users selected an internet plan and submitted their address, the prices of two out of three available plans were quietly reduced. No visual indicator or message communicated the change, emulating a common real-world dynamic pricing tactic. This manipulation created two naturally occurring user conditions: those who noticed the price drop and those who did not, allowing for a comparative analysis of user reactions across awareness levels.

The structure of the study was designed to mirror a typical online subscription experience. Task 1 allowed participants to explore the website freely and become familiar with the interface. In Task 2, participants selected an internet plan based on their needs. This is where the critical manipulation occurred: after submitting their address, they were shown the same plan layout, but with reduced prices for two of the three plans. Importantly, the visual presentation remained identical, ensuring the change could go unnoticed unless participants made a mental comparison (Fig. 2).

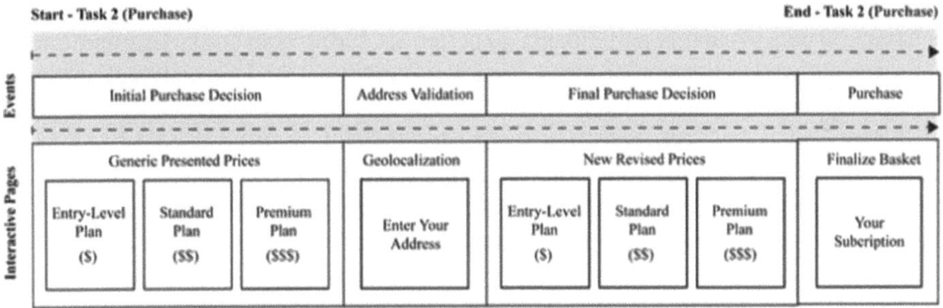

Fig. 2. Sequential Representation of Task 2.

4.2 Study Stimulus and Tasks

The study stimulus consisted of real interface elements from an active Canadian telecommunications website. Hence, its structure and commercial logic provided an ecologically valid environment for simulating an online subscription journey. Participants navigated this live website during the tasks, which ensured ecological validity and realistic decision-making conditions.

Two tasks were developed to reflect a typical customer journey. The first task, referred to as the familiarization task, allowed participants to explore the site freely without a purchase objective. This phase served to reduce novelty effects and simulate casual browsing behaviour. The second task required participants to choose an internet plan for their household, thereby engaging with the website in a more goal-directed manner.

During this second task, a key manipulation was introduced: after the user validated their address, the prices of two of the three available plans were silently reduced. The interface remained visually identical, with the plan layout and design unchanged. This lack of explicit signaling allowed for the spontaneous detection of the price change, emulating how dynamic pricing strategies often operate in real-world e-commerce environments.

4.3 Participants

A total of 22 participants (12 men, 10 women; M age $= 37.0$, $SD = 13.6$; age range: 18–62) were recruited for the study. Participants were drawn from two separate recruitment sources: the university's internal participant panel and an external recruitment firm. This dual-sourcing approach was used to diversify the sample, as the internal panel primarily comprised younger students, while the external firm focused on recruiting individuals from older age brackets.

Eligibility criteria included being at least 18 years old, fluent in French (spoken and written), and having made at least one online purchase within the past three months. Participants were also required to hold primary responsibility for their household's telecommunications services to ensure contextual relevance.

4.4 Measures

The study combined self-reported questionnaires, physiological monitoring, and behavioural data to capture participants' experiences during both tasks. This multimodal approach allowed us to examine users' cognitive, emotional, and navigational responses with precision and contextual depth.

Self-reported data were collected at the end of each task using standardized instruments. These included the Net Promoter Score (NPS) to assess satisfaction, the Customer Effort Score (CES) to evaluate perceived task difficulty, and selected items from the WebQual scale to measure informational clarity and fit to task. Affective Slider was used to report momentary arousal and valence levels, along with a confidence-in-decision item to reflect on their final plan choice. All scales used a 10-point response format.

Physiological signals were recorded throughout the session using electrodermal activity (EDA) and electrocardiogram (ECG) sensors. These allowed us to observe fluctuations in emotional arousal during specific moments of the interaction, especially before and after the unannounced price change.

Behavioural data were gathered through eye-tracking, screen recordings, and clickstream logs. This enabled us to reconstruct the navigation path, examine visual attention to pricing elements, and analyze how participants responded to the pricing interface after the manipulation.

4.5 Analytical Approach

Data analysis combined physiological, behavioural, and self-reported metrics to evaluate participants' experiences across the two tasks.

Participants were classified into two groups based on their post-task interviews: those who explicitly noticed the price reduction (price-aware) and those who did not (non-aware). This grouping enabled a comparative analysis of how awareness of the pricing manipulation affected emotional responses and user experience.

Physiological data (EDA and ECG) were preprocessed to reduce noise and aligned with key interaction timestamps to isolate arousal shifts before and after the pricing change. Clickstream data and screen recordings were reviewed to reconstruct participants' decision pathways and detect whether they revisited pricing information after the manipulation.

Self-reported measures were summarized using descriptive statistics and, where appropriate, compared across the two participant groups. This multi-method approach allowed for the triangulation of findings and the identification of subtle differences in how participants perceived and responded to unannounced price changes.

5 Results

5.1 Navigation Paths and Exposure to Price Changes

To understand how participants encountered the pricing manipulation, we analyzed their browsing recordings to trace each step of their decision journey. This analysis revealed two distinct navigation paths: a conventional path, which aligned with the intended structure of the experiment, and an unconventional path, which bypassed key stages in the task.

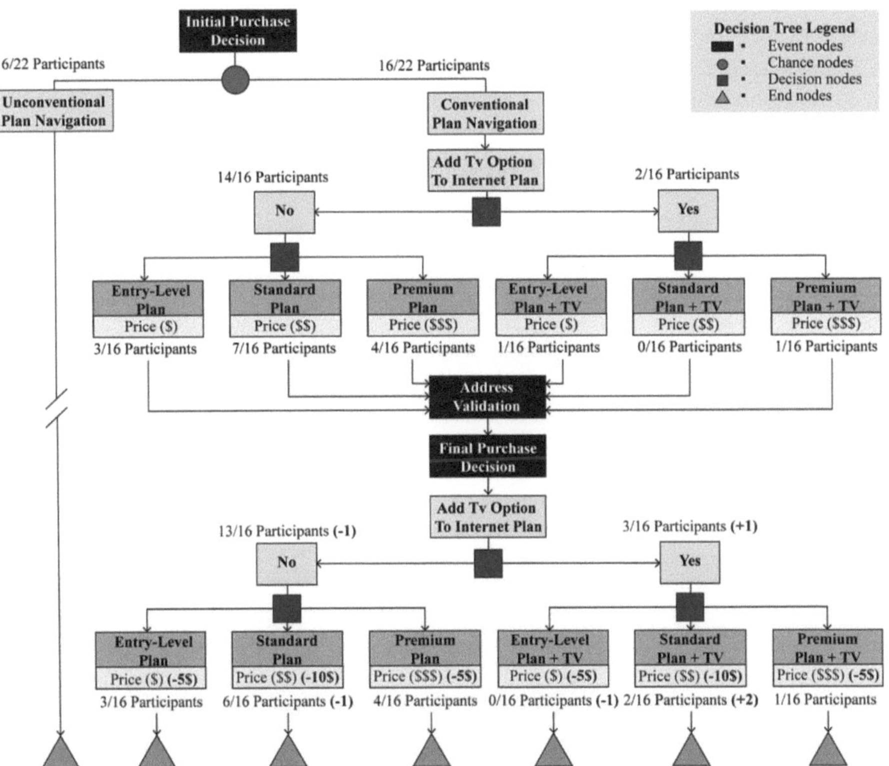

Fig. 3. Navigation Path Decision Tree.

The conventional path was followed by participants who began their journey through the website's main header navigation. This structured route guided them through the address validation step, after which a subtle price change was introduced. These participants were exposed to both versions of the plan offerings, before and after the pricing update, and directly interacted with the dynamic pricing element embedded in the flow.

In contrast, six participants followed an unconventional path, beginning their journey through alternative entry points that bypassed the website's header. As a result, they skipped the address validation step entirely and only encountered one version of the internet plan offerings, either before or after the price change. Because they were not exposed to the pricing manipulation, they were excluded from the primary analysis.

This filtering process reduced the analytical sample from 22 to 16 participants. The remaining participants followed the complete intended flow and experienced the full pricing sequence necessary for evaluating the impact of the dynamic price change.

For those exposed to the manipulation, the pricing update included a $5 reduction for the entry-level and premium plans, and a $10 reduction for the standard plan. Despite these favourable changes, 14 out of 16 participants retained their original selection, suggesting that the price reduction may have enhanced the perceived value of their chosen plan rather than prompting them to switch. To illustrate this process, Fig. 3 presents a decision tree mapping participants' navigation behaviour, initial plan choices, and final outcomes.

At the initial decision point, 14 participants selected internet-only plans, 3 chose the entry-level plan, 7 selected the standard plan (the most popular), and 4 opted for the premium plan. Two participants selected internet plans that included the TV option. By the final decision screen, one additional participant upgraded to include TV, bringing the total to 3 with TV bundles and 13 with internet-only plans.

Two participants changed their original selection, both by upgrading to a more expensive option. One participant added TV to their standard plan, and another upgraded from entry-level + TV to standard + TV. These outcomes suggest that while most participants remained with their initial choice, the price reductions may have helped reinforce those decisions or encouraged selective upgrades when the added value justified the change.

5.2 Awareness and Responses to Price Change

To assess how dynamic pricing influenced customer experience, we examined whether participants noticed the price change and how this awareness shaped their emotional and behavioural responses. Of the 16 participants exposed to the manipulation, six were classified as price change–aware based on whether they spontaneously identified the price reduction during the task or interview. Ten participants made no mention of any pricing difference and were classified as unaware. To visualize how awareness aligned with participant sentiment, we created a timeline of emotional responses across key task stages, coded on a scale from positive (2), to indifferent (1), to negative (0). Table 1 summarizes these trajectories across four moments: the initial plan selection, the address validation step, the final selection, and post-purchase reflection.

Table 1. Timeline of Participant Awareness and Emotional Response.

	Event 1	Event 2	Event 3	Post Experience
	Initial Purchase Decision	Address Validation	Final Purchase Decision	Finalized Purchase
	Response_Initial_Decision	Address_Validation_Awareness	Price_Change_Awareness	Response_Final_Purchase
P01	2	1	1	2
P03	1	1	1	2
P05	1	0	1	1
P11	0	1	1	0
P14	1	1	1	0
P18	1	0	1	0
P19	1	1	0	1
P21	2	0	0	2
P22	2	0	0	2
P23	1	0	0	2
P30	0	0	0	1
P33	0	0	0	0
P35	2	0	0	2
P42	2	0	0	2
P43	2	0	0	2
P47	2	0	0	2

Positive (2) = 7	Yes(1) = 5	Yes (1) = 6	Positive (2) = 9
Indifferent (1) = 6	No (0) = 11	No (0) = 10	Indifferent (1) = 3
Negative (0) = 3			Negative (0) = 4

Among the aware group, all six participants acknowledged noticing a pricing change. P01 said, "I have the impression that my address and the price have gone down. Instead of $70, it was $65, so I didn't understand why it went down, but it convinced me to continue," expressing both awareness and acceptance. P11 reflected, "It's different from the price you're offered at the start, which changes when you enter your address, and then it's another price again when you make the final purchase. That's a bit complex." P14 noted, "Among other things, and we already have this when you select the address and the offer changes in relation to the offer on the screen, it already gives me questions about customer service for me, about why it's different from the initial price."

All six also reported confusion. P05 shared, "By the way, I didn't quite understand everything; I mean, because there are different prices presented when I first clicked on it, it said $50 a month, then I guess $50 included the $12." P03 added, "That wasn't clear at first. I had to play with parameters to see if the price changed, and when I saw that it was included, I was satisfied." Notably, six of the ten unaware participants also reported confusion, despite not detecting the price change. P21 remarked, "When I understood all the details and the discount, it wasn't clear [...] I would have had to spend more time unpacking it all, or call to chat." Four others in this group did not express any confusion.

As shown in Fig. 5, emotional responses evolved differently across the two groups. In the aware group, four participants were initially indifferent, one positive, and one negative. By the end, two reported positive experiences, one remained indifferent, and three became negative. The unaware group showed greater stability: six began with a positive view, two were indifferent, and two had a negative view. By the end, seven were positive, two remained indifferent, and only one was negative (Fig. 4).

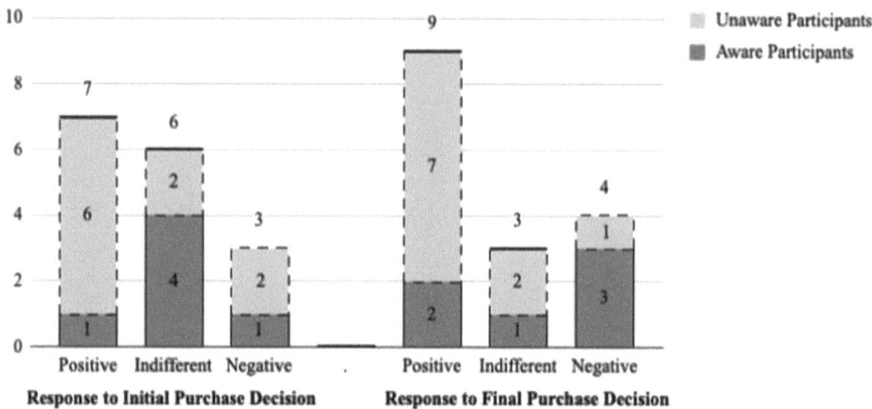

Fig. 4. Visualization of Emotional Responses to Purchase Decisions by Awareness

The most significant shifts occurred among those who were initially indifferent. Of the six participants in this category, one became positive, two remained indifferent, and three shifted to negative. This suggests that indifferent participants were more sensitive to contextual ambiguity and less anchored in their decision.

Despite emotional shifts, behavioural responses remained mostly stable. Figure 5 summarizes final product choices and payment changes by group. Among aware participants, five retained their original plan, and one upgraded by adding services. In the unaware group, nine kept their plan and one upgraded. No participants in either group downgraded their selection.

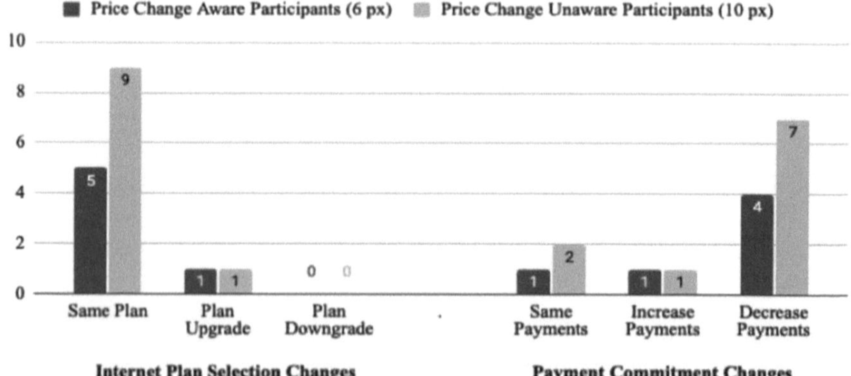

Fig. 5. Visualization of Product Selection Outcomes Based on Price Awareness

Regarding payment outcomes, four aware participants saw a cost reduction, one increased their payment due to an upgrade, and one saw no change. Among the unaware participants, seven reduced their payment, two saw no change, and one paid more after upgrading. These results suggest that while emotional experiences were shaped by awareness, most participants reaffirmed their original selection or made small adjustments. Subtle price reductions often served to reinforce confidence, particularly among those who did not detect the change.

5.3 Emotional Experience: Arousal and Valence

This section presents the physiological data collected during the purchasing task, focusing on participants' emotional valence (positivity vs. negativity) and arousal (emotional intensity) across the three key stages of the purchase journey: the initial plan selection, the address validation step (where the price change occurred), and the final plan confirmation. Participants were divided based on whether or not they noticed the price change, and the results reflect how awareness influenced their lived emotional experience.

As shown in Table 2, participants who noticed the price change (n = 6) started with a mean valence of −.187, which declined further to −.217 at the address validation stage, suggesting a rise in negative emotion. However, this was reversed slightly by the final purchase decision (−.169), indicating partial recovery. The standard deviation also decreased from .137 to .083, suggesting increasingly consistent responses among this group as the task progressed. In contrast, participants who did not notice the price change (n = 10) began with a less negative valence (−.110), which steadily improved across events to −.008 by the final decision. This trend suggests a progressively more positive experience for unaware participants. Please refer to Fig. 6 for a visual comparison.

Table 2. Progression of Valence During the Customer Purchase Journey.

Groups	Events	Mean Valence	Std Dev Valence
Price Change Aware Participants (6 px)	Initial Purchase Decision (Event 1)	-.187	.137
	Address Validation (Event 2)	-.217	.117
	Final Purchase Decision (Event 3)	-.169	.083
Price Change Unaware Participants (10 px)	Initial Purchase Decision (Event 1)	-.110	.142
	Address Validation (Event 2)	-.102	.100
	Final Purchase Decision (Event 3)	-.008	.192

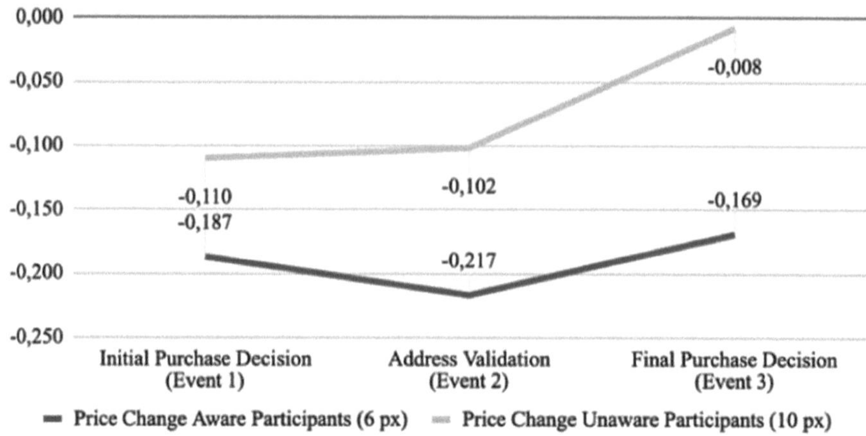

Fig. 6. Mean Valence in the Customer Journey.

A Friedman test showed no significant change in valence across events for the aware group, $\chi2(2) = 3.000$, p = .223, while the difference for the unaware group approached significance, $\chi2(2) = 5.600$, p = .061. Mann-Whitney U tests revealed no significant difference between groups at the initial decision stage (U = 18.000, p = .212, r = .330). However, by the address validation stage, the difference was significant (U = 10.000, p = .033, r = .540), and it remained significant at the final decision (U = 6.000, p = .011, r = .650), with unaware participants reporting more positive emotional states. These results suggest that detecting the price change introduced a drop in emotional positivity that lingered through the end of the purchase.

In terms of arousal, shown in Table 3, the price-aware group exhibited a gradual increase in emotional intensity, rising from .029 at the initial decision to .050 during address validation and peaking at .061 by the final decision. Variability was highest during the price change event (SD = .062), indicating differing reactions to the manipulation. In contrast, the unaware group began with a substantially higher arousal level (.277), which peaked during address validation (.489) before dropping to .240 by the final step. Standard deviations followed a similar curve (from .208 to .796 to .285), reflecting greater emotional fluctuation among this group. These results are illustrated in Fig. 7.

Table 3. Progression of Arousal During the Customer Purchase Journey.

Groups	Events	Mean Arousal	Std Dev Arousal
Price Change Aware Participants (6 px)	Initial Purchase Decision (Event 1)	.029	.021
	Address Validation (Event 2)	.050	.062
	Final Purchase Decision (Event 3)	.061	.041
Price Change Unaware Participants (10 px)	Initial Purchase Decision (Event 1)	.277	.208
	Address Validation (Event 2)	.489	.796
	Final Purchase Decision (Event 3)	.240	.285

Mann-Whitney U tests confirmed that the price change-unaware group exhibited significantly higher arousal than the aware group at each task stage: Event 1 ($U = 3.000$, $p = .004$, $r = .730$), Event 2 ($U = 4.000$, $p = .005$, $r = .710$), and Event 3 ($U = 11.000$, $p = .044$, $r = .520$).

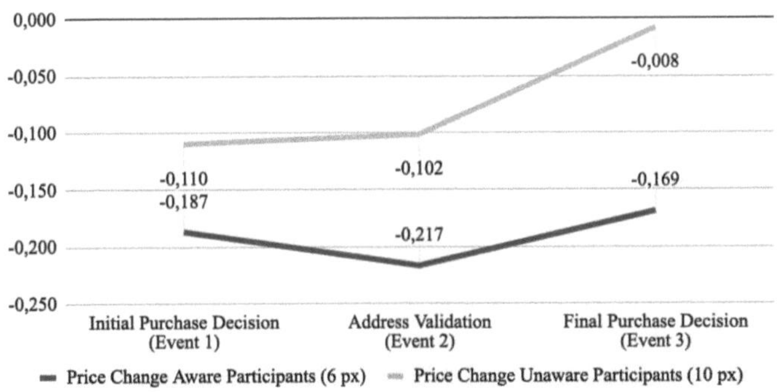

Fig. 7. Mean Arousal in the Customer Journey.

These results highlight two distinct emotional profiles. The aware group experienced a more regulated but emotionally subdued journey, with valence dipping during the price change and arousal rising only slightly. In contrast, the unaware group showed more intense emotional engagement, peaking during the address validation step, even though they did not consciously register the price change. Together, these findings suggest that both the presence and absence of pricing awareness shape customer experience in meaningful and measurable emotional ways.

5.4 Self-Reported Measures: Net Promoter Score

NPS scores revealed a clear divergence between awareness groups. As shown in Table 4, participants who noticed the price change reported a negative NPS of −33, reflecting a more critical customer experience. This group included 1 promoter, 2 passives, and 3 detractors. In contrast, the group that did not notice the price change reported a positive NPS of +30, with 4 promoters, 5 passives, and only 1 detractor, indicating a more favourable experience overall.

Table 4. Net Promoter Score (NPS).

Groups	Task	Mean Score	Standard Deviation
Price Change Aware Participants (6 px)	Purchase (T2)	-33.00	2.811
Non-Price Change Aware Participants (10 px)	Purchase (T2)	30.00	1.135

A Wilcoxon rank-sum test confirmed the statistically significant difference ($U = 18.000$, $p = .031$, $r = .330$). While both groups completed the same purchase task and selected similar plans, participants who remained unaware of the price change were more likely to recommend the service. This finding reinforces the idea that even beneficial price adjustments, when perceived as unclear or unexplained, can erode brand sentiment.

6 Discussion

6.1 Summary of Main Findings

This chapter examines how subtle dynamic pricing influences customers' online purchase journeys, decision-making processes, emotions, and brand perceptions. Small price reductions introduced during the purchase process tended to reinforce participants' initial plan selection rather than prompting reconsideration, with 14 out of 16 participants remaining with their initial choice after the price drop.

However, awareness of the price change induced emotional complexity and cognitive strain, actively shaping participants' customer journeys. The six participants who noticed the price change exhibited fluctuating emotional responses characterized by increased arousal and declining valence at key stages. These responses reflected confusion, skepticism, and a decline in trust.

While both groups reported similarly high confidence in their final purchase decisions, their NPS scores revealed a clear divide. Unaware participants had a smoother, more positive journey and a higher NPS score, indicating a greater willingness to recommend or engage with the brand in the future. In contrast, aware participants had lower NPS scores, suggesting diminished brand advocacy.

These findings suggest that while subtle dynamic pricing can reinforce decision confidence when unnoticed, consumers' awareness of such tactics can complicate user experience, guide skepticism, and reduce brand loyalty.

6.2 Theoretical Contributions

This study reinforces anchoring theory in digital contexts where prices shift mid-journey. Despite a favourable price reduction introduced after the address validation step, 14 out of 16 participants maintained their original plan selection. Consistent with prior research [25, 34], the initial price appeared to serve as a benchmark, influencing subsequent evaluations. The lower price was interpreted as reinforcing value rather than prompting reassessment. These findings extend anchoring effects to dynamic pricing environments, showing that first price exposures continue to shape final decisions even as new information is introduced.

In addition, while previous research often focuses on price increases, this study adds nuance by examining unannounced price reductions. Although reductions are generally perceived positively [5, 7], the results show that when such changes are noticed without explanation, they can trigger confusion and affect trust. Participants who noticed the price drop reported slightly lower post-decision confidence and weaker brand advocacy [35]. These findings highlight that fairness perceptions are shaped not just by the financial outcome but by how transparently the change is introduced, positioning awareness as a key mediating factor.

The study also underscores the role of information architecture in moderating exposure to dynamic pricing. Only participants who followed the conventional navigation flow, using the homepage and filtering options, encountered the price manipulation. Those who navigated via shortcuts bypassed it entirely. While prior work has explored how price information is displayed [19, 36], less has addressed how journey structure affects pricing exposure. These findings suggest that navigation behaviour is central to how users experience pricing strategies, reinforcing the impact of site design on perception and behaviour [37].

6.3 Practical Implications

Dynamic pricing is often designed to trigger switching or urgency [23], but the findings suggest another role: reinforcing confidence in decisions already made. In this study, 14 of 16 participants stayed with their initial plan despite encountering a lower price later in the journey. Rather than prompting reconsideration, the reduced price seemed to validate their original choice. This aligns with anchoring theory, where early price exposure forms the basis for future evaluations[25, 34]. For practitioners, subtle reductions may be used not to redirect choice, but to enhance perceived value, confidence, and satisfaction at the moment of final decision.

Moreover, even favourable pricing adjustments can introduce confusion if presented without explanation. Participants who noticed the price change expressed slight uncertainty about why it occurred, reporting lower post-decision confidence. This suggests that clarity and contextual framing are essential, not just the benefit itself. Research on fairness emphasizes the need for perceived procedural legitimacy and transparency [5, 23]. In dynamic environments, organizations should consider embedding cues (e.g., tied to time, demand, or location) to help explain price changes and preserve trust.

Furthermore, the effectiveness of dynamic pricing depends not only on the strategy itself but on whether users encounter it. In this study, only participants who followed the full navigation path, including the address validation step, experienced the price change. Those taking shortcuts bypassed the manipulation entirely. This underscores the importance of information architecture in shaping exposure to pricing interventions [19, 38]. Pricing tactics must be embedded into user flows to ensure they are encountered as intended, without disrupting clarity or user control [37].

Lastly, while both awareness groups reported similar levels of confidence in their final decisions, physiological and NPS data revealed a more complex picture. Aware participants showed more emotional fluctuation, higher arousal and confusion, paired with lower brand advocacy scores. This highlights that pricing strategies affect not only transactional outcomes but also long-term brand perceptions [39]. Emotional responses to unclear pricing tactics may undermine trust, even when the price is favourable. Organizations should weigh the timing, framing, and transparency of pricing tactics not just for conversion, but for their impact on loyalty and advocacy.

6.4 Limitations and Future Research

Two limitations of this study should be acknowledged. First, the absence of real monetary transactions may have reduced the emotional stakes of the decision-making process, potentially influencing the intensity of participants' reactions to the price changes. Second, only 16 participant responses were used in the final analysis. Six participants were excluded after taking an unconventional path that caused them to bypass the section of the purchase journey where the dynamic price change occurred. While their exclusion ensured consistency among those who encountered the manipulation, it reduced the overall sample and limited generalizability.

Future research could study how natural, unprompted browsing behaviour interacts with dynamic pricing strategies could offer nuanced insights. Studying how users who miss pricing triggers experience the interface may inform better design strategies for engagement. Future research could also explore the use of real-time communication elements, such as price change notifications or explanatory tooltips, to examine how transparency moderates fairness perceptions and trust. Finally, longitudinal studies could investigate how repeated exposure to dynamic pricing affects long-term customer sentiment, decision confidence, and brand loyalty.

7 Conclusion

As e-commerce evolves, so does the complexity of pricing strategies shaping online customer experiences. This study showed how subtle, unannounced price reductions can influence user perception, decision-making, and brand sentiment, positioning dynamic pricing as a strategic UX element rather than a purely economic one.

The research investigated the impact of dynamic pricing, specifically subtle price reductions, on emotional, cognitive, and behavioural responses in a realistic online environment. Awareness of the price change played a central role: while most participants did not alter their choice, those who noticed the change reported more emotional ambivalence and reduced trust. Conversely, unaware participants described a smoother journey, higher confidence, and stronger brand advocacy. While group-level differences in self-reports were not statistically significant, they aligned with physiological and qualitative data offering a nuanced view of user experience.

The study contributes to theory by showing how mechanisms like anchoring and reference pricing persist even when prices change mid-journey, and how awareness can alter both perception and emotion in real time.

For practice, the findings underscore the importance of integrating pricing strategies into the design of user journeys. Whether noticed or not, price changes can influence perception and trust. Transparency and contextual cues can mitigate uncertainty when users detect changes. Organizations should consider the interplay between pricing design, timing, and navigation to foster both confidence and clarity.

This study also highlights the value of combining physiological, behavioural, and qualitative data to gain deeper insight into the user experience of dynamic pricing.

In closing, this study emphasized that UX is shaped by what users see and do, and how they feel and interpret events along their journey. Pricing, often considered a backend consideration, is a vital aspect of that experience. How it is introduced, adjusted, or withheld can either build or erode trust. By viewing pricing as an experience rather than a final detail, organizations can create journeys that are clearer, more respectful, and better aligned with the expectations of today's users.

Acknowledgements. This work was supported by the Natural Sciences and Engineering Research Council of Canada (NSERC) Alliance Léger (ALLRP 575332 - 22) and PROMPT (Prompt Project 180, Léger).

References

1. Elmaghraby, W., Keskinocak, P.: Dynamic pricing in the presence of inventory considerations: research overview, current practices, and future directions. Manag. Sci. **49**, 1287–1309 (2003). https://doi.org/10.1287/mnsc.49.10.1287.17315
2. Shiller, B.R.: First-Degree Price Discrimination Using Big Data (2014)
3. Gibbs, C., Guttentag, D., Gretzel, U., Yao, L., Morton, J.: Use of dynamic pricing strategies by Airbnb hosts. Int. J. Contemp. Hosp. Manag. **30**, 2–20 (2018). https://doi.org/10.1108/IJCHM-09-2016-0540
4. Grewal, D., Hardesty, D.M., Iyer, G.R.: The effects of buyer identification and purchase timing on consumers' perceptions of trust, price fairness, and repurchase intentions. J. Interact. Mark. **18**, 87–100 (2004). https://doi.org/10.1002/dir.20024
5. Xia, L., Monroe, K.B., Cox, J.L.: The price is unfair! a conceptual framework of price fairness perceptions. J. Mark. **68**, 1–15 (2004). https://doi.org/10.1509/jmkg.68.4.1.42733
6. Haws, K.L., Bearden, W.O.: Dynamic pricing and consumer fairness perceptions. J. Consum. Res. **33**, 304–311 (2006). https://doi.org/10.1086/508435
7. Bolton, L.E., Warlop, L., Alba, J.W.: Consumer perceptions of price (Un)Fairness. J. Consum. Res. **29**, 474–491 (2003). https://doi.org/10.1086/346244
8. Grewal, D., et al.: Strategic online and offline retail pricing: a review and research agenda. J. Interact. Mark. **24**, 138–154 (2010). https://doi.org/10.1016/j.intmar.2010.02.007
9. Lemon, K.N., Verhoef, P.C.: Understanding customer experience throughout the customer journey. J. Mark. **80**, 69–96 (2016). https://doi.org/10.1509/jm.15.0420

10. Hamilton, R., Chernev, A.: Low prices are just the beginning: price image in retail management. J. Mark. **77**, 1–20 (2013). https://doi.org/10.1509/jm.08.0204

11. Priester, A., Robbert, T., Roth, S.: A special price just for you: effects of personalized dynamic pricing on consumer fairness perceptions. J. Revenue Pricing Manag. **19**, 99–112 (2020). https://doi.org/10.1057/s41272-019-00224-3

12. Hannak, A., Soeller, G., Lazer, D., Mislove, A., Wilson, C.: Measuring price discrimination and steering on e-commerce web sites. In: Proceedings of the 2014 Conference on Internet Measurement Conference, pp. 305–318. ACM, Vancouver (2014). https://doi.org/10.1145/2663716.2663744

13. L. Ferguson, J., Scholder Ellen, P.: Transparency in pricing and its effect on perceived price fairness. J. Prod. Brand Manag. **22**, 404–412 (2013). https://doi.org/10.1108/JPBM-06-2013-0323

14. Garbarino, E., Lee, O.F.: Dynamic pricing in internet retail: effects on consumer trust. Psychol. Mark. **20**, 495–513 (2003). https://doi.org/10.1002/mar.10084

15. Martin, K.D., Murphy, P.E.: The role of data privacy in marketing. J. Acad. Mark. Sci. **45**, 135–155 (2017). https://doi.org/10.1007/s11747-016-0495-4

16. Bambauer-Sachse, S., Young, A.: Consumers' intentions to spread negative word of mouth about dynamic pricing for services: role of confusion and unfairness perceptions. J. Serv. Res. **27**, 364–380 (2024). https://doi.org/10.1177/10946705231190871

17. Malc, D., Mumel, D., Pisnik, A.: Exploring price fairness perceptions and their influence on consumer behavior. J. Bus. Res. **69**, 3693–3697 (2016). https://doi.org/10.1016/j.jbusres.2016.03.031

18. Chen, K., Zha, Y., Alwan, L.C., Zhang, L.: Dynamic pricing in the presence of reference price effect and consumer strategic behaviour. Int. J. Prod. Res. **58**, 546–561 (2020). https://doi.org/10.1080/00207543.2019.1598592

19. Mazumdar, T., Raj, S.P., Sinha, I.: Reference price research: review and propositions. J. Mark. **69**, 84–102 (2005). https://doi.org/10.1509/jmkg.2005.69.4.84

20. Roy, R., Rabbanee, F.K., Sharma, P.: Exploring the interactions among external reference price, social visibility and purchase motivation in pay-what-you-want pricing. Eur. J. Mark. **50**, 816–837 (2016). https://doi.org/10.1108/EJM-10-2014-0609

21. Mazumdar, T., Papatla, P.: Loyalty differences in the use of internal and external reference prices. Mark. Lett. **6**, 111–122 (1995). https://doi.org/10.1007/BF00994927

22. Tanford, S., Choi, C., Joe, S.J.: The influence of pricing strategies on willingness to pay for accommodations: anchoring, framing, and metric compatibility. J. Travel Res. **58**, 932–944 (2019). https://doi.org/10.1177/0047287518793037

23. Weisstein, F.L., Monroe, K.B., Kukar-Kinney, M.: Effects of price framing on consumers' perceptions of online dynamic pricing practices. J. Acad. Mark. Sci. **41**, 501–514 (2013). https://doi.org/10.1007/s11747-013-0330-0

24. Furnham, A., Boo, H.C.: A literature review of the anchoring effect. J. Socio-Econ. **40**, 35–42 (2011). https://doi.org/10.1016/j.socec.2010.10.008

25. Simonson, I., Drolet, A.: Anchoring effects on consumers' willingness-to-pay and willingness-to-accept. J. Consum. Res. (2004)

26. Armstrong, M.: Price discrimination. MPRA Paper. University Library of Munich, Germany (2006)

27. Anderson, E.T., Dana, J.D.: When is price discrimination profitable? Manag. Sci. **55**, 980–989 (2009). https://doi.org/10.1287/mnsc.1080.0979

28. Kosinski, M., Stillwell, D., Graepel, T.: Private traits and attributes are predictable from digital records of human behavior. Proc. Natl. Acad. Sci. **110**, 5802–5805 (2013). https://doi.org/10.1073/pnas.1218772110

29. Wu, Z., Yang, Y., Zhao, J., Wu, Y.: The impact of algorithmic price discrimination on consumers' perceived betrayal. Front. Psychol. **13**, 825420 (2022). https://doi.org/10.3389/fpsyg. 2022.825420
30. Carter, R.E., Curry, D.J.: Transparent pricing: theory, tests, and implications for marketing practice. J. Acad. Mark. Sci. **38**, 759–774 (2010). https://doi.org/10.1007/s11747-010-0189-2
31. Chen, H., Bolton, L.E., Ng, S., Lee, D., Wang, D.: Culture, relationship norms, and dual entitlement. J. Consum. Res. **45**, 1–20 (2018). https://doi.org/10.1093/jcr/ucx118
32. Popescu, I., Wu, Y.: Dynamic pricing strategies with reference effects. Oper. Res. **55**, 413–429 (2007). https://doi.org/10.1287/opre.1070.0393
33. Viglia, G., Mauri, A., Carricano, M.: The exploration of hotel reference prices under dynamic pricing scenarios and different forms of competition. Int. J. Hosp. Manag. **52**, 46–55 (2016). https://doi.org/10.1016/j.ijhm.2015.09.010
34. Zong, Y., Guo, X.: An experimental study on anchoring effect of consumers' price judgment based on consumers' experiencing scenes. Front. Psychol. **13**, 794135 (2022). https://doi.org/ 10.3389/fpsyg.2022.794135
35. Reichheld, F.F.: The one number you need to grow. Harv. Bus. Rev. (2003)
36. Lynch, J.G., Ariely, D.: Wine online: search costs affect competition on price, quality, and distribution. Mark. Sci. **19**, 83–103 (2000). https://doi.org/10.1287/mksc.19.1.83.15183
37. Tuch, A.N., Bargas-Avila, J.A., Opwis, K., Wilhelm, F.H.: Visual complexity of websites: effects on users' experience, physiology, performance, and memory. Int. J. Hum.-Comput. Stud. **67**, 703–715 (2009). https://doi.org/10.1016/j.ijhcs.2009.04.002
38. Chandrashekaran, R., Grewal, D.: Anchoring effects of advertised reference price and sale price: the moderating role of saving presentation format. J. Bus. Res. **59**, 1063–1071 (2006). https://doi.org/10.1016/j.jbusres.2006.06.006
39. Chaudhuri, A., Holbrook, M.B.: The chain of effects from brand trust and brand affect to brand performance: the role of brand loyalty. J. Mark. **65**, 81–93 (2001). https://doi.org/10. 1509/jmkg.65.2.81.18255

Tourism Demand Forecasting: Precision with Mamba-iTransformer Multidimensional Analysis

Jiao Feng[1], Yingjie Bai[2], Zhendong Li[1,2(✉)], Jing Zhao[2], and Hao Liu[2,3]

[1] School of Innovation and Entrepreneurship, Ningxia University,
Yinchuan 750021, China
`lizhendong@nxu.edu.cn`
[2] School of Information Engineering, Ningxia University, Yinchuan 750021, China
[3] Ningxia Key Laboratory of Artificial Intelligence and Information Security for
Channeling Computing Resources from the East to the West, Yinchuan, China

Abstract. This study introduces a novel hybrid framework, termed Mamba-iTransformer, designed for tourism demand forecasting. The framework synergistically integrates the linear time complexity and long-range dependency modeling capabilities of Mamba with the multivariate correlation capturing and non-linear representation learning strengths of iTransformer. By leveraging this integration, Mamba-iTransformer adeptly captures both long- and short-term dependencies, thereby enhancing the accuracy of time series forecasting while maintaining computational efficiency in processing extended sequence data. Empirical evaluations reveal that Mamba-iTransformer achieves superior predictive performance across multiple real-world datasets, significantly outperforming existing state-of-the-art methodologies. This research contributes a highly efficient and precise approach to tourism demand forecasting, demonstrating robust generalization capabilities and adaptability.

Keywords: Tourism demand forecasting · Long and Short-term Dependencies · Time Series Prediction

1 Introduction

Tourism is regarded as one of the most promising drivers of economic development, capable of fostering the flow of people, goods, capital, and information within specific regions, while also creating employment opportunities for society. Despite the steady growth of the tourism industry over the past decade, the China Tourism Association reported [1] that by 2020, the total number of domestic tourists in China had reached 2.88 billion, and domestic tourism revenue amounted to 2.23 trillion RMB, reflecting a decrease of 52.1% and 53.8% respectively from the previous year, primarily due to the impact of the COVID-19 pandemic. This inherent volatility and susceptibility to random factors render tourism demand forecasting particularly challenging.

F. F.-H Nah and K. L. Siau (Eds.): HCII 2025, LNCS 16343, pp. 224–238, 2026.
https://doi.org/10.1007/978-3-032-13167-6_16

Tourism planners require precise predictions of tourist arrivals [2–4]. Similarly, all stakeholders within the destination and tourism value chain, such as transportation departments, travel agencies, accommodation providers, event organizers, and retailers, need accurate forecast data to make short-term operational decisions and to develop long-term strategies for analyzing market trends, setting priorities, and managing risks. Given its significance, tourism demand forecasting continues to garner substantial attention [4–6].

In recent years, tourism demand forecasting models have been extensively applied and studied. The prevalent models can be broadly categorized into two main types: time series analysis models and machine learning models [7]. Both types of models aim to learn the characteristics of time series data to compare the effectiveness of tourism demand forecasts across different regions. Typically, time series analysis models adhere strictly to statistical assumptions, necessitating the design of appropriate feature extraction methods to transform raw data into features that comply with these assumptions. For machine learning models, enhancing feature learning efficiency through methods such as principal component analysis [8], embedding extraction [9], and hashing [10] is a common practice.

Despite the utility of existing literature in aiding tourism managers to formulate management strategies, several limitations persist. Time series analysis models assume that tourism activities are linear and stable, which may lead to an incomplete representation of these activities [11]. Furthermore, these models often employ feature learning methods to convert raw data into equivalent stationary time series, potentially resulting in the loss of original information. The performance of machine learning models similarly hinges on the feature identification process. Due to the heterogeneity and dynamic nature of tourism activities, a strategy proposed for one case may not be applicable to another. Consequently, tourism managers must assess the effectiveness of strategies before implementation, as tourism recovery is a time-consuming and costly process [12].

To address these limitations, the attention mechanism in machine learning is considered a suitable approach for estimating tourism demand [13]. The attention mechanism enables models to design and apply simulations of complex real-world systems [14]. Additionally, different scenarios can be set and results calculated within the attention framework. Existing research has demonstrated the feasibility of the attention mechanism in evaluating non-stationary time series forecasts [15]. However, current attention-based methods are optimized through the backpropagation of errors, which can render the models inefficient and prone to overfitting.

Despite the success of Transformers in natural language processing, several challenges arise when applying them to time series forecasting:

Computational Complexity: The self-attention mechanism in Transformers has quadratic complexity, leading to high computational costs when handling long time series [16]. **Capturing Multivariate Relationships:** Traditional Transformers may struggle to effectively capture relationships between variables in multivariate time series, resulting in suboptimal performance [17].

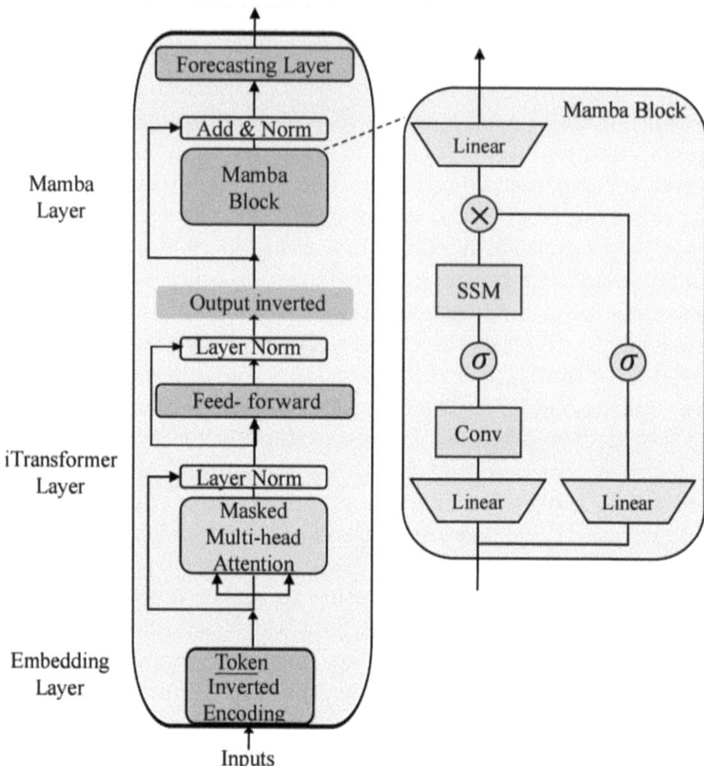

Fig. 1. Overall Structure of the Mamba-iTransformer Model. (a) Embedding Layer: Raw input series are inverted and encoded as tokens. (b) iTransformer Layer: Masked multi-head attention is applied to the encoded tokens, followed by layer normalization and feed-forward network. (c) Mamba Layer: The output from the iTransformer layer is fed into the Mamba block, which includes a linear transformation, convolution, and SSM (State Space Model) operation. The Mamba block's output is then normalized and added back to the input of the layer. (d) Forecasting Layer: The final output is produced by the forecasting layer after the Mamba block.

Temporal Order Information: The permutation-invariant nature of the self-attention mechanism may impair its ability to capture the sequential information inherent in time series data [18].

To tackle these challenges, the iTransformer has been proposed [19], addressing the inadequacies of Transformers in capturing relationships among variables in multivariate time series. Additionally, to overcome the limitations of Transformers in long-sequence forecasting, the Mamba method was introduced, which enhances efficiency in handling long time series by incorporating linear time complexity and long-range dependency modeling capabilities [20].

Research indicates that state space models (SSM) and Transformers have complementary strengths in language modeling. To verify if this holds true for time series data, a hybrid architecture named Mambaformer [21] was proposed, combining SSM and Transformers to achieve superior performance in time series forecasting.

Building on this foundation, we propose a hybrid framework named Mamba-iTransformer for tourism demand forecasting. This framework integrates the linear time complexity and long-range dependency modeling capabilities of Mamba with the multivariate correlation capturing and nonlinear representation learning abilities of iTransformer. By combining the strengths of Mamba and iTransformer, Mamba-iTransformer can simultaneously capture both short- and long-range dependencies, thereby enhancing the accuracy of time series forecasts while maintaining efficient computational performance for long-sequence data.

Experimental results demonstrate that Mamba-iTransformer achieves state-of-the-art predictive performance across multiple real-world datasets, significantly outperforming existing advanced methods [2,22–24]. This study provides an efficient and accurate new method for tourism demand forecasting, showcasing its robust generalization capabilities and adaptability. Accurate tourism demand forecasting is crucial not only for the growth and sustainable development of the tourism industry but also for the economic prosperity and well-being of global communities [25].

By integrating the advantages of Mamba and iTransformer, Mamba-iTransformer Fig. 1 addresses the computational complexity and multivariate relationship modeling limitations of traditional Transformers in time series forecasting. Its linear complexity, selective memory mechanism, and enhanced multivariate relationship modeling capabilities make Mamba-iTransformer a powerful tool for time series prediction. Experimental results further validate its effectiveness, demonstrating its superior performance on diverse time series data. See Fig. 1 for more details.

2 Preliminaries

2.1 Problem Statement

In the context of long-short range time series forecasting, we are given historical time series data with a look-back window $L = (x_1, x_2, \ldots, x_L)$ of length L. Each $x_t \in \mathbb{R}^M$ at time step t comprises M variables. Our objective is to predict the next F future values $F = (x_{L+1}, x_{L+2}, \ldots, x_{L+F})$ with a length of F. Additionally, we assume that associated temporal context information $(c_1, c_2, \ldots, c_L)$ with dimension C is known, such as the day of the week and the hour of the day. It is important to note that this work operates under a rolling forecasting setting, where after completing a forecast for F, the look-back window B moves forward by F steps into the future, allowing the models to perform the next forecast.

2.2 State Space Models

The State Space Model (SSM) is a modern class of sequence modeling frameworks that are broadly related to RNNs, CNNs, and classical state space models [26]. S4 [27] and Mamba [20] are two notable examples of SSMs. These models are inspired by a continuous system that maps an input function or sequence $x(t) \in \mathbb{R}$ to an output function or sequence $y(t) \in \mathbb{R}$ through an implicit latent state $h(t) \in \mathbb{R}^N$ as follows:

$$h'(t) = Ah(t) + Bx(t) \tag{1}$$

$$y(t) = Ch(t) \tag{2}$$

where $A \in \mathbb{R}^{N \times N}$, $B \in \mathbb{R}^{N \times 1}$, and $C \in \mathbb{R}^{1 \times N}$ are learnable matrices. SSM can be discretized from continuous signals into discrete sequences by a step size Δ. The discretized version is as follows:

$$h_t = Ah_{t-1} + Bx_t \tag{3}$$

$$y = Ch_t \tag{4}$$

where the discrete parameters (A, B) can be derived from the continuous parameters (A, A, B) using a discretization rule, such as the zero-order hold (ZOH) rule $A = \exp(\Delta A)$, $B = (\exp(\Delta A) - I) \cdot AB$. After discretization, the model can be computed in two ways: either as a linear recurrence for inference as shown in Equation (2), or as a global convolution for training as shown in Eq. (3):

$$K = (CB, CAB, \ldots, CA^k B, \ldots) \tag{5}$$

$$y = x * K \tag{6}$$

where K is a convolutional kernel.

2.3   iTransformer

Overview of iTransformer. iTransformer [19] employs an encoder-only architecture, which includes an embedding layer, a projector layer, and several Transformer blocks (TrmBlocks). Multiple blocks can be stacked to model multivariate time series data.

Variable-Centric Feature Representation. For multivariate time series X with length T and V variables, we define X_t to represent all variables at a specific time point, while X_v represents the entire sequence of a specific variable. Unlike traditional methods, iTransformer treats X_v as sequences with consistent semantics and measurement units. The embedding layer learns the sequential feature representation for each variable, referred to as Variate Tokens. These tokens interact through the self-attention mechanism in subsequent layers. Layer normalization and feed-forward networks standardize the feature distribution of different variables and perform fully connected feature encoding. Finally, the projector layer maps each Variate Token to the prediction results. Both the embedding and projector layers are implemented using multi-layer perceptrons (MLPs). Since the order of time points is inherently captured by the arrangement of neurons, additional positional encoding is not required.

Module Analysis Layer Normalization: In traditional Transformers, layer normalization is applied across multiple variables at the same time step, which may introduce noise. In iTransformer, layer normalization is applied within each Variate Token, standardizing the feature distribution across different variables, mitigating differences in measurement units, and addressing non-stationarity issues.

Feed-Forward Network: Leveraging the universal approximation theorem of multi-layer perceptrons, the feed-forward network operates on the entire sequence, extracting intrinsic properties such as amplitude, periodicity, and frequency spectrum, thereby enhancing generalization.

Attention Layer: The attention mechanism models the relationships between different Variate Tokens. By analyzing attention maps, it reveals the correlations among variables. In the Softmax-weighted operation, highly correlated variables receive greater emphasis, making it suitable for complex prediction scenarios driven by physical knowledge.

3   Methodology

3.1   Overview of Mamba-iTransformer

Drawing on the advantages of hybrid architectures in language models [28,29], we propose Mamba-iTransformer, which combines the strengths of Mamba and iTransformer. This hybrid model is capable of capturing both long-term and short-term dependencies in time series data, thereby enhancing performance. Mamba-iTransformer employs an encoder-only structure similar to that of iTransformer.

3.2   Variate Token and Data Embedding

Focusing on the integrity of variables, we introduce the Variate Token, which emphasizes association modeling centered around variables. This approach is well-suited for high-dimensional time series data with numerous and interrelated variables. The tokens are transposed before input. To integrate positional information into the embedding layer, we preprocess the sequence using the Mamba module. This process embeds order information within the input tokens. Mamba can be viewed as a type of RNN, where the hidden state at the current time step t is updated based on the hidden state from the previous time step $t - 1$. This recursive mechanism allows Mamba to naturally consider the sequential order of the data. Therefore, unlike iTransformer, which does not require positional encoding, Mamba-iTransformer replaces positional encoding with the Mamba preprocessing module. The Mamba preprocessing module can be expressed as:

$$H_0 = \text{Embedding}(X) \tag{7}$$

where H_0 is a hybrid vector that includes token embeddings, temporal embeddings, and positional information.

3.3 Self-attention Layer

To inherit iTransformer's excellent performance in capturing multivariate correlations, we utilize masked multi-head attention layers to capture the relationships between tokens. In each attention head h, the attention layer transforms the embedding H_0 into queries Q, keys K, and values V using learnable matrices W_Q, W_K, and W_V. The scaled dot-product attention is then computed as:

$$\text{Attention}(Q, K, V) = \text{softmax}\left(\frac{QK^T}{\sqrt{d_k}}\right) V \qquad (8)$$

The outputs from each head are concatenated to form the output vector H_1, with an embedding dimension of d. Using a learnable projection matrix W_o, we obtain the output of the attention layer:

$$H_1 = \text{Concat}(\text{Attention}_1, \dots, \text{Attention}_h)W_o \qquad (9)$$

A masking mechanism is employed to prevent positions from attending to subsequent positions. We set h following the standard Transformer configuration.

3.4 Core Structure: Alternating Layers

The core structure of the Mamba-iTransformer layer alternates between Mamba layers and self-attention layers. This design leverages the strengths of both Mamba and iTransformer to facilitate long- and short-term time series prediction while effectively capturing multivariate correlations.

3.5 Mamba Layer

To overcome the computational challenges of Transformers and surpass their performance, we integrate the Mamba layer into our model, enhancing its ability to capture long-term dependencies in time series data. The Mamba block is a sequence-to-sequence module with matching input and output dimensions. Specifically, Mamba accepts the input H_1 and expands its dimensions through two linear projections. For one of the projections, Mamba processes the expanded embeddings through convolution and SiLU (Sigmoid Linear Unit) activation, then feeds them into the core State Space Model (SSM). The discretized SSM module is capable of selecting relevant information related to the input while filtering out irrelevant data. The other projection undergoes SiLU activation and serves as a residual connection, combining with the output of the SSM module through a multiplicative gating mechanism. Finally, Mamba produces the output H_3 through an output linear projection:

$$H_2' = \mathrm{Linear}_1(H_1) \tag{10}$$

$$H_2'' = \mathrm{Linear}_2(H_1) \tag{11}$$

$$H_{\mathrm{conv}} = \mathrm{SiLU}(\mathrm{Conv}(H_2')) \tag{12}$$

$$H_{\mathrm{SSM}} = \mathrm{SSM}(H_{\mathrm{conv}}) \tag{13}$$

$$H_{\mathrm{res}} = \mathrm{SiLU}(H_2'') \tag{14}$$

$$H_{\mathrm{mamba}} = H_{\mathrm{res}} \odot H_{\mathrm{SSM}} \tag{15}$$

$$H_3 = \mathrm{Linear}_3(H_{\mathrm{mamba}}) \tag{16}$$

3.6   Forecasting Layer

In this layer, we leverage a linear transformation to map the high-dimensional embedding space back to the original dimensionality of the time series data, thereby obtaining the prediction results, as illustrated below:

$$\widehat{X} = \mathrm{Linear}(H_3) \tag{17}$$

where $\widehat{X} \in \mathbb{R}^{B \times L \times M}$ represents the predicted outcomes.

4   Experiments

4.1   Datasets and Evaluation Metrics

To evaluate the Mamba-iTransformer series models, we employed two popular real-world benchmark datasets, including HK2012–2018 [24] and Macau2018 [2]. These datasets are categorized as multivariate time series. The statistical information of the datasets is summarized in Table 1 and Table 2.

In addition, we utilized our own dataset, namely the Ningxia Yinchuan City tourist flow data. Our objective was to first validate the model using the benchmark datasets, and subsequently use the validated model to predict the tourist flow data for Yinchuan City. The statistical information of the Yinchuan dataset is summarized in Table 3. We use the MAPE (Mean Absolute Percentage Error) and MAE (Mean Absolute Error) metrics to assess the Mamba-iTransformer.

Table 1. Overview of the HK2012-2018 Dataset

Attribute	Description
Dataset Name	HK2012–2018
Coverage Time	From 2012 to 2018, a total of 72 months of data
Data Composition	Tourist arrival data and Search Intensity Index (SII) data
Tourist Arrival Source	Hong Kong Tourism Board (HKTB)
SII Data Source	Google Trends and Baidu Index, targeting specific tourist markets
Keyword Categories	Food and Beverage, Accommodation, Transportation, Tourism, Shopping, Entertainment, etc.

Table 2. Overview of the Macau2018 Dataset

Attribute	Description
Dataset Name	Macau2018
Coverage Time	From 2011.1 to 2018.8, a total of 72 months of data
Data Composition	Monthly tourism arrival volume and Search Intensity Index (SII) data
Tourist Arrival Source	Statistics and Census Service of the Macao Special Administrative Region Government (DSEC)
SII Data Source	Google Trends and Baidu Index, collected for selected visitor markets
Keyword Categories	Dining, Lodging, Transportation, Tour, Shopping, and Recreation

Table 3. Overview of the Macau2018 Dataset

Attribute	Description
Dataset Name	Macau2018
Coverage Time	From 2011.1 to 2018.8, a total of 72 months of data
Data Composition	Monthly tourism arrival volume and Search Intensity Index (SII) data
Tourist Arrival Source	Statistics and Census Service of the Macao Special Administrative Region Government (DSEC)
SII Data Source	Google Trends and Baidu Index, collected for selected visitor markets
Keyword Categories	Dining, Lodging, Transportation, Tour, Shopping, and Recreation

4.2 Forecasting Results

In this section, we undertook extensive empirical experiments to assess the forecasting capabilities of our proposed model, comparing it against a set of sophisticated benchmarks within the realm of deep learning-based forecasting. Our model was evaluated using the HK2012–2018 dataset [24], with comparisons made to the following abbreviated benchmark models: STL-DADLM, DADLM, DLM, ANN, ARIMA, XGBTR, SVR, ETS, and Naïve.

AU, GB, PH, TH, SG, and US represent subsets of the HK2012–2018 dataset, corresponding to arrivals in Hong Kong from Australia, the United Kingdom, the Philippines, Thailand, Singapore, and the United States, respectively. Figures 2, 3, 4, 5, 6, 7, 8, 9, 10, 11, 12 and 13 show the forecasting results for these subsets.

Table 4. Overview of the Ningxia Yinchuan City Dataset

Attribute	Description
Dataset Name	Ningxia Yinchuan City
Coverage Time	From 2023 to 2024
Data Composition	Tourist flow data
Data Source	Local tourism authorities

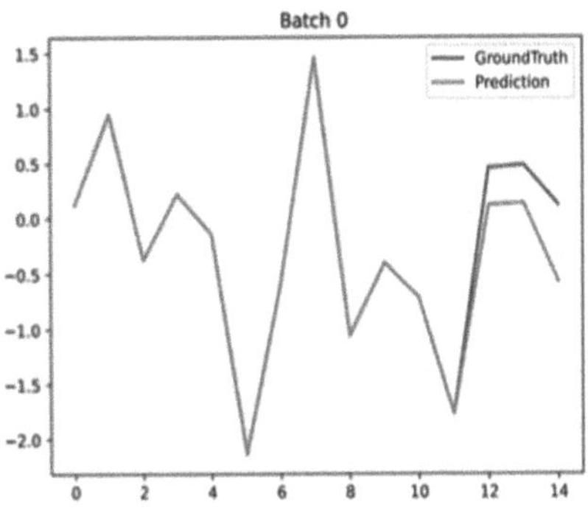

Fig. 2. AU3Months.

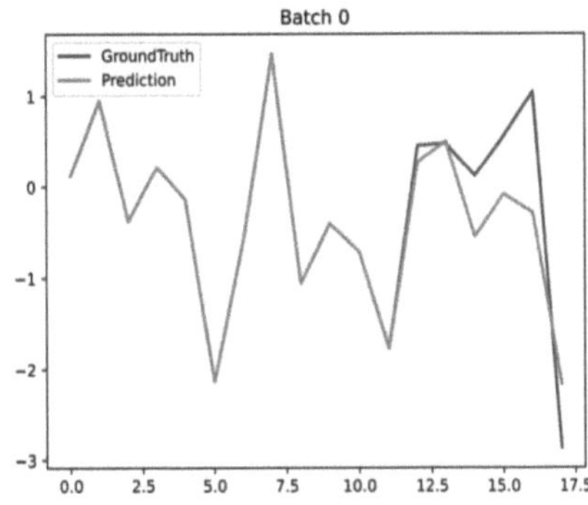

Fig. 3. AU6Months.

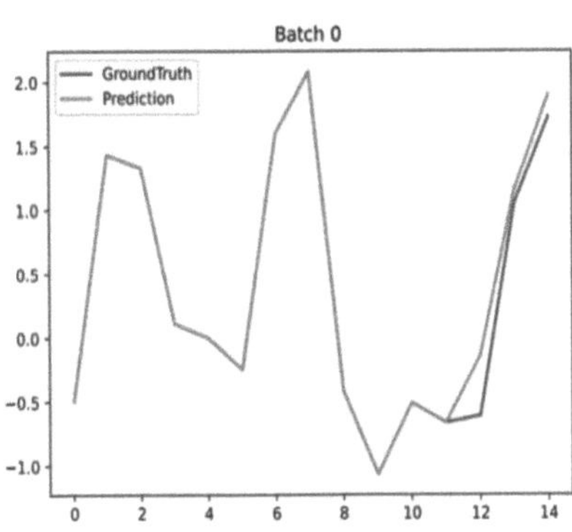

Fig. 4. GB3Months.

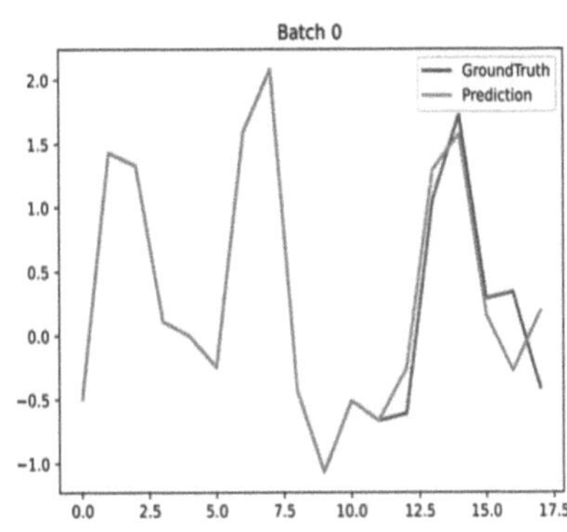

Fig. 5. GB6Months.

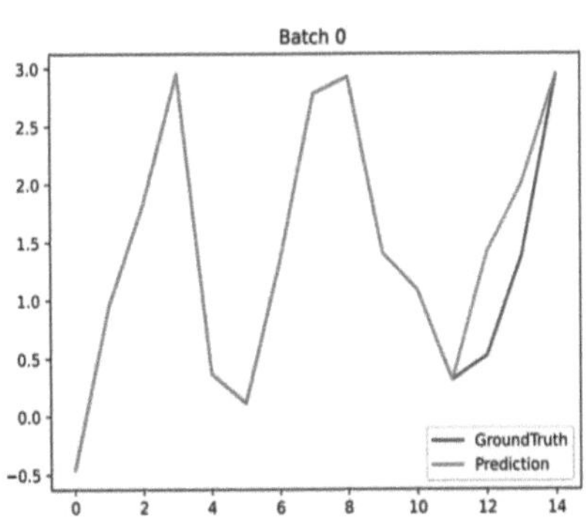

Fig. 6. PH3Months.

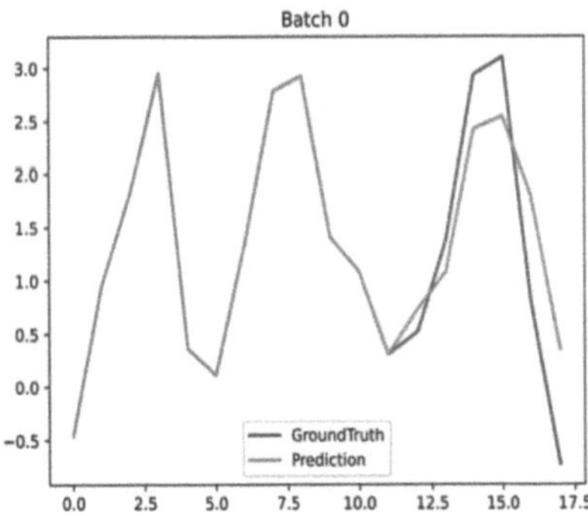

Fig. 7. PH6Months.

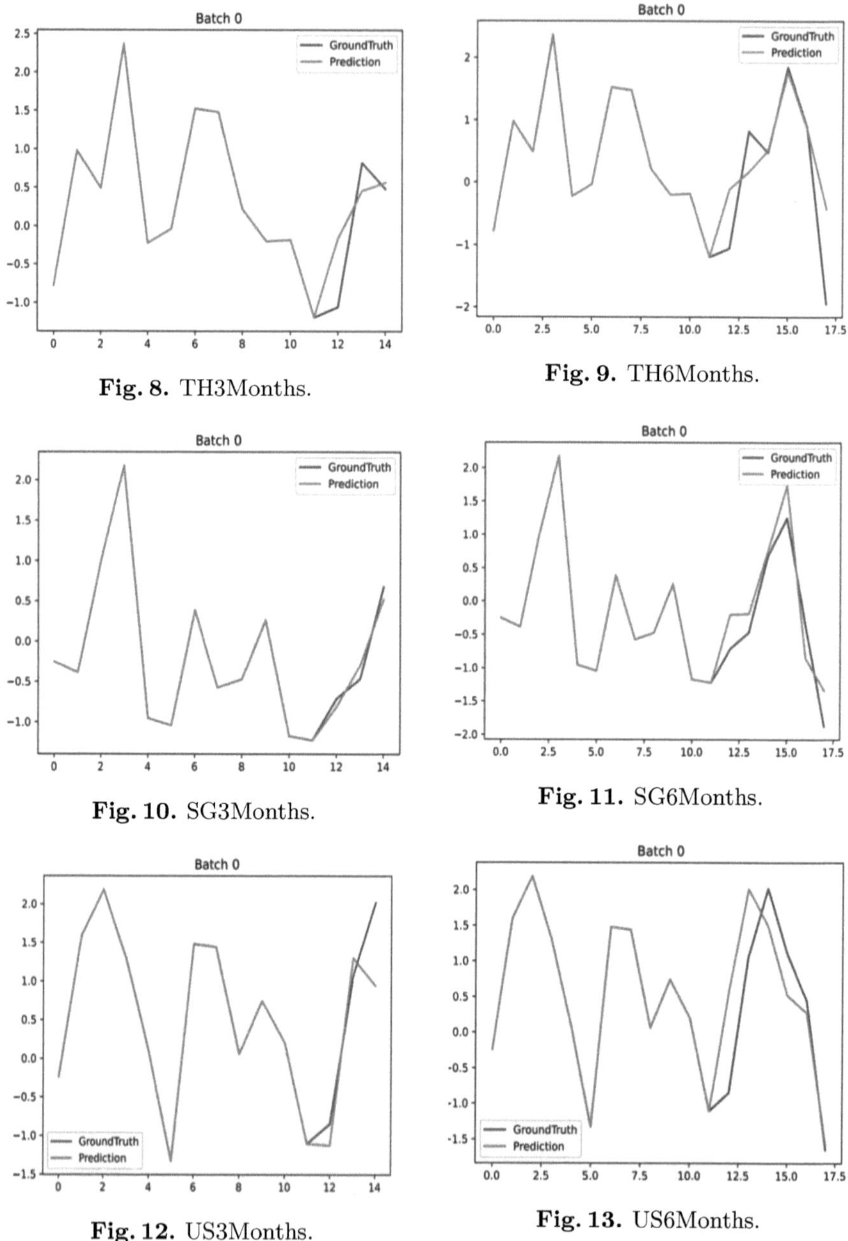

Fig. 8. TH3Months.

Fig. 9. TH6Months.

Fig. 10. SG3Months.

Fig. 11. SG6Months.

Fig. 12. US3Months.

Fig. 13. US6Months.

It is evident that Mambaformer does not transpose the input, resulting in insufficient capture of multivariate correlations. This limitation hinders its ability to fully exploit the relationships between different variables in the dataset. On the other hand, while Mamba possesses linear time complexity and strong long-range dependency modeling capabilities, it does not integrate with the Transformer class of models. Consequently, it lacks the sophisticated attention mechanisms that Transformers offer, which are crucial for capturing intricate patterns in the data.

Similarly, although iTransformer excels in capturing multivariate correlations, it does not incorporate the advantages of Mamba. This results in suboptimal performance when dealing with long time series data, as it cannot leverage Mamba's efficiency and long-distance dependency modeling.

In contrast, our approach, the Mamba-iTransformer, effectively combines the strengths of both iTransformer and Mamba. By integrating iTransformer's ability to capture multivariate correlations with Mamba's linear time complexity and robust long-range dependency modeling, Mamba-iTransformer achieves superior performance. This hybrid model not only captures intricate relationships between multiple variables but also handles long time series data efficiently.

Therefore, it is clear that Mamba-iTransformer's dual capability is reflected in its outstanding performance metrics, making it the best-performing model in our comparative experiments. The synergy between the two models' strengths results in a more comprehensive and efficient approach to time series forecasting, setting Mamba-iTransformer apart as the superior choice (Table 5).

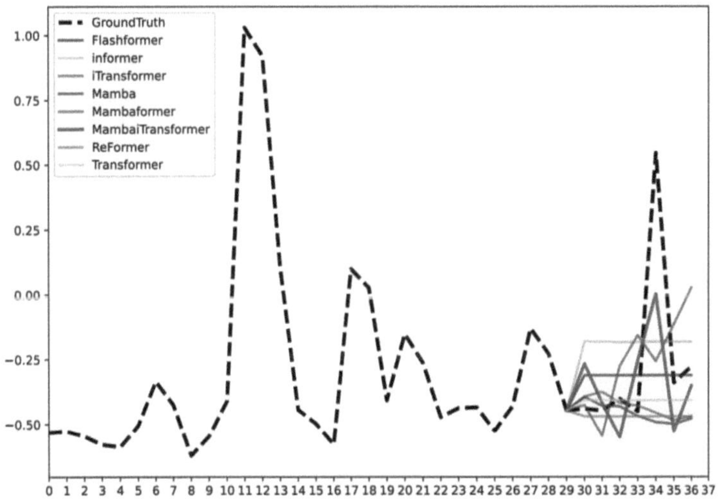

Fig. 14. Comparison of Prediction Results.

Based on the analysis of Fig. 14, it is evident that different models exhibit varying levels of accuracy in time series forecasting. The Transformer and Informer models perform well at certain peak points but lack precision in other areas. The Mamba model captures overall trends reasonably but struggles with detailed fluctuations. The Reformer model shows relatively poor performance,

Table 5. Long-Term Forecasting MAPE Comparison for Four Years in the Six Source Markets

Method	MAPE				
	AU	GB	PH	TH	SG-US
Mamba-iTransformer-3 months (OURS)	0.86	0.28	0.79	0.66	0.35–0.54
STL-DADLM-3 months	4.48	4.54	5.04	6.21	6.33–4.12
DLM-3 months	5.60	5.31	6.97	7.41	6.37–4.55
ANN-3 months	6.19	5.92	7.89	9.18	7.33–5.16
ARIMA-3 months	8.99	7.28	9.13	10.33	8.09–6.18
XGBTR-3 months	7.12	7.79	8.33	11.23	9.17–10.13
SVR-3 months	8.22	7.83	8.93	9.13	7.56–10.18
ETS-3 months	9.20	9.11	10.31	12.11	10.09–11.33
Naive-3 months	10.22	10.02	11.23	13.01	13.10–12.08
Mamba-iTransformer-6 months (OURS)	0.54	0.29	0.80	0.66	0.35–0.54
STL-DADLM-6 months	4.57	4.05	4.65	8.97	8.03–4.50
DLM-6 months	5.74	5.72	5.47	8.91	8.47–6.33
ANN-6 months	5.89	6.33	7.17	9.23	9.02–7.82
ARIMA-6 months	9.12	9.33	8.19	10.32	10.11–11.14
XGBTR-6 months	11.12	12.32	9.76	9.39	10.35–12.63
SVR-6 months	10.25	11.18	9.98	9.95	11.76–11.83
ETS-6 months	12.30	13.21	11.35	11.09	12.78–13.88
Naive-6 months	12.92	13.56	12.60	12.93	13.02–13.90

with a lower degree of alignment between predicted and actual data. Mambaformer performs better than standalone Mamba and Transformer models but still has inaccuracies. In contrast, the Mamba-iTransformer demonstrates superior performance, accurately capturing both overall trends and detailed fluctuations, with the highest alignment between predicted and actual data. Overall, the Mamba-iTransformer effectively combines the strengths of Mamba and iTransformer, offering enhanced prediction accuracy and balanced performance, making it the best choice for time series forecasting tasks.

References

1. China Tourism Association: China's tourism market size forecast in 2020 (2020). https://www.askci.com/news/chanye/20190201/1458221141173.shtml
2. Law, R., Li, G., Fong, D.K.C., Han, X.: Tourism demand forecasting: a deep learning approach. Ann. Tour. Res. **75**, 410–423 (2019). https://doi.org/10.1016/j.annals.2019.01.014
3. Li, X., Law, R.: Forecasting tourism demand with decomposed search cycles. J. Travel Res. **59**(1), 52–68 (2020)

4. Wan, S.K., Song, H.: Forecasting turning points in tourism growth. Ann. Tour. Res. **72**, 156–167 (2018)

5. Sun, S., Law, R.: Forecasting tourist arrivals with machine learning and internet search index. Tour. Manag. **70**, 1–10 (2019)

6. Shen, S., Li, G., Song, H.: Combination forecasts of international tourism demand. Ann. Tour. Res. **38**(1), 72–89 (2011)

7. Jiang, P., et al.: Inbound tourism demand forecasting framework based on fuzzy time series and advanced optimization algorithm. Appl. Soft Comput. **92**, 106320 (2020)

8. Zheng, H., Fu, L., Ye, Q.: Flexible capped principal component analysis with applications in image recognition. Inf. Sci. **614**, 289–310 (2022)

9. Fan, S., et al.: Multi-attention deep neural network fusing character and word embedding for clinical and biomedical concept extraction. Inf. Sci. **608**, 778–793 (2022)

10. Xie, Y., et al.: Online deep hashing for both uni-modal and cross-modal retrieval. Inf. Sci. **608**, 1480–1502 (2022)

11. Xie, G., Qian, Y., Wang, S.: A decomposition-ensemble approach for tourism forecasting. Ann. Tour. Res. **81**, 102891 (2020)

12. Claveria, O., Torra, S.: Forecasting tourism demand to Catalonia: neural networks vs. time series models. Econ. Model. **36**, 220–228 (2014)

13. Song, H., Qiu, R.T.R., Park, J.: Progress in tourism demand research: theory and empirics. Tour. Manag. **94**, 104655 (2023)

14. Liu, X., et al.: Self-attention negative feedback network for real-time image super-resolution. J. King Saud Univ.-Comput. Inf. Sci. **34**(8), 6179–6186 (2022)

15. Zheng, W., Huang, L., Lin, Z.: Multi-attraction, hourly tourism demand forecasting. Ann. Tour. Res. **90**, 103271 (2021)

16. Vaswani, A., et al.: Attention is all you need. In: Advances in Neural Information Processing Systems, vol. 30 (2017)

17. Li, S., et al.: Enhancing the locality and breaking the memory bottleneck of transformer on time series forecasting. In: Advances in Neural Information Processing Systems, vol. 32 (2019)

18. Zhou, H., et al.: Informer: beyond efficient transformer for long sequence time-series forecasting. In: Proceedings of the AAAI Conference on Artificial Intelligence, vol. 35, no. 12 (2021)

19. Liu, Y., et al.: itransformer: inverted transformers are effective for time series forecasting. arXiv preprint arXiv:2310.06625 (2023)

20. Gu, A., Dao, T.: Mamba: linear-time sequence modeling with selective state spaces. arXiv preprint arXiv:2312.00752 (2023)

21. Park, J., et al.: Can mamba learn how to learn? a comparative study on in-context learning tasks. arXiv preprint arXiv:2402.04248 (2024)

22. LeCun, Y., Bengio, Y., Hinton, G.: Deep learning. Nature **521**(7553), 436–444 (2015)

23. Ma, X., et al.: Dimensionality-driven learning with noisy labels. In: International Conference on Machine Learning. PMLR (2018)

24. Zhang, Y., et al.: Tourism demand forecasting: a decomposed deep learning approach. J. Travel Res. **60**(5), 981–997 (2021)

25. Bi, J.-W., Han, T.-Y., Li, H.: International tourism demand forecasting with machine learning models: the power of the number of lagged inputs. Tour. Econ. **28**(3), 621–645 (2022)

26. Gu, A., et al.: Combining recurrent, convolutional, and continuous-time models with linear state space layers. In: Advances in Neural Information Processing Systems, vol. 34, pp. 572–585 (2021)
27. Gu, A., Goel, K., Ré, C.: Efficiently modeling long sequences with structured state spaces. arXiv preprint arXiv:2111.00396 (2021)
28. Fathi, M., et al.: Block-state transformer. arXiv preprint arXiv:2306.09539 (2023)
29. Lieber, O., et al.: Jamba: A hybrid transformer-mamba language model. arXiv preprint arXiv:2403.19887 (2024)

Investigating the Use of AI in E-Business by the Shoprite Holdings Group

Zahraa Khan⬤, Beverley Saurombe⬤, and Rhulani Maluleka⁽⊠⁾⬤

University of Johannesburg, Johannesburg, South Africa
{222212131,224117941}@student.uj.ac.za, rmaluleka@uj.ac.za

Abstract. Since the early 2000s, increasing digitalization across various economic sectors has led to the growth of the field of e-Business. Currently, artificial intelligence (AI) technologies have been increasingly integrated into various sectors, often reshaping the way workflows have been conducted. In the field of e-Business, AI technologies have a wide range of applications, within domains such as marketing, supply chain management, fraud detection, customer interaction, and process automation. In this research paper, a case study is conducted on South African retail group Shoprite Holdings and its use of AI in e-Commerce and broader e-Business is conducted. The various AI techniques used within different areas of the business's operations are identified, and the factors influencing the business's use of AI are investigated through the application of the PESTEL framework. It is found that legal and economic factors are the most salient when considering the group's use of AI, and the importance of interpreting the results within a local legal and economic context is emphasized. Recommendations are provided on potential future AI applications on the part of the business.

Keywords: e-Business · Artificial Intelligence · PESTEL Analysis · Shoprite Holdings

1 Introduction

Since the advent of the Internet in the late 20th century, the business sector has become increasingly digitalized, giving rise to the concept of e-Business. E-Business can be defined broadly as the conduction of business operations through the Internet or other electronic mediums. It is a subject that focuses on the intersection of organizational activity and information and communication technology [2].

Artificial intelligence was first incorporated into the retail sector when traditional processes and tools could no longer meet the growing demand for services and goods to be supplied to consumers. As concepts such as mass customization gained prominence [44], it became necessary to maintain the efficiency and economies of scale associated with mass production.

A solution to address this demand was found in the adoption of AI technologies. AI allowed for the automation of labor-intensive tasks when there was

F. F.-H Nah and K. L. Siau (Eds.): HCII 2025, LNCS 16343, pp. 239–253, 2026.
https://doi.org/10.1007/978-3-032-13167-6_17

a shortage in the workforce, and retailers started incorporating artificial intelligence into their businesses to help them better understand customer needs and preferences [14]. AI technologies have also had utility in areas where human analytic capacity has failed [21].

Although previous research has explored the applications of AI by large multinational corporations, less research has been conducted to investigate how smaller and more localized businesses have used these technologies to conduct business activities. The objective of this investigation is, through the conduction of a case study, to identify the ways in which the South African retail group, Shoprite Holdings, incorporates artificial intelligence tools and techniques into its business operations and to apply the PESTEL framework to examine the various factors influencing the group's usage of AI. In doing so, the investigation seeks to inform further efforts in the industry to implement AI, as well as to contribute to ongoing academic discourse within the field of e-Business.

In the following section, Sect. 2, a brief background of the subject chosen for the case study is given. In order to contextualize the case study and inform the subsequent analysis, in Sect. 3, a literature review will be performed on the role that artificial intelligence plays in the field of e-Business, with a particular focus on its applications within e-Commerce. An overview and justification of the research methodology (including the analytical framework) chosen for the study will follow in Sect. 4. The findings of the analysis will be outlined and discussed in Sects. 5 and 6 respectively. Finally, in Sect. 7, the study will provide recommendations for further efforts by the group and other companies seeking to incorporate artificial intelligence into business operations, along with recommendations for further research.

2   Shoprite Holdings: A Background

Shoprite Holdings, the parent company of Shoprite and Checkers, was founded in 1979 [39]. Barney Rogut and Basil Geller, who were considered seasoned retailers, founded the first eight-store grocery chain. PEP Stores later purchased the grocery chain from them. However, it was Christoffel Wiese who transformed Shoprite Holdings from a single supermarket in South Africa into the Shoprite Holdings that is known today when he took over in 1981 [41].

During its early expansion, Shoprite Holdings focused on the middle to lower income market [1]. In 1983, it had gained 21 stores and 33 outlets in various provinces by 1986, and was listed on the Johannesburg Stock Exchange (JSE) with a market capitalization of R29 million [41].

Wiese's vision and leadership enabled him to spearhead Shoprite Holdings' growth and continental expansion into the largest supermarket retailer in Africa. The first international store was in Windhoek, Namibia, in 1990 and in 2002 it launched a secondary listing on the Namibian Stock Exchange (NSX). The 2000s marked further expansion into Zimbabwe, Uganda, Egypt, Malawi, Lesotho, and acquisitions in Madagascar and Tanzania [37]. Today, it is operational in a total of ten African countries [5].

Although Covid-19 sped up the use of AI in e-Commerce, Shoprite's previous AI integration in its operations laid the groundwork for sophisticated AI adoption in the subsequent years. These included demand prediction and inventory management, customer relationship management (CRM) and loyalty programs, inventory optimization, and price optimization. In response to increasing digital demand and competitive pressure, the group invested heavily in e-Commerce platforms, most notably Checkers Sixty60 [4].

3   Literature Review

This objective of this section is to discuss the various ways in which artificial intelligence has been applied in e-Business over the past decade and in doing so, to further contextualize this case study and inform the subsequent analysis and recommendations. In general, these applications fall within one of six realms: customer experience and satisfaction, marketing and sales optimization, operations and supply chain management, fraud detection and risk management, process automation, and human resources.

The use of artificial intelligence for grocery retail in chains in particular has been discussed in previous literature. Neurauter [28] identifies that AI technologies paired with an omnichannel approach are a driver of success in grocery stores. Wolniak et al. [47] identify AI as a "key player" in the transformation of grocery shopping, also citing inventory management optimization and smart recommendations as reasons for this.

3.1   Customer Experience

As e-Business as a field has progressed, customers have come to expect and demand the personalization and ease of use that AI-driven algorithms offer through custom recommendations and predictive analytics.

AI technologies have improved customer interaction quality in various ways. A review by Sulastri [40] focused in particular on the impact of AI-driven personalization and the use of AI chatbots. It was revealed that machine learning algorithms used to predict customer preferences and provide customized offers had increased customer engagement, as demonstrated by an increased likelihood of repeat purchases and positive feedback in the form of ratings. In addition, chatbots with natural language processing (NLP) abilities were found to have increased customer service efficiency through their ability to manage simultaneous interactions, provide instant responses, and be available 24/7.

When consumers began to demand customization experiences, legacy systems could not deliver on scale [44]. There was a need for a system that could keep up with demand. A solution was found in AI-driven recommendation engines that could analyze a large number of data sets that included browsing behavior and purchase history. Such systems can make recommendations in real time with high accuracy, leading to increases in conversion rates and loyalty [42]. An investigation by Yin et al. [50] further investigated the impact of AI-driven recommendations on customer engagement in e-Commerce, finding that these personalized recommendations significantly influenced customer click intentions.

3.2 Security and Risk Management

Another area in which AI technologies can be utilized within an e-Business context is security and risk detection and management. Machine learning and data mining techniques have the ability to identify patterns within fraudulent data, thereby highlighting potential fraud and managing risk within a business.

Mutemi and Bacao conducted a systematic review of the literature [26] to investigate how machine learning techniques have been applied in e-Commerce for fraud detection. Artificial neural networks in particular were widely used for the task.

AI has also been applied to the problem of physical security. To solve the problem of shoplifting, smarter surveillance was needed as traditional CCTV surveillance was insufficient. Using AI-powered video analytics that detect suspicious behaviors and automate alerts allowed retailers to strengthen security [16].

3.3 Task Automation

Many processes in e-Business can potentially be positively impacted by AI automation. In the retail sector, this can often be seen in the implementation of self-checkout systems. Self-checkout systems can make customer shopping experiences smoother while reducing the need for human cashiers. Cui et al. found that self-checkout systems lead to more favorable perceptions of the store atmosphere and a higher intention to purchase, among customers [7].

3.4 Supply Chain Management

Although AI techniques are often used in the context of business-customer interaction, they also have significant utility in logistic operations, including supply chain management (SCM). Applications in this domain include inventory management and optimization, logistic routing, and demand forecasting.

The primary application area discussed in academic literature is production optimization, including the sub-areas of inventory and routing optimization. Most investigations on the application of AI in SCM focus on machine learning. For example, both deep learning ensemble models and reinforcement learning models are effective when applied to automated inventory management, and in particular demand forecasting and decision making for inventory replenishment, displaying the potential to significantly increase sales and revenue [8,20]. Dynamic route scheduling is another area in which AI solutions - genetic algorithms, ant colony optimization algorithms, and reinforcement learning - have proven to be highly effective [8].

The Covid-19 pandemic exposed weaknesses in supply chains that were in place because traditional methods had huge carrying costs and retailers would lose sales [16]. AI's inventory-optimization systems and demand forecasting systems allow retailers to forecast demand spikes, minimizing stock-outs and overstocks [19].

4   Methodology

This investigation will take the form of a case study. It is crucial that studies on the use of AI in e-Business be carried out not only within the theoretical realm, but also to assess the real-life deployment and impact of AI technologies by corporations. Furthermore, since existing studies tend to focus on larger, global corporations, there is a need for case studies of smaller, geographically localized enterprises.

As academic literature on the subject of the case study, Shoprite Holdings, is limited, this investigation primarily utilizes secondary sources of information such as articles accessed from the group's website, as well as reports done on the group by various South African news outlets.

The PESTEL framework was chosen to perform the analysis. Originally developed from the research of Francis J. Aguilar, the framework aims to provide a view of the environment in which a business operates by examining the political, economic, social, technological, environmental, and legal influences that act on the business [45]. It has been chosen for this investigation because of the broad and comprehensive outlook it enables, as well as its frequent and well-established usage as a strategic management tool within the business sector.

5   PESTEL Analysis

5.1   Political Influences

This subsection discusses the ways in which South African policies and initiatives, or lack thereof, have influenced or could influence the group's adoption of AI in e-Business.

For South African companies seeking to incorporate AI into their business operations, a crucial policy to consider is South Africa's National AI Policy Framework [11]. The framework was published in 2024 by the Department of Communications and Digital Technologies (DCDT). Its main focus is to promote inclusive growth by striking a balance of building capacity, responsible AI deployment, and a human-centered approach [10].

The framework outlines the strategic pillars of the policy. The first of these stated is the development of talent. Along with educational recommendations, this pillar highlights the need for industry collaboration—the cultivation of partnerships between the industrial and academic sectors.

Another pillar outlined in the policy is research and development. Funding usually comes from the government, that is, incentives such as grants and subsidies. However, UNESCO highlighted concerns about uneven incentives, arguing that actual funding for the adoption of AI is still lacking [43]. This suggests that the framework is still high-level, indicating the possibility of a slow AI uptake for most small-to-medium enterprises (SMEs).

The framework in general suggests the creation of public-private partnerships, that is, collaborative efforts between government and industry. The pillars mentioned suggest avenues for the group's further use of AI—for instance, Shoprite could potentially collaborate with academics within the field of artificial intelligence to test the deployment of new algorithms or AI technologies within the real world.

Another political influence that has affected the group's use of AI is the purchase rationing policies that were implemented during Covid-19 to impose quantity limits on staples according to government guidelines to prevent hoarding [25]. The group's use of AI in inventory management operations could have facilitated their compliance with these policies.

5.2 Economic Influences

These are influences that affect market economics, cost structures, and supply chain economics. Incorporating AI techniques into business operations can involve costs such as the acquisition or hiring of hardware to train machine learning models, the hiring of machine learning engineers, or the training of employees. Consequently, another factor for the business to consider is whether the business can afford to incorporate AI given the local economy, and whether the return on investment (ROI) is sufficiently high to warrant these costs.

In the context of artificial intelligence, ROI initiatives measure the financial and strategic benefits gained from investing in AI technologies compared to cost [15]. One of the benefits of investing in AI is that it is innovative and increases business efficiency, which ultimately increases ROI [30].

Factors influencing the ROI of AI technologies include cost savings, speed and accuracy, revenue growth, productivity gains, and scalability. Cost savings affect AI ROI through the reduction of operational costs by automating tasks, improving efficiency, and reducing errors. AI-powered tools can increase speed and accuracy by improving decision-making and reducing downtime in business operations. AI can help increase revenue by improving the customer experience, driving sales, and enabling data-driven decision-making [18]. The use of AI can also result in productivity gains by helping employees focus on higher-value tasks by handling repetitive work [32]. Finally, AI enables businesses to scale operations with minimal additional investment [24].

The ROI of AI investments is likely to be large, as it has the potential to increase sales, make business operations more efficient, and save resources by optimizing resource allocation (for instance, through inventory optimization), thereby reducing costs in the long run. However, it is possible that the ROI will not be immediate, as AI techniques may need to be deployed for a while before resulting in a significant impact [31].

As mentioned in Sect. 2, Shoprite operates within 10 African countries— multiple of which face economic issues such as income equality and low employment rates [6]. As a result, citizens of these countries could be particularly vulnerable to job losses resulting from the application of AI to task automation (seen, for instance, in the group's experimentation with an AI-powered self-checkout system [12]). Since low-skilled jobs are most likely to be automated, the relatively low educational attainment rates in some of these countries means that the economic impact of AI automation could be particularly severe.

5.3   Social Influences

As discussed in the previous subsection, socioeconomic inequality is prevalent within South Africa and various other African countries in which the group operates, which makes the social influences of the adoption of AI by businesses, particularly retailers such as the group that cater to various socioeconomic demographics, a concern.

A significant social issue is the digital divide that exists within the country [27]. An over reliance on new technologies in favor of more conventional means of commerce could negatively impact those who are unable to access those technologies, or who have not had the requisite education to understand how to use them.

Currently, Shoprite uses AI technology for a pricing tool that was designed by Boston Consulting Group to help keep its prices low for their customers. This technology ensures that more people can afford to buy from Shoprite within their own means, catering to more socioeconomic groups [3].

During Covid-19, Shoprite extended its operating hours and workforce support by hiring temporary staff that were put on rotation and made extended shifts possible. This was done to maintain service levels and to help prevent panic buying [23]. Shoprite Holdings adopted transparent customer communication using SMS and social networks to inform customers about safe shopping protocols [17].

5.4   Technological Influences

Technological developments in recent years have had a significant impact on group policies and have the potential to further influence their adoption of AI technologies. The most notable example of this is the group's e-Commerce platform: their grocery delivery service app, Sixty60. The company uses machine learning algorithms to determine which routes and regions are optimal [36]. In addition, the app includes an AI-driven recommendation system, which is used to recommend grocery products to customers based on individual historical purchasing data. During Covid-19, Shoprite Holdings tripled its back-end order processing to increase its delivery capacity on Sixty60 [22].

The group has also used technological developments to aid in logistics, broader supply chain management, and store layout [36]. This included repurposing dark stores—stores that only sell to consumers online—for e-Commerce into dedicated online order picking zones to accelerate delivery [35].

Another example of how technology has facilitated Shoprite's business operations is found in Shoprite's clothing brand, UNIQ by Checkers, which offers radio frequency identification-based self-service (RFID) checkouts in its standalone stores. It was introduced in March 2023, making it the first clothing retailer in South Africa to offer such a service and the use of smart tags [38]. The advantage of this, in addition to automating repetitive labor-intensive tasks, is reduced queue times, as RFID allows the simultaneous scanning of multiple items. This speeds up the checkout process as it eliminates the need to scan items individually [33].

In August 2021, Shoprite introduced a fully automated cashierless concept store located in Brackenfell, Capetown called "Checkers Rush". It used AI camera technology to identify products and then proceeds to bill customers automatically when exiting. However, this was not a public store as it was only accessible to employees [12].

5.5   Environmental Influences

By reducing resource waste, AI-driven logistics can have a positive impact on the sustainability of the company. Food waste is a significant problem in South Africa, with more than 10 million tonnes of food going to waste each year [49]. This has led to pressure on food retailers to ensure that wastage is minimized.

Through the application of predictive analytics to predict demand within supply chain management, along with the use of AI-driven algorithms to optimize inventory levels in inventory management, as discussed in the review of the literature. Consequently, the group has joined many other companies in using machine learning algorithms to predict sales and automatically place replenishment orders, thus reducing the amount of potential surplus stock that can result in food waste [34].

Another environmental factor affecting the group's use of AI is route optimization [36]. Not only does route optimization streamline business operations by saving time, shorter delivery routes result in decreased fossil fuel usage, enabling the business to reduce its carbon footprint and promoting sustainability.

The ecological impact of the choice of sources is also worth considering. In this regard, Shoprite Holdings decided to reduce its transport footprint by sourcing locally, reducing the intensity of carbon from supply [29].

Although Shoprite has exhibited social consciousness in its environmental policies, the creation and deployment of large machine learning models raises the question of the environmental impact of model training. The computation carried out to train large ML models has high energy costs and generates large amounts of carbon emissions [9]. It is uncertain whether the machine learning models currently used by Shoprite for inventory management and data analytics are trained on a scale that would result in a significant environmental impact. However, the company primarily operates—and thus potentially utilizes data centers in—developing regions, some of which may be particularly vulnerable to environmental harm, due to their relatively significant reliance on natural resources. These considerations, then, should be factored into decisions about the scaling of existing models as well as the training of new ones.

5.6   Legal Influences

Machine-learning algorithms underpin many of the AI technologies that are applied in the context of e-Business. However, in order to train machine learning models for the purposes of predictive analytics or personalized recommendations, data must be collected from customers. This can raise concerns about data privacy, informed consent, and laws surrounding data protection. The most relevant framework in this regard is the Protection of Personal Information Act (POPIA) [13].

POPIA which is similar to the General Data Protection Regulation (GDPR), governs the processing of personal data and includes its use in AI platforms. It outlines the conditions for the informed consent of the individual whose data is collected, the necessity of the data being collected, and the protection of the data by responsible parties to protect data from loss or unauthorized access. The Information Regulator, responsible for data protection in South Africa, recognizes the need to understand the implications of AI for the protection of personal information, as there is currently no legislation governing the use of AI in South Africa [46].

The absence of any legislation governing the use of AI in South Africa as well as in various other African countries where Shoprite Holdings operates raises various concerns. The lack of explicit laws surrounding AI usage could result in impeded decision-making, or else the making of ethically or legally gray decisions on the part of the group or other corporations utilizing AI in e-Business. Another concern is data processing—although conditions for this are outlined in POPIA, the act does not contain any clauses pertaining specifically to AI data processing, which may pose different challenges or concerns.

During June 2022, following a cyberattack on the business, the group had an opportunity to demonstrate its dedication to protecting its customers' data privacy. Customer data was compromised and sold on the dark Web. In response to this, Shoprite Holdings took measures to increase its cybersecurity posture by investing in Omnisient, a privacy protection startup, to ensure that it secures customer data using bank-grade encryption technology [48].

6   Discussion

6.1   Interpretation of Key Influences

The PESTEL analysis revealed various factors that inform or have the potential to inform the ways in which AI technologies are being used by Shoprite Holdings. As can be seen in Fig. 1, economic and legal factors emerged as the ones with the greatest impact, due to the current socioeconomic realities in South Africa, as well as the increasing regulation with regard to data protection, respectively.

In general, the company has successfully incorporated AI technologies into many of its business operations. These include logistics, through machine learning-driven delivery route optimization, and inventory management through the application of predictive analytics. Additionally, the group's e-Commerce

Political	Economic	Social	Technological	Environmental	Legal
AI Policy Framework	ROI of AI	Digital Divide	Recommendation System	Food Waste Reduction	Absence of Legislation
Lack of Government Funding	Automation-related Job Loss	Price Optimisation	e-Commerce (Sixty60)	Demand Prediction	AI Data Processing Concerns
Purchase Rationing Policies			Self-Service Checkout	Fuel Reduction	Cybersecurity Posture
				Model Training Costs	

Fig. 1. Summary of the various PESTEL factors' influence on Shoprite Holdings' AI usage. Green and yellow indicate significant and modest positive impact respectively, while red and orange indicate significant and modest negative impact respectively. (Color figure online)

platform, that is, the grocery delivery app Sixty60, utilizes AI technologies through the use of their product recommendation system.

Economic factors play an important role within a company's business operations, and while the implementation of AI can be costly, findings suggest that Shoprite has deemed the investments to be worthwhile.

Although environmental considerations are often considered less important in the context of AI deployment, the group has taken a proactive approach in this regard through their deployment of technologies to reduce food waste.

The legal and social factors surrounding the group's use of AI were notable. The company's data collection policies force it to comply with POPIA. Furthermore, digital and socioeconomic inequalities often impact how AI technologies are deployed and received by customers. Increasing technological complexity can run the risk of excluding less digitally literate customers. However, the Shoprite Holdings group has instead shown social responsibility by using the technologies in an attempt to help lower income customers.

Several themes discussed in this case study show similarities with those in the existing literature, primarily with regard to technical implementations of AI. For example, AI technologies were found to be commonly applied in logistics and supply chain management and [50] found that recommendation systems were one of the most common ways companies applied AI technologies.

However, many of the factors influencing the group's adoption and usage of AI technologies are not covered in existing literature. The primary reason for this is that most existing literature focuses on the use of AI by multinational corporations, while the group's application of AI is better understood and analyzed in a local South African context.

For example, due to the significant socioeconomic inequality in the country, South African businesses could be viewed as having a unique responsibility to ensure that the incorporation of AI technologies into business operations promotes equity rather than exacerbate existing disparities. Furthermore, local South African legislation on AI and data privacy must inform the ways South African businesses deploy these technologies.

6.2   Implications and Recommendations for the Group

Although the company has already succeeded in the application of AI-driven technologies to business operations, the literature reviewed suggests that there are even more avenues for the application of AI to streamline business operations and increase sales within the domain of e-Business. For example, the group could make use of a chatbot on the Sixty60 app, employing natural language processing and generative AI techniques in order to improve customer service.

The group can also expand its offer of real-time insights to suppliers and franchisees through APIs using Insights-as-a-Service (IaaS). It works by providing Shoprite Holdings with a cloud-based solution that uses advanced analytics and AI to extract meaningful insights from the data. The group could also employ augmented reality algorithms to enable virtual try-ons for customers of its fashion outlet, Uniq.

6.3   Avenues for Future Research

The literature investigating the application of AI in e-Business is abundant; but there appears to be a lack of case studies investigating how smaller and medium enterprises (SMEs) and more localized companies incorporate AI into their workflows. Research on companies operating in developing regions is also lacking.

It is crucial that this domain be further explored; smaller companies and those operating within developing regions may have different factors to consider when deciding how to incorporate AI in their businesses and different use cases for AI. Such investigations, then, will enable similarly sized and located enterprises to make more informed decisions when incorporating AI into their own workflows.

7   Conclusion

The investigation carried out in this paper intended to examine how Shoprite Holdings has incorporated artificial intelligence into its various e-Business operations. A literature review of AI in e-Business was performed, after which a case study was carried out and the PESTEL framework employed to analyze various factors influencing the business's deployment of AI technologies.

The purpose of this case study was to add to the growing body of academic literature investigating the application of AI within e-Business and to inform future efforts in the industry through the analysis of a real-world use case, in particular, the case of a localized South African retail group.

Economic and legal factors were found to be the most influential in the business's usage of AI. Some of the group's approaches to AI incorporation were similar to previous applications within e-Business, such as the utilization of an AI-powered recommendation system on their e-Commerce platform and the use of predictive analytics for inventory optimization. However, some of the ways in which the group applied AI technologies distinguished it from other corporations, namely its socially conscious approach to algorithmic pricing and its application of AI to approach business operations sustainably. Similarly located retailers can look towards the group's use of AI in e-Business as an exemplification—of both the successful implementation of established technologies within an African context and the social and environmental consciousness displayed in this implementation.

Future research should conduct similar case studies through the use of direct interviews with company employees or IT professionals. Furthermore, future research could then involve the comparison of similar enterprises such as local African or South African retail groups, with respect to AI applications within e-Business.

References

1. Badal, A.: A case study of shoprite holdings limited, 2021. J. Manag. Policy Pract. **22**(3) (2021)
2. Beynon-Davies, P.: eBusiness. Bloomsbury Publishing (2017)
3. Business, I.: Shoprite is using AI tech to help customers save (2024). https://www.iol.co.za/business/shoprite-is-using-ai-tech-to-help-customers-save-3e5d0495-ec36-4326-88a3-361c820833f9. Accessed 22 Mar 2025
4. CA Programme Faculty of Economic and Management Sciences, University of Pretoria: Retail industry report 2024 (2024). https://www.studocu.com/en-za/document/university-of-pretoria/business-acumen/retail-industry-report-final/94698442
5. Cambaza, K.: Shoprite holdings ltdcase study: challenges for expansion in Africa. REVES - Revista Relações Sociais **7**(2), 19553 (2024). https://doi.org/10.18540/revesvl7iss2pp19553, https://periodicos.ufv.br/reves/article/view/19553
6. Chancel, L., Cogneau, D., Gethin, A., Myczkowski, A., Robilliard, A.S.: Income inequality in Africa, 1990–2019: measurement, patterns, determinants. World Dev. **163**, 106162 (2023)
7. Cui, Y., van Esch, P., Jain, S.P.: Just walk out: the effect of AI-enabled checkouts. Eur. J. Mark. **56**(6), 1650–1683 (2022)
8. Daios, A., Kladovasilakis, N., Kelemis, A., Kostavelis, I.: AI applications in supply chain management: a survey. Appl. Sci. **15**(5) (2025). https://doi.org/10.3390/app15052775, https://www.mdpi.com/2076-3417/15/5/2775
9. Delort, E., Riou, L., Srivastava, A.: Environmental impact of artificial intelligence. Ph.D. thesis, INRIA; CEA Leti (2023)
10. Department of Communications and Digital Technologies. https://www.dcdt.gov.za/. Accessed 11 May 2025
11. Department of Communications and Digital Technologies (2024). https://fwblaw.co.za/wp-content/uploads/2024/10/South-Africa-National-AI-Policy-Framework-1.pdf
12. Ellis, M.: Checkers rush: shoprite launches automated, cashierless concept store in cape town (2021). https://memeburn.com/2021/08/checkers-rush-shoprite-launches-automated-cashierless-concept-store-in-cape-town/. Accessed 10 May 2025
13. Government of South Africa: Chapter 3

14. Hariguna, T., Ruangkanjanases, A.: Assessing the impact of artificial intelligence on customer performance: a quantitative study using partial least squares methodology. Data Sci. Manag. **7**(3), 155–163 (2024). https://doi.org/10.1016/j.dsm.2024.01.001, https://www.sciencedirect.com/science/article/pii/S2666764924000018
15. Investopedia: Return on investment (ROI) (2025). https://www.investopedia.com/terms/r/returnoninvestment.asp. Accessed 21 Mar 2025
16. Kulkarni, N.D., Bansal, S.: Utilizing gen AI and computer vision for applications in the retail sector. Online Sci. Res. (2023). https://www.onlinescientificresearch.com/articles/utilizing-gen-ai-and-computer-vision-for-applications-in-the-retail-sector.html
17. Lee, D.: Crisis communication strategies of supermarkets during COVID-19. J. Retail Manag. **12**(3), 150–162 (2020). https://doi.org/10.1016/j.jretman.2020.08.004
18. Lopez, S.: Optimizing marketing ROI with predictive analytics: harnessing big data and AI for data-driven decision making. J. Artif. Intell. Res. **3**(2), 9–36 (2023)
19. Lu, H.P., Cheng, H.L., Tzou, J.C., Chen, C.S.: Technology roadmap of AI applications in the retail industry. Technol. Forecast. Soc. Chang. **195**, 122778 (2023)
20. Ma, X., Zeyu, W., Ni, X., Ping, G.: Artificial intelligence-based inventory management for retail supply chain optimization: a case study of customer retention and revenue growth. J. Knowl. Learn. Sci. Technol. ISSN: 2959-6386 (online) **3**(4), 260–273 (2024). https://doi.org/10.60087/jklst.v3.n4.p260
21. McKinsey, Company: The state of AI: global survey. Technical report, McKinsey and Company (2025). https://www.mckinsey.com/capabilities/quantumblack/our-insights/the-state-of-ai
22. Mokgola, C.: Checkers sixty60 doubles capacity to meet lockdown demand. ITWeb (2020). https://www.itweb.co.za/content/WnzADrGvE6Wq7Hyp
23. Moodley, S.: Supermarkets boost staff as panic buying continues. IOL (2020). https://www.iol.co.za/business-report/companies/supermarkets-boost-staff-as-panic-buying-continues-45612367
24. Moro-Visconti, R.: Artificial intelligence-driven digital scalability and growth options. In: Artificial Intelligence Valuation: The Impact on Automation, BioTech, ChatBots, FinTech, B2B2C, and Other Industries, pp. 131–204. Springer (2024). https://doi.org/10.1007/978-3-031-53622-9_3
25. Mufson, S.: South Africa's retailers impose limits on food as panic buying intensifies. Reuters (2020). https://www.reuters.com/article/us-health-coronavirus-safrica-groceries-idUSKBN21403S
26. Mutemi, A., Bacao, F.: E-commerce fraud detection based on machine learning techniques: systematic literature review. https://www.sciopen.com/article/pdf/10.26599/BDMA.2023.9020023.pdf?ifPreview=0. Accessed 12 May 2025
27. Ndulu, B., Ngwenya, N.X., Setlhalogile, M.: The digital divide in South Africa: insights from the COVID-19 experience and beyond. In: Qobo, M., Soko, M., Xenia Ngwenya, N. (eds.) The Future of the South African Political Economy Post-COVID 19, pp. 273–295. Springer, Cham (2022). https://doi.org/10.1007/978-3-031-10576-0_11
28. Neurauter, C.: The future of grocery stores: omnichannel and AI technologies and next-generation brick-and-mortar grocery stores. Master's thesis, Universidade Catolica Portuguesa (2022)
29. Nkosi, B.: Local suppliers keep South Africa's shelves stocked. SAfm Bus. Daily (2020). https://www.safm.co.za/local-suppliers-stock
30. van Orlé, C.: Market value of AI: does investing in AI pay off? Master's thesis, University of Twente (2024)

31. Pandey, S., Gupta, S., Chhajed, S.: ROI of AI: effectiveness and measurement. SSRN Electron. J. (2021). https://doi.org/10.2139/ssrn.3858398
32. Ramachandran, K., Mary, A.A.S., Hawladar, S., Asokk, D., Bhaskar, B., Pitroda, J.: Machine learning and role of artificial intelligence in optimizing work performance and employee behavior. Mater. Today: Proc. **51**, 2327–2331 (2022)
33. Retailer, S..: Retail automation and payment solutions 2023 - taking care of business in an automated world (2023). https://supermarket.co.za/index.php/feature-articles/5937-retail-automation-and-payment-solutions-2023-taking-care-of-business-in-an-automated-world. Accessed 10 May 2025
34. Shoprite Holdings: From reducing shopping queues to delivery times: how the Shoprite Group innovates using AI. https://www.shopriteholdings.co.za/newsroom/2022/the-shoprite-group-innovates-using-ai.html. Accessed 21 Mar 2025
35. Shoprite Holdings: 2020 sustainability report (2020). https://www.shopriteholdings.co.za/docs/shp-sustainability-report-2020.pdf, describes conversion of retail space for e-fulfilment during lockdown
36. Shoprite Holdings: How the Shoprite Group is redefining shopping in South Africa—shopriteholdings.co.za (2023). https://www.shopriteholdings.co.za/newsroom/2023/retail-store-of-the-future.html. Accessed 20 Mar 2025
37. Shoprite Holdings: Our story (2024). https://www.shopriteholdings.co.za/group/story.html. Accessed 08 May 2025
38. Shoprite Holdings Newsroom: How the shoprite group is redefining shopping in South Africa. Shoprite Holdings Newsroom (2023). https://www.shopriteholdings.co.za/newsroom/2023/retail-store-of-the-future.html. Accessed 10 May 2025
39. Smith, A., Smit, H., Campus, U.B.P.: Case study: Shoprite (2010)
40. Sulastri, L.: The role of artificial intelligence in enhancing customer experience: a case study of global e-commerce platforms. Int. J. Sci. Soc. **5**(3), 451–469 (2023). https://doi.org/10.54783/ijsoc.v5i3.1257
41. Thorne, S.: The man who built South Africa's biggest retail empire (2024). https://businesstech.co.za/news/business/787575/the-man-who-built-south-africas-biggest-retail-empire/. Accessed 28 Apr 2025
42. Topics, E.: 55+ new generative AI stats (2024) (2025). https://explodingtopics.com/blog/generative-ai-stats
43. UNESCO: Country profile: South Africa – global AI ethics and governance observatory (key insights) (2025). https://www.unesco.org/ethics-ai/en/southafrica
44. U.S., E., Canada: Improve customer experience (cx). Epicor Blog (2023). https://www.epicor.com/en-us/blog/industries/the-pros-and-cons-of-ai-adoption-in-retail/
45. Vilas Belsare, H.: Pestle analysis. Int. J. Adv. Res. **13**(02), 608–612 (2025). https://doi.org/10.21474/IJAR01/20411
46. de Wet, P., Fourie, J.: South Africa: AI and data privacy regulations – the complexities of AI technologies and processing personal information. VDT Attorneys Inc. (2024). https://vdt.co.za/artificial-intelligence/south-africa-ai-and-data-privacy-regulations-the-complexities-of-ai-technologies-and-processing-personal-information/. Accessed 11 May 2025
47. Wolniak, R., Stecuła, K., Aydın, B.: Digital transformation of grocery in-store shopping-scanners, artificial intelligence, augmented reality and beyond: a review. Foods **13**(18) (2024). https://doi.org/10.3390/foods13182948, https://www.mdpi.com/2304-8158/13/18/2948

48. Writer, S.: Shoprite backs local tech start-up omnisient. https://www.itweb.co.za/article/shoprite-backs-local-tech-start-up-omnisient/KWEBbvyLLlNqmRjO. Accessed 11 May 2025
49. WWF: wwf.org.za. https://www.wwf.org.za/?21641/Food-Loss-and-Waste-Facts-and-Futures-Report. Accessed 22 Mar 2025
50. Yin, J., Qiu, X., Wang, Y.: The impact of AI-personalized recommendations on clicking intentions: evidence from Chinese e-commerce. J. Theor. Appl. Electron. Commer. Res. **20**(1), 21 (2025). https://doi.org/10.3390/jtaer20010021

AI Adoption in Emerging E-Commerce Markets: A Strategic Comparison of Takealot and Global Leaders

Shavir Sejal Morar and Rhulani Maluleka[(✉)] [ID]

University of Johannesburg, Johannesburg, South Africa
{222028506,rmaluleka}@uj.ac.za

Abstract. Artificial intelligence (AI) is transforming e-business globally, yet its adoption in emerging markets poses distinct challenges. This paper examines AI integration strategies within e-commerce in developing economies, focusing on South Africa's Takealot as a core case study. We compare Takealot's approach to those of global leaders Amazon and Alibaba, and regional peer Jumia, to identify how AI can be effectively adopted under infrastructure constraints, regulatory frameworks, and diverse consumer contexts. We propose a novel framework, ADAPT (Assessment, Development, Adaptation, Phased implementation, Tracking), tailored to guide AI adoption in emerging market e-commerce. Through a literature review and comparative analysis, we demonstrate how Takealot's measured, context-aware adoption of AI aligns with best practices and addresses local barriers. The ADAPT framework and accompanying principles (contextual intelligence, infrastructure-aware design, gradual capability building, trust-centric implementation, and localized metrics) provide actionable guidance for e-business platforms in similar markets. Our findings underscore that successful AI deployment in developing economies requires not a direct transplantation of solutions from mature markets, but rather strategic adaptation to local conditions. The paper's contributions include a structured framework for AI adoption in resource-constrained e-commerce environments and insights bridging global AI innovations with emerging market needs.

Keywords: e-Commerce · Artificial Intelligence · Takealot

1 Introduction

E-commerce platforms worldwide increasingly leverage artificial intelligence to enhance customer experience, optimize operations, and drive growth. Industry giants like Amazon and Alibaba have pioneered AI-driven solutions—from recommendation engines to automated logistics—that contribute substantially to their success [3]. However, the context of emerging markets differs markedly: infrastructure is less robust, regulatory environments and consumer behaviors diverge, and firms often operate under resource constraints. This raises a critical question: How can e-businesses in developing economies effectively adopt

F. F.-H Nah and K. L. Siau (Eds.): HCII 2025, LNCS 16343, pp. 254–271, 2026.
https://doi.org/10.1007/978-3-032-13167-6_18

AI technologies to remain competitive and improve performance, despite these challenges?

This paper addresses the question by examining AI adoption strategies in emerging market e-commerce, using South Africa's largest online retailer, Takealot, as a focal case. Takealot's experience is contrasted with global leaders (Amazon, Alibaba) and a regional peer (Jumia in Africa) to derive insights on best practices and pitfalls [7]. Takealot provides a compelling study: operating in an environment characterized by intermittent connectivity, a patchwork of digital literacy levels, and data privacy regulations like the Protection of Personal Information Act (POPIA), Takealot cannot simply replicate Amazon's playbook. Instead, it has had to innovate and adapt AI solutions to local realities. Similarly, Jumia – often dubbed "the Amazon of Africa" – has encountered hurdles in trying to scale an Amazon-like model across African countries, underscoring the need for context-specific strategies.

The objective of this research is to develop a framework for effective AI adoption in developing e-commerce markets that accounts for these unique constraints and opportunities. By synthesizing literature and case evidence, we propose the ADAPT framework as a stepwise approach to guide e-businesses through AI implementation – from initial readiness assessments to continuous performance tracking. We critically evaluate this framework against real-world practices and provide recommendations for practitioners and contributions to academic discourse on AI in e-business.

2   Problem Background

Leading e-commerce companies in advanced markets have harnessed AI at scale to drive performance. Amazon's recommendation algorithms, for instance, account for a significant portion of sales, while Alibaba's AI-driven logistics system optimizes delivery routes and warehouse operations [8]. These AI implementations have yielded impressive gains – Amazon's recommendation engine is reported to generate roughly one-third of overall revenue, and Alibaba's smart logistics platform has cut delivery costs by around 30.

However, the environment in which global giants operate enables these AI advances in ways not readily replicable in developing economies. Amazon and Alibaba benefit from extensive high-quality data, reliable broadband infrastructure, abundant AI talent, and supportive regulatory regimes. By contrast, emerging market e-commerce firms face distinct challenges that complicate AI adoption. In South Africa, Takealot operates amid infrastructure constraints – broadband connectivity is improving but remains uneven, and many customers access the platform via mobile networks that can be slow or unreliable. Power outages (load-shedding) and rural connectivity gaps further impede consistent digital engagement. Data quantity and quality are more limited due to a smaller online user base and less extensive digital footprints, restricting the training of accurate AI models. Additionally, compliance with strict data protection laws like POPIA adds complexity to data management and AI-driven personalization [1].

The customer base in emerging markets tends to be highly diverse in language, culture, and digital literacy. South Africa's consumers, for example, speak 11 official languages and range from tech-savvy urban buyers to first-time online shoppers in townships and rural areas. Designing AI systems (such as recommendation engines or chatbots) that cater to such diversity is non-trivial – algorithms must accommodate multilingual content and varying levels of user familiarity with e-commerce. Trust and user adoption are also hurdles: many consumers are new to e-commerce and may be wary of fully automated services, requiring a careful balance between AI automation and the reassurance of human support. Payment preferences (e.g., cash on delivery in some regions) and address verification issues demand adapted AI solutions in order fulfillment and fraud detection compared to markets with ubiquitous digital payments.

These challenges are evident in the experiences of regional players like Jumia, a pan-African e-commerce platform. Jumia initially attempted to emulate Amazon's model across African countries, but encountered infrastructural voids and institutional barriers that curtailed its growth [7]. The company struggled with unreliable logistics networks, low internet penetration in target markets, and a lack of established consumer trust in online shopping. As a result, Jumia had to modify its strategy – investing in basic delivery infrastructure, embracing cash payments, and engaging in extensive consumer education – to survive in its operating environment. Academic analysis of Jumia's trajectory confirms that nonmarket factors (such as weak infrastructure, informal economies, and policy voids) forced it to adjust tactics beyond the standard e-commerce playbook. This reinforces the notion that direct transplantation of AI strategies from developed markets often fails in emerging contexts. Instead, local e-businesses must innovate within their constraints: for example, by using simpler AI tools that work offline or on low-end devices, and by gradually introducing AI features alongside efforts to build customer trust.

Takealot's context exemplifies these dynamics. As South Africa's e-commerce leader, Takealot has a relatively advanced operation but still contends with the country's infrastructural and socio-economic limitations. The company cannot rely on the assumption of ubiquitous high-speed connectivity or fully automated processes without oversight. Early in its growth, Takealot focused on establishing basic e-commerce capabilities (catalog management, a user-friendly mobile app, and nationwide delivery logistics) before venturing into sophisticated AI projects. Only after strengthening its data infrastructure and accumulating sufficient transaction data did Takealot begin deploying AI-driven features such as personalized product recommendations and dynamic pricing. Moreover, Takealot has approached AI adoption cautiously and adaptively: recommendation algorithms have been tuned to local buying patterns (incorporating, for instance, regional product preferences and seasonal demand fluctuations unique to South Africa), and the platform's mobile app is optimized to handle intermittent connectivity – caching content and enabling offline browsing of previously loaded pages to some extent. In customer service, Takealot introduced AI chatbots for basic inquiries but retained human agents for complex issues, reflecting an understanding of customers' comfort levels with automation [6].

3   Literature Review

Significant research and industry evidence demonstrate that AI technologies can substantially enhance e-commerce performance. For example, a study by Prokopenko and Järvis [8] reports that Amazon's recommendation system contributes roughly 35% of the company's revenue, while Alibaba's AIdriven logistics platform has reduced delivery costs by about 30%. These figures underscore AI's ability to drive sales through personalization and to streamline operations via optimization algorithms. Likewise, Davenport et al. [3] note that AI-driven personalization and targeting can boost conversion rates by up to 30%, indicating major marketing gains from machine learning in understanding customer behavior. Beyond these headline numbers, various successful applications of AI in leading e-commerce firms have been documented: from chatbots providing 24/7 customer support, to automated inventory management and demand forecasting systems that minimize stockouts and improve supply chain efficiency. Collectively, the literature establishes AI as a transformative force in online retail, capable of improving both front-end user experience and back-end productivity.

Implementing AI in developing market e-commerce, however, presents unique challenges that have been the focus of a growing body of research. Benbya et al. [1] observe that organizations often face barriers like limited access to quality data, shortages of skilled AI talent, and inadequate infrastructure when trying to adopt AI innovations. These issues tend to be exacerbated in emerging economies, where reliable large-scale datasets may not be available and investment in digital infrastructure lags behind that in developed regions. Moreover, there are challenges specific to African e-commerce, including intermittent connectivity, low levels of digital literacy, and regulatory uncertainties, which are key impediments to technology adoption. For instance, if consumers or employees lack experience with digital tools, even an AI recommendation engine might not be effective or trusted. Similarly, ambiguous or evolving regulations around data privacy and AI (such as how South Africa's POPIA will be enforced in practice) can create hesitation and compliance burdens for companies looking to deploy AI-driven personalization or data mining. These findings from the literature make it clear that a straightforward importation of AI solutions into developing markets is fraught with difficulty – instead, targeted strategies are required to overcome contextual barriers.

Researchers have proposed that e-commerce firms in developing environments follow a maturation and adaptation approach to AI adoption. Borges et al. [2] conducted a systematic review and suggest a staged model of building AI capabilities, wherein organizations first establish foundational technological infrastructure and basic analytics before pursuing advanced AI applications. This maturity model aligns with the intuitive idea that prerequisites – such as data collection processes, cloud infrastructure, and internal expertise – must be in place to effectively leverage sophisticated AI.

Another theme in the literature is the need for a holistic, multidisciplinary perspective when implementing AI. Dwivedi et al. [5] argue that successful AI deployment requires addressing a spectrum of factors – not just technical feasibility, but also organizational readiness, user acceptance, and policy implications. This is especially pertinent in emerging markets where institutional voids and social factors play a large role. Companies must combine technological innovation with change management, training, and perhaps new business models tailored to local realities. The importance of organizational and human factors is echoed by studies highlighting trust and cultural acceptance as crucial to AI adoption. For example, ensuring transparency of AI decisions and maintaining human oversight can be vital in building user trust in markets new to e-commerce technologies.

Meanwhile, research has catalogued the key application areas of AI in ecommerce that any aspiring platform – developed or emerging – would consider. Duan et al. [4] identify core domains such as product recommendation systems, demand forecasting, dynamic pricing optimization, and customer service automation as primary use-cases for AI in online retail. These applications directly impact revenue and efficiency: recommendation algorithms personalize the shopping experience to increase basket sizes; predictive analytics anticipate stock requirements and consumer trends; pricing algorithms adjust to market conditions in real-time; and AI chatbots or voice assistants handle routine inquiries, improving customer support scalability. In developing markets, each of these applications remains relevant but often must be modified – for instance, recommendation engines might need to factor in sparse purchasing data and be hybridized with domain expertise, or chatbots might need to operate in multiple local languages and hand off to humans when queries surpass their understanding. Nonetheless, this taxonomy of AI uses provides a checklist for emerging e-commerce firms aiming to modernize their operations: it points to what is technologically possible and proven, even if the path to implementation must be tailored.

Finally, recent scholarship is beginning to converge on frameworks specific to AI adoption in developing contexts. A systematic review by Malapane and Ndlovu [6] on AI in South African e- commerce stresses the alignment of AI projects with an organization's innovation capacity and strategic goals. Their findings suggest that companies benefit from carefully assessing their digital readiness and adopting a frugal innovation mindset – essentially making the most of limited resources and identifying high-impact, low-cost AI interventions. This underscores a gap in the literature: while general models for technology adoption exist, there is room for a dedicated framework that guides e-businesses in emerging markets through the AI implementation journey under local constraints. Our work addresses this gap by synthesizing the above insights – the necessity of contextual assessment, phased capability-building, and user-centric design – into a coherent framework. In the next section, we present the proposed ADAPT framework, which draws from these literature-driven principles and the comparative case analysis of Takealot and its peers.

4   Proposed Framework

Drawing on the comparative analysis of Takealot's strategy and global best practices, we propose the ADAPT framework as a structured approach for adopting AI in developing market e-commerce. ADAPT is an acronym encapsulating five sequential stages – Assessment, Development, Adaptation, Phased Implementation, and Tracking – that together form a roadmap for gradual and context-aware AI integration. This framework is tailored to the realities of emerging markets, aiming to help e-business platforms build AI capabilities effectively while mitigating risks and resource limitations. Each stage of ADAPT is described below, along with its rationale and how Takealot exemplifies its implementation.

Assessment: The process begins with a comprehensive evaluation of the current state of the business's technology and environment. Before introducing any AI solution, a company should rigorously assess its existing infrastructure, data assets, and organizational readiness. Key questions include: What quality and quantity of data are available for AI models? Are the IT systems (e.g. databases, servers, cloud services) robust enough to support AI workloads? Does the staff have or can acquire the necessary skills to manage AI tools? This assessment also involves identifying pain points and opportunities where AI could have the most impact. In Takealot's case, early assessments pinpointed areas suitable for AI enhancement – such as improving product recommendations and warehouse logistics – that were feasible given the data at hand. Crucially, Takealot's management identified "high-impact, low-barrier" entry points for AI: for instance, implementing a basic collaborative-filtering recommendation engine using their growing transaction dataset, which was a manageable project in a data-constrained setting. At the same time, they recognized what was not yet viable (such as fully autonomous delivery drones, given regulatory and infrastructural hurdles). By conducting this upfront assessment, Takealot ensured that its AI initiatives were grounded in reality and aligned with the company's strategic priorities and capacity. This stage sets the foundation and prevents wasted effort on incompatible or overly ambitious projects – a vital step for emerging market firms with little slack for experimentation failure.

Development: After assessing needs and readiness, the next stage focuses on developing the necessary foundational capabilities. This goes beyond procuring technology; it involves building up the data infrastructure, human talent, and internal processes required to support AI. For Takealot, the development phase meant significant investment in data collection and management systems. The company improved how it captured user interaction data on its platform, established scalable data storage solutions, and introduced analytics tools to begin extracting insights. Parallel to technical development, Takealot concentrated on human capital – hiring data scientists and upskilling existing employees (through training programs and collaborations with external AI experts). This stage is about creating an environment in which AI can thrive: algorithms are only as good as the data and platform they run on. By fortifying its back-end systems (for example, implementing a cloud-based data lake to consolidate customer and product information) and instilling a data-driven culture in its teams,

Takealot laid the groundwork for more advanced AI down the line. For emerging e-businesses, this development step may also involve piloting simple analytics projects that build confidence and organizational know-how. It is essentially a capacity-building phase. Notably, skipping this phase or giving it short shrift is dangerous – deploying AI without adequate data or expertise often leads to failures or underperformance, which can set back AI adoption significantly.

Adaptation: The third stage emphasizes adapting global best practices to local conditions. Rather than importing AI solutions "as is" from developed market counterparts, businesses should modify and tailor these tools to fit their environment. Adaptation can take many forms. For algorithms, it might mean retraining models on local data or adjusting parameters to account for different user behavior patterns. For user-facing AI features, it could involve customizing language and content to local languages or cultural norms. In the Takealot case, adaptation was critical in its recommendation systems. While the underlying concept of a recommender engine was inspired by those at Amazon, Takealot fine-tuned its algorithms to reflect South African consumers' preferences and constraints. For example, Takealot's team discovered that due to smaller data volumes, a hybrid approach (combining collaborative filtering with content-based recommendations and even incorporating domain knowledge like seasonal trends in South Africa) yielded better results than a purely collaborative filtering approach that works well for Amazon with its massive user base. Additionally, Takealot's recommendation and search algorithms were designed to be bandwidth-aware – offering simpler default suggestions if the system detected a slow network, thereby ensuring a smoother experience for users on patchy connections. Another adaptation was compliance with local regulations: any AI-driven personalization on Takealot had to be vetted for alignment with POPIA's privacy requirements, leading to the adoption of more transparent data handling practices and opt-out features for customers. This stage acknowledges that context matters – economic, cultural, and legal factors in emerging markets necessitate changes to how AI is implemented. Firms that adapt technology cleverly can overcome constraints; those that do not risk deploying solutions that misfire or even alienate users.

Phased Implementation: With preparations and adaptations in place, the next step is to implement AI solutions in a phased, incremental manner. A big-bang rollout of multiple AI systems is ill-advised, especially in developing contexts where organizations and customers alike need time to adjust. Instead, Takealot adopted a gradual implementation path: it introduced AI features one by one, starting with lower-complexity applications and then advancing to more complex ones as confidence grew. Initially, the company launched a basic "Customers who viewed this also viewed..." recommendation widget – a relatively simple algorithm that nonetheless added noticeable value to the shopping experience. After monitoring its performance and gathering feedback, Takealot expanded to more sophisticated personalized recommendations and later to AIdriven logistics optimizations (like route planning for deliveries). This incremental rollout allowed the company to manage risk and learn continuously.

Early successes built momentum and buy-in within the organization, while early failures (or unexpected outcomes) could be contained and addressed without derailing the entire AI program. Importantly, phased implementation also helps in building customer trust: Takealot did not abruptly replace human customer service with AI, for example, but gradually introduced a chatbot for FAQ support while keeping live agents readily available. Over several years, Takealot's AI capability matured stepwise – from rudimentary product recommendations and simple automated emails to advanced features like dynamic pricing adjustments and an AI-powered complementary product recommender using generative techniques (rolled out in 2024). Each phase acted as a proof-of-concept for the next, ensuring the organization was ready (in terms of both infrastructure and skill) to progress. This approach resonates strongly with the literature on technology adoption in emerging markets, which advocates pilot programs and iterative scaling to account for learning curves and to accommodate any needed course corrections.

Tracking: The final component of the ADAPT framework is ongoing tracking and evaluation of AI performance using context-appropriate metrics. Once AI solutions are deployed, it is crucial to continuously monitor their outcomes and impact, especially in dynamic emerging markets. Traditional e-commerce KPIs (Key Performance Indicators) – such as conversion rate uplift, click-through rates on recommendations, or order fulfillment time reductions – are certainly relevant. However, they may need to be augmented or adjusted to fully capture local realities. Takealot, for example, developed specialized metrics to track AI effectiveness while accounting for South Africa's market specificities. In addition to measuring recommender click-through rates, Takealot monitored metrics like the percentage of sessions with slow connectivity where the recommender still managed to display results (a measure of robustness), and the chatbot resolution rate for users in different languages (to see if the AI performed equally well across English and local languages). The company also kept an eye on customer satisfaction indicators and trust signals – for instance, tracking the volume of customer complaints or confusion related to AI features (such as any backlash against personalized targeting) – to ensure that the introduction of AI was positively received. This tracking stage enables a feedback loop: if an AI model's performance dips or exhibits bias (say, failing to recommend products popular in rural areas due to underrepresentation in data), the team can detect it and take corrective action (perhaps by retraining the model or supplementing data from those user segments). By establishing clear metrics and monitoring processes, Takealot ensured that AI adoption translated into tangible benefits and that any negative side effects or contextual misalignments of AI were promptly addressed. For emerging e-businesses, this emphasis on measurement is vital – it not only justifies the investments into AI by showing results, but also highlights areas where the approach might need refinement or further localization. In summary, "tracking" closes the ADAPT loop by tying AI initiatives back to business objectives and local market conditions, fostering a cycle of continuous improvement.

In conclusion, the ADAPT framework provides a stepwise strategy for ecommerce platforms in developing countries to adopt AI responsibly and effectively. It captures the importance of starting with a realistic understanding of one's environment (Assessment), building necessary foundations (Development), tailoring solutions to fit the local puzzle (Adaptation), rolling them out judiciously (Phased Implementation), and vigilantly ensuring they deliver value (Tracking). This framework is not purely theoretical – it is derived from observing what worked for Takealot as well as aligning with recommendations from prior research. In the next section, we justify why each element of ADAPT is critical and examine the framework's strengths and potential limitations when applied in practice.

5   Justification and Critical Evaluation

The ADAPT framework addresses the core challenges identified in the literature and case analysis by breaking the AI adoption journey into manageable, contextsensitive stages. Each component of ADAPT can be justified both on theoretical grounds and by its practical merits, particularly as evidenced by Takealot's experience and similar cases. Here we discuss why ADAPT is an appropriate model for emerging market e-businesses and critically evaluate its assumptions and potential limitations.

Firstly, Assessment is justified by the high stakes of AI projects and the resource constraints typical in developing markets. Unlike tech giants with budgets for experimentation, smaller emerging market firms cannot afford to invest blindly in AI initiatives that might not align with their capabilities or immediate needs. By conducting a thorough initial assessment, companies ensure a strategic fit for AI – targeting use-cases that solve pressing problems and are feasible with available data and technology. This stage mitigates the risk of AI becoming a costly fad or a failed pilot project. It also resonates with innovation adoption theories that emphasize organizational readiness as a prerequisite for successful implementation (Dwivedi et al., 2021). A critical perspective might argue that extensive assessment could delay action or become a bureaucratic hurdle. However, in the context of limited resources, this upfront diligence is arguably necessary. The key is to balance analysis with agility: the assessment should be time-bound and focused on decision-enabling insights. In practice, Takealot's assessments did not paralyze progress; rather, they guided the company to quick wins (e.g. a simple recommender) that proved AI's value early, thereby securing internal support for subsequent investments. Without proper assessment, companies risk either overreaching (attempting complex AI without groundwork, leading to failure) or underutilizing AI (fearing the unknown and missing opportunities). ADAPT's emphasis on assessment is thus well-founded for emerging markets, as it grounds innovation in reality.

The Development phase is justified as a necessary investment in future capabilities. One might question whether firms in emerging economies have the luxury to spend time and resources on capacity-building before seeing immediate returns. However, AI systems are not plug-and-play – their success heavily depends on the underlying data infrastructure and human expertise. Takealot's phased investments in data warehousing and talent development paid off by enabling more sophisticated AI projects down the line that competitors without such foundations could not attempt (Gillwald et al., 2023). From a critical standpoint, it is possible to over-invest in infrastructure without clear ROI if one is not careful (the so-called "IT spend trap"). ADAPT guards against this by tying development to the assessment's findings: companies build what they specifically need for the identified AI opportunities. Another important aspect is knowledge transfer – developing local talent and know-how means that AI solutions can be maintained and evolved internally, rather than relying perpetually on expensive foreign consultants or off-the-shelf products that might not adapt well. This capacity-building has long-term benefits, contributing to the sustainability of AI initiatives. That said, a potential limitation is the availability of talent; emerging markets often suffer from brain drain and shortages of skilled data scientists. Firms may need to be creative, such as partnering with universities or using remote expertise, during this development phase. The framework assumes that with effort, foundational gaps can be filled – an assumption that generally holds, but may require ecosystem-level support (e.g., policies to improve internet infrastructure or education) beyond the control of an individual firm.

Adaptation is perhaps the linchpin of the framework, and its justification lies in the mantra "one size does not fit all." The need to adapt AI solutions to local context is strongly supported by both theory (e.g., contingency theory in IS, which posits that technology effectiveness depends on fit with environment) and by observed outcomes – notably Jumia's struggles when it tried to directly copy Amazon's model without modification (Peprah et al., 2024). By modifying AI to account for local languages, behaviors, and constraints, companies greatly improve the relevance and acceptance of those systems. Takealot's adaptive tweaks, such as simplifying features for low connectivity scenarios, are prime examples of contextual innovation that made AI workable in practice. A critical evaluation might note that adaptation requires local knowledge and perhaps additional development effort (customizing off-the-shelf AI or creating new training data), which can be challenging. Furthermore, excessive customization could reduce the ability to benefit from global AI advancements if a company diverges too far from standard platforms. ADAPT implicitly encourages a balance: use global best practices as a starting point, then localize thoughtfully. The framework assumes that companies can strike this balance. In practice, seeking input from local users and stakeholders is crucial during adaptation – a practice Takealot followed by incorporating feedback from its South African customer base when refining its recommendation algorithms. Another aspect of adaptation is regulatory compliance: emerging market regulators may impose different rules (or none at all). Adhering to local laws (like POPIA) is non-negotiable, and ADAPT's adaptation stage explicitly accounts for such requirements, thus preventing legal and ethical pitfalls that could arise from naïve implementation of foreign AI solutions (for example, using customer data in ways that violate local privacy norms). In essence, the adaptation stage ensures cultural and regulatory legitimacy of AI initiatives, which is a strong justification for its necessity.

The Phased Implementation stage is justified by change management principles and risk mitigation. Introducing AI incrementally allows both the organization and its customers to gradually embrace change. For employees, a phased approach provides time to upskill and adapt workflows as AI tools come online one by one. For customers, it prevents a sudden shock or alienation – for instance, phasing in an AI chatbot while still keeping human support ensures that customers are not left frustrated by an immature AI system. Moreover, small-scale implementations (proofs of concept or pilot programs) generate evidence of success that can be leveraged to secure buy-in for broader AI adoption. This tactic is well-supported by innovation diffusion research, which highlights the value of trialability and observability in accelerating adoption (Duan et al., 2019). A potential criticism of phased implementation is that it might slow down the realization of full benefits – a firm might take years to reach the AI sophistication that competitors elsewhere already have. However, this "slower" pace is a prudent trade-off in environments where doing too much too soon could backfire (e.g., launching a complex AI without understanding local nuances could cause failures that set the whole initiative back). Additionally, phased rollout does not preclude being ambitious; it simply means sequencing the ambition. Takealot, for example, had a long-term vision to apply AI across many areas, but it deliberately ordered the execution such that simpler projects (with quick returns and fewer points of failure) came first. Each phase built the case – and the infrastructure – for the next. In evaluating this approach, one sees that it fostered an iterative learning culture: mistakes or unexpected outcomes in early phases could be corrected and informed later phases. The framework does assume that management has the patience and strategic outlook to implement AI stepwise rather than chasing immediate, flashy outcomes. Given the often short-term pressures on businesses, this assumption may be tested; however, the sustained growth of Takealot relative to some fast-but-faltering competitors illustrates the merit of a disciplined, phased strategy in emerging markets.

Finally, the Tracking stage is justified by the need for accountability and continuous improvement. By measuring AI performance with relevant metrics, companies ensure that the AI initiatives remain aligned with business goals and actually deliver value. In emerging markets, where there may be skepticism about advanced technologies, demonstrating clear benefits (e.g., an uplift in sales from a recommendation engine, or cost savings in logistics) is crucial to maintain organizational and stakeholder support. Tracking also helps catch any negative consequences early - for instance, if an AI pricing algorithm inadvertently started suggesting prices that were too high for certain customer segments, monitoring key indicators would reveal the issue and prompt an intervention (such as adjusting the algorithm or adding a rule to prevent that outcome). A thorough evaluation of this stage recognizes that choosing the right metrics is itself a challenge. If a company focuses only on metrics easily improved by AI (say, website click-through rates) but ignores harder-to-measure outcomes (like long-term customer satisfaction or brand trust), it might get a false sense of success. ADAPT advocates for context-specific KPIs, which implies a mix of standard e-commerce metrics and locally meaningful measures. Takealot's use of metrics like service uptime during connectivity issues or customer service resolution rates in multiple languages exemplifies tailoring measurement to context (Malapane Ndlovu, 2022). A limitation could be the capacity to perform such monitoring - smaller firms might not have advanced analytics to compute these metrics. However, the very AI tools being implemented can often assist in measurement (e.g., AI can help analyze customer sentiment from feedback to gauge trust). Another critique might be that continuous tracking adds overhead; yet, in dynamic markets, not tracking can lead to stagnation or misallocation of effort. The feedback loop created by tracking ensures that AI adoption is not a one-off project but an ongoing process of refinement - which is essential because both the technology and the market environment keep evolving.

In critically evaluating the ADAPT framework as a whole, its strength lies in providing a systematic yet flexible approach. It is systematic in that it forces consideration of all key facets - from initial conditions to final outcomes - rather than jumping straight into technical implementation. At the same time, it is flexible and not overly prescriptive; different companies can execute each stage in ways that suit their scale and sector (for example, the specific metrics in Tracking will differ between a fashion e-tailer and a grocery delivery service, but the principle of monitoring remains). One potential limitation is that ADAPT may appear resource- or time-intensive, which could be daunting for very small enterprises. However, even for SMEs, the core ideas (assess first, start small, adapt to local needs, etc.) are applicable and can be scaled to their capacity. Another consideration is the external environment: ADAPT implicitly assumes that if a company follows these steps, it can overcome challenges, but some external factors (like sudden regulatory changes or economic shocks) might disrupt the sequence. For example, a regulatory change might force a company back to the Adaptation stage to re-tool an AI system for compliance. The framework could accommodate this by iterating stages as needed - ADAPT is not strictly linear; in practice, feedback from Tracking might send a firm back to Adaptation or even to re-assess certain assumptions as the environment changes. This iterative potential is a valuable aspect, even if not explicitly spelled out in the acronym. In conclusion, the justification for ADAPT is strong in the context of emerging market e-commerce: it directly tackles the identified needs for careful planning (Assessment), capacity-building (Development), contextualization (Adaptation), prudent execution (Phased Implementation), and validation (Tracking). Each stage is grounded in both academic insights and pragmatic considerations. While no framework can guarantee success, ADAPT provides a roadmap that significantly increases the likelihood of effective AI adoption by aligning the process with the realities on the ground. Companies like Takealot that have unwittingly followed elements of this approach have achieved measurable benefits from AI, lending credence to the framework. The critical evaluation suggests that companies should remain aware of potential pitfalls – such as underestimating the time required or over-customizing solutions – but these are manageable with strong leadership and a clear vision. In the next section, we discuss broader implications of our findings, offer advice for e-business practitioners, and outline the contributions of this research to the field of e-business strategy.

6   Discussion and Recommendations

The analysis of Takealot's AI adoption journey, in comparison with global leaders and regional peers, yields several key principles that e-commerce businesses in emerging markets should heed. These principles form the essence of the advice we offer to practitioners and also represent the broader contribution of this research to understanding AI in e-business strategy. The five principles outlined below encapsulate the critical success factors for AI implementation under the challenging conditions of developing economies, and they align closely with the stages of the ADAPT framework proposed in this paper.

(i) Contextual Intelligence: Successful AI adoption begins with a deep understanding of the local context and the development of solutions tailored to that context. Rather than treating AI as a one-size-fits-all technology, e-business firms must exercise contextual intelligence – an acute awareness of local market conditions, consumer behavior, and limitations. Takealot's approach exemplifies this principle: the company recognized that South African consumers have unique purchasing patterns (for example, a mix of online and offline shopping influences, regional product preferences, and sensitivity to data costs) and it built its AI systems accordingly. One striking outcome of this was Takealot's hybrid recommendation strategy that incorporated offline purchasing insights (such as trends gathered from brick-and-mortar retail data in South Africa) into its online recommendation algorithm, compensating for sparse purely online data. This allowed the AI to function effectively despite data limitations, demonstrating that integrating local knowledge can greatly improve AI relevance. For practitioners, the takeaway is clear – invest time in studying and engaging with your market. AI projects should begin not with technology, but with questions: "What local problem are we solving? What local nuances must the solution respect?" By answering these, businesses can ensure their AI initiatives are grounded in reality and deliver genuine value to their customers.

(ii) Infrastructure-Aware Design: AI systems deployed in emerging markets must be designed to perform under less-than-ideal infrastructure conditions. This principle emerged strongly from Takealot's experience: the company's technical teams deliberately built features that could gracefully handle connectivity issues, given that many South African users might have patchy internet access. For instance, Takealot's mobile app was optimized so that essential functionalities (like viewing one's cart or product details that were previously loaded) remain available even if the connection drops, thereby maintaining basic service continuity. In a similar vein, AI algorithms were tuned to be lightweight when needed – for example, using on-device caching or simpler models during instances of low bandwidth, then updating when a stable connection resumes.

This infrastructure-aware design ensures that the benefits of AI are not lost when users are in low-resource settings. For other e-commerce firms, this could mean prioritizing AI features that do not require real-time cloud processing for every interaction, or developing fallbacks for when network or power infrastructure fails. Embracing this principle may involve additional engineering effort, but it pays off in user experience and reliability. It acknowledges a reality of developing markets: robustness can be more important than cutting-edge sophistication.

(iii) Gradual Capability Building: Patience and incremental progress are virtues when building AI capabilities in emerging market organizations. The case study analysis shows that Takealot's step-by-step progression from basic to advanced AI applications allowed it to cultivate internal expertise and stakeholder buy-in over time. Each successful implementation (like the initial recommender system) built the team's confidence and demonstrated value, which justified the next project (such as an AI-driven warehouse routing system). This gradual capability building aligns with well-known maturity models and appears to be a prudent path in environments where companies cannot marshal large AI programs all at once. A rushed or overly ambitious attempt to deploy multiple complex AI systems simultaneously could overwhelm an organization and lead to failures, especially if employees are not yet fully comfortable with AI tools. By scaling up in stages, as ADAPT's Phased Implementation advocates, firms can ensure that their organizational learning curve keeps pace with technological advancements. The principle here for practitioners is to treat AI adoption as a journey, not a one-time project. Set long-term goals, but implement through a series of short-term projects that each yield learning and improvements. Over time, the accumulation of skills and technological assets will enable tackling more sophisticated AI challenges. Moreover, gradual implementation helps in change management - staff and customers adapt progressively, reducing resistance and smoothing the transition to an AI-enhanced mode of operation [2].

(iv) Trust-Centered Implementation: Building and maintaining stakeholder trust is a cornerstone of successful AI integration, particularly in markets where digital commerce is relatively new and consumers may be apprehensive. Takealot's trajectory underscored the importance of transparency and human-centered design in AI deployment. The company adopted a human-in-the-loop approach in sensitive areas like customer service: its AI chatbot handles simple queries, but transparently hands over to a human agent for more complex or sensitive issues. This approach reassures customers that AI is there to assist, not to alienate or frustrate them. Additionally, Takealot has been mindful of privacy and consent, explicitly informing users about personalization features and allowing them to opt out - a practice that aligns with POPIA and generally good ethical standards. By prioritizing trust, Takealot avoids the scenario where customers feel uneasy or exploited by AI (for example, feeling that price optimizations are unfair or that recommendations are intrusive). For businesses in similar markets, trust-centered implementation means engaging in open communication about AI use, ensuring AI decisions are explainable when possible, and blending AI with a human touch. It may also involve culturally sensitive

AI behavior - for example, tuning the tone of an AI assistant to match local communication styles, as a way to make the interaction feel more natural. Ultimately, trust is what will determine user acceptance: an advanced AI feature that is mistrusted will be disabled or avoided by users, nullifying its benefits. Therefore, companies should measure trust-related outcomes (customer feedback, churn rates after introducing an AI feature, etc.) as part of their tracking, and be prepared to iterate on AI designs to address trust gaps. This principle contributes to the broader discourse by highlighting that technological success (accuracy, efficiency) alone is insufficient; social acceptance is equally vital in technology adoption, especially in developing contexts with potentially greater skepticism [5].

(v) Localized Metrics: The final principle derived from our findings is the need to define and use performance metrics that reflect local market conditions and business objectives. Conventional e-commerce metrics are a starting point, but they might not tell the full story in an emerging market scenario. Takealot developed context-specific Key Performance Indicators (KPIs), as discussed earlier, to evaluate its AI systems. For example, beyond tracking recommendation click-through rates, they considered metrics like engagement from users on slower networks and the retention rate of new online shoppers (to see if AI personalization was aiding or possibly overwhelming first-time e-commerce users). This focus on localized metrics ensured that Takealot measured what truly mattered for growth in South Africa, rather than blindly following metrics that are benchmarks in Silicon Valley but less pertinent locally. The recommendation here for practitioners is to align metrics with the realities of their customer base and strategic goals. If an e-commerce platform operates in a region where trust in online services is low, then an increase in repeat purchase rate or reduction in call-center complaints might be a more telling success measure for an AI chatbot than, say, the raw number of queries handled by the bot. Localized metrics also feed back into iterative improvement: they can reveal, for instance, if certain groups of users (perhaps rural vs. urban, or different language speakers) are benefiting less from an AI feature, indicating a need for further adaptation. This principle reinforces that success criteria for AI projects must be locally defined. It is a contribution to e-business strategy literature in that it urges a departure from universal metric standards and advocates for metrics that capture developmental impact (like broadened access to services, inclusion of new customer segments, etc.) which are highly relevant in emerging markets [6].

Together, these five principles form a blueprint for e-commerce companies seeking to navigate the complexities of AI adoption in emerging markets. They also represent the key contributions of this research. At a practical level, we provide a guide for managers: by following ADAPT and these guiding principles, businesses can better manage the risk-reward equation of AI projects. For instance, a manager at an online retailer in an emerging economy can use ADAPT to formulate a phased AI adoption plan, and use the principles to ensure the plan remains grounded in local reality and customer-centric. At a theoretical level, our work contributes a nuanced understanding that technologies like

AI do not diffuse uniformly; instead, their adoption requires a strategic fit with local context to succeed. We add to the literature by articulating a framework (ADAPT) that encapsulates this understanding and by distilling lessons from a real-world case that can inform future studies and models.

It is also worth discussing the broader implications and potential generalization of our findings. While our focus has been on e-commerce in South Africa and similar developing markets, the approach may hold insights for other sectors in emerging economies – such as banking (fintech AI solutions facing trust and literacy issues) or healthcare (AI diagnostic tools in low-resource settings). The ADAPT framework's emphasis on readiness, adaptation, and phased rollout can be translated to those domains as well. Furthermore, as AI becomes more prevalent, even companies in developed markets might find value in some principles like trust-centered implementation, which is increasingly important globally. However, the unique contribution here is explicitly framing these strategies for emerging market conditions, which have been underrepresented in mainstream AI adoption discourse.

In concluding this discussion, we advise e-business leaders in emerging markets to approach AI not as a shiny object or a simple off-the-shelf enhancement, but as a strategic transformation that must be nurtured within the fertile soil of local understanding. Patience, adaptation, and vigilance are virtues in this journey. By following frameworks like ADAPT and adhering to the principles outlined, companies can avoid common pitfalls (such as misaligned technology or customer pushback) and steadily unlock the transformative potential of AI. In doing so, they contribute not only to their own competitiveness but also to the broader digital development of their economies – demonstrating that, with the right strategy, emerging markets can leapfrog into the AI-powered future on their own terms.

7   Conclusion

This study set out to examine how e-commerce platforms in developing markets can successfully adopt artificial intelligence, using Takealot's experience in South Africa as a central case and drawing comparisons with global leaders like Amazon and Alibaba and regional competitors like Jumia. The objective was to derive strategies and a framework that address the unique challenges faced by e-businesses in emerging economies – including infrastructure limitations, regulatory constraints, and varying consumer readiness – while capitalizing on the proven benefits of AI in e-commerce.

The core contribution of this paper is the ADAPT framework, which we proposed and elaborated as a guideline for AI adoption in e-commerce under emerging market conditions. ADAPT – encompassing Assessment, Development, Adaptation, Phased Implementation, and Tracking – offers a structured yet flexible roadmap that any similar platform can follow. Each stage of the framework addresses specific aspects identified as critical: from evaluating readiness and focusing on capacity-building, to customizing solutions, gradually rolling them out, and continuously monitoring their impact. When applying ADAPT to Takealot's journey, we found that it effectively encapsulated the key steps the company took (whether implicitly or explicitly) to integrate AI in a sustainable and effective manner.

The findings of this study carry implications beyond the immediate case. They suggest that embracing AI in developing markets is possible and advantageous, but only through a strategy that is patient, adaptive, and human-centric. The narrative of technology leapfrogging often touted for emerging economies is nuanced by our research: leapfrogging with AI is achievable, yet it requires stepping stones (investments in data and skills, small pilot successes, etc.) that build up to the leap. By sharing Takealot's story and our framework, we contribute to demystifying how a resource-constrained player can join the AI revolution. This is a positive message for many emerging market firms that might feel daunted by the gulf between them and the Amazons of the world.

In conclusion, the integration of AI into e-business in emerging markets should be approached as a strategic evolution rather than a simple plug-in of technology. Takealot's measured, context-aware implementation demonstrates that e-commerce platforms operating in constrained environments can effectively leverage AI to enhance their competitiveness and customer satisfaction. The ADAPT framework and accompanying principles provided in this paper aim to serve as a blueprint for such endeavors. Future research can build on this work by applying and testing the framework in other markets and sectors, or by quantifying the impact of following these strategies versus not doing so. As AI continues to advance and spread, we hope that frameworks like ADAPT will help ensure its benefits are inclusive – extending to consumers and businesses in all corners of the globe, not just those in tech-rich environments. By meeting the unique needs of emerging markets, AI can truly become a tool for broad-based digital empowerment and growth.

References

1. Benbya, H., Pachidi, S., Jarvenpaa, S.: Artificial intelligence in organizations: implications for information systems research. J. Assoc. Inf. Syst. **22** (2021). https://doi.org/10.17705/1jais.00662
2. Borges, A.F., Laurindo, F.J., Spínola, M.M., Gonçalves, R.F., Mattos, C.A.: The strategic use of artificial intelligence in the digital era: systematic literature review and future research directions. Int. J. Inf. Manag. **57**, 102225 (2021). https://doi.org/10.1016/j.ijinfomgt.2020.102225, https://www.sciencedirect.com/science/article/pii/S0268401219317906
3. Davenport, T., Guha, A., Grewal, D., Bressgott, T.: How artificial intelligence will change the future of marketing. J. Acad. Mark. Sci. **48**, 24–42 (2020)
4. Duan, Y., Edwards, J.S., Dwivedi, Y.K.: Artificial intelligence for decision making in the era of big data – evolution, challenges and research agenda. Int. J. Inf. Manag. **48**, 63–71 (2019). https://doi.org/10.1016/j.ijinfomgt.2019.01.021, https://www.sciencedirect.com/science/article/pii/S0268401219300581
5. Dwivedi, Y.K., et al.: Artificial intelligence (AI): multidisciplinary perspectives on emerging challenges, opportunities, and agenda for research, practice and policy.

Int. J. Inf. Manag. **57**, 101994 (2021). https://doi.org/10.1016/j.ijinfomgt.2019.08.002, https://www.sciencedirect.com/science/article/pii/S026840121930917X
6. Malapane, T.A., Ndlovu, N.K.: The adoption of artificial intelligence in the south African e-commerce space: a systematic review. In: 2022 Systems and Information Engineering Design Symposium (SIEDS), pp. 7–12 (2022). https://doi.org/10.1109/SIEDS55548.2022.9799403
7. Peprah, A.A., Atarah, B.A., Kumodzie-Dussey, M.K.: Nonmarket strategy and legitimacy in institutionally voided environments: the case of Jumia, an African e-commerce giant. Int. Bus. Rev. **33**(2), 102169 (2024)
8. Prokopenko, O., Järvis, M.: AI-driven transformation: mapping the course for future business landscapes. Teadmus OÜ, Tallinn (2024)

How Do Display Cues Affect Purchase Intention in the Live-Streaming Context: The Moderating Role of Perceived Value

Xin Wen[✉], Zirui Tang, and Haorun Song

School of Design, Shanghai Jiao Tong University, Shanghai 200240, People's Republic of China
wenxin99@sjtu.edu.cn

Abstract. An increasing amount of evidence indicates that product display cues are crucial in consumers' online purchasing behavior. As a special category of online sales, agricultural products have their characteristics and needs that distinguish them from other products. The current body of research examining the influence of agricultural product presentation in live-streaming on individuals' purchase intention is rather limited. This study explored the display cues of agricultural products in live-streaming Drawing on the Stimulus-Organism-Response (S-O-R) model and integrating the Perceived Value Theory, to analyze the factors affecting consumers' perceived benefits and purchase intention. The outcomes revealed that display visibility and cue multiplicity in agricultural products live-streaming offer significant advantages in terms of perceived benefits. The variables of display visibility and cue multiplicity jointly augmented consumers' perceived quality, while cue multiplicity had no discernible impact on consumers' perceived entertainment. Furthermore, consumers' purchase intentions were strengthened by perceived quality, perceived entertainment, and perceived value. This study will broaden the application scope of the S-O-R model and the perceived value theory. It will help us better understand how product display cues affect purchase intentions during live-streaming, and provide theoretical backing and practical advice for successful online marketing.

Keywords: Display cues · Agricultural products · Purchase intention · Live-streaming · Perceived value

1 Introduction

In the current context of deepening digitization and informatization, live-streaming e-commerce combines the features of traditional e-commerce with streaming media technology, has emerged. It offers consumers with a more immersive and interactive experience with visibility, interactivity, and entertainment. In contrast to traditional e-commerce, live-streaming e-commerce provides consumers with product displays in real-time videos. It is able to present more detailed product information through streamer interaction and consumer group interaction, which quickly enhances consumers' knowledge of the products [48]. Based on the 52nd Statistical Report on China's Internet

F. F.-H Nah and K. L. Siau (Eds.): HCII 2025, LNCS 16343, pp. 272–295, 2026.
https://doi.org/10.1007/978-3-032-13167-6_19

Development, by June 2023, the number of live-streaming users in China reached 765 million. This represented an increment of 14.74 million compared to December 2022 and accounted for 71.0% of the total Internet user population, showing its strong market prospects.

Unlike general consumer goods and services, agricultural products are non-standardized, and traditional sales of agricultural products face many problems, such as a single market channel, asymmetric information, and too many intermediate links. In the face of increasing consumer demand for high product quality, quality origin traceability and flexible purchasing methods, the traditional sales model has made it challenging to satisfy consumers' various demands. Live-streaming of agricultural products realizes the direct docking between agricultural producers and consumers, minimize the gap between supply and demand, and improve the efficiency and transparency of agricultural sales. Despite the various advantages of agricultural products live-streaming, and the fact that it is in the stage of booming development, improving consumer satisfaction and increasing the conversion rate is still a significant challenge for retailers. In addition, compared with other live-streaming, agricultural e-commerce has the public welfare of helping farmers, and the consumer decision-making scene is given a specific social nature. Therefore, in the agricultural products live-streaming shopping, consumers expect to reduce consumer decision-making bias and realize satisfactory consumption during the purchase process while achieving the goal of helping agriculture and other social values.

As agricultural product live-streaming e-commerce becomes increasingly popular, academics have launched many studies on enhancing live-streaming strategies to help farmers from various perspectives, such as the current status of agricultural products live-streaming, scene characteristics, consumer trust, and marketing system. In macro research, based on scene marketing related theories, scholars have put forward feasible countermeasures, such as optimizing the quality of agricultural products, live scene, content, and data, to enhance the scene-based marketing strategy for agricultural products [1]. In terms of consumer trust, the information exchange mechanism and information transfer asymmetry between streamers and consumers, makes it possible to provide quality endorsement of agricultural products through the reputation of officials' streamers and to show consumers the supply chain of agricultural products through diversified information [38]. In the context of live-streaming e-commerce marketing characteristics, it constructs the marketing process and mode of agricultural products under the promotion of live-streaming e-commerce. It puts forward optimization strategies in terms of reconstructing the live-streaming marketing system, planning the overall marketing scheme and constructing the live-streaming marketing ecosystem [11]. On this basis, more in-depth research has also been carried out on the agricultural products live-streaming room, such as the situational interaction in the live-streaming environment, the on-site arrangement in the spatial scene, the richness of the product introduction, the emotional arousal of the streamer traits and the social proximity of the scenario atmosphere, and many other factors can exert varying degrees of impact on the effect of agricultural products live-streaming. Regarding the impact of streamer characteristics on consumers' intentions, streamer popularity, professionalism, authenticity, interactivity, individual attributes, etc., can all influence consumers' purchase intentions.

However, with the depth of the research, the current live-streaming of agricultural products still has certain problems. First, in the context of e-commerce live-streaming, the streamer occupies an absolutely dominant position, which has a pivotal and direct impact on the quality of live- streaming, product conversion rate and user stickiness. Some live-streaming have exaggerated propaganda, low standardization and low consumer trust. This requires e-commerce streamers to have the ability to live-streaming expertise, providing consumers with sufficient and adequate information [35]. Moreover, in the current agricultural products live-streaming situation, with a professional background in e-commerce, live-streaming talent is relatively scarce, and there need for a practical ability to quickly learn the live strategy to streamer professional live training to enhance live skills and professional quality [30]. Secondly, the important advantage of live-streaming as one type of e-commerce lies in the real-time information display and interaction, which brings consumers intuitive, accurate display and sufficient information about commodity-related cues [17]. At present, the theoretical and practical research on how problems such as unclear expression of product traceability, low authenticity, unintuitive product display, and too little commodity-related cue information of live agricultural products affect consumers' consumption experience and purchasing decision is still insufficient. The lack of theoretical models for the traits of agricultural products and the guidance of the display skills and display strategies in practice affects the conversion of agricultural products into consumption to a certain extent.

Based on this, this study focuses on consumers' explicit demand for product quality and consumption experience, looks at the product display cues of agricultural products live-streaming, and explores the mechanism of the influence of product display attributes of agricultural products live-streaming on consumers' purchase intentions by integrating the S-O-R model and the perceived value theory, with the mediation of consumers' perceived value, and enhances the merchants' understanding of the consumers. The study enriches the results of theoretical research on agricultural products live-streaming, and guides practical strategies. Therefore, in this study, we attempt to address the following research questions:

RQ1: How do product presentation attributes affect consumer-perceived value in agricultural products live-streaming?

RQ2: How does consumer-perceived value affect purchase intention in agricultural products live-streaming?

RQ3: How does perceived value mediate between product presentation attributes and purchase intention?

By solving the above three problems, our study can enrich the theoretical model of agricultural products live-streaming e-commerce research, explore the optimization path through an in-depth analysis of the traits of agricultural products live-streaming, explore the breakthrough point of agricultural products live-streaming at the level of product display, put forward a more targeted strategy of agricultural products live-streaming, and offer theoretical backing and practical direction for the effective online marketing of agricultural products.

2 Literature Review and Theoretical Background

2.1 Live-Streaming E-Commerce of Agricultural Products

Recently, the expansion of the live-streaming market and the fast advancement of live-streaming technology have led to a new business model, live e-commerce, in which streamers present in real-time via video to discuss and respond to viewers' questions [55], and sell goods and services directly to their customers through the online visual media. Compared to traditional e-commerce, it provides consumers with a highly interactive and novel shopping experience, which generates more significant incentives to drive consumer behavior. The brisk growth of live e-commerce also provides new sales channels for traditional industries such as agricultural products.

Compared with other product categories, consumers are becoming more circumspect when it comes to purchasing agricultural products. The traditional sales model has high communication costs, and consumers' concerns about product quality and product sources are not conducive to transactions. Agricultural products e-commerce live-streaming combines the strengths of multiple media, provides consumers with more prosperous and more vivid stimulus cues, realizes the optimization from static pictures to real-time dynamic video, highly visual interface from multiple senses to increase the consumer's sense of immersion and sense of presence, the streamer can also communicate with consumers about how they feel and what the product looks or smells which affects the consumer's product price, quality, characteristics and other perception. In addition, for consumers of agricultural products, the multi-dimensional dynamic information display capability of the agricultural live platform can transmit the growing environment, production process, product characteristics and other information of agricultural products to the audience in a clipless manner, presenting a "what you see is what you get" offline shopping environment, and enhancing the consumer's sense of trust. Compared with traditional e-commerce, rely on customer service response and user feedback after the interaction mode, live-streaming e-commerce supports consumers and streamers and viewers' real-time interaction; information feedback is more rapid, accurate, and personalized and can effectively help consumers make a purchase decision. The real-time intervention of the streamer can help consumers obtain product information more quickly and efficiently.

For the live-streaming of agricultural products, the existing research mainly researches the product supply chain model, development model and consumers' purchase intentions. The research on product supply chain and development model is relatively macroscopic. In contrast, the specific refinement to the optimization strategy research on live-streaming, the analysis of consumers' purchase intentions can effectively understand the factors affecting consumer experience and decision-making to improve the quality of live-streaming. Researchers have discussed the effect of e-commerce streamer characteristics on consumers' purchase intentions, such as credibility, interactivity and professionalism. However, considering the unique attributes of agricultural products, the purchasing decisions made by consumers hinge not merely on the ultimate quality of the product, but also on the online selling scenario, the environment, and the presentation format [50]. Therefore, further clarification is needed on how agricultural product presentation cues influence consumers' purchase intention and consumers' perceptual experience in agricultural product live-streaming rooms.

2.2 The Stimulus-Organism-Response Model

In order to conduct a scientific and systematic research on the influencing factors and mechanisms of agricultural consumers' purchase intention, this paper adopts the Stimulus-Organism-Response (S-O-R) theoretical model. Psychology which was first proposed by Mehrabian and Russell in 1974 [30]. The model is effective in explaining the influence of the external environment on human behavior and is also extensively applied in environmental psychology in retail environments [14]. Where S stands for the stimulus of the external environment (Stimulus), O stands for the organism with cognition (Organism) and R stands for the action-wise and psychological response (Response).

In the shopping environment, stimulus variables belong to the external influences that cause changes in consumers' emotions and cognition, and are composed of marketing variables and other environmental factors; organism variables are composed of individuals' perceptual, mental, and thinking activities and include both emotional and cognitive dimensions, in which perceived entertainment, satisfaction, etc. in the realm of emotion, while perceived benefits, etc. belong to the category of cognition; response variables are consumers' under the influence of various stimuli The final output of the psychological or behavioral response, such as direct order, add to cart and other purchase decisions [12].

With the development of marketing science, the S-O-R model has been widely used with different scenarios such as retailing and online shopping, and is also applicable to the live- streaming context. There have been some research results to explore the mechanism of the external environment stimulating individuals to generate purchase intention internally in the context of agricultural products live-streaming e-commerce. From the aspect of live atmosphere, the live interactive atmosphere and supportive atmosphere in the agricultural products live-streaming e-commerce context have a significant positive effect on consumers' perceived trust, perceived entertainment and perceived usefulness, which in turn influences consumers' purchase intentions; from the perspective of consumer cognition, the normality, authenticity, visibility, quality value, public welfare, etc., presented in the agricultural products live-streaming room can augment consumers' perceived value and perceived trust, and it is conducive to improving consumers' purchase intentions and subsequent repeat purchase intentions; from the perspective of streamer attributes, when consumers face the streamer with high trust, high interactive attributes and strong professional ability, their emotional experience when watching live-streaming e-commerce to help agricultural products will also be enhanced, which will improve their purchase intentions and viewing viscosity.

At present, the application of the S-O-R model to analyze specific product categories, such as agricultural products with unique characteristics, etc., is less research. In the study of agricultural products live-streaming lack of live agricultural products information display attributes on consumer experience and purchase intentions of in-depth research.

2.3 Perceived Value Theory

Perceived Value Theory originated in business research and was first proposed by Zeithaml in 1988 [43]. The model of Perceived Value Theory concludes that perceived value represents a customer's comprehensive assessment of the utility of a product or service, which is founded on the perceived benefits and costs, so that increasing the perceived value of a customer can be achieved by either increasing the perceived benefits or decreasing the perceived costs of the customer.

The model proposed by Zeithaml [44] divides elements into three levels: low-level attributes, perception of low-level attributes and high-level attributes. The theoretical model of perceived value in the aspect of e-commerce live-streaming consists of four levels: low-level attributes, low-level perception, high-level cognitive attributes, and purchase intention/decision-making, in which the low-level attributes are the attributes of the live-streaming room; the low-level perception is the consumer's perception of the attributes of the live-streaming room; the high-level cognitive attributes include the consumer's perceived benefits and perceived costs, and the combination of both of these attributes is the perceived value; this ultimately affects the purchase intentions.

The key concepts in the perceived value theoretical model include perceived benefits, perceived payments and perceived value. Among these, perceived benefits are the positive effects or benefits that consumer feel when using or owning a product or service. These advantages can be useful (e.g., the utility and performance of the product), emotional (e.g., the pleasure and satisfaction that comes from using the product), and social (e.g., the social status and identity that comes from using the product). Consumers consider these benefits together in the decision-making process to assess whether the product or service can fulfil their demands and expectations. Perceived payments refer to the various costs or prices consumers must pay to acquire a product or service. These payments include not only monetary costs (the price of the product) but also a variety of non-monetary costs, such as time costs (the time it takes to buy and use the product), psychological costs (the psychological pressure and uncertainty in the decision-making process), and effort costs (the cost of the effort and learning required to use the product), and so on. Perceived value is a consumer's overall evaluation of a product or service after considering perceived benefits and perceived payments. After weighing the benefits and payments, it reflects the consumer's subjective value perception after weighing the benefits and payments. In e-commerce live-streaming scenarios, perceived value directly affects consumers' purchasing decisions and satisfaction and is an important basis for merchants to develop live-streaming marketing strategies.

The perceived value theoretical model has been used extensively in online shopping and live e-commerce (as shown in the Table 1). There are specific research results to explore how the attributes of the live-streaming room in the context of live e-commerce affect the perceived value, which in turn influences the customer's intention to participate or purchase. From the aspect of streamer features, when consumers face highly credible, interactive, professional streamers, they will have trust in them, so that the emotional experience of watching live e-commerce to help agricultural products will be enhanced, and their purchase intentions and viewing viscosity will be improved. From the perspective of product display, product knowledge, product display, product and background matching degree in the live e-commerce context plays a crucial positive role in affecting consumer perceived entertainment, and perceived value, which in turn influences consumer purchase intention. From the perspective of consumer perception, the attributes of live-streaming can improve consumers' perceived usefulness, perceived entertainment and symbolic value, which is conducive to increasing consumers' purchase intentions and subsequent repeat purchase intentions.

For the agricultural products live-streaming, consumers' experience of functionality and emotion in perceived benefits is the most prominent, i.e., perceived quality and perceived entertainment are considered. Therefore, this study focuses on perceived quality and perceived entertainment in perceived benefits and combines the comprehensive analysis of perceived value as a cognitive organism (O) to analyze the influence mechanism of the display attributes of agricultural products live-streaming on consumers' purchase intentions mediated by consumers' perceived value.

Table 1. Related Research Variables of Perceived Value Theory.

Main influence factors	Authors	Main Research Variables
Characteristics of live streamers	Meng & Lin (2023)	Professionalism, Credibility, Attractiveness, Interactivity, Perceived Value, Trust, Satisfaction
	Zhou & Huang (2023)	Professionalism, Attractiveness, Interactivity, Image Matching, Perceived Practical Value, Perceived Emotional Value
	Lee & Chen (2021)	Attractiveness, Trustworthiness, Expertise, Perceived Enjoyment, Perceived Usefulness
Product display	Zhang (2023)	Product Showcase, Time Pressure
	Shang, Ma & Wang (2023)	Product-background fit, Perceived pleasure, Purchase intention
	Wongkitrungrueng et al. (2020)	Perceived usefulness value, perceived entertainment value, perceived symbolic value, trust in product/streamer

3 Research Model and Hypotheses

The research model of this study is presented in Fig. 1. Drawing on the S-O-R model and perceived value theory, the product display information (including display visibility and cue multiplicity) is regarded as the external stimulus S; consumers' perceived gain is taken as the organism O, including perceived quality, perceived entertainment, and perceived value. Drawing on the S-O-R model and perceived value theory, the product display information (including display visibility and cue multiplicity) is taken as the external stimulus S; consumers' perceived gain is taken as the organism O, including perceived quality, perceived entertainment, and perceived value; and purchase intention is taken as the response R. In addition, the gender, income, age, and education background of consumers are considered as control variables.

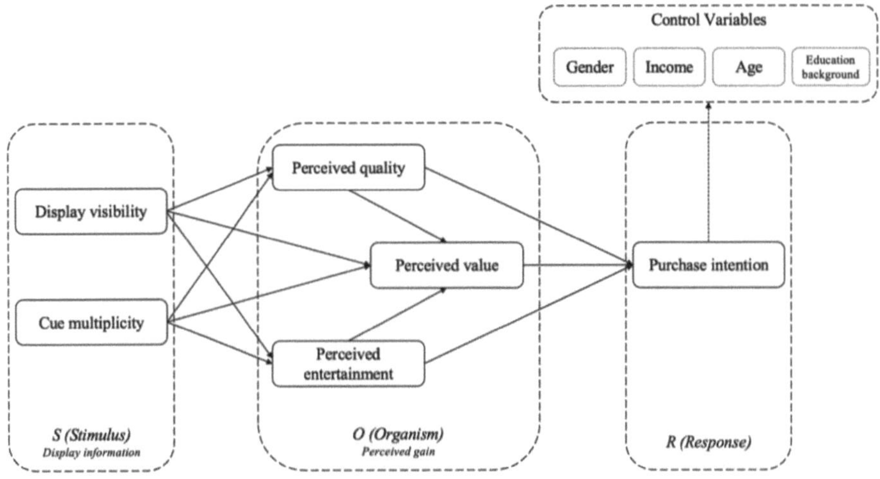

Fig. 1. The research models.

3.1 Relationship Between Product Display Information and Consumers' Perceptions

A comprehensive display of products is required in the agricultural live-streaming context to provide consumers with comprehensive visualized information and multi-sensory cues, so this study selects display visualization and cue multiplicity for the agricultural display information.

Display visibility in live e-commerce refers to the degree of visual perception of the consumer of the product and the degree of visualization of the product information when watching the live-streaming, including the interactivity, immersion, and conception of the live-streaming [2]. Live-streaming through the form of real-time video allows consumers to have a more intuitive understanding of the commodity, the streamer through the direct display of commodity details and with multifaceted explanations to enhance the consumer's awareness of the product and the immersion in the process of watching the live-streaming [19]. In the agricultural products e-commerce live-streaming, the streamer's display and introduction of an agricultural product can be carried out from various aspects, such as: combining with the edible scene using the corresponding utensils to contain the food for display, describing the flavor of the food such as the aroma and the taste of the food when tasting, and displaying the details of the appearance of the goods in detail, and so on. According to the theory of mind flow, when consumers' attention is focused on one thing, its perceived value will be enhanced [13].

Compared with traditional online shopping, live-streaming can bring consumers rich three-dimensional visibility and provide diversified display methods, thus significantly improving the perceived quality of the product and the perceived entertainment in the viewing.

Cue multiplicity refers to using multiple cues or factors to explain a phenomenon or relationship in a study. In consumer behavior research, cue multiplicity refers to the diversity of information that consumers need to face when making online purchases, i.e., the information from multiple channels and sources that consumers are subjected to when searching, browsing, and learning about a product [21]. Consumers will have difficulty in making decisions when these conflicting information and evaluations of a product from different websites, platforms, and social media, and when these information about a product from multiple perspectives and sources all point positively to the product's strengths, it will improve the consumer's perceptions of the product.

In the context of agricultural products live-streaming e-commerce, the delivery of cue information has channel diversity, and consumers can not only understand the product information through the text and pictures in the product detail page but also combine the verbal and non-verbal information of the streamer [43]. Among them, the streamer's introduction of an agricultural product can often be carried out from multiple aspects, such as the cultural knowledge of the source region of the agricultural product, the planting and growing information of the agricultural product, and the various processing and eating methods of the agricultural product, and so on. These multiple aspects of information and cues related to agricultural products will affect the consumer's understanding of the product and the perception of the atmosphere of the live-streaming room. The multifaceted information of commodities in the same scene can complement each other, thus forming a strong explanation of commodities, bringing multifaceted and effective information stimulation to consumers, improving their perception of commodities [30], and positively affecting perceived entertainment.

Based on this, the following assumptions are made:

H1a. Display visibility has positive influences on consumers' perceived quality.

H1b. Display visibility has positive influences on consumers' perceived entertainment.

H1c. Display visibility has positive influences on consumers' perceived value.

H2a. Cue multiplicity has positive influences on consumers' perceived quality.

H2b. Cue multiplicity has positive influences on consumers' perceived entertainment.

H2c. Cue multiplicity has positive influences on consumers' perceived value.

3.2 Consumers' Perceptions

Agricultural products are distinguished from other product categories by their non-standardization and hierarchical quality. Consumers need to confirm the quality of the product to obtain a positive experience of consumption. The streamer will provide support for consumers to confirm the quality of the product by introducing the relevant and practical information about each stage of the product for consumers to reduce the possibility of poor viewing and consumption experience caused by consumers' concern and distrust of the quality of the product.

Entertainment is the pleasure objectively felt by an individual while performing a particular behavior or activity [36]. Research has shown that entertainment marketing activities (e.g., publishing entertainment content) can influence consumer attitudes and behaviors [39]. In agricultural products live-streaming, streamers will utilize interesting and helpful technologies (e.g., virtual reality) to demonstrate products, etc. In addition, some streamers will use humor to make communication with their customers and make them feel cozy and happy in the live-streaming. Since the streamers will present information about the agricultural products in an entertainment interaction, the consumers will get some degree of utilitarian value in the entertainment interaction.

Based on this, the following hypotheses were put forward for this study.

H3. Perceived quality has positive influences on perceived value.

H4. Perceived entertainment has positive influences on perceived value.

3.3 Relationship Between Consumers' Perceptions and Purchase Intention

In agricultural live e-commerce, perceived quality indicates to the degree to which the consumer, through the description, characteristics, and price of the goods shown in the live-streaming room and the actual situation, including the quality of the goods, features, size, and other aspects of the product quality judgment. Compared with traditional online shopping, live e-commerce can present the goods in an accurate and complete way, with a high degree of product reproduction to consumers. At the same time, the live-streaming of the streamer's real-time introduction, interaction, and other behaviors will also enhance the consumer's perception and confirmation of product quality [56]. In the live-streaming of agricultural products e-commerce, the streamer's introduction of the authenticity of a commodity can be carried out in many ways, such as introducing the source information of agricultural products, demonstrating the freshness of agricultural products, and making reliable quality assurance and commitment.

The perceived quality of agricultural products directly influences consumers' purchase decisions and consumption experience [30]. On the one hand, if during the live-streaming, consumers find that the streamer or the product detail page conveys product information that is inconsistent with reality, they will have a sense of mistrust, lowering their trust in the streamer and the product, which in turn affects the purchase intention; on the other hand, if consumers find that the product is inconsistent with the description in the live-streaming after they have purchased it, it will lead to a decline in consumer satisfaction, an increase in the rate of return, and the formation of a negative word of mouth about the e-commerce platform and the streamer. When consumers are more positive about the perceived quality of agricultural products, they are more likely to recognize the live-streaming and the streamer. They are more willing to immerse themselves in the entertainment atmosphere of the live-streaming [15].

Consumer-perceived entertainment refers to a sense of mental, psychological satisfaction generated in the process of consumers experiencing a product or service, emphasizing the pleasure brought by this experience process itself rather than just the gains brought by the results. When consumers watch e-commerce live-streaming, their goal is not only to buy the goods they want at a low price in the center of the live-streaming room but also to obtain a pleasurable viewing and shopping experience and emotional value. In live e-commerce, consumers' perceived entertainment will receive the influence of streamer, pop-up area comments, other consumers' interactive behavior, and a variety of interactive games such as live red packets, etc. A variety of forms of product introduction, the lively and active atmosphere of the pop-up area, the positive interaction of other viewers to grab the purchase behavior and high frequency, high participation in the grabbing of the red packets, etc., will improve the perceived entertainment of the consumers while watching e-commerce live-streaming. This kind of interesting and diverse live content is often more able to attract the attention of consumers and enhance their pleasure, which in turn increases the length of time consumers watch the live-streaming, improves the exposure rate of products, and thus promotes the purchase intention.

Research has demonstrated that perceived entertainment plays a crucial role in consumer decision-making and purchasing processes, influencing consumers' purchase intentions and continued usage behavior. Koo & Ju [23] demonstrated that consumers' perceived entertainment during the experience process significantly influences their purchase intentions. In addition, other scholars have proved that consumers' perceived entertainment has positive influences on their satisfaction with the entire purchasing behavior, increasing their intentions to make a second purchase and their trust in the merchant after completing the transaction chain [20].

Perceived value represents a consumer's comprehensive assessment of a product or service's utility during the acquisition process. It comes from the consumer's consideration of both the benefits obtained and the costs incurred due to the purchase behavior [53]. Sweeney and Soutar [44] suggest that perceived value is the increasing effect of social self-concept brought by a consumer when purchasing a product with exceptional social value. In the live-streaming scenario of agricultural products, the perceived value of consumers can be divided into two aspects: one is the purchase of original, high-quality, original and high-quality agricultural products at a lower price, and the other is the psychological fulfillment of consumer poverty alleviation that consumers get from purchasing agricultural products to contribute to the cause of poverty alleviation in poverty-stricken areas, and so on. These together constitute the perceived value of agricultural products to live consumers.

The assessment of perceived value is a dynamic process which is influenced by consumers' personal characteristics, purchasing environment, and other factors, thus affecting their purchasing intentions and behavior. Jin, Lee & Lee [22] stated that consumers' perceived value of an important determinants of consumers' purchasing decisions.

Based on this, the following assumptions are made:

H5. Perceived quality has positively influence on consumers' purchase intentions.

H6. Perceived value has positively influence on consumers' purchase intentions.

H7. Perceived entertainment has positively influence on consumers' purchase intentions.

4   Methodology

4.1   Variables and Measurements

This study empirically tests the proposed theoretical model using a questionnaire based on the methodology of previous studies. By reviewing previous studies, we found a validation scale corresponding to the model variables proposed in this paper and validated by scholars. We adjusted and modified this to create a scale that is more in line with the characteristics of agricultural products live-streaming. The measure of display visibility draws on Liu et al. [29] with three question items; the measure of cue multiplicity draws on Vickery et al. [45] with three question items; the measure of perceived quality draws on Beverland et al. [6] with three question items; the measure of perceived entertainment is measured by Shen et al. [41] and consists of 3 items; perceived value is measured by Davis et al. [10] and consists of 3 items; and purchase intention is measured by Creyer [9] and others and consists of 3 items. All item scales were measured using a five-point Likert scale, where 1 indicates complete disagreement, and 5 indicates complete agreement. Participants were asked to answer truthfully. The variables and scales are shown in the Table 2.

Table 2. Variables and measurements

Variables	Measurements	References
Display visibility (DV)		
DV1	I thought the appearance of the agricultural products in the live-streaming room was comprehensive and transparent in its presentation	Liu et al. (2013)
DV2	The descriptions of the different sensory experiences in the live- stream gave me a fuller understanding of the agricultural products	
DV3	Using the corresponding utensils to display the agricultural products helped me visualize the serving scenario	
Cue multiplicity (CM)		
CM1	I want the streamer to introduce culture to increase my understanding of the agricultural products	Vickery et al. (2004)
CM2	I want the streamer to present information about the production to increase my understanding of the agricultural products	
CM3	I would like the live-streaming room to introduce a variety of serving methods to increase my knowledge of the agricultural products	
Perceived quality (PQ)		
PQ1	When watching a live-streaming of agricultural products, I want to learn about the source of the agricultural products	Beverland et al. (2008)
PQ2	When watching a agricultural products live-streaming, I consider the freshness and style flavors of the products	
PQ3	I expect reliable quality assurance and commitment from live sellers	
Perceived entertainment (PE)		
PE1	I had a great time watching the streamers bring in the agricultural products	Shen et al. (2010)

(*continued*)

Table 2. (*continued*)

Variables	Measurements	References
PE2	I thought the streamer's presentation of the agricultural products was very original and unique	
PE3	I'd like to watch the agricultural products live-streaming as a pastime	
Perceived value (PV)		
PV1	Buying agricultural products on the live feed can make my daily life easier	Davis et al. (1989)
PV2	I can shop for a wider variety of agricultural products in the live-streaming	
PV3	I can feel the advantage of buying agricultural product in the live-streaming over buying it at the supermarket	
Purchase intention (PI)		
PI1	I'm willing to add agricultural products to my cart when watching the live-streaming	Creyer (1997)
PI2	I'm willing to order agricultural products right off the live-streaming	
PI3	I'm willing to buy back agricultural products in the live-streaming many times over	

4.2 Data Collection

This study builds on previous research by using a questionnaire to collect data, a survey data collection method that is recognized in management science as a reliable method for collecting large amounts of individual-level data [3, 5]. The questionnaire for this study was created using the Questionnaire Star platform (https://www.wjx.cn/) to ensure data collection reliability and randomization. Questionnaire Star is a platform that provides questionnaire creation and data collection services. The questionnaire was distributed to potential customers through WeChat, China's leading social media channel. The link to the questionnaire is shared across multiple WeChat groups. Users can voluntarily answer the questionnaire, and each user ID can only answer the questionnaire once. Participants who fill out the questionnaire will be paid a certain amount. The restriction on recruiting participants must be at least 18 years old.

The online questionnaire was divided into four sections. The first section introduced the source and topic of the questionnaire and outlined the survey's objectives. The aim was to eliminate the respondents' defenses and guide them to answer sincerely based on the actual situation. In the second part, to ensure the questionnaire's validity, platform screening questions were set up according to the research theme, limiting the respondents to consumers of live e-commerce who watched agricultural products live-streaming or purchased products in the live- streaming room. The third part deals with the respondents' personal information, including gender, age, occupation, education level, monthly income, etc. The fourth part is the main structure of the questionnaire, which contains the research variables of the proposed dimensions and consists of 18 questions.

The questionnaire was collected from May-June 2024. A pre-survey was first conducted to test the applicability of the questionnaire questions; this was followed by data collection from a large sample. With 413 participants, we first excluded consumers who had watched agricultural products live-streaming. In addition, invalid correspondences were excluded (e.g., too long or too short completion time, duplicates or too many outliers, etc.). The final number of valid questionnaires was 337, with a validity rate of 81.6%. This sample size is considered acceptable in live research [7]. Among all the respondents, 57.0% were female, and 43.0% were male; most of the respondents were between 18 and 30 years old (62.61%), which is the same as the age group of the current Chinese e-commerce consumers; most of the respondents had an education of bachelor's degree or below (83.68%); and the respondents' incomes were centered on 3,000–8,999 RMB (64.1%). This study believes that the data of this questionnaire reflects the basic situation of current e-commerce on-site consumers more realistically, which is representative to a certain extent and can support the subsequent research and analysis.

4.3 Control Variables

Four control variables were incorporated into the study to guarantee the reliability of the results. These control variables limit the effects of unrelated.

This may disrupt the strength and direction of the link between stimulus, organism, and response. Based on previous studies [24]. We used demographic variables such as gender, age, educational background, and income as control variables.

5 Data Analysis Results

5.1 Reliability and Validity

SPSS 25.0 was used to analyze the data for reliability, and AMOS 28.0 was used to validate the factor analysis. The overall Cronbach's α of the scale was 0.886, and the Cronbach's α of each variable was more significant than 0.7, indicating that the observed variables can better explain the variables. The factor loadings for each variable were higher than 0.7, indicating that the variables can be better explained by the observed variables. An analysis of the aggregation validity of the scale revealed that the AVE of each variable was greater than 0.5, and the combined reliability was greater than 0.7, indicating that the scale has good aggregation validity. In addition, the square root of the AVE for each variable was higher than the correlation coefficient, indicating that the discriminant validity of the scale was high (as shown in the Table 3).

Table 3. Loadings, AVE, and CR.

Constructs	Items	Loadings	Cronbach's α	AVE	CR
Display visibility (DV)	DV1	0.705	0.815	0.5977	0.8162
	DV2	0.811			
	DV3	0.799			
Cue multiplicity (CM)	CM1	0.762	0.794	0.5627	0.7942
	CM2	0.760			
	CM3	0.728			
Perceived quality (PQ)	PQ1	0.824	0.821	0.6044	0.8206
	PQ2	0.741			
	PQ3	0.765			
Perceived value (PV)	PV1	0.752	0.836	0.6013	0.8187
	PV2	0.749			
	PV3	0.823			
Perceived entertainment (PE)	PE1	0.800	0.815	0.6306	0.8366
	PE2	0.805			
	PE3	0.777			
Purchase intention (PI)	PI1	0.754	0.827	0.6121	0.8255
	PI2	0.812			
	PI3	0.780			

From the results of the structural equation modeling (SEM) fitness test in the Table 4, it can be seen that the RMSEA value is 0.062, which is in the range of 0.05 ~0.08, indicating that the model fits well; the chi-square degrees of freedom ratio ($\chi2/df$) is 2.343, which is less than 3, indicating that the hypothesized model fits well with the actual sample data; the values of TLI, NFI, IFI, and CFI are all greater than 0.9, which reached the fitness standard, indicating that the model constructed in this paper fits well with the actual collected data. The results show that the model constructed and the hypotheses proposed in this paper fit well with the actual data.

Table 4. Model Fitness results

Adaptation index	$\chi2/df$	PGFI	PNFI	RMSEA	TLI	NFI	IFI	CFI
Recommended	< 3	> 0.5	> 0.5	< 0.08	> 0.9	> 0.9	> 0.9	> 0.9
Model	2.343	0.665	0.730	0.062	0.926	0.900	0.940	0.940
Conclusion	Supported	Supported	Supported	Supported	Supported	Supported	Supported	Supported

5.2 Hypothesis Testing

The research model was estimated using AMOS 28.0 to obtain the structural equation model path (as shown in the Fig. 2). The parameter estimation of the structural equation model was organized according to the above results. The original hypotheses, regression paths, standardized path coefficients, p-values, and results of hypothesis testing are listed in the Table 5. Among the 11 hypotheses, only hypothesis H2b is not supported, indicating that cue multiplicity in the agricultural products live-streaming has no impact on consumers' perceived entertainment. ($\beta = 0.063$, $p = 0.402$). From the support path, display visibility and cue multiplicity have positive influences on consumers' perceived quality, and display visibility has positive influences on consumers' perceived entertainment; consumers' perceived quality, perceived value, and perceived entertainment have positive influences on consumers' purchase intentions, with the influences of perceived value being more significant ($\beta = 0.38$, $p = 0.000$).

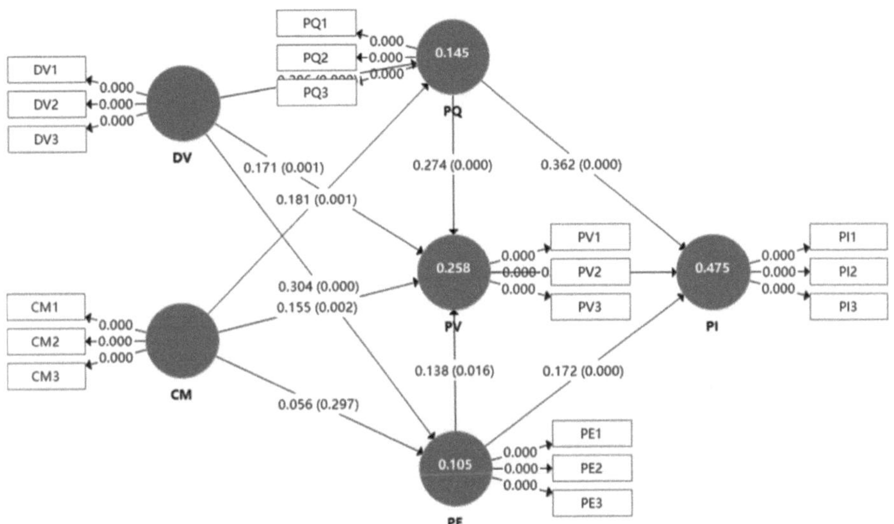

Fig. 2. Model with path coefficients.

Table 5. Model Path Coefficients and Hypothesis Test

Hypothesis	Relationship	Estimates	P-value	Conclusion
H1a	Display visibility - > Perceived quality	0.286	0.000	Supported
H1b	Display Visibility - > Perceived Entertainment	0.171	0.002	Supported
H1c	Display visibility - > Perceived Value	0.304	0.000	Supported
H2a	Cue multiplicity - > Perceived quality	0.181	0.001	Supported

(continued)

Table 5. (continued)

Hypothesis	Relationship	Estimates	P-value	Conclusion
H2b	Cue multiplicity - > Perceived Entertainment	0.155	0.002	Unsupported
H2c	Cue multiplicity - > Perceived Value	0.056	0.293	Supported
H3	Perceived quality - > Perceived Value	0.274	0.000	Supported
H4	Perceived Entertainment - > Perceived Value	0.138	0.015	Supported
H5	Perceived quality - > Purchase Intention	0.362	0.000	Supported
H6	Perceived Entertainment - > Purchase Intention	0.37	0.000	Supported
H7	Perceived Value - > Purchase Intention	0.172	0.000	Supported

Note: *, ** and *** indicate significant at the 10%, 5% and 1% statistical levels, respectively

Table 6. Mediating effect results

Relationship	Estimates	P-value
CM - > PE - > PI	0.01	0.367
DV - > PE - > PI	0.052	0.002
CM - > PQ - > PI	0.066	0.004
DV - > PQ - > PI	0.103	0.000
CM - > PV - > PI	0.057	0.006
DV - > PV - > PI	0.063	0.005
CM - > PE - > PV - > PI	0.003	0.364
PE - > PV - > PI	0.051	0.018
DV - > PE - > PV - > PI	0.016	0.032
CM - > PQ - > PV - > PI	0.018	0.011
PQ - > PV - > PI	0.101	0.000
DV - > PQ - > PV - > PI	0.029	0.000
CM - > PE - > PV	0.008	0.366
DV - > PE - > PV	0.042	0.031
CM - > PQ - > PV	0.05	0.010
DV - > PQ - > PV	0.078	0.000

In order to further test whether the mediating variables (perceived quality, perceived value, and perceived entertainment) mediate the effects of external variables (display visibility, cue multiplicity) on purchase decisions, this study used the Bootstrap mediation effect test to test whether the mediation effect is significant. AMOS 28.0 was used in the testing process, and the significance and coefficients of the product of the mediating effect coefficients of perceived quality, perceived entertainment, and perceived value were calculated using the nonparametric percentile Bootstrap method. Setting a sample of 5000 times, if the confidence interval does not contain zero at a confidence level of 95%, the coefficient product is significant, and there is a mediating effect.

The results are shown in the Table 6. Each mediating effect model passes the test at the 95% probability level.

6 Conclusion and Discussions

This study applies the S-O-R model, combined with the Perceived Value Theory, to explain the effects of product display cues on consumers' perceived value and purchase intention in the agricultural products live-streaming. In this study, the attributes of product display visibility and cue multiplicity in the agricultural products live-streaming are taken as stimuli, the perceived quality, perceived value, and perceived entertainment, which represent the factors of consumer experience, are taken as organisms, and the consumers' purchase intentions in the live-streaming is taken as reaction. The study results show that the expressions of cue multiplicity of commodity information in the agricultural products live-streaming have no impact on consumers' entertainment. Display visibility and cue multiplicity jointly augmented consumers' perceived quality, and display visibility has positive influence on consumers' perceived entertainment; consumers' perceived quality, perceived value, and perceived entertainment have positive influences on consumers' purchase intentions, and the effect of perceived value is more significant.

In the S-O-R model, stimuli can trigger an individual's perception. Display visibility and cue multiplicity in the agricultural products live-streaming can enhance consumers' perceived benefits. The actual display of agricultural products in the live-streaming and the streamer's commitment to the quality of the product can convey the quality and value of the product and enhance the consumer's perception of the value of the product through the live-streaming, the consumer can directly see the specific details of the agricultural products, and this intuitive display allows the consumer to comprehend the product more intuitively and accurately, which will enhance the consumer's perceived benefits in the purchase; the streamer in the live-streaming of the agricultural products related to other cues in the live-streaming such as: production location, production methods, consumption methods, etc. can provide consumers with more product information, thus enhancing the perception of product value.

The display of visibility in the live-streaming of product e-commerce can enhance the consumer's perception of entertainment. Live show of the real scene and the real production process so that consumers can feel the live-streaming of the growth of agricultural products, picking, and other processes; this life experience can trigger the emotional resonance of consumers, increase the sense of participation and interactivity, so that consumers are more willing to participate in and invested in live-streaming, thus enhancing the perceived entertainment when watching live-streaming; live-streaming of real-time display of high-definition images and colorful The real-time display of high-definition images and colorful images of agricultural products in the live-streaming can bring visual, intuitive feelings to consumers in the live-streaming, and this visual immersion can improve the viewing experience of consumers and enhance the perceived entertainment. The effect of cue multiplicity in live- streaming on consumers' perceived entertainment is insignificant and is considered to have no effect. The possible reason is that the introduction and display of other product-related information in the agricultural products live-streaming is too dull to be combined with entertaining information and cannot cause consumers to be entertained when watching.

Consumers' perceived benefits in agricultural products live-streaming can enhance their purchase intentions in the live-streaming room. E-commerce live-streaming not only provides product information but also accompany various preferential activities, limited-time discounts and so on. Consumers watching the agricultural products live-streaming agricultural products can feel the value of the product itself and the public welfare value of supporting the cause of helping farmers. This increase in perceived value stimulates the consumer's desire to buy.

Consumers' perceived entertainment in agricultural live-streaming e-commerce can enhance their purchase intentions in the live-streaming room. Entertainment, an important feature of e-commerce live-streaming, provides consumers with an easy and interesting shopping experience. In the live-streaming process, the streamer will usually use humorous language, vivid expressions, and actions to introduce the product; through the entertaining content display and explanation, the streamer can transfer the complex product information to the consumer in a simple and easy-to-understand way, making it easier for consumers to understand and accept, and enhancing consumer pleasure. This sense of pleasure can increase the interest of consumers in live content so that they are more willing to stay in the live-streaming room, further understand the product, and produce purchase intentions.

6.1 Theoretical Implications

The live-streaming e-commerce market is growing rapidly, and while there are many academic studies on the influence of live e-commerce on consumer purchasing decisions, consumer behavior is still evolving in the context of the emerging and innovative live e-commerce market. Moreover, there is still a lack of in-depth research on agricultural products, a product category with its product characteristics. Thus, this study aims to address the research gap by exploring the relationship between the display information of agricultural products and consumers' perceptions and purchase intentions based on the characteristics of agricultural products.

6.2 Managerial Implications

The results of this study also provide practical insights for live-streaming managers and platforms. Our findings suggest that comprehensive visual product information needs to be provided in agricultural live-streaming. High-definition photography and video equipment can be used to ensure that consumers can clearly see the details of agricultural products, including color, shape, and texture, and that all aspects and details of the agricultural products are displayed through multi-angle displays and lens zooms to provide consumers with a more comprehensive understanding of the appearance and characteristics of the products. Combining text, pictures, videos, and other media to provide consumers with a comprehensive introduction.

To enhance multi-sensory-based cue multiplicity, the production methods and planting techniques of agricultural products can be introduced during the live-streaming, so that consumers can better understand the production standards and quality assurance measures of the products; the consumption methods and cooking suggestions of agricultural products can be provided, including recipe recommendations and food combinations, so that consumers can better understand the diversified uses and nutritional value of the products; the features and advantages of agricultural products can be demonstrated through comparison and demonstration, such as taste Through comparisons and demonstrations, we demonstrate the characteristics and advantages of agricultural products, such as taste, nutritional value, variety, etc.; and share consumers' use cases and experiences, including word-of-mouth evaluations and purchasing feelings, so as to enable consumers to obtain cues and insights from other people's real experiences, and to increase the sense of trust in the products.

In an increasingly homogenized live-streaming environment, it is critical to incorporate advanced technologies to create live-streaming environments that satisfy consumers' positive perceptions of agricultural product quality, attractiveness, and entertainment benefits. These optimization strategies can improve the display and design elements associated with agricultural products live-streaming to increase consumer conversions during live-streaming and ultimately increase sales.

6.3 Limitations and Future Research Directions

There is a large variety of agricultural products, and no detailed studies are conducted according to specific categories. Live-streaming platforms are diverse, and there are refinement possibilities for different platforms and different consumer types. Perceived benefit, positive impact perspective, no perceived loss incorporated in modeling.

While the results of this study provide relevant theoretical and practical contributions, there are limitations that provide guidance and opportunities for future research directions. Due to the cost and time constraints of the study, this study sampled from the audience of live e-commerce in China, and investigating a broader sample would allow for more generalizability of the results. Although our sample is representative, the sample size is limited and may not fully reflect the purchasing behavior of all consumers. In addition, in terms of product categories, agricultural products cover a wide range of specific product categories, and the specific needs of different product categories vary.

In terms of theoretical modeling, this study does not refine the different types of live- streaming platforms. The multiplicity of streamer types and product types of live-streaming merchants makes their operation models, audience groups, and consumers' purchasing decision paths different. Future research can analyze different types of live-streaming platforms in depth, establish more refined theoretical models, and better explain and predict the path of influence of different types of live-streaming e-commerce attributes on consumers' purchase decisions. In addition, this study only analyzes the perceived benefits of consumers in the agricultural products live-streaming, lacks the study of perceived losses in the research model, and has not analyzed the role of live-streaming of agricultural products in social benefits, which can be used as a focus for future research.

Disclosure of Interests. The authors declare that they have no known competing financial interests or personal relationships that could have appeared to influence the work the authors declare that they have no known competing financial interests or personal relationships that could have appeared to influence the work.

References

1. Addo, P.C., Fang, J., Asare, A.O., Kulbo, N.B.: Customer engagement and purchase intention in live-streaming digital marketing platforms. Serv. Ind. J. **41**(11), 767–786 (2021)
2. Ambadar, Z., Cohn, J.F., Reed, L.I.: All smiles are not created equal: morphology and timing of smiles perceived as amused, polite, and embarrassed/nervous. J. Nonverbal Behav. **33**, 17–34 (2008)
3. Baabdullah, A.M., Alalwan, A.A., Rana, N.P., Kizgin, H., Patil, P.: Consumer use of mobile banking (M-Banking) in Saudi Arabia: towards an integrated model. Int. J. Inf. Manage. **44**, 38–52 (2019)
4. Barsade, S.G., Coutifaris, C.G.V., Pillemer, J.: Emotional contagion in organizational life. Res. Organ. Behav. **38**, 137–151 (2018)
5. Bawack, R.E., Bonhoure, E., Kamdjoug, J.R.K., Giannakis, M.: How social media live streams affect online buyers: a uses and gratifications perspective. Int. J. Inf. Manage. **70**, 102621 (2023)
6. Beverland, M.B., Lindgreen, A., Vink, M.W.: Projecting authenticity through advertising: consumer judgments of advertisers' claims. J. Advert. **1**, 5–15 (2008)
7. Chen, C.C., Lin, Y.C.: What drives live-stream usage intention? the perspectives of flow, entertainment, social interaction, and endorsement. Telemat. Inform. **35**(1), 293–303 (2018)
8. Chen, N., Fang, Y.: The role of influencers in live streaming e-commerce: influencer trust, attachment, and consumer purchase intention. J. Theor. Appl. Electron. Commer. Res. **18**(3), 1601–1618 (2023)
9. Creyer, E.H.: The influence of firm behavior on purchase intention: do consumers really care about business ethics? J. Consum. Mark. **14**(6), 421–432 (1997)
10. Davis, F.D., Bagozzi, R.P., Warshaw, P.R.: User acceptance of computer technology: a comparison of two theoretical models. Manage. Sci. **8**, 982–1003 (1989)
11. Dong, X., Zhao, H., Li, T.: The role of live-streaming e-commerce on consumers' purchasing intention regarding green agricultural products. Sustainability **14**(7), 4374 (2022)
12. Eroglu, S.A., Machleit, K.A., Davis, L.M.: Atmospheric qualities of online retailing: a conceptual model and implications. J. Bus. Res. **54**(2), 177–184 (2001)
13. Fei, M., Tan, H., Peng, X., Wang, Q., Wang, L.: Promoting or attenuating? an eye-tracking study on the role of social cues in e-commerce livestreaming. Decis. Support. Syst. **142**, 113466 (2021)
14. Fiore, A.M., Kim, J.: An integrative framework capturing experiential and utilitarian shopping experience. Int. J. Retail Distrib. Manage. **35**(6), 421–442 (2007)
15. Fu, J.R., Hsu, C.W.: Live-streaming shopping: the impacts of para-social interaction and local presence on impulse buying through shopping value. Ind. Manag. Data Syst. **123**(7), 1861–1886 (2023)
16. Gironda, J.T., Korgaonkar, P.K.: ISpy? tailored versus invasive ads and consumers' perceptions of personalized advertising. Electron. Commer. Res. Appl. **29**, 64–77 (2018)

17. Hewei, T., Youngsook, L.: Factors affecting continuous purchase intention of fashion products on social e-commerce: SOR model and the mediating effect. Entertain. Comput. **41**, 100474 (2022)

18. Horic-Asselin, D., Brosseau-Liard, P., Gosselin, P., Collin, C.A.: Effects of temporal dynamics on perceived authenticity of smiles. Atten. Percept. Psychophys. **82**, 3648–3657 (2020)

19. Hsu, C.L., Chang, K.C., Chen, M.C.: The impact of website quality on customer satisfaction and purchase intention: perceived playfulness and perceived flow as mediators. IseB **10**(4), 549–570 (2012)

20. Jacoby, J.: The emerging behavioral process technology in consumer decision-making research. Adv. Consum. Res. **4**(1) (1977)

21. Jin, N.P., Lee, S., Lee, H.: The effect of experience quality on perceived value, satisfaction, image and behavioral intention of water park patrons: new versus repeat visitors. Int. J. Tour. Res. **17**(1), 82–95 (2015)

22. Koo, D.M., Ju, S.H.: The interactional effects of atmospherics and perceptual curiosity on emotions and online shopping intention. Comput. Hum. Behav. **26**(3), 377–388 (2010)

23. Kumar, S., Yadav, R.: The impact of shopping motivation on sustainable consumption: a study in the context of green apparel. J. Clean. Prod. **295**, 126239 (2021)

24. Lee, C.H., Chen, C.W.: Impulse buying behaviors in live streaming commerce based on the stimulus-organism-response framework. Information **12**(6), 241 (2021)

25. Li, C., Xia, Z., Liu, Y., et al.: Is online shopping addiction still a depressive illness?—the induced consumption and traffic trap in live e-commerce. Heliyon **10**(9) (2024)

26. Li, Q., Zhao, C., Cheng, R.: How the characteristics of live-streaming environment affect consumer purchase intention: the mediating role of presence and perceived trust. IEEE Access (2023)

27. Lin, Q., Jia, N., Chen, L., Zhong, S., Yang, Y., Gao, T.: A two-stage prediction model based on behavior mining in livestream e-commerce. Decis. Support. Syst. **174**, 114013 (2023)

28. Liu, J., Li, K.: Exploring the mechanism of live streaming e-commerce anchors' language appeals on users' purchase intention. Front. Psychol. **14** (2023)

29. Liu, Y., Hongxiu, L., Feng, H.: Website attributes in urging online impulse purchase: an empirical investigation on consumer perceptions. Decis. Support. Syst. **3**, 829–837 (2013)

30. Liu, Y., Sun, X.: Tourism e-commerce live streaming: the effects of live streamer authenticity on purchase intention. Tourism Rev. **79**(5), 1147–1165 (2023)

31. Luo, H., Cheng, S., Zhou, W., Yu, S., Lin, X.: A study on the impact of linguistic persuasive styles on the sales volume of live streaming products in social e-commerce environment. Mathematics **9**(13), 1576 (2021)

32. Ma, X., Chen, H., Lang, X., et al.: Research on the impact of streamers' linguistic emotional valence on live streaming performance in live streaming shopping environments. J. Retail. Consum. Serv. **81**, 104040 (2024)

33. Mehrabian, A., Russell, J.A.: A verbal measure of information rate for studies in environmental psychology. Environ. Behav. **6**(2), 233 (1974)

34. Meng, L.M., Duan, S., Zhao, Y., et al.: The impact of online celebrity in livestreaming e-commerce on purchase intention from the perspective of emotional contagion. J. Retail. Consum. Serv. **63**, 102733 (2021)

35. Meng, Z., Lin, M.: The driving factors analysis of live streamers' characteristics and perceived value for consumer repurchase intention on live streaming platforms. J. Organ. End User Comput. **35**(1), 1–24 (2023)

36. Moon, J.W., Kim, Y.G.: Extending the TAM for a world-wide-web context. Inform. Manag. **38**(4), 217–230 (2001)

37. Parboteeah, D.V., Valacich, J.S., Wells, J.D.: The influence of website characteristics on a consumer's urge to buy impulsively. Inf. Syst. Res. **20**(1), 60–78 (2009)

38. Peng, L., Lu, G., Pang, K., et al.: Optimal farmer's income from farm products sales on live streaming with random rewards: case from China's rural revitalisation strategy. Comput. Electron. Agric. **189**, 106403 (2021)

39. Schreiner, M., Fischer, T., Riedl, R.: Impact of content characteristics and emotion on behavioral engagement in social media: literature review and research agenda. Electron. Commer. Res. **21**, 329–345 (2021)

40. Shang, Q., Ma, H., Wang, C., et al.: Effects of background fitting of e-commerce live streaming on consumers' purchase intentions: a cognitive-affective perspective. Psychol. Res. Behav. Manag. 149–168 (2023)

41. Shen, Y.C., Huang, C.Y., Chu, C.H., et al.: Virtual community loyalty: an interpersonal-interaction perspective. Int. J. Electron. Commer. **15**(1), 49–74 (2010)

42. Sun, B., Zhang, Y., Zheng, L.: Relationship between time pressure and consumers' impulsive buying—role of perceived value and emotions. Heliyon **9**(12), e23185 (2023)

43. Sun, Y., Shao, X., Li, X., et al.: A 2020 perspective on "How live streaming influences purchase intentions in social commerce: an IT affordance perspective." Electron. Commer. Res. Appl. **40**, 100958 (2020)

44. Sweeney, J.C., Soutar, G.N.: Consumer perceived value: the development of a multiple item scale. J. Retail. **77**(2), 203–220 (2001)

45. Vickery, S.K., Droge, C., Stank, T.P., et al.: The performance implications of media richness in a business-to-business service environment: direct versus indirect effects. Manage. Sci. **50**(8), 1106–1119 (2004)

46. Wang, C., Liu, T., Zhu, Y., et al.: The influence of consumer perception on purchase intention: evidence from cross-border e-commerce platforms. Heliyon **9**(11) (2023)

47. Wang, L., Li, X., Zhu, H.Y., et al.: Influencing factors of livestream selling of fresh food based on a push-pull model: a two-stage approach combining structural equation modeling (SEM) and artificial neural network (ANN). Expert Syst. Appl. **212**, 118799 (2023)

48. Wongkitrungrueng, A., Assarut, N.: The role of live streaming in building consumer trust and engagement with social commerce sellers. J. Bus. Res. **117**, 543–556 (2020)

49. Xie, F., Luo, J.: Research on the influence of live streaming commerce affordances on consumers' impulse purchase intention based on SPSS25.0 and Amos23.0. In: Proceedings of the 2021 2nd International Conference on E-Commerce and Internet Technology (ECIT) (2021)

50. Xin, M., Liu, W., Jian, L.: Live streaming product display or social interaction: how do they influence consumer intention and behavior? a heuristic-systematic perspective. Electron. Commer. Res. Appl. **67**, 101437 (2024)

51. Xu, P., Cui, B., Lyu, B.: Influence of streamer's social capital on purchase intention in live streaming e-commerce. Front. Psychol. **12**, 748172 (2022)

52. Yin, J., Huang, Y., Ma, Z.: Explore the feeling of presence and purchase intention in livestream shopping: a flow-based model. J. Theor. Appl. Electron. Commer. Res. **18**(1), 237–256 (2023)

53. Zeithaml, V.A.: Consumer perceptions of price, quality, and value: a means-end model and synthesis of evidence. J. Mark. **52**(3), 2–22 (1988)

54. Zhang, M., Alan, G., et al.: The impact of live video streaming on online purchase intention. Serv. Ind. J. **40**(9–10), 656–681 (2019)

55. Zhang, N.: Product presentation in the live-streaming context: the effect of consumer perceived product value and time pressure on consumer's purchase intention. Front. Psychol. **14**, 1124675 (2023)

56. Zhang, Y., Xu, Q.: Consumer engagement in live streaming commerce: value co-creation and incentive mechanisms. J. Retail. Consum. Serv. **81**, 103987 (2024)

57. Zheng, S., Chen, J., Liao, J., et al.: What motivates users' viewing and purchasing behavior motivations in live streaming: a stream-streamer-viewer perspective. J. Retail. Consum. Serv. **72**, 103240 (2023)

58. Zhou, Y., Huang, W.: The influence of network anchor traits on shopping intentions in a live streaming marketing context: the mediating role of value perception and the moderating role of consumer involvement. Econ. Anal. Policy **78**, 332–342 (2023)

Digital Transformation of Business and Governance

Technological Approach to Managing Transparency in Electronic Government Procedures

Jorge Hochstetter-Diez$^{(\boxtimes)}$, Jaime Díaz-Arancibia ,
Mauricio Diéguez-Rebolledo , Marlene Negrier-Seguel ,
Ana Bustamante-Mora , and Claudio Navarro-Cruces

Depto. Cs. de la Computación e Informática, Universidad de La Frontera, Temuco,
Chile
{jorge.hochstetter,jaimeignacio.diaz,mauricio.dieguez,
marlene.negrier,ana.bustamante,claudio.navarro}@ufrontera.cl

Abstract. Integrating information technologies in public management has marked a change in how governments operate and relate to citizens. This article examines the significant impact of this technological integration on the transparency of government procedures, paying particular attention to e-government platforms. The article presents an innovative electronic platform that allows government entities to self-assess their transparency about electronic procedures. This tool is based on a maturity model that integrates elements of e-government and open government, emphasizing organizational learning characteristics for effective measurement and improvement of transparency. The usefulness of maturity models is highlighted in formulating specific and targeted recommendations that encourage cultural change toward continuous and transparent practices. The study concludes by highlighting the need to implement sound policies and develop indicators that evaluate the effectiveness of these initiatives to combat persistent problems such as corruption and strengthen trust in government operations. This approach provides a straightforward methodology for evaluating and improving transparency and drives an ongoing dialogue on the importance of a culture of transparency in public administration.

Keywords: Electronic Procedures · Mature Models · Transparency

1 Introduction

In the modern digital era, the integration of information technology within government operations has significantly transformed public sector transparency and service delivery. Over the past two decades, numerous governments have embraced e-government platforms to enhance the quality of public services and elevate the transparency of their operations [1]. This shift typically begins with implementing IT-focused legislation to support, enable, and streamline public sector functions [2].

F. F.-H Nah and K. L. Siau (Eds.): HCII 2025, LNCS 16343, pp. 299–310, 2026.
https://doi.org/10.1007/978-3-032-13167-6_20

With substantial public resources at stake, particularly in procuring goods and services and recruiting public personnel—collectively referred to here as electronic procedures—the need for effective and efficient electronic procurement systems is paramount. In many countries, these systems are centralized through web portals to demonstrate a transparent procurement process [3].

However, the integration of these technologies introduces numerous challenges. Governments must fully adopt technology within public systems [5], establish policies to ensure the delivery of high-quality services, develop comprehensive legal and regulatory frameworks, adopt robust management practices, and build adequate institutional structures. Furthermore, training for public officials and operators is crucial to the success of these initiatives [6].

E-government systems that manage public electronic procedures are critical to national transparency agendas. Effective control over procurement processes ensures active transparency and optimizes vendor interactions, thus reducing corruption, enhancing public trust, boosting procurement efficiency, and attracting new business partners [4].

Despite these advancements, challenges such as corruption persist within public sector procurement [7,8]. To tackle these issues, governments need to implement policies and laws to improve transparency and develop metrics to evaluate their effectiveness. More than simply enacting laws is required to guarantee true transparency [11]. The pivotal role of information technologies in enhancing transparency and improving public service delivery is recognized worldwide. These technologies, often supported by legislative frameworks, are essential for maintaining transparent and efficient electronic procedures [12].

To initiate adequate transparency, it is crucial to provide mechanisms that allow entities to efficiently manage and monitor their progress toward achieving required transparency standards. Such tools enable self-diagnosis of transparency levels in procurement processes, assessment of organizational maturity regarding transparency, and formulation of actionable recommendations for improvement. This framework serves as an initial assessment tool and lays the groundwork for ongoing enhancements. Over time, it aims to foster a cultural shift towards greater transparency, considering each public agency's unique dynamics. By integrating these mechanisms into existing structures, governments can more effectively foster an environment of openness and trust, which is essential for the robust functioning of public institutions.

This article presents an electronic platform that enables government entities to self-assess their transparency concerning electronic procedures. This platform incorporates a maturity model that blends elements of e-government and open government initiatives with specific electronic procedures and organizational learning characteristics, offering a tailored approach to measuring and enhancing transparency.

2   Background

2.1   Transparency

Transparency refers to providing information by public institutions to the populace, standing in contrast to the secrecy and opacity typical of the 18th century [16]. For transparency to be adequate, the information shared must be accessible, relevant, high-quality, and dependable [21]. It is a critical tool for enforcing public accountability and ensuring governmental responsibility towards society [22]. Transparency makes specific types of information available and allows public participation in decision-making processes [23]. In the public sector context, transparency is closely linked to accountability; without it, there is no basis for public scrutiny as information and activities are intentionally obscured [16]. The term transparency encompasses various concepts associated with the metaphor of visibility, including ethical decision-making, appropriate conduct by officials, public reporting, integrity, accountability, and the upholding of democratic values [23]. However, it is essential to note that while these attributes may reflect the potential virtues of social systems, transparency today is often pursued as an objective facilitated by digital technologies, regardless of the angle from which it is analyzed.

2.2   Electronic Procedures

Public electronic procedures, facilitated by e-government systems, are crucial to national government programs because they aim to ensure active transparency and enhance efficient interactions with suppliers [17]. These systems are anticipated to enhance transparency, potentially reducing corruption [27–30], and boosting confidence in the procurement system. Additionally, they are expected to improve the productivity of purchasing and service operations and attract new vendors interested in conducting business with the government [31]. As bidding for goods, services, and public tenders is often perceived as a hotspot for corruption, transparent electronic procedures in these areas are likely to encourage citizen oversight [9, 27]. Furthermore, as a culture of transparency becomes more ingrained, individuals are believed to naturally adopt practices that support transparent processes in their professional activities [32].

2.3   Maturity Models

Maturity models delineate a pathway for evolutionary advancement within an organization, guiding it from inconsistent processes to highly mature ones [6]. These models facilitate the evaluation of an organization's current state of development or a specific business process, helping to define improvement strategies to meet set goals clearly and pinpointing critical areas for enhancement [33]. Many researchers utilize these models to conduct organizational diagnostics and to set benchmarks for progress [34–37]. Employing a maturity model suggests an ingrained discipline of learning within an organization [38]. This implies that participants acknowledge the importance of adopting specific actions or practices. They set standards and regulations that guide and evaluate their actions, practices, and strategies, leading to modifications, changes, and innovations that enhance procedures, techniques, technologies, skills, competencies, and overall effectiveness [39]. In the field of software, the most recognized maturity models are the Capability Maturity Model (CMM) and CMM Integration (CMMI), both developed by the Software Engineering Institute (SEI) in the USA. These models primarily focus on developing, maintaining, and acquiring software products and services. Their structured approach to assessing capacity and maturity has been emulated by numerous other models in various domains [35].

2.4 Organizational Learning

Organizational learning involves participants within processes understanding the necessity to develop and refine specific procedures. They set standards to guide and assess their performance, practices, and strategies, facilitating adjustments, changes, and innovations that enhance procedures, techniques, technologies, skills, and overall effectiveness. This enhancement hinges on fundamentally learning-based processes, and it is crucial to grasp the full scope of learning for all stakeholders involved—both within an individual organization and across different organizations. These stakeholders must adeptly adjust to their surroundings, a vital challenge where learning is indispensable for continually updating their environmental knowledge and improving their competencies in specific operational areas [24].

Staff members or adaptive agents learn to create and share mental models that dictate strategies and rules for strategic behavior based on regular, consistent interactions. These strategies and rules, which are patterns of interaction, are dynamically modified, allowing agents to use this information to predict situations, act in particular ways, and adapt to one another in a self-organized and endogenous manner [25]. Agent decision-making is influenced by typical environmental structures, interpreted through heuristics that serve as cognitive rules for processing information [26].

3   Proposed Solution

The proposed solution comprises two interconnected components: a methodology for diagnosing transparency in public entities' electronic procedures and a prototype web platform that implements this methodology to enable autonomous evaluations by public entities.

The framework is anchored in an established maturity model detailed in [40]. This model utilizes observable organizational elements and behaviors across various dimensions derived from multiple organizational ontology theories. A set of questions, each corresponding to a different level of maturity, is generated for these dimensions. The responses to these questions are then classified to ascertain the maturity level within each dimension.

Our prototype web platform facilitates the application of this diagnostic methodology, allowing public entities to assess their transparency practices independently. This platform guides users through a structured evaluation process based on the maturity model. It defines specific measurement levels and criteria for each dimension, detailing compliance requirements for achieving each maturity level.

The solution includes a systematic approach to perform diagnostics based on objective criteria, which are analyzed within this project's scope. As illustrated in Fig. 1, this process integrates various elements to determine maturity levels and generate tailored recommendations for improvements. Entities using this methodology are encouraged to develop activities and tasks based on these recommendations, promoting ongoing enhancements in transparency.

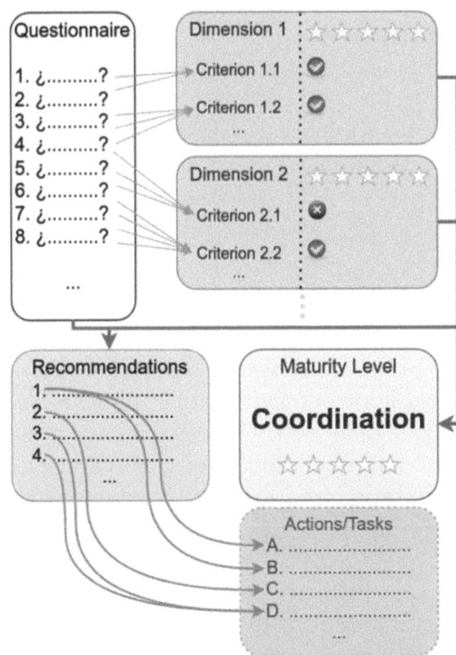

Fig. 1. Diagnostic methodology operation diagram.

3.1 Diagnostic and Recommendation Mechanism

The solution includes a systematic approach to perform diagnostics based on objective criteria, which are analyzed within this project's scope. As illustrated in Fig. 1, this process integrates various elements to determine maturity levels and generate tailored recommendations for improvements. Entities using this methodology are encouraged to develop activities and tasks based on these recommendations, promoting ongoing enhancements in transparency. To address the challenge of recommending improvement actions, we approach it as an optimization problem. Here, we propose adapting the model from Diéguez et al. [41], which uses optimization models to suggest the most effective set of actions or controls. This adaptation will consider the specific actions and constraints relevant to our project's context.

The main value of this proposal lies in the implementation of a systematic approach that carries out diagnoses based on objective criteria adapted to each organization's specificities. Organizations adopting this method can develop activities and tasks aligned with these recommendations, fostering continuous improvements in transparency. This model, designed as an optimization problem, seeks to provide the most effective solution to address the specific challenges identified in the diagnosis, thus maximizing the benefits of transparency within existing organizational constraints.

The proposal is divided into two main phases. The first is related to the organization's classification in the level of maturity of its transparency processes. The second phase focuses on determining a schedule for advancing towards higher levels of maturity through recommendations for implementing transparency practices that are adapted to the conditions and restrictions of each particular organization.

Diagnostic. In the diagnostic stage, a process is carried out to understand and evaluate how information and processes are managed and disseminated within the organization. This process establishes a precise reference point from which targeted and measurable improvements can be implemented.

The diagnostic stage begins with the definition of clear and objective metrics that reflect the fundamental aspects of transparency, such as information accessibility, clarity of internal and external communications, and effectiveness of disclosure policies. In our proposal, the metrics are given in the associated maturity model.

The diagnostic process focuses on collecting data to evaluate the metrics defined in the model. This step involves various methods, including employee and stakeholder surveys, interviews with management and other key employees, and analysis of documents and records. Direct observation of work practices can also provide valuable insights into how transparency is promoted or inhibited in day-to-day operations.

The data collected through quantitative and/or qualitative analysis techniques is examined to identify trends, gaps, and areas of strength and weakness in relation to transparency metrics. This analysis allows us to determine the organization's current level of transparency maturity and highlights areas that require attention. This information serves as the basis for the next stage of the process: the formulation of specific, customized recommendations. These recommendations are intended to address the deficiencies identified during the diagnostic and to improve the organization's overall level of transparency.

Recommendation. The recommendation stage defines a methodological framework to incorporate optimization techniques to solve the problem of recommending and implementing transparency practices based on the state identified in the diagnosis. This involves considering the recommendation of an improvement plan for advancing transparency levels as an optimization problem, in which an objective must be defined, and the organization's restrictions must be identified.

However, the decision regarding the transparency practices to be implemented to achieve progress in the maturity model in the context of limited resources is a complex task since it implies considering multiple variables and restrictions. These variables include risk levels, costs and time required for implementation, human resources limitations, and internal and external policies. This means that decisions about which transparency measures to implement to reduce the gap become a complex challenge, given the numerous goals and constraints. This challenge is intensified when seeking to optimize the organization's resources, i.e., finding the best solution that fits the available resource constraints.

As stated in [42], the recommendations stage can be divided into three sub-stages:

Optimization Problem Identification: This sub-stage seeks to clarify the optimization problem to be applied for its subsequent modeling. To this end, it is necessary to determine (i) the objective to be achieved, (ii) the constraints to be taken into account, and (iii) the parameters of the variables that define both the objective and the constraints inherent to the organization.

The definition of the objective should specify the expected results or desired benefits of the recommendation. Examples of appropriate objectives include:

- Maximize the number of transparency practices to be adopted,
- Maximize the benefits derived from the implementation of transparency practices,
- Minimize the risk associated with the lack of implementation of transparency practices,
- Minimizes the time required to implement transparency practices.

Another element to consider is the specific conditions or constraints of the organization when making a recommendation. These constraints are usually linked to the organization's resource availability to execute an improvement plan. Examples of these constraints include:

- a set budget,
- a specific time frame for carrying out the implementation project,
- a specific level of risk that the organization seeks to reduce and

Finally, it is necessary to establish some relevant parameters for the modeling, such as:

- implementation cost of each transparency practice,

– implementation time of each transparency practice,
– benefit associated with the implementation of each transparency practice,
– risk associated with each transparency practice.

The second step consists of formulating the current situation as an optimization problem. The product of this effort is a mathematical model created using conventional Operations Research methods.

From the point of view of modeling an optimization problem, when approaching the resolution through Operations Research Techniques and specifically considering linear programming, the definition of the objective is aligned with the model's Objective Function. The specific constraints of the organization act as constraints in the model, and the parameters are linked to the variables of the objective function and the constraints.

Then, mathematically, the model would be represented as follows:

$$MAX \left(\sum_{i>0} P_i X_i \right) \tag{1}$$

s.t.

$$\sum_{i>0} C_i X_i - B \leq 0 \tag{2}$$

In the Eq. 1, the objective function is represented, in this case, a maximization of the variable X together with its parameter P. Furthermore, it is subject to constraints, Eq. 2 where the summation of the variable X by its parameter C must not exceed the threshold B.

Finally, the third process consists of solving the proposed model using various optimization problem-solving techniques applied in Operations Research. Several computer tools can help solve the problem, such as GAMS [43] and NEOS-SERVER [44]. This last process results in the set of practices that will constitute the recommended improvement plan to increase organizational transparency.

The information necessary for modeling and solving the problem comes from the organization's diagnosis and the conditions defined by those in charge or responsible for transparency management through questionnaires.

3.2 IT Platform

The IT platform has become essential for developing transparency management and control processes. First, the platform also serves as a management tool, featuring a dashboard displaying diagnostic results. This enables public entities to conduct comparative analyses of successive diagnostics, identifying areas of progress and those needing attention. Figure 2 provides a visual representation of the diagnostic process facilitated by the platform.

In addition, it becomes an essential tool for automating the process since it can contribute significantly to the modeling and resolution of the recommendations problem, integrating, through the answers to the questionnaires, the definitions of parameters, objectives, and constraints, and solver tools for the resolution of the optimization model.

3.3   Limitations and Future Directions

While this proposal aims to enhance transparency management within governmental organizations and foster cultural changes toward transparency, it is crucial to note the limitations regarding the immediate assessment of cultural impact. Cultural transformations are gradual and vary by organization. Nevertheless, we will include a Methodology Adoption Intention study to evaluate the readiness and willingness of stakeholders to integrate this process into regular organizational practices.

This solution stands out in a political landscape that increasingly values transparency but lacks effective methodologies for assessing and enhancing it across diverse public entities (such as municipalities, military forces, hospitals, and schools). It supports compliance with transparency laws and reduces the risk of corruption by providing clear, actionable insights for public managers.

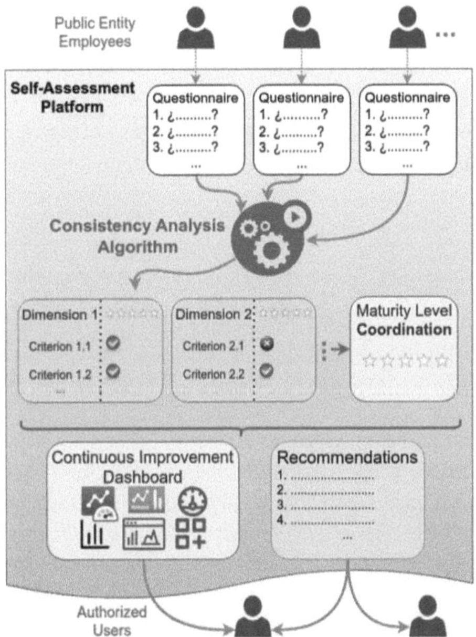

Fig. 2. Functional diagram of the prototype platform for transparency diagnostics.

4   Conclusions and Future Work

Implementing e-government platforms has significantly improved transparency in public processes, especially in contracting and acquiring services. However, despite these advances, challenges such as corruption persist, suggesting that more than technology adoption is needed. A solid regulatory framework and effective implementation and monitoring are required to guarantee natural and sustainable transparency.

It is essential to use maturity models to evaluate and improve transparency in public entities. These models offer a clear path for development and continuous improvement, allowing organizations to evaluate their current state and establish specific improvement strategies based on detailed diagnoses and personalized recommendations.

The process of increasing transparency is continuous and requires cultural change within government organizations. Adoption of organizational learning practices is crucial to this end, allowing entities to constantly adapt and improve their transparency processes and policies through self-assessment and the implementation of new technologies and procedures.

Acknowledgments. The authors thank the American University of Europe and its Ph.D. Program in Computer Science. Jorge Hochstetter-Diez is suported by Grant ANID, Chile, FONDECYT DE INICIACIÓN EN INVESTIGACIÓN, Project No 1124-0115, Jaime Díaz-Arancibia is supported by Grant ANID, Chile, FONDECYT DE INICIACIÓN EN INVESTIGACIÓN, Project No 11230141. Ana Bustamante-Mora is supported by Universidad de La Frontera, project PEG23-0007.

Disclosure of Interests. The authors have no competing interests to declare that are relevant to the content of this article.

References

1. Shahab, M., Antoni, D., Akbar, M.: Public private partnership e-government in improving service quality in community health. In: Sriwijaya International Conference on Information Technology and its Applications (SICONIAN 2019), pp. 92–96 (2020)
2. Arshad, S., Khurram, S.: Can government's presence on social media stimulate citizens' online political participation? Investigating the influence of transparency, trust, and responsiveness. Gov. Inf. Q. **37**, 101486 (2020)
3. Adjei-Bamfo, P., et al.: An e-government framework for assessing readiness for public sector e-procurement in a lower-middle income country. Inf. Technol. Dev. **26**, 742–761 (2020)
4. Rivera, J.: Transparencia y democracia: claves para un concierto (IFAI, 2008)
5. Manurung, N., Amin, M., Warjio, W.: Analysis of e-Government implementation towards Asahan smart city. Int. J. Multicultural Multireligious Understand. **7**, 661–670 (2020)
6. Lemke, F., Taveter, K., Erlenheim, R., Pappel, I., Draheim, D., Janssen, M.: Stage models for moving from e-government to smart government. In: Electronic Governance and Open Society: Challenges in Eurasia: 6th International Conference, EGOSE 2019, St. Petersburg, Russia, 13–14 November 2019, Proceedings 6, pp. 152–164 (2020)

7. Glyptis, L., Christofi, M., Vrontis, D., Del Giudice, M., Dimitriou, S., Michael, P.: E-Government implementation challenges in small countries: the project manager's perspective. Technol/ Forecast. Soc. Change **152**, 119880 (2020)
8. Cruz-Rubio, C.: Participación ciudadana y compras públicas en América Latina: marco conceptual, análisis de casos y factores de éxito (2020)
9. Hapuhennedige, S., Bernsen, E., Kohler, J.: Exploring accountability and transparency within international organizations: what do we know and what do we need to know? Integrity, Transparency Corruption Healthc. Res. Health **I**, 125–139 (2020)
10. Mackey, T., Cuomo, R.: An interdisciplinary review of digital technologies to facilitate anti-corruption, transparency and accountability in medicines procurement. Glob. Health Action **13**, 1695241 (2020)
11. Navarro, F.: Qué transparencia requiere el gobierno abierto? Revista De Gestión Pública. **2**, 303–333 (2013)
12. Yildiz, M.: E-government research: reviewing the literature, limitations, and ways forward. Gov. Inf. Q. **24**, 646–665 (2007)
13. Ronaghan, S.: Benchmarking e-government: a global perspective. In: Assessing the Progress of the UN Member States. United Nations Division for Public Economics and Public Administration and American Society for Public Administration (2002)
14. Shareef, M., Kumar, V., Kumar, U., Dwivedi, Y.: e-Government Adoption Model (GAM): differing service maturity levels. Gov. Inf. Q. **28**, 17–35 (2011)
15. Gutiérrez, M., Casetti, M.: Una mirada a la ley de transparencia en Chile: aspectos que condicionan su logro en lo municipal. Via Inveniendi Et Iudicandi. **9**, 41–59 (2014)
16. Mabillard, V., Pasquier, M.: Transparency and trust in government (2007–2014): a comparative study. NISPAcee J. Publ. Admin. Policy **9**, 69–92 (2016)
17. Concha, G., Naser, A.: El desafio hacia el gobierno abierto en la hora de la igualdad. Comisión Económica Para América Latina Y El Caribe (CEPAL) **18** (2012)
18. Iribarren, M., et al.: Capability maturity framework for eGovernment: a multidimensional model and assessing tool. International Conference on Electronic Government, pp. 136–147 (2008)
19. Concha, G., Astudillo, H., Porrua, M., Pimenta, C.: E-Government procurement observatory, maturity model and early measurements. Gov. Inf. Q. **29**, S43–S50 (2012)
20. Krishnan, S., Teo, T., Lim, V.: Examining the relationships among e-government maturity, corruption, economic prosperity and environmental degradation: a cross-country analysis. Inf. Manag. **50**, 638–649 (2013)
21. Ruijer, E., Détienne, F., Baker, M., Groff, J., Meijer, A.: The politics of open government data: understanding organizational responses to pressure for more transparency. Am. Rev. Pub. Admin. **50**, 260–274 (2020)
22. Naessens, H.: Ética pública y transparencia. In: XIV Encuentro De Latinoamericanistas Españoles: Congreso Internacional, pp. 2113–2130 (2010)
23. Matheus, R., Janssen, M.: A systematic literature study to unravel transparency enabled by open government data: the window theory. Publ. Performance Manag. Rev. **43**, 503–534 (2020)
24. Argote, L., Hora, M.: Organizational learning and management of technology. Product. Oper. Manag. **26**, 579–590 (2017)
25. Congleton, R.: Understanding institutional diversity (JSTOR, 2007)
26. Poteete, A., Janssen, M., Ostrom, E.: Working Together: Collective Action, the Commons, and Multiple Methods in Practice. Princeton University Press (2010)

27. Gründler, K., Potrafke, N.: Corruption and economic growth: new empirical evidence. Eur. J. Polit. Econ. **60**, 101810 (2019)
28. Walker, S., Archbold, C.: The New World of Police Accountability. Sage Publications (2018)
29. Balla, S., Gormley Jr., W.: Bureaucracy and Democracy: Accountability and Performance. CQ Press (2017)
30. Hochstetter, J., Vairetti, C., Cares, C., Ojeda, M., Maldonado, S.: A transparency maturity model for government software tenders. IEEE Access **9**, 45668–45682 (2021)
31. Higuera-Molina, E., Zafra-Gómez, J., Plata-Dıaz, A., Campos-Alba, C.: Ciclos polıÌẠticos y factores explicativos de la externalización de servicios públicos en los gobiernos locales. Revista De Estudios Regionales. **112**, 105–123 (2018)
32. Hochstetter, J., GarcıÌẠa, M., Cares, C.: Socio-technical factors in electronic software biddings. J. Theor. Appl. Electron. Commerce Res. **14**, 34–60 (2019)
33. Lopes, D., Carvalho, J., Gonçalves, C.: Maturity models as instruments for the optimization of electronic business in the tourism industry. In: Advances in Tourism, Technology and Systems: Selected Papers from ICOTTS20, Volume 1, pp. 278–287 (2021)
34. Goncalves Filho, A., Waterson, P.: Maturity models and safety culture: a critical review. Saf. Sci. **105**, 192–211 (2018)
35. Proença, D., Borbinha, J.: Maturity models for data and information management. In: Méndez, E., Crestani, F., Ribeiro, C., David, G., Lopes, J.C. (eds.) TPDL 2018. LNCS, vol. 11057, pp. 81–93. Springer, Cham (2018). https://doi.org/10.1007/978-3-030-00066-0_7
36. Ifenthaler, D., Egloffstein, M.: Development and implementation of a maturity model of digital transformation. TechTrends **64**, 302–309 (2020)
37. Sandoval-Almazan, R., Gil-Garcia, J.: Are government internet portals evolving towards more interaction, participation, and collaboration? Revisiting the rhetoric of e-government among municipalities. Gov. Inf. Q. **29**, S72–S81 (2012)
38. Leite, J., Cappelli, C.: Software transparency. Bus. Inf. Syst. Eng. **2**, 127–139 (2010)
39. Garzón Castrillón, M., Fisher, A.: Modelo teórico de aprendizaje organizacional. Pensamiento & Gestión, 195–224 (2008)
40. Hochstetter, J., Diaz, J., Dieguez, M., Espinosa, R., Arango-López, J., Cares, C.: Assessing transparency in eGovernment electronic processes. IEEE Access **10**, 3074–3087 (2021)
41. Diéguez, M., Cares, C., Cachero, C., Hochstetter, J.: MASISCo–methodological approach for the selection of information security controls. Appl. Sci. **13**(2), 1094 (2023)
42. Diéguez, M., Bustos, J., Cares, C.: Mapping the variations for implementing information security controls to their operational research solutions. ISEB **18**(2), 157–186 (2020). https://doi.org/10.1007/s10257-020-00470-8
43. GAMS Development Corporation: General Algebraic Modeling System. Disponible en http://www.gams.com/. Accedido el 20 de abril de 2024
44. NEOS Server. NEOS Guide. Disponible en https://neos-server.org/neos/. Accedido el 19 de abril de 2024

Research on Market Competition Information Mining Method Based on Multi-source Text Data Mining

Shengqing Huang[(⊠)], Huiying Xue, Miao Zheng, Zhijie Zhu, and Yingfu Liu

Gannan Normal University, Ganzhou, People's Republic of China
hsq_0702@163.com

Abstract. Market competition information is an important basis for small and medium enterprises (SMEs) decision-making when conducting iterative product design, which included information on competitive analysis, user experience and satisfaction, production capacity, and R&D capability. In the previous New Product Development (NPD) process, Customer Requirements (CRs) and Market Competition Information (CIs) often need to be corrected through market surveys and questionnaires. To explore how to analyze competitors' products by mining the market sales, user reviews and other data of Internet shopping platforms, which plays a crucial role in product iteration decision making, this paper proposes an Apriori-Latent Dirichlet Allocation (A-LDA) competitive information mining model based on multi-source text data, which uses text mining and analysis to obtain the competitive information contained in users' online reviews by generalizing and summarizing the syntactic structure and candidate word sets of market-oriented competitive information. By summarizing and summarizing the syntactic structure and candidate word sets for MCI, the model uses text mining and analysis to obtain objective information about user needs and market competition contained in users' online comments, so as to analyze competitors' product-related information, thus obtaining decision-making information about product design iteration for the enterprise. Finally, through the empirical analysis of product attributes, online comments, and sales data of countertop dishwashers of four different brands, the results show that this method can provide a reference for enterprises to obtain the market competition information for product iteration design decision-making.

Keywords: New Product Development · Market Competition Information · Multi-Source Text Data Mining · Topic Model

1 Introduction

Enterprise product developers listen to the voice of the user is the consensus in the field ofIt is a consensus in the product design field that enterprise product developers listen to the voice of the user, and it is also the starting point and driving force for most enterprises in product design and development. Products are ultimately used and

F. F.-H Nah and K. L. Siau (Eds.): HCII 2025, LNCS 16343, pp. 311–328, 2026.
https://doi.org/10.1007/978-3-032-13167-6_21

evaluated by customers, and the user's experience and needs can provide an effective direction for the evolution and development of the product. However, there is a huge gap between user requirements (CRs) and product realization. In the actual product design process, excess and insufficient functions, excess and insufficient quality may exist at the same time, and it is necessary to transform or transform user requirements accordingly in order to produce a mapping relationship with the engineering characteristics, and to find the direction of product development, and the requirement transformation stage is an indispensable part of the product design process. The transformation stage is one of the indispensable stages in the product design process.

Demand transformation stage is the main perspective of enterprise product development decision-making, the main purpose is to identify the mapping relationship between user demand and product engineering characteristics, convert user demand into product innovation and design issues or product characteristics of Engineering Characteristics (ECs), and ultimately the process of development decision-making. The implementation process requires comprehensive consideration of the relationship between user needs, market competition information (CIs) and product engineering characteristics. For small and medium-sized enterprises (SMEs), they rely on research and expert experience to make judgments at this stage, and lack of channels to understand market competition information, which leads to low efficiency in making product development decisions, and the phenomenon of single decision maker often occurs, with a high risk of failure, which is detrimental to the sound development of SMEs. Aiming at the above problems, this paper aims to solve the problem of poor access to competitive information in the demand transformation stage of product development for small and medium-sized enterprises (SMEs) by mining and analyzing multi-source text data based on online reviews, product market attributes and sales data.

1.1 Methods of Analyzing Competitive Intelligence in Business Decision-Making

Enterprises in the development of new products often need to pay attention to competitors' product development strategy, to understand the situation of competitive products, the content of the relevant competitive intelligence mainly involves two aspects [1], on the one hand, competitors competing products analysis, on the other hand, their own products and internal environment analysis. Among them, competitor analysis is the soul of the product competitive intelligence analysis work, but also the core work, which includes two levels, the first is the strategic level, such as the identification of competitors, competitors' current goals, the way to participate in the competition, as well as the market positioning, through the mastery of the above information can be predicted competitor's future direction; the second is the product level, including the strengths and weaknesses of competing products, through the market share, The second is the product level, including the strengths and weaknesses of competing products, analyzing the core competence and development direction of competitors' products through the market share, coverage of sales channels, production capacity, and research and development capability. The analysis of competitors is to accurately grasp the position of the enterprise in the market, so as to find the product positioning designation development strategy. By adding competitive information, the relationship between user needs and design features of the constructed demand transformation model can be more accurate to support product development decisions.

The methods of competitor analysis mainly include core competitiveness analysis, inverse engineering method, tracking analysis method, etc., and its own competitiveness analysis mainly retains SWOT analysis, customer satisfaction survey, product life cycle, customer value analysis, etc., and the above mentioned analysis methods require enterprises to pay a large amount of manpower cost to conduct research and analysis, and the channels of the information sources are also relatively lack of, and are not easy to obtain. In the context of the information age, this paper proposes the use of online review data for competitive analysis on the one hand can help enterprises to understand the market trends and user demand hotspots, on the other hand, can help the enterprise's field experts to better understand the internal and external environment of the enterprise and the product so as to judge the direction of product development to provide support [2].

1.2 Online Review Mining Method Based on Multi-Source Text Data

User demand acquisition based on multi-source text big data mostly takes user online reviews as the data source, and mainly mines the two aspects of product feature extraction and user sentiment analysis contained in this data source. In terms of feature extraction, Chen et al. proposed a product feature acquisition method based on Latent Dirichlet Allocation (LDA) [3]; Ma Bozhang et al. used the Latent Dirichlet Distribution Probabilistic Topic Model text training model to extract the review information and extract the product features in the reviews, which proved that the LDA model can realize the effective web review mining [4]; Zhang Guofang et al. used TF-IDF to extract product features, and based on the BERT pre-training model for text sentiment analysis, to grasp user feedback information to grasp the direction of product design [5]; Yang Deqing et al. used the Kano model to dynamically screen the content of user community reviews, and obtained the product feature information in the user's review [6]; Hu et al. used the Apriori association rule of frequent frequent terms of Apriori association rules to screen product features, and obtained information to guide design activities by extracting adjectives describing product features as evaluation words [7]; Zhang et al. used Word2Vec to cluster similar product features in online reviews [8]; Kangale et al. summarized the product reviews, not only counting the product's each feature's The proportion of positive and negative opinions is not only counted, but also allows users to view the relevant original reviews [9]; Yang Cheng et al. constructed an evaluation index system using online reviews as a data source, which is used as a basis for obtaining product attributes that need to be improved, and obtaining suggestions for improvement by analyzing negative reviews [10]. However, mining and analyzing methods that focus on using online review information to obtain enterprise competition information are rare.

From the reviewed literature, new product development at this stage faces challenges such as increased competition and difficulty for enterprises to obtain competitive information. The online review mining technology based on multi-source text has been relatively mature, but the existing research pays less attention to the competition information that enterprises need urgently. In the process of demand transformation engineering characteristics, enterprises need to use the demand transformation model to search for the mapping relationship between the user's demand or the competition information and the design characteristics, and at the same time, they need to choose the appropriate calculation method in the case of fewer resources available to be deployed. In this process, the competitive information will greatly affect the final result of the mapping relationship in the transformation model, especially the defective positioning of the product itself, by comparing with other competitors, we can speculate the position of the existing products in the market as well as the strengths and weaknesses of the product itself, so as to judge the defective information of the product, how to obtain the competitive information that is effective for the decision of the product innovation and design and input into the transformation model is the challenge of this paper. Challenge of this paper.

Therefore, this study aims to propose feasible solutions for practical gaps by exploring the following questions:

Q 1: How to mine online reviews to objectively capture coarse-grained CRs?

Q 2: How to mine CIs based on multi-source texts that are needed by companies and analyzed to help them make decisions?

In order to investigate the above problems, this study uses LDA topic model, Apriori association algorithm for mining and analyzing user online reviews and corporate product information to obtain CRs and CIs, which can help product developers in identifying important CRs, and the obtained results can effectively help corporations and product developers to improve the accuracy of their decision-making in new product development decisions and reduce the R&D cost.

2 Methodology

2.1 Analysis of Text Data Mining Tasks in the Requirements Transformation Phase

According to the above analysis, the main research content of this phase is to obtain product competition information task analysis, product competition information mining mainly focuses on user review information and product attribute information, in which the user review information is the main source of information including the identification of competitors and mining of competitors' product user review information, online review information includes the same type of products of different brands of different models and prices of different feedback information from the user, this information contains hidden product competition information that can reflect the differences in the use of the product. The online review information includes different feedback information of the same type of products of different brands, different models and prices, which contains hidden competitive information of the products and can reflect the differences of the products in the use of the users, through the mining of the user experience of different competitors, we can understand the competition of the product in the market, such as which functions or features of the product are of concern to the users, whether the product form is the user's preference, whether the product has the advantage of the price, whether the product has the advantage of the market share, whether the product and service meet the needs of consumers and so on. Whether the service satisfies the consumer's needs, etc. This competitive information is more helpful for product design demand transformation. Product attribute information is a covariate, through the horizontal comparison analysis of the functions and hardware of different competing products can help domain experts to obtain more information, so as to judge the market positioning of the product and the disadvantages of the product compared with similar products, and assist domain experts to locate the defects of the product.

However, online review information contains a large amount of irrelevant noise information, the use of topic models for text analysis will lead to valuable information submerged in a large amount of irrelevant information, the data structure of the product attribute information is more dispersed, and the most valuable part of the mining and acquisition of competitive information is often the correlation information between the data, due to the differences in the structure of the data, the correlation between the data mining and processing methods are more Difficulty. Previous studies have analyzed and mined users' attitudes toward product features with sentiment classification or topic models, but the sentiment classification model can only obtain a good or bad representation of users' attitudes toward product features, and when users comment on a certain product, there may be a mixture of completely opposite attitudes toward different features in the same comment, e.g., "I was impressed by I was impressed by how *quiet* the wash cycle is. Sitting 10 feet away, I almost could not hear it. The discharge cycle is VERY loud… Nothing is wrong with the machine. It just could use better soundproofing around the pump. Nothing is wrong with the machine. It just could use better soundproofing.", from the real online user reviews, it can be observed that users think that they are satisfied with the quietness of the product during the washing process, but they think that the pump is too loud during the draining process, which affects their life and needs more soundproofing materials. This makes the sentiment classification model also can not get in-depth access to the user's actual attitude towards the product features, and may even cause misjudgment, purely using the LDA topic model is also unable to directly mine the data contained in this type of competing information, the use of the topic model for text analysis often ignores the mining of this information. The reason is that many user documents usually contain a small number of sentences that are inconsistent with or irrelevant to the final topic, and the information contained in these sentences may be related to the defects of the product's functionality or the attitude towards the product's features, which is still of great significance in the analysis of the market competition of the target product, and it can better help the product developers to understand the attitude of the users and the defects of the product, and the text mining at the document level often misses this information. Mining often misses this information, and the functional advantages and disadvantages of the product need to classify and mine the user's sentiment, which requires word-level text mining techniques for complementary analysis, so as to retain the semantic information of the text and identify the latent information of the text.

According to the characteristics of competitive information data and the means of mining competitive information described above, it can be seen that competitive information data involves the correlation of multi-dimensional factors working together, such as brand, market, price and other factors, and how to mine the correlation information of multi-dimensional factors is an extremely challenging task. Because it involves more text data sources, and data types have different characteristics, such as user comments for the user's natural language is unstructured data, product attributes and prices are structured data, competitive information is hidden in the two data types, and it is more difficult to combine the two data types, the key to mining the competitive information hidden in the text data lies in mining the intrinsic connection between the data, and the product area The demand for mining competitive information from the perspective of the product domain is mainly focused on the performance of specific products in various aspects, involving only feature extraction, theme extraction, classification, clustering, association analysis and semantic level to the word as a unit of similarity and correlation between the information content of the mining analysis, does not involve the strategic level of the enterprise and other multi-level information mining, so the main task of mining competitive information on the product focuses on the clustering, classification and association analysis, and relatively speaking, it does not need to be a key to mining competitive information hidden in text data, the key is to mine the intrinsic connection between the data, and the product domain. Therefore, the main task of product competition information mining focuses on information clustering, classification and correlation analysis, and relatively speaking, it does not need to deal with a large amount of data, and it is suitable for the analysis and acquisition strategy based on information content mining, combining quantitative and qualitative analysis methods to excavate the potential information content and correlation information, and then converting the results of the excavation into the required data through logical reasoning by human beings.

2.2 Competitive Information Mining Model Construction Based on Apriori-LDA

This paper combines the analysis method of competitive intelligence in the field of enterprise management, the analysis means and the data characteristics of the task of competitive information demand in the product field, this chapter proposes to select the competitive information mining model suitable for the product field in accordance with the analysis process of "clustering-categorization-association". This chapter proposes to follow the analysis process of "clustering-categorization-association" and select the competitive information mining model suitable for the product domain, and classify the same type of products of different product brands based on the product price and sales volume as a reference to complete the mining and screening of the product separation corpus, and proposes the competitive information mining model based on Apriori-LDA suitable for the product design domain, which consists of three phases. The second stage is to use the LDA topic model to mine user needs and feedbacks of different brand products; the third stage is to use the Apriori association algorithm to filter the key topics and finally determine the key user needs, so as to prepare for the next logical reasoning of user needs and competitive information into the form of data suitable for inputting into the QFD, and thus to construct the mapping relationship matrix between user needs, competitive information and engineering characteristics.

The product developers first mine the online review data in the shopping platform, then pre-process the data and input them into LDA-Kano user demand acquisition model and LDA-Apriori competitive information acquisition model respectively, to obtain the original user demand, the performance of the target product in the market as well as the performance of the competitive products in the market, and then form a team to conduct the user and expert surveys based on the obtained information. Combined with the interval gray number algorithm to obtain the initial importance of CRs and the initial performance of target and competitive products in CRs.

The product developers first mine the online review data in the shopping platform, then pre-process the data and input them into LDA-Kano user demand acquisition model and LDA-Apriori competitive information acquisition model respectively, to obtain the original user demand, the performance of the target product in the market as well as the performance of the competitive products in the market, and then form a team to conduct the user and expert surveys based on the obtained information. Combined with the interval gray number algorithm to obtain the initial importance of CRs and the initial performance of target and competitive products in CRs (Fig. 1).

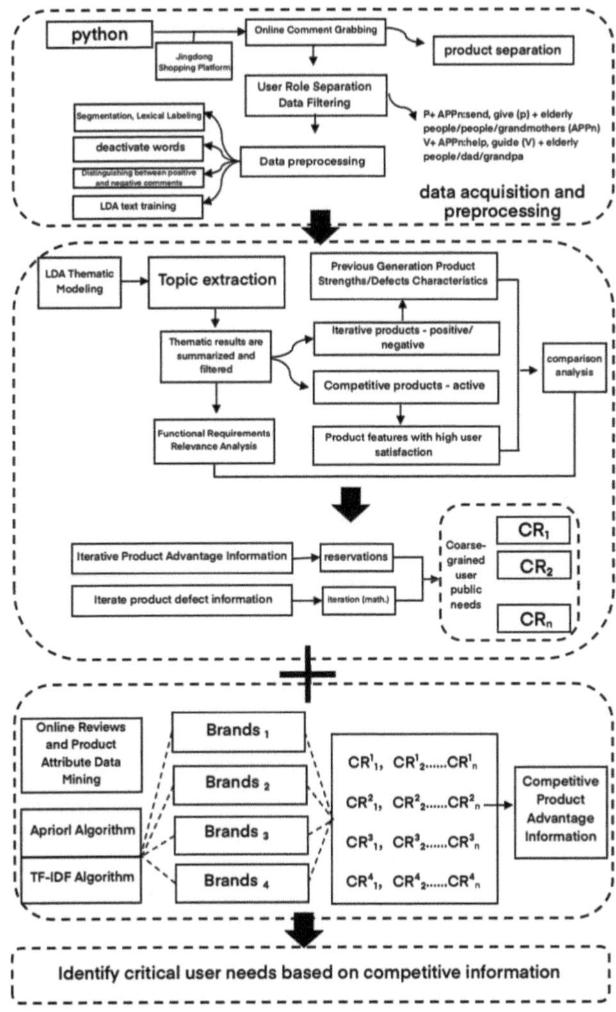

Fig. 1. Complete flowchart of competitive information mining model based on Apriori- LDA.

The product developers first mine the online review data in the shopping platform, then pre-process the data and input them into LDA-Kano user demand acquisition model and LDA-Apriori competitive information acquisition model respectively, to obtain the original user demand, the performance of the target product in the market as well as the performance of the competitive products in the market, and then form a team to conduct the user and expert surveys based on the obtained information. Combined with the interval gray number algorithm to obtain the initial importance of CRs and the initial performance of target and competitive products in CRs.

Based on the above analysis, the LDA-Apriori competitive information mining model is constructed. It is specifically divided into three concrete steps, the mining method of coarse-grained user demand driven by online comments under the separation perspective is divided into three phases, the first phase of online text mining through the octopus collector, followed by the necessary preprocessing of the mined raw data, such as deleting invalid and duplicate comments, deleting punctuation, etc.; the second phase of the use of the LDA theme model on the mined online comments of users to carry out the Theme extraction to obtain users' description of the theme, analyze and filter the extracted theme results separately to get the advantages/disadvantages of each brand's product, and finally obtain the market performance of different features of the product according to the frequency of the theme's appearance. The extraction of themes in this study is done by implementing the LDA theme model through scripts written in the Python programming language. It is worth noting that in this framework, the text preprocessing and topic discovery parts can be automated using a program, while the topic naming and analysis processes are classified through experts. The specific steps are as follows:

Step 1: Data preprocessing. The online review information of products on Jingdong online shopping platform is collected, and the original corpus is obtained by mining on the principle of product separation. Pre-processing of data such as de-weighting, standardization, word splitting, de-discontinued words, etc. is carried out to make the obtained comment data have a higher credibility; products of different brands are classified to build a corpus of user comments, followed by mining of the original corpus with the principle of role separation, and deleting the comment information that does not conform to the principle, as shown in Table 1.

Table 1. User role separation mining data format.

Part of Speech (noun, verb, adjective etc.)	Typical Example
APPn	*Dads, grandpas, seniors, family members, etc*
p + APPn	*To send, give (p) + elderly/grandmother(APPn)*
v + APPn	*Help, guide (v) + older person/dad, etc.(APPn)*

注:n for noun; v for verb; APPn stands for Appellation Noun; p is for preposition.

From the lexical point of view, the candidate set of words for mining of role-separated consumption behavior is set as:

$$CandidateWords = \{Appellation\ noun,\ verb,\ preposition\} \qquad (2\text{-}1)$$

The corpus acting on the topic model is obtained by filtering the database to obtain comment segments with role separation attributes [17]. Step 2: Mining user requirements. The processed user online review data are fed into the LDA topic model pairs for topic extraction. The basic idea of the LDA model is to represent a document as a random mixture over potential topics, where each topic is characterized by a distribution over words [20].

The LDA topic model consists of two main steps: text generation and Gibbs sampling [18], (1) Text generation is divided into four steps: first, for a topic z, obtain a polynomial distribution vector φ of words in the topic according to the Dirichlet distribution Dirichlet (β);

Second, obtain the total number of words in the text N according to the Poisson distribution;

Third, obtain a subject distribution probability vector θ for that text according to the Dirichlet distribution Dirichlet (α);

Fourth, for each word Wn out of the total N words of that text: randomly select a topic z from the multinomial distribution of θ, and then select a word from the polynomial conditional probability distribution of z as Wn.

(2) Gibbs sampling: parameter estimation is needed when constructing the LDA model, through the estimation of φ and θ, we can obtain the relevant information of the topics contained in the corpus, and their proportion in each document, Gibbs sampling algorithm is the most popular extraction algorithm of the LDA model, so Gibbs sampling is used for parameter estimation, the steps are as follows:

First, the parameter values are obtained by parameter estimation, and the probability value of a particular text is obtained according to the graph model:

$$p\left(\frac{w}{\alpha,\beta}\right) = \int p\left(\frac{\theta}{\alpha}\right) \prod_{n=1}^{N} \sum_{z_n} p\left(\frac{z_n}{\theta}\right) p\left(\frac{w_n}{z_n,\beta}\right) d\theta \tag{2-2}$$

Next, since Collapsed Gibbs sampling samples the themes of each monad by integrating them, and thus counting the frequency to calculate the parameters, i.e., to calculate the conditional probability of a sequence of themes under a sequence of words, the formula is as follows:

$$p\left(z_i = k \,/\, \overrightarrow{z_{\neg i}}, \overrightarrow{w}\right) = \frac{p\left(\overrightarrow{w}, \overrightarrow{z}\right)}{p\left(\overrightarrow{w}, \overrightarrow{z_{\neg i}}\right)} \propto \frac{n_{k,\neg i}^{t} + \beta_t}{\sum_{t=1}^{V} n_{k,\neg i}^{t} + \beta_t} \left(n_{m,\neg i}^{t} + \alpha_k\right) \tag{2-3}$$

In Eq. (2–3), z_i denotes the topic variable corresponding to i words; $\neg i$ denotes the ith item excluded from it; denotes the number of occurrences of lexical item t in topic k; β_t is the Dirichlet prior for lexical item t; n_m^k denotes the number of occurrences of topic k in text m; α_k is the Dirichlet prior for topic k.

After obtaining the topic labeling for each word, the values of φ and θ are finally computed:

$$\varphi_{k,t} = \frac{n_k^t + \beta_t}{\sum_{i=1}^{V} n_k^t + \beta_t} \tag{2-4}$$

$$\theta_{m,k} = \frac{n_m^k + \alpha_k}{\sum_{k=1}^{K} n_m^k + \alpha_k} \tag{2-5}$$

where $\varphi_{k,t}$ denotes the probability of the lexical item t in the topic k; θ denotes the probability of the topic k in the text m.

Finally, the number of topics K was determined by analyzing the computation of the perplexity degree, the value was set to 50/K, the value β was set to 0.01, and its value was set to an empirically taken value. Lower perplexity can reflect better generalization [20].

$$\text{Perplexity}(D_{\text{test}}) = \exp\left\{ -\frac{\sum_{d=1}^{M} \ln(p(W_d))}{\sum_{i=1}^{M} N_d} \right\} \tag{2-6}$$

By sorting the probability values obtained from the calculation, the vocabulary contained under each topic is obtained, i.e., each topic and the vocabulary to which it belongs, and the relationship between each document and the topic it contains can also be obtained, and the number of topics contained in the corpus is determined by the perplexity calculation. By extracting the topics from the online comments of the users, the user needs focused by the users can be obtained.

The third step is competitive information mining. Apriori algorithm is applied to analyze the user requirements obtained in step 2 in different branded corpora in a competitive comparison to find the relationship between topics and user attitudes.

Apriori algorithm uses breadth-first search and hash tree structure to compute candidate itemsets efficiently [19]. The basic process of the algorithm is: according to the frequent itemset to generate candidate itemsets, first scan the database to simply count the support frequency of each candidate itemset, obtain all the subsets in the corpus, combined with the nature of the association to delete the candidate itemsets with infrequent subsets, to get the one-dimensional maximum frequent itemset formed by the candidate itemsets that meet the minimum support, and then start the cycle of processing, filtering the frequent itemsets through the minimum confidence level, until there is no more frequent itemsets generated, so as to find the k-dimensional frequent itemset and obtain the strong association rules. Until no more frequent itemsets are generated, thus finding the k-dimensional frequent itemsets and obtaining the strong association rules. Minimum support and minimum confidence measure the association rules in the database, which represent the certainty and usefulness, respectively, as in Eqs. (2–7) and (2–8). Lift is a complement to the association rules, which reflects the value of the association rules, as in (2–9):

$$\text{sup port}(A \Rightarrow B) = P(A \cup B) \tag{2-7}$$

$$\text{confidence}(A \Rightarrow B) = P(B|A) = \frac{\text{sup port}(A \cup B)}{\text{sup port}(A)} = \frac{\text{sup port\_count}(A \cup B)}{\text{sup port\_count}(A)}, \tag{2-8}$$

$$\text{lift}(A \Rightarrow B) = \frac{\text{confidence}(A \Rightarrow B)}{\text{sup port}(B)} \tag{2-9}$$

where *A* and *B* denote the itemsets (subject terms), $A \Rightarrow B$ denote the association rules that are greater than the minimum support value minsup, and S denotes the proportion of all topics that contain both subject terms *A* and *B*.

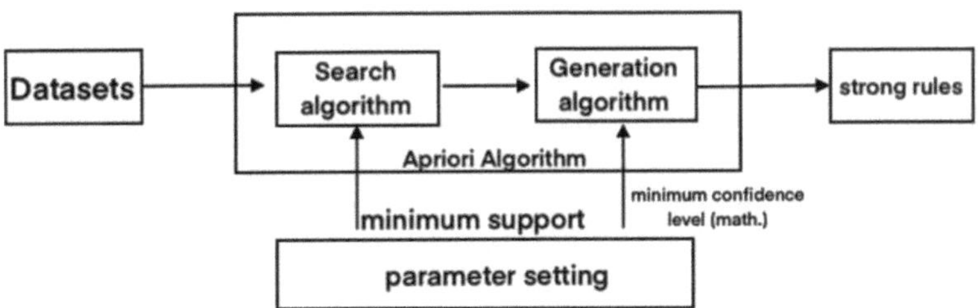

Fig. 2. Process Diagram for Association Mining.

The main task of association mining is to find strong association rules from a given corpus with minimum support and minimum execution given by the user. The itemsets corresponding to the derived strong association rules A → B are frequent itemsets, and the confidence of the association rules A → B derived from the frequent itemsets A ∪ B can be calculated from the support of the frequent itemsets A and A ∪ ·B. The association mining process can be divided into two parts. Therefore, the association mining process can be divided into two parts, the search algorithm searches the frequent itemsets and the generation algorithm produces association rules. The strong rule result set obtained by setting the minimum support threshold and minimum confidence threshold in the parameters corresponds to the search algorithm and the generation algorithm respectively. As shown in Fig. 2.

3   Results

3.1   Example Validation of Competitive Information Mining for Countertop Dishwashers

Based on the above model, the online reviews are respectively correlated and analyzed according to brands to obtain the keywords of user attitudes that are strongly associated with features, combined with the attributes of the products and price information as covariates output as the performance information of different brands of products in the same type of CRs, however, document-level text mining often misses some information, and word-level text mining loses a large amount of semantic information, which leads to the text's true meaning is lacking or wrong, and sentence-level text mining achieves the best balance between retaining semantic information and recognizing latent information of the text. Therefore, we try to reconstruct the corpus after reviewing the original sentences with the list of topic words obtained from the LDA model, reuse the Apriori algorithm to analyze the words that frequently match with the topic words, so as to locate the semantic relationships before and after the key words in the reviews, and finally apply TF-IDF word frequency analysis to review the frequent occurrences of keywords reflecting the attitudes of the CRs within the products of different brands Finally, TF-IDF word frequency analysis is used to review and sort the frequent occurrence of keywords reflecting the attitude of CRs within different brands, compare the current information on the market performance of different brands, the more frequent the occurrence indicates that users of the brand are more concerned about the CRs, and ultimately locate the users' attitudes towards specific user needs, and preliminarily judge the performance of the products in the market based on the differences in the attitudes of the users of the products of different brands, and then place the information into the expert survey questionnaire as the pre-information, so that we can get the importance rating of the CRs and the market status of CRs. The information is placed into the expert questionnaire as pre-information to obtain the CRs importance score and CRs market position, and then the CIs information is obtained by analyzing the position of each competitor's individual CRs in the market, and in the second stage, expert research is required to make appropriate judgments on the importance of user needs based on experience, so as to prepare pre-input data for the construction of the QFD conversion matrix.

According to the above steps a countertop dishwasher is selected as the research object to experimentally validate the method proposed in this section.

1. Data Collection

First, mining online review text data. The Octopus crawler software was used to collect online review data of dishwasher products in the price range of US$289.9-410 on the Amazon platform, and a total of 4,272 online reviews were collected and saved in xls format, and a comparison of the sales of four dishwashers produced by the four companies with the highest sales volume, including the target company, on the Amazon platform reveals that the sales of the target company's products with the same performance are the least compared with the other four companies. Sales are the least compared to the other four companies for the same performance. The raw data were preprocessed to remove invalid and duplicate reviews, delete punctuation marks, and process the online review data of the four companies separately. After preprocessing, we got a total of 4,066 valid comments, of which the target company got 418 valid comments, company 1 got 798 valid comments, company 2 got 961 valid comments, and company 3 got 486 valid comments.

Next, user requirements are acquired. The user requirement topic extraction process is carried out by applying the LDA-Kano user requirement acquisition model proposed in Chapter III. The number of topics K is determined according to the perplexity formula (2–6), the parameters of α and β are not estimated accurately, and the defined parameters are smoothed at 50/K and 200/M. K is the number of topics of the LDA topic model, M is the total number of training sample documents in LDA which is 3,252 (80%), and the test sample of the LDA model which is 813 (20%). The results of perplexity are shown in Fig. 3; to avoid over-clustering and improve the clustering results, the trade-off between topic similarity and model perplexity is made by setting the number of topics of the whole market data to 75, and the number of topics of other companies to 40, with a better generalization ability of its topic number model. Set the number of iterations to 6000. Classify and analyze the output results of all reviews in LDA to summarize (Table 2), combine the Kano model to obtain the original user requirements of the product through a small amount of research, summarize the obtained user requirements, and obtain the 14 results of the requirements that users pay more attention to the product by summarizing and screening the results (Table 3), but the results can't be directly inputted into the QFD framework.

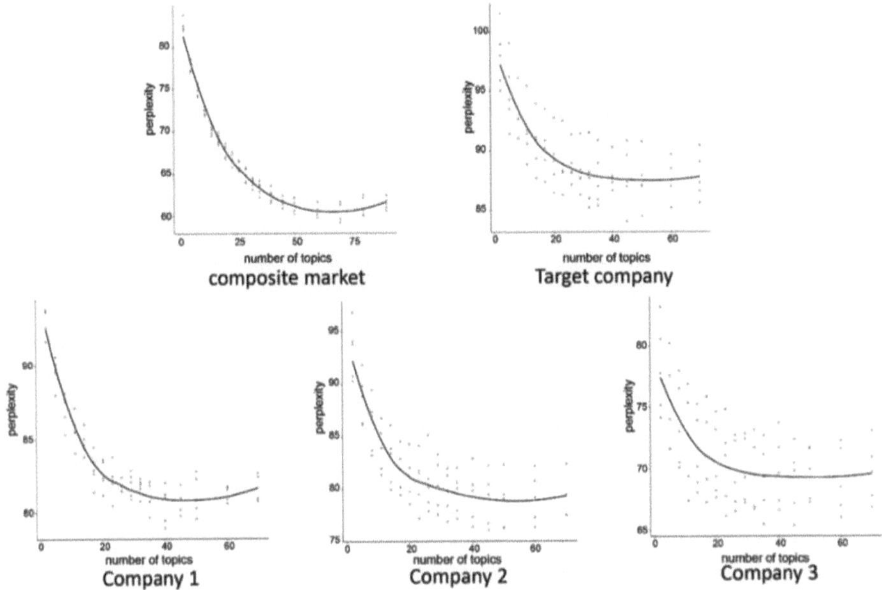

Fig. 3. Confusion Values of Different Companies.

Table 2. Inductive topics.

Serial number	Topic Classification	Thematic generalization results
1	Service and after-sales	warranty, delivery, damaged, troubleshooting, installed, broke
2	Product Features	dry, sound, space, leak, hose, adapter, model, drain, connects, system, control, heating, setup
3	product pattern	Fit, material, wire, heavy
4	Product Price	Brand, danby, cheap, fantastic, attractive, price, performance, excellent, expensive

Finally, the competitive information is obtained. First, the Apriori algorithm is applied to calculate the association of the topics output from LDA. The output results are combined with the demand screening in step 2 to reduce the redundancy of QFD data, and the screening results are summarized into 9 categories of user demands (Table 3);

Table 3. Result of User Requirement Information Filtering for Desktop Dishwasher Market

Categorization of first-level user requirements	Categorization of secondary user requirements	Categorization of user requirements at the three-tier level
After-sales and service	After-sales service and logistics	Convenient after-sales service
		No damage to logistics and packaging
Product Features	drying function	Rapid drying
	quiet	Noise reduction
	spatial	increase space
		Bowl Basket Personalization
	Bowl Basket Personalization	Multiple dishwashing modes
		Easy to operate
	drainage system	Increase drainpipes
		Reduced water leakage
Appearance and quality	Appearance quality	Appearance is beautiful and generous
		materials
Brands and Prices	branding	famous brand
	quality-price ratio	inexpensive

secondly, the product review corpus of four companies is established separately, and input into the LDA topic model, and the LDA results of each key company contain 40 topics, and each topic contains 10 topic words. The LDA results of each key company contain 40 topics, and each topic contains 10 topic words. The output topic words are used to locate the user comments, such as through the keyword "dry" to locate the user comments "There is no drying cycle so the dishes just partially dry from the heat that was left from the hot water. They never ever come out completely dry", etc. The raw data is pruned and analyzed using the Apriori association algorithm implemented in python language, with the parameter of minimum support set to 0.005, and the minimum confidence set to 0.5. When the minimum confidence level is 0.5, we get in (Table 4) the strong association rules of CR2 about company 1, which are described in 7 ways to represent the same CR; we can adjust the order of words in these strong association rules to get easy-to-understand and low noise sentences, and correspond the results to 9 important CRs, so as to understand the user's attitude towards each CRs (Table 5).

Table 4. Example of strong rules (Target company CR2)

Strong association rules	Key Sentences/Phrases	Degree of support	Degree of confidence	Degree of promotion
['dry'] = > ['dishes']	Dishes dry	0.0623	0.7875	1.915
['dry'] = > ['not']	Not dry	0.0594	0.75	1.58
['dry'] = > ['water']	Water no dry	0.0398	0.503	2.13
['dry', 'not'] = > ['water']	Water not dry	0.0319	0.5375	2.275
['out', 'dry'] = > ['dishes']	Dishes no dry	0.03487	0.8056	1.697
['hot'] = > ['water', 'not']	Water not hot	0.0304	0.7409	4.567
['out', 'dry', 'not'] = > ['dishes']	Dishes out not dry	0.0302	0.9037	2.197

Table 5. Representative CRs.

NO.	Customer requirement	Customer attitude
CR_1	After-sales and logistics	warranty is worthless/ arrived damaged
CR_2	drying function	Can not dry the water on dishes
CR_3	Appearance and materials	No different external appearance/wire
CR_4	Easy to operate	Easy to operate/install different faucet adapter
CR_5	quiet	No noise, super quite/loud noise/ horrible noise
CR_6	spatial	Small space/ limited space
CR_7	Program Control Mode	cycle too long / clean cycle great
CR_8	Brands and Prices	Product expensive/cheap
CR_9	drainage system	Drain out quick/ hose leaks water

4   Discussion

Due to the differences in the products, the users' concerns and opinions about the CRs of each company are not consistent. Will be compared through the data of the four companies, we analyze the attitudes of users of different companies to CRs when using the product and the frequent number of times the theme appears, to determine the current situation of the market performance of different companies' products information, the more frequent the number of times indicates that the more users are concerned about the last to obtain the performance of all the company's products in the demand of the situation of the for the reference as in Table 6.

Table 6. User attitudes towards CRs in different companies.

NO	CRs	target company	frequency	Company 1	frequency	Company 2	frequency	Company 3	frequency
CR_1	After-sales and logistics	worthless	2	worthless	2	arrived damaged	4	arrived damaged	1
CR_2	drying function	dish not dry	6	dish not dry	5	dish not dry	5	dish not dry	4
CR_3	Appearance and materials	normal	1	heavy	1	excellent	1	Nice appearance	5
CR_4	Easy to operate	Faucet no adapter	7	Easy set	8	Faucet no adapter	7	Faucet no adapter	6
CR_5	Quite	super quite	1	super quite	5	Small amount of noise	2	Loud noise	4
CR_6	spatial	small space	6	small space	8	limited space	5	limited space	2
CR_7	recurrent mode	clean cycle great	9	clean cycle great	6	error in the cycle	10	error in the cycle	9
CR_8	Brands and Prices	Product expensive	1	Product expensive	1	Product cheap	2	Product expensive	1
CR_9	drainage system	hose leaks water	7	hose leaks water	4	Drain out quick	4	hose leaks water	8

According to the results obtained by the proposed method, as shown in Table 6, it can be clearly observed that the users of the target company pay more attention to CR6 (recirculation mode) and have a positive attitude, mostly positive emotions, and also pay more attention to CR2 (drying function), CR4 (easy operation), CR6 (space), and CR9 (draining system), but most of them are negative; the users of Company 1 pay frequent attention and mostly positive evaluations in CR4 (easy operation) and CR5 (quiet), and CR6 (cycle mode) were frequently concerned and mostly positively evaluated, while performing poorly in CR2 (drying function), and CR6 (space); Company 2 users were most frequently concerned in CR6 (cycle mode) and were mostly negatively emotional, believing that the Company 2 product performs poorly in this area and in CR2 (drying function), CR4 (easy operation), CR6 (space) are not effective, human-computer interaction is not satisfactory enough, but in CR9 (drainage system) is the product of the user feedback is better; Company 3 Users in the CR2 (drying function), CR4 (easy operation), CR5 (mute), CR6 (recirculation mode), CR9 (drainage system) negative attention is high, and compared with the other companies CR3 (appearance and materials) in terms of users are mostly favorable. Some market competition information can be obtained through the generalization and summary of the information, such as the market countertop dishwasher users of CR2 (drying function), CR4 (easy operation), CR6 (space), CR9 (drainage system) aspects of the feedback more negative emotions, may be the next stage of the product needs to be improved aspects. Combined with the mined product attribute data (e.g., Fig. 4), the obtained information is input into the expert research as the antecedent information, and the expert is required to make appropriate judgment on the importance of the user's demand based on experience, and can o prepare accordingly for the construction of the QFD demand transformation matrix in the next step.

Product Dimensions :19.69 x 21.65 x 17.24 inches
Noise:52 dB
Material Type :Steel
Roomy Interior: 6 place setting capacity with a silverware basket
Annual Energy Consumption :203 Kilowatt Hours Per Year
Easy Set Up: The quick connect feature;
Six Convenient Wash Cycles: Choose from Intensive, Normal, Economy, Rapid, Glass and Soak
Item Weight : 46.3 pounds

Product Dimensions :21.7 x 19.7 x 17.2 inches
Noise:none
Material Type :Stainless Steel
Roomy Interior: the six-place setting capacity and includes folding down rack shelves and a cutlery basket
Easy-to-use controls: the LED digital controls
Seven Convenient Wash Cycles: seven wash programs - heavy, Normal, baby care, light, glass, Speed 45 min, self clean
Item Weight : 63.8 pounds

Product Dimensions :21.6 x 19.6 x 17.2 inches
Noise:none
Material Type :Stainless Steel
Roomy Interior: 6 standard place setting
Easy-to-use controls: quick connect assembly with accessories including inlet and drain hose and a faucet adapter for water lines
Six Convenient Wash Cycles: heavy, normal, ECO, glass, speed, and rinse for your different dishwashing needs. Delay button light to postpone wash cycle
Item Weight : 44 pounds

Product Dimensions :19.63 x 21.63 x 17.31 inches
Noise:52.3 dB
Material Type :Stainless Steel
Roomy Interior: Six (6) standard place setting capacity / Includes dish rack, cup shelf, and cutlery basket
Easy-to-use controls: Quick connect adapter fits standard sized kitchen faucets / Beautiful digital display
Seven Convenient Wash Cycles
Warranty: 1 year parts;
Item Weight : 44 pounds

Fig. 4. Information on the attributes of different companies' products.

5   Conclusions and Future Works

The main goal of this paper is to mine user requirements and product competitive information contained in text data to help product developers identify important CRs, ECs and provide useful product design suggestions. Using LDA topic model and Apriori association algorithm to mine and analyze user requirements and competitive information of online reviews in English context, it is found that the information processing of different languages can provide experts with richer competitive information, solving the problem of the difficulty of mining competitive information in text data, and helping to solve the problem of traditional QFD in the user requirements and competitive information acquisition from questionnaires, which is too difficult to solve. By using natural language processing technology, it helps to solve the problem of traditional QFD in user demand and competitive information acquisition with questionnaire as the main source, which is too subjective and consumes human cost; and by analyzing the examples, it verifies the validity of the method proposed in this chapter. In the future, the method proposed in this paper provides effective support for the determination of product defect localization in the demand transformation stage of product innovation design from the perspective of integrating competitive information mining, and can provide effective defect localization information for the next stage of design proposal generation.

References

1. Chen, M.J.: Competitor analysis and interfirm rivalry: toward a theoretical integration. Acad. Manag. Rev. **21**(1), 100–134 (1996)
2. Jun, Q.: A hierarchical framework of enterprise competitive intelligence analysis methods. Libr. Intell. Work **11**(5), 43–47 (2006)
3. Chen, K., Kou, G., Shang, J., et al.: Visualizing market structure through online product reviews: Integrate topic modeling, TOPSIS, and multi-dimensional scaling approaches. Electron. Commer. Res. Appl. **14**(1), 58–74 (2015)
4. Bozhang, M., Zhijun, Y.: A feature extraction method for online review products based on potential Dilitrean distribution model. Comput. Integr. Manufact. Syst. **20**(1), 96–103 (2014)
5. Guofang, Z., Jiaojiao, K., Linghua, C.: A text-driven automotive design planning method for web reviews. Mech. Des. **38**(2), 139–144 (2021)
6. Yang, D., Zhang, J., Guo, W., et al.: Research on the construction of Kano model for dynamic user requirements based on online product community. Mech. Des. **35**(3), 12–19 (2018)
7. Hu, M., Liu, B.: Mining opinion feature in customer reviews. Am. Assoc. Artif. Intell. **69**(4735), 755–760 (2004)
8. Zhang, D., Xu, H., Su, Z., et al.: Chinese comments sentiment classification based on word2vec and SVMperf. Expert Syst. Appl. **42**(4), 1857–1863 (2015)
9. Kangale, A., Kumar, S.K., Naeem, M.A., et al.: Mining consumer reviews to generate ratings of different product attributes while producing feature-based review-summary. Int. J. Syst. Sci. **47**(13), 3272–3286 (2016)
10. Cheng, Y., Kun, T., Chunyang, Y.: Improvement of cell phone products based on review big data. Comput. Integrat. Manufact. Syst. **26**(11), 1–19 (2020)
11. Nielsen, J.: Usability engineering. In: Zhengjie, L. (ed.) Translation. Machinery Industry Press, Beijing (2004)
12. Agrawal, R., Srikant, R.: Fast algorithms for mining association rules. In: Proceedings of the 20th International Conference on Very Large Data Bases, Santiago, SM, Chile, vol. 1215, pp. 487–499 (1994)
13. Borgelt, C., Kruse, R.: Induction of association rules: Apriori implementation. In: Compstat: Proceedings in Computational Statistics, pp. 395–400. Physica-Verlag HD (2002)
14. Guo, Y., Wang, M., Li, X.: Application of an improved Apriori algorithm in a mobile e-commerce recommendation system. Ind. Manag. Data Syst. **117**(02), 287–303 (2017)
15. Sun, Y.G., Qiang, H.Y., Xu, J.Q., et al.: Internet of things-based online condition monitor and improved adaptive fuzzy control for a medium-low-speed maglev train system. IEEE Trans. Industr. Inf. **16**(4), 2629–2639 (2020)
16. Liu, Y.: Study on application of apriori algorithm in data mining. In: Proceedings of the 2010 Second International Conference on Computer Modeling and Simulation, Sanya, China, vol. 3, pp. 111–114 (2010)
17. Shi, L., Qiang, Y., Yijun, L., et al.: Mining product characteristics and emotional tendencies of Chinese online customer reviews. Comput. Appl. Res. **27**(8), 3016–3019 (2010)
18. Wang, Z.Z., He, M., Du, Y.P.: Text similarity calculation based on LDA topic model. Comput. Sci. **40**(12), 68–71 (2013)
19. He, B., Agrawal, D.P.: An identity-based authentication and key establishment scheme for multi-operator maintained Wireless Mesh Networks. In: The 7th IEEE International Conference on Mobile Ad-hoc and Sensor Systems, pp. 71–78. IEEE (2010)
20. Blei, D.M., Andrew, Y.N., Jordan, M.I.: Latent Dirichlet allocation. J. Mach. Learn. Res. **3**(1), 993–1022 (2003)

Implementation of Artificial Intelligence for Tax Processes: Bibliometric Analysis from an International View

Evaristo Navarro[1], Isabel Cristina Yepes[2], Joaquin Sierra[3], Johny Garcia-Tirado[4], Javier Alfonso Ramírez[4(✉)], and Carlos Barros[5]

[1] Universidad de la Costa, 58 Street #55-66, Barranquilla, Colombia
enavarro3@cuc.edu.co
[2] Universidad Simón Bolívar, 59 Street #59-65, Barranquilla, Colombia
[3] Universidad Libre de Colombia, Seccional Cartagena, 177 Street #30-20, Bolívar, Colombia
[4] Corporación Universitaria Taller Cinco, 58 North Highway Kilometer 19, Chia, Colombia
jramirez07papers@gmail.com
[5] Institución Universitaria de Barranquilla, 45th Avenue #48-31, Barranquilla, Colombia

Abstract. Current research focuses on analyzing existing scientific production and exploring emerging trends in the application of AI in the tax field. The ability of machine learning algorithms to process large volumes of data at high speed has opened up new possibilities in the tax space. From accurately detecting tax evasion patterns to personalizing tax services, AI is radically transforming the way tax administrations interact with taxpayers and manage tax systems. Using bibliometric methods and the Scopus database, this study aims to identify new scientific trends regarding the impact of artificial intelligence on taxation processes. The results showed an average annual growth of 7.56%, indicating a positive trend. The data showed a constant growth in scientific production since 2019 (91) until reaching a peak in 2022 (139). Regarding the sources found, Lecture Notes in Networks and Systems is the most relevant with 27 documents, followed by Advances in Intelligent Systems and Computing with 20 documents and Lecture Notes in Computer Science (including subseries) with 19 documents. According to the results found, both Kumar R and LI J share the first place in terms of number of published papers, with 5 publications each; the rest of the most relevant authors have 4 publications each, with the exception of Almada M (3). With 12 associated articles, Aalborg University is positioned as the institution with the greatest presence in the search results, followed by the Rostov State University of Economics, with 11 associated articles. In conclusion, this bibliometric study lays the foundation for future research in this interdisciplinary area. The results obtained can be useful for researchers, professionals and decision makers interested in understanding the implications of artificial intelligence in the tax field.

Keywords: Artificial Intelligence · Taxation · Bibliometric analysis · Finance

F. F.-H Nah and K. L. Siau (Eds.): HCII 2025, LNCS 16343, pp. 329–340, 2026.
https://doi.org/10.1007/978-3-032-13167-6_22

1 Introduction

The tax landscape is transforming due to the capacity of machine learning algorithms to analyze massive amounts of data quickly. The AI realm is changing how tax systems are administered and how taxpayers are treated from accurately identifying tax avoidance tendencies to even tailoring tax services [1]. AI can perform ordinary duties such as case-by-case analysis of tax returns, allowing tax experts to devote their time to more critical and difficult challenges. Moreover, AI models are able to sift through large databases to analyze and identify factors that pose a risk and detect unusual activities that suggest fraudulent behavior [2].

A major benefit of AI in taxation comes in the form of enabling tax authorities to make projections in the future based on previously acquired information. In spite of that, the use of AI in taxation comes with its fair share of difficulties. There are troubling issues such as data security, algorithm opacity and potential algorithmic discrimination that require a proper approach to ensure that such technology is applied in an ethical manner [3]. Furthermore, the development of appropriate regulatory measures to control the growth of AI in taxation is also critical.

When AI is applied to the processes of taxation the emerging trends indicate that certain AI tools are being employed around the world to determine the amount of value-added tax (VAT) collection [4]. This applies more to developing nations, where there is a possibility of automating the VAT collection process, which is a hurdle to tax avoidance. Such systems improve the clarity of the procedure via the utilization of big data and machine learning which is directed towards predicting what is deemed as abnormal behavior in VAT reporting [5].

But then again, there is a serious point of contention to be brought up in the discussions around these new technologies being incorporated in the decision making of the political actors in charge of fiscal systems which is the very backbone of many nations. This raises the questions about the ethics and morality of giving taxation management to AI [6]. From the view of the accounting profession, while it is an innovative technology, these changes represent a significant leap towards modernizing accountancy practices. The harnessing of new technologies for more effective and efficient forensic and tax audits helps transform accountants into powerful analyzers using these technologies rather than being held back by them [7].

The necessity to adapt tax and financial systems to the new problems and restrictions has led to significant advancements in scientific study in recent years [8]. This study offers a number of guiding tools for comprehending the extent and significance of research on artificial intelligence in tax procedures using the bibliometric technique. An examination of the current scientific output would provide insight into the future top contributors, collaboration creators, and global trends in this area [9]. A thorough explanation of publishing patterns, author productivity, regional distribution, and institutional effect has been made feasible by the use of sophisticated bibliometric tools, specifically R and VOSviewer [10]. Moreover, a thorough comprehension of author contributions and journal importance for this topic is made possible by the application of Lotka's and Bradford's rules [11].

The research is significant because it provides a close-up perspective of scientific advancements in this subject, making it feasible to identify knowledge gaps and future research possibilities. Since the industry encounters problems that are more specific to it than to others, it is imperative that academics, policymakers, and practitioners understand the present status of artificial intelligence in tax procedures in order to foster innovation [12]. The paper discusses the innovation of tax and financial systems through this bibliometric analysis, and it provides a platform for more relevant research that may be attempted to improve tax procedures.

2 Materials and Methods

This bibliometric study delves into the intersection between artificial intelligence and tax processes, analyzing existing scientific production and exploring emerging trends in the application of AI in the tax field. The main areas of research, key actors and the implications of this symbiotic relationship for governments, businesses and citizens were examined. Through an exhaustive search in the Scopus database, this research identifies trends, authors, institutions and key publications in this emerging area.

To carry out this analysis, a search strategy was designed in Scopus using key terms related to both concepts (taxation and artificial intelligence), through the search equation: (TITLE-ABS-KEY ("taxation") OR TITLE -ABS-KEY ("tax") OR TITLE-ABS-KEY ("imposition") AND TITLE-ABS-KEY ("artificial intelligence") OR TITLE-ABS-KEY ("IA") OR TITLE-ABS-KEY ("Automation")) AND PUBYEAR > 2018 AND PUB-YEAR < 2025. This equation identified documents that in their titles, summaries or keywords addressed the topics of taxation and artificial intelligence.

The search results were processed to extract relevant information such as the total number of documents, annual growth rate, average age of documents, average citations per document and total references. On the other hand, keywords, authors, institutional affiliations and document types were searched into this analysis, carried out on documents published between 2019 and 2024, covering a period of five years.

3 Results

The analysis was carried out on documents published between 2019 and 2024, covering a period of five years. In total, 502 sources (journals, books, etc.) were consulted and 750 relevant documents were identified, showing that scientific production in this field has experienced an average annual growth of 7.56%, indicating a positive trend. The majority of the documents analyzed are scientific articles (375), followed by conference chapters (226) and books (19) (Table 1).

The data show constant growth in scientific production since 2019 (91) until reaching a peak in 2022 (139). Starting that year, a slight decrease is observed in the number of articles published in 2023, followed by a stabilization in 2024 (131), as is shown in Table 2.

The Lotka law can be used to chart the production curve based on the number of authors to gain a clearer insight into their contributions to knowledge. 94.6% of authors wrote one document, 4.2% wrote two or fewer, and 0.7% wrote three or fewer, as shown in Table 3 and Fig. 1.

Table 1. Description of main information.

Main information about data	
Timespan	2019:2024
Sources (Journals, Books, etc.)	502
Documents	750
Annual Growth Rate %	7.56
Document Average Age	2.33
Average citations per doc	6.537
References	28904
DOCUMENT TYPES	
Article	375
Book	19
book chapter	68
conference paper	226
conference review	31
Erratum	2
Letter	1
Note	5
Review	1
short survey	22
DOCUMENT CONTENTS	
Keywords Plus (ID)	3690
Author's Keywords (DE)	2208
AUTHORS	
Authors	2030
Authors of single-authored docs	171
AUTHORS COLLABORATION	
Single-authored docs	185
Co-Authors per Doc	2.9
International co-authorships %	15.07

Source: author using R software based on information from Scopus (2025).

The Bradford Law, which separates journals into three performance zones, each with an increase in the number of journals and a corresponding proportion of articles, is used to provide the most relevant sources based on the frequency of publications on the topic and through the percentiles. Table 4 shows the percentages that correlate to each

Table 2. Annual scientific production.

Year	Articles
2019	91
2020	122
2021	131
2022	139
2023	136
2024	131

Source: own elaboration (2025).

Table 3. Lotka's Law.

Documents written	Number of Authors	Proportion of Authors
1	1921	0.946
2	86	0.042
3	14	0.007
4	7	0.003
5	2	0.001

Source: own elaboration (2025).

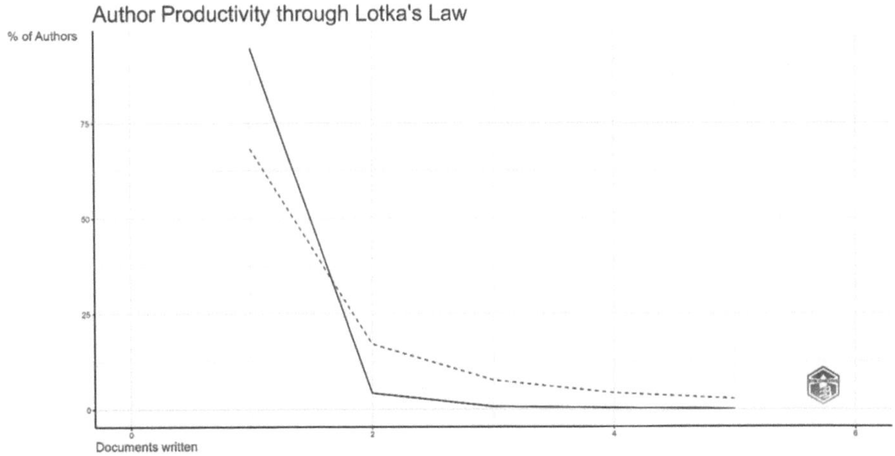

Fig. 1. Lotka's Law, source: author based on information from Scopus (2025).

Bradford Law zone. Zones 2 and 3 exhibit similar numbers of articles, however they are dispersed throughout 208 and 247 journals, respectively, whereas Zone 1 comprises 33.07% of the papers published in just 47 journals (Table 5).

Table 4. Bradford's Law.

Zone	No. Journals	No. Titles	Percentages
Zone 1	47	248	33.07%
Zone 2	208	255	34.00%
Zone 3	247	247	32.93%

Source: own elaboration (2025).

Table 5. Most relevant authors.

Authors	Articles	Fractional articles
KUMAR R	5	1.08
LI J	5	1.53
IONESCU L	4	3.17
JR	4	0.82
LI H	4	2.58
LI X	4	1.12
LI Y	4	0.92
PICA LM	4	4.00
ZHANG J	4	1.78
ALMADA M	3	0.51
BENTLEY D	3	3.00
BORANGIU T	3	1.08
FAÚNDEZ-UGALDE A	3	1.17
FETTKE P	3	0.87
GÓRSKI Ł	3	0.51
MELLADO-SILVA R	3	1.17
OBERSON X	3	3.00
TYLIŃSKI K	3	0.51
WANG X	3	1.20
WANG Y	3	1.17
ZHANG L	3	0.67
ZHANG X	3	0.87
ZHOU Y	3	1.33

Source: own elaboration (2025).

Regarding the sources found, Lecture Notes in Networks and Systems is the most relevant with 27 documents, followed by Advances in Intelligent Systems and Computing

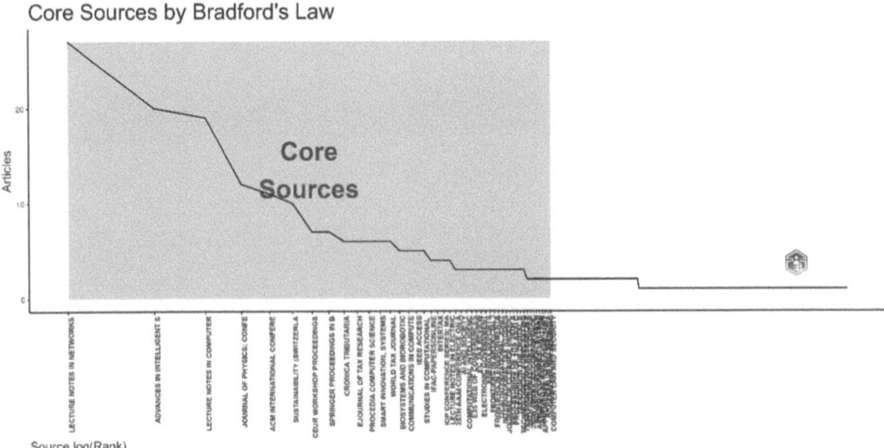

Fig. 2. Bradford's Law, source: author based on information from Scopus (2025).

with 20 documents and Lecture Notes in Computer Science (including subseries) with 19 documents. Among the three sources mentioned there are 66 publications, that is, 52.8% of the documents found. Based on the graphs obtained, it can be concluded that the graph shows that scientific production in the investigated study area follows a pattern similar to that described by Bradford's Law. Most articles are concentrated in a small group of sources, while the vast majority of sources contribute few articles (Figs. 2 and 3).

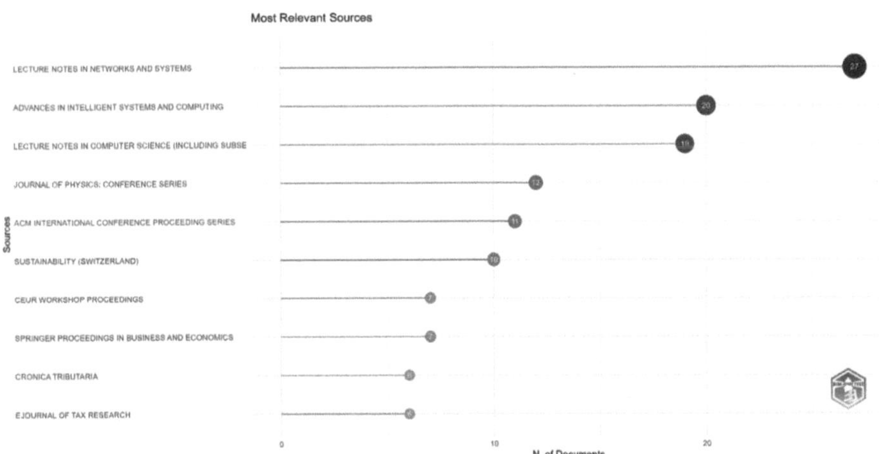

Fig. 3. Most relevant sources, source: author based on information from Scopus (2025).

With 12 associated articles, Aalborg University is positioned as the institution with the greatest presence in the search results. On the other hand, the NOTREPORTED category (12) groups together documents that do not specify an institutional affiliation.

Next is the Rostov State University of Economics, with 11 associated articles (Figs. 4 and 5).

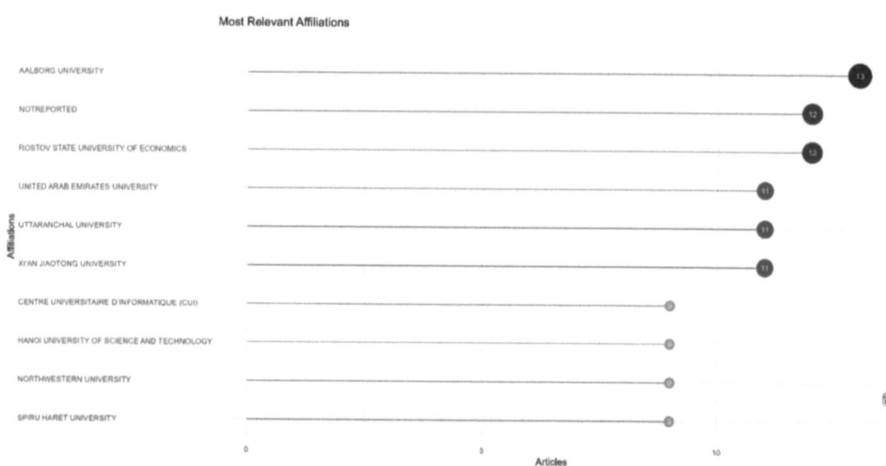

Fig. 4. Most relevant affiliations, source: author based on information from Scopus (2025).

According to the results found, Kumar R is the most productive author of all those presented with a total of 5 documents; He is followed in productivity by the author LI J, with 5 publications. Both Kumar R and LI J share the first place in terms of number of published papers. The rest of the most relevant authors have 4 publications each, with the exception of Almada M (3).

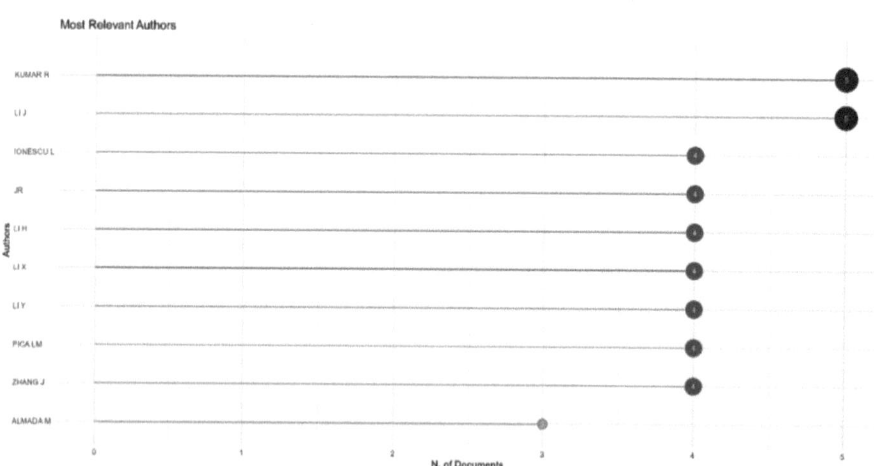

Fig. 5. Most relevant authors, source: author using R software based on information from Scopus (2025).

However, productivity ratings change when looking at fractional articles, which take into account each author's proportional contribution to a multi-author work. Although Pica LM has only 4 publications, he has a high article count of 4.00, meaning he is the sole author of all of their published work or have published only single-authored articles. In the same way, Bentley D and Oberson X scored 3.00, indicating that they were the primary or sole authors of their papers, even though they had only three publications in total.

In contrast, Kumar R has only 1.08 papers, indicating that although he is the leader in total publications, his contributions are spread across several collaborative works. When co-authorship is taken into account, similar trends are observed for authors with lower contributions, such as JR (0.82) and Almada M (0.51).

The results of this bibliometric study show that artificial intelligence is playing an increasingly important role in the field of taxation. With an annual growth rate of 7.56%, the steady increase in the number of scientific publications shows that experts and scholars are still interested in the relationship between AI and tax activities. Bradford's Law states that the concentration of research evidence in a small number of sources means that particular journals and conferences will influence the discussion of a topic. The large but fragmented research environment is also reflected in Lotka's Law, whereby research is often distributed among many authors and only a few scientists publish many papers.

The literature review clearly shows the growing importance of AI in tax administration and compliance. AI-based models are used especially in developing countries for tax fraud detection, tax revenue forecasting, and automated VAT collection. The significant benefits of these innovations include increased accuracy, improved efficiency and reduced operational costs for tax authorities. But they also bring issues such as algorithmic transparency, ethical dilemmas and the need to put in place a legal framework to ensure the ethical use of AI in tax.

The leadership of kier AI tax research is presented by Aalborg University and Rostov University of Economics, which shows the major academic centers in this field. Few global research studies are targeted at wider audiences, which make it problematic to solve specific tax problems that vary from one region to the other politically and economically. Future research should be more inclusive with regards to institutional interactions to better assess the boundaries of the role AI can play in taxations across jurisdictions.

One of the key findings of this research is the discrepancy, which exists between scientific and practical work. There is expansion of advanced theory and modeling of AI, but little focus on applying it to policy changes and other practical areas. To close this gap facilitates the need to better integrate moral and practical AI taxation systems. To design such systems, taxes, academic institutions, technology developers, and more importantly, the authorities need to work together.

In addition, the ethical challenges of using AI for tax purposes cannot be ignored. This surrounds the issue of algorithmic discrimination, data security, and control by certain classes of taxpayers on AI powered decision-making. Especially when everything is controlled remotely, stakeholders should not risk obfuscating the yardstick of transparency and accountability in tax administration through the application of AI technologies. Therefore, legislators together with AI specialists should define unambiguous standards for the application of AI in tax systems.

Our bibliographic analysis indicates several more interesting research areas. Addressing the knowledge gap will involve research analyzing the comparative effectiveness of various AI models for tax compliance, the use of AI integrated with Blockchain technology for securing tax transactions, and the socio-economic ramifications of AI based taxation systems. Finally, further evidence based interdisciplinary studies that explore legal and ethical boundaries, as well as technical parameters, will be instrumental in most AI usage boundaries in taxation predetermined systems in future.

To date, very little research has been done on the implications of tax AI usage on small and medium sized enterprises (SMEs) and that needs to be further developed. However, the costs involved, technological sophistication required, and even regulatory compliance may pose extensive barriers for SMEs. Usually, larger firms have the resources to freely use AI for their tax compliance needs. When considering the barriers and benefits of AI for SMEs, a far more constructive and effective strategy toward AI aided tax management will emerge.

Further research into the impact of AI on tax professionals and tax jobs is also important. It is important to assess how this technological revolution may impact job roles, skill requirements and workforce motivation as AI systems become increasingly adept at handling complex tax tasks. To ensure a smooth transition and reduce the likelihood of staff attrition, research should focus on identifying ways to upskill tax professionals and redefine their responsibilities in an AI-enabled tax environment.

In short, AI has the potential to radically transform tax administration, increasing accuracy and efficiency. To prevent abuse, its implementation must be supported by strict ethical standards and regulatory controls. The results of this bibliographic analysis highlight the need for further research and collaboration to fully integrate AI into taxation while minimizing risks. Stakeholders can ensure that AI is used as a tool to create fairer and more efficient tax systems around the world by encouraging interdisciplinary discussions and international collaboration.

4 Conclusions and Discussions

This study's bibliometric analysis attempts to create suitable regulatory frameworks to go along with the development of artificial intelligence in the tax domain and its connection to scientific output. Examining the primary study topics, important players, and the ramifications of this mutually beneficial relationship for governments, corporations, and individuals, it highlights some noteworthy findings that advance current understanding in the subject and suggest new lines of inquiry. Using Scopus data, a bibliometric analysis of 750 papers on the effects of case management sustainability models on healthcare organizations produced the findings mentioned below.

Scientific papers made up the majority of the examined literature (375), followed by conference chapters (226) and books (19). Between 2019 and 2024, the number of authors increased by 7.56% year, reaching 2030. According to the statistics, scientific output has been steadily increasing from 2019 (91) and peaked in 2022 (139). Following that year, there is a minor decline in the quantity of articles produced in 2023, which is followed by a leveling off in 2024 (131). 94.6% of writers created one document, 4.2% wrote two or fewer, and 0.7% wrote three or fewer, in accordance with Lotka's law. Bradford's law also states that 47 journals make up 33.07% of the literature.

The three biggest sources in this field are Lecture Notes in Computer Science (including subseries) with 19 documents, Lecture Notes in Networks and Systems with 27 documents, and Advances in Intelligent Systems and Computing with 20 papers. With 12 related papers, Aalborg University was the organization that made the largest contribution to the study field. Second position goes to the NOTREPORTED category, which has 12 related items and compiles materials without an institutional affiliation. With eleven related articles, Rostov State University of Economics comes next. Lastly, with a total of five documents, Kumar R is the most productive author. He shares the top spot with author LI J, who has five publications as well.

Researchers, experts, and decision-makers who want to comprehend the effects of artificial intelligence in the tax domain may find the results helpful. Regarding the new developments in artificial intelligence in taxes, it is noteworthy that a variety of AI technologies are being used all over the world to efficiently compute value-added tax collection. This is especially important in developing nations, because preventing tax fraud is made more difficult by the possibility of automating VAT collection.

By using big data and machine learning to examine and forecast anomalous trends in VAT reporting, this solution improves process transparency. The discussion over integrating these new technologies into the decision-making processes of political actors in charge of fiscal systems—which form the basis of many states—raises important issues, though. This brings up questions regarding the morality and ethics of giving artificial intelligence power over taxes.

Lastly, from the standpoint of the accounting industry, these developments mark a critical turning point in the evolution of conventional responsibilities. In order to increase the efficacy and efficiency of forensic and tax audit procedures, innovative technologies are becoming indispensable instruments. By collaborating with these new technologies, modern accountants may become more capable analysts.

References

1. Rahman, S., Sirazy, M.R.M., Das, R., Khan, R.S.: An exploration of artificial intelligence techniques for optimizing tax compliance, fraud detection, and revenue collection in modern tax administrations. Int. J. Bus. Intell. Big Data Anal. 7(3), 56–80 (2024). https://n9.cl/lccii
2. Agrawal, S.: Enhancing payment security through AI-Driven anomaly detection and predictive analytics. Int. J. Sustain. Infra. Cities Soc. 7(2), 1–14 (2022). https://vectoral.org/index.php/IJSICS/article/view/99
3. Daneshjou, R., Smith, M.P., Sun, M.D., Rotemberg, V., Zou, J.: Lack of transparency and potential bias in artificial intelligence data sets and algorithms: a scoping review. JAMA Dermatol. 157(11), 1362–1369 (2021). https://doi.org/10.1001/jamadermatol.2021.3129
4. Yordanova, Z.: Supporting Digitalization of ERP (SAP) value-added tax management through data analytics tools. In: Kostavelis, I., Folinas, D., Aidonis, D., Achillas, C. (eds.) Supply Chains. ICSC 2024. Communications in Computer and Information Science, vol. 2110. Springer, Cham (2025). https://doi.org/10.1007/978-3-031-69344-1_16

5. Nuryani, N., Yahya, I., Lestari, A.: Premature ventricular contraction detection using swarm-based support vector machine and QRS wave features. Int. J. Biomed. Eng. Technol. **16**(4), 306–316 (2014). https://doi.org/10.1504/IJBET.2014.066224

6. Mökander, J., Schroeder, R.: Artificial intelligence, rationalization, and the limits of control in the public sector: the case of tax policy optimization. Soc. Sci. Comput. Rev. **42**(6), 1359–1378 (2024). https://doi.org/10.1177/08944393241235175

7. Chávez-Díaz, J.M., Aquiño-Perales, L., De-Velazco-Borda, J.L., Villagómez-Chinchay, J. A., Flores-Sotelo, W.S.: Artificial intelligence in accounting and auditing: bibliometric analysis in Scopus 2020–2023, **36**(2), 1329–1318 (2024). https://doi.org/10.11591/ijeecs.v36.i2.pp1 319-1328

8. Adeoye, O.B., et al.: Fintech, taxation, and regulatory compliance: navigating the new financial landscape. Finan. Account. Res. J. **6**(3), 320–330 (2024). https://doi.org/10.51594/farj.v6i3.858

9. Beck, S., et al.: The open innovation in science research field: a collaborative conceptualisation approach. Indust. Innov. **29**(2), 136–185 (2022). https://doi.org/10.1080/13662716.2020.179 2274

10. Ramirez, J., Gallego, G., Niebles-Núñez, W., Tirado, J.G.: Blockchain technology for sustainable supply chains: a bibliometric study. J. Distrib. Sci. **21**(6), 119–129 (2023). https://doi.org/10.15722/jds.21.06.202306.119

11. Basu, A., Dutta, B.: An analytical study of alternative method for solving Lotka's law with Simpson's 1/3 rule. J. Sci. Res. **13**(2), 466–474 (2024). https://doi.org/10.5530/jscires.13.2.37

12. Lescrauwaet, L., Wagner, H., Yoon, C., Shukla, S.: Adaptive legal frameworks and economic dynamics in emerging technologies: navigating the intersection for responsible innovation. Law Econ. **16**(3), 202–220 (2022). https://doi.org/10.35335/laweco.v16i3.61

From a On-Premises-Centered to a Cloud Ecosystems: Lessons Learned from a Success Story in the Chilean Financial Sector

Felipe Vásquez[1,2]([✉])(iD), Juan Lagos[1]([✉])(iD), Fernanda Gutiérrez[1]([✉])(iD), Francisco Escobar[1]([✉])(iD), and Jorge Hochstetter-Diez[1]([✉])(iD)

[1] Depto. Cs. De la Computación e Informática, Universidad de La Frontera, Temuco, Chile
{felipe.vasquez,juanmanuel.lagos,fernanda.gutierrez,francisco.escobar,
jorge.hochstetter}@ufrontera.cl
[2] Universidad de Alicante, Alicante, Spain

Abstract. Digital transformation has become a key driver of innovation and competitiveness in the financial sector, particularly in the context of cloud computing and data-driven decision-making. This study presents a case analysis of a Chilean bank that transitioned from an on-premises infrastructure to a cloud-based ecosystem, deployed over Microsoft Azure technologies. The research examines the challenges, processes, and outcomes associated with this transformation, highlighting the role of advanced data management techniques, such as MLOps, in optimizing business intelligence and operational efficiency. The transition involved restructuring data ingestion, processing, and visualization workflows, integrating tools like Azure Data Factory, Azure Databricks, and Data Lake Storage to improve scalability, automation, and security. The study discusses key improvements, including enhanced real-time data access, better orchestration of analytics pipelines, and increased transparency through Identity and Access Management (IAM) systems. Findings indicate that migrating to a cloud framework not only enhances system efficiency but also strengthens regulatory compliance, risk management, and customer trust. The research underscores digital transformation as a strategic pillar in modern banking, demonstrating how cloud-native architectures can drive operational resilience, data governance, and innovation in financial services.

Keywords: Digital Transformation · Cloud Computing · MLOps · Financial Services · Data Governance · Business Intelligence

F. F.-H Nah and K. L. Siau (Eds.): HCII 2025, LNCS 16343, pp. 341–353, 2026.
https://doi.org/10.1007/978-3-032-13167-6_23

1   Introduction

Digital transformation has emerged as a key process for organizational improvement [29], driving companies to adapt to an ever-changing competitive environment. This process involves not only the adoption of advanced technologies but also the reconfiguration of business models, organizational structures, and internal processes to create more agile, innovative, and customer-oriented organizations [25,30].

Notably, the COVID-19 pandemic accelerated the digital transformation journey [15], highlighting the necessity for banks to adapt swiftly to changing consumer behaviors and their reliance on digital channels [24]. The competitive landscape has further intensified as fintech companies introduce innovative solutions that disrupt established banking practices, prompting traditional banks to embrace a more agile approach to remain relevant. This evolving scenario underscores the urgent need for banks to invest in technology and redefine their customer engagement strategies to navigate the complexities of a digital economy.

In this context, an organization's ability to extract value from its data becomes a fundamental pillar [1]. Digital transformation empowers decision-makers through advanced data processing tools and techniques that enable more precise and timely analysis of information.

Technologies such as MLOps (Machine Learning Operations), which integrate machine learning models into production workflows, play a crucial role in ensuring that predictive and prescriptive models are scalable, reliable, and aligned with organizational goals [7]. This approach significantly enhances data-driven business strategies and decision-making [16].

The present study examines the digital transformation case of a banking company that previously operated under a on-premises-centered framework as its functional model. It will analyze the stages of the transformation process, the challenges faced during the transition to a cloud digital model, and the outcomes achieved in terms of operational efficiency, customer satisfaction, and data-driven decision-making.

This analysis aims to show how digital transformation can have a significant impact when it is implemented holistically, highlighting the importance of advanced data processing techniques as key enablers of organizational success.

2   Background

Digital transformation is a process of organizational change, encompassing operations, business models, and organizational culture, that uses digital technologies to improve productivity and competitiveness [18,32]. The implementation of digital transformation strategies generates several benefits, such as cost reduction, improved production processes and increased customer satisfaction [11].

However, the impact of digital transformation is not always linear, and to successfully address factors such as organization size, industry and organizational culture, specific capabilities need to be developed throughout the process, adapting to changing needs as the transformation progresses [9]. Technologies such as big data, artificial intelligence and cloud solutions enable better analytics and forecasting, facilitating informed decision making [8,17].

Optimizing business performance and creating new opportunities are made possible by digital transformation, enabling organizations to leverage data analytics for prediction, decision support and the development of innovative business strategies [2,19]. Advanced data processing techniques can significantly improve decision making in various domains [5] while intelligent techniques such as expert systems, artificial neural networks, fuzzy systems and data mining can be employed to enrich decision making processes where the choice of technique depends on the problem domain and the complexity of the data [4].

Within the framework of digital transformation, technological infrastructure plays an essential role in enabling more agile and effective processes, especially for financial institutions [21,26]. Digital transformation in financial services embraces the adoption of IT infrastructures, social media, mobile technologies and big data to improve efficiency and customer satisfaction [3,10]. The choice between solutions with on-premises or cloud services depends on specific business needs, security requirements and cost structures [6], influencing not only the ability to process large volumes of data, but also the integration of advanced techniques such as MLOps to optimize data-driven decision making [22,26].

While on-premises services, with their focus on locally hosted structures, offer a higher degree of customization, configuration control and data sovereignty, they often come with high upfront costs, greater complexity in maintenance and, consequently, a limited ability to adapt to changing demands [6,31].

On the other hand, cloud services, operating under pay-per-use models, provide greater scalability, flexibility and cost-effectiveness, reducing economic barriers and the need for substantial physical infrastructure [6,14,22]. Although security risks and limited customization capabilities raise challenges for cloud adoption [31], in high security loss environments cloud services may have lower average expected losses compared to on-premises services [31]. However, while cloud services tend to have favorable costs, a thorough financial comparison should take into account factors such as the cost of capital, interest, intensity of use and duration of use.

Over the technology infrastructure layer, methodologies such as MLOps, an extension of DevOps designed for machine learning, is gaining popularity as organizations implement more structured approaches to data analytics [23,28]. This methodology streamlines the development, deployment, and maintenance of machine learning models, enhancing business outcomes through optimized processes, technology integration, and effective team management, and ensuring quality through monitoring, validation, and governance [23,28].

A key element of digital transformation is data transparency and governance, aspects that ensure the traceability, integrity and accessibility of information in digital environments [13]. The implementation of advanced cloud architectures, combined with auditing and monitoring tools, allows organizations to record, control and justify every interaction with data, ensuring regulatory compliance and reducing risks of fraud or operational errors. In addition, role-based access management strengthens security and protects sensitive information. In the financial sector, these practices are essential to maintain the trust of customers and regulators, while optimizing process efficiency and improving strategic decision making [27].

3   Study Case: Bank Industry Transformation

In 2021, in the middle of the COVID-19 global crisis, a Chilean bank started an interesting digital transformation process, which involved from modifications at the technological infrastructure level to the remodeling of processes linked to software development, business processes and generation of data subproducts.

3.1   Technological Infrastructure

In general terms, the migration from a on-premises-centered framework for processes and cloud data storage, which interacted in a decoupled way, to a unified technological ecosystem that allows data storage, processing and generation of sub-processes within the same platform was addressed.

Old Architecture. Figure 1 presents a data processing flow typical of the old architecture that supported the banking institution's processes. The system involves multiple components and processes such as:

1. Data Sources: There are data sources, which are consumed according to their nature, in real time or near-real-time (NRT), where there are services that send messages to a data consumption channel; or in periodic batch execution that connect to FTP servers, database systems or access stored files.
2. Message Producer: A message producer generates data in real time, which is then consumed by a component called Message Consumer through a streaming or NRT mechanism. This message producer includes different sources and services that fit this generalization.
3. Message Consumer and Data Insertion: The Message Consumer receives data in real time and inserts it into a Cloud Data Lake, which acts as a centralized storage for processing and analyzing data. The Kafka tool was used for this.
4. Pivotal on-premises Server: The critical component of this infrastructure is detected in the Pivotal on-premises Server, which centralizes and is responsible for several activities. Firstly, it is the connection server with which the Data Engineers interact, developing in it the data manipulation and processing tasks by means of .sh scripts that structure the step-by-step of the process to be performed.

   This server is characterized for being a connection point for multiple users, therefore it is usually limited in its performance, with a tendency to run out of resources such as RAM or storage, hence the need to set purge processes of the data already processed and ingested in the Data Lake to liberate space on the machine.

5. Orchestration: The server is also responsible for maintaining the orchestration of processes through the Control-M tool, which although it aims at automating activities, often failed in its purpose, forcing manual intervention for the execution of processes.
6. Data Consumer: It is the user or system that uses the refined data stored in the Data Lake to make decisions or generate sub-products such as reports or dashboards.

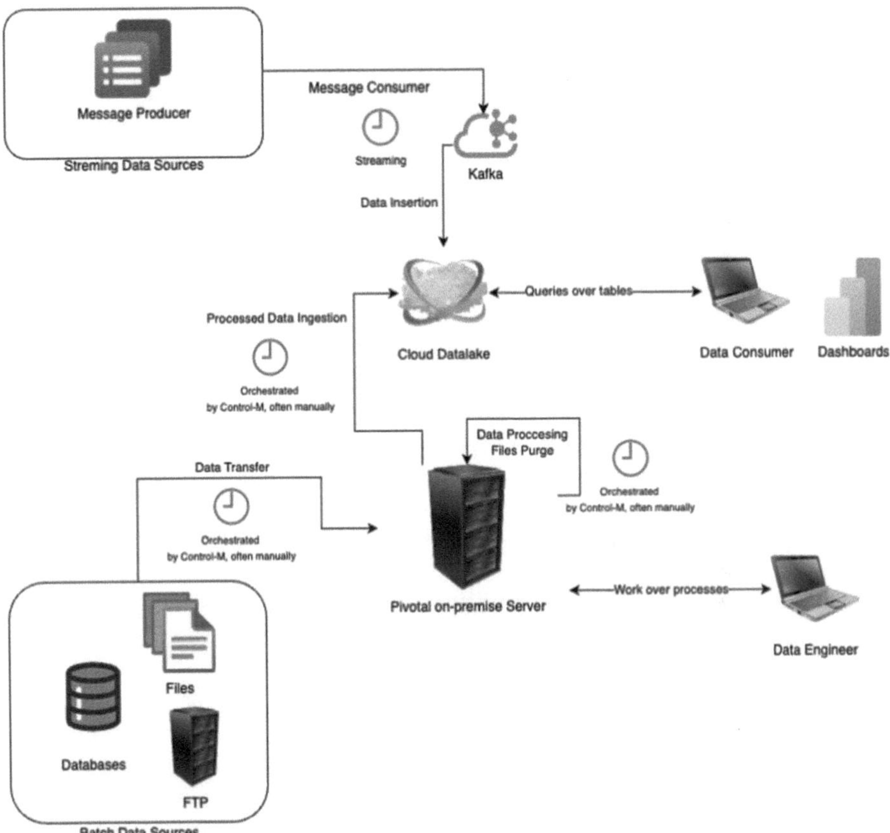

Fig. 1. Old architecture used in the banking company with a on-premises-centered framework.

New Architecture. The new architecture implemented by the bank, which is shown in Fig. 2, establishes a first key decision: to bring both data storage and processing to the cloud. There are common components here with the old architecture seen in Fig. 1: the streaming and batch data sources are the same, as they are inputs to the system. The changes that the new architecture introduces mainly point to the use of more coupled and natively interoperable tools as the Microsoft Azure ecosystem, using Azure Data Lake to store the data and Azure Databricks for processing, consumption and generation of sub-products as detailed below:

1. Azure Data Factory: This Azure tool becomes the key to batch data inges- tion. With its own orchestrator, it is able to automate the execution of pipelines that end with the storage of new data in the Data Lake. In addi- tion, it links with GitHub in an organic way to be able to version the pipelines developed by the data engineer.

2. Azure Databricks: It is a third-party application integrated into the Microsoft Azure ecosystem. It provides the functionality to visualize the data stored in the Data Lake through Data Catalogs, Schemas and Tables. In addition, it provides access management through the integration of Azure's Active Directory, contributing to data governance and security.

3. Message Consumer and Data Insertion: The Message Consumer is directly a Databricks job, with a notebook operating in real time with built-in fault tolerance, constantly listening to the messages emitted and integrating them into the data lake. The messages emitted by the Message Producer have a unique ID and a configurable life time in days, so in case of any failure in the consumption process, it is able to start up again, know which was the last message processed and resume the next ones automatically.

4. Data Lake Storage: This type of storage is used to store data, using a hierar- chy of containers that implements the principles of zone architecture accord- ing to [20].

5. Data Consumer: It is the user or system that utilizes the refined data stored in the Data Lake to make decisions with them or generate sub-products such as reports or dashboards. In addition, through databricks they can develop sub-products with external tools such as those native to the platform.

6. Batch Data Ingestion: The batch data ingestion processes are established on the basis of an architecture that summarizes its internal components coinciding with [12], allowing to systematize the design of these pipeline in reusable and general archetypes (parametric data ingestion templates built in Azure Data Factory).

7. Data Processing: Databricks computation clusters are used to execute the code notebooks. These notebooks are:
   - Multi-language, being able to include Python, R, Scala, SQL and Mark- down.
   - Configurable: being able to include the use of parameters whose value is given by the pipeline that call their execution.
   - Orchestrable: being able to be run through the Internal scheduling of Azure Data Factory.

8. Databricks Notebooks: Instead of .sh files, the notebooks structure and sys- tematize routines such as schema and table management (CRUD), populat-

ing tables with data stored in the datalake and executing scripts for data manipulation.

9. Data Access: Processed data are stored in Databricks Schemas, where they are available for queries. Data Consumers use these schemas to perform queries directly from Databricks notebooks. The robustness of Databricks adds layers of security, data governance and risk management by regulating at the catalog, schema and table level who can access the data and with what read or write privileges.

10. Data Analysis: Using the notebooks stored in Databricks, it is possible to carry out basic analysis such as queries, EDA, view creation, to more complex routines such as the creation, training and use of machine learning models under the umbrella of MLOps.

11. Data visualization: Having technologies such as Python and all its libraries, plus the distributed processing power of Spark, allows the generation of products such as graphics (even embedded in notebooks), reporting, internal dashboards in Databricks as well as external with other tools, to be very easy to achieve, share and regulate their access, being able to provide decision makers with valuable inputs.

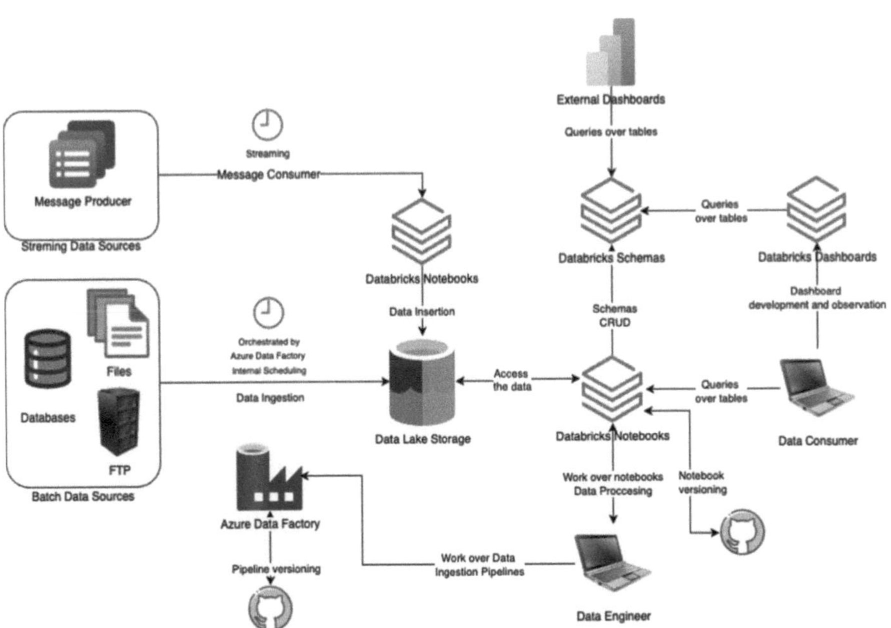

Fig. 2. New architecture used in the banking company with a full cloud framework.

3.2   Processes

In parallel to the modifications in the technological infrastructure, significant changes were implemented in the interaction between actors and the processes in the new technological architecture adopted. These adjustments not only optimize data management, but also strengthen information governance and security.

First, a regulated access way was established to the data sources, which were previously available through the on-premises pivot server. With the new infrastructure, access to this data is only possible through Databricks' data catalog and Identity and Access Management (IAM) system. This strategy allows consolidating the "single source of truth" principle, ensuring that all data-driven decisions are based exclusively on the information stored and processed in the data lake, eliminating direct access to the original sources.

Also, data ingestion processes, previously executed through .sh scripts on the on-premises server, were replaced by automated pipelines through Azure Data Factory (ADF). These new workflows ensure traceability at all stages, from creation to production deployment, thanks to integration with GitHub and Azure DevOps. In addition, ADF's internal monitoring provides a detailed log history that allows auditing the execution of processes.

Finally, all data extraction, transformation and loading (ETL), query and manipulation operations are managed exclusively through Databricks notebooks, executed in clusters whose access and privileges configuration is strictly regulated. In this way, the possibility of data manipulation by unauthorized users is restricted. In addition, the production deployment of notebooks, jobs and job clusters in Databricks follows a management process using Azure DevOps, aligned with established practices for the implementation of pipelines in Azure Data Factory.

The main differences can be seen by comparing the old process flow in Fig. 3 versus the new flow in Fig. 4.

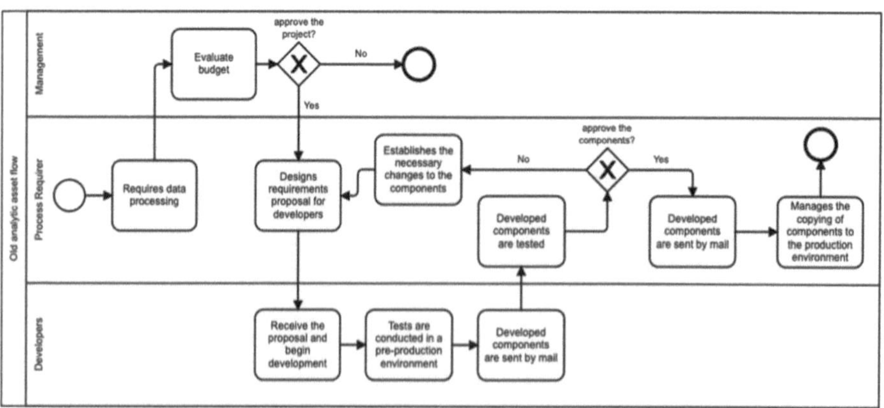

Fig. 3. Abstraction of a development process in the old technological architecture.

It is critical how the old process shown in Fig. 3 is highly manual, going to the extreme of sharing components by e-mail. Also, quality assurance and testing are the responsibility of the developers, with a risk of bias and malpractices when auditing a proprietary product.

In contrast, the new flow shown in Fig. 4 remarks how responsibilities are formalized in different actors, through more automated, subject to audit and traceable processes.

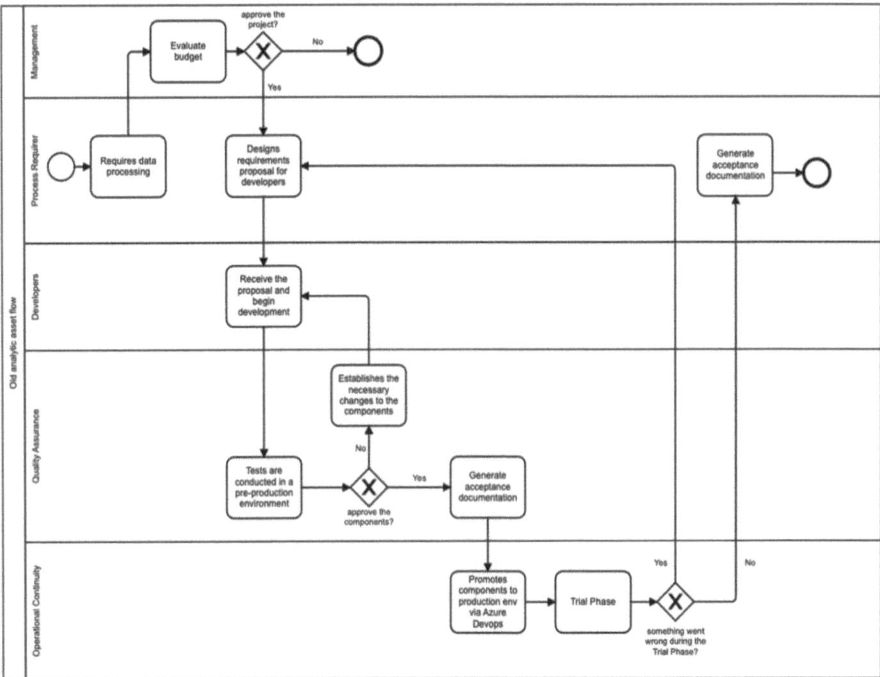

Fig. 4. Abstraction of a development process in the new technological architecture.

4   Discussion

A key aspect of digital transformation in the financial sector is the improvement of transparency in data management and operational processes. Migrating to a cloud-based architecture not only optimizes the efficiency and scalability of systems, but also introduces mechanisms for auditing, traceability and real-time access to information. Tools such as Azure Data Factory and Databricks allow every interaction with data to be logged, ensuring that modifications and accesses are documented and subject to audit.

This is particularly relevant in the ability to track and justify data-driven decisions, which is critical for customer confidence and regulatory oversight. In addition, integration with identity and access management (IAM) systems in the cloud strengthens information governance, allowing role-based permissions and access levels to be defined, which reduces the risk of internal fraud and improves the security of banking processes. In this sense, digital transformation not only responds to the need for efficiency, but also becomes a strategic pillar to ensure transparency and trust in digital banking.

The implementation of a centralized data lake within the cloud architecture —designed to store raw and processed data without rigid schemas— has enhanced data traceability, uniqueness, and veracity in the studied Chilean bank. By consolidating all data sources into a unified Azure Data Lake, the bank eliminated siloed on-premises systems prone to manual errors and fragmentation. Tools like Azure Data Factory and Databricks ensure full auditability, with role-based access (via Azure Active Directory) and pipeline versioning in GitHub attributing every modification to specific users.

The "single source of truth" principle minimizes duplication and subjective interpretations, aligning with the theoretical definition of a data lake as a governed, flexible ecosystem. These measures not only strengthen data integrity for strategic decisions but also address financial sector demands for regulatory compliance, where transparency and audit trails are critical.

The achievement of objectives in a digital transformation project can be approached from various perspectives. From a technical approach, as discussed in the previous chapter, the impact of the data management architecture on the elimination of bottlenecks, the improvement of elasticity to meet variable service demands, and the mitigation of critical points, such as the old on-premises server, stand out. This server, which previously represented a breaking point in the infrastructure, was identified as a negative differentiating factor in the performance of the banking platform.

Additionally, a component that was not considered in previous iterations is introduced: an advanced reporting tool. This tool allows daily monitoring of executed processes, identifying those that were successfully completed, as well as failures, interruptions or cancellations, along with their respective causes.

This level of visibility is fundamental to implement continuous improvement strategies in organizations. Accurate identification of errors in the digital infrastructure facilitates opportunities for statistical analysis, process optimization, and improved banking services. In this way, the system not only corrects deficiencies, but also enables a framework for innovation and operational excellence, aligning with the strategic goals of digital transformation.

5   Conclusion

This study analyzed the digital transformation of a Chilean bank that migrated from an on-premises infrastructure to a Microsoft Azure-based cloud ecosystem, addressing critical challenges such as data fragmentation, error-prone manual processes, and scalability limitations.

The adoption of tools like Azure Data Factory, Databricks, and Data Lake Storage enabled centralized storage, automated ingestion and processing workflows, and strengthened governance through role-based access controls and embedded auditing. Results demonstrated significant improvements in operational efficiency (reduced processing times), transparency (full data traceability), and innovation capacity (MLOps implementation for predictive models). This case emphasizes that cloud migration is not merely a technological upgrade but a strategic repositioning to compete in digital economies.

The Chilean bank's experience provides a replicable model for financial institutions seeking to modernize their infrastructures. The proposed architecture—based on scalable cloud solutions and managed services—is particularly viable for medium-to-large entities facing growing demands for agility and regulatory compliance.

Tools like Azure Active Directory and Data Factory can adapt to diverse regulatory contexts, while the standardization of pipelines and notebooks in Databricks facilitates gradual adoption without disrupting critical operations. However, success depends on factors such as cloud technology training, alignment with local security policies, and integration of data-driven organizational cultures. Banks in emerging markets, where digitization is nascent but accelerating, could particularly benefit from this approach.

Future research could explore:

- **Advanced Analytics Integration**: Leveraging generative AI or *edge computing* to optimize real-time predictive models.
- **Governance Automation**: Implementing *Data Observability* solutions to automatically monitor data quality, ethical use, and drift.
- **Proactive Security**: Evaluating *zero-trust* architectures or homomorphic encryption techniques for multi-cloud environments.
- **Sustainability**: Measuring the environmental impact of cloud migration and strategies to reduce carbon footprint in mass processing.

Additionally, it would be valuable to compare this case with migrations in non-financial sectors or regions with divergent regulatory frameworks, identifying universal patterns and context-specific factors. The convergence of MLOps, DevOps, and FinOps emerges as a critical area to ensure digital transformation is both technically and economically sustainable.

Acknowledgments. This research was partially funded by Universidad de La Frontera, research direction, research project DIUFRO DI25-0084.

Jorge Hochstetter-Diez is suported by Grant ANID, Chile, FONDECYT DE INICIACIÓN EN INVESTIGACIÓN, Project No 1124- 0115.

Disclosure of Interests. The authors declare no conflicts of interest.

References

1. Aboiron, E., Aboiron, J.: Digital transformation as a tool for organizational change and value creation. Int. J. Appl. Res. Bus. Manage. **3**, 29–36 (2022)

2. Arsal, R.E., Durdu, H.T., Tongarlak, M.H.: Organizational enablers of data-driven digital transformation: A case study from banking industry. In: 2022 IEEE Technology and Engineering Management Conference (TEMSCON EUROPE), pp. 210–216. IEEE (2022)

3. Chan, J.: Digital transformation in the era of big data and cloud computing. Int. J. Intell. Inf. Syst. **9**, 16 (2020). https://doi.org/10.11648/j.ijiis.20200903.11

4. Das, T.: Intelligent techniques in decision making: a survey. Indian J. Sci. Technol. **9**(12), 1–6 (2016)

5. Deepa, S., Radhika, M., Diwakar, M., Rufina, P., Nithya, A., Mohanapriya, M.: Data fusion and analysis techniques for enhanced decision-making in IoT environments. In: 2023 7th International Conference on Electronics, Communication and Aerospace Technology (ICECA), pp. 1513–1518. IEEE (2023)

6. Gaianu, M.: On premise data center vs cloud. In: 2023 International Conference on Computational Science and Computational Intelligence (CSCI), pp. 1068–1071 (2023). https://doi.org/10.1109/CSCI62032.2023.00176

7. Heinz, D., Hunke, F., Breitschopf, G.F.: Organizing for digital innovation and transformation: bridging between organizational resilience and innovation management. In: Ahlemann, F., Schütte, R., Stieglitz, S. (eds) Innovation Through Information Systems: Volume II: A Collection of Latest Research on Technology Issues, pp. 548–564. Springer, Cham (2021). https://doi.org/10.1007/978-3-030-86797-3_36

8. Kommisetty, P., et al.: Leading the future: big data solutions, cloud migration, and AI-driven decision-making in modern enterprises. Educ. Adm. Theory Pract. **28**(03), 352–364 (2022)

9. Konopik, J., Jahn, C., Schuster, T., Hoßbach, N., Pflaum, A.: Mastering the digital transformation through organizational capabilities: a conceptual framework. Digit. Bus. **2**(2), 100019 (2022)

10. Kraus, S., Jones, P., Kailer, N., Weinmann, A., Chaparro-Banegas, N., Roig-Tierno, N.: Digital transformation: an overview of the current state of the art of research. SAGE Open **11**(3), 21582440211047576 (2021). https://doi.org/10.1177/21582440211047576

11. Kretschmer, T., Khashabi, P.: Digital transformation and organization design: an integrated approach. Calif. Manage. Rev. **62**(4), 86–104 (2020)

12. Lagos, J., Cravero, A.: Reference architecture for data ingestion in data lake. In: 2023 18th Iberian Conference on Information Systems and Technologies (CISTI), pp. 1–9 (2023). https://doi.org/10.23919/CISTI58278.2023.10211281

13. Mokhtar, S., Hussin, N., Tokiran, N.S., Wahab, H., Ibrahim, A.: Digital transformation in information management. Int. J. Acad. Res. Bus. Soc. Sci. **10**(11), 1453–1460 (2020)

14. Mydyti, H., Ajdari, J., Zenuni, X.: Cloud-based services approach as accelerator in empowering digital transformation. In: 2020 43rd International Convention on Information, Communication and Electronic Technology (MIPRO), pp. 1390–1396. IEEE (2020)

15. Nagel, L.: The influence of the Covid-19 pandemic on the digital transformation of work. Int. J. Sociol. Soc. Policy **40**(9/10), 861–875 (2020)

16. Oladele, T.C.: Digital transformation in finance and banking sectors. In: Moloi, T. (eds) Digital Transformation in South Africa: Perspectives from an Emerging Economy, pp. 23–38. Springer, Cham (2024). https://doi.org/10.1007/978-3-031-52403-5_8

17. Paramesha, M., Rane, N.L., Rane, J.: Big data analytics, artificial intelligence, machine learning, internet of things, and blockchain for enhanced business intelligence. Partners Univ. Multidisc. Res. J. **1**(2), 110–133 (2024)

18. Riasanow, T., Setzke, D.S., Böhm, M., Krcmar, H.: Clarifying the notion of digital transformation: a transdisciplinary review of literature. J. Competences, Strategy Manage. **10**(1), 5–31 (2019)

19. Roedder, N., Dauer, D., Laubis, K., Karaenke, P., Weinhardt, C.: The digital transformation and smart data analytics: an overview of enabling developments and application areas. In: 2016 IEEE International Conference on Big Data (Big Data), pp. 2795–2802. IEEE (2016)

20. Sawadogo, P., Darmont, J.: On data lake architectures and metadata management. J. Intell. Inf. Syst. **56**(1), 97–120 (2020). https://doi.org/10.1007/s10844-020-00608-7

21. Sebastian, I.M., Ross, J.W., Beath, C., Mocker, M., Moloney, K.G., Fonstad, N.O.: How big old companies navigate digital transformation. In: Strategic Information Management, pp. 133–150. Routledge (2020)

22. Sen, V.V., Hussein, S., Sumaru, M.R., Ali, S., Ali, F.: Cloud-based service versus on-premise services: a comparative study at a local organization in Fiji. In: 2023 IEEE Asia-Pacific Conference on Computer Science and Data Engineering (CSDE), pp. 1–5 (2023). https://doi.org/10.1109/CSDE59766.2023.10487723

23. Soh, J., Singh, P., Soh, J., Singh, P.: Machine learning operations. Data science solutions on Azure: tools and techniques using Databricks and MLOps, pp. 259–279 (2020)

24. Mamadiyarov, T., Adhambek ugli Sulaymanov, Z., Anvar ugli Askarov, S., Bakhtiyor kizi Uktamova, D.: Impact of Covid-19 pandemic on accelerating the digitization and transformation of banks. In: Proceedings of the 5th International Conference on Future Networks and Distributed Systems, pp. 706–712 (2021)

25. Vărzaru, A.A., Bocean, C.G.: Digital transformation and innovation: the influence of digital technologies on turnover from innovation activities and types of innovation. Systems **12**(9), 359 (2024)

26. Vial, G.: Understanding digital transformation: a review and a research agenda. Managing Digit. Transformation, pp. 13–66 (2021)

27. Vishwanath, T.: Towards transparency in finance and governance. Tech. rep., Working Paper (1999)

28. Watson, H.J., Larson, D.: MLOps: from a cottage industry to a factory approach. Int. J. Bus. Intell. Res. (IJBIR) **15**(1), 1–22 (2024)

29. Wulan, T.S., Devi, P.A.P., Kurniati, D., et al.: Digital tranformation and impact on organizational change and performance. J. Econ. Educ. Entrepreneurship Stud. **5**(1), 188–196 (2024)

30. Zare, J., Persaud, A.: Digital transformation and business model innovation: a bibliometric analysis of existing research and future perspectives. Manage. Rev. Q., 1–34 (2024)

31. Zhang, Z., Nan, G., Tan, Y.: Cloud services vs. on-premises software: competition under security risk and product customization. Inf. Syst. Res. **31**(3), 848–864 (2020)

32. Ziyadin, S., Suieubayeva, S., Utegenova, A.: Digital transformation in business. In: Ashmarina, S., Vochozka, M., Mantulenko, V. (eds) Digital Age: Chances, Challenges and Future, vol. 7, pp. 408–415. Springer, Cham (2020). https://doi.org/10.1007/978-3-030-27015-5_49

Design of University Fees and Financial Management System

Shengying Ye[✉] and Mengjia Li

Gannan Normal University, Ganzhou, China
`gs62480@student.upm.edu.my`

Abstract. The aim of this study is to design an efficient and reliable university fee and financial management system, which adopts a four-layer structure design, including a presentation layer, business logic layer, persistence layer, and data layer, to address the complexity and business requirements of the system. In terms of system function design, the focus is on building the charging module, salary management module, and cashier management module, ensuring the efficient operation of core functions such as tuition collection, faculty salary payment, and financial report generation. In addition, the system also integrates advanced hardware configuration and software environment, for example, using IBM X3850 server and MySQL database management system, to enhance data processing ability and the user experience. Through strict test, the system in terms of functionality and performance to achieve the intended target, effectively improve the efficiency and accuracy of the university financial management. The research results indicate that the system design is reasonable and can adapt to the diverse needs of financial management in universities, providing a modern and automated financial management solution for universities.

Keyword: Universities · Financial Management · System Construction

1 Introduction

In today's digital age, the efficiency, accuracy, and scientificity of financial management in universities are crucial for their stable operation and development. With the enlargement of university scale, the number of students and teachers are also on the increase, financial data quantity also in explosive growth. The traditional financial management mode is facing the huge challenge. University tuition and financial management involves tuition fee collection, salary payment, fund management and other key links. Any problem in any link may affect the normal operation of the school and the vital interests of teachers and students.

At present, although some universities have introduced financial management systems, there are still many shortcomings. The coupling degree between existing system functional modules is high, resulting in poor maintainability of the system. Once a module needs to be adjusted, it may cause a ripple effect and affect the stability of the entire system. At the same time, in terms of fee management, untimely data sharing leads to delayed information updates, which can easily result in inconsistent data; In salary management, the salary calculation standards are not flexible enough to adapt to complex and changing personnel policies; The cashier management process is cumbersome and lacks an effective risk warning mechanism [1–3].

Given the shortcomings of existing research, this article aims to design a fully functional, structurally sound, efficient, and reliable university fee and financial management system. By deeply analyzing Existing system function module coupling between high, resulting in poor maintainability of the system. Once the module needs to be adjusted, ripple effects may occur, affecting the stability of the entire system. The financial management needs of universities and adopting an advanced four-layer architecture design concept, the system is divided into a presentation layer, a business logic layer, a persistence layer, and a data layer to achieve independent operation and collaborative work of each layer, reduce the coupling degree between modules, and improve the scalability and maintainability of the system. In the design of each function module, optimize the charging module, data sharing and processing enhanced the flexibility of compensation management module, improve the cashier management module of the risk control mechanism, the rational allocation of hardware and software environment, to ensure the high-efficiency and stable operation of the system, providing strong support for the financial management of universities and promoting the development of intelligent and information-based financial management in universities.

2   Overall System Structure Design

Based on the requirements analysis of the university financial management system, this system design adopts a four-layer structure to cope with the complexity and business needs of the system. The overall structure of the system is shown in Fig. 1 [4].

1. Representation layer

The data stream receives user input information and operation instructions, such as salary query conditions or tuition payment operations, preprocesses them, and passes them to the business logic layer. The data processed by the business logic layer is received, converted into page styles, and presented to the user. The interface definition provides the user interface, such as login box, salary query input box, etc., implemented through HTML, CSS and JavaScript. The protocol uses HTTP protocol to transmit data, constructs page structure using HTML, designs CSS styles, and implements dynamic interaction using JavaScript.

2. Business logic layer

Data flow from the presentation layer receives data and instructions, according to the business functions to deal with it, calls to obtain or update data persistence layer function, and return the results to the presentation layer. Interface definition defines the interaction with the presentation layer and persistent layer interface methods, such as salary management operation interface (addEmployee, updateSalary, queryWage). The protocol and technology are written in Java language for business logic, and the Spring framework is used to implement component management and dependency injection, decoupling each layer.

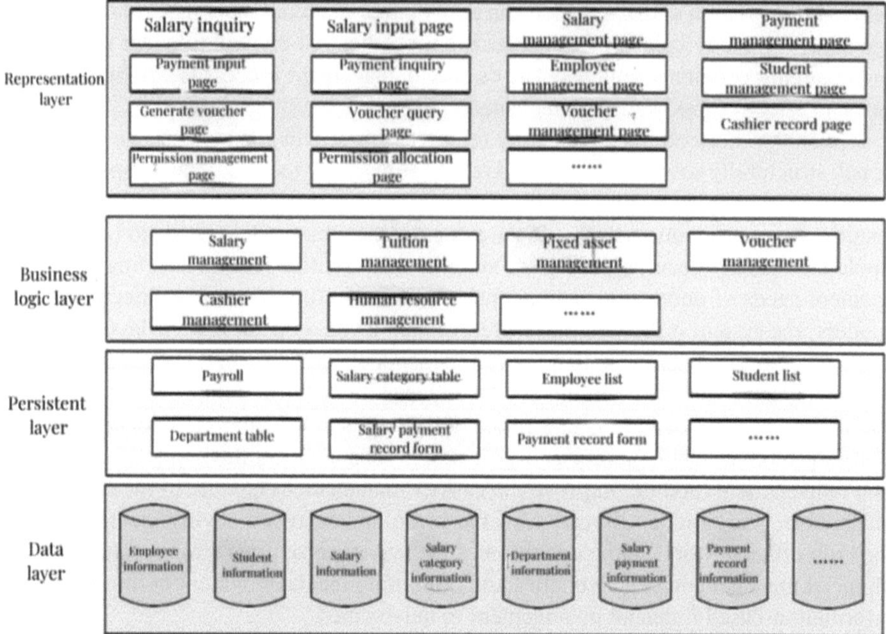

Fig. 1. Structure design of university financial management system.

3. Persistent layer

The data stream receives function calls and parameters from the business logic layer, interacts directly with the database, performs addition, deletion, query, and modification operations, and returns the results to the business logic layer. The interface definition defines the database operation interface methods, such as update, query, delete, insert. The ORM is realized by using Hibernate framework of this agreement, and connect to the database through JDBC technology, simplifies database operations.

4. Data layer

The data flow is responsible for the information access of the basic database, storing persistent layer data in corresponding tables or reading data from tables and passing it back to the persistent layer. The interface definition defines the mapping between database table structures and entity classes, such as between payroll and payroll entity classes. The protocol uses MySQL database management system to define and query data through SQL language.

3 System Function Design

3.1 Charging Module Design

The system fee module in the design of the university fee and financial management system is mainly built around student tuition fees and other expenses. In view of the difficulty in managing the payment information of nearly ten thousand students in a university, this module directly obtains the basic information of students such as name, grade, major and student ID through the data sharing mechanism with the academic system, avoiding tedious manual statistics and data entry errors. At the same time, for newly enrolled students, the function of independently adding personal information in the academic or financial system is provided to ensure the real-time and accuracy of the data [5].

The tuition management module not only manages core information such as students' payable tuition fees, paid tuition fees, and payment time, but also covers detailed records such as whether there are outstanding fees over the years, and supports changing and saving this information at any time. The tuition fee management process is shown in Fig. 2. The student management sub-module realizes the addition, deletion, modification and query of student information, providing a convenient operation interface for financial personnel. The payment input submodule is responsible for recording and registering students' newly paid fees, and sending payment information to the voucher management submodule in real time to generate electronic payment vouchers, which improves work efficiency and accuracy.

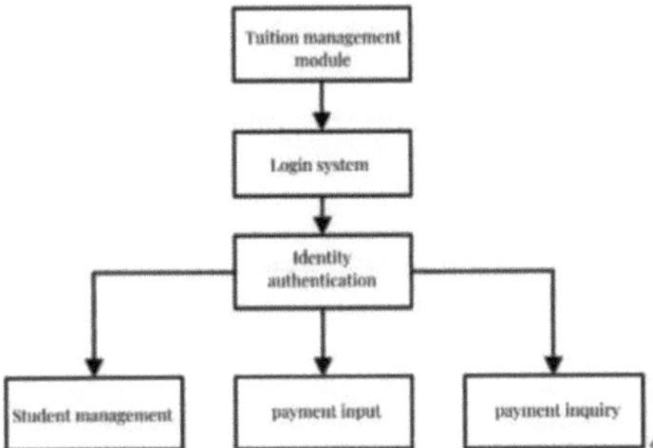

Fig. 2. Tuition management process.

The payment inquiry submodule is an important component of the tuition management module. It can not only accurately query the payment status of students, but also perform statistical analysis on the payment status of all students in the school, such as generating a list of unpaid students, providing strong support for financial decisions. In order to cope with the tedious reimbursement process and the difficulty of signing paper documents in H University, the system designed an optimization plan. By introducing OCR recognition technology, paper bills are converted into electronic files, edited and reviewed before being registered into the accounting system, and finally authenticated as electronic bills.

3.2 Salary Management Module Design

The salary management module is not only responsible for handling the personal information management of all faculty and staff in the school, but also covers many aspects such as setting, publishing and querying salary standards. In personal information management, the system should be able to store and maintain each teacher's detailed information, including but not limited to the teaching experience, working time, contact information and education background. These pieces of information are crucial for subsequent salary calculations and need to support flexible query methods to enable users to retrieve relevant information based on different criteria. In addition, considering the importance of personal privacy protection, all sensitive data should be properly stored through encryption technology to ensure that only authorized personnel can access it.

As for the formulation of salary standards, the unified guidelines issued by the state should be followed, and corresponding adjustments should be made according to the specific situation of the school. As one of the main factors affecting basic salary, the classification of job categories is mainly based on factors such as teachers' professional background, scientific research achievements, service years, and current job level [6].

The salary management process designed in this article is shown in Fig. 3. The module should include the following key sub-functions: first, employee information management, for adding, modifying or deleting specific employee files; The second is the salary input interface, where you can input the specific monthly income amount of each teacher, and support batch import and export operations; The third is the query service, which not only opens self-inspection rights for ordinary users to view salary details, but also provides management services for comprehensive data analysis, such as calculating total expenses by department; Finally, there is the editing function, which grants the user with the appropriate permissions to modify the error record.

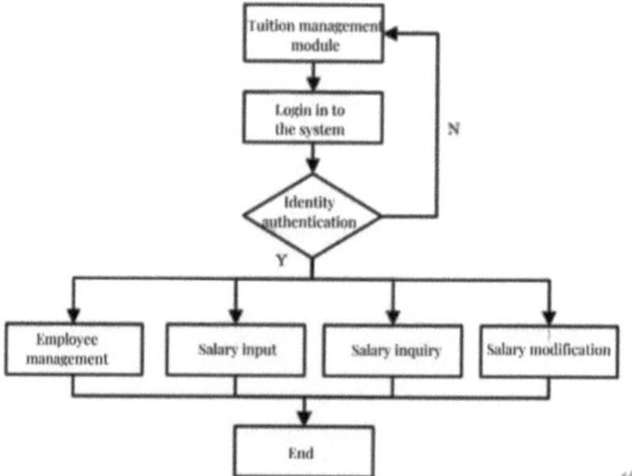

Fig. 3. Salary management process.

3.3   Cashier Management Module Design

The cashier management module is responsible for handling all transactions related to cash. The module is designed to ensure the security, compliance and efficient operation of funds, as shown in Fig. 4. First of all, the report management functions allows the system to automatically generate monthly, quarterly and annual financial reports. These reports not only reflect the school's overall financial condition, also includes teachers participate in external capital flows of the project, provide decision support for management. Secondly, check management involves registering all checks received by teachers in a unified manner and arranging dedicated personnel to go to the bank to complete the withdrawal process. This step is crucial for ensuring timely funding.

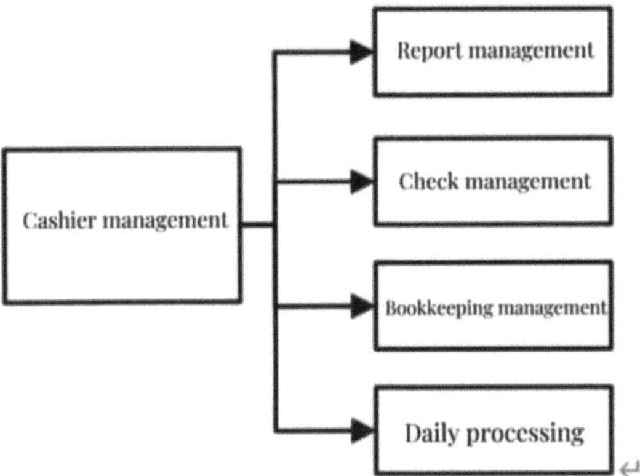

Fig. 4. Cashier management module.

As another important aspect, account management involves the establishment of detailed accounting records to track the income and expenditure of each cash transaction, including but not limited to the use of tuition fees and research grants, so that the specific amount and trend of the current cash stock can be accurately understood at all times. In addition, daily processing covers a wide range of basic operations, such as cash deposit and withdrawal, expense reimbursement approval, and stamping and authentication of relevant documents, which are essential parts of maintaining the normal operation of the institution. The entire cashier management system also integrates strict internal control mechanisms, such as a dual audit system, to ensure that every transaction complies with national laws and regulations and can effectively prevent potential financial risks. All in all, a comprehensive and detailed cashier management system, help improve the financial management of the school level, promoting the healthy and stable development of the school.

3.4 Data Transmission Encryption

In the design of university financial management systems, security is extremely critical and is mainly ensured through the following measures:

1. SSL/TLS protocol data transmission encryption

The SSL/TLS protocol constructs a secure encrypted channel between the client and server to ensure the confidentiality and integrity of data transmission. When users access the system, they first engage in an SSL/TLS handshake to negotiate encryption algorithms and key exchange methods, such as generating symmetric encryption keys using RSA or ECDHE. Then, data is encrypted and transmitted using this key to prevent theft and tampering. Taking a university in Chengdu as an example, both user login information and financial data transmission are encrypted using SSL/TLS. If a teacher checks their salary and requests encrypted transmission of data, both ends can decrypt and view it with a key to ensure security.

2. Strict user authentication and access control mechanisms

Adopting multi factor authentication, in addition to username and password, combined with SMS verification code, fingerprint recognition, etc. If financial personnel need to use the password login and message code, password must have the strength requirement, and prompted to change regularly, to prevent cracking.Use of RBAC model, for financial administrators, teachers, students, etc. Define roles and permissions. If the financial administrator can operate the core module, the permissions of teachers and students are restricted. The business logic layer verifies request permissions based on roles and resources, and rejects and prompts if they do not match.

3. System operation log security audit

Record user operation logs, including login time, operation module, content, results, and IP address. If the finance staff changes the salary data, record the details. Periodically audit and analyze logs using data mining techniques. If a login or operation exception is found, such as frequent abnormal operations or suspicious IP login within a short period of time, the system will send an alarm and notify security personnel to investigate to ensure system security and stability. These measures comprehensively guarantee the security of university financial management systems from encryption, authentication, auditing, and other aspects, ensuring their stable and reliable operation, effectively preventing various security risks, and safeguarding the security of financial data and system stability.

4 Detailed Structural Design of the System

In the process of system design, multi-dimensional factors such as hardware, software and network environment are comprehensively considered to ensure that the system can operate efficiently and has powerful data processing capabilities. As the main user group of the system is concentrated in the campus network, a large number of business data needs high processing speed, the hardware configuration of the server side must show advanced performance and powerful processing ability. From a hardware perspective, in order to meet the needs of high concurrency access and massive data processing, the server should adopt high-performance processors, large capacity memory, and high-speed storage devices. This hardware configuration ensures that the system can maintain fast response even when handling a large number of requests, effectively improving the user experience.

In terms of software, the system should adopt efficient algorithms and optimized data structures to reduce the consumption of computing resources and improve the speed of data processing. At the same time, the software should also have good scalability and compatibility, so that it can easily meet the challenges of future business growth and technological change. In addition, considering the impact of network environment on system performance, stable and reliable network connection methods should be selected, and network transmission protocols should be optimized to reduce network latency and improve data transmission efficiency. This helps ensure the stable operation of the system within the campus network, meeting users' requirements for real-time and accuracy.

In terms of hardware environment design, IBM X3850 is adopted as the core server platform of the system. The server not only integrates advanced gigabit network card, but also has excellent data processing capability and efficient data transmission rate, making it easy to handle real-time processing and transmission tasks of massive data. Even under extreme system pressure or high concurrency access, it can still maintain efficient and stable operation, ensuring business continuity and data integrity.

In addition, the design of IBM X3850 fully considers the needs of future technological development, demonstrating high scalability and flexibility. This means that with the expansion of business scale or new requirements brought by technological progress, users can easily upgrade and expand existing systems without worrying about compatibility issues, effectively extending the service life of the system and reducing long-term operation and maintenance costs. At the same time, its outstanding performance in reliability, including redundant power supply design, hot swappable components, and fault warning mechanisms, provides strong guarantees for the continuous and stable operation of the system, and lays a solid foundation for future system maintenance and upgrade work.

In terms of software environment configuration, this system adopts MySQL as the core database management system, and the database code design is shown in Fig. 5. To further optimize the user experience and improve work efficiency, the Windows server 2010 operating system is installed on both the server and all client computers. This server specific operating system launched by Microsoft integrates the most cutting-edge technological achievements at that time and supports multiple communication protocol standards including TCP/IP and HTTP, which enables it to seamlessly integrate various types of applications and services, greatly enhancing the flexibility and compatibility of the system.

```python
import mysql.connector

# Connect to database
mydb = mysql.connector.connect(
    host="localhost",
    user="your_username",
    password="your_password",
    database="university_finance"
)

mycursor = mydb.cursor()

# Create student table (example)
mycursor.execute("""
CREATE TABLE IF NOT EXISTS students (
    student_id INT AUTO_INCREMENT PRIMARY KEY,
    student_name VARCHAR(255),
    grade INT,
    major VARCHAR(255),
    tuition_due DECIMAL(10, 2),
    tuition_paid DECIMAL(10, 2),
    payment_date DATE
)
""")

# Insert student data
sql = "INSERT INTO students (student_name, grade, major, tuition_due,
tuition_paid, payment_date) VALUES (%s, %s, %s, %s, %s, %s)"
val = ("John Doe", 3, "Computer Science", 5000.00, 2000.00, "2023-09-15")
mycursor.execute(sql, val)
mydb.commit()

# Query student data
mycursor.execute("SELECT * FROM students")
result = mycursor.fetchall()
for row in result:
    print(row)

# Update student payment information
sql = "UPDATE students SET tuition_paid = %s WHERE student_name = %s"
val = (3000.00, "John Doe")
mycursor.execute(sql, val)
mydb.commit()

# Delete student data (example, proceed with caution)
sql = "DELETE FROM students WHERE student_name = %s"
val = ("John Doe",)
mycursor.execute(sql, val)
mydb.commit()

# Close connection
mycursor.close()
mydb.close()
```

Fig. 5. Database code design.

In order to maintain consistency and compatibility with the existing operating system of the school, the network connection and antivirus software configuration of this system follow the unified standards and system within the school, without separate processing or settings. By adopting unified network security measures and anti-virus strategies in the school, external threats and internal risks can be effectively resisted, and data security and integrity in the financial management system can be protected. Second, the design simplifies the system maintenance and management. Due to consistency with the existing system of the school, it is possible to more efficiently utilize the school's existing resources and support services during system upgrades, patch updates, and daily maintenance, reducing additional workload and maintenance costs. In addition, this integration method also helps to improve the coordination and efficiency of the overall

IT environment, enabling better collaboration between various systems and providing users with a smoother and more convenient user experience.

5   System Testing Results

After a comprehensive system test, our tuition and financial management system has shown corresponding effectiveness in all stages. In the module testing phase, each module is tested according to user requirements, and the test results are shown in the table. Test scenarios were set for common data types with critical values, and the system output results were basically consistent with expectations, demonstrating good stability and fault tolerance (Table 1).

Table 1. Testing results.

Test examples	Testing procedure	Testing results
System login	Enter account and password to log in to the system	The system is running normally
Staff management	Add, modify, and delete personnel information	The system is running normally
Salary management	Add, modify, and delete salary information	The system is running normally
Invoicing	Enter information and issue an invoice	The system is running normally
Financial inquiry	Income and expenditure query, check if the structure is correct	The system is running normally
Exit	System exits normally	The system is running normally

6   Conclusion

This study successfully designed a university tuition and financial management system, which is based on a four-layer structure, including a presentation layer, business logic layer, persistence layer, and data layer. Each layer has a clear division of labor and cooperation, which effectively realizes modularity and hierarchical decoupling, and improves the maintainability and scalability of the system. In terms of function design, the charging module obtains student information through data sharing with the academic system, optimizes the payment process, and provides query and statistical functions; The salary management module covers employee information management, salary standard setting and salary inquiry, etc., while taking into account personal privacy protection and flexible inquiry needs; The cashier management module ensures the safety, compliance, and efficient operation of funds, integrates report management, check management, reconciliation management, and daily processing functions, and has strict internal control mechanisms.

In the system design process, fully consider hardware, software, and network environment factors. The system test results show that both the functionality and performance have reached the predetermined goals, the interface is friendly, the permission management is effective, the multi module data processing is accurate, and it exhibits good response speed, stability, and reliability when simulating multi-user access.

Future research could further deepen the functions of the system, such as enhancing data analysis capabilities to provide a more accurate basis for university financial decisions; Optimize the integration of the system with other campus systems to improve the overall level of campus information management; Continue to pay attention to the development of network security technology, and constantly strengthen the data security protection capability of the system to adapt to the growing financial management needs of colleges and universities and the complex and changing environment.

Acknowledgments. This work was supported by the Provincial Project on Teaching Reform Research in Higher Education Institutions in Jiangxi Province under [JXJG-22-51-9].

References

1. Haiyan, W.: Research on the informationization of financial management in higher education institutions under the digital background. China Manag. Inform. **26**(19), 69–72 (2023)
2. Haoming, W., Feng, Y.: The application of management accounting in financial management of universities. Cont. Bridge View (11), 84–86 (2022)
3. Yan, S.: Construction of university financial management system based on SWOT analysis. Shanghai Manag. Sci. **45**(04), 120–125 (2023)
4. Shujing, L.: Reflections on the application of management accounting in university financial management. Market Outlook (14), 48–50 (2023)
5. Huazhi, D.: A brief analysis of the design and practice of intelligent financial management system in colleges and universities. J. Zhejiang Voc. Tech. College Comm. **22** (01), 88–92 (2023)
6. Runling, Z.: Exploration into the optimization of financial information management processes in higher education institutions in the Era of "Big Intelligence Moving Cloud". Financ. Econ. (08), 134–136 (2023)

Envisioning the Futures of Digital Provisioning Platforms for Sustainable Consumption in Mobility and Food

Hakan Yılmazer, Sumru Deniz, and Aykut Coşkun

Koç University-Arçelik Research Center for Creative Industries, 34450 İstanbul, Turkey
{hyilmazer18,aykutcoskun}@ku.edu.tr

Abstract. Digital platforms offer substantial potential for sustainable consumption. Ridesharing platforms facilitate the sharing of rides, providing a convenient and cost-effective alternative to personal car usage. This reduction in personal car usage contributes to the mitigation of carbon dioxide emissions associated with mobility. Surplus food platforms facilitate the redistribution of surplus food, thereby addressing food waste. However, the utilization of these platforms in food and mobility provision does not necessarily guarantee these benefits. Furthermore, as they transform and disrupt existing consumption models, they may inadvertently lead to unintended consequences, such as increased consumption. Design fiction serves as an appropriate methodology to explore the potential benefits and drawbacks of Digital Provisioning Platforms (DPP) and their implications for sustainable consumption. In this paper, we present four food and mobility DPP fictions that address various aspects of sustainable consumption in food and mobility (i.e., Yesil Yarınlar, Mom-AI, Road Buddies, and Communa). These fictions were developed through two design fiction workshops conducted with 12 participants. Their reflections on these fictions revealed several tension points, which we categorized into three areas: Scalability and Impact, Cultural and Social Dimensions of Platforms, and Potential Rebound Effects on Sustainability. While presenting an alternative future for digital food and mobility DPP through design fictions, our work serves as a valuable resource for the design of new DPP in these domains.

Keywords: Digital Provisioning Platforms (DPP) · Sustainable Consumption · Food · Mobility · Design Fiction

1 Introduction

Sustainable consumption practices such as ride-sharing and purchasing locally produced food have become an important consideration in our daily lives. Various technological interventions have emerged recently to help users follow such practices. Being one of these interventions, Digital Provision Platforms (DPP) provide technology-enabled exchange systems that facilitate interactions between producers (e.g. farmers) and consumers, connecting the latter with resources, services, or products while promoting sustainable and local consumption practices.

F. F.-H Nah and K. L. Siau (Eds.): HCII 2025, LNCS 16343, pp. 365–387, 2026.
https://doi.org/10.1007/978-3-032-13167-6_25

In the context of food provision, allowing a direct connection between producers and consumers promotes the use and awareness of local produce and the mitigation of waste that emerges from logistics chains or over-consumption. For example, platforms like REKO-rings [18] aim to reduce the environmental impact of food logistics by providing digital store-fronts for local producers and cooperatives to reach consumers. Similarly, platforms like Too Good To Go [48] aim to minimize food waste by allowing consumers to purchase unsold food at discounted prices, which would otherwise be discarded. These initiatives are contributing to a more circular food economy, improving the sustainability of food systems.

Similarly, DPP that focus on urban mobility aim to decrease the environmental impact of transportation, by the means of promoting eco-friendly options. For instance, platforms offering alternative transportation options, such as Lime [49], provide micro-mobility solutions like e-scooters, which have been shown to reduce car dependency, lowering greenhouse gas emissions in urban areas [20]. Additionally, platforms like BlaBlaCar [50] offer ride-sharing services, providing a middle ground between traditional public transport and private car ownership. These services help decrease the number of private vehicles on the road, leading to less congestion, lower emissions, and better urban air quality [24].

While there are studies that focus on the environmental and societal impact of these platforms, there might be unintended consequences from the services they provide that hinder their effectiveness. For example, several cities banned the use of e-scooters upon the rising number of injuries and fatalities including Paris, London, and Melbourne [9, 16, 36]. Surplus food platforms often sell surplus meals at a lower price. However, recent research shows that though such applications can reduce food waste, this effect can be offset by the rebound effects; people tend to buy more when food prices are lower [15]. Furthermore, though purchasing surplus food boxes at discount prices can help tackle food waste and help consumers save money, being unaware of a box's content harms their shopping experience [21].

One of the ways to foresee and mitigate these unintended consequences is futuring [8]. Future narratives allow the exploration of potential benefits and hazards of a system by creating fictive scenarios that amplify the impact of these benefits or hazards. One of the methods in creating future narratives is design fiction [7, 31], which uses storytelling and prototyping to envision scenarios that anticipate the impact of emerging technologies and how they can transform society. Using future narratives can help identify potential flaws in DPP and allow adjustments to ensure they more effectively align with long-term sustainability goals. In the literature, there are very few studies that use these methods to analyze and reflect on the use of digital technologies for promoting sustainable behaviors. To the best of our knowledge, no study has explored food and mobility DPP through design fiction.

This paper presents the results of a study in which four design fictions for DPP in mobility and food were created to discuss their potential implications on food and mobility-related consumption practices. The fictions focused on the city of Istanbul, Turkey. With a population of 15.7 million [45], the city exhibits unique urban challenges and opportunities, serving as an ideal setting for exploring the impact of digital tools on sustainable consumption. The residents are increasingly turning to technology to make more sustainable food and mobility choices [6]. There have been various food and mobility apps created for sustainable consumption, responding to a growing cultural and institutional push towards environmental responsibility.

We conducted two workshops with 12 participants within the scope of an international research project, SSCP2022 Belmont Forum, which aims to examine the impact of DPP on sustainable consumption in food and mobility practices. During the workshops, working in groups of three, the participants created future narratives based on their personal experiences and societal, technological, and legislative trends, as well as four DPP concepts that are situated in these narratives. We later turned these concepts into DPP fictions, which were presented to the participants to gather insights into their implications on mobility and food practices. In this paper, we present these design fictions and discuss key issues that should be considered for the design of future DPP based on the workshop results and insights gathered from our participants. These key issues (i.e., Scalability and Impact, Cultural and Social Dimensions of the Platforms, and the Possible Rebound Effects on Sustainability) reveal how DPPs could reshape consumption patterns by fostering community engagement, promoting responsible food choices and encouraging more sustainable mobility behaviors. Our analysis contributes to a deeper understanding of how DPP can be designed to support sustainable practices while addressing the challenges that may hinder their long-term effectiveness, such as platform misuse or unintended consequences, highlighting the need for evaluating the interaction between these platforms and the communities they serve.

2 Related Work

2.1 Digital Platforms for Encouraging Sustainable Consumption in Food and Mobility Domains

Food and mobility play a significant role in environmental degradation. While food production contributes a substantial share of global greenhouse gas emissions, accounting for approximately 26% [28], with food loss and waste accounting for %8–10 [42], vehicles, particularly cars, and vans, contribute around 10% of global CO_2 emissions [47].

Food and mobility practices are dynamic; we have recently witnessed many changes in the way we produce, purchase, cook, and eat food, as well as how we move in the city. During and after the COVID-19 pandemic, various digital platforms have been introduced to the market, connecting consumers with service providers in food (e.g., purchasing food online) and mobility (calling a taxi or planning a trip). We call such platforms Digital Provisioning Platforms (DPP), which refer to systems that provide technology-enabled exchange systems to facilitate interactions and transactions between producers and consumers, promoting sustainable and local consumption practices.

Among these platforms, some stood out with their ambition to address the environmental impact of food and mobility practices. For example, in the food sector, platforms like Too Good to Go [48] redistribute surplus food or enable users to purchase unsold items at discounted prices. Similarly, Good Eggs [51] encourages local food consumption to promote sustainability. Previous work has recognized the effectiveness of these platforms in addressing food waste [2, 19, 27]. In the mobility sector, ride-sharing apps like

BlaBlaCar [50] and bike-sharing/scooter systems like Lime [49] aim to reduce personal car dependency and promote shared transportation. These platforms connect passengers and drivers based on shared routes, with more advanced platforms optimizing routes using real-time traffic data to enhance efficiency [33]. In short, by facilitating cooperation between producers and consumers, they connect users with resources, services, or products in ways that minimize waste [17, 19, 23], help lower carbon emissions, reduce resource consumption, and engage communities in sustainable practices [29].

While the food and mobility sectors have been populated with DPP that have various business models, and there are studies focusing on the environmental impact of these platforms, the literature lacks studies that explore their potential future implications (e.g., unintended consequences like encouraging over-purchase of food), and how they can be reconsidered in light of recent technological, societal, economic and political changes.

2.2 Using Design Fiction to Explore Digital Technologies for Supporting Sustainable Consumption in Food and Mobility

Design fiction uses creative storytelling and speculative design to explore possible futures, not by predicting what will happen but by crafting tangible glimpses into what could happen. Through the development of prototypes, videos, fictional artifacts, and alike, this method aims to spark critical discussion about the impact of technology and social trends.

Design fiction has been recognized as an important tool in various fields, including but not limited to HCI, Design, and Business. Gomez-Corona et al. [11] emphasize the significance of design fiction and speculation for studying consumer behavior and suggest that they guide discussions about technological innovations, ethical issues, and consumption behaviors. This method is not only valuable for discussing the potential implications of emerging technologies but also for creating a strategic vision for companies [34].

There are several studies at the intersection of digital technologies and sustainability consumption in relation to food and mobility practices. For example, Hebrok and Mainsah [14] explored how design fiction can provoke discussions about sustainable food futures by creating a fictional service called "Bird", which was designed to align dietary choices with personal ambitions in health and aesthetics. In another work, Oogjes et al. [26] proposed "Lyssna," a design fiction that generates unique sounds for different food items, which change over time, reflecting their freshness and encouraging cooking creativity, and discussed how it can influence domestic food practices to reduce waste. Furthermore, Ballie and Bruce [3] created three design fictions for sustainable mobility (i.e., The digital Twin of Dundee city, Community Hubs for Smart Cities, and 20 min Neighborhoods) and gathered insights from citizens on the future of mobility practices through Design Imaginariums (i.e., collaborative spaces that facilitate creative problem-solving and active citizen involvement).

Despite this interest in using design fiction and speculative design, there has been no attempt to explore the future of DPP with sustainability goals, i.e., how these technologies would shape and shaped by future mobility and food practices.

2.3 Food and Mobility DPP from the Turkish Context

Both food production and mobility practices in Turkey have a significant environmental impact. Being the second most resource-intensive sector, food production is responsible for the largest carbon footprint [1]. Furthermore, household food waste in Turkey was 8.7 million tons per year, according to UN FAO's Food Waste Index Report [42]. As for mobility, with 30 million commutes a day, transportation accounts for 28% of the total CO_2 emissions of Istanbul, the largest city in Turkey. 31.6% of commuters rely on private vehicles and shuttles [39]. These statistics indicate problems that could be addressed by DPP, such as ride-sharing apps, surplus food platforms or local food provisioning platforms.

In fact, within the last decade, several DPP operating in food and mobility domains have been introduced. An example of a food DPP is Fazla [52], which brings together consumers and food provisioning companies (retailers, restaurants, distributors) through its mobile app. Consumers can buy surplus food from these companies at discounted prices. Another DPP in food is Yenir [53], which sells products nearing their best-before dates at discounted prices through online channels and physical stores. An example of mobility DPP is Martı [54], a super mobility app that provides multiple transportation services to its users., such as ride-sharing, e-scooters, and e-bikes. Aside from these local initiatives, there are global platforms that also offer services in Turkey. One such example is BlaBlaCar [50], which connects drivers and passengers traveling to similar destinations through a mobile app.

In the last few years, there have been multiple developments that could present some challenges but also provide some opportunities for the operation of DPP in Turkey. Starting with mobility, recent reports showed that the number of personal vehicles administered, especially motorcycles, has increased compared to 2023 [44]. Similarly, due to the need for a driver's license, while using motorcycles (and electric variants) that are below certain power is lifted, the possibility for consumers to use these variants more in the future has increased [40]. These trends indicate that emissions associated with personal vehicle usage will continue to be a major problem for major cities like Istanbul. In addition, some municipalities and various institutions have been trying to improve the city's sustainability with their actions. Local municipalities transition to electric-powered buses [43], and institutions' campaigns about awareness, such as WRI Sustainable Cities Network Turkey's project with the aim of using bicycles for collecting urban waste, help adapt these practices to the daily lives of Istanbul citizens [37]. These developments provide a fertile ground for mobility DPP to develop further. However, there have also been instances where such a development could be hindered. For instance, there isn't still active legislation for ride-sharing apps in Turkey, despite the efforts of platform owners [41]. The tension between taxi drivers and drivers of ride-sharing platforms further makes the operation of these ridesharing DPP problematic.

In food practices, digital platforms that allow consumers to order food online have been around for more than 10 years in Turkey. The usage of these platforms significantly increased during the pandemic, and this increase persists [13]. For example, 47.5% ordered deliveries from restaurants, fast food chains, and catering companies, while 34% purchased food products in the first quarter of 2024 [38]. Furthermore, Turkish consumers have started to adopt healthier and special eating habits [55], and nutrition brands have started to include more products with healthier components [46]. This is mainly due to achieving a wider market reach; even so, it also raises more awareness among consumers, indicating a consumer base that is prone to choose products with "green" aspects. On the other hand, although online shopping has increased, 80% of consumers still prefer to purchase food in person, choosing items by seeing and selecting them directly, especially when selecting fresh produce, fish, and meat in-store [55]. Furthermore, while there is a tendency to consume healthy, local, and sustainable food, consumers are still not so much interested in learning more about the quality of these foods since reading the packaging has decreased over the years [10, 12].

While the number of food and mobility DPP are increasing in Turkey, their wider adoption is still slow, hindering their sustainability potential. Consequently, we believe it is imperative to explore the future of these platforms to comprehend their potential applications and facilitate their seamless integration of sustainable practices into daily routines. In short, Turkey emerges as a pertinent case study for DPP, as it presents the opportunity to adapt these platforms amidst a diverse set of challenges.

3 Methodology

In this study, we explored the futures of food and mobility DPP in Turkey through two design fiction workshops. We conducted the workshops on August 1, 2024 and Sep 30, 2024 with 12 participants. The workshops were organized within the scope of an international research project supported under the Belmont Forum SSCP framework (https://uni.oslomet.no/disco-project/). In the first phase of this project, in-depth interviews were conducted with 60 users of DPP in food and mobility. The workshop invitations were sent to individuals who participated in these interviews. Since the workshops involved the task of creating fictions, the research team has extended these invitations to designers and design researchers from their own network, prioritizing the ones with previous experience in using DPPs (See Table 1 for participant details). In each workshop, there were two groups, one working on the food DPP and the other on mobility DPP. Each group included three participants, one moderator, and one note-taker/image creator. The authors' university email directory, daily event list, and authors' social media circles were used to recruit participants.

Table 1. Participant Details.

Workshop	Theme	Participant ID	Gender	Age	Occupation
1	Food	1	Female	27	Design researcher
1	Food	2	Female	25	Design researcher
1	Food	3	Female	25	Industrial Designer
1	Mobility	4	Female	28	Design Researcher
1	Mobility	5	Female	33	Design researcher
1	Mobility	6	Male	28	Design researcher
2	Food	7	Male	44	Service Designer
2	Food	8	Female	28	Housewife
2	Food	9	Female	27	Designer
2	Mobility	10	Female	42	Service Designer
2	Mobility	11	Male	23	Undergraduate Student
2	Mobility	12	Male	34	Manager

The design fiction workshops lasted approximately 3,5 h. They were conducted online in Zoom [56] and by using templates prepared in Miro [57], an online collaboration platform [The Miro templates can be accessed via the following anonymous link: https://osf.io/exafr/?view_only=84bf4b31eeeb4ace9c0af07327369a84]. The workshop had five phases: Familiarization and synthesis of signals and drivers, Exploration of impacts across different scales and scopes, Envisioning potential futures, and Reflecting on the DPP fictions. While the first four phases were conducted synchronously, the last phase was done asynchronously.

Phase 1: Familiarization and Synthesis of Signals and Drivers (45 min). This phase is designed to familiarize the participants with the concept of DPP, drivers and signals, and local trends that might influence the future of these platforms. Drivers refer to broader technological trends, social changes, environmental trends, and political tendencies such as 'aging population,' 'digital divide,' 'climate change,' or 'artificial intelligence.' Signals refer to specific and distinct events that anticipate changes in the current situation, such as the launch of ChatGPT or legislation against banning scooters. local trends refer to new legislations, changes in consumer behavior, political events, and campaigns that happen in the local context and that might influence how individuals use DPP in their consumption practices. Signals, drivers, and trends were determined through desk research. In this phase, participants start reading the drivers, signals, and local trends we identified, as well as discussing and taking note of their own experiences with food and mobility DPP. During this phase, the participants were also invited to share their own observations and insights into how DPP are used in the local context.

Phase 2: Exploration of Impacts Across Different Scales and Scopes (45 min). In the second phase, the participants were asked to think about the potential implications of drivers, signals, and the local trends on sustainable consumption in mobility and food across various scales of change (i.e., individual/household, neighborhood, city and country) and various impact categories (i.e., economical, societal, environmental, political, and technological). They used a mandala template to map potential implications. Each participant individually wrote down the implications they would think of and then discussed them with the group.

Phase 3: Envisioning Potential Futures (60 min). In this phase, the participants were asked to choose one chain of trends/drivers and their implications from the mandala template and start creating a desired future narrative, i.e., how they imagine the future of DPP in light of drivers, signals, trends and their implications on consumption practices in food and mobility. They were also encouraged to think about the possible barriers or facilitators they could face to bring out this desired narrative. We told them to choose a year that is about 5–10 years into the future to create this narrative. The reason was to let them speculate about the possible futures of the DPP without being too concerned about the present issues (technical challenges, legislations, etc.) and to prevent them from creating scenarios for too-distant futures. During this stage, as the facilitators, we used generative AI tools (i.e., Midjourney [58]) to create images of the topics they were discussing to spark their imaginations and help them solidify their narrative in their minds. After the creation of the narrative, they were asked to create a how might we question (HMW) to create ideas that can help reach this desired future.

Phase 4: Defining, Ideating, and Refining Concepts (60 min). This phase followed the flow of a typical ideation process where participants created personas, scenarios, and ideas as a response to their HMW question linked to their desired future. During the idea generation, they first individually created ideas and then engaged in a group discussion where they selected compelling and relevant ones. At the End of This Phase, They Were Asked to Refine Their Ideas into one concept to present the description of the concept, its core features, how these features are implemented, and key stakeholders that influence and are influenced by it.

Phase 5: Reflecting on the DPP Fictions. The concepts created in the previous phase were transformed into design fictions by the research team[1]. The sources of the fictions included the concept descriptions presented at the end of previous phase, participants' discussions during the entire session and the notes of the research team. The process was also iterative: right after the second author created a fiction, it was discussed among the research team, identifying inconsistencies and helping refine the fictions further. During this phase, we used generative AI tools (i.e., Midjourney [58]) to create the scenarios for each concept, and to create supportive visuals to communicate the core ideas and features better. Each fiction contains the background scenario outlining why and how it addresses the user needs, a description of core features, and their positive and negative implications. These design fictions were later put into a separate Miro file, and presented to the participants, allowing them to read and comment on all fictions created from the workshops. This way, it was possible to get feedback from all the

---

[1] While preparing the fictions, the authors paid special attention to reflecting the ideas generated by the participants as much as possible. Furthermore, we would like to clarify that the design fictions presented in this paper do not represent the authors' conceptions of DPP; rather, they are re-interpretations of what participants created within the workshop..

participants about all the fictions. During this post-workshop phase, the participants were asked to consider the following questions when they reflect on each fiction: what would be the implications of this design fiction for our mobility/food consumption practices? How would it influence our relationship with food/mobility? what would be the implications for the food/mobility system in the local context? what would be the unexpected consequences of this design fiction? Participants' answers to these questions were analyzed by the authors, using affinity diagramming, i.e., grouping them according to their thematic proximity and identifying the relationship between different groups.

4 Fictions

As a result of the workshops, four fictions, two for food and two for mobility, were created. The food provisioning fictions were called Yeşil Yarınlar and Mom AI. The former is a platform aimed at bringing consumers and producers together while encouraging consumers to become producers themselves and learn food production practices through interacting with farmers. The latter fiction is an AI assistant aimed at helping consumers decide the best food for their body, allowing them to follow a personalized diet and facilitating decision-making when they feel uncertain about food-related decisions.

The mobility provisioning fictions were RoadBuddies and Communa. Both fictions were focused on creating a community around ridesharing. While the former aims to do this by allowing riders to customize their scooters and wearable accessories (e.g., helmets), the latter aims to do so by reward systems and matching riders according to their preferences.

During the workshops, we observed that while the participants started thinking about the current and future state of DPP, which was in line with our initial framing of the workshop, they discussed broader issues pertaining to the way we produce, distribute, cook, and eat food as well as the way we commute in the city for work and leisure. In other words, the participants did not feel obliged to create ideas for future DPP; rather, they explored how digital technologies could support future consumption practices in the food and mobility domain. Thus, the fictions created in the workshops reflect this approach.

The remainder of this section presents each of these fictions in detail, describing a baseline scenario, the core features, and their positive and negative implications. [A high-resolution of the images of the fictions can be accessed via the following link: https://osf.io/exafr/?view_only=84bf4b31eeeb4ace9c0af07327369a84].

4.1 Food Fiction 1: Yeşil Yarınlar

Yeşil Yarınlar is a service that brings people who want to grow their own produce and local farmers together in the hard reality surrounding food in the speculative future of 2028. Consuming sustainable and healthy food has become vital for consumers. However, due to the cost of producing such food, the prices of "authentic" organic food have skyrocketed. In the harvesting land, surplus food increases as the farmers find it difficult to sell their produce. However, even with this surplus, as the income gap increases, there are many who cannot access healthy and organic food. This creates a setting where food prices have gone up significantly, whereas nutritional value plummets. Meanwhile, because of the advancements in technology, people also become more digitally literate, encouraging many to search for the real nutritional value of the food they are consuming. Still, as the misinformation about the quality of food increases, they struggle to make a decision when buying food.

In this nutrition-scarce, high-price food crisis, Yeşil Yarınlar tries to create a community and make eating healthy in this climate easier (Fig. 1). The service has both physical and digital components to promote a sustainable lifestyle. Its starting kit helps city residents gain momentum in growing their own fruits and vegetables by giving them the necessities they need in an apartment. Also, Yeşil Yarınlar's mobile application connects consumers with primary producers to ensure the quality of the produce if they want to buy from the local farmers, as well as creating a mentor-mentee relationship between people with no experience trying to grow their produce and local farmers who have been doing this professionally for years.

Yeşil Yarınlar also aims to strengthen trust, build a community, and strengthen local economies. To spread these aims to a bigger audience, the urban agriculture magazine called EkoYaşam published an article about Yeşil Yarınlar in one of their volumes. This article explains the innovative and easy way for Yeşil Yarınlar to produce at the comfort of home (Fig. 1, left top corner). Meanwhile, sustainability influencers who are very popular in 2028, share their own experiences with Yeşil Yarınlar and try to promote it by showing how easy it is for them to grow vegetables and fruits (Fig. 1, right upper corner). While this helps the platform to attract new consumers, it also triggered some concerns for both existing consumers and producers who believe that the expansion of the user group to non-enthusiasts could risk the community feeling nurtured by the platform. Other users also share their own experience of Yeşil Yarınlar on a forum that they created called YeşilDostlar (Fig. 1, bottom). Apart from the service's own connection of mentor-mentees, in YeşilDostlar website, all users share tips, ask questions, and explain their own experiences.

Fig. 1. The components of Yeşil Yarınlar, a service to connect consumers with producers.

4.2 Food Fiction 2: Mom AI

In the year 2035, AI has almost been fully integrated with every part of daily life. In the food domain, as people have been concerned about health, sustainability, and food waste, highly customized AI companions are on the rise. One of these technologies is Mom AI. It is a context-aware and personalized wearable product that knows the user's preferences, dislikes, and needs regarding food, even in some cases better than the user's. It promotes healthy living by seamless integration into the users' daily lives, monitoring what they eat, and predicting the body's nutritional needs. By perfectly matching the users' nutritional needs and food options, it also aims to prevent food waste that occurs due to expectation mismatch in palate and portion size. It has an "inner voice" feature where Mom AI can get context clues and help them make food-related decisions.

After its initial release, three additional types of Mom AI have been created (Fig. 2, top). The first one is the Basic Mom AI, which has all the aforementioned features, making it suitable for daily use. The second version is the Mobile Mom AI, which has additional features for people with visual or tactile impairments to make it easier to adapt Mom AI to their everyday lives. The third one is the Gourmet Mom AI, which has multiple semi- or full-professional features for users who want to increase their cooking and tasting abilities or enjoy high-quality recipes. The last one is the Deluxe Mom AI, which has more technological features and is fitted for bigger families.

However, despite the benefits of facilitating healthy and sustainable food choices, Mom AI has triggered some concerns. For some users, personalization comes with the cost of violation of their privacy. One concerned user discusses this issue on their blog, explaining that they used it but then noticed how much of their personal data is actually going in so that the AI could work efficiently. They express their concerns on the topic of data security of Mom AI (Fig. 2, bottom).

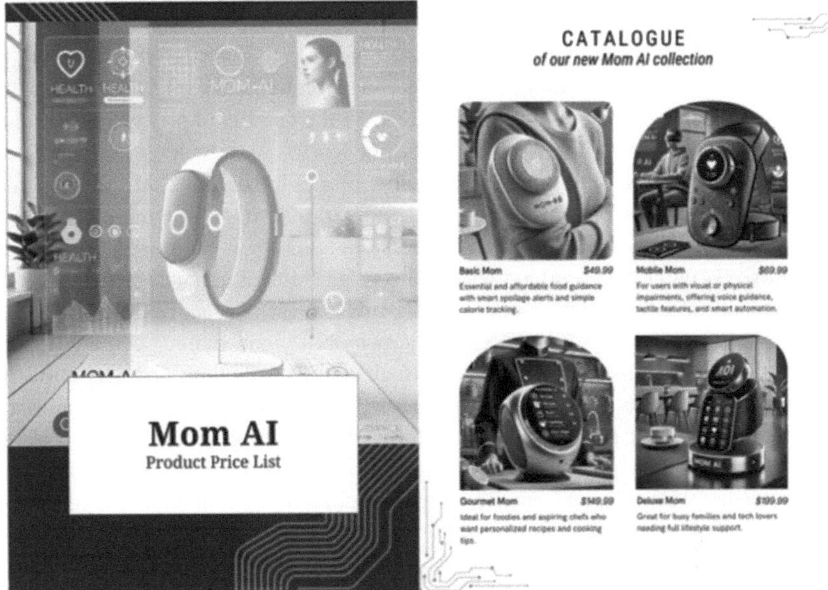

Mom AI Product Catalogue

A blog entry about Mom AI

Fig. 2. The components of Mom-AI, an AI-supported assistant for food decision-making.

4.3 Mobility Fiction 1: RoadBuddies

Istanbul in 2030 has more than its fair share of traffic problems due to increasing population and infrastructural problems. People choose individual cars rather than sharing them due to the lack of trust in the communities. As the number of private cars continued increasing, the city's mobility problem only got worse. As a remedy to this problem, some citizens of Istanbul rediscovered the potential of ride-sharing platforms and micro-mobility solutions. However, they later remembered that this on-demand practice also came with its downsides, such as security concerns (e.g., being exposed to harassment by other drivers and riders) and hygiene issues (e.g., riding a used scooter). These challenges opened up a space for a new ride-sharing platform. RoadBuddies is designed to create a community of riders who use micro-mobility and shared scooters in certain parts of the city. Just like Yeşil Yarınlar, RoadBuddies uses both physical and digital components to achieve its goal. It promotes wearables such as helmets or glasses to ensure the rider's security and to build the foundation of the community into a physical object. In the mobile application, users can find people who live in a close vicinity and travel the same route to spend time together and combat the mundaneness of everyday life.

To support the effect of RoadBuddies and overcome its possible hygiene problem, the company offered a complementary solution, ScootShield, which is a sanitization spray for shared scooters (Fig. 3, left). Additionally, RideCharms comes into the picture in order for users to express themselves while in this community (Fig. 3, right). With RideCharms, anyone can find items such as stickers or attachable charms to their wearables to express their styles and show their belonging to a specific rider community. This way, riders can even find people whose style is similar to them. With the help of ScootShield and RideCharms, RoadBuddies' turns mobility into a whole experience rather than trying to get to a destination.

4.4 Mobility Fiction 2: Communa

In the year 2035, after a decade of stagflation, the economy of the country has relatively recovered, and employment rates have started to increase. People find it very hard to own their personal cars as the prices are quite high. Another problem is that people who already own personal cars find it difficult to maintain them. This created a demand for car-sharing. As the owners of the cars found it as another source to maintain their cars, people who couldn't afford them had an easier way of transportation. Of course, the problems of trust and lack of security in car-sharing practices continue.

Within such a setting, Communa has been introduced to the market as a car-sharing service to address the increasing need for a trustworthy and innovative car-sharing experience. It aims to provide a safe platform for ridesharing, encouraging this sustainable practice by awarding points to users based on their reduced carbon footprints. Also, in a crowded city like Istanbul, Communa has a goal of building a community to create a safe space for riders and drivers.

Fig. 3. The components of RoadBuddies, a ride-sharing platform for community building.

Although the reward systems of Communa motivated many individuals to participate in car-sharing (both as a rider and driver), in time, they have realized that there are also ways to earn these points without committing to sustainability actions. On the application's review page, some users have commented on how easy it is to benefit from this point system without fully committing to the app's aims (Fig. 4, bottom). Another concerned user also shares her point of view on the safety of Communa. She explains that there might be leaks through the playlist feature of the app relating to her location, bringing light to the data security issue (Fig. 4, top right). These concerns show that Communa needs to improve its systems to protect user data and make sure the points system supports its goals. Fixing these issues can help build trust and create a safer, more reliable community as they have intended from the beginning.

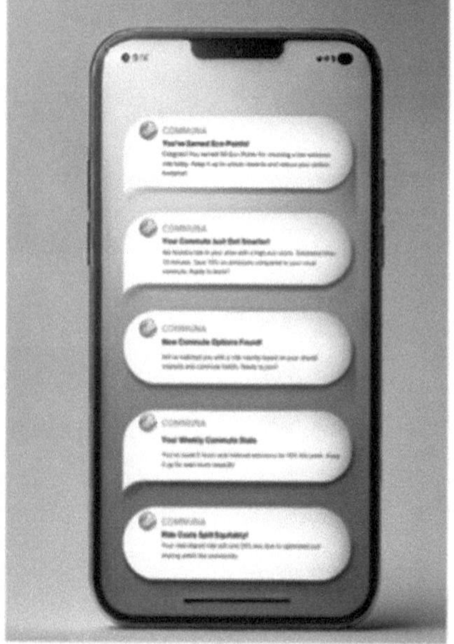

Notifications of Communa

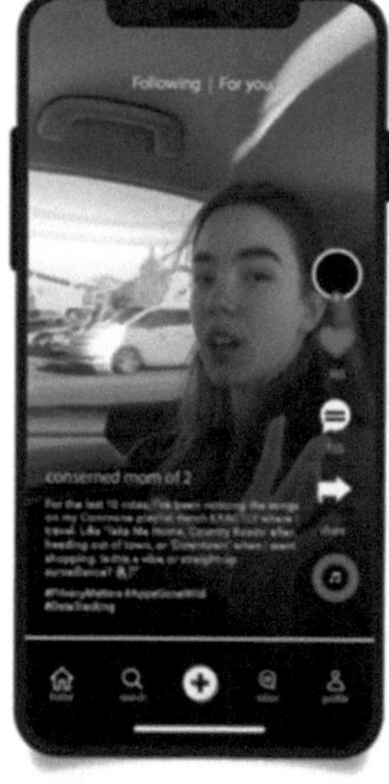

A user of Communa expressing concerns on social media

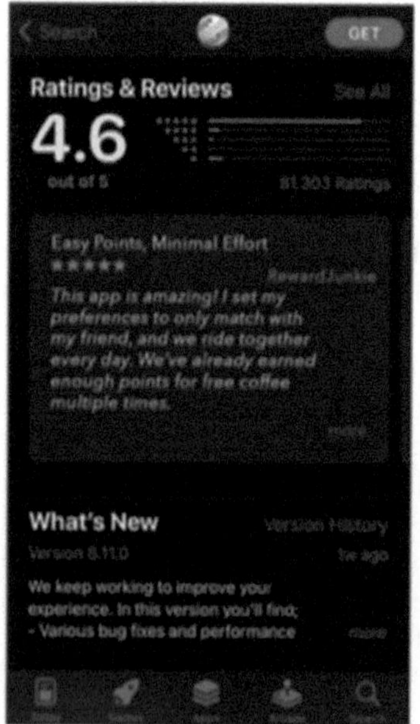

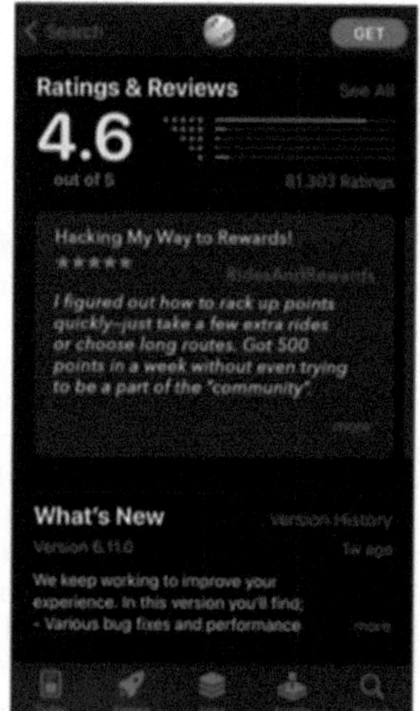

App reviews of Communa

Fig. 4. The components of Communa, a reward-based car-sharing service.

5 Discussion

Digital provisioning platforms can potentially motivate sustainable behaviors in food and mobility by facilitating sharing rides, renting scooters, shopping for local food, and reducing food waste. These platforms influence and even disrupt existing provision service systems in these domains. They not only bring sustainability benefits but also raise some concerns. Hence, exploring the potential implications (both negative and positive) of these platforms is key to devising a new DPP. Utilizing the power of design fiction to explore such implications, and based on two design workshops with 12 participants, this paper presents four DPP design fictions in mobility and food domains (Yeşil Yarınlar, Road Buddies, Communa, and Mom-AI).

These DPP extend beyond simply offering products for provision and purchase, highlighting the broader impact of sustainability and illustrating that provisioning systems are not solely about environmental conservation. Instead, they reflect a more holistic approach, encompassing social, economic, and cultural dimensions. This was evident in the fictions created by the participants. For example, while the participants initially focused on the current and future state of DPP, they also delved into broader issues related to food production, distribution, cooking, and consumption. Additionally, they explored how digital technologies could support future consumption practices in the food and mobility domains. They didn't feel compelled to generate ideas for future DPP; instead, they sought to understand how digital technologies could facilitate these practices. As a result, the fictions created during the workshops touched upon social aspects (e.g. community building in Yeşil Yarınlar, Road Buddies, and Communa), economic (e.g., enabling comfortable and cost-effective commuting in Communa), and cultural aspects (e.g., guiding food decisions based on personal preferences and cultural values in Mom AI).

We gathered insightful comments from our participants during the last stage of the workshop, where they were invited to reflect on each fiction according to a set of questions. These comments, along with their discussion during the workshops, helped us identify several issues that are worth discussing in the paper. Grouped under Scalability and Impact, Cultural and Social Dimensions of Platforms, and Possible Rebound Effects on Sustainability, this section elaborates on these issues. While we acknowledge the value of proposing solutions that address the negative side effects of DPP in food and mobility, within the scope of this paper, we discuss the platforms with both their positive and negative aspects from the perspective of users. Thus, specific solutions are not within the scope of this paper.

5.1 Scalability and Impact of DPP

In terms of scalability, the fictions created in the workshops were mostly local or city-level. For the food platform of Yeşil Yarınlar, the primary focus is on nurturing a community-driven approach to urban farming, which has the potential to transform the food system at a city scale. While this can promote awareness of food systems and encourage localized food production, its ability to scale beyond small-scale gardening is constrained [32]. Unless users adopt more extensive practices or partner with food companies, it may not fully address the larger issue of sustainable food provision. Similar local constraints can be noted in RoadBuddies, a micro-mobility platform with its community-building approach. While charms could enhance local community engagement and encourage residents to choose micro-mobility solutions, their impact would be restricted unless they succeed in shifting broader mobility patterns, such as decreasing private car usage. The platform's potential for growth is further hindered by its dependence on a niche user base, those who are inspired by the community aspects and the novelty of charms.

Both platforms face the challenge of scaling from local or city-specific solutions to broader, more transformative models. Widespread adoption and application require deeper cultural and infrastructural changes, such as overcoming entrenched habits. As for the cultural barriers, one prominent issue is privacy and safety. Existing mobility platforms, such as Uber, provide various methods for a secure experience; however, they still do not eliminate the unwillingness of female users to use a ride-sharing app alone [22]. A more community-based approach that necessitates self-regulation from its users (as in RoadBuddies) may have drawbacks compared to a centrally controlled platform, as it might require more systematic change. Still, there are additional potential benefits of a community-based approach as well, such as leveraging social media trends to promote growth. However, this also paves the way for competitors to offer more convenient and affordable alternatives, leading consumers to withdraw from the platform. Unless both platforms can address these barriers towards scalability, ranging from community engagement to system-wide support, they risk remaining small-scale interventions with limited long-term impact.

Another point regarding the scalability of these platforms is the issue of lifespan. The lifespan of the DPP, such as Yeşil Yarınlar, RoadBuddies and Communa, is inherently tied to their ability to sustain user engagement, adapt to evolving needs, and scale effectively. Any platform that connects producers and consumers always carries the risk of being obsolete, as consumers initiate their own interactions and even transactions with producers. For Yeşil Yarınlar, alongside the inherent difficulties of keeping up with a routine for small-scale gardening, empowering users can also give them the agency to stop using the platform after a while. Similarly, Communa might struggle to maintain long-term interest if its novelty wears off or if it fails to integrate into existing transportation systems. In addition, small communities that form thanks to the system can start to have their own agency and become self-sustaining social circles [4]. While RoadBuddies does not suffer from the same concerns, due to the integration of incentives for using the system in the form of points, the potential of users spinning off to create their own platforms is a risk. The platform would need to keep bringing new incentives or means of utilizing the existing points system to keep users engaged.

5.2 Cultural and Social Dimensions of DPP

The social implications of the DPP extend beyond their sustainability goals to encompass important aspects of cultural engagement, community building, inclusivity, and awareness of systems. By promoting interactions between producers and consumers, they highlight the impact of these social aspects on sustainable consumption [35]. In the cases of Yeşil Yarınlar and RoadBuddies, the platforms recognize the value of social and cultural dimensions in shaping sustainable behaviors. Yeşil Yarınlar encourages users to engage with food production in a more hands-on and community-driven way, turning food from a commodity into a cultural experience. Participants in workshops emphasized that urban farming could strengthen social bonds by involving people in the growing, purchasing, and consuming of locally produced food. This direct engagement fosters greater awareness of the time, effort, and resources required to grow food, potentially shifting food consumption from convenience to a more meaningful, ritualistic practice. It also creates an opportunity for people to connect with local farmers, deepening the sense of community and enhancing cultural connections to food [30]. Similarly, Road-Buddies seeks to build social ties by promoting shared transportation. By associating users with neighborhood-specific charms, the platform could foster a sense of belonging and encourage more sustainable mobility practices.

However, the cultural implications of both platforms are not without tension. Communa, which focuses on lifestyle matching for ride-sharing to create a "safer" environment for some passengers, may inadvertently exclude certain groups. While Communa and RoadBuddies aim to build communities, they must also address these issues of exclusion to be truly inclusive. On the other hand, the Mom-AI concept, for example, which guides food choices through technology, faced resistance from some participants who felt that technology's intrusion into personal food decisions could diminish the emotional and cultural significance of eating. This resistance highlights the concern over the potential negative impact of technology on cultural rituals and personal agency [5]. One of the examples of the agency problem was the case of "bad habits." Since participants sometimes chose to break the rules by selecting less sustainable or unhealthy options instead of AI suggestions, and they did not want to be judged based on these decisions. Another was the participants' concerns regarding the potential loss of diversity in food types, as they believed that the Mom AI concept would make similar suggestions over time, leading to the standardization of consumers' food choices.

5.3 DPP's Possible Rebound Effects on Sustainability

While these DPP fictions aim to promote sustainable consumption habits, their individual approaches can also cause unexpected rebound effects that undermine this aim. For example, RoadBuddies could foster a sense of community and reduce overall personal vehicle use. However, the emphasis on social interactions could also lead to preference away from more sustainable means of public transport, as people prioritize socializing through shared rides, thus increasing transportation demand. Similarly, the ScootShield concept within the RoadBuddies fiction aims to provide better sensorial experiences during shared rides. However, this concept may also inadvertently encourage overconsumption or waste if not carefully used with resource use in mind. These two concepts, together, can shift the perception towards private cars from symbols of status to functional community vehicles, potentially reducing car ownership and emissions, and could also lead to an increased demand for more high-tech vehicles or more frequent use of shared services, which may offset environmental benefits.

DPP that focus on food provision are also susceptible to these rebound effects. Yeşil Yarınlar, encouraging homegrown food production, achieves its sustainability goals by reducing food miles and promoting local production. However, encouraging every user to adopt such practices could also result in increased household water demand or overall productivity since more systematic change is required to realize this transition, such as redesigning people's houses to accommodate urban farming activities [25]. Additionally, inefficient practices by inexperienced growers and potential frustration experienced by them can cause unexpected resentment towards DIY practices.

In all these scenarios, while the design fictions aim to create more sustainable behaviors, they also illustrate how shifts in behavior and consumption patterns can have complex, sometimes contradictory, effects that must be carefully considered to ensure long-term sustainability benefits from DPP.

6 Conclusion

Despite their potential to encourage sustainable consumption, the implementation of DPP in food and mobility provision does not guarantee sustainability benefits and even leads to unintended consequences. In this paper, we explored the potential benefits and drawbacks of DPP and their implications for sustainable consumption by creating and reflecting on four DPP fictions together with 12 participants. The fictions reveal how DPP could reshape consumption patterns by fostering community engagement, promoting responsible food choices, and encouraging more sustainable mobility behaviors. Participants' reflections on these fictions revealed several tension points, which we categorized into three areas: Scalability and Impact, Cultural and Social Dimensions of Platforms, and Potential Rebound Effects on Sustainability. Thus, our analysis contributes to a deeper understanding of how DPP can be designed to support sustainable practices while addressing the challenges that may hinder their long-term effectiveness, such as platform misuse or unintended consequences, highlighting the need for evaluating the interaction between these platforms and the communities they serve.

Acknowledgments. This study was funded by the Scientific and Technological Research Council (TUBITAK) with grant number 123N041, under the framework of BELMONT FORUM, the Systems of Sustainable Consumption and Production Collaborative Research Action (2022).

Disclosure of Interests. Authors declare that they have no competing interests.

References

1. Aktürk, E., Gültekin, S.: The impact of food production on ecological footprint in Turkey: an analysis across agriculture, livestock, and aquaculture. Environ. Dev. Sustain., May 2024. https://doi.org/10.1007/s10668-024-04944-4
2. Apostolidis, C., Brown, D., Wijetunga, D., Kathriarachchi, E.: Sustainable value co-creation at the Bottom of the Pyramid: using mobile applications to reduce food waste and improve food security. J. Market. Manag. **37**, 856–886, 9–10 June 2021. https://doi.org/10.1080/0267257X.2020.1863448
3. Ballie, J., Bruce, F.: Reimagining sustainable mobility futures: exploring design imaginariums for city-wide challenges, 24 June 2024. https://doi.org/10.21606/drs.2024.288

4. Başdar, S.: The formal and the informal in Istanbuls taxi sector. Master of Arts. Boğaziçi University, Atatürk Institute for Modern Turkish History (2011). https://ata.bogazici.edu.tr/ma-theses/sinem-basdar

5. Boström, M.: Social relations and everyday consumption rituals: barriers or prerequisites for sustainability transformation? Front. Sociol. 723464, 6 August 2021. https://doi.org/10.3389/fsoc.2021.723464

6. Çavuş, O.: Gıda İsrafının Önlenmesinde Teknolojinin Gücü: Dijital Uygulamalar. J. New Tourism Trends 2(2021), 83–96 (2021)

7. Coulton, P., Lindley, J., Sturdee, M., Stead, M.: Design fiction as world building, 4230036 Bytes (2019). https://doi.org/10.6084/M9.FIGSHARE.4746964

8. Fry, T.: Design Futuring: Sustainability, Ethics and New Practice (1st ed.) Bloomsbury Publishing Plc (2009). https://doi.org/10.5040/9781350036079

9. Gill, M.: London, we tried but it's time to end the experiment and ban e-scooters. Standard (2024). https://www.standard.co.uk/comment/escooter-experiment-failed-ban-lime-madrid-melbourne-paris-b1181689.html

10. Gökçen, M., Seylam Küşümler, A.: Yetişkinlerde Gıda Etiketi Okuma Bilgi Düzeyi ile Davranışa Geçirme Arasındaki İlişki. Online Türk Sağlık Bilimleri Dergisi 6, 82–91, 1 March 2021. https://doi.org/10.26453/otjhs.794408

11. Gomez-Corona, C., Wathelet, O., Minvielle, N.: How to think about the future of food? speculative design and design fiction applied to consumer research. Curr. Opin. Food Sci. 60(2024), 101226 (2024). https://doi.org/10.1016/j.cofs.2024.101226

12. Güneş, E.F., Aktaç, Ş., İrem, B., Korkmaz, O.: Tüketicilerin Gıda Etiketlerine Yönelik Tutum ve Davranışları. Akademik Gıda 12, 30–37, 3 September 2014

13. Güney,O.I., Sangün, L.: How COVID-19 affects individuals' food consumption behaviour: a consumer survey on attitudes and habits in Turkey. BFJ 123, 2307–2320, 7 June 2021. https://doi.org/10.1108/BFJ-10-2020-0949

14. Hebrok, M., Mainsah, H.: Skinny as a bird: design fiction as a vehicle for reflecting on food futures. Futures 141, 102983, August 2022. https://doi.org/10.1016/j.futures.2022.102983

15. Hegwood, M., et al.: Rebound effects could offset more than half of avoided food loss and waste. Nat Food 4, 585–595, 7 July 2023. https://doi.org/10.1038/s43016-023-00792-z

16. Kelly, C.: Hundreds of Lime and Neuron e-scooters trucked out of Melbourne as ban deadline looms. The Guardian (2024). https://www.theguardian.com/australia-news/2024/sep/23/hundreds-of-lime-and-neuron-e-scooters-trucked-out-of-melbourne-as-ban-deadline-looms

17. Łobejko, S., Bartczak, K.: The role of digital technology platforms in the context of changes in consumption and production patterns. Sustainability 13, 8294, 15 July 2021. https://doi.org/10.3390/su13158294

18. Oscar Lorentzon. REKO-rings. https://northsearegion.eu/reframe/online-resource-centre/regional-organization-in-a-cooperative-structure/reko-rings/

19. Martínez-Peláez, R., et al.: Role of digital transformation for achieving sustainability: mediated role of stakeholders, key capabilities, and technology. Sustainability 15, 11221, 14 July 2023. https://doi.org/10.3390/su151411221

20. McQueen, M., Abou-Zeid, G., MacArthur, J., Clifton, K.: Transportation transformation: is micromobility making a macro impact on sustainability? J. Plann. Lit. 36, 46–61, 1 February 2021. https://doi.org/10.1177/0885412220972696

21. Meaker, M.: I Spent a Week Eating Discarded Restaurant Food. But Was It Really Going to Waste? *Wired* (2024). https://www.wired.com/story/too-good-to-go-app-week-food-waste/

22. Meshram, A., Choudhary, P., Velaga, N.R.: Assessing and modelling perceived safety and comfort of women during ridesharing. Transp. Res. Proc. 48(2020), 2852–2869 (2020). https://doi.org/10.1016/j.trpro.2020.08.233

23. Michelini, L., Principato, L., Iasevoli, G.: Understanding food sharing models to tackle sustainability challenges. Ecol. Econ. **145**, 205–217, March 2018. https://doi.org/10.1016/j.eco lecon.2017.09.009

24. Mitropoulos, L., Kortsari, A., Ayfantopoulou, G.: A systematic literature review of ride-sharing platforms, user factors and barriers. Eur. Transp. Res. Rev. **13**, 61, 1 December 2021. https://doi.org/10.1186/s12544-021-00522-1

25. Nicholls, E., Ely, A., Birkin, L., Basu, P., Goulson, D.: The contribution of small-scale food production in urban areas to the sustainable development goals: a review and case study. Sustain. Sci. **15**, 1585–1599, 6 November 2020. https://doi.org/10.1007/s11625-020-00792-z

26. Oogjes, D., Bruns, M., Wakkary, R.: Lyssna. In: Proceedings of the 2016 ACM Conference Companion Publication on Designing Interactive Systems - DIS 2016 Companion (2016). https://doi.org/10.1145/2908805.2909401

27. Ozdemir, C., Sultan Kaman, G., Yilmaz, H.: Smart food waste fighters: insights from mobile apps and users. JHTI, August 2024. https://doi.org/10.1108/JHTI-04-2024-0324

28. Poore, J., Nemecek, T.: Reducing food's environmental impacts through producers and consumers. Science **360**(6392), 987–992, June 2018. https://doi.org/10.1126/science.aaq0216

29. Schanes, K., Stagl, S.: Food waste fighters: what motivates people to engage in food sharing? J. Clean. Prod. **211**, 1491–1501, February 2019. https://doi.org/10.1016/j.jclepro.2018.11.162

30. Secer, A., Masotti, M., Iori, E., Vittuari, M.: Do culture and consciousness matter? a study on motivational drivers of household food waste reduction in Turkey. Sustain. Prod. Consum. **38**, 69–79, June 2023. https://doi.org/10.1016/j.spc.2023.03.024

31. Sterling, B.: Design fiction. Interactions **16**, 20–24, 3 May 2009. https://doi.org/10.1145/151 6016.1516021

32. Türkkan, C.: Urban gardens vs. community gardens: tensions and trajectories for urban agriculture in Istanbul. Moment **10**, 30–47, 1 July 2023. https://doi.org/10.17572/mj2023.1.3047

33. Turno, F.M., Yatskiv Jackiva, I.: Mobility-as-a-service: literature and tools review with a focus on personalization. Transport **38**, 243–262, 4 December 2023. https://doi.org/10.3846/transp ort.2023.20997

34. Wathelet, O., Minvielle, N.: Studying future food scenarios with design fiction. In: Gómez-Corona, C., Rodrigues, H. (eds.) Consumer Research Methods in Food Science. Methods and Protocols in Food Science. Humana, New York (2023). https://doi.org/10.1007/978-1-0716-3000-6_23

35. Weber, H., Loschelder, D.D., Lang, D.J., Wiek, A.: Connecting consumers to producers to foster sustainable consumption in international coffee supply – a marketing intervention study. J. Market. Manag. **37**, 1148–1168, 11–12 July 2021. https://doi.org/10.1080/0267257X.2021.1897650

36. Yanatma, S.: Paris officially the first city in Europe to ban e-scooters. What are the rules in other countries? euronews (2023). https://www.euronews.com/next/2023/09/01/electric-sco oters-what-are-the-rules-across-europe-and-where-are-injuries-highest

37. Bisikletin atık yönetiminde kullanılması devrim niteliğinde bir hareket olacak. WRI Sustainable Cities (2018). https://thecityfixturkiye.com/bisikletin-atik-yonetiminde-kullanilm asi-devrim-niteliginde-bir-hareket-olacak/

38. Survey on Information and Communication Technology (ICT) Usage in Households and by Individuals 2023. https://data.tuik.gov.tr/Bulten/Index?p=Hanehalki-Bilisim-Teknolojileri-(BT)-Kullanim-Arastirmasi-2023-49407

39. İstanbul'da Sürdürülebilir Ulaşıma Doğru. İPA - İstanbul Planlama Ajansı (2023). https://ipa.istanbul/yayinlarimiz/genel/istanbulda-surdurulebilir-ulasima-dogru/

40. B Sınıf Ehliyetle 122CC Motosiklet Kullanabilecekler. Turkey Ministry of Internal Affairs (2024)

41. Martı, "Paylaşımlı Yolculuk Yönetmeliği" için 376 bin dilekçeyi İBB'ye teslim etti. AA - Anatolian Agency (2024). https://www.aa.com.tr/tr/gundem/marti-paylasimli-yolculuk-yon etmeligi-icin-376-bin-dilekceyi-ibbye-teslim-etti/3149155
42. Food Waste Index Report 2024. UNEP - UN Environment Programme. https://www.unep. org/resources/publication/food-waste-index-report-2024
43. ABB'NİN ELEKTRİKLİ OTOBÜSLERİNE BAŞKENTLİLERDEN TAM NOT. EGO - Ankara Electricity, Gas and Bus Operations Organization (2024). https://www.ego.gov.tr/ tr/haber/5849/abbnin-elektrikli-otobuslerine-baskentlilerden-tam-not
44. Road Motor Vehicles, April 2024. TUIK. https://data.tuik.gov.tr/Bulten/Index?p=Motorlu-Kara-Tasitlari-Nisan-2024-53456
45. The Results of Address Based Population Registration System, 2023. TUIK. https://data. tuik.gov.tr/Bulten/Index?p=The-Results-of-Address-Based-Population-Registration-Sys tem-2023-49684&dil=2
46. Food Trends in Turkey. Innova Market Insights (2024). https://www.innovamarketinsights. com/trends/food-trends-in-turkey/
47. Global CO2 emissions by year 1940–2024. Statista. https://www.statista.com/statistics/276 629/global-co2-emissions/
48. Too Good To Go. https://www.toogoodtogo.com/en-us
49. Lime. https://www.li.me/
50. BlaBlaCar. https://www.blablacar.com.tr/
51. Good Eggs. https://www.goodeggs.com/home
52. Fazla Gıda. https://fazla.com/en/
53. Yenir. https://www.yenir.com/
54. Martı. https://www.marti.tech/
55. Türkiye'nin Yeme ve İçme Alışkanlıkları Araştırması. Metro. https://www.metro-tr.com/hak kimizda/basin-bultenleri/turkiyede-yeme-ve-icme-aliskanliklari-basin-bulteni
56. Zoom. https://www.zoom.com/en
57. Miro. https://miro.com/
58. Midjourney AI. https://www.midjourney.com/home

Digital Transformation Chatbot (DTchatbot): Integrating Large Language Model-Based Chatbot in Acquiring Digital Transformation Needs

Jiawei Zheng$^{(\boxtimes)}$, Gokcen Yilmaz , Ji Han ,
and Saeema Ahmed-Kristensen

DigitLab, University of Exeter, London, UK
`{J.Zheng2,G.Yilmaz,J.Han2,S.Ahmed-Kristensen}@exeter.ac.uk`

Abstract. Many organisations pursue digital transformation to enhance operational efficiency, reduce manual efforts, and optimise processes by automation and digital tools. To achieve this, a comprehensive understanding of their unique needs is required. However, traditional methods, such as expert interviews, while effective, face several challenges, including scheduling conflicts, resource constraints, inconsistency, etc. To tackle these issues, we investigate the use of a Large Language Model (LLM)-powered chatbot to acquire organisations' digital transformation needs. Specifically, the chatbot integrates workflow-based instruction with LLM's planning and reasoning capabilities, enabling it to function as a virtual expert and conduct interviews. We detail the chatbot's features and its implementation. Our preliminary evaluation indicates that the chatbot performs as designed, effectively following predefined workflows and supporting user interactions with areas for improvement. We conclude by discussing the implications of employing chatbots to elicit user information, emphasizing their potential and limitations.

Keywords: Digital transformation · Chatbot · Large Language Models · Workflow-based Interview

1 Introduction

Digital transformation is a strategic imperative for organisations seeking to integrate digital technologies into different aspects of their business models, which can fundamentally change how organisations operate and deliver value to customers. It is a process that aims to improve an organisation by triggering changes to its properties through combination of information, computing and communication technologies [19]. For example, in inventory management, deploying Internet of Things (IoT) devices such as sensors enables real-time monitoring of stock levels, allowing automated reordering and seamless communication with suppliers. This reduces manual efforts, enhances inventory accuracy, and minimises

F. F.-H Nah and K. L. Siau (Eds.): HCII 2025, LNCS 16343, pp. 388–403, 2026.
https://doi.org/10.1007/978-3-032-13167-6_26

delays in replenishment [11]. To ensure effective and efficient digital transformation, we must begin with a comprehensive understanding of an organisation's needs, challenges, and current operational practices.

Currently, organisations' digital transformation needs are typically elicited through one of three methods: 1) workshops or interviews, where information is captured via audio recording devices or handwritten notes; 2) engagement with external digital consultants to provide strategic advice and recommendations; and 3) internal assessments led by organisational staff [3]. While these methods can be effective under certain cases, they also come with several challenges that make them less suitable for the fast-paced and resource-constrained environment of current businesses [6,8,15]. For instance:

- **Time Consuming**: Data collected during these sessions is typically recorded using voice recording devices or documented as written notes. Transcribing audio recordings into written text or analysing handwritten notes requires significant effort and time, introducing complexity, increasing workloads, and causing delays.
- **High Costs**: Engaging with digital transformation experts can be resource-intensive for organisations, especially for Small and Medium-sized Enterprises (SMEs).
- **Limited Scalability**: Traditional workshops and interviews are inherently one-off events, requiring significant coordination and effort to schedule and execute.
- **Fragmented Communication**: In multilingual organizations, the lack of a shared language or communication platform can hinder meaningful dialogue, leaving critical needs misunderstood or overlooked entirely. Moreover, once workshops or consultations conclude, businesses often lack mechanisms for iterative follow-up or ongoing support. This can impede the organization's ability to adapt strategies as new challenges emerge.

In response, online questionnaires have been adopted to elicit information [20]. While these tools can be provided 24/7 to access and complete in their own space, regardless of geographic location, these questionnaires lack interactive features, which results in survey-taking fatigue [4]. This problem is exacerbated with open-ended questions, which is an important method to collect valuable information and deeper insights. Formulating and typing responses to such questions requires significant time and effort from respondents, increasing their cognitive burden. As a result, respondents are more likely to skip such questions or provide low-quality or even irrelevant answers. This, in turn, compromises the quality and reliability of the data collected. Additionally, analysing and consolidating responses from open-ended questions is a time-intensive task for researchers.

The advent of chatbots, enhanced by increasingly powerful conversational capabilities, offers a compelling alternative to traditional online questionnaires [20]. While retaining the benefits of online questionnaires, chatbots introduce an interactive and dynamic dimension that can enhance participant engagement and improve the quality of responses. Recent advancements in Large Language Models (LLMs) further amplify the potential of chatbots, equipping them with diverse domain knowledge and the ability to deliver human-like interactions and effectively manage complex conversations. For instance, LLM-powered chatbots can assist participants by clarifying questions, guiding them through the conversation, and encouraging more thoughtful responses.

This paper investigates whether LLM-powered chatbots can enhance the user experience in understanding and navigating the digtal transformation of organisations. We introduce DTchatbot, a conversational agent designed to guide organizational representatives through a structured dialogue aimed at uncovering their unique challenges, goals, and transformation priorities. We present the design and development of DTchatbot. The chatbot employs a workflow-based approach to guide users through a series of questions, meticulously designed to identify the challenges, needs, and goals unique to their organizations. To enhance accessibility and usability, the system integrates a Speech-to-Text model that seamlessly transcribes participants' audio responses into text, enabling natural and intuitive interactions. To the best of our knowledge, we are the first to develop and use the LLM-powered chatbot for conducting expert consulting sessions. A preliminary user study with two SMEs and two experts indicates that the DTchatbot effectively conducts conversational interviews and supports insightful user engagement.

2   Related Work

Digital transformation is a critical process for modern organisations, involving the adoption of digital technologies to enhance operational efficiency, drive innovation, and improve customer experiences. It brings new business and operating models across all sectors and requires organisations to fundamentally rethink their workflows, strategies, and current practices. Many studies and industries highlight and demonstrate the benefits of digital transformation [3,8,15]. For example, studies have shown that adopting IoT technologies can lead to increased operational efficiency, such as reducing production costs through automation or optimising supply chain management [16]. The success of digital transformation depends heavily on a deep understanding of an organisation's needs.

Recent advancements in conversational AI and chatbots have paved the way for innovative approaches to understanding users' needs. Conversational AI and chatbots have long been of interest to the Human-Computer Interaction (HCI) community due to their various interaction benefits, such as the application of learning and driving assistant [5,9] and customer service agent [21]. One key advantage is that conversational interfaces provide a natural and intuitive way for users to express themselves, which in turn improves the usability of a system. Unlike traditional online questionnaires and surveys, conversational interactions offer flexibility and can accommodate diverse user requests without forcing users to adhere to predefined workflow [17]. This adaptability makes conversational AI particularly effective for engaging with users and eliciting complex information.

Many researchers have investigated the use of conversational AI for eliciting user information through a one-on-one, text-based conversation. For example, Cranshaw et al. introduce a conversational agent designed to assist with scheduling events by eliciting key information from dialogue [7]. Moreover, conversational AI has been successfully applied in job interview settings [10]. These findings highlighted the potential of conversational AI to perform human-liked interactions and collect nuanced and contextually rich data.

Building on existing work, we focus on investigating the use of a chatbot to conduct interviews with organisational stakeholders, Our aim is to facilitate the elicitation of information crucial for guiding their digital transformation.

3 DTchatbot Features

Instead of building the chatbot into existing chat applications, such as WhatsApp, Slack, etc., and other third-party chatbot platforms, e.g., juji [20], we decided to implement a fully web-based platform. This was guided by: 1) it has the freedom to implement new functionalities and allows for better adaptability, since existing platforms often come with inherent limitations, including restrictions on customisations, data access, and integration with external tools, and 2) these platforms are often closed source, thus leaving little opportunity to implement and test our own functionalities.

Our chatbot is fully developed based on open-source components, which allows easy adoption by other researchers and industries. The architecture of the DTchatbot is shown in Fig. 1, including two main components, *chatbot interface* and *backend*. Users, typically organisational representatives, such as product mangers or engineers, interact with DTchatbot through the *interface* by answering questions that were designed to identify their digital transformation needs. We describe the details next.

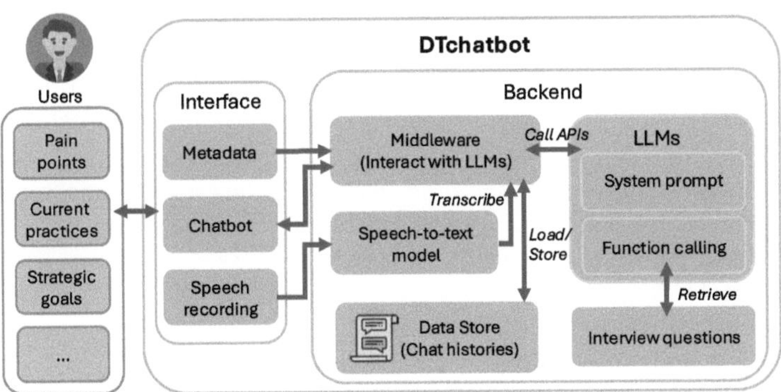

Fig. 1. The architecture of the Consulting Chatbot.

3.1   Chatbot Interface

It is designed with two primary features to facilitate the identification of digital transformation needs. First, it enables recording client information, such as company name, client name, industry type and size, and job title. This structured data allows for the categorisation of consulting workflows based on job titles, providing a tailored approach to addressing client needs. For instance, within a single organisation, expert consultations may involve professionals from various departments, and the job title serves as a critical attribute to distinguish the interactions. This categorisation ensures that the focus of the needs identification is aligned with the specific expertise of each client, fostering a more effective and targeted engagement. This recorded information also enables clients to revisit and continue conversations that were not completed in previous sessions, which is described in more detail in Sect. 3.2.

Second, the interface supports multilingual and multimodal inputs, e.g., text and speech, ensuring accessibility and flexibility for diverse users. For textual interactions, the DTchatbot leverages the capabilities of LLMs, like OpenAI's GPT-4 [12], which supports over 90 languages. This allows seamless communication across linguistic boundaries. Additionally, DTchatbot integrates an speech-to-text model, such as OpenAI Whisper model [14], which supports over 50 languages [13], to process voice inputs from users. This multimodal and multilingual support broadens accessibility and enhances the user experience (see Fig. 2b). This designed feature addresses the limitations of traditional workshops, particularly those stemming from language barriers and reliance on voice recording devices.

3.2   Backend

The backend of the chatbot is instructed to ask questions based on a pre-defined workflow, ensuring a structured and systematic method for collecting information. The questions are designed and organised according to the workflow, which guides the conversation in a logical sequence. The workflow begins by asking users to identify their priorities across five key domains of digital transformation: *corporate governance, customer and market management, research and development, supply chain,* and *production management.* Based on these priorities, the chatbot dynamically presents targeted interview questions within each domain to elicit organisation-specific information. Figure 2a shows that the DTchatbot follows our predefined workflow to conduct interviews.

We adopt D3A questions, developed by Bogazici University, as our interview questions, which are used nationally by TUBITAK through certified consultants to evaluate firms' digital transformation capability levels and create roadmaps [18]. They are designed for in-depth interviews, with responses scored on a 0–4 scale. These questions form the core input for a chatbot aimed at streamlining digital transformation assessments. The chatbot uses the same logical flow to guide users, ensuring consistent and comprehensive data collection. The questions have been pilot-tested with SMEs working in Istanbul Dudullu and nearby industrial zones, including over 146 SMEs across key sectors (around 16,500 employees) [2]. The complete set of questions [2], detailed for each category, is provided in the Appendix A.

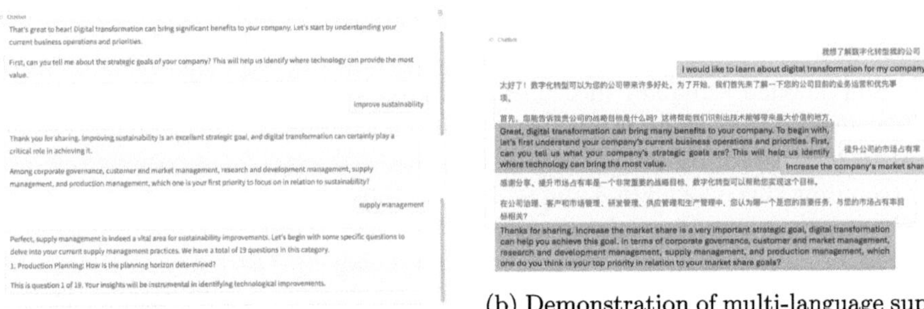

(a) Demonstration of workflow-based interview questions.

(b) Demonstration of multi-language support (Chinese and its English translation).

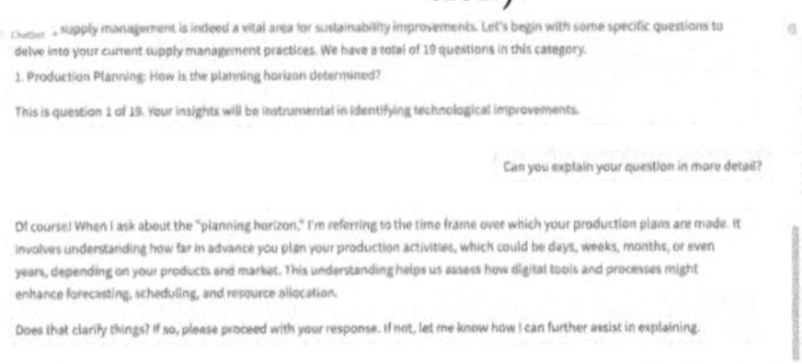

(c) Demonstration of client guidance.

Fig. 2. Demonstration of DTchatbot.

By leveraging the capabilities of LLMs, DTchatbot provides real-time support for technical clarifications and guidance, improving the experience of the information collection process. For example, if a user mentions a need for implementing a cloud-based solution but is unsure about the differences between public, private, and hybrid cloud models, the bot can offer a clear explanation if the user asks a question like "Can you explain to me the differences among public, private and hybrid cloud services?" The chatbot can generate accurate responses. Similarly, if a client references a specific technology, without fully understanding its potential applications in a domain, the chatbot can provide tailored insights, examples, and even recommendations based on best practices. This enhances user engagement by making the experience more interactive, supportive, and personalized.

This capability is further expanded to provide guidance to users on how to effectively answer interview questions, ensuring that they articulate their needs and priorities. For instance, if a user is unsure how to respond to a strategic question, DTchatbot can offer examples or prompts to help them frame their objectives. By offering this guidance, DTchatbot not only improves the quality of the input but also encourages deeper reflection, enabling a more thorough and insightful exploration of their digital transformation needs. Figure2c demonstrates this feature.

Upon completing the conversation, DTchatbot automatically generates a comprehensive summary report outlining current practises, identified challenges, and strategic goals, providing a holistic view to inform digital strategy.

The full conversation history of the consulting process is stored on the web server in a structured format. The conversation history is systematically organised and labelled using key metadata, including the company name, interviewee name, and job title, as inputted through the user interface. This labelling ensures that each consultation session is uniquely identifiable and contextually relevant. By recording this information and storing the interaction history, users can seamlessly pick up where they left off, without the need to repeat or reintroduce their queries or responses. This feature not only enhances the user experience but also supports a more efficient and customised information collection, as the bot retains context and builds on previous discussions. The messages within the conversation are clearly distinguished, with labels explicitly indicating whether a message was provided by the user or generated by the DTchatbot. This structured format enhances traceability and simplifies subsequent analysis, such as tailored recommendations and iterative refinement of transformation strategies.

3.3   Implementation

We utilise Gradio [1], an open-sourced framework for building web applications, to build the *user interface*. Gradio provides a suite of off-the-shelf tools that accelerate the creation of responsive interfaces. Using Gradio, we design an interface that supports both text-based and audio-based interactions with the chatbot. This interface acts as the primary medium for collecting user input and delivering responses.

The *backend* includes a middleware that bridges the user interface and the LLMs. It processes and packages the text input into structured requests that are sent to the LLMs through APIs for processing. For audio inputs, we integrate the OpenAI Whisper model [14], which transcribes spoken responses into text. The text is then sent to the middleware for communicating with LLMs.

We use the capabilities of LLMs to conduct interviews aligned with predefined questions designed to acquire digital transformation needs. The bot operates based on carefully crafted system prompts, which guide its behaviour during the interview process. The function-calling capabilities of LLMs are utilised to dynamically retrieve interview questions from a predefined question list, ensuring seamless adaptability during the information collection process. This question list operates as a modular plug-in for the chatbot, allowing for effortless customisation and editing based on the specific stage of the consultation or the requirements of different interviews. An excerpt of the prompt is shown in Fig. 3. We interact with LLMs via API request, enabling flexibility in selecting and utilising different LLMs as needed. Specifically, in our study, the OpenAI GPT-4 model is used to process user queries and generate responses. The chat scripts are stored on the Web server, referred to as the *Data Store*, in a structured JSON format.

Prompt for LLMs

System Message

You are an expert digital transformation consultant, and your role is to interview clients to deeply understand their business needs, challenges, and opportunities for digital transformation. Your objective is to gather comprehensive information about their current processes, goals, and vision for future improvements, focusing on areas where technology can bring the most value. You need to ask questions following the below routine.

1. Ask a question: What is your top priority in the categories of corporate governance, customer and market management, research and development management, supply management, and production management?

2. Ask questions returned from *retrieve_question* function in corresponding category. Until it returns "All questions completed".

Provide real-time updates on the progress of the interview as you ask each question, clearly indicating how many questions have been completed and how many remain.
Encourage the client to remain patient and engaged throughout the process.
Note: If the client speaks other languages, then you ask the question in the corresponding language.

User [Client]
{Response by client }

Fig. 3. An excerpt of prompt for LLMs.

4   Preliminary User Study

We conducted a preliminary user study to evaluate the capability of DTchatbot in identifying the digital transformation needs of organisations. The study involved two digital transformation experts and representatives from two SMEs, enabling us to gather insights from both expert and client perspectives. The primary objectives of the evaluation were to investigate both the effectiveness and the experience of using the chatbot following: **Obj1**: How do digital transformation experts perceive the use of a chatbot for acquiring organisations' needs? **Obj2**: How do users from SMEs reflect on their experience with the DTchatbot?

Obj1 involves expert interactions with DTchatbot, where participants were asked to provide feedback (see Appendix B) on two key aspects: 1) reduction of effort, and 2) enhancement of functionality and usability. For the **obj2**, the participants interacted with the DTchabot and they were asked to provide feedback, using the targeted questions (see Appendix C). These questions focused on four key areas: *perceived benefits, interaction and usability, data input and analysis,* and *perceived limitations.* The profiles of SME representatives are: 1) human resource manager in an engineering solution company, 2) production director of a manufacturing company. Other information is detailed in Appendix D.

4.1 Expert's Opinions

Both experts agreed that the DTchatbot helps support digital transformation initiatives and effectively reduces effort. *Expert 1* highlighted that the chatbot is user-friendly and offers a logical question sequence, which aids in the initial identification of gaps. While it is limited to detailed analysis, it provides a good starting point for understanding the specific needs of organisations. *Expert 2* found the chatbot particularly useful for providing suggestions, strategies, and implementation steps, helping users focus on their transformation goals. The digital tool recommendations save significant time and effort by eliminating the need for extensive manual searches, enabling users to concentrate on higher-priority tasks.

Experts also suggested several enhancements to improve the chatbot's functionality and usability:

- **Interactive Features**: *Expert 1* suggested re-organising the question sequence dynamically based on user inputs for better contextual alignment. *Expert 2* recommended introducing selection boxes for common responses, reducing the need for manual input and making interactions more efficient.
- **Visualisation and Reporting**: *Expert 2* proposed that the chatbot generate flowcharts to visually represent the suggested digital transformation processes, enhancing user comprehension. At the end of the conversation session, the chatbot could provide a detailed report summarising its recommendations to better assist users.
- **Analytical Depth**: Expert 1 suggested that integrating the analysis of diverse data types would enable the chatbot to deliver more detailed and insightful results. Moreover, including explanatory examples within the questions would improve user understanding and facilitate accurate responses.

4.2 Client's Reflections

Client reflections are categorized into four areas as follows:

Perceived Benefits: Participants found the chatbot interaction beneficial, particularly in raising awareness about their gaps in the early stages of digital transformation. They appreciated its ability to identify deficiencies and guide decision-making, highlighting its potential as a diagnostic tool that complements expert consultancy. One participant stated, "It is beneficial for SMEs to raise awareness about understanding their gaps in the initial stages of the digital transformation. If there is an ongoing process, the chatbot might help observe areas for improvement".

Interaction and Usability: All participants emphasised the voice transcription functionality and quick response time. These features were particularly appreciated for their ability to streamline interactions and reduce the effort required for communication. However, one participant suggested that introducing an **answer auto-completion** feature could further enhance the user experience. They stated, "Suggestions could be provided for each question. For example, after writing short keywords for responses, automatic sentence completion or sentence improvement could enhance the interaction". This feedback highlights the potential to integrate intelligent text assistance into the chatbot, allowing users to provide more structured and detailed responses with less effort.

Data Input and Analysis: The participants appreciated the ability of the DTChatbot to maintain meaningful conversations through logical follow-up questions. Additionally, they valued the chatbot's capability to provide technical clarifications and guidance on answering questions, stating, "It analyses customer complaints in-depth and provides answers, which is helpful". However, participants also identified opportunities for improvement in usability. They suggested enhancing the chatbot by enabling it to accept diverse inputs beyond text, such as workflows or structured data entries. One participant remarked, "Instead of answering the chatbot's questions with text, allowing inputs such as workflows and data entries would make it more user-friendly and practical for generating digital solution suggestions".

Perceived Limitations: The participants highlighted that although the chatbot is effective for initial awareness and identifying gaps, it may not be sufficient to fully support digital transformation efforts. They stated, "It is good for understanding ourselves in the initial stages, but it is not sufficient for a complete digital transformation process. For example, it could be integrated into a digital system like an Enterprise Resource Planning (ERP) to increase usability".

It is important to note that data privacy and security are critical considerations for the DTChatbot, given the sensitive nature of organisations' current practices and challenges discussed during consultations. To address these concerns, the DTChatbot ensures that all client data, including chat histories, is securely stored with a robust access control system.

5   Discussion and Future Work

The DTchatbot offers significant advancements in the process of eliciting digital transformation needs through its multimodal and multilingual capabilities. It provides a highly scalable and accessible solution for acquiring information. Its integration of advanced LLMs, ensures context-aware guidance and technical clarification, providing a highly personalised and insightful consulting experience. Additionally, its structured workflow-based design ensures that consultations are systematic and aligned with pre-defined instructions. The ability to record interaction histories facilitates downstream tasks, like the generation of actionable insights and detailed reports. The integration of the OpenAI Whisper audio-to-text model streamlines the process by enabling seamless handling of audio inputs, enhancing overall efficiency.

This work demonstrates the potential of LLM-powered chatbots to provide dynamic, context-aware, and domain-specific interactions. Beyond digital transformation, the structured and interactive capabilities of the DTChatbot suggest broader applicability to general expert interviews and consulting tasks across industries, underscoring its versatility as a tool for knowledge acquisition and user engagement. It highlights the implications of employing chatbots to address the challenges of engagement and scalability.

Despite these advancements, several challenges and constraints remain. One critical concern is ensuring data privacy and security, as the DTchatbot processes sensitive client information. Addressing this limitation requires the implementation of strict data governance practices, including the deployment of locally hosted LLMs to mitigate risks associated with data disclosure. Moreover, while LLMs are powerful, they can occasionally generate responses that are inaccurate or overly generic, particularly when faced with highly specialized or nuanced queries. This highlights the need for fine-tuning LLMs to better cater to specific domains, such as digital transformation.

Future work will focus on accommodating reflections from both experts and SME users, such as integrating multiple data input formats, like images, documents, etc., to further improve usability. We also plan to extend its functionality to support detailed analysis, enabling the generation of tailored reports for organisations.

Acknowledgement. This work is funded by DIGITLab, UKRI Next Staged Digital Economy Centre (EP/T022566/1).

Appendix

A   Interview Question List

Table 1. The list of interview questions in each category.

Category	Question
Corporate Governance	How are management decisions made?
	Is there a written strategic plan?
	Is there a strategy for digitalisation?
	Are business processes defined?
	What is the level of cooperation between units?
	How are financial records created?
	Who is responsible for information systems?
	Are there cybersecurity systems in the organisation?
	Is it possible to access company data remotely?
	How is the training and development of employees managed?
	What is being done to improve digital competencies of employees?
	How are new ideas collected within the company?
Customer and Market Management	How are sales and marketing activities carried out?
	How do you make sales forecasts?
	How is sales data shared with other business units?
	How do you create quotes?
	What can your customers do through digital media?
	How are customer conversations and related information stored?
	How do you receive orders from your customers?
	How is the dealer network monitored?
	How are customer projects tracked?
	How is the sales team's performance monitored?
	How is distributor performance monitored?
	How do you track customer feedback and issues such as after-sales returns, technical service, complaints?
Research and Development Management	Is there a P&D or R&D department?
	Are there any patents and/or patent applications?
	Is there any cooperation with academic institutions in product development and innovation?
	Is there an externally supported R&D project?
	How are product/process/material design - development - engineering studies done?
	Who is involved in product/process/material design - development - engineering studies?
	Do you produce the technologies used or buy them ready-made?
	Is there hardware on products to collect data (e.g., sensors, chips)?
	ow is the need to develop new products, new services and processes determined?
	Is it possible to customise the product?

(continued)

Table 1. (*continued*)

Category	Question
Supply Management	Production Planning: How is the planning horizon determined?
	Production Planning: How is production planning done?
	What happens when it is necessary to make changes in the production plan due to a disruption or need caused by the supplier, customer or institution?
	How are batch sizes determined in production?
	How is capacity management carried out in the enterprise?
	How do you determine material requirements?
	Purchase Orders: How do you purchase materials?
	Purchase Orders: How is communication with suppliers ensured?
	How do you choose suppliers?
	How is supplier performance evaluated?
	How is information shared with other company functions (sales, purchasing, production, storage, shipment)?
	How is information shared with external supply chain partners (suppliers, logistics, customers)?
	How is raw material stock planning done?
	How are raw material stocks tracked?
	How is warehouse management done (raw materials, components, finished products)?
	How is line feeding done: physically conveying materials?
	How is line feeding done: material demand of production?
	How are logistics work orders created?
	How are logistics managed?
Production Management	How do you forward production work orders to the line?
	How do you forward bills of materials to production?
	How is scheduling/rescheduling done?
	How do you track production?
	How do you monitor machines and downtime during production?
	How is workforce monitoring done?
	How do you keep track of material movements in production area?
	How do you monitor production performance?
	How is production information shared internally?
	How is Quality Management done?
	How do you handle quality problems related to materials, products and/or processes (problem assessment)?
	How do you handle quality problems related to materials, products and/or processes (nonconformity record)?
	How do you evaluate quality control data related to your materials?
	How do you evaluate quality control data related to your finished products?
	How do you evaluate quality control data related to your processes?
	How do you evaluate quality control data related to your semi-finished products?
	How is maintenance management carried out?
	What methods are used for machine maintenance?
	How are maintenance planning and scheduling done?
	How is energy consumption monitored?

B   Questions for Collecting Experts' Opinions

1. How effective is the DTchatbot in reducing user effort and supporting digital transformation?
2. What additional features and functionalities could improve the usability and analytical capabilities of the DTchatbot?

C   Questions for Collecting SME Clients' Opinions on DTchatbot

1. Perceived Benefits
   - Did the chatbot help you identify gaps in your digital transformation journey? How?
   - Were the chatbot's questions helpful in understanding your organisation's needs?
2. Interaction and Usability
   - Was the chatbot easy to use? What aspects could be improved?
   - Did the follow-up questions enhance the conversation?
3. Data Input and Analysis
   - Would it be useful if the chatbot allowed different types of inputs, like workflows or data files?
   - How should the chatbot process and present information to better meet your needs?
4. Perceived Limitations
   - Is the chatbot sufficient for a complete digital transformation, or does it need additional features (e.g., system integration)?
5. General Feedback
   - What single improvement would make the chatbot more useful for your organisation?

D   Participants Profile

Digital transformation experts:

- Expert 1: Early career researcher and academic in Supply Chain Management, expert on Industry 4.0, digital transformation, sustainability, sustainable supply chain management.
- Expert 2: Senior researcher and academic in Design and Innovation, expert on Design creativity, product innovation, design management.

Representatives of SMEs:

- The Human Resource Manager of an SMEs specialising in advanced engineering solutions for the defence industry, including remote-controlled detonators and unmanned systems.
- The Production Director of a manufacturing SME known for its production of engine cooling systems, including viscous fan clutches and system solutions for industrial and automotive applications.

References

1. Abid, A., Abdalla, A., Abid, A., Khan, D., Alfozan, A., Zou, J.: Gradio: Hassle-free sharing and testing of ml models in the wild. arXiv preprint arXiv:1906.02569 (2019)
2. Akarun, L.: Boğaziçi Üniversitesi Endüstri 4.0 Platformu Raporu.Türkiye'de Dijital Dönüşüm Değerlendirme Aracı (D3A) 2019 - 2020 Sonuç Raporu, https://www.istka.org.tr/media/132472/türkiye-de-dijital-dönüşüm-değerlendirme-arac\T1\i-d3a-2019-2020-sonuç-raporu.pdf
3. Bellantuono, N., Nuzzi, A., Pontrandolfo, P., Scozzi, B.: Digital transformation models for the I4.0 transition: lessons from the change management literature. Sustainability **13**(23), 12941 (2021). https://doi.org/10.3390/su132312941
4. Ben-Nun, P., et al.: Respondent fatigue. Encyclopedia Surv. Res. Methods **2**, 742–743 (2008)
5. Cai, Z., Park, S., Nixon, N., Doroudi, S.: Advancing knowledge together: integrating large language model-based conversational AI in small group collaborative learning. In: Extended Abstracts of the CHI Conference on Human Factors in Computing Systems, pp. 1–9. CHI EA '24, Association for Computing Machinery (2024). https://doi.org/10.1145/3613905.3650868
6. Cozmiuc, D.C., Pettinger, R.: Consultants' tools to manage digital transformation: the case of PWC, Siemens, and Oracle. J. Cases Inf. Technol. (JCIT) **23**(4), 1–29 (2021). https://doi.org/10.4018/JCIT.20211001.oa7
7. Cranshaw, J., Elwany, E., Newman, T., Kocielnik, R., Yu, B., Soni, S., Teevan, J., Monroy-Hernández, A.: Calendar.help: designing a workflow-based scheduling agent with humans in the loop. In: Proceedings of the 2017 CHI Conference on Human Factors in Computing Systems, pp. 2382–2393. CHI '17, Association for Computing Machinery, New York, NY, USA (2017). https://doi.org/10.1145/3025453.3025780
8. Furjan, M.T., Tomičić-Pupek, K., Pihir, I.: Understanding digital transformation initiatives: case studies analysis. Bus. Syst. Res. J. **11**(1), 125–141 (2020). https://doi.org/10.2478/bsrj-2020-0009
9. Huang, S., Zhao, X., Wei, D., Song, X., Sun, Y.: Chatbot and fatigued driver: exploring the use of LLM-based voice assistants for driving fatigue. In: Extended Abstracts of the CHI Conference on Human Factors in Computing Systems, pp. 1–8. CHI EA '24, Association for Computing Machinery (2024). https://doi.org/10.1145/3613905.3651031
10. Li, J., Zhou, M.X., Yang, H., Mark, G.: Confiding in and listening to virtual agents: the effect of personality. In: Proceedings of the 22nd International Conference on Intelligent User Interfaces, pp. 275–286. IUI '17, Association for Computing Machinery, New York, NY, USA (2017). https://doi.org/10.1145/3025171.3025206
11. Mastos, T.D., et al.: Industry 4.0 sustainable supply chains: an application of an IoT enabled scrap metal management solution. J. Cleaner Prod. **269**, 122377 (2020). https://doi.org/10.1016/j.jclepro.2020.122377
12. OpenAI: ChatGPT. https://chatgpt.com/ (2024). Accessed 15 Dec 2024
13. OpenAI: Whisper. https://github.com/openai/whisper?tab=readme-ov-file#available-models-and-languages (2024). Accessed 15 Dec 2024
14. Radford, A., Kim, J.W., Xu, T., Brockman, G., McLeavey, C., Sutskever, I.: Robust speech recognition via large-scale weak supervision. In: Proceedings of the 40th International Conference on Machine Learning. ICML'23, JMLR.org (2023)

15. Schneider, S., Kokshagina, O.: Digital transformation: what we have learned (thus far) and what is next. Creativity and Innov. Manage. **30**(2), 384–411 (2021). https://doi.org/10.1111/caim.12414
16. Taj, S., Imran, A.S., Kastrati, Z., Daudpota, S.M., Memon, R.A., Ahmed, J.: IoT-based supply chain management: a systematic literature review. Internet Things **24**, 100982 (2023). https://doi.org/10.1016/j.iot.2023.100982
17. Traum, D.: Computational approaches to dialogue. In: The Routledge Handbook of Language and Dialogue, vol. 1, pp. 143–161 (2017)
18. TÜSSİDE, T.: DDX Dijital Dönüşüm Değerlendirme Modeli. https://ddx.tubitak.gov.tr/ddx-nedir/
19. Vial, G.: Understanding digital transformation: a review and a research agenda. J. Strateg. Inf. Syst. **28**(2), 118–144 (2019). https://doi.org/10.1016/j.jsis.2019.01.003
20. Xiao, Z., et al.: Tell me about yourself: using an AI-powered chatbot to conduct conversational surveys with open-ended questions. ACM Trans. Comput.-Hum. Interact. **27**(3), 15:1–15:37 (2020). https://doi.org/10.1145/3381804
21. Xu, A., Liu, Z., Guo, Y., Sinha, V., Akkiraju, R.: A new chatbot for customer service on social media. In: Proceedings of the 2017 CHI Conference on Human Factors in Computing Systems, pp. 3506–3510. CHI '17, Association for Computing Machinery, New York, NY, USA (2017). https://doi.org/10.1145/3025453.3025496

Author Index